D0146845

INTERNATIONAL
BIOGRAPHICAL DICTIONARY OF
COMPUTER
PIONEERS

INTERNATIONAL
BIOGRAPHICAL DICTIONARY OF
COMPUTER
PIONEERS

Editor

J. A. N. LEE

CHICAGO • LONDON

For information, write to:
FITZROY DEARBORN PUBLISHERS
70 East Walton Street
Chicago, Illinois 60611
U.S.A.

or

FITZROY DEARBORN PUBLISHERS
11 Rathbone Place
London W1P 1DE
England

Library of Congress Cataloging-in-Publication Data

Lee, J.A.N.
    International Biographical Dictionary of Computer Pioneers / J.A.N. Lee.
       p.   cm.
    Includes index.
    ISBN 1-884964-47-8
    1. Computers – Biography.   I. Title
QA76.2.A2L44   1995
004 ' . 092' 2 – dc20
[B]   94-40232
                    CIP

British Library Cataloguing in Publication Data

International Biographical Dictionary of
Computer Pioneers
  I. Lee, J. A. N.
  004.0922

  ISBN 1-884964-47-8

First published in the U.S. and U.K., 1995
Printed by Braun-Brumfield, Inc.

Cover design by Peter Aristedes

CONTENTS

C

G

H

I

J

K

L

M

T

U

V

W

Y

Z

INTRODUCTION

"Those who forget the lessons of history are doomed to repeat it"—Arnold Toynbee, 1919

The history of computing is founded on people. While one can create a chronological history of the field based on the artifacts and concepts that provided the stepping stones from the first simple counting tables to modern (super) computers, behind every intellectual concept there is a person, and from that person we can learn special personal lessons. From our experience in editing the *Annals of the History of Computing,* many of the manuscripts submitted for consideration lack two most important elements—a review of the environment in which an artifact or concept is born, and the downstream impact of the introduction of that artifact or concept in the field of computing and computation. One significant element of the environment in which computational elements are created is the people who inhabit the field. This book looks at those pioneers, their qualifications, their activities, and the recognition accorded them by our industry.

The source of many biographies is the *Annals of the History of Computing,* either from the biographical data provided when the pioneer wrote a paper for publication, or, regrettably, from an obituary when the pioneer died. In some cases, the biography was the subject of a scholarly paper in the *Annals* or in another journal; where possible, edited versions of these articles are reprinted here. A major starting point for selecting this set of pioneers was the listing created by this author and Eric Weiss for the tenth anniversary issue of the *Annals.* That list was derived from one major source—pioneers whose name appeared in the index for the first ten volumes three or more times. The new list has been extended considerably, especially in the recognition of pioneers outside the US.

Collecting a list of pioneers whose biographies should be included in this volume is akin to selecting persons to be honored in a Hall of Fame. And in consonance with various established "Halls of Fame," I have attempted to include not only those whose contributions have been central to the progression of the field of computing, but also those who played supportive roles as enlightened managers, financiers, or educators. To distinguish between a "pioneer" and a "significant contributor" has been difficult. My general guideline has been that a pioneer is one who introduced a new element, concept, or direction to the field.

Each biography is accompanied by a list of publications in which the reader may find more information about the accomplishments of the pioneer. Each bibliography is divided into two sections—biographical entries and significant publications. The former includes autobiographical and biographical articles as well as (where appropriate) obituaries. Where a pioneer has written about his accomplishments much later than the time of the work, it is classified as biographical; a report written at the time of the work is listed as a significant publication. In many cases the biographical information is reprinted from an obituary or an eloge; in those cases where the original author included a set of references for the work, these have been included separately.

It is to be expected that reviewers of this collection of biographies will comment on the unevenness of the presentations. Where a pioneer has written an autobiographical article, we have chosen at least to incorporate portions in the biography printed here. Throughout the work on this collection we have tried to give credit where credit is due, and to recognize that it is not the number of words that measure the quality of a pioneer's contributions to our field. Some of our pioneers have had much written about them, and their lives have been opened up to meticulous scrutiny, while others, working in the background, are unnoticed because their work is not quite so exciting. Some of our pioneers had lives that extended far beyond their well-known activities in computing or computer science, and while we have not emphasized these activities, we have included notes on them when they show their personalities. Hopefully I have balanced the attention to the homosexuality of Alan Turing with the Catholicism of Gerry Weeg and the nationalistic pride of Grace Hopper. We would hope that in future editions, more complete biographies of some of our pioneers can be added to match those of their peers.

We need to nurture and recognize our pioneers more frequently. One of the interesting fall-outs from the activity of recording biographies was to notice how many of our pioneers have not been honored by our professional societies or by their countries. Where possible I have not restricted the list of pioneers to those who have been recognized by such designations as fellows of societies, or as members of academies. Perhaps the award committees of our societies and academies will be prompted to recognize some of our pioneers and to reward them after this publication.

ACKNOWLEDGMENTS

The origin of this work is the set of one-liners that were created by Eric Weiss, Biographies Department editor of the *Annals of the History of Computing*, Michael Williams, Assistant Editor-in-Chief for

Departments, and myself. That set of approximately 200 entries was published in the 10th-anniversary issue of the journal. From that beginning grew my inspiration to do a more complete job of recognizing our pioneers. Eric has continued to serve as the editor of the Biographies Department of the *Annals*; several of the biographies contained herein were authored by him, subjected to my heavy-handed editing and extended to include formal (*Who's Who* style) biographies, and listings of publications. My thanks to Eric for his contributions. My son Stuart helped me get started on this second project to identify the pioneers of our field, by doing much of the library searches for existing biographical materials. Many thanks to the several typists who have helped out in the preparation of this set of biographies, including Kellie Ross, Lisa Cox, and Molly Rich. I am also extremely grateful for permission to include excerpts from their original works by the following authors:

EDITED FROM THE ANNALS OF
THE HISTORY OF COMPUTING:

Addie, Robin, "Memories of Alan Turing," *Ann. Hist. Comp.*, Vol. 15, No. 1, 1992, pp. 59–60.

Addison, J. W., "Eloge: Alfred Tarski, 1901–1983," *Ann. Hist. Comp.*, Vol. 6, No. 4, 1984, pp. 335–336.

Auerbach, Isaac L., "Eloge: Niels Ivar Bech, 1920–1975," *Ann. Hist. Comp.*, Vol. 6, No. 4, 1984, p. 332.

Auerbach, Isaac L., "Eloge: Dov Chevion, 1917–1983," *Ann. Hist. Comp.*, Vol. 7, No. 1, Jan. 1985, pp. 4–6.

Auerbach, Isaac L., "Harry H. Goode, June 30, 1909–October, 1960," *Ann. Hist. Comp.*, Vol. 8, No. 3, July 1986, pp. 257–260.

Berry, Jean R., "Clifford Edward Berry, 1918–1963: His Role in Early Computers," *Ann. Hist. Comp.*, Vol. 8, No. 4, Oct. 1986, pp. 361–369.

Blum, Joseph, Robert L. Kirby, and Jack Minker, "Eloge: Walter W. Jacobs, 1914–1982," *Ann. Hist. Comp.*, Vol. 6, No. 2, 1984, pp. 100–101.

Campaigne, Howard, From the Foreword to Flowers, Thomas H., "The Design of Colossus," *Ann. Hist. Comp.*, Vol. 5, No. 3, July 1983.

Campbell-Kelly, Martin, "Christopher Strachey, 1916–1975: A Biographical Note," *Ann. Hist. Comp.*, Vol. 7, No. 1, Jan. 1985, pp. 19–42.

Cohn, H., "Reminiscences of a True Believer," *Ann. Hist. Comp.*, Vol. 16, No. 1, 1994, pp. 71–76.

Curtis, Kent K., N. C. Metropolis, William G. Rosen, Yoshio Shimamoto, and James N. Snyder, "John R. Pasta, 1918–1981: An Unusual Path Toward Computer Science," *Ann. Hist. Comp.*, Vol. 5, No. 3, July 1983.

La Porte, Deidre, and George R. Stibitz, "Eloge: E.G. Andrews, 1898–1980," *Ann. Hist. Comp.*, Vol. 4, No. 1, 1982, pp. 4–5.

Phillips, Norman A., "Eloge: Jule G. Charney, 1917–1981," *Ann. Hist. Comp.*, Vol. 3, No. 4, 1981, pp. 308–309.

Ramunni, Girolamo, "Louis Couffignal, 1902–1966: Informatics Pioneer in France," *Ann. Hist. Comp.*, Vol. 11, No. 4, 1989, pp. 247–256.

Randell, Brian, "From Analytical Engine to Electronic Digital Computer: The Contributions of Ludgate, Torres, and Bush," *Ann. Hist. Comp.*, Vol. 4, No. 4, 1982, pp. 327–341.

Rosin, Robert R., "Philip Dorn," *Ann. Hist. Comp.*, Vol. 15, No. 4, 1993, pp. 84–85.

Santemases, José Garcia, "Early Computer Developments in Madrid," *Ann. Hist. Comp.*, Vol. 4, No. 1, 1982, pp. 31–34.

Stern, Nancy, "John William Mauchly: 1907–1980," *Ann. Hist. Comp.*, Vol. 2, No. 2, 1980, pp. 100–103.

Todd, John, "John Hamilton Curtiss, 1909–1977," *Ann. Hist. Comp.*, Vol. 2, No. 2, 1980, pp. 104–110.

Tonik, Albert B., "Eloge: Herman Lukoff: 1923–1979," *Ann. Hist. Comp.*, Vol. 2, No. 3, 1980, pp. 196–197.

Tropp, Henry. S., "Leslie John Comrie," Anecdotes Dept., *Ann. Hist. Comp.*, Vol. 4, No. 4, Oct. 1982, pp. 371–372.

Turski, Wladylaw, "Obituary: Andrei Ershov," *Ann. Hist. Comp.*, Vol. 15, No. 2, 1993, p. 55.

Tweedale, Geoffrey, "Bertram Vivian Bowden," *Ann. Hist. Comp.*, Vol. 12, No. 2, 1990, pp. 138–140.

Weiss, E. A., "John Grist Brainerd: Obituary," *Ann. Hist. Comp.*, Vol. 10, No. 1, 1988, pp. 78–79.

Weiss, E. A., "Richard P. Feynman: Obituary," *Ann. Hist. Comp.*, Vol. 10, No. 2, 1988, pp. 141–142.

Weiss, Eric A., "Saul Gorn: Obituary," *Ann. Hist. Comp.*, Vol. 14, No. 3.

Weiss, Eric A., "Jan A. Rajchman," *Ann. Hist. Comp.*, Vol. 11, No. 4, 1989, p. 328.

Weiss, Eric A., "Obituary," *Ann. Hist. Comp.*, Vol. 11, No. 3, 1989, p. 225.

Weiss, Eric A., "Grace Brewster Murray Hopper," *Ann. Hist. Comp.*, Vol. 14, No. 2, 1992, pp. 56–58.

Weiss, Eric A., "Ida Rhodes," *Ann. Hist. Comp.*, Vol. 14, No. 2, 1992, pp. 58–59.

Weiss, Eric A., "John E. Parker—Obituary," *Ann. Hist. Comp.*, Vol. 14, No. 4, 1992.

Weiss, Eric A., "Obituary: Neil MacDonald," *Ann. Hist. Comp.,* Vol. 10, No. 3, 1988, p. 217.

Weiss, Eric A., "Obituary: John H. Dessauer," *Ann. Hist. Comp.,* To be published.

Wilkes, Maurice V., "Babbage's Expectations for his Engines," *Ann. Hist. Comp.,* Vol. 13, No. 2, 1991, pp. 141–146.

Williams, Michael R., "Joseph Clement: The First Computer Engineer," *Ann. Hist. Comp.,* Vol. 14, No. 3, 1992, p. 55ff.

Williams, Michael R., "From Napier to Lucas: The Use of Napier's Bones in Calculating Instruments," *Ann. Hist. Comp.,* Vol. 5, No. 3, July 1983, pp. 279–296.

Zemanek, Heinz, "Eloge: Victor Mikhaylovich Glushkov, 1923–1982," *Ann. Hist. Comp.,* Vol. 4, No. 2, 1982, pp. 100–101.

Zemanek, Heinz, "Eloge: Adriaan van Wijngaarden (1916–1987)," *Ann. Hist. Comp.,* Vol. 11, No. 3, 1989, pp. 210–225.

Zemanek, Heinz, "Johanna Piesch," *Ann. Hist. Comp.,* Vol. 15, No. 3, 1993, p. 72.

EDITED FROM OTHER SOURCES:

Cohen, I. B., "Howard Aiken, Harvard University, and IBM: Cooperation and Conflict," in Elliott, Clark A., and Margaret W. Rossiter, eds., *Science at Harvard University: Historical Perspectives,* Lehigh University Press, Bethlehem; Associated University Presses, London and Toronto, 1992, pp. 251–284.

Folkart, Burt A., "John Bardeen; Physicist Won 2 Nobels," *Los Angeles Times,* Jan. 31, 1991.

Froehlich, Leopold, "Babbage Observed," *Datamation,* Cahners/Ziff Pub. Assoc., Mar. 1985.

Hilton, Peter, "Obituary—M.H.A. Newman," *Bull. London Math. Soc.,* Vol. 18, 1986, pp. 67–72.

Jerger, Ronald K. "John Cocke: Vision with Enthusiam," *IEEE Spectrum,* Dec. 1991, pp. 33–34.

Lindstrom, Gary, "Elliott I. Organick: 1925–1985," *Comm. ACM,* Vol. 29, No. 3, Mar. 1986, p. 231.

Perry, Tekla S., "Richard W. Hamming," *IEEE Spectrum,* May 1993, pp. 80–82.

Rees, Mina, "Warren Weaver," *Biographical Memoirs,* Vol. 57, National Academy of Sciences, 1983, pp. 493–530.

Zemanek, Heinz, "Marcel Linsman, 1912–1989," *IFIP Newsletter,* Vol. 6, No. 3, 1989, p. 8.

A significant source of information about members of staff of the IBM Corporation was:

Pugh, Emerson W., Lyle R. Johnson, and John H. Palmer, *IBM's 360 and Early 370 Systems,* MIT Press, Cambridge, Mass., 1991.

While this book does not contain specific biographies of IBM pioneers, there are a number of anecdotes about them, and I have drawn extensively on this source to provide information on a number of persons included herein.

EDITED FROM UNPUBLISHED CONTRIBUTIONS BY THE FOLLOWING AUTHORS:

Fritz Jörn on Heinz Billing
Staff of LLNL on Sidney Fernbach
Harry Huskey on Derrick Lehmer
Jill Fain Lehman on Allen Newell
Jamie Pearson on Kenneth Olsen
Margaret Paull on David Packard
John Rice on Saul Rosen
Carolyn E. Tajnai on Arthur Samuel
Henry S. Tropp on George Stibitz

The sources of these excerpts are included with each biography.
The following pioneers edited their own biographies and provided material that was edited by me into the entry in this collection:

John Vincent Atanasoff	William Atchison
Isaac Auerbach	Charles Bachman
Friedrich Bauer	Laszlo Belady
Gwen Bell	Robert Bemer
James Birkenstock	Garrett Birkhoff
Erich Bloch	Andrew Booth
Charles Bradshaw	Tony Brooker
Gordon Brown	Arthur Burks
Arthur C. Clarke	Edgar Codd
Arnold Cohen	Harvey Cohn
Larry Constantine	James Cooley
Allen Coombs	Donald W. Davies
Peter Denning	B. O. Evans
Aaron Finerman	I. Jack Good
Ralph Griswold	Jerrier A. Haddad

William Hewlett
Cuthbert Hurd
Kenneth Iverson
Brian David Josephson
Donald Knuth
Daniel D. McCracken
Donald Michie
Donn Parker
Alan Perlis
James Pomerene
Anthony Ralston
Douglas Ross
Allan Scherr
Samuel Snyder
Maurice Wilkes

C.A.R. Hoare
Harry Huskey
John Jacobs
Tom Kilburn
Thomas Kurtz
Nicholas Metropolis
Kristen Nygaard
John T. Parsons
John Pierce
Emerson Pugh
Mina Rees
Gerard Salton
Herbert A. Simon
Joseph Traub
Konrad Zuse

Last, but by no means least, my sincere thanks to the many pioneers listed in this collection who responded so readily to my inquiries about their lives. In most cases they were extremely modest and were not overly happy to be credited with anything even slightly more than they credited themselves. I attempted to give them a sample biography to follow, but was hesitant to use the biography of a living pioneer. Giving them an obituary of a pioneer was not the most tactful concept either. I did my best not to put a hex on them, but regrettably in a few cases their contribution became the basis for their obituary.

J.A.N. Lee
Blacksburg, VA

JEANNE CLARE ADAMS

Born June 15, 1921, Utica, N.Y.; Chairman of the ANSI Fortran Standards Committee that developed the controversial Fortran 9X proposal, which introduced array and vector processing to the language.

Education: BS, economics, University of Michigan, 1943; MS, telecommunications and electrical engineering, University of Colorado, 1979.

Professional Experience: systems analyst, Army Air Corps, 1943–1946; research statistician, Research Program, Harvard University, 1947–1949; National Center for Atmospheric Research, Boulder, Colo., 1960–1981, 1984–present; CYBER 205 project coordinator, Institute for Computational Studies, Colorado State University, 1982–1984.

Jeanne Adams, who holds a master's degree in electrical engineering and telecommunications from the University of Colorado, is a long-time computer-user support manager for the National Center for Atmospheric Research in Boulder, Colo. For a brief period she coordinated the CYBER 205 project for Colorado State University's Institute for Computational Studies. Adams went to CSUI in February 1982 from the National Center for Atmospheric Research, where she had been deputy head of the Computing Division, assistant for planning, and manager of university liaison. She was a research statistician for a project on juvenile delinquency at Harvard University and served as systems service analyst for the Army Air Force. She is chair of the International Standards Organization Committee on Programming Languages (TC97/SC5) and the ANSI Fortran Standards Committee (X3J3). Adams has written reference manuals for a variety of computer equipment, including the CYBER 205.

BIBLIOGRAPHY

Significant Publications

Adams, Jeanne C., Walter S. Brainerd, and Charles H. Goldberg, *Programmer's Guide to Fortran 90*, McGraw-Hill, New York, 1990.

Adams, Jeanne C., Walter S. Brainerd, J. Martin, B. Smith, and J. Wagener, *Fortran 90 Handbook*, McGraw-Hill, New York, 1992.

HOWARD HATHAWAY AIKEN

Born 1900; died 1973. Designer and developer of the first large-scale operating relay calculator in the US

Education: SB, electrical engineering, University of Wisconsin, 1923; SM, physics, Harvard University, 1937; PhD, physics, Harvard University, 1939.

Professional Experience: Madison Gas & Electric, Westinghouse, 1919–1932; Harvard University: instructor, associate professor of applied mathematics, 1937–1961, director, Computation Laboratory, 1946–1961; US Navy, Commander, Naval Mine Warfare School, 1941–1944, Harvard/Navy Computation Laboratory, 1944–1946; University of Miami, professor, 1961–1973; after retirement from Harvard, he created Howard Aiken Industries.

Honors and Awards: IEEE Computer Society Pioneer Award, 1980.

Aiken was the leader in developing four large-scale calculating machines (the word "computer" was never applied to his devices), but his accomplishments reached far beyond machine design and construction. His primary focus was *computation*; he built and used machines to solve problems. He directed research in switching theory, data processing, and computing components and circuits. He initiated one of the earliest graduate programs in computer science at Harvard University: fifteen doctoral degrees and many master's degrees were earned under his supervision. The publications of the Computation Laboratory are contained in 24 volumes of *Annals*. Scientists across the world were welcomed into his laboratory, and he did much to stimulate interest in computers in Europe. Truly a giant in early development of automatic computation, Aiken left perhaps his greatest legacy, the many people whom he influenced—particularly the members of his staff at the Computation Laboratory at Harvard.

Aiken's Shift from Electron Physics to Computing[1]

Although Howard Hathaway Aiken achieved world fame as a computer pioneer, when he entered Harvard's Graduate School of Arts and Sciences in 1933 as a candidate for the PhD in physics, he had no idea that he would devote his career to computing. Then 32, older than

---

[1] Much of the following essay on Aiken is extracted with permission from Cohen 1992.

most graduate students, he had obtained his undergraduate degree in electrical engineering from the University of Wisconsin and had worked as a power engineer before coming to Harvard.

During Aiken's initial years as a Harvard graduate student, he followed the usual program of studies. He then shifted his allegiance to the field of electronics, the physics of vacuum tubes, and the properties of circuits, working directly under Professor E. Leon Chaffee, who became (and remained) his primary academic sponsor. He began teaching in his second year as a graduate student and, after receiving his PhD in 1938, was appointed a faculty instructor, the name of the rank then introduced by Harvard to replace that of assistant professor. Aiken never published any of the results of his thesis research; all of his published writings dealt with one or another aspect of computing and computers.

Aiken's Background in Computing and Gadgetry

In an autobiographical letter to Warren Weaver in September 1940, Aiken stated that his "chief research for the past six years has been the construction of an automatic calculating machine for scientific purposes." This would place the beginnings of his interest in a "calculating machine" in 1935, when he had begun his thesis research.

His training as an electrical engineer and as a graduate student in physics would have exposed him to a generous amount of pure and applied mathematics. In those days, scientists advanced from slide-rule calculations to using electromechanical desktop calculations—chiefly Monroe, Burroughs, and Marchant machines. Aiken mastered this kind of calculating, as well as the mathematics of ordinary and partial differential equations, vector analysis, and matrices. In this he was in no way different from dozens of other students in pure and applied physics.

One feature of Aiken's writings shows him to have been very different from most other physicists and applied mathematicians: Aiken always had an interest in the history of his subject, and he joyfully paid tribute to his illustrious predecessors. This feature has led to a severe misunderstanding of his knowledge of the work of some predecessors, notably Charles Babbage; as a result, Aiken's originality has been seriously misjudged by assuming that he had depended heavily on Babbage's ideas.

Aiken's 1937 proposal for a calculating machine began with a series of paragraphs devoted to an account of the pioneers in machine calculation: Pascal, Moreland, Leibniz, and—above all—Babbage. This same historical homage characterizes the series of articles in *Electrical Engineering* in 1946. The whole of the first chapter of the *Manual of*

Operations for Mark I was a historical chronicle, stressing the work of Charles Babbage; one of the illustrations even showed a set of calculating wheels from Babbage's never-completed Difference Engine. The result was that Aiken's machine was often considered to be indebted to Babbage's ideas; L.C. Comrie, the leading figure in British computing, referred to the Mark I as "Babbage's Dream Comes True."

Planning for the Mark I/ASCC[2]

Aiken's 1937 proposal is a fairly long document, filling twenty-three double-spaced typed pages. It opens with a brief history of "aids to calculation," concluding in a major discussion of Babbage's engines, plus a brief statement of Hollerith's invention of punched-card "tabulating, counting, sorting, arithmetical machinery." Aiken observed that the machines "manufactured by the International Business Machines Company" have made it possible to do "daily in the accounting offices of industrial enterprises all over the world" the very "things Babbage wished to accomplish." Aiken then turned to the "need for more powerful calculating methods in the mathematical and physical sciences."

The next section was crucial to the organization of a calculating machine. Aiken specified four design features that are different for punched card accounting "machinery" and "calculating machinery as required in the sciences." First, a machine intended for mathematics must "be able to handle both positive and negative quantities," whereas accounting machinery is designed "almost entirely" for "problems of positive numbers." Second, calculating machinery for mathematical purposes must "be able to supply and utilize" many kinds of transcendental functions (e.g., trigonometric functions): elliptic, Bessel, and probability functions. Third, for mathematics, a calculating machine should "be fully automatic in its operation once a process is established." In calculating the value of a function in its expansion in a series, the evaluation of a formula, or numerical integration (in solution of a differential equation), the process, once established, continues "indefinitely until the range of the independent variables is covered"—usually "by successive equal steps." Fourth, calculating machinery designed for mathematics "should be capable of computing lines instead of columns," since very often in the numerical solution of a differential equation, the computation of a value will be found to depend on preceding values. This is actually "the reverse" of the way in which "existing calculating machinery" is capable of evaluating a function by steps.

---

[2]Automatic Sequence Controlled Calculator, the IBM designation for the calculator.

The proposal was obviously geared directly toward IBM's operative elements. But it is also clear that, at the general level of Aiken's actual text, the only demands for functional elements were that they be digital; that they be capable of performing the four fundamental operations of arithmetic; that they could be linked and controlled so as to perform their operations in a predetermined sequence; that they could store numbers (either constants or intermediate results) and to introduce them at a specified stage in the automatic sequence, and that they print out the final results in tabular form. IBM engineers could readily understand the function of each of the operative elements and could design circuits that would permit these operations to be performed in sequence according to predetermined commands entered on punched cards or perforated tape. These engineers could, and did, transform Aiken's ideas into an electromagnetic level of machine reality that allowed the calculator to be designed for construction.

A factor in the later disagreement that arose between Aiken and IBM, however, was that Aiken always discussed his machine in terms of the higher level mathematical problems he had designed it to solve. A full and comprehending reading of Aiken's proposal thus required a level of mathematical literacy that was several degrees beyond the capacity of almost everyone on the engineering staff of IBM at that time. Not many of the engineers in 1937 were even college graduates. Clair D. Lake, the engineer who was put in charge of Aiken's project, was a distinguished inventor who came to IBM in 1915 from the automotive field; his "credentials were based on performance, not education" (after the eighth grade he had gone to a manual training school rather than a high school). Francis E. (Frank) Hamilton, who directed the work on the Aiken project, had a distinguished career at IBM. He became a member of the company as a draftsman in 1923, when it was still known as CTR; in 1937, Hamilton was an assistant to Lake. The third member of the working team for Aiken's machine was Benjamin Durfee, who had been with IBM since 1917 (in the CTR days) and who had spent a year in the company training school, after which he developed "a reputation for diligence in servicing tabulators" (a job consisting "mainly of checking machine adjustments, oiling and cleaning, and replacing worn parts").

The enormous intellectual gulf between Aiken and the IBM engineers with whom he was in contact transcended the level of mere mathematical training. Lake, Hamilton, and Durfee were from a wholly different world, and they had no understanding of Aiken's scientific and intellectual values. Aiken often tended to think of this IBM trio as mere mechanics, supergadgeteers, clever at their work but in no possible sense his peers. They, in turn, considered "their machine" to be their invention, admitting only that Aiken had supplied the initial broad outlines and the occasion for the project. Naturally, these men (and everyone else at IBM) would resent any later move by Aiken to present himself as principal inventor, on a different and more fundamental level of creativity than Lake, Hamilton, and Durfee. In retrospect we can see an inevitable head-on collision that would necessarily arise when it came time to apportion the credits for the great invention.

IBM Agrees to Build the Machine

By March 31, 1939, the final agreement had been drawn up and signed. IBM agreed (1) "to construct for Harvard an automatic computing plant comprising machines for automatically carrying out a series of mathematical computations adaptable for the solution of problems in scientific fields." Harvard agreed (2) to furnish "without charge" the structural foundation, and (3) to appoint "certain members of the faculty or staff or student body" to cooperate with "the engineering and research divisions of IBM in completing the design and testing." It was agreed (4) that all Harvard personnel assigned to this project would sign a standard "nondisclosure" agreement to protect IBM's proprietary technical and inventive rights. IBM (5) would receive no compensation, nor were any charges to be made to Harvard. The finished "plant" would become "the property of Harvard." A letter from Dean Westergaard confirmed the "understanding that the computing plant will be for the use of Harvard in scientific fields and that no commercial use will be made of it by Harvard." On May 10, 1939, about a year and a half after Aiken's first approach to IBM, James Bryce wrote Aiken that all the papers had been signed and that he was now "engaged in getting an appropriation put through." He would then "issue the shop orders" and "begin the actual work of designing and constructing the calculating machine." It may be noted that Bryce quietly shifted the language from "calculating plant" to "calculating machine." By May 12, the first appropriation had been made and the project was at last under way.

In January 1943, the Harvard machine was completed in the North Street Laboratory at Endicott, N.Y., and ran a test problem. But only in December 1943 was the machine demonstrated to members of the Harvard faculty. The machine was then disassembled and shipped to Harvard, where it was housed in a large basement room in the

Physics Research Laboratory, known as the Battery Room because it then housed a giant wet-cell battery.[3]

Excitement rippled through the Physics Department on February 1, 1944, as the trucks arrived and the parts of the huge machine, many of them in large crates, were transported to the Battery Room. To record the event, the Cruft Laboratory photographer Paul Donaldson was on hand to make still photographs and to capture the entrance of the crates on 16-mm film with his newly acquired Kodak Ciné Special motion picture camera.

By early spring the giant machine was in full operation, under the direction of Robert Campbell. Aiken himself was not in residence. A reserve officer in the Navy, Aiken had been called to active duty in 1941 and had been sent to the Naval Mine Warfare School in Yorktown, Va. His assignment was to prepare Navy technicians for using mines.

The Dedication of the ASCC/Mark I

When the machine had been turned over to the Navy for operation during wartime, Campbell became a lieutenant in the Navy and was joined by Lt. Richard M. Bloch and Lt. Grace Murray Hopper (who had been a professor of mathematics at Vassar College), plus other naval personnel including Lt. Comdr. Hubert A. Arnold, Ens. Ruth A. Brendel, Lt. Harry Goheen, and Lt. Brooks J. Lockhart. There was also the usual complement of naval "ratings." When Aiken himself was transferred to Cambridge, he became the first naval officer in history to command a computer.

On April 17, 1944, Harvard's president, James Bryant Conant, reported to IBM's president, Thomas J. Watson, Sr., that "the calculating machine" had been "put into operative condition." Expressing his appreciation for "the speed with which the machine has been installed" and noting that it "is already being used for special problems in connection with the war effort," Conant nevertheless regretted that the covering sheath was "still to be completed," thus delaying the "public announcement of the machine and its purpose." Watson replied on April 21 that he had "given orders to rush the completion of the cabinet for the machine." He concluded in an expression of the "great pleasure and inspiration" it had been for his "organization to cooperate with you and your associates in connection with this machine." He

---

[3]As an aside, I may mention that as a very junior member of the wartime staff of the Physics Department I participated in the faculty vote to turn over the Battery Room to Aiken and IBM for the new calculator. The vote stipulated that at the end of the war the room would be restored to its original function, something that—to the regret of some members of the department—was never done. This vote was my first formal contact with Howard Aiken and his machine.—I. Bernard Cohen

was "looking forward to being present at the dedication." On July 24 Conant wrote about the arrangements for the dedication, to take place on Monday, August 7. A luncheon at the Fogg Museum of Art would be followed by ceremonies in University Hall. Conant hoped that Watson would "say a few words."

The Harvard News Office, in close consultation with Aiken, prepared a news release. It was evidently not considered necessary to clear the release with IBM, even though what used to be called "common courtesy" might have seemed to demand such action. According to IBM's historians, "Watson [would have] assumed that he and Aiken would agree in a press release." The release was headed "World's greatest mathematical calculator" and bore the statement: "The NAVY, which has sole use of the machine, has approved this story and set this release date [Monday papers, August 7, 1944]." The first five paragraphs (occupying almost two of the eight pages) stated that the machine would be presented to Harvard by IBM, that it would solve many types of mathematical problems, that the presentation would be made "by Mr. Thomas J. Watson, president of International Business Machines Corporation," that the machine was "new in principle," and was an "algebraic super-brain." Then followed the bold unqualified statement that "In charge of the activity . . . is the inventor, Commander Howard H. Aiken, U.S.N.R," who "worked out the theory which made the machine possible." It may be observed that not only was Aiken designated "the inventor," but no reason had been given thus far for IBM being the donor—it had not even been mentioned that IBM had actually constructed the machine. In fact, in the whole eight pages, the only reference to IBM's contribution was a single paragraph later on in the release.

Two years of research were required to develop the basic theory. Six years of design, construction, and testing were necessary to transform Commander Aiken's original conception into a completed machine. This work was carried on at the Engineering Laboratory of the International Business Machines Corporation at Endicott, N.Y., under the joint direction of Commander Aiken and Clair D. Lake. They were assisted in the detailed design of the machine by Frank E. Hamilton and Benjamin M. Durfee.

It is said that when Watson arrived in Boston accompanied by his wife and first saw the news story, he became so irate that he even planned to return to New York without attending either the ceremonial luncheon or the formal dedication ceremonies. When Watson arrived at his hotel, he telephoned—so the story goes—to his Harvard hosts, threatening to boycott the ceremonies on the following day.

Conant and Aiken thereupon rushed from Cambridge to Boston to placate Watson, who launched into a furious tirade against Aiken and (presumably) Harvard. Evidently Conant and Aiken succeeded in calming Watson, who did attend the dedication on the following day and gave a star performance.

The Aftermath of the Dedication

About a month after the dedication, on September 20, 1944, Aiken wrote a letter of apology and explanation to Watson,[4] which was acknowledged by Watson in his reply to Aiken dated October 3, 1944. Watson thanked Aiken both for his letter and for "your kind remarks about me at the dedication of the Harvard machine." Watson mentioned a letter that Aiken had written to Lake, of which he had "just seen a copy," in which Aiken had referred "to the unpleasantness that had unfortunately occurred." Watson then restated his strong feelings about the "original press statements given out, identifying you as sole inventor of the machine" and not giving Lake, Hamilton, and Durfee credit "for their very important and untiring efforts." Watson therefore felt the need of telling Aiken that "it would have been a gracious gesture on your part" and "very much appreciated" by Lake, Hamilton, and Durfee if Aiken's "letter to Mr. Lake had contained an acknowledgment of the sincere regret over such unfortunate and erroneous publicity."[5]

Conclusion

The IBM ASCC (the Harvard Mark I) was the first of a series of four computers associated with Howard Aiken. Mark I and Mark II were electromagnetic, using relays, but Mark III and Mark IV had a variety of electronic components, including vacuum tubes and solid-state transistors. Of the four, Mark I was the most memorable because it produced such reliable results, and could run continuously for 24 hours a day, seven days a week. Thus, although it was very slow compared with any of the electronic machines, it produced a huge output since—unlike its electronic rivals, which had long "downtimes"—it ran continuously. Mark I also had a long life span, serving students and researchers at Harvard for more than a decade. Mark I was also notable for its very existence, proving that complex calculators or computers were feasible and could reliably follow a complex sequence of commands.

---

[4] I have not been able to locate a copy.—I. Bernard Cohen

[5] I have not as yet been able to find the text of the letter from Aiken to Lake.—I. Bernard Cohen

Howard Aiken's place in the history of computers, however, is not to be measured by these four machines, interesting and important as they may have been. He recognized from the start that the computers being planned and constructed would require mathematicians to program them, and he was aware of the shortage of such mathematically trained men and women. To fill this need, Aiken convinced Harvard to establish a course of studies leading to the master's degree, and eventually also the doctorate, in what was to become computer science. Just as Aiken—by the force of his success, abetted by his ability to find outside funding for his programs—achieved tenure and rose to become the first full professor in the new domain of computer science, so he inaugurated at Harvard what appears to have been the first such academic program anywhere in the world. The roster of his students contains the names of many who became well known in this subject, including Gerrit Blaauw, Frederick Brooks, Jr., Kenneth Iverson, and Anthony Oettinger. As other later programs came into being, they drew directly or indirectly on Aiken's experience at Harvard.

Aiken is sometimes held to be reactionary because he was always wary of the concept of the "stored program" and did not incorporate it into any of his later machines. This stance did put him out of step with the main lines of computer architecture in what we may call the post-Aiken era, but it must be kept in mind that there are vast fields of computer application today in which separate identity of program must be maintained, for example, in telephone technology and what is known as ROM ("read-only memory"). In fact, computers without the stored-program feature are often designated today (for instance, by Texas Instruments Corporation) as embodying "Harvard architecture," by which is meant "Aiken architecture."

In assessing Aiken's fundamental contributions to the computer, many computer scientists and historians would stress his bold pioneering achievement of introducing computers into a university environment and inaugurating an academic program in computer science. Others would give primacy of place to the Harvard Mark I (the IBM Automatic Sequence Controlled Calculator), not as a machine that set design standards for an industry, but rather as a first real demonstration that such machines were practicable. It is a fact of historical record that Mark I was the machine that first proved to the world at large that a complex calculating engine could function automatically, performing operations in sequence, and could follow a predetermined program from the entry of the data to the production of the final results. The worldwide publicity attendant on these achievements, aggrandized by the stark fact of its regular and continuous operation to produce reliable and accurate results, convinced any last doubters that large-scale, automatically sequenced calculators were practical and could perform a major role in the technical world. In this sense, it is certainly correct to say that when the switch on Mark I was thrown, the Computer Age began.

Aiken's Calculators[6]

The four large-scale calculators which Aiken developed were:

Automatic Sequence Controlled Calculator (the Harvard Mark I, known within IBM as the ASCC): conceived by Aiken in 1937, designed by IBM engineers and by Aiken, built by IBM as a gift to Harvard. The Mark I was used at Harvard by a US Navy crew that included Grace Murray Hopper and Richard Bloch. Aiken was extremely conservative in his use of well-tested, well-understood elements, using electro-mechanical decimal rotary counters and relays, punched tape for the input of instructions, and tables of functions. Punched cards, as well as modified electric typewriters, were also used for input/output. The major purpose of this calculator was to calculate tables of values.

Mark II: Designed and built at Harvard for the Naval Proving Ground at Dahlgren, Va., for the development of ballistics tables. While this machine used basically the same components as the Mark I, it actually contained two complete identical calculators.

Mark III: Like Mark II, this machine was designed and built at Harvard for Dahlgren. Unique in utilizing separate magnetic drums for data and instructions and some vacuum tube circuitry for such components as registers, this calculator also used magnetic tape for input/output. The tapes were transferred to off-line electric typewriters for hard copy. At first the Mark III seemed to be a highly unreliable machine, but it was discovered that many of the problems were created by closing the machine down each weekend and restarting on Mondays. Once the machine was left up continually, the system became very reliable.

Mark IV: Designed, built, and operated at Harvard for the US Air Force, it incorporated the magnetic drums and tapes of the Mark III

---

[6]Prepared by the 1983 National Computer Conference Pioneer Day Committee.

but added core memory shift registers for working data storage. For the first time this machine contained semiconductor diode circuitry as well as vacuum tubes.

Component	Mark I	Mark II	Mark III	Mark IV
Detailed Design Began	1939	1945	1948	1950
Implementation Complete	1944	1948	1950	1952
Retired from Use	1958	1956	1956	1962
Data Word[7]	23 dd+s	10 dd+s+e	16 dd+s	16 dd+s
Memory-Data-Slow Access[8]	72	96	4,000	4,000
Memory-Data-Fast Access	0	0	360	230
Memory-Instructions	paper tape	paper tape	4,000	10,000
Basic Add Time[9]	300	200	4	1.2
Basic Multiply Time	6,000	1,000	12	12

[7] dd = decimal digit; s = sign; e = exponent in floating-point notation.

[8] Words

[9] Milliseconds (both Add and Multiply)

QUOTATION

"The president of IBM can't tell the president of Harvard what to do."

BIBLIOGRAPHY

Biographical

Berkeley, Edmund C., *Giant Brains or Machines That Think*, John Wiley, New York, 1949.

Chase, George C., "History of Mechanical Computing Machinery," *Ann. Hist. Comp.*, Vol. 2, No. 3, 1980, pp. 198–226.

Cohen, I.B., "Howard Aiken and the Computer," in Nash, Stephen. G., ed., *A History of Scientific Computing*, ACM Press History Series, ACM, New York, 1990, pp. 41–53.

Cohen, I.B., "Howard Aiken, Harvard University, and IBM: Cooperation and Conflict," in Elliott, Clark A., and Margaret W. Rossiter, eds., *Science at Harvard University: Historical Perspectives*, Lehigh Univ. Press, Bethlehem, Pa., 1992, pp. 251–284.

Oettinger, Anthony G., "Retiring Computer Pioneer—Howard Aiken," *Comm. ACM,* Vol. 5, No. 6, 1962, pp. 298–299, 359.

Ritchie, David, *The Computer Pioneers,* Simon and Shuster, New York, 1986.

Salton, Gerard, "Howard Aiken's Children: The Harvard Computation Laboratory and Its Students," *Abacus,* Vol. 1, No. 3, 1984, pp. 28–34.

Slater, Robert, *Portraits in Silicon,* MIT Press, Cambridge, Mass., 1987.

Tropp, Henry S., "Howard Aiken," in Ralson, A., and C.L. Meek, eds., *Encyclopedia of Computer Science and Engineering,* Petrocelli/Charter, New York, 1976, pp. 34–35.

Significant Publications

Aiken, H.H., "Proposed Automatic Calculating Machine," Nov. 1937, reprinted in *IEEE Spectrum,* Aug. 1964, pp. 62–69.

Aiken, H.H., and Grace Murray Hopper, "The Automatic Sequence Controlled Calculator," *Electrical Engineering,* Vol. 65, 1946, pp. 384–391, 449–454, 552–528.

Aiken, H.H., "A Manual of Operation for the Automatic Sequence Controlled Calculator," *Annals of the Computation Laboratory of Harvard University,* Harvard Univ. Press, Cambridge Mass., 1946.

Block, R.M., "Mark I Calculator," *Proc. Symp. Large-Scale Digital Calculating Machinery, 1947, Annals of the Computation Laboratory of Harvard University,* Harvard Univ. Press, Cambridge, Mass., 1948.

Campbell, R.V.D., "Mark II Calculator," *Proc. Symp. Large-Scale Digital Calculating Machinery, 1947, Annals of the Computation Laboratory of Harvard University,* Harvard Univ. Press, Cambridge, Mass, 1947.

SAMUEL N. ALEXANDER

Director of the Standards Eastern Automatic Computer (SEAC) project at the National Bureau of Standards.

Honors and Awards: IEEE Computer Society Pioneer Award, 1980.

BIBLIOGRAPHY

Significant Publications

Alexander, Samuel, "Input and Output Devices for Electronic Digital Calculating Machinery," *Proc. Symp. Large-Scale Digital Calculating Machinery,* Harvard Univ. Press, Cambridge, Mass., 1948, pp. 248–253.

Wegstein, Joseph H., and Samuel N. Alexander, "Programming Scientific Calculators," *Control Engineering,* Vol. 3, May 1956, pp. 89–92.

MUKHAMMAD IBN MUSA AL-KHOWARIZMI

Ninth-century Eastern Persian whose books on astronomy, algebra, and Indian numbers became the origin of European mathematics in the twelfth century. He was the transmitter of the Hindu art of reckoning to the Arabs and thus to Europe, from whose name comes the word "algorithm."

BIBLIOGRAPHY

Biographical

Zemanek, Heinz, "Al-Khorezmi: His Background, His Personality, His Work, and His Influence," *Symp. Algorithms in Modern Mathematics and Computer Science,* Urgench, Uzbek, USSR, Sept. 1979.

Zemanek, Heinz, "Al-Khorezmi Anniversary in Turkestan," *Ann. Hist. Comp.,* Vol. 6, No. 3, July 1984, pp. 314–315.

Gene M. Amdahl

Born November 16, 1922, Flandreau, S.D.; A designer of the IBM System/360, and of the machines that bear his name.

Education: BSEP, South Dakota State University 1948; MS and PhD, theoretical physics, University of Wisconsin 1952.

Professional Experience: project engineer, IBM, 1952 to 1955; Ramo Wooldridge and Aeronutronic, Inc., 1955–1960; IBM, 1960–1970; IBM fellow, 1965; director, Advanced Computing Systems Laboratory, Menlo Park, Calif., IBM, 1965–1970; founded Amdahl Corporation,1970–1980; created Trilogy Systems Corporation, chairman, 1980–present.

Honors and Awards: IEEE Computer Society W. Wallace McDowell Award, 1976; Data Processing Management Association Computer Science Man of the Year, 1976; IEEE Computer Society Pioneer Award, 1980; AFIPS Harry Goode Award, 1983; ACM/IEEE Eckert-Mauchly Award, 1987; member, National Academy of Engineering; fellow, IEEE; distinguished fellow, British Computer Society; Information Processing Hall of Fame, Infomart, Dallas, Texas, 1985.

Although not a computer science graduate, Amdahl designed his first computer as part of his PhD dissertation. Eventually the machine, the Wisconsin Integrally Synchronized Computer (WISC), was built by successive generations of students. Amdahl first worked for IBM as a project engineer from 1952 to 1955. He became a leader in the design of the IBM 704 but resigned in 1955 after having lost the struggle for design control of the Stretch computer.[10] After employment at Ramo Wooldridge and Aeronutronic, Inc., he returned to IBM in 1960 and was successively appointed as IBM fellow and laboratory director.

During his two terms at IBM (1952–1955, 1960–1970), Amdahl was a leader in the design of several computers, most notably the IBM System/360. Although he and project manager Fred Brooks clashed occasionally, they shared strict objectivity, broad knowledge, and persuasive skill. Amdahl's value to the project stemmed from his ability to represent and defend the emerging plan, as well as his technical contributions to it. In 1965 he was named an IBM fellow and was subsequently appointed director of IBM's Advanced Computing Systems Laboratory in Menlo Park, Calif.

He founded the Amdahl Corporation in 1970 but lost control to Japanese investors in 1979. In 1980 he created Trilogy Systems Corporation to design, manufacture, and market large-scale, high-performance computer systems. In 1985 Trilogy acquired ELXSI, Ltd., for its principal computer system entry, and Amdahl became its chair-

---

[10]From Pugh, Emerson W., Lyle R. Johnson, and John H. Palmer, *IBM's 360 and Early 370 Systems*, MIT Press, Cambridge, Mass., 1991.

man. Trilogy Systems Corporation was the world's largest start-up company, having raised $230 million before developing its first product. Dr. Amdahl was cited in 1987 by the Eckert-Mauchly Award Committee for his "outstanding innovations in computer architecture, including pipelining, instruction lookahead, and cache memory."

BIBLIOGRAPHY

Biographical

Amdahl, Gene M., "Recollections of the 701A," *Ann. Hist. Comp.*, Vol. 5, No. 2, Apr. 1983, pp. 213–217.

Slater, Robert, *Portraits in Silicon*, MIT Press, Cambridge, Mass., 1987.

Significant Publications

Amdahl, Gene M., *The Logical Design of an Intermediate Speed Digital Computer*, unpublished PhD dissertation, Univ. of Wisconsin, Madison, Wis., 1952.

ERNEST GALEN ANDREWS

Born January 10, 1898, Topeka, Kan.; died October 13, 1980, Hanover, N.H.; 1940s designer of the relay computers at the Bell Telephone Laboratories; founding member of the Association for Computing Machinery.

Education: BS, mathematics, William Jewell College, Liberty, Mo., 1922.

Professional Experience: Installation Department, Western Electric Company, 1922–1925; Bell Telephone Laboratories, 1925–1959; Sanders Associates, Inc., Nashua N.H., 1959–1969.

Following service aboard the USS Kansas during World War I, Andrews attended William Jewell College in Liberty, Mo., where he received a bachelor's degree in mathematics in 1922.[11] In that same year, he accepted a position with the installation department of the Western

---

[11]From La Porte and Stibitz, 1982.

Electric Company in Kansas City, from which he was transferred to Atlanta and then to New York City.

In 1925, Andrews joined Bell Telephone Laboratories upon its formation out of the engineering department of Western Electric. Here he worked for many years on installation and maintenance requirements in the switching-development organization. In 1941, with the onset of World War II, he was made responsible for the design of radar trainers and the preparation of radar instruction manuals. (Bell Telephone Laboratories had begun work on the development and production of radar in 1937, at the invitation of the US Navy.)

Andrew's involvement with computing machinery began in 1943 and continued through the development and construction of five successive models of early large-scale electromechanical computers. After the war, he worked on the development of automatic message accounting systems for dial-central offices, but the focus of Andrew's activities was on the planning and programming of military systems, first as a member of the military communications department and finally with a study group in the military systems engineering department.

Following his retirement from Bell Telephone Laboratories in June 1959, Andrews joined Sanders Associates, Inc., in Nashua, N.H., where he became manager of preliminary design.

Andrews held several patents and was the author of a number of articles on early Bell Telephone Laboratories computing machinery.

Andrews' principal contributions to early computer technology included his work in the design and construction of the relay computers at Bell Telephone Laboratories and his efforts on behalf of the Association for Computing Machinery. His work on the relay computers started in 1942 with the BTL Models II and III, and continued through all the subsequent models of this series. He cooperated with Samuel B. Williams on the later models and was especially helpful in the design of the duplicate $250,000 copies of the Model IV, used at NASA's Langley Field and at the Army's Aberdeen Proving Ground.

"Andy" was a founding member of ACM and served for several years as an officer and a member of committees in that organization.[12] He wrote several very early articles dealing authoritatively with the history and development of binary computers. Andrew and the group of engineers he supervised contributed many useful concepts and embodiments of those concepts in the development of binary computers. One of these contributions led to a true multiplier for the Model III Computer. The multiplier stored and called out on demand the

---

[12]Contributed by George R. Stibitz.

two-decimal products of all digits of the multiplicand by a digit of the multiplier. The scheme permitted many shortcut methods of calculation. He contributed to the development of the automatic accounting system of the Bell System, where he made use of his experience in the relay computer field.

After two retirements, he was by no means ready to vegetate. He was interested in the mechanism of the heart, and tried unsuccessfully to establish a connection with people working in that field. He retained an interest in developments in that and many other areas of applied science and communications up to the time of his death.

BIBLIOGRAPHY

Biographical

La Porte, Deidre, and George R. Stibitz, "Eloge: E.G. Andrews, 1898–1980," *Ann. Hist. Comp.*, Vol. 4, No. 1, 1982, pp. 4–5.

Significant Publications

Andrews, E.G., and H.W. Bode, "Use of the Relay Digital Computer," reprinted in *Ann. Hist. Comp.*, Vol. 4, No. 1, 1982, pp. 5–13.

Andrews, E.G., "Telephone Switching and the Early Bell Laboratories Computers," reprinted in *Ann. Hist. Comp.*, Vol. 4, No. 1, pp. 14–19.

MORTON MICHAEL ASTRAHAN

Born December 5, 1924, Chicago; died June 2, 1988, Los Gatos, Calif.; instrumental in the development of the I/O interrupt; organizer and first chairman, IRE Professional Group on Electronic Computers (forerunner of the IEEE Computer Society).

Education: BS, Northwestern University, 1945; MS, California Institute of Technology, 1946, PhD, electrical engineering, Northwestern University, 1949.

Professional Experience: joined IBM 1949 and remained with the corporation until his retirement on January 1, 1985.

Honors and Awards: fellow, IEEE, 1969; AFIPS Distinguished Service Award, 1975; Northwestern University Merit Award, 1984; IEEE Centennial Award, 1984.

Astrahan joined IBM on graduation from Northwestern University in 1949 and a year later was involved in the specification and logic design of IBM's 701 computing system (the Defense Calculator), which was also the company's first commercial stored-program binary computer. By 1952 he had complete responsibility for the I/O system development and the prototype testing for the AN/FSQ7 computer at IBM Poughkeepsie. The computer—developed for the SAGE Air Defense System, which was still in use in 1983—was the world's first large-scale special-purpose time-sharing system and the first to use active/stand-by duplexing. He contributed to the concepts of index registers for parallel computers, associative memory, and the I/O interrupt, which led to three patents. He moved to San Jose, Calif. in 1956, where his work included directing research in multiterminal communications systems and multiplexing systems. This work led to the first typewriter style terminal and one of the first text editors. In 1962 he worked at IBM World Trade in Paris, returning after two years to Los Gatos, where he worked on the definition and early development of a computer-aided instruction system in cooperation with Stanford University. In 1969 he worked with Raj Reddy and Arthur Samuel on speech recognition. In 1970 Astrahan turned his hand to database systems (including work on the Data Independent Accessing Model development of SQL), to System R, high-performance optimization, and highly available systems.

Mort Astrahan was deeply involved in the AFIPS Joint Computer Conference organization, serving on the Conference Committee for 34 years commencing in 1952.

BIBLIOGRAPHY

Biographical

Anon., "Morton Michael Astrahan," *Ann. Hist. Comp.,* Vol. 11, No. 1, 1989, p. 49.

Armer, Paul, et al., "Reflections on a Quarter Century: AFIPS Founders," *Ann. Hist. Comp.,* Vol. 8, No. 3, July 1986, pp. 225–256.

Astrahan, M.M., et al., "History of the Design of the SAGE Computer—The AN/FSQ-7," *Ann. Hist. Comp.,* Vol. 5, No. 4, Oct. 1983, pp. 340–349.

Significant Publications

Astrahan, M.M., and N. Rochester, "The Logical Organization of the New IBM Scientific Calculator," *Proc. ACM Nat'l Conf.*, ACM, N.Y., 1952, pp. 79–83.

Astrahan, M.M., et al., "Logical Design of the Digital Computer for the SAGE System," *IBM J. Research and Development*, Vol. 1, 1957, pp. 76–83.

JOHN VINCENT ATANASOFF

Born October 4, 1903, Hamilton N.Y.; inventor of the Atanasoff Berry Computer (ABC) with Clifford Berry, predecessor of the 1942 ENIAC, a serial, binary, electromechanical, digital, special-purpose computer with regenerative memory.

Education: BSEE, University of Florida, 1925; MS, Iowa State College (now University), 1926; PhD, physics, University of Wisconsin, 1930.

Professional Experience: graduate professor at Iowa State College (now University), 1930–1942; US Naval Ordnance Laboratory, 1942–1952; founder, Ordnance Engineering Corp., 1952–1956; vice-president, Atlantic Dir., Aerojet General Corp., 1950–1961.

Honors and Awards: US Navy Distinguished Service Award 1945; Bulgarian Order of Cyril and Methodius, First Class, 1970; doctor of science, University of Florida, 1974; Iowa Inventors Hall of Fame, 1978; doctor of science, Moravian College, 1981; Distinguished Achievement Citation, Alumni Association, Iowa State University, 1983; Foreign Member, Bulgarian Academy of Science, 1983; LittD, Western Maryland College, 1984; Pioneer Medal, IEEE Computer Society, 1984; Appreciation Award, EDUCOM, 1985; Holley Medal, ASME, 1985; DSc (Hon.), University of Wisconsin, 1985; First Annual Coors American Ingenuity Award, Colorado Association of Commerce and Industry, 1986; LHD (Hon)., Mount St. Mary's College, 1990; US Department of Commerce, Medal of Technology, 1990[13]; IEEE Electrical Engineering Milestone, 1990.

Special Honors: Atanasoff Hall, named by Iowa State University; Asteroid 3546—Atanasoff—named by Cal Tech Jet Propulsion Laboratory and Bulgarian Academy.

---

[13]Presented by President George Bush.

"Advent of Electronic Digital Computing"[14]

Introduction

I am writing a historical account of what has been an important episode in my life. During the last half of the 1930s I began and, later with Clifford E. Berry, pursued the subject of digital electronic computing. Included were my conceptions of computing, and the construction both of a prototype and of what I later called the Atanasoff Berry Computer (ABC), to honor the memory of Dr. Berry's extraordinary competence. But my contacts with computing began much earlier.

The year 1913 made an impression on my mind because so much seemed to happen then. My family lived in a new house in Polk County, Florida on the premises of a phosphate mine where my father was an electrical engineer. Early that year, my father decided that his position required him to have a better slide rule than the one he had. Now, my father did not really need that new slide rule. So the new slide rule was left for me, with its book of instructions. That slide rule was my meat. In two weeks or thereabouts, I could solve most simple problems with it.

Can you imagine how a boy of nine-plus, with baseball on his mind, could be transformed by this knowledge? Baseball practice was reduced to zero and a stern study of logarithms was substituted. By the age of ten I became an expert in computing logarithms and many other mathematical and scientific problems.

Early in high school, I decided to study theoretical physics as my life's work. However, at the University of Florida I studied Electrical Engineering, since it was the most theoretical course given.

In September 1925, I started my graduate work in mathematics at Iowa State College (now University) at Ames, Iowa.

In the period between 1925 and 1928, I taught mathematics at Iowa State College, and continued graduate work in mathematics and physics. I received a master's degree in mathematics in 1926 at Iowa State College. In March 1929, I went to the University of Wisconsin to continue my work for the doctorate. I received my PhD in physics in July 1930. My thesis was titled *The Dielectric Constant of Helium*.

This was my first experience in serious computing. Such calculations required many weeks of hard work on a desk calculator such as the Monroe, which was all that was available at the time. I was also impressed that the process of approximating the solution of partial dif-

---

[14]Adapted by J. V. Atanasoff from his original manuscript submitted to *Annals of the History of Computing*, 1983.

ferential equations required a great many calculations, a fact that ultimately motivated my work in automatic computing.

After receiving my doctorate, I returned to Iowa State College where I became assistant professor of Mathematics. There I gave increased attention to the International Business Machines equipment located in the statistics department. While this equipment did not permit the mathematical dexterity of the Monroe, it nevertheless represented the largest calculator of the day.

As the only person in theoretical physics at ISU, I did not have much competition. I was soon made assistant professor of both mathematics and physics and then, not too much later, an associate professor in both departments. At about that time (1934), I commenced to give attention to the formal process of approximating the solution of partial differential equations.

State of the Computing Art

As I came to feel the basic need for more powerful means of computing, I examined, in more detail, the types of apparatus that were available. I soon determined that computers could be divided into two classes, analog and digital.

In analog computers, a number is represented by a physical quantity in the machine as measured by some system of units. A digital computer also requires some entity to represent numbers. Here, however, the representation is not a simple one-to-one relationship, but is determined by a kind of algorithm called the Hindu-Arabic number system. While historically this system used numbers to the base ten, we intend no such restriction, for in theory any whole number greater than unity can be used as the base. My own device and most modern computers use the base two.

It seemed very clear to me that the advantages of the analog approach had been largely explored and found wanting, except in some special cases not requiring relatively high accuracy. For most of the purposes of technology and science, we were left with a digital approach. But to make this fully effective would require a new and original art.

I thought I knew how a computer should work. First, the computer would have to add and subtract, and later, one could expand these operations into multiplication and division. At the time, I wondered if anyone had devised a definition of multiplication that was not based on addition, but the four elementary operations of arithmetic are interrelated and all computing theoreticians have had to go along with that fact. From the start, I was interested in carry-over; it is the crux of the digital method.

What are the characteristics with which the digital numbers are to be represented? In those days I had little precedent as to the architecture of a new digital computer of a larger size, that is, capacity. The only attempt at a machine of sufficient capacity for my purposes was the differential analyzer, an analog device which, as I have said, did not seem promising. In simple computers and even in the tabulators, the medium of representation was always mechanical, often the rotation of a shaft, and I must admit that I was inclined to follow this precept.

Even at this early stage, the principal other medium that occurred to me was an electrical state of a circuit. I had studied electrical engineering and physics, and I had also studied and experimented with electronics, then in its infancy. So it was perhaps natural that my mind turned to this medium in which I had my greatest expertise.

At an early point in my thinking about digital computers, I commenced to think about the effects of a change in the base of the number system. Now I had to visualize how a change in base would affect computing structures. At that time, I had only a very vague idea of a computing machine. I hoped that the nature of the arithmetic for the various bases would indicate which one would be most advantageous for a computer. These thoughts led to a conclusion which has stood the test of time.

In looking over the 1936 art in computing, I had become convinced that a new computer should provide for a much larger retention of data. Almost from the start, I called this "memory." The word seemed natural to me, as I suppose that it did to others, since it is still in use today in a wide field including computers.

I now continue with a quotation from my transcript of testimony which I gave in federal court on 1971 June 15:

"Well, I remember that the winter of 1937 was a desperate one for me because I had this problem and I had outlined my objectives but nothing was happening, and as the winter deepened, my despair grew and I have told you about the kinds of items that were rattling around in my mind and we come to a day in the middle of winter when I went out to the office intending to spend the evening trying to resolve some of these questions and I was in such a mental state that no resolution was possible. I was just unhappy to an extreme degree, and at that time I did something that I had done on such occasions—I don't do it anymore—I went out to my automobile, got in and started driving over the good highways of Iowa at a high rate of speed.

"I remember the pavement was clean and dry, and I was forced to give attention to my driving, and as a consequence of that, I was less nervous, and I drove that way for several hours. Then I sort of became aware of my surroundings. I had, of course, been aware of the road before, but then I became aware of where I was and I had reached the Mississippi River, starting from Ames and was crossing the Mississippi River into Illinois at a place where there are three cities, one of which is Rock Island.

"I drove into Illinois and turned off the good highway into a little road, and went into a roadhouse there which had bright lights. It was extremely cold and I took my overcoat. I had a very heavy coat, and hung it up, and sat down and ordered a drink, and as the delivery of the drink was made, I realized that I was no longer so nervous and my thoughts turned again to computing machines.

"Now, I don't know why my mind worked then when it had not worked previously, but things seemed to be good and cool and quiet. There were not many people in the tavern, and the waitress didn't bother me particularly with repetitious offers of drinks. I would suspect that I drank two drinks perhaps, and then I realized that thoughts were coming good and I had some positive results.

"During this evening in the tavern, I generated within my mind the possibility of the regenerative memory. I called it 'jogging' at that time. I'm thinking about the condensers for memory units, and the fact that the condensers would regenerate their own state, so their state would not change with time. . . . During that same evening, I gained an initial concept of what is called today the 'logic circuits.' That is a non-ratcheting approach to the interaction between two memory units, or, as I called them in those days, 'abaci.'"

During that evening in the Illinois roadhouse, I made four decisions for my computer project.

- I would use electricity and electronics as the media for the computer;
- In spite of custom, I would use base-two numbers (binary) for my computer;
- I would use condensers for memory, but "regenerate" to avoid lapse;
- I would compute by direct logical action, not by enumeration.

I am now amazed and pleased to find that each of my four decisions relates to structures that are in use in modern computers.

It is true that I did not invent the modern dynamic memory but this memory uses capacitors (condensers) for memory, and the refresh cycle directly derived from my jogging or regenerative ideas.

So far, the work on the computer had been done by me in my spare time. Since the trip to Illinois, I had used more than a year working mostly on jogging and logic circuits for adding and subtracting. I now felt much more confident that the project would be a success and I knew that I could not go on alone. So, early in the spring of 1939, I made an application for a grant from the dean of the graduate school. I planned to hire an assistant and to have a small budget for materials and shop work.

In selecting an assistant, I felt that I should choose an electrical engineer, since most students entering graduate work in physics did not have the mechanical or electronic skill. Soon after having these thoughts, I met Dr. Harold Anderson, a professor of electrical engineering, on the sidewalk in the center of the campus and told him of my need. He already knew of my interest in computers, and he answered in a moment, "I have your man—Clifford Berry."

We started actual work at the beginning of the fall quarter of 1939. Our first effort was to try to prove the feasibility of this new method of computing that I had developed using theory only.

The Prototype Computer

Even before the fall quarter had begun, Clifford had studied my plans and we were soon involved in a discussion of how we should proceed. We both agreed that the theoretical aspect of these plans, however necessary it had been, would have to be reduced to practice. Each portion of my design would have to be built, examined and fully tested. In the end, we would compose these parts to form a prototype of a computer to see if the portions would co-act as I had planned. There were parts of the whole that were not fully designed and we would have to devise them and bring them to fruition.

As I have said, I chose condensers (or capacitors) as the element for memory, because a condenser can give a good voltage to actuate a vacuum tube, and because the vacuum tube will give enough voltage to recharge the condenser.

We next had to study how condensers would operate as memory elements, and we soon learned that almost any condenser would work. We selected paper capacitors of about 0.0015 microfarads capacity.

I suppose the reader will have gathered that I was delighted with the concept of jogging. Jogging is reminiscent of the little boy going to the grocery store and reciting, "a dozen eggs, a pound of butter," over and over, hoping to arrive at the store before his memory has failed. Jogging may be employed when a memory element has two states and when they deteriorate over time, we can cause it to pass from one state to the other.

In the 1930s vacuum tubes were the only active element available for electronics. It was hard to get a low-voltage, direct-current source, and so we wished to use alternating current for our tubes. This limited us to heater type tubes. The only objection was that the heater types used much more power for the heat source.

Almost as soon as the prototype was completed, it began to work very well. Our visitors who understood what was going on were surprised to find so much structure giving additions and subtractions that were correct. Of course, our explanation to them had to cover base-two number theory.

There is little doubt that the prototype, which was the first electronic digital computer, was completed near the end of 1939. My memory said November 1939. Much later, during cross examination in court, counsel for defense (Sperry-Rand) showed me material which purported that this was not until early in 1940. In re-cross, material was adduced by counsel for the plaintiff (Honeywell) which showed that the first demonstration was in October 1939.

The prototype was, of course, a relatively crude device. It could just add and subtract the binary equivalents of decimal numbers having up to eight places. Nevertheless, Clifford Berry and I regarded this machine as a great success. It settled many doubts about how an electronic computer should be built:

- The device was digital, not analog like the differential analyzer;
- While the clock system was mechanical, all computing was electronic;
- For the first time, vacuum tubes were used in computing;
- The very advantageous base-2 number system was first used;
- Logic systems were first employed in computing;
- All computation was done in a serial manner;
- Capacitors (or condensers) were used as memory elements;
- A rotating drum memory contained the capacitors;
- What I called jogging (which others now call regeneration or refreshing) was first used in computation.

Clifford E. Berry and I were very pleased to have access to a method of computing with such power. Once our prototype had proved successful, we both knew that we could build a machine that could do almost anything in the way of computation.

During the early years, our computer had a title relating to the solution of large systems of linear algebraic equations. About 1968, I became aware that it would be discussed at length, and, since Berry was dead, I wanted a title that would honor him for his extraordinary ability and effort in developing this computer. Accordingly, I renamed it the Atanasoff Berry Computer . . . the ABC.

In order to get started fast, I decided to take a chance and estimate the size of the machine. I knew a few dimensions of the various parts that were to go into it. I was repeatedly trying to estimate the number of vacuum tubes I would need for this digital electronic computer. Arbitrarily, we had decided that it would operate over 30 fields, and so would require 30 add-subtract mechanisms. Without very much figuring, I made an estimate of the size of the total machine and arrived at roughly the size of an office desk. So, I ordered a lot of angle iron for the frame. People saw these irons at the back entrance of the physics building and wondered about them. I heard someone replying to a question, "Oh, Atanasoff thinks he is going to make a computer out of those angle irons."

At that time, the largest digital computer was the IBM tabulator. The one we had at Iowa State College could tabulate and sum 40 columns of the 80 that the punched card provided. But we knew there existed machines which could tabulate and add the full 80 columns, divided into ten fields of eight columns each. . . . We planned a machine of 3000 fields of memory, which would in fact calculate at a speed of about 30 times that of the largest IBM tabulator.

When one starts a new and strange project, one must expect that it will be in financial trouble from the start. I had received some aid from Iowa State College, and expected and did receive more from time to time. However, I knew that I should seek some other source for the funds necessary to complete the computer project.

In my requests to Iowa State College, I had used a two-page write-up, but in asking others for help, I needed something better. During the spring and summer of 1940, I used my spare time to write not only what we had done, but also what we proposed to do during the remainder of the project. This paper, finished on August 14, 1940, has been reprinted by Brian Randell in his book *The Origins of Digital Computers* (1982).

I felt that the work we were doing on computers should be patented, and so, at an early stage, I had investigated the subject of patents at Iowa State College. It seemed clear to me that there was no firm policy on the subject. I learned that the Iowa State College Research Foundation (ISCRF), whom I consulted concerning a patent application, did not regard their own patent counsel as adequate for this task. I was referred to Mr. Richard R. Trexler, a Chicago patent attorney.

When ultimately ISCRF and I entered into a contract for the proceeds of a patent on my invention, they agreed, in principle at least, to use Mr. Trexler as our patent attorney.

No official pronouncement was made on the terms of a contract, or even on the necessity for a contract, until Dr. Friley, president of Iowa State College, received the letter of March 24, 1941, from President Howard Poillon of Research Corporation granting $5330, a considerable amount of money in those days. Then, from a seeming absence of any policy, the situation changed drastically and Iowa State College policy was suddenly firm. I am still not exactly sure how it all came about, but I have since seen a letter from Dr. Friley to ISCRF saying that Iowa State College should hold onto rights to the patent on my invention. I very soon heard from ISCRF. The first words came to me verbally; in substance, I would not be allowed to use the grant until I signed a patent contract with ISCRF. I signed the contract in July 1941.

At the time I first contacted Trexler (August 6, 1940), I was finishing my manuscript on "Computing Machines for the Solution of Large Systems of Linear Algebraic Equations," and I supplied him with a copy. This did not satisfy Mr. Trexler, so with some help from me, he drew up a rather extensive specification covering the details of the patent, and together we directed a draftsman in making the patent drawings.

At this state in my scientific career, I usually attended the winter meeting of the American Association for the Advancement of Science, which in those days was scheduled between Christmas and New Year's. So, late in 1940, I turned my car eastward with my family and after other activities, on December 26 I attended the meetings in Philadelphia for three days. My interests were rather wide, and I frequently moved between the sessions of the various societies which would meet with the AAAS. There were, of course, no papers on computing in the modern sense, but I was interested in calculation in general. As a consequence of this, I visited what I clearly remember was a more than ordinarily dusty, chalk-filled classroom assigned to Dr. John W. Mauchly for giving a paper on an application of a harmonic analyzer, which he had constructed, to some weather phenomena. After the paper was over, I advanced to the podium.

He was very enthusiastic about his analog electrical system for doing Fourier transforms, which had been the subject of his paper. We talked for most of an hour in this first meeting. In the end, we shook hands and promised to write.

Dr. Mauchly made good on his promise to write. My files do not have his first letter, but they do have a letter from me dated January

23, 1941, answering him and inviting him to come and see me. Mauchly was well pleased with my invitation and there were a succession of letters between us. My memory is that he arrived about dark on Saturday, June 14, 1941, accompanied by his young son Jim.

My memory is very clear that he first saw the computer with his son and my family. There was no one else around, this being Sunday, and this checks with his letter saying he might spend Friday at Iowa City. The computer was covered with a sheet to prevent dust from settling on it, but I quickly removed this obstruction and he saw the ABC for the first time. The machine was in process of construction at this point.

I believe that Dr. Mauchly and his son left Ames early on Friday, June 20. Meanwhile, two-thirds of our waking time was spent talking about computers. He read my manuscript and would have liked to take a copy home with him, but I did not allow him to do that. He read all parts of this description of our machine and discussed it with me. Sam Legvold was a graduate student of mine working on another of my projects in a room next to the computer. Much later, he told the federal court in Minneapolis of Mauchly having his coat off and working with the machine, when I was otherwise employed. Mauchly took the manuscript to my home with him, and he took notes on white bond paper which I gave him, at his request.

Mauchly and I had a very cordial relationship while he was at Ames, and after he left we still corresponded, though at less frequent intervals. On September 30, 1941, he wrote a letter to me which contained the question, ". . . would the way be open for us to build an 'Atanasoff Calculator' (à la Bush analyzer) here?" In my answer of October 7, I had to tell him:

> Our attorney has emphasized the need of being careful about the dissemination of information about our device, but it does require that we refrain from making public any details for the time being. It is, as a matter of fact, preventing me from making an invited address to the American Statistical Association.

On December 7, 1941, the Japanese bombed Pearl Harbor and the US was involved in that terrible holocaust. The future of everyone had to be adjusted to meet this emergency. Soon it became evident that Berry would be drafted unless he were engaged in a war-related project. Our computer work did not have such a preferred status, and although I did what I could to get him deferred, the draft board had never heard of our project. As a result, Mr. Berry started to look for a position for which he could be deferred. He was so able that he quickly found a suitable position with Consolidated Engineering Corporation of Pasadena, Calif. He married my secretary, Jean Reed, and on July 1, 1942, he left Iowa State College.

During the spring and summer of 1942, I continued to work with the ISCRF and Mr. Trexler to get the patent under way. There always seemed to be some reason why it should be put off, however, and put off it was. The patent was never applied by Iowa State College, probably due to short-term financial considerations.

US Naval Ordnance Laboratory (1942–1948)

I began work at the Naval Ordnance Laboratory (NOL) late in September. The NOL was the research laboratory of the Bureau of Ordnance. It had responsibility for depth charges, and mines and various other projects, as assigned. Historically, it had been located in the US Naval Gun Factory, beside the Anacostia River, and there it remained until the war was over and a new laboratory was constructed north of Washington, D.C., at White Oak, Md.

Although acoustics had not been one of my particular fields of interest, I was a theoretical physicist, and so I was put in charge of acoustical testing of mines for the Navy Ordnance Laboratory.

My first objective was to get acquainted with the subject of acoustics. My next objective was to acquire a staff. I was able to get the services of David Beecher. He had not been my major graduate student (at Iowa State College) but I knew him well, and he had on occasion, worked on the ABC. Later I was able to get both Dr. Herman Ellingson, who was on the staff of Luther College in Decorah, Iowa, and my former major student, Sam Legvold. The rest of my staff came from various other sources.

Although I do not have the date, I think that early in 1943 I was seated at my desk in my noisy, dirty space in Bld. 184, when I felt someone approaching me from the right. It was Dr. Mauchly. By some means, he had become attached to the NOL, his security clearance was satisfactory, and somehow he attached himself to my staff. The exact basis of his employment with NOL was never known to us. I introduced him to my superior, but he had no more knowledge than I. I did not know how much money he received for his consulting services and I was too busy to find out. He said he was still employed by the Moore School, but he came back once or twice a week. At first, I planned various things for him to do; later, I attached him to Dr. Ellingson's statistical group. I do believe, however, that every time he came in, he stopped by to see me briefly.

One such occasion, he told me that he and J. Presper Eckert had devised a new way to compute. I remember that I was very busy, but I asked him to tell me about it. His reply was simple: "I cannot, the subject is classified."

The visits of Mauchly continued sporadically until the end of the war. On August 30, 1944, both Mauchly and Eckert visited me in the Gun Factory. I believe that at least Eckert did not have proper security clearance for the area and so they were escorted. They had arranged through the Army and the Navy to obtain my services on quartz transducers. Although I agreed to help them, they filled their needs elsewhere. This was the only time I ever saw J. Presper Eckert.

In a period from September, 1942 until the war ended, I was in Ames every few months, and I took the time to see some member of Iowa State College and discuss the prospect of filing a patent application on our work on computers. At various times, I also wrote to Counselor Trexler and to the ISCRF. During the first year or two, I really believed that a patent would be applied for. Much later, Mr. Trexler said he had never been authorized to proceed.

I have in my files an Iowa State College interoffice memo without signature, written, I believe, by Dean R. E. Buchanan, of Iowa State College, and it is concerned with the patent situation. The date was June 26, 1948, but I did not see it for perhaps twenty years. The author speaks of seeing me at the NOL, and I do remember seeing Dean Buchanan at about that time. He speaks of "Atanasoff's saying that the computer was probably largely obsolete." This was clearly incorrect; I spoke, rather, of the need for moving rapidly if anything was to be salvaged from our work. The memo gives no explanation of the delay in executing the patent contract between Iowa State College and me.

About September 1945, while I was attending a staff meeting at the Gun Factory, my superior, Dr. L. H. Rumbaugh, told us that the Bureau of Ordnance was going to build a computer. Of course the research department would do the work. It was over three years since I had left computing at Iowa State College, and I had not spoken of this part of my history; it was known, however, and so I was selected to head the project.

Dr. John Mauchly came to see us for the first time in several months. In the last years of his life, he claimed that on this occasion I asked him how to build a computer. I do not remember doing this and do not believe I did; in any case, I do remember that as always we talked of many things but I heard nothing from him about computers.

The computer project seemed to be doing very well except for understaffing, but in a short time my superior and I were called to the office of the chief of research of the Bureau of Ordnance and we were told that the Bureau wished to discontinue this project. As is usual in such cases, no basic reason was given. After the conclusion of the computer project, Dr. John Mauchly no longer came to the NOL and I saw him again only once, at a much later date, when he came to my house with Laurence B. Dodds, Counsel for Sperry-Rand.

The Ordnance Engineering Corporation (1952–1961)

Early in 1952, I was thinking of the types of experience I had encountered. I was 48 years old and I knew that if I wanted to be involved in private enterprise, the time had come; one of my friends, in fact, had told me that I was already too old. However, with a few firm friends, I incorporated The Ordnance Engineering Corporation (TOEC) in the state of Maryland.

During the first years of this corporation, we rented space in Rockville, Md. On June 15, 1954, we received a visit from Mr. A.J. Etienne, who was a patent attorney for International Business Machines Corporation. As soon as I learned that we were going to discuss patents, I called David Beecher, our vice president, into the conference. Mr. Etienne announced his purpose by saying in substance, "If you will help us, we will break the Mauchly-Eckert computer patent; it was derived from you."

I hesitated to reply to Mr. Etienne. I was looking back over the years that had passed since Mauchly had told me (in 1943) that he and Eckert had invented a "new method of computing, different from yours," and I had believed him. This was the first substantial item to the contrary that I had encountered. I did not know of the patent to which Mr. Etienne was referring, that is, the Regenerative Memory patent 2,629,827, issued the previous year (1953). (The ENIAC patent, applied for in 1947, was not issued until 1964.)

I remember wondering if Etienne was correct.

In 1956, we sold the corporation to Aerojet General Corporation, with principal offices in Azusa, Calif. After our incorporation into Aerojet General (AGC), we were called the Atlantic Division. In 1959, I was made vice president of AGC and managed the Atlantic Division.

As the US changed to peace conditions after the Korean War, I used my experience in computing to shift the activity of the Atlantic Division toward the invention and manufacture of automatic equipment for parcel handling and sorting. By this time, I had found being a "corporation man" not to my liking. Accordingly, I resigned as vice president of Aerojet General Corporation early in 1961.

During these years, I was well aware of the growing interest in computing. Even before Mr. Etienne's visit, I knew that certain companies were making inquiries of anyone skilled in the art, including Dr. Clifford E. Berry and myself.

From time to time during the twenty-plus years that had elapsed after Berry had left Ames, I visited Clifford and Jean in their home in Altadena. Nearly every time that my business called me to California, I took an evening to spend with them and their family. During, say, the first two-thirds of this period, I was told of his interest in and success with his work, and of his rapid advancement with his company. I do not know exactly when this picture changed; perhaps by 1960, though, Clifford, while still excited with his work, was less satisfied with the position he held with his company. I also noticed a slight cynicism in his general attitude, which I took to be a natural consequence of aging.

Late in 1963, I was overwhelmed to get a letter from Jean Berry, saying that Clifford had resigned his position, taken a place with a company in Long Island, and had died one night at his apartment.

In late 1967, still feeling unhappy over his death, I made a personal investigation of it. I located his apartment and talked with the man who had first found him. I also visited the police of the county, since his death was not natural; he had been found in bed with a plastic sack over his head but with his bedclothes smoothly over his arms, which were by his sides. An autopsy revealed that his brain plasma had 0.12% alcohol content, which would have permitted him to drive a car in some jurisdictions. He had been taking dilantin because of recent epilepsy, and so his blood and brain were carefully examined for this and other drugs; none was found. Suicide, said the authorities.

Preliminaries of Litigation
On April 26, 1967, I was visited by Mr. Allen Kirkpatrick, a patent attorney of Washington, who represented Control Data Corporation (CDC). He had learned of me by reading a book, *Electronic Digital Systems,* by R. K. Richards. Mr. Richards had seen our computer with Clifford Berry. I soon was told that Sperry-Rand Corporation was suing CDC, and was given a quick summary of the issues. Later, Mr. Kirkpatrick furnished me copies of the patents involved, and suggested that I scan their claims to find any that were developed in my own work.

During his April visit, Mr. Kirkpatrick also told me that Sperry-Rand was going to sue Honeywell (my notes say that the Honeywell suit was begun on May 26, 1967). More specifically, Honeywell was to be sued by Illinois Scientific Developments, Inc. (ISD), a subsidiary of Sperry-Rand. Kirkpatrick gave me some information on the Honeywell suit as well. At about this time, I also was contacted by Henry Hanson,

D. Dennis Allegretti, Charles G. Call, patent attorneys, and Henry Halladay, trial attorney, all of whom represented Honeywell in that case. I agreed to do consulting work for both CDC and Honeywell.

Then, not long after Mr. Kirkpatrick came to see me, I was approached by attorneys George Eltgroth, Norman Fulmer, and H. Mial Dustin of General Electric. Fulmer had been at Iowa State College and had actually worked on the ABC. When these men visited me, I had partially read the ENIAC patent and I knew that certain claims were derived from my work.

Law is not my specialty, although I had spent some 2000 hours studying patent law over the years, and I append the following from hearsay. Sperry-Rand, having acquired certain patents from Mauchly and J. Presper Eckert, in particular the ENIAC patent 3,120,606 and the Regenerative Memory patent 2,629,827, felt that they had a basic patent control of the computing machine field, and sought to levy royalties on those companies in violation of the claims of their patents. I have heard these royalties were estimated at one billion dollars, all told.

To begin this legal process, Sperry-Rand chose to sue CDC over the Memory patent and Honeywell over the ENIAC patent, since both CDC and Honeywell had resisted paying royalties; Honeywell counter-sued for anti-trust violation and became the plaintiff in a combined ENIAC suit.

The Memory patent had been applied for in 1947 and was issued in 1953. The ENIAC patent had been applied for in 1947 and was issued in 1964. For some legal reasons and/or the desire of judges, the suit of Sperry-Rand *vs.* CDC was to be held in Baltimore and the suit of Honeywell *vs.* Sperry-Rand was planned for Minneapolis.

It was soon clear to everyone that these lawsuits would become monumental in computing machine history and would take some years before coming to trial.

After learning from the attorneys of Honeywell and CDC how seriously they regarded the litigation, I made a careful search of my papers. I had just moved into a new house and had a collection of boxes which had not been opened for many years. Some of these had been with me and some had been in storage. In two of these boxes, I found my files for the computing machine. These represented hundreds of items which were later used in the litigation.

I was interested, but slightly amused, that I had found myself in the mesh of the federal court system of our nation. I have always been intrigued by the law and our patent system, but jurisprudence is far removed from the fields in which I have labored. Watching these two cases unfold in our federal courts gave me a little deeper feeling of how man gets along with man.

Formal Litigation
We use the term "formal litigation" for the two processes, deposition and trial, by which evidence is produced for the judge (or jury) to use in reaching a verdict. This part of litigation is the major part; in important cases, the records become voluminous. In the matter of computer litigation being considered here, there were only two cases at that time, the Memory case and the ENIAC case; even so, the legal documents numbered in the thousands.

In the early years while the trials were pending, there were many depositions, including those of the principal witnesses and of many other witnesses who would not attend the trial. I was deposed once for each of the two trials. While my first deposition, on the Memory case, was rather short, the second, on the ENIAC case, lasted approximately two weeks, beginning on November 11, 1968. In both cases, Dodds was counsel for Sperry-Rand.

Among the witnesses deposed (of personal interest to me) were myself, both trials; Mauchly, both trials; J. Presper Eckert, both trials; Lura Meeks Atanasoff, both trials; and Sam Legvold, both trials; as well as many other people. Clifford Berry was not alive at the time of the deposition, but in a way a letter he wrote to R.K. Richards[14] on March 22, 1963, quoted again and again in the trial, served as a statement by him of the situation when Mauchly came to Ames.

The deposition of Dr. John W. Mauchly October 11, 12, 13, 1967, was taken on behalf of the defendant, CDC, in the suit by Sperry-Rand on the so-called Memory patent 2,629,827 and certain other patents.

Mauchly spoke of his visit to see our machine. He spoke of being cordially received, but hinted that no one was willing to tell him all about the machine. He claimed that nothing worked except the motor. There was no demonstration of the action of the machine, he asserted.

He said he had no time with the machine: perhaps half-an-hour. Later: perhaps 1½ hours.

He saw one cylinder of condensers, he said. He learned that memory was retained by the use of regeneration, but said he was not told how the regeneration worked.

Both Sam Legvold (a former student and employee) and myself, on deposition and in trial testimony, stated under oath (and Berry in his 1963 letter to Richards corroborated), that when Mauchly visited the computer laboratory at Ames, he was given the full details of the project and he was given much more than anyone else; that he was given the complete current operational test of the computer; that he

---

[14]See Biography of Clifford Berry, p. 89.

spent a length of time with the machine in excess of 16 hours, took his coat off to work on the machine in his shirtsleeves and held certain parts of the machine in his hands; and that he saw our current memorandum (August 1940) on the machine and took notes.

Honeywell versus Sperry-Rand

This trial was held in the federal court at Minneapolis, with Judge Earl R. Larson presiding. It began June 1, 1971. Knowing that I would be an early witness, I went to Minneapolis on June 7. For the moment, I spent my time listening to the court testimony and having private briefings by counsel for Honeywell.

This being my first testimony in a federal court, I took it very seriously. The total record associated with my presence on the witness stand was 1,338 pages long. Of this, the major portion was describing the computer; one of the last parts related to the period when Mauchly was working for me at the NOL, and I have covered that in my historical summary of the case.

It was late on Friday, June 25, 1971, and I was through testifying, after nine days on the witness stand. I took time to say good-bye to some of the staff, including the court reporters, who had stood by and prepared good copy in spite of technical words and low tones.

Then I looked over at the table for Sperry-Rand and there was (Counselor) Mr. Ferrill, alone, picking up some papers. I do not want to be lacking in manners, and so I advanced with my hand extended to say good-bye to him. I find it hard to describe what happened for the next few seconds; I felt that I was looked over in some minute detail. In the end, though, he reluctantly took my hand. He did not look happy; perhaps he knew better than I of the effects of my testimony.

The trial in the ENIAC case ended on March 13, 1972; it had taken 135 days or parts of days. A total of 77 witnesses were heard. The total trial transcript was 20,667 pages. After the trial ended, Judge Larson took some time to reach his decision, which was finally issued on October 19, 1973. Of course, this was a decision that should have received major press coverage; the press, however, was occupied with other matters, because October 20 was the date of the Saturday Night Massacre of Watergate fame.

The decision itself comprised 248 pages of legal paper, with an appendix of 60-plus pages. The judge found 17 specific claims on the ENIAC patent invalid on a variety of grounds, including two claims taken to be representative of the subject matter derived from me by Mauchly and Eckert. He found the entire patent invalid on three grounds unrelated to actual inventorship: public use, sales, and published disclosure, all dated more than one year prior to the ENIAC patent filing date of June 26, 1947. Of greater significance to me is the fact that he also found the entire patent invalid on the ground of derivation from my prior electronic digital computer. I quote relevant passages from Judge Larson's decision:

> "The subject matter of one or more claims of the ENIAC was derived from Atanasoff, and the invention claimed in the ENIAC was derived from Atanasoff."
>
> "Eckert and Mauchly did not themselves first invent the automatic electronic digital computer, but instead derived that subject matter from one Dr. John Vincent Atanasoff."
>
> "Between 1937 and 1942, Atanasoff, then a professor of physics and mathematics at Iowa State College, Ames, Iowa, developed and built an automatic electronic digital computer for solving large systems of simultaneous linear algebraic equations."
>
> "This breadboard model machine, constructed with the assistance of a graduate student, Clifford Berry, permitted the various components of the machine to be tested under actual operating conditions."
>
> "The discussions Mauchly had with both Atanasoff and Berry while at Ames were free and open and no significant information concerning the machine's theory, design, construction, use or operation was withheld."
>
> "Prior to his visit to Ames, Iowa, Mauchly had been broadly interested in electrical analog calculating devices, but had not conceived an automatic electronic digital computer."
>
> "Eckert and Mauchly did not themselves first invent 'the automatic electronic digital computer,' which Sperry-Rand and ISD contend to be the subject matter of the ENIAC patent, but instead derived that broad subject matter from Dr. John V. Atanasoff, and the ENIAC patent is thereby invalid."

After thus spelling out the conduct of Mauchly and Eckert in regard to me and my work, Judge Larson presented the other side of the picture, including a lack of action by me, and found Honeywell not entitled to antitrust damages for willful and intentional fraud on the Patent office.

In addition to his findings on the derivation of the ENIAC from me, Judge Larson now ruled that the Regenerative Memory Patent No. 2,629,827 at issue in the CDC case in Baltimore, was derived from me.

Disposition of the Two Cases

Everyone expected that Judge Larson's decision would be appealed, but rather quickly it was settled by the payment of money and an agreement between the parties that each would support the judge's decision of 1973. I have been told that Sperry-Rand paid $3,500,000, sufficient to reimburse Honeywell for the cost of the trial. Thus ended this important case.

As to the Computer Memory case in Baltimore, I acted as a witness in it after the ENIAC trial was over. The trial in that case was active for only a few days; then it was abandoned from lack of interest of principals or counsel. In 1981, nine years later, some important judge insisted that the case be settled, and so it too was settled by a contractual agreement, this time between CDC and Sperry-Rand. I was told that a payment of money was made here also, by Sperry-Rand, but the amount and other terms were not disclosed. The matter was moot, because the patent had expired.

BIBLIOGRAPHY

Biographical

Atanasoff, John V., "Advent of Electronic Digital Computing," *Ann. Hist. Comp.*, Vol. 6, No. 3, 1984, pp. 229–282.

Burks, Alice R., and Arthur W. Burks, *The First Electronic Computer: The Atanasoff Story*, University of Michigan Press, Ann Arbor, Mich., 1988.

Burks, Arthur W., and Alice R. Burks, "The ENIAC: First General Purpose Electronic Computer," *Ann. Hist. Comp.*, Vol. 3, No. 4, 1981, pp. 310–399.

Finerman, A., ed., "The Origins of Modern Computing," *Comp. Revs.*, Sept. 1990, pp. 449–481.

Larson, E.R., *Findings of Fact, Conclusions of Law and Order for Judgment*, File No. 4-67 Civ. 138, Honeywell Inc. *vs.* Sperry-Rand Corporation and Illinois Scientific Developments, Inc., US District Court, District of Minnesota, Fourth Division, Oct. 19, 1973.

Mauchly, John W., "Amending the ENIAC Story," *Datamation*, Vol. 25, No. 11, 1979, pp. 217–219.

Mollenhoff, Clark R., "Atanasoff, John Vincent" in Ralston, Anthony, and Edwin D. Reilly, Jr., *Encyclopedia of Computer Science and Engineering*, Van Nostrand Reinhold Co., New York, 1983.

Mollenhoff, Clark R., *Atanasoff: The Forgotten Father of the Computer*, Iowa State Univ. Press, Ames, Iowa, 1988.

Ritchie, David, *The Computer Pioneers*, Simon and Shuster, New York, 1986, Chapter 6.

Slater, Robert, *Portraits in Silicon*, MIT Press, Cambridge, Mass., 1987, Chapter 6.

Significant Publications

Atanasoff, John V., "Computing Machine for the Solution of Large Scale Systems of Linear Algebraic Equations," reprinted in Randell, Brian, *Origins of Digital Computers: Selected Papers,* Springer-Verlag, Berlin and Heidelberg, 1982, pp. 315–336.

WILLIAM ATCHISON

Born April 7, 1918, Smithfield, Ky.; computer science educator who was a major contributor to, and influence on the development of, "Curriculum 68," which in turn set the standards for computer science curricula throughout the US.

Education: BA, mathematics and chemistry, Georgetown College, Kentucky, 1938; MA, mathematics, University of Kentucky, 1940; PhD, mathematics, University of Illinois, 1943; post-doctoral studies, mathematics, Harvard University, 1950–1951.

Professional Experience: laboratory assistant, Physics Laboratory, Georgetown College, 1936–1938; assistant, mathematics, University of Kentucky, 1939–1940; University of Illinois: teaching assistant and instructor, mathematics, 1940–1944, instructor and assistant professor, mathematics, 1946–1955; Georgia Institute of Technology: research associate professor, 1955–1963, research professor, mathematics, 1963–1966, head, programming and coding group, Rich Electronic Computer Center, 1956–1957, chief, Rich Electronic Computer Center, 1957–1966, acting director, School of Information Science, 1963–1964, professor, Information Science, 1963–1966; University of Maryland: director, Computer Science Center, 1966–1973, acting chairman, Department of Computer Science, 1973–1974, professor, computer science, 1966–1988, professor emeritus, 1988–present; senior computer scientist, National Institute of Education, 1974–1975.

Honors and Awards: ACM Distinguished Service Award, 1973; Chester Morrill Memorial Award, Chesapeake Division, Association for Systems Management, 1975; Special Award, IFIP WG 3.1, 1974; First ACM SIGCSE[15] Award for

---

[15]Special Interest Group on Computer Science Education.

Outstanding Contributions to Computer Science education, 1981; Distinguished Alumni Award, Georgetown College, 1982; honorary member, IFIP WG 3.1, 1992.

Atchison's principal contributions to the field of computer science were in the areas of computer science education and curriculum. He was chair of the Association for Computing Machinery Curriculum Committee on Computer Science (C^3S), which produced "Curriculum 68" [Atchison et al. 1968] and its predecessor, "An Undergraduate Program in Computer Science," published in 1965. Curriculum 68 served as the basis for most undergraduate programs in the US as well as for computer science programs in many overseas countries. Atchison made many presentations on Curriculum 68 both in the US and abroad. He wrote "The Development of Computer Science Education" for Vol. 24 (1985) of the series entitled *Advances in Computers.*

Atchison was very active in several professional societies including ACM, American Federation of Information-Processing Societies (AFIPS), the National Council of Teachers of Mathematics, and EDUCOM, from 1956 until his retirement in 1988. He was particularly interested in promoting computer education in secondary and primary schools, as well as in colleges. He was also interested in helping developing nations enhance their computer education efforts.

He served as a member of the AFIPS Education Committee, serving as chair for several years. He was the AFIPS representative to the International Federation for Information Processing (IFIP) Education Committee, serving as vice-chair of the Education Committee (TCh-3), and chair of the Secondary Education Working Group (WG 3.1). Through this medium he organized three international working conferences on the use of computers in secondary education. While the representative of the University of Maryland to EDUCOM, Atchison was elected to serve as chair of the Interuniversity Communication Council for the 1972–73 period.

Atchison's computer experience started on the ILLIAC at the Univ. of Illinois in 1951. He programmed the ILLIAC to do random walks in simulation of long chain rubber modules; several papers, written jointly with two physical chemists, resulted from this work.

Atchison spent two years in the US Navy (1944–1946), serving as Educational Services Officer on the island of Guam. While there, he and his staff ran 22 college courses for the GIs about to return home from service.

BIBLIOGRAPHY

Biographical

William Atchison is listed in the following biographical books: *American Men of Science; Who's Who in America; Who's Who in the East; Who's Who in Computer Education and Research; Personalities of the South; Who's Who in Computers and Data Processing; Who's Who in American Education; The Blue Book, Leaders of the English Speaking World; Dictionary of International Biography; Business Leaders of Maryland.*

Significant Publications

Atchison, William F., et al., "Recommendations for Academic Programs in Computer Science," *Comm. ACM*, Vol. 12, No. 3, 1968.

Atchison, William F., "Computer Science as a New Discipline," *Proc. Inaugural Conf. on Computing, Statistics, and Scientific Research*, Cairo University, Cairo, Egypt, 1969.

Atchison, William F., "The Development of Computer Science Education," in *Advances in Computers*, Academic Press, New York, 1985, pp. 319–377.

ISAAC L. AUERBACH

Born October 9, 1921, Philadelphia, Pa.; died December 24, 1992, Narberth, Pa.; first president and founder of the International Federation for Information Processing (IFIP).

Education: BSEE, Drexel University, 1943; MS, applied physics, Harvard University, 1947.

Professional Experience: research engineer, Univac Division, Sperry-Rand Corp., 1947–1949; manager, Defense Space and Special Products Division, Burroughs Corp., 1949–1957; president, Auerbach Associates, Inc., 1957–1976; president, Auerbach Publishers Inc., 1960–1981, chairman, 1981–1986.

Honors and Awards: National Academy of Engineering; president, IFIP, 1960–1965; fellow, IEEE; fellow, AAAS; distinguished fellow, British Computer Society; DEng (Hon.), Drexel University.

Isaac Auerbach was a member of the original team for the design of the BINAC and Univac I in the late 1940s. He directed the development of the first transistorized guidance computer used in the US Space Program. He developed an extraordinarily reliable magnetic core encryption/decryption communication system. He founded many companies in the computer field, including Auerbach Associates, the first computer consulting company, which grew into a multinational organization responsible for the design of command and control systems for the Pacific and Indian Oceans; and Auerbach Publishers, a leading source of electronic data processing and management information services. He was the biographer of several IFIP and AFIPS personalities—Victor Glushkov, Niels Ivar Bech, Dov Chevion, and Harry Goode. In 1994 IFIP created a new service award in his name.

QUOTATION:

"I am not a great writer, although a decent, innovative, and creative entrepreneur, and a competent editor."

BIBLIOGRAPHY

Biographical

Armer, Paul, et al., "Reflections on a Quarter Century: AFIPS Founders," *Ann. Hist. Comp.*, Vol. 8, No. 3, July 1986, pp. 225–256.

Auerbach, Isaac L., "The Start of IFIP—Personal Recollections," *Ann. Hist. Comp.*, Vol. 8, No. 2, 1986, pp. 180–192.

Significant Publications

Auerbach, Isaac L., J.P. Eckert, R.F. Shaw, and E.B. Shepperd, "Mercury Delay Line Memory Using a Pulse Rate of Several Megacycles," *Proc. IRE*, Vol. 37, No. 8, Aug. 1949, pp. 855–861.

Auerbach, Isaac L., and J.O. Paivinen, "Design of Triode Flip-Flops for Long-Term Stability," *IRE Trans. Elec. Comp. PGEC*, Vol. 2, No. 2, June 1953, pp. 14–26.

Auerbach, Isaac L., "Magnetic Elements in Arithmetic and Control Circuits," *AIEE Winter General Meeting*, AIEE, New York City, Feb. 3, 1955.

Auerbach, Isaac L., "Systems Engineering," *IRE WESTCON Convention Record*, Vol. 1, No. 10, Aug. 1957, pp. 62–67.

Auerbach, Isaac L., "Magnetic Core Circuits for Digital Applications," *Automatic Control,* Vol. 11, No. 2, Aug. 1959, pp. 48–55.

Auerbach, Isaac L., "European Electronic Data Processing: A Report on the Industry and the State of the Art," *Proc. IRE,* Vol. 49, No. 1, Jan. 1961, pp. 330–348.

Auerbach, Isaac L., "Need for an Information Systems Theory," *The Skyline of Information Processing, Proc. 10th Anniv. Celebration of the Int'l Fed. Information Processing,* Amsterdam, The Netherlands, 1970.

CHARLES BABBAGE

Born December 26, 1791, in Teignmouth, Devonshire, UK; died 1871, London; known to some as the "Father of Computing" for his contributions to the basic design of the computer through his Analytical Engine. His previous Difference Engine was a special purpose device intended for the production of tables.

While he did produce prototypes of portions of the Difference Engine, it was left to Georg and Edvard Schuetz to construct the first working devices to the same design, which were successful in limited applications.

Significant Events in His Life: 1791, born; 1810, entered Trinity College, Cambridge; 1814, graduated Peterhouse; 1817, received MA from Cambridge; 1820, founded the Analytical Society with Herschel and Peacock; 1823, started work on the Difference Engine through funding from the British Government; 1827, published a table of logarithms from 1 to 108000; 1828, appointed to the Lucasian Chair of Mathematics at Cambridge (never presented a lecture); 1831, founded the British Association for the Advancement of Science; 1832, published "Economy of Manufactures and Machinery"; 1833, began work on the Analytical Engine; 1834, founded the Statistical Society of London; 1864, published *Passages from the Life of a Philosopher*; 1871, died.

OTHER INVENTIONS:

The cowcatcher, dynamometer, standard railroad gauge, uniform postal rates, occulting lights for lighthouses, Greenwich time signals, heliograph ophthalmoscope. He also had an interest in cyphers and lock-picking, but abhorred street musicians.

Babbage Observed[1]

Near the northern pole of the moon there is a crater named for Charles Babbage. When he died in 1871, however, few people knew who he was. Only one carriage (the Duchess of Somerset's) followed in the burial procession that took his remains to Kensal Green Cemetery. The Royal Society printed no obituary, and the [London] *Times* ridiculed him. The parts of the Difference Engine that had seemed possible of completion in 1830 gathered dust in the Museum of King's College.

---

[1]Reprinted with permission from *Datamation*, March 1985 (edited) ©1985 by Cahners/Ziff Publishing Associates, L.P.

In 1878 the Cayley committee told the government not to bother constructing Babbage's Analytical Engine. By the 1880s Babbage was known primarily for his reform of mathematics at Cambridge. In 1899 the magazine *Temple Bar* reported that "the present generation appears to have forgotten Babbage and his calculating machine." In 1908, after being preserved for 37 years in alcohol, Babbage's brain was dissected by Sir Victor Horsley of the Royal Society. Horsley had to remind the society that Babbage had been a "very profound thinker."

Charles Babbage was born in Devonshire in 1791. Like John von Neumann, he was the son of a banker—Benjamin (Old Five Percent) Babbage. He attended Trinity College, Cambridge, receiving his MA in 1817. As the inventor of the first universal digital computer, he can indeed be considered a profound thinker. The use of Jacquard punch cards, of chains (sequences of instructions), and subassemblies, and ultimately the logical structure of the modern computer—all emanated from Babbage.

Popularly, Babbage is a sort of Abner Doubleday of data processing, a colorful fellow whose portrait hangs in the anteroom but whose actual import is slight. He is thought about, if at all, as a funny sort of distracted character with a dirty collar. But Babbage was much more than that. He was an amazing intelligence.

The Philosopher
Babbage was an aesthete, but not a typical Victorian one. He found beauty in things: stamped buttons, stomach pumps, railways and tunnels, man's mastery over nature.

A social man, he was obliged to attend the theater. While others dozed at Mozart, Babbage grew restless. "Somewhat fatigued with the opera [Don Juan]," he writes in the autobiographical *Passages From the Life of a Philosopher,* "I went behind the scenes to look at the mechanism." There, a workman offered to show him around. Deserted when his Cicerone answered a cue, he met two actors dressed as "devils with long forked tails." The devils were to convey Juan, via trapdoor and stage elevator, to hell.

In his box at the German Opera some time later (again not watching the stage), Babbage noticed "in the cloister scene at midnight" that his companion's white bonnet had a pink tint. He thought about "producing colored lights for theatrical representation." In order to have something on which to shine his experimental lights, Babbage devised "Alethes and Iris," a ballet in which sixty damsels in white were to dance. In the final scene, a series of dioramas were to represent Alethes' travels. One diorama would show animals "whose remains are contained in each successive layer of the earth. In the lower portions, symptoms of increasing heat show themselves until the centre is reached, which contains a liquid transparent sea, consisting of some fluid at white heat, which, however, is filled up with little infinitesimal eels, all of one sort, wriggling eternally."

Two fire engines stood ready for the "experiment of the dance," as Babbage termed the rehearsal. Dancers "danced and attitudinized" while he shone colored lights on them. But the theater manager feared fire, and the ballet was never publicly staged.

Babbage enjoyed fire. He once was baked in an oven at 265° for "five or six minutes without any great discomfort," and on another occasion was lowered into Mt. Vesuvius to view molten lava. Did he ponder hell? He had considered becoming a cleric, but this was not an unusual choice for the affluent graduate with little interest in business or law. In 1837 he published his *Ninth Bridgewater Treatise,* to reconcile his scientific beliefs with Christian dogma. Babbage argued that miracles were not, as Hume wrote, violations of laws of nature, but could exist in a mechanistic world. As Babbage could program long series on his calculating machines, God could program similar irregularities in nature.

Babbage investigated biblical miracles. "In the course of his analysis," wrote B.V. Bowden in *Faster than Thought* (Pitman, London, 1971), "he made the assumption that the chance of a man rising from the dead is one in 10^{12}." Miracles are not, as he wrote in *Passages From the Life of a Philosopher,* "the breach of established laws, but . . . indicate the existence of far higher laws."

The Politician

Of all his roles, Babbage was least successful at this one. He had himself to blame: he was too impatient, too severe with criticism, too crotchety. Bowden wrote that in later life Babbage "was frequently and almost notoriously incoherent when he spoke in public." What ultimately kept him from building an Analytical Engine was not his inability to finish a project, but his inadequacies as a political man, as a persuader. His vision was not matched by his judgment, patience, or sympathy.

Babbage was a confusing political figure. A liberal republican, he was pro-aristocratic and strongly antisocialist. Friend to Charles Dickens and to the workman, he was a crony to the Midlands industrialist. The son of a Tory banker, he supported the cooperative movement and was twice an unsuccessful Whig candidate to Parliament. But his liberalism waned during the 1840s; by 1865, he was a conservative utilitarian for whom capitalism and democracy were incompatible.

In July 1822, Babbage wrote a letter to the president of the Royal Society, describing his plan for calculating and printing mathematical tables by machine. By June 1823 Babbage met with the Chancellor of the Exchequer, who granted money and told Babbage to proceed with the engine (which he did, starting work in July). But no minutes were made of this initial meeting.

In August 1827, Babbage's 35 year-old wife, Georgiana, died. Babbage traveled to the Continent. By the end of 1828 he returned to England, the initial £1,500 grant gone. Babbage was financing the construction himself. And the exchequer could not recall promising further funds.

Convincing the government to continue with two tons of brass, hand-fitted steel, and pewter clockwork was not easy. In 1829 a group of Babbage's friends solicited the attention of the Duke of Wellington, and then the Prime Minister. Wellington went to see a model of the engine, and in December ordered a grant of £3,000. Engineer Joseph Clement[2] was hired to construct the engine for the government, and to oversee the fabrication of special tools. By the end of 1830 Babbage wanted to move the engine's workshop to his house on Dorset Street. A fireproof shop was built where Babbage's stables had stood. A man of great ego, Clement refused to move from his own workshop, and made, according to Babbage, "inordinately extravagant demands." Babbage would not advance Clement further money, so Clement dismissed his crew, and work on the Difference Engine ceased.

This did not seem to perturb Babbage. His initial scheme for the Difference Engine called for six decimal places and a second-order difference; now he began planning for 20 decimal places and a sixth-order difference. "His ambition to build immediately the largest Difference Engine that could ever be needed," wrote Bowden, "probably delayed the exploitation of his own ideas for a century."

With Clement and his tools gone, Babbage wanted to meet with Prime Minister Lord Melbourne in 1834 to tell him of a new machine he had conceived—the Analytical Engine, an improved device capable of any mathematical operation. He contended it would cost more to finish the original engine than to construct this new one. But the government did not wish to fund a new engine until the old one was complete. "He was ill-judged enough," wrote the Reverend Richard Sheepshanks, a secretary of the Royal Astronomical Society, "to press

[2]See separate biography of Joseph Clement, p. 168.

the consideration of this new machine upon the members of Government, who were already sick of the old one." (Sheepshanks was Babbage's archenemy. In 1854 he published a vituperative 100-page work, "Letter to the Board of Visitors of the Greenwich Royal Observatory, in Reply to the Calumnies of Mr. Babbage," at its meeting in June 1853, and in his book entitled *The Exposition of 1851*.)

For the next eight years Babbage continued to apply to the government for a decision on whether to continue the suspended Difference Engine or begin the Analytical Engine, seemingly unaware of the social problems that preoccupied Britain's leaders during what Macauley called the Hungry Forties. Although £17,000 of public money had been spent, and a similar amount by Babbage, the Prime Minister avoided him. "It is nonsense," wrote Sheepshanks, "to talk of consulting a Prime Minister about the kind of Calculating Machine that he wants." Prime Minister Robert Peel recommended that Babbage's machine be set to calculate the time at which it would be of use. "I would like a little previous consideration," wrote Peel, "before I move in a thin house of country gentlemen a large vote for the creation of a wooden man to calculate tables from the formula $x^2 + x + 41$."

Finally, in November 1842, the Chancellor of the Exchequer, having sought the opinion of Sir George Airy on the utility of the machine, and having been told it was "worthless," said he and Peel regretted the necessity of abandoning the project. On November 11, Babbage finally met with Peel and was told the bad news.

By 1851 Babbage had "given up all expectation of constructing the Analytic Engine," even though he was to try once more with Disraeli the next year. He wrote in the vitriolic *Exposition of 1851*: "Thus bad names are coined by worse men to destroy honest people, as the madness of innocent dogs arises from the cry of insanity raised by their villainous pursuers."

Some believed Babbage had "been rewarded for his time and labor by grants from the public use," according to biographer Moseley Maboth (*Irascible Genius*). "We got *nothing* for our £17,000 but Mr. Babbage's grumblings," wrote Sheepshanks in his "Letter to the Board of Visitors of the Greenwich Royal Observatory." "We should at least have had a clever toy for our money."

Peel, however, declared in Parliament that Babbage "had derived no emolument whatsoever from the government." Offered a baronetcy in recognition of his work, Babbage refused, demanding a life peerage instead. It was never granted.

The Music Hater

Lady Lovelace wrote that Babbage hated music. He tolerated its more exquisite forms, but abhorred it as practiced on the street. "Those whose minds are entirely unoccupied," he wrote with some seriousness in *Observations of Street Nuisances* in 1864, "receive [street music] with satisfaction, as filling up the vacuum of time." He calculated that 25% of his working power had been destroyed by street nuisances, many of them intentional. Letters to the *Times* and the eventual enforcement of "Babbage's Act," which would squelch street nuisances, made him the target of ridicule.

The public tormented him with an unending parade of fiddlers, Punch-and-Judys, stilt-walkers, fanatic psalmists, and tub-thumpers. Some neighbors hired musicians to play outside his windows. Others willfully annoyed him with worn-out or damaged wind instruments. Placards were hung in local shops, abusing him. During one 80-day period Babbage counted 165 nuisances. One brass band played for five hours, with only a brief intermission. Another blew a penny tin whistle out his window toward Babbage's garden for a half hour daily, for "many months."

When Babbage went out, children followed and cursed him. Adults followed, too, but at a distance. Over a hundred people once skulked behind him before he could find a constable to disperse them. Dead cats and other "offensive materials" were thrown at his house. Windows were broken. A man told him, "You deserve to have your house burnt up, and yourself in it, and I will do it for you, you old villain." Even when he was on his deathbed, the organ-grinders ground away implacably.

In Babbage's relation with "the Mob," we see his curious naïveté in matters social. Although he was far above the rabble—"not unknown" to the Duke of Wellington and Lord Ashley—he seemed unaware of it at times. He expected the same civility from a drunken brothel-keeper as he would from a gentleman. In 1860, the London of the multitudinous poor was far from gentle. Yet, in his ingenuousness, he could fathom neither bums nor bamboozlers. He would cross town to check the tale of a mendicant, and frequently was surprised to encounter deceit.

Babbage once met a man who claimed not to have eaten for two days. Babbage invited him to breakfast. The next morning he called at Babbage's house, claiming hard times. Eventually, the man hired on as a steward on a small West Indian ship. "A few evenings after the ship had supposed to have sailed, he called at my house," wrote Babbage, "apparently much agitated and stated that, in raising the anchor, an accident had happened, by which the captain's leg had been broken." Babbage later tried to verify this tale, but found his steward "had been living riotously at some public-house in another quarter, and had been continually drunk."

Babbage never understood that the growth and crowdedness of London resulted from the industrial expansion he championed. By 1850 industry had taken over in Britain. "Many years before, I had purchased a house in a very quiet locality," he wrote in 1864. Then came a hackney stand, and beer shops and coffeehouses, and people. The din beneath his window, the German bands, the pickpockets, came with industry. The railroad and factory brought crowds to London, and with them came meanness and thievery.

The Newtonian

Like Newton, Babbage was Lucasian professor of mathematics at Cambridge. He founded both the British Association's Statistical Society and the Royal Astronomical Society. His Difference Engine calculated by Newton's method of successive differences, and would even accomplish "operations of human intellect" by motive power. Babbage believed in a world where, once all things were dutifully quantified, all things could be predicted. As such, he was a perfect Newtonian.

Nature, according to Question 31 of Newton's *Opticks,* is "very consonant and conformable to herself." Newton's program was official in Babbage's time. Science "consisted in isolating some central, specific act, and then using it as the basis for all further deductions concerning a given set of phenomena," writes Ilya Prigogine in *Order Out of Chaos.* The Marquis Laplace, an avid Newtonian and friend of Babbage, said that if a mind could know everything about particle behavior, it could describe everything: "Nothing would be uncertain, and the future, as the past, could be present to our eyes."

Babbage wanted to quantify everything. Fact and data intoxicated him. He tried handicapping horse races mathematically. Babbage's love of numbers was well known: in the mail he received requests for statistics. He would preserve any fact, simply because he thought "the preservation of any *fact* might ultimately be useful."

He would stop to measure the heartbeat of a pig (to be listed in his "Table of Constants of the Class Mammalia"), or to affix a numerical value to the breath of a calf. In 1856 he proposed to the Smithsonian Institution that an effort be made to produce "Tables of Constants of Nature and Art," which would "contain all those facts which can be expressed by numbers in the various sciences and arts."

Babbage delighted in the thought of having a daily account of food consumed by zoo animals, or the "proportion of sexes amongst our poultry." He proposed tables to calibrate the amount of wood (elm or oak) a man would saw in ten hours, or how much an ox or camel could plow or mow in a day.

Babbage's unflagging fascination with statistics occasionally overwhelmed him, as is seen in the animation of his Smithsonian proposal. "If I should be successful," he wrote, ". . . it will thus call into action a permanent cause of advancement toward truth, continually leading to the more accurate determination of established fact, and to the discovery and measurement of new ones."

In *Mechanics Magazine* in 1857 Babbage published a "Table of the Relative Frequency of the Causes of Breaking of Plate Glass Windows," detailing 464 breakages, of which "drunken men, women, or boys" were responsible for fourteen. Babbage thought the table would be "of value in many respects," and might "induce others to furnish more extensive collections of similar and related facts."

Babbage faced significant problems with mechanical techniques. He had to invent the tools for his engine. His thought is so thoroughly modern that we wonder why he did not pursue electromechanical methods for his engines (especially after Faraday's 1831 discovery of induction, and Babbage's own electrical experiments). It is easy to forget how long ago Babbage worked.

Even under the best of circumstances, the limitations of Newtonian physics might have prevented Babbage from completing any Analytical Engine. He did not know the advances of Maxwell (and could not know those of Boltmann, Gödel, and Heisenberg). Although he knew Fourier socially, Babbage did not seem to grasp the importance of his 1811 work on heat propagation, nor did he seem to know of Joule's efforts with heat and mechanical energy.

The reversibility of attraction is a basic tenet of Newtonian mechanics. A body, or piece of information, may retrace its path and return to where it started. In Babbage's design for the Analytical Engine, the discrete functions of mill (in which "all operations are performed") and store (in which all numbers are originally placed, and, once computed, are returned) rely on this supposition of reversibility.

In his 1824 essay on heat, Carnot formulated the first quantitative expression of irreversibility, by showing that a heat engine cannot convert all supplied heat energy into mechanical energy. Part of it is converted to useful work, but most is expelled into a low-temperature reservoir and wasted.

From this observation came William Thomson's discovery of the Second Law of Thermodynamics in 1852, and Rudolf Clausius' discovery of entropy in 1865. In ideal reversible processes, entropy remains constant. But in others, as Eddington showed with his "arrow of time," entropy only increases; thus, information cannot be shuttled between mill and store without leaking (some possibility of error), like faulty sacks of flour. Babbage did not consider this problem, and it was perhaps his greatest obstacle to building the engine.

It is easy to forget that Babbage was essentially a child of the Enlightenment, and that his epoch was much different from our own. He resided in an era of wood and coal, and the later era of steel and oil would not begin for perhaps a decade after his death.

The Industrialist

"Faith in machinery," wrote Matthew Arnold in *Culture and Anarchy* in 1869, "is our besetting danger." The Whiggery of the mid-Victorian era optimistically endorsed the principle of progress. Britain changed from the relatively pastoral society of 1820 to the brutishly materialistic one of the 1840s and 1850s.

Babbage shared his era's enthusiasm for industry. His finest work, *On the Economy of Manufactures,* was published in 1832. In it, with watch in hand, Babbage discovers operational research, the scientific study of manufacturing processes. It is a tour of the manufacturing processes of the period, from needle-making to tanning. Babbage detailed how things both ornamental and functional were made in mid-nineteenth century Britain. His characteristically blunt analysis of the printing trade caused publishers to refuse his books.

Babbage worked when industry was in a frenzy to improve and expand. Increases in manufacturing and population were viewed as "absolute goods in themselves," noted Matthew Arnold. In *Das Kapital,* Marx quoted from *Economy of Manufactures* on this rage to improve: "Improvements succeeded each other so rapidly, that machines which had never been finished were abandoned in the hands of their makers, because new improvements had superseded their utility."

Babbage disliked Plato, according to his friend Wilmot Buxton, because of Plato's condemnation of Archytas, "who had constructed machines of extraordinary power on mathematical principles." Plato thought such an application of geometry degraded a noble intellectual exercise, "reducing it to the low level of a craft fit only for mechanics and artisans."

Babbage loved practical science, and was among the first to apply higher mathematics to certain commercial and industrial problems. He took no part in what Anthony Hyman (in his book, *Charles Babbage*) called the era's "growing divorce between academic science and engineering practice."

Babbage had a forge built in his house on Devonshire Street, and accomplished, with his draftsmen, pioneering work in precision engineering. Because conventional mechanical drawing proved inadequate for his engines, he had to develop his own abstract notation. He called his work with mechanical notation "one of the most important additions I have made to human knowledge."

With the die-cast pewter gear wheels of his Difference Engine, and with his design of lathes and tool-shapers, Babbage did much to advance the British machine tool industry. Joseph Whitworth (later Sir), foreman in Babbage's shop, was responsible for the introduction of the first series of standard screw threads.

The expansion of the railways marked the grandest phase of the industrial revolution. Railroads freed manufacturing from its dependence on water transport, and opened new markets. When the first public railroad, the Stockton & Darlington, opened on September 27, 1823, Babbage was 34. By 1841 there were over 1,300 miles of rail in Britain, and 13,500 miles by 1870. J.D. Bernal wrote in *Science and Industry in the Nineteenth Century*, that "Babbage seems to have been one of the few who interested themselves scientifically in its [the railroad's] working." Babbage's life was intertwined with the railroad. He invented a cow catcher in 1838, apparently the first in Britain. He was present for opening ceremonies of George Stephenson's Manchester & Liverpool line in 1830. Of the cheering crowds at the initial run, he wrote, "I feared . . . the people madly attempting to stop by their feeble arms the momentum of our enormous train."

Babbage's great formal association with railroads came in 1837 and 1838, when he conducted experiments for I.K. Brunel's Great Western Railway, which ran from London to Bristol. Babbage argued for the superiority of Brunel's wide-gauge track. His research into the safety and efficiency of the line was, according to Bernal, "100 years ahead of his time."

Babbage rode the rails like a river pilot road the Mississippi, knowing every turn on the route, every crossing, every intersection. "My ear," he wrote, "had become peculiarly sensitive to the distant sound of an engine."

The Misanthrope

Babbage was known as a "mathematical Timon." In his later years he came to suffer from a mechanist's misanthropy, regarding men as fools and grubby thieves. By 1861 he said he had never spent a happy day in his life, and would gladly give up the rest of it if he could live three days 500 years thence.

Laughed at by costermongers and viscounts, met with diffidence by his lessers, the impatient Babbage grew angry, like the cave-dwelling Timon, with a changing world. Nevertheless, as his friend Lionel Tollemache wrote, "there was something harmless and even kindly in his misanthropy, for . . . he hated mankind rather than man, and his aversion was lost in its own generality."

Like Shakespeare's Timon, Babbage would have made a fascinating leader. (Sheepshanks, of course, disagreed: "I don't know any Government office or any other office for which he is fit, certainly none which requires sense and good temper.")

What a delightful, if distracting, place it would be where Babbage was in charge. Consider his plan in *Economy of Manufactures* for a "simple contrivance of tin tubes for speaking through." (Babbage calculated it would take 17 minutes for words spoken in London to reach Liverpool.) Or his plan for sending messages "enclosed in small cylinders," along wires suspended from high pillars (he thought church steeples could be used for this purpose.)

In *Passages,* Babbage relates how, as a youth, he nearly drowned while testing his contrivance for walking on water. In *Conjectures on the Conditions of the Surface of the Moon,* we find him describing his 1837 experiments in cooking a "very respectable stew of meat and vegetables" in blackened boxes (with window glass) buried in the earth. Toward the end of his life we find him mulling the prevention of bank note forgery and working in marine navigation. We realize that, with his harlequin curiosity about all things, and with his wonderfully human sense of wonder, Babbage escapes pathos and attains greatness.

QUOTATIONS

"Some of my critics have amused their readers with the wildness of the schemes I have occasionally thrown out; and I myself have sometimes smiled along with them. Perhaps it were wiser for present reputation to offer nothing but profoundly meditated plans, but I do not think knowledge will be most advanced by that course; such sparks may kindle the energies of other minds more favorably circumstanced for pursuing the enquiries." (*On the Economy of Machinery and Manufactures,* 1832, preface to second edition)

"Every moment dies a man/Every moment 1 $\frac{1}{16}$ is born."
(A correction to Tennyson's "Ev'ry moment a man dies/Ev'ry moment one is born.")

"If unwarned by my example, any man shall undertake and shall succeed in really constructing an engine . . . upon difference principles or by simpler means, I have no fear of leaving my reputation in his charge, for he alone will be fully able to appreciate the nature of my efforts and the value of their results."[3]

BIBLIOGRAPHY

Biographical

Babbage, Henry P., ed., *Babbage's Calculating Engines: Being a Collection of Papers Relating to Them, Their History, and Construction,* E. and F.N. Spoon, London, 1889.

Babbage, H.P., "Babbage's Analytical Engine," reprinted in Randell, Brian, ed., *Origins of Digital Computers: Selected Papers,* Springer-Verlag, Berlin Heidelberg, 1982, pp. 19–54.

Babbage, Neville F., "Autopsy Report on the Body of Charles Babbage ("the father of the computer")," *Medical J. Australia,* Vol. 154, 1991, pp. 758–759.

Bromley, Alan G., "Charles Babbage's Analytical Engine," *Ann. Hist. Comp.,* Vol. 4, No. 3, 1982, p. 196.

Buxton, W.H., *Memoir of the Life and Labours of the Late Charles Babbage Esq. F.R.S.,* Vol. 13, Charles Babbage Institute Reprint Series of the History of Computing, MIT Press, Cambridge, Mass., 1988.

Campbell-Kelly, Martin, "Charles Babbage's Table of Logarithms," *Ann. Hist. Comp.,* Vol. 10, No. 3, 1988, p. 159ff.

Campbell-Kelly, Martin, ed., *The Works of Charles Babbage,* Pickering and Chatto, London, 1989, 11 Volumes.

Cohen, I. Bernard, "Babbage and Aiken," *Ann. Hist. Comp.,* Vol. 10, No. 3, 1988, p. 171ff.

Davies, Donald Watts, "Babbage's Friend," (CQD), *Ann. Hist. Comp.,* Vol. 12, No. 2, 1990, p. 147ff.

Dubbey, J. M., *The Mathematical Work of Charles Babbage,* Cambridge Univ. Press, New York, 1978.

Froehlich, Leopold, "Babbage Observed," *Datamation,* Cahners/Ziff Pub. Assoc., Mar. 1985.

Gridgeman, N. T., *The Mathematical Work of Charles Babbage* (review), *Ann. Hist. Comp.,* Vol. 1, No. 1, 1979.

Halacy, Dan, *Charles Babbage, Father of the Computer,* Macmillan, New York, 1970.

Harrison, Thomas J., "Charles and the Computer," *Measurement and Control,* Vol. 19, Apr. 1986, pp. 84–91.

---

[3] Quoted in the Babbage exhibit at the Science Museum, Kensington; attributed to Babbage in 1864.

Hyman, Anthony, *Charles Babbage, Pioneer of the Computer,* Princeton Univ. Press, Princeton, N.J.,1982.

Hyman, Anthony, "Babbage Studies," (CQD), *Ann. Hist. Comp.,* Vol. 11, No. 3, 1989, p. 225ff.

Huskey, Harry and Velma, "Lady Lovelace and Charles Babbage," *Ann. Hist. Comp.,* Vol. 2, No. 4, 1980, pp. 299–329.

Huskey, Harry and Velma, "Charles Babbage and Lady Lovelace," (anecdote), *Ann. Hist. Comp.,* Vol. 3, No. 4, 1981, p. 414ff.

Huskey, Velma, "Who Was the Mysterious Countess?," (anecdote), *Ann. Hist. Comp.,* Vol. 7, No. 1, 1985, p. 58ff.

Kean, David W., *The Author of the Analytical Engine,* Thompson Book Co., Washington D.C., 1966.

Morrison, Philip and Emily, *Charles Babbage and his Calculating Machines,* Dover Publications, New York, 1961.

Nagler, Harry, "Napier and Babbage," (anecdote), *Ann. Hist. Comp.,* Vol. 2, No. 2, 1980, p. 186ff.

Robert, C.J.D., "Babbage's Diff. Eng. No.1 and . . . Sine Tables," (CQD), *Ann. Hist. Comp.,* Vol. 9, No. 2, 1987, p. 210ff.

Slater, Robert, *Portraits in Silicon,* MIT Press, Cambridge, Mass., 1987.

Smillie, K.W., "Mr. Babbage's Calculating Machine," (CQD), *Ann. Hist. Comp.,* Vol. 2, No. 3, 1980, p. 268ff.

van Sinderen, Alfred, "The Printed Papers of Charles Babbage," *Ann. Hist. Comp.,* Vol. 2, No. 2, 1980, pp. 169–185.

van Sinderen, Alfred, "The Trinity House," (correction), *Ann. Hist. Comp.,* Vol. 3, No. 1, 1981, p. 73.

van Sinderen, Alfred, "A. Hyman: *Charles Babbage*" (review), *Ann. Hist. Comp.,* Vol. 5, No. 1, 1983, p. 76.

van Sinderen, Alfred, "Babbage's Letter to Quetelet, May 1835," *Ann. Hist. Comp.,* Vol. 5 No. 3, 1983, p. 263ff.

van Sinderen, Alfred, "Babbage and the Scheutz Machine . . . ," (anecdote), *Ann. Hist. Comp.,* Vol. 10, No. 2, 1988, p. 133ff.

van Sinderen, Alfred, "Babbage and Bowditch," (CQD), *Ann. Hist. Comp.,* Vol. 10, No. 3, 1988, p. 218ff.

Wilkes, Maurice V., "Babbage, Charles" in Ralston, Anthony, and Edwin D. Reilly, Jr. *Encyclopedia of Computer Science and Engineering,* Van Nostrand Reinhold Co., New York, 1983.[4]

Wilkes, Maurice V., "Babbage's Expectations for the Diff. Engine," (anecdote), *Ann. Hist. Comp.,* Vol. 9, No. 2, 1987, p. 203ff.

---

[4]Also in the 3rd edition 1992.

Wilkes, Maurice V., "Babbage and the Colossus," (CQD), *Ann. Hist. Comp.*, Vol. 10, No. 3, 1988, p. 218ff.

Wilkes, Maurice V., "Babbage's Expectations for his Engines," *Ann. Hist. Comp.*, Vol. 13, No. 2, 1991, pp. 141–146.

Wilkes, Maurice V., "Pray, Mr. Babbage . . . ," A Play, *Ann. Hist. Comp.*, Vol. 13, No. 2, 1991, pp. 147–154.

Wilkes, Maurice V., "Charles Babbage—The Great Uncle of Computing?," *Comm. ACM*, Vol. 35, No. 3, 1992, pp. 15–16, 21.

Significant Publications

Babbage, Charles, "Observations on the Application of Machinery to the Computation of Mathematical Tables," *Memoirs of the Astronomical Society*, Vol. 1, No. 2, 1825, pp. 311–314.

Babbage, Charles, *Economy of Machinery and Manufactures*, Charles Knight, London, 1832.

Babbage, Charles, "On the Mathematical Powers of the Calculating Engine," unpublished MS, reprinted in Randell, B., ed., *The Origins of Digital Computers: Selected Papers*, Springer-Verlag, Berlin, 1973, pp. 19–54.

Babbage, Charles, *Passages from the Life of a Philosopher*, Longmans and Green, London, 1864, reprinted with introduction by Martin Campbell-Kelly, IEEE Press, Piscataway, N.J., 1994.

CHARLES BACHMAN

Born December 11, 1924, Manhattan, Kan.; proposer of a network approach to storing data as in the Integrated Data Store (IDS) and developer of the OSI Reference Model.

Education: BS, mechanical engineering, Michigan State University, 1948; MS, mechanical engineering, University of Pennsylvania, 1950.

Professional Experience: Dow Chemical Corporation, 1950–1960; General Electric Company, 1960–1970; Honeywell Information Systems, 1970–1981; Cullinet, 1981–1983; founder and chairman, BACHMAN Information Systems, 1983–present.

Honors and Awards: ACM Turing Award, 1973; distinguished fellow, British Computer Society, 1978.

Bachman began his service to the computer industry in 1958 by chairing the SHARE Data processing Committee that developed the IBM 709 Data Processing Package (9PAC), and which preceded the development of the programming language Cobol. He continued this development work through the American National Standards Institute SPARC Study Group on Data Base Management Systems (ANSI/ SPARC/DBMS) that created the layer architecture and conceptual schema for database systems. This work led to the development of the international "Reference Model for Open Systems Integration," which included the basic idea of a seven-layer architecture, the basis of the OSI networking standard. Bachman received the 1973 ACM Turing Award for his development of the Integrated Data Store, which lifted database work from the status of a specialty to first-class citizenship in computing. IDS provided an elegant logical framework for organizing large on-line collections of variously interrelated data. The system had pragmatic significance also in taking into account advice on expected usage patterns, to improve physical data layouts. The facilities of IDS were fully integrated into the Cobol language and so became available for full-scale practical use. Bachman was cited for the completeness of this conception—from the underlying modeling to installation in the field—and for its proven impact on data processing. In 1983 he founded Bachman Information Systems, Inc., whose products pioneered the concepts of reverse engineering.

BIBLIOGRAPHY

Significant Publications

Bachman, C., "The Programmer as a Navigator," *Comm. ACM,* Vol. 16, No. 11, 1973, p. 653ff.

JOHN WARNER BACKUS

Born December 3, 1924, Philadelphia, Pa.; leader of the IBM team that created the programming language Fortran; inventor of the metalanguage BNF, known variously as Backus-Normal or Backus-Naur Form; currently proponent of improved methods of programming such as the functional approach.

Education: BS, mathematics, Columbia University, 1949; AM, mathematics, Columbia University, 1950.

Professional Experience: IBM Corp.: programmer, Pure and Applied Science Departments, 1950–1953, manager, Programming Research Department, 1954–1958, IBM Research Staff, 1958–1963, IBM fellow, 1963–1991; adjunct professor of information sciences, University of California, Santa Cruz, 1974; visiting professor, University of California, Berkeley, 1980, 1985.

Honors and Awards: IBM fellow, 1963; W.W. McDowell Award, IEEE, 1967; National Medal of Science, 1975; ACM Turing Award, 1977; IEEE Computer Society Pioneer Award, 1980; member, National Academy of Sciences; member, National Academy of Engineers; Charles Stark Draper Award, National Academy of Engineering (NAE), 1993.

John Backus was employed by IBM as a programmer for the Selective Sequence Electronic Calculator (SSEC) in 1950, after receiving his Master's degree in mathematics from Columbia University.[5] Later he headed the development of the Speedcoding interpretive system for the IBM 701. He also took part in the design of the IBM 704, and was the original advocate for its built-in floating-point operations. From early 1954 until late 1958, he was manager of the programming research group (later department) in IBM during its development of Fortran.

While Backus was a member of the committees that designed Algol 58 and Algol 60, he joined IBM Research. In the course of efforts to define Algol 58 more precisely, he employed the syntax description technique known as BNF; this technique was improved and used by Peter Naur to describe the syntax of Algol 60 in the Algol Report.

After his work on Algol, Backus spent a number of years working on the mathematics of families of sets. Between 1970 and 1978 he developed a functional style of programming and its associated algebra of programs. This work became the topic of his 1978 Turing Award Lecture, "Can Programming be Liberated from the von Neumann Style? A Functional Style and Its Algebra of Programs."

---

[5]Adapted from the biography that accompanied John Backus' paper in Wexelblat 1981.

In 1963 Backus was appointed an IBM fellow. He resides in San Francisco, Calif. He retired on October 31, 1991, and is associated with the IBM Almaden Research Center as a consultant.

On February 22, 1994, the National Academy of Engineers awarded Backus the third Draper Award "for the development of Fortran—FORmula TRANslation—the first general-purpose, high-level computer language, which ushered in the computer software revolution."

QUOTATIONS

"It [Fortran] is an incredible achievement that 25 years ago these people designed and produced a compiler that has remained the best overall optimizer for not 5 years, not 10 years, but 20 years."

"I myself have had many failures and I've learned that if you are not failing a lot, you are probably not being as creative as you could be, you aren't stretching your imagination enough.[6]

BIBLIOGRAPHY

Biographical

Anon., "The Man Behind Fortran," *Computing Report,* IBM Corp., New York, Vol. 2, No. 4, 1966, pp. 7–19.

Backus, John, "Programming in America in the 1950s—Some Personal Impressions," in N. Metropolis, J. Howlett, and Gian-Carlo Rota, *A History of Computing in the Twentieth Century,* Academic Press, New York, 1980, pp. 125–136.

Backus, John, "The History of Fortran I, II and III," in Wexelblat, Richard L., ed., *History of Programming Languages,* Academic Press, New York, 1981, pp. 25–74.

Lee, J.A.N., and Henry Tropp, eds., "25th Anniversary of Fortran," Special Issue, *Ann. Hist. Comp.,* Vol. 6, No. 1, 1984.

Slater, Robert, *Portraits in Silicon,* MIT Press, Cambridge, Mass., 1987.

Stegman, Claire, "Pathfinder," *Think,* IBM Corp., Armonk, N.Y., 1979, pp. 18–24.

---

[6]On the occasion of receiving the Draper Award, February 22, 1994.

Significant Publications

Backus, John W., and Harlan Herrick, "IBM 701 Speedcoding and other Automatic-Programming Systems," ONR Symp. Automatic Programming for Digital Computers, ONR, Washington D.C., 1954, pp. 106–113.

Backus, J.W., R.J. Beeber, S. Best, R. Goldberg, L.M. Haibt, H.L. Herrick, R.A. Nelson, D. Sayre, P.B. Sheridan, H. Stern, I. Ziller, R.A. Hughes, and R. Nutt. *Programmer's Reference Manual, The Fortran Automatic Coding System for the IBM 704 EDPM,* IBM Corporation, New York, 1956.

Backus, John W., "The Syntax and Semantics of the Proposed International Algebraic Language of the Zurich ACM-GAMM Conference," *Proc. First Int'l. Conf. Information Processing,* Butterworth, London, 1960, pp. 125–132.

Backus, John W., "Can Programming be Liberated from the von Neumann Style? A Functional Style and Its Algebra of Programs," *Comm. ACM.,* Vol. 21, 1978, pp. 613–641.

Charles L. (Chuck) Baker

Software engineer responsible for the early JOSS II on-line computer services.

Education: BS, physics, MIT, 1951.

Professional Experience: Douglas Aircraft Company: 1951–1956, computing specialist, Santa Monica Engineering Department, 1953–1956; Rand Corp., Santa Monica, 1956–1967; IBM Corp., Washington, D.C.; International Computing Co.; Ocean Data Systems, senior software engineer, Science Applications, Inc.

Baker joined the Douglas Aircraft Co. in 1951, and in 1953 was a computing specialist in the Santa Monica, Calif. engineering department. In 1955 he was a delegate to the Project for the Advancement of Coding Techniques (PACT). In 1956 he moved to the Rand Corporation in Santa Monica. Among his activities was project leadership for the JOSS II on-line computer service—coordinating the research to develop the nature and extent of computer problem-solving support required. Technical activities included the design and specification of the JOSS II remote typewriter console, interfaced to the computer through a unique private-wire installation which distributed "JOSS computer power" automatically to any of 300 individual wall outlets in the Rand complex. During the period 1956–1961 he programmed the Information Processing Language Five (IPL-V) system for the IBM 704, 709, 7090 and the 7044 series of machines, and specified many features of the final, complete system. As the first acting secretary of SHARE, he organized the SHARE Operating System working group, which produced the first large-scale operating system—SOS—for the IBM 709. He relocated to the Washington, D.C., area in 1967 and worked at IBM, the International Computing Company, and Ocean Data Systems. He is currently senior software engineer at Science Applications, Inc.

BIBLIOGRAPHY

Biographical

Baker, Charles L., "JOSS—JOHNNIAC Open-Shop System," in Wexelblat, Richard L., ed., *History of Programming Languages,* Academic Press, New York, 1981, Chapter X.

Significant Publications

Baker, Charles L., "The PACT I Coding System for the IBM Type 701," *J. ACM,* Vol. 3, 1956, pp. 272–278.

JOHN BARDEEN

Born May 23, 1908, Madison, Wis.; died January 30, 1991, Boston, Mass.; co-inventor in 1947 of the transistor, with William Shockley and Walter Brattain.

Education: BS, physics: University of Wisconsin, 1928; MS 1929; PhD, Princeton University, mathematics and physics, 1936.

Professional Experience: worked as a geophysicist with the Gulf Research and Development Corp., 1930–1933; junior fellow, Harvard University, 1935–1938; assistant professor of physics, University of Minnesota, 1938–1941; physicist, US Naval Ordnance Laboratory, Washington D.C., 1941–1945; research physicist, Bell Telephone Laboratories, 1945–1951; professor, electrical engineering and physics, 1951–1978, emeritus professor of electrical engineering and physics, University of Illinois, Urbana, Ill., 1975–1991.

Honors and Awards: Nobel Prize, physics, 1956 and 1972, the only scientist ever to receive two Nobel Prizes in the same field; Fritz London Award, 1962; National Medal of Science, 1965; Michelson-Morley Award, 1968; Medal of Honor, IEEE, 1971; Lomonosov Prize from the Soviet Academy of Science, 1988; Third Century Award, 1990; member, National Academy of Science; member, American Academy of Arts and Science; fellow, American Physics Society; fellow, IEEE.

John Bardeen, the last surviving member of the three-man team that developed the transistor, and who twice won the Nobel Prize, died Wednesday [January 30, 1991].[7] Catherine Foster, a spokeswoman for the University of Illinois, where Bardeen was Professor Emeritus, said he died at Brigham and Women's Hospital in Boston. "He had gone to see a doctor and had had exploratory surgery [Tuesday] and seemed to come through fine, I understand," she said. "But this morning he suffered cardiac arrest."

Bardeen, an electrical engineer and physicist, won the Nobel prize in 1956 as the co-inventor of the transistor, and again in 1972 as co-developer of the theory of superconductivity at low temperatures. He was the last living member of the Bell Telephone Laboratories transistor research team, which included Walter Brattain, who died in 1987, and William P. Shockley, who died in 1989. Their work, completed in 1947, made the vacuum tube obsolete. Direct descendants of the transistor are the integrated circuits on devices ranging from the space shuttle to videocassette recorders and from calculators to computers.

Bardeen once told a reporter that "I knew the transistor was important, but I never foresaw the revolution in electronics it would bring." Yet it was the development of the theory of low-temperature superconductivity (with Leon Cooper and J. Robert Schrieffer) of which he was most proud. "Superconductivity was more difficult to solve and it required some radically new concepts," Bardeen said after the announcement of his second Nobel Prize. Superconductivity, in which electricity travels with little or no resistance, helped researchers develop such medical diagnostic tools as magnetic imaging, and made high-speed computers possible.

Among Bardeen's other honors were the 1965 Medal of Science, the 1976 Presidential Medal of Freedom, and the 1988 Lomonosov Prize from the Soviet Academy of Science. He also held membership in 14 professional societies and had received 16 honorary doctorates.

In 1990 *Life Magazine* named him one of the 100 most influential Americans of the 20th century, and President Bush made him one of

---

[7]From Folkart, Burt A., "John Bardeen; Physicist Won 2 Nobels," *Los Angeles Times,* January 31, 1991.

11 recipients of the Third Century Award for creative contributions to America.

He taught at the University of Minnesota, did research at the Naval Ordnance Laboratory in Washington D.C., and joined the Bell research group in physics at Murray Hill, N.J. He joined the University of Illinois faculty in 1951 and retired in 1975.

In 1983, Japan's Sony Corporation donated $3 million to endow a John Bardeen research and teaching chair in electrical and computer engineering at the University of Illinois.

BIBLIOGRAPHY

Significant Publications

Bardeen, John, Walter Brattain, and William Shockley, *Nobel Lectures—Physics, 1942–62,* Elsevier, New York, 1964.

JOEL BARR, AKA IOSIF VENIAMINOVICH BERG

Born 1916; US citizen who emigrated to the Soviet Union and became one of the fathers of Soviet microelectronics.

After a long search following his graduation from the City College of New York, Barr's career finally took off thanks to America's World War II industrialization. But after the war he was fired from a high-paying job at Sperry Gyroscope, a defense contractor, when it was learned that he was a member of the Communist Party.

He later traveled to Europe, first to Paris, and then to Prague, where he got a glimpse of socialism in action.

In Czechoslovakia, he was joined by a friend and former colleague, Alfred Sarant. By now calling himself Joseph Berg from Johannesburg, South Africa, Barr married a Czech woman and started a family. He kept his real identity secret even from his wife, Vera, who learned the truth only after 20 years of marriage.

Then-Soviet leader Nikita Khrushchev invited the two American engineers to Russia in 1956 and set them up in their institute in Leningrad. Russian colleagues credit Barr and Sarant with being the fathers of Soviet microelectronics, which enabled the regime to compete in the Cold War arms race and thereby strengthen its position at home.[8]

BIBLIOGRAPHY

Biographical

Shogren, Elizabeth, "Soviet Defense Pioneer Trades Communism for Social Security," *Roanoke Times and World News,* Oct. 15, 1992.

FRIEDRICH (FRITZ) L. BAUER

Born June 10, 1924, Regensburg, Bavaria, Germany; early German computer scientist responsible for the STANISLAUS and for the stack method of expression evaluation, known in German as the "Keller" (Cellar) method.

Education: University of Munich, 1946–1951; State Teacher Examination, 1949; PhD, University of Munich, 1952.

Professional Experience: high school teacher, 1949–1951; Munich University of Technology: lecturer, 1954–1958, reader, mathematics, 1955–1958; Gutenberg University, Mainz: associate professor, applied mathematics, 1958–1962, professor, 1962–1963; Munich University of Technology: chair, mathematics, 1963–1972, chair, computer science, 1972–present.

Honors and Awards: member, Bavarian Academy of Sciences, 1968; Bavarian Order of Merit, 1971; DSc (Hon.), University of Grenoble, 1974; Austrian Wilhelm Exner Medal, 1978; Cross of Merit (First Class), Federal Republic of Germany, 1982; member, Leopoldina Academy, Halle, 1984; Bavarian Maximilian Order of Science and Art, 1986; IEEE Computer Pioneer Medal, 1988; DSc (Hon.), University of Passau, 1989.

Fritz Bauer started to work as a highschool teacher in 1949 and at the same time continued his studies at the Munich University. He was promoted to lecturer in 1954, and reader for mathematics at the Munich University of Technology in 1955. In 1958 he joined Gutenberg

---

[8]From Shogren 1991.

University in Mainz as associate professor of applied mathematics. In 1962 he was promoted to full professor at Mainz, but returned to the Munich University of Technology in 1963 where he accepted a newly created chair. In 1972 Bauer moved from the chair of mathematics to a new chair of computer science, the field he had prepared and built up at Munich. He has authored a number of books, some of which have been translated into English, Russian, and other languages.

In 1950 he designed STANISLAUS, a parallel calculator for propositional formulae typed in Polish parenthesis-free form. Based on this technology, he and Klaus Samelson developed in 1955 the stack method of expression evaluation.

Bauer has received many national and international honors. He received honorary doctorates from the University of Grenoble and from the University of Passau. He was awarded the Austrian Wilhelm Exner medal and recently the IEEE Computer Pioneer Medal. He was also awarded the Bavarian Order of Merit (First Class) of the Federal Republic of Germany. He is a member of the Bavarian Academy of Sciences and of the Leopoldina Academy in Halle. His highest awards have been the Bavarian Maximilian Order of Science and Art, and the Cross of Merit.

BIBLIOGRAPHY

Biographical

Bauer, F.L., "The Cellar Principle of State Transition and Storage Allocation," *Ann. Hist. Comp.*, Vol. 12, No. 1, 1990, pp. 41–49.

Significant Publications

Bauer, F.L., "Zür Darstellungstheorie der Spingruppen," *Math. Annalen*, Vol. 128, 1954, pp. 228–256.

Bauer, F.L., "Ein direktes Iterationsverfahren zür Hurwitzerlegung eines Polynoms," A.E.Ü, Vol. 9, 1955, pp. 285–290.

Bauer, F.L., and K. Samelson, *Automatic Computing Machines and Method of Operation,* US Patent No. 3047228, filed March 28, 1958; patent awarded July 31, 1962.

Bauer, F.L., "The Formula-Controlled Logical Computer 'Stanislaus'," *Math. Tables Aids Comp.*, Vol. 14, 1960, pp. 64–67.

Bauer, F.L., "On the Field of Values Subordinate to a Norm," *Numer. Math*, Vol. 4, 1962, pp. 103–113.

Bauer, F.L., "Fields of Values and Gershgorin Disks," *Numer. Math.*, Vol. 12, 1968, pp. 91–95.

Bauer, F. L., "Konvexe Kegel und die Oszillation," *Wiss. Z. TU Desden*, Vol. 17, 1968, pp. 1127–1142.

Bauer, F.L., "Angstl's Mechanism for Checking Well-Formedness of Parenthesis-Free Formulae," *Math. Comp.*, Vol. 31, 1977, pp. 318–320.

Bauer, F.L., "Between Zuse and Rutishauser—The Early Development of Digital Computing in Central Europe," in Metropolis, N., J. Howlett, and Gian-Carlo Rota, *A History of Computing in the Twentieth Century*, Academic Press, New York, 1980, pp. 505–524.

Bauer, F.L., "Cryptology: Methods and Maxims," in Beth, T., ed., *Cryptology*, Lecture Notes in Computer Science, No. 149, Springer-Verlag, Berlin, 1983.

Bauer, F.L., and M. Wirsing, "Crypt-Equivalent Algebraic Specifications," *Acta Informatica*, Vol. 25, 1988, pp. 111–153.

Samelson K., and F.L. Bauer, "Sequential Formula Translation," *Comm. ACM*, Vol. 2, Feb. 1960, pp. 76–83.

Niels Ivar Bech

Born 1920 Lemvig, Denmark; died 1975; originator of Danish computer development.

Niels Ivar Bech was one of Europe's most creative leaders in the field of electronic digital computers.[9] He originated Danish computer development under the auspices of the Danish Academy of Technical Sciences and was first managing director of its subsidiary, Regnecentralen, which was Denmark's (and one of Europe's) first independent designer and builder of electronic computers.

Bech was born in 1920 in Lemvig, a small town in the northwestern corner of Jutland, Denmark; his schooling ended with his graduation from Gentofte High School (Statsskole) in 1940. Because he had no further formal education, he was not held in as high esteem as he deserved by some less gifted people who had degrees or were university professors.

During the war years, Bech was a teacher. When Denmark was occupied by the Nazis, he became a runner for the distribution of ille-

---

[9]Reprinted from Auerbach 1984.

gal underground newspapers, and on occasion served on the crews of the small boats that perilously smuggled Danish Jews across the Kattegat to Sweden. After the war, from 1949 to 1957, he worked as a calculator in the Actuarial Department of the Copenhagen Telephone Company (Kobenhavns Telefon Aktieselskab, KTA).

The Danish Academy of Technical Sciences established a committee on electronic computing in 1947, and in 1952 the academy obtained free access to the complete design of the computer BESK (Binar Electronisk Sekevens Kalkylator) being built in Stockholm by the Swedish Mathematical Center (Matematikmaskinnamndens Arbetsgrupp). In 1953 the Danish academy founded a nonprofit computer subsidiary, Regnecentralen.

Bech was assigned by KTA to the project and assisted in building DASK (Dansk BESK), a slightly modified copy of BESK, in a concentrated effort by a devoted group of people who assembled the parts by hand. In 1957 DASK became operational, and Bech was named managing director of Regnecentralen, serving in that capacity until 1971.

During these fourteen years, the most productive phase of his life, Bech was the senior Dane in computers—the spokesman for both Regnecentralen and the Academy of Technical Sciences. He was the leader of everything that Regnecentralen did, in hardware and software. For example, he guided some students from the DASK coding courses, which were started in 1955, to develop a library of subroutines, thus laying the foundation for later software projects at Regnecentralen.

Immediately after the completion of DASK in 1959, Regnecentralen developed a prototype of the GIER computer and by the end of 1962 had produced eighteen GIER systems. Bech made substantial efforts to strengthen and formalize Regnecentralen's connections with Danish universities. He tried to make permanent collaboration contracts, including a provision that Regnecentralen would establish computing centers at Danish universities. He convinced the government to acquire and install a GIER in every major university in the country, thus creating a network of university computers.

Bech recognized the value of long-standing Danish contacts with the East and saw that the antipathy between the US and the nations of Eastern Europe offered Regnecentralen some unique commercial opportunities. In 1964 he sold an early GIER to the University of Warsaw. Shortly thereafter, Regnecentralen's equipment and know-how were introduced into Czechoslovakia, Hungary, and Bulgaria, and later into Rumania, the Democratic German Republic, and Yugoslavia.

BIBLIOGRAPHY

Biographical

Sveistrup, Poul, Peter Naur, H.B. Hansen, and C. Gram, *Niels Ivar Bech—en epoke edb-udviklingen i Danmark*, DATA, Copenhagen, 1976, p. 144.

Auerbach, Isaac L., "Eloge: Niels Ivar Bech, 1920–1975," *Ann. Hist. Comp.*, Vol. 6, No. 4, 1984, p. 332.

LASZLO A. BELADY

Born April 29, 1928, Budapest, Hungary; proponent and implementor of virtual machine architectures and the "Belady" algorithm.

Education: BS, mechanical engineering, MS, aeronautical engineering, 1950, Technical Univ. Budapest.

Professional Experience: IBM Corp.: T.J. Watson Research Center, 1961–1981, program manager for software technology, IBM Headquarters, 1981–1983; manager of software engineering, Japan Science Institute (now Tokyo Research Laboratories), 1983–1984; vice president and director of the software technology and advanced computer technology programs, Microelectronics and Computer Technology Corp. (MCC), 1984–1991; chairman, Mitsubishi Electric Research Laboratories, Cambridge, Mass., 1991–present.

Honors and Awards: IBM Outstanding Contribution Awards, 1969 and 1973; J. D. Warnier Prize for Excellence in Information, 1990; fellow, IEEE "for contributions to the design of large software systems," 1988.

Belady did early work in operating systems, virtual machine architectures, program behavior modeling, memory management strategies, computer graphics, and data security. He co-designed and built the experimental M44/44X machine, the first computer with multiple virtual machine organization, and later participated in the design of the TSS-67, one of the earliest commercial time-sharing systems. In academic circles, Belady is best known for the OPT (or MIN) Page Replacement Algorithm, also know as the "Belady Algorithm": Given the ordered string of memory references which an executing program generates, and a given memory which is subdivided into equal-sized pages, the memory being smaller than necessary to contain the entire program material, the algorithm calculates the minimum number of page loads necessary to complete the program execution. The number is useful in order to (a) estimate system performance, and (b) compare "feasible" page replacement algorithms.

His own memories were expressed at a meeting where he was honored for his early work in 1991:

"It is really unusual for me to look back; I spend too little time reminiscing. I am now, however, forced to recall for you what I consider the most memorable aspects of my life.

"I grew up in a small town in Hungary, where my father was employed by the government as a civil engineer, designing and supervising the construction of roads and bridges. He worked often at home with compass and slide rule, tools that fascinated me. Often, he took me to the site and even today, I have the irresistible urge everyday to go to a neighboring office from which I can view the progress of a new four-level intersection being built next to our company.

"At school my favorite subjects were mathematics, the history of arts, and philosophy. I hated Latin and the study of languages in general but loved physical activity: running and biking with friends, fencing, boxing, gymnastics, skiing, skating. For years, my fondest memory was when during a school break I went out skiing, in bright sunshine, alone. It was indeed beautiful—not another soul around.

"In the meantime, WWII came to a finish. Towards its end I was once so hungry—and undernourished, weighing only about 110 pounds—that I dug up the potatoes in the field which were sown for the next crop and ate them raw. During this period, I finished my last year in high school by working first as an automobile mechanic apprentice and then (because it paid more), during the winter of 1945/46, at the salvaging of the bridges on the Danube which were blasted by the retreating Germans. We went to work by walking on ice floes, sometimes dipping in the icy waters, but we got special rations of sugar and lard. Otherwise, these items were only available on the black market. In the summer of 1946, I took my high school exams. I passed but not with honors!

"I was barely accepted to the Technical University of Budapest, because children of the intelligentsia were not favored by the then-rising Communist regime. I started in mechanical engineering. The first year was tough because I cut classes and went to swim instead, as I thought that I already knew all the mathematics that was needed (we learned calculus in the last two grades in high school in Hungary). But by my final year, which was in my chosen field, aeronautical engineering, I was at the top of the class. Upon graduation, almost all aeronautics graduates were drafted and became officers of the Air Force technical staff. After three years, I finally escaped military service, but even my civilian employment was the design of special equipment for MIG-15 fighter planes. It was during this time that I received my first patents.

"The 1956 revolution interrupted my new adventure—working towards an M.S. in electronics engineering. During the revolution, my friends and I planned for the new Hungarian aircraft industry and made serious attempts to contact Western firms. As the Russians returned, I and exactly one-third of my fellow aeronautics graduates left Hungary. They are still living in the US (including myself) and Western Europe.

"I spoke German, and a peculiar 'one-way' English; I understood and could read almost everything, but had difficulty speaking the language. My reading skill was due to the fact that, during college years, I supported myself by translating English technical literature into Hungarian. After having escaped Hungary by walking 30 miles through the swamps to the Austrian border, I settled in Cologne, Germany where I became a draftsman at Ford Motor Company, the only position for which they thought a Hungarian engineer was qualified. After a few months, they "discovered" me, and for the next two years, I was designing front-end suspension systems. I became restless, as I liked airplanes better than automobiles! A friend introduced me to Theodor van Karman, the world-famous father of supersonic aerodynamics from Cal Tech (he was originally from Hungary) who helped me to find a job at Dassault in Paris as an aerodynamics engineer.

"I married an Hungarian and she has been my wife for more than 30 years. We had not known each other in Hungary, but met on our first day of freedom in Austria. At the Dassault job, I did more programming on the IBM 650, 1620, and 704 to solve equations than anything else, although I still used my beloved slide rule extensively. I was satisfied with the company and the job, but it was clear that we would never be accepted by French society even though my son was born there in 1961. We applied for immigration to the US and arrived in New York in the same year.

"From friends, I learned that you need a white shirt and dark suit for job interviews. I bought the clothing and, after distributing about 100 resumes and getting only four or five unsuccessful interviews, I gave up presenting myself as an engineer and applied as a programmer. This worked and IBM hired me into their brand-new, but empty, Yorktown research facility as a "building filler."

"I was lucky to land among an incredibly smart group, John Backus' people, who just finished their work on Fortran and its compilers. Memory management was identified as the next problem. Then, over the next few years, we designed and built IBM's first experimental virtual machine, the M44/44X, software first. The project was headed by Bob Nelson, who later became one of the first IBM fellows. Unfortunately, he died of his fourth heart attack around his 60th birthday in 1990. This man, while unknown to the non-IBM world, was a deep thinker and a very broadly read intellectual, but was of a rather shy nature. We became close friends, and to him I owe everything I learned about computers and programming.

"This work on virtual machines and paging paid off well. My paper written in 1965 became the Citation Index most-referenced paper in the field of software over a 15-year period. But by 1968, I was in computer graphics, as I was tremendously motivated by visualizing software, as other engineering artifacts are visual. Unfortunately, two years later IBM gave up on interactive graphics. After placing my fifteen people in other research groups, I went to Berkeley for a year and taught graduate courses in computer structures and memory management. Upon returning to Yorktown, I found IBM very interested in data security, and my friend, Manny Lehman, was interested in analyzing the unpredictability of operating system development. So, I managed a group in data security which produced a few interesting results—among them a signature verification system, a virtual machine penetration study and a cryptographic effort which later led to a US government standard.

"The Program Evolution Dynamics work with Manny Lehman was even more interesting. For the following several years, we produced many papers, and organized conferences and workshops. Much of the material produced at this time was later published in a joint book (1985). Indeed, we were quite often criticized by our peers for this unusual effort as we were prophets trying to make some sense out of the large system complexity phenomenon and maintenance—it was heresy. I spent 1974 at Imperial College/London University with Manny Lehman, who is still there. I became more interested, however, in not only studying the phenomenon but also in doing design better. In the mid 1970s, I organized a group to utilize on practical systems the concept of data abstraction (today called object-oriented design). IBM, again, was not sufficiently enthusiastic, and I left for more administrative duties in IBM World Headquarters in Armonk. I was responsible for software technology, reporting to B.O. Evans, IBM vice president for Engineering, Programming and Technology. He was one of the greatest guys for whom I have ever worked.

"By the 1980s Japan emerged as a fascinating technical culture, and I became strongly interested in what makes them tick. The best way to find out was to live there for a while. When Hisashi Kobayashi, now Dean of Engineering at Princeton, invited me to join him at the new IBM research facility in Tokyo, I went gladly in early 1983. The next year and a half was terrific.

"For a while, I had been flirting with the idea of retiring from IBM and teaching. I finally made a deal with Georgia Tech to start teaching in the fall of 1984. But Admiral Bobby Inman intercepted me and offered me the job of software chief of the new MCC. During that summer, my wife and I sat around our kitchen table in Tokyo discussing our future, while Inman was calling weekly. Finally, I accepted his offer and joined MCC in September 1984.

"I am happy with what we have been doing in the Software Technology Program (STP) in spite of the obvious difficulties being experienced by the country, the computer industry and, thus, MCC. On balance, I am a lucky guy—as are you—to have the chance of living in such incredibly rich and interesting times."

Since that time, Belady has left MCC and is now with the Mitsubishi Electric Research Lab in Cambridge, Mass.

BIBLIOGRAPHY

Significant Publications

Belady, Laszlo A., "A Study of Replacement Algorithms for a Virtual Storage Computer," *IBM Systems Journal*, Vol. 5, No. 2, June 1966, pp. 78–10.[10]

Belady, Laszlo A., and Meir L. Lehman, *Program Evolution, Processes of Software Change*, Academic Press, London, 1985.

---

[10]This paper on Virtual Memory Management became the *Citation Index Classic* in 1983 as most referenced publication in computer software.

CHESTER GORDON BELL

Born August 19, 1934, Kirksville, Mo.; DEC designer of the PDP line of computers; with wife Gwen, founder of the Computer Museum, Boston.

Education: BSEE, MIT, 1956; MSEE, MIT, 1957.

Professional Experience: research engineer, Research Laboratory for Electronics, MIT, 1959–1961; manager, computer design, Digital Equipment Corp., 1961–1966; associate professor of computer science, Carnegie-Mellon University, 1966–1978; professor, electrical engineering and computer science, 1978; senior consultant, Stardent Computers, Sunnyvale, Calif.

Honors and Awards: Mellon Institute Award, Carnegie Mellon University, 1973; fellow, IEEE, 1974; IEEE W. Wallace McDowell Award, 1975; National Academy of Engineering, 1977; IEEE Computer Society Pioneer Award, 1980; ACM/IEEE Eckert/Mauchly Award, 1982; National Medal of Technology, 1991; IEEE John von Neumann Medal, 1992.

Bell's citation for the award of the IEEE Fellowship reads: "For contributions to the design of time-sharing computer systems, and for education in the understanding of computer structures."

Bell designed the first minicomputers and time-sharing computers at Digital Equipment Corp., and led the development of the company's VAX minicomputers. His other achievements include start-ups at Encore Computer, where he was responsible for one of the first multiple microprocessors, and at Ardent Computer, where he built the first graphics supercomputer. A director of several companies and a co-founder of the Computer Museum in Boston, Bell has received many prizes. President George Bush awarded him the National Medal of Technology "for his continuing intellectual and industrial achievements in the field of computer design, and for his leading role in establishing cost-effective, powerful computers that serve as a significant tool for engineering, science, and industry."

BIBLIOGRAPHY

Biographical

Slater, Robert, *Portraits in Silicon,* MIT Press, Cambridge, Mass., 1987, Chapter 19.

Significant Publications

Bell, C.G., and A. Newell, *Computer Structures: Readings and Examples,* McGraw-Hill, New York, 1971.

GWEN BELL

Born July 20, 1934, Elkader,[11] Iowa; founding president, Computer Museum, Boston, Mass.

Education: BA, University of Wisconsin, Madison, 1955; MURP, Harvard University, 1957; PhD, geography, Clark University, 1967.

Professional Experience: Graduate School of Public and International Affairs, University of Pittsburgh, 1966–1973; founder, Computer Museum, Boston, 1980.

Honors and Awards: president, ACM, 1992–1994.

While on a Fulbright scholarship in Australia, Bell was introduced to the English Electric DEUCE, a computer designed after the Pilot ACE of Alan Turing. Returning to Cambridge, Mass., she used the TX-0 at MIT to analyze a redevelopment area of Boston, being the first person to develop a "geographic information system" on a computer and to produce a variety of maps. After receiving her doctoral degree she taught at the Graduate School of Public and International Affairs, University of Pittsburgh. During the 1970s she was active as a United Nations consultant on planning; she also edited a journal and three books. In 1978 Ken Olsen (President of DEC) asked Bell whether the TX-0 could possibly be recreated faithfully at a Marlboro facility of DEC. This got her started on collecting and exhibiting the artifacts relating to the history of computing. By 1980 she saw the need for a true computer museum and in 1981 applied for non-profit status, which was given to the muse-

---

[11]The town was the most northerly outpost of Spanish settlement in America, originally with the Spanish name El Kadir.

um in 1982. She moved the museum to downtown Boston and opened the new facility in 1984.

ROBERT W. BEMER

Born February 8, 1920, Sault Ste. Marie, Mich.; programmer extraordinaire; inventor of many terms in common usage and contributor to Cobol and Fortran.

Education: AB, mathematics, Albion College, 1940; certificate, aeronautical engineering, Curtiss-Wright Technical Institute of Aeronautics, 1941.

Professional Experience: programmer, Rand Corp., 1949–1951; group leader, mathematical analysis, Lockheed Corporation, Burbank, Calif., 1951–1952; manager, numerical analysis group, Marquardt Aircraft, 1952–1954; manager, mathematical analysis department, Lockheed Missile Systems Division, 1954–1955; IBM Corp.: assistant manager, programming research, 1955–1957, manager, programming systems, 1957–1960, manager, Corporate Logical Systems Standards, 1960–1961, director of programming standards, 1961–1962; director, systems programming, Univac Division, Sperry-Rand Corp., 1962–1965; consultant to general manager, Bull GE, 1965–1966; manager, systems and software engineering integration, General Electric Co., 1966–1970; staff consultant to vice president, ASTO, 1970–1974; editor, *Honeywell Computer Journal,* 1972–1974; senior consulting engineer, 1974–1982; president, Bob Bemer Software Inc., 1982–present.

Honors and Awards: fellow, British Computer Society; three times AFIPS NCC Pioneer Day Honoree—Cobol, Fortran, and SHARE.

Bemer is the inventor of the words "Cobol," and "CODASYL," six ASCII characters, and the concepts of registry and escape sequences in character codes. He also invented the term and defined the nature of the "software factory." At IBM he developed the first load-and-go system (PRINT I) and also was responsible for the implementation of the programming system FORTRANSIT, which provided a quick first compiler for the IBM 650 computer, and was the first programming language to run both decimal (IBM 650) and binary (IBM 704) computers. For the support of commercial programming Bemer developed PRINT I; in the late 1950s he developed XTRAN, a step towards Algol, and "Commercial Translator," which became a significant input to Cobol. His major Cobol innovations were the IDENTIFICATION and ENVIRONMENT divisions, and the PICTURE clause.

Bemer is probably best known for his contributions to ASCII (American Standard Code for Information Interchange). He was not the inventor of ASCII; a hard-working committee surveyed many candidates for a code for information interchange, but instead of selecting one, it generated a code that did not exist before it began its work. Bemer represented IBM in this work, even though IBM still favored EBCDIC. At the time the hardware permitted the use of only seven bits, and thus any alphabet was limited to 128 characters and symbols. While hardware circuitry used eight bits, one bit was used for distinct check-bit, or error-bit, purposes. The American Standards Committee X3.2 recognized the limit of 128 symbols as being a significant barrier to the general acceptance of the code, and thus sought a solution. Bemer proposed the concept of an "escape sequence" that would allow the information system to break out of one alphabet and enter another that would be identified by the 7-bit identifiers following the escape code 0011011. As of 1991, 150 such extra-ASCII alphabets have been defined and registered, including Greek, Cyrillic, Arabic, and Japanese.

The escape sequence is the basis of many technologies, such as cursor movement and color on video screens, laser printers, photo-composition, video games, and computer-generated movies.

Bemer's forceful articulation and demonstration of the simplicity of the "escape sequence" solution achieved acceptance of a US standard that rendered as nonstandard *all* existing computer designs, software systems, and telecommunications hardware, including the whole repertoire of IBM equipment that used EBCDIC (Extended Binary Coded Decimal Interchange Code). Remarkably, ASCII and its companion parallel codes have survived for almost 30 years, along with only a few programming languages such as Fortran and Cobol. Very few such basic technologies have managed to survive through so many generations of machines. Since personalized automobile license plates became available, Bemer's cars have carried the tags "ASCII," "ESC SEQ," "Cobol 1," and "Cobol 2."

QUOTATION

"There is something wrong with a profession in which the only way to get anything done is to find a bearded wonder, lock him in a closet, and slip him crackers under the door." (From first COINS Symposium, Miami, Fla., 1971)

BIBLIOGRAPHY

Biographical

Bemer, R.W., "Nearly 650 Memories of the 650," *Ann. Hist. Comp.,* Vol. 8, No. 1., Jan. 1986, pp. 66–69.

Significant Publications

Bemer, R.W., "A Proposal for a Generalized Card Code [of] 256 Characters," *Comm. ACM,* Vol. 2, No. 3, Mar. 1959, pp. 8–13.

Bemer, R.W., "ESCape—A Proposal for Character Code Compatibility," *Comm. ACM,* Vol. 3, No. 2, Feb. 1960, pp. 71–72.

Bemer, R.W., "Survey of Modern Programming Techniques," *The Computer Bulletin,* 1961, pp. 127–135.

Bemer, R.W., "A Politico-Social History of Algol," *Ann. Rev. in Automatic Program,* Vol. 5, Pergamon Press, New York, 1969, pp. 151–238.

EDMUND C. BERKELEY

Born March 21, 1909, New York City; died March 7, 1988, Newton, Mass.; founder of ACM and author of the early book Giant Brains, Or Machines that Think, *the first popularization of computers; as editor of* Computers and People, *also known as Neil D. MacDonald.*

Education: BA mathematics and logic, Harvard University, 1930.

Professional Experience: actuarial clerk, Mutual Life Insurance of New York, 1930–1934; chief research consultant, Prudential Insurance of America, 1934–1942, 1946–1948; US Navy, Dahlgren Laboratory and Harvard Computational Center, 1942–1946; president, Berkeley Associates, 1948–1988.

Edmund Callis Berkeley, founder and lifelong editor/publisher of *Computers and People,* the oldest computing periodical still in existence, died of cancer after months of illness on March 7, 1988, just 2 weeks short of his 79th birthday. Berkeley was part of Howard H. Aiken's Harvard Mark II team; was the founder and first member of the Association for Computing Machinery (ACM); wrote the first book to popularize computers, *Giant Brains, Or Machines that Think*; and devoted his life to the mental improvement of his readers, the prevention of nuclear war, and the saving of the world.

Throughout his life Berkeley was a didactic writer, editor, and publisher, first in the field of computers in their earliest technical aspects, later in regard to their interrelations with people (when he changed the name of his magazine from *Computers and Automation* to *Computers and People*), and finally in an effort to bring sanity to a world seemingly determined to destroy itself with nuclear weapons. He was active and vigorous in using publications to teach his fellows and improve his world until ill health slowed him down and forced him to adopt the title of editor emeritus of his magazine. Even then he looked on the months remaining to him as an opportunity to tie up loose ends and, perhaps, as a friend put it, to unravel a few new ones.

Berkeley was born in New York City in 1909, graduated with an AB *summa cum laude* in mathematics and logic from Harvard College in 1930, entered the computer field in 1938 as an actuary using punched-card machines for the Prudential Insurance Company of America, and worked with Howard Aiken during the war as an active-duty naval reserve officer. After demobilization, he returned briefly to Prudential, where he participated in studies that led to the purchase of a Univac I. In 1947, he invited seven friends to a meeting that resulted in the establishment of the ACM (then known as the Eastern Association for Computing Machinery). Of this founding group only Robert V. D. Campbell and Harry E. Goheen survive in 1994. Berkeley was the first secretary of ACM, holding that office until 1953, and continued as a member until his death.

In 1948 he went into business for himself as Edmund C. Berkeley and Associates (later Berkeley Enterprises), started *Computers and Automation* in 1951, consulted for industry, and devised and sold several relay computers and small robots (Simon, Squee, Relay Moe, and so on) as educational projects in kit form.

In 1949 he wrote the first carefully crafted and widely accepted popularization of computers, *Giant Brains, Or Machines that Think,* a book that fastened the "brain" name on computers and presented a somewhat optimistic view of what computers could do or would do soon. Berkeley never recanted and insisted all his life that he had it right in his first book. *Giant Brains* was followed in 1956 by *Computers—Their Operations & Applications,* and 13 other books that had total sales in excess of $110,000. The objective of all his writing and editing was not to entertain but to educate, uplift, and improve his readers, although he sometimes despaired of being able to do so. His later books and articles were often concerned with the problems of how to think clearly and act wisely. His language, in writing and speaking, reflected his mind: precise, careful, and crisp—determined to be both correct and clear, not just brief, amusing, or acceptable.

In 1972 ACM honored Berkeley as its singular founder at its 25th anniversary dinner. His acceptance speech was a direct denunciation of those in computing who worked on the killing devices used in the Vietnam war, or computing companies that made such horrors, and of ACM for ignoring this immorality. He said that it was a "gross neglect of responsibility" that ACM was not investigating whether computer applications were good or evil and how computers could be used to increase the good of society. Several prominent ACM members, employees of the firms and government military agencies that Berkeley had pointed to, ostentatiously walked out of the banquet room while he was speaking. The leaders of ACM were clearly embarrassed by their honoree, and ACM never publicly referred to his speech in any way.

Berkeley's lifetime goal, only partly achieved at his death, was to educate his readers so that they could do as he did: think clearly about important matters, reach wise conclusions, and act bravely in support of their principles. He aspired to be, and was accepted by many as, the conscience of the computer industry because of his devotion to the idea that computers should work for the good of and not the destruction of mankind.

QUOTATIONS

The last issue of *Computers and People* to which he contributed, January–February 1988, contains this note: "There will be zero computer field and zero people if the nuclear holocaust and nuclear winter occur. Every city in the United States and the Soviet Union is a multiply-computerized target. Radiation, firestorms, soot, darkness, freezing, starvation, megadeaths, lie ahead. Thought, discussion, and action to prevent this earth-transforming disaster is imperative. Learning to live together is the biggest variable for a computer field future."

It is also significant that Berkeley indicated his views on pacifism in his 1952 article on Machine "Intelligence": "An automatic computing machine which has developed a wonderful facility in this particular kind of problem [the meaning of words] is the military deciphering machine, *of which persons like myself, who do not wish to be contaminated with classified information, know very little.*" [Emphasis added.]

BIBLIOGRAPHY

Biographical

Adams, Jim, "Edmund C. Berkeley," *Comm. ACM,* Vol. 31, No. 6, June 1988, pp. 781–782.

Anon., "Edmund Callis Berkeley," *Ann. Hist. Comp.,* Vol. 10, No. 3, 1988, pp. 216–217.

Anon, "Neil D. MacDonald," *Ann. Hist. Comp.,* Vol. 10, No. 3, 1988, p. 217.

Significant Publications

Berkeley, Edmund C., *Giant Brains or Machines That Think,* John Wiley and Son, New York, 1949.

Berkeley, Edmund C., "Machine 'Intelligence'," *Astounding Science Fiction,* Jan. 1952, pp. 82–85.

CLIFFORD EDWARD BERRY

Born 1918; died October 30, 1963, Long Island, N.Y.; with John V. Atanasoff, the developer of the earliest known electronic computer for the solution of linear systems—the ABC.

Education: BS, physics, Iowa State College, 1939; MS, physics, Iowa State College, 1941; PhD, physics, Iowa State College, 1948.

Professional Experience: Consolidated Engineering Corp., Pasadena, 1942–1963; director of advanced development, Vacuum-Electronics, Huntington, Long Island, N.Y.

Introduction[12]

A remarkable team of two scientists, John V. Atanasoff and Clifford E. Berry, together invent-ed the world's first electronic digital computer. Atanasoff came up with the concept of using the digital approach one winter night at a small tavern in Illinois.[13] The need for a fast computer had been on his mind for some time, as a way to help his graduate students at Iowa State College (now University) speed their calculations. He needed someone with a talent for inventing and a thorough knowledge of electronics to work with him on this project. Atanasoff recalls the exact spot on the campus—where the sidewalk leaving Beardshear Hall and heading toward the bookstore crossed the walk leading to Engineering—that he met the head of the Engineering Department and stopped to chat. Atanasoff said that he had managed to get some financial backing, and he asked if the dean could suggest an electrical engineering graduate with a thorough knowledge of electronics to work with him. Without a second's hesitation, the dean suggested Clifford Edward Berry, a bril-liant, hard-working budding scientist with an impressive history of awards and achievements. They met, and the team of Atanasoff and Berry—two entirely different but gifted physicists—was born.

The following reminiscences by Jean Berry, wife of Clifford, include two items not included in Atanasoff's biography. One is a let-ter, describing the ABC, that Berry wrote to R.K. Richards, the author of *Electronic Digital Systems,* shortly before Berry died. The other item

---

[12]Adapted from Berry 1986.

[13]See the biography of J.V. Atanasoff, p 27.

contains recollections written by Robert L. Mather who, at the time of the construction of the ABC, was an undergraduate helping Berry.

Clifford Berry and the ABC
Clifford Berry graduated from Marengo (Iowa) High School in 1934 at the age of 16. He had a straight "A" average and was class valedictorian. Because he was so young, his family thought he should wait a year before starting college. He spent that year taking more science courses and working on his ham radio setup. He was an Eagle Scout and an assistant scoutmaster. He loved classical music. For financial reasons, his widowed mother moved to Ames so that all four children could attend Iowa State College. Cliff earned money for college by working for Gulliver Electric, but in spite of this outside work he maintained an extremely high grade average, and was elected to four honorary fraternities: Sigma Xi, Eta Kappa Nu, Phi Kappa Phi, and Pi Mu Epsilon. In his junior year he was given a special award for making the highest scholastic record in the Department of Electrical Engineering during his freshman and sophomore years.

Although we lived just a few blocks apart in Ames, Cliff and I did not meet until October 1941, when his laboratory mate arranged a blind date. Cliff had graduated from ISC in 1939 and begun work on his graduate degrees in physics and mathematics, and on the computer that was later named the ABC.

In a 1940 issue of *EE News*, an ISC electrical engineering newsletter, Berry wrote:

> I am still working on the calculating machine [the prototype had been completed in 1939] and we can see the end in view, though some months off. I grow more enthusiastic about it as time goes on—it is so basically new that a continual stream of ramifications emerges from the central idea.

He was awarded a master's degree in physics in 1941. His thesis was based on one of his contributions to the invention of the ABC, and was entitled, "Design of an Electrical Data Recording and Reading Mechanism." In the thesis, Berry wrote:

> The present work was undertaken in conjunction with the development of a high-speed computing machine. . . . In order to realize to the fullest extent the high-speed capabilities of the computing machine proper, it is necessary to record and read numbers on cards at rates of the order of 60 holes per second. This seems plainly beyond the limits of practicability in so far as the usual mechanical methods

are concerned; hence, the method to be described was developed to meet this need.

After graduating from ISC, I taught at a local school for a year. Teaching did not appeal to me, so I obtained a position at ISC as a secretary in the English Department. A few weeks after I met Berry, he told me about an opening as secretary to John V. Atanasoff, on the missile project he headed. I became JV's secretary in November 1941, and worked for him on the missile project until Cliff and I married on May 30, 1942.

Berry and Atanasoff worked well together. They were both very busy in addition to completing the computer—Atanasoff with his teaching and his supervision of the missile project, and Berry with his graduate studies and, and in early 1942, his courting of me, which took an increasingly greater amount of his spare time. Frequently Cliff worked all night on the computer and then snatched a few hours of sleep on a cot in the basement of the physics building.

I agree heartily with Atanasoff, who said in 1983 at ISU that without the ABC, computers would have been delayed by perhaps ten years. I also agree with Atanasoff's statement in the *Annals* (1984): *"I feel that the choice of Clifford E. Berry was one of the best things that could have happened to the project. After he had worked for a short time, I knew that he had the requisite mechanical and electronic skills—and that he had vision and inventive skills as well"* (p. 241).

We left Ames at the end of June 1942, one month after our wedding. Berry had a job waiting for him in Pasadena at Consolidated Engineering Corporation. He had completed most of the course work for his PhD in physics, but he did not resume work on it until World War II ended. From the beginning, he made swift progress in his career. He wrote technical publications, patents, and internal company reports, and made speeches at various societies. He was listed in *American Men of Science, Leaders in American Science,* and *Who's Who on the West Coast.*

The 30–103 Analog Computer

In 1945, just three years after we left Ames, Cliff developed an analog computer. He had been thinking about it for some time, according to Consolidated scientists with whom I have since talked. When he finally figured it out, he wasted no time, taking everybody in the research department off current projects and putting them to work building a prototype of the computer. His superior was out of town, and Cliff later said that he had needed a lot of courage to take it upon himself to put the entire department on this computer. Consolidated named it the 30-103 and formed a new company called ElectroData to manufacture it. ElectroData did not exist long as a separate entity—it soon merged with Burroughs—but it was, I believe, the beginning of the California computer industry.

The analog technique had been used during the war, but not until Cliff invented the 30-103, (and Consolidated applied for a patent and put it on the market) was a computer available for industry that could solve linear simultaneous equations. According to J.C. Pemberton, the project engineer, the 30-103 was invented for an urgent reason: Consolidated needed something to untangle simultaneous data that came out of the mass spectrometer. This same J.C. Pemberton, by the way, had contributed something to the building of the Atanasoff-Berry Computer: he made a set of dies that formed the radial brass contacts for the rotating memory drum of the ABC. It was an unpaid contribution.

The 30-103 aroused a great deal of excitement in the scientific community. Cliff presented a paper on it at the January 12, 1946 meeting of the American Physical Society; a report appeared in the January 19, 1946 issue of *Science News Letter.* On February 5, 1946, Cliff was the speaker of the evening at a dinner meeting of the California Instrument Society, where he showed and described the 30-103.

In April 1946, the 30-103 was featured on the cover of the *Journal of Applied Physics* and was described in a lengthy article (Berry et al., 1946). Although it has been nearly forgotten in the constantly changing computer world, it was an important first.

In the summer of 1946 we were visiting Sam Legvold of ISC. He had been one of the group working with Atanasoff on the missile project. He asked Cliff how near to completion of his PhD he was, and I was astounded to find out that he had completed all but his orals and thesis. Sam and I persuaded Cliff to finish the work for his PhD. Aside from two courses he took at Cal Tech, and the French and German requirements, which he did by correspondence, my husband spent the following year studying for his orals, which he took in June 1947. The second year was spent doing the research for his thesis, which was completed in time for him to receive his PhD the following summer, 1948. This thesis was based on mass spectrometry, in which he was building an international reputation. It was a busy time for me; we had a daughter when he resumed work on his PhD and a son by the time he received it, so the child care was left to me.

Cliff's career flourished. He was one of the charter members of Committee E-14 of the American Society of Testing Materials. He was a member of the American Physical Society, the American Association for the Advancement of Science, and the American Vacuum Society. He presented papers at the meetings of these societies as well as the Instrument Society of America, the American Chemical Society, the American Optical Society, the Gordon Research Conference on Instrumentation (he was the chairman in 1959), the Max Planck Institut für Kohlenforschung, the National Bureau of Standards Symposium on Mass Spectrometry, the American Institute of Electrical Engineers, and the Western Spectrometry Association. He was guest lecturer at Ohio State University during a summer session. One of his most distinguished inventions was the Isatron (derived from Ion Source Analyzer), considered the heart of the mass spectrometer. At the time of his death, only 21 years after he began his professional career, Clifford Berry had over 30 patents issued and a number still pending, a total of 47, of which 46 were in the field of mass spectrometry. The patent on the 30–103 analog computer was entitled Linear Simultaneous Equation Solver, number 2,557,070. It was issued June 19, 1951.

Clifford Edward Berry died October 30, 1963. He had been dissatisfied with this work after Consolidated merged with Bell and Howell, which occurred around 1959 or 1960. In 1963, when he heard of an opening for director of advanced development at Vacuum-Electronics in Huntington, Long Island, he applied and was hired. He spent one week of that October fixing up our house and garden for sale, and another week at a vacuum conference. He lived in Long Island for only two weeks, during which he bought a new Chevrolet and looked at a number of houses. I remained in California to sell our house. His death remains a mystery. The coroner's report called it "possible suicide." The police kept his room locked for the three weeks while they sought clues. Some time later, Atanasoff, having driven to Long Island in search of clues about the cause of death, told me that the landlord had torn the plastic bag off Cliff's face with no difficulty. When I told a physician what I knew, he said that Cliff could not possibly have killed himself—he was murdered: *"It's like trying to hold your breath; you can't."* In magazine and newspaper articles, Atanasoff has referred to Berry's death as *"foul play."* From the information I have, I believe him. Nothing can bring my husband back, however, so I hope these brief remarks will put all further speculation to rest.

Letter from Clifford E. Berry to Richard K. Richards of Iowa State University

A few weeks after Cliff's death, I came across a carbon of a letter dated July 2, 1963, that he had written to R.K. Richards (1966) who was writing a book on early computers.

Dear Dr. Richards:

Thank you for your letter of April 30, 1963. It is unfortunate that Dr. Atanasoff has not responded, since he must have stored away somewhere, my notebooks, various reports, and drafts of his patent applications (I do not recall the names of the attorneys). I shall try to answer your questions as best I can from memory.

The machine was designed for a single purpose, namely to solve large sets of linear simultaneous algebraic equations (up to 30 x 30). It used binary arithmetic internally, with a word length of 50 bits. The basic mathematical procedure used was the successive elimination of coefficients from pairs of equations so as to eventually reduce the original square matrix to a triangular one. Since the internal memory of the computer only held the coefficients of two equations at a time, intermediate results (i.e., the single equations resulting from the linear combination of two so as to reduce by one the number of variables) were stored on special punched cards each of which held 30 fifty-place binary numbers. These cards were then read back into the machine at a later step in the process. A card could be punched or read in one second, but had to be inserted manually.

The maximum time required, in the worst possible case, for the machine to eliminate a variable between two equations, was about 90 seconds; the average was much less.

Within the machine there were two storage units, one for the coefficients of each of the equations of the pair being combined. These storage units consisted of rotating drums filled with small capacitors, each capacitor being connected to a small brass contact on the drum surface. Five-sixths of the drum periphery was occupied by these contacts (30 rows of 50 each), the other sixth being blank to provide time for other operations. The drums were driven by a geared-down synchronous motor so as to rotate at exactly 1 rps. Thus, the rate at which contacts passed a reading brush was 60 per second. The polarity of the charge on the capacitor indicated whether it represented a "one" or a "zero," and each capacitor was recharged immediately after it was read so that it never had to hold a charge for more than one second. All words were handled in parallel, but within each word the digits were handled serially. It is interesting to note parenthetically that before designing the capacitor memory units we seriously considered using magnetic drums, but we abandoned this approach because of anticipated low signal levels.

There were 30 identical units which were essentially binary adders. Each consisted of a set of direct-coupled vacuum tubes (seven twin triodes) so interconnected that they performed binary addition. Each unit had three inputs, two for the digits being added (or subtracted) and one for the carry over from the previous place, and two outputs, one for the result in that place and one for the carry over to the next place.

Initial data input to the machine was by IBM cards which were read by a special reader of our design. Each card carried five 15-place decimal numbers and was read in 15 seconds. The machine converted decimal numbers to binary numbers by means of a rotating drum (rear left corner of the machine) which carried contacts arranged to represent the binary equivalents of 1, 2, –9, 10, 20, –9 x 10^{14}. Final output of decimal numbers utilized the same apparatus in reverse and the decimal results appeared on a mechanical counter.

The above material more or less answers your questions 1 and 2. I will try to answer your remaining questions briefly.

3) Design and construction began in September, 1939, when I began my graduate work. It is amusing to recall that Prof. Atanasoff instructed me to build a framework for the machine during the first month before we had any real idea of what was going to go in the machine. As a result, the machine "grew" as work progressed, rather than being first designed and then constructed.

4) The only major element that was not completed when work stopped in the middle of 1942, was the reading circuits for the binary cards. The basic computing part of the machine had been completed and operating for more than a year, but it was of little use without means for storing the intermediate results.

5) The most important circuit developed was that of the adders. We initially tried flip-flops, but were discouraged by their unreliability and response to stray transients. The basic type of circuit which we finally evolved proved to be extremely reliable and non-critical.

The grids of the input tubes floated on small capacitors which were charged by momentary contact with a storage capacitor. A positive charge simply drained off through the grid and left the grid at ground potential so that the tube was conducting. A negative input blocked the tube so that the plate rose to the supply voltage. The output tubes were coupled: resistor $R^\wedge$. was selected so that tube A was blocked if either or both inputs were positive; this gave the carry over. The actual circuit with three inputs was considerably more complicated and required 14 triode elements. Changing a bias potential at one point in the circuit. All input capacitors were discharged to zero after each operation through individual neon bulbs connected to a half-wave 60 cycle source.

6) Prof. Atanasoff had thought about computing machines for several years, and had made an attempt to modify an IBM accounting machine to solve large sets of simultaneous equations. He soon recognized that the operation would be too slow and abandoned this approach. I am sure he was aware of the early work in the field and I recall that we were at least aware of Aiken's "relay" computer although we may not have known much about it.

7) The newspaper clipping was from one of the Des Moines papers—either the "Register" or the "Tribune." Incidentally, the object I was holding was not a "memory" but rather a set of 90 triode elements used in conjunction with one of the memory drums to shift the numbers so as to divide by powers of two.

I am sorry to have taken so long to write this and I hope it is not too late to be of help. Incidentally, I remember that several years ago Sam Legvold had one of the memory drums under his desk! There are undoubtedly a number of parts scattered around the Physics Department somewhere.

Sincerely,

Clifford E. Berry

I wrote to Richards to find out more about the book that led to the correspondence, and I quote part of his answer: *"Yes, I am writing a book on computers, and Cliff is to be mentioned in it in connection with Dr. Atanasoff's computer inasmuch as Dr. Atanasoff had told me on the telephone that many of the ideas in the machine, as well as the actual construction, should be credited to Cliff."* The book (Richards 1966) begins, after the introduction, with the words: *"The ancestry of all electronic digital systems appears to be traceable to a computer which will here be called the Atanasoff-Berry Computer. This computer was built during the period from about 1939–1942."*

Mather's Recollections on the ABC at Iowa State

Over the years we had kept in touch with most of the men who had worked on the project. One was Robert L. Mather, now retired from work with the Navy, who wrote the following letter to me in 1984:

In the 1940s a germinal entity existed at Iowa State University (then, Iowa State College, Ames, Iowa). Today known as the Atanasoff-Berry Computer (ABC), it can be said to be a predecessor of today's digital computer. Who were Atanasoff and Berry? Their names are not now found in common reference books, yet the stamp of the computer is on everyone's life.

I knew these men first as an upper-level undergraduate student, then as an electronic technician (1941–1942), and later as friends. One cannot describe them as they were some 40 years ago without being aware that the milieu of the day differs drastically from that of today. In 1941 JV [Atanasoff] was 37, Cliff was 24, and I was 20. I realize from the August 1940 paper of JV (see later) that I came too late on the scene to know which ideas were contributed by JV and which by Cliff—no doubt that paper had contributions by both men. Both men were brilliant and either of them could have generated any of the key concepts.

The craftsman in the Atanasoff-Berry team was Clifford E. Berry. Cliff had graduated from ISC in 1939 as an electrical engineer and was working with JV as a graduate student when I first met him in 1940. He had a knack for electronics design which he learned as a radio amateur. When I first knew him he was also well learned in graduate physics, and I was impressed that he thoroughly knew all the aspects of the computer that he was working on.

Cliff was my admirable older brother, so to speak, while John Vincent Atanasoff (whom was always called JV) was more distant—not quite a father figure but an authority figure and also older. Cliff could make things and could make them work. He valued home, children, and a stable marriage, yet aggressively sought new insights in every direction. I valued his friendship for the rest of his life.

Together, JV and Cliff designed and built the Iowa State computer (later to be called the ABC) in a small basement alcove of the physics building. It is credited with being the first electronic digital computer—a claim that lies buried in patent litigation of the early 1970s, a claim that was established by the court but that resulted in no financial gain to them or to Iowa State, and I believe, had little financial impact on the burgeoning computer industry.

One should realize that the IBM machines of those days were extremely cumbersome for calculations of any significant complexity. Their only competition was the electrically driven Monroe or Marchant mechanical calculator combined with pencil and paper (and don't forget the eraser!).

One should perhaps mention that at that time, IBM had an arrangement with the college that allowed Snedecor's lab to use their equipment at reduced cost (a common arrangement). JV had made some overtures to IBM about some financial assistance for building his computer. He felt that IBM wanted more out of such assistance than they deserved. At any rate he chose that more difficult task of finding funds elsewhere. Probably the greatest fault with the computer project was that it was seriously underfunded. There were too many cost-cutting decisions that sacrificed component reliability. There were not funds that would have carried the project through the debugging stage and into useful application. There was too much dependency on student-wage labor who were readily drawn away when jobs developed. In fact, even JV was drawn away—faculty salaries were pretty low, also.

JV did have ready application for such a machine, if it had been usable, in the graduate research his other students were doing. Erwin Kammer was investigating the elastic constants of beta quartz, and at one point in the reduction of his data, systems of linear equations had to be solved. It was an appalling defect of the USA in the 1930s that supporting funds for advanced development of useful tools were not available—a defect we learned more about in the 1940s.

The ABC was designed to solve systems of linear equations up to systems of 30 equations in 30 unknowns. Modern computer terminology allows succinct description of the process. The numerical theory is very clearly described in Chapter 9 of the book by Anthony Ralston, *A First Course in Numerical Analysis* (New York, McGraw-Hill, 1965). The process may be known to the reader as classical Gaussian elimination. Each coefficient was represented by a fixed-point 50-bit number (15-digit precision). The number was represented electronically by 50 plus or minus charges on 50 capacitors. The charges were read by vacuum tubes once per second and either replenished or modified according to the arithmetic process being implemented. Addition and subtraction were done by an electronic AND/OR circuit. Multiplication and division were done by electronic bit-shifting.

A detailed description of the computer by Atanasoff himself is in Section 7.2 (p. 305) of *The Origins of Digital Computers—Selected Papers,* edited by Brian Randell (New York, Springer-Verlag, 1973). This is a reproduction of a paper JV prepared to justify a grant of $5,000 for the machine—written in August 1940. I remember reading it in July 1941 as one of Cliff's ways of introducing me to the machine after I started working for him. Some of the photographs were added later—in fact, I think I may have taken some of them.

I recall my hourly wage as 50 cents per hour. One of my first tasks was sorting screws and nuts in the basement student shop, and later with some coaching and supervision from Cliff I moved up to punching and wiring on the computer. The picture on page 325 of Randell's book showing the final state of the computer in May 1942 is very meaningful to me as I clearly remember cinching up those waxed-string lacings on the wire bundles over to the base-2 to base-10 conversion drum. A similar bundle shows on the thyratron chassis beneath the IBM card reader. That chassis with 30 thyratrons was my creation. Those thyratrons drove the transformers, which punched the holes in the paper cards for the intermediate memory of the coefficients. I've always wondered about the transients that would have resulted when the punching called for all 30 to fire simultaneously!

The 50 capacitors for each coefficient were mounted radially to a row of 50 pins on the surface of a phenolic bakelite drum. There were 32 such rows on each drum (giving a spare row or two). The drums revolved once per second under the stationary metal brushes leading to the electronics. All of the reading, computation, etc., was done in synchrony with the 60 Hertz power mains. The 10/60 second of dead time was used for various housekeeping chores of the computation. Each drum had the coefficients of one linear equation. A switch allowed a pair of corresponding coefficients from the two drums to be chosen for elimination. One set of coefficients was subtracted from the other (the arithmetic was done in parallel for all 30 coefficients) until the remainder turned positive. Then divided, subtracted—and so on until the coefficient had been completely eliminated. The remaining coefficients were then put into punch-card memory. The process was repeated until the last unknown was given a numerical value, which could then be substituted in the next-to-last pair of equations to evaluate a second unknown, and so on until all the unknowns were evaluated.

This process in not significantly different from modern-day computer procedure. As Ralston's book points out, there is an optimum sequence for the elimination of coefficients and there are cumulative-numerical rounding errors that can be estimated. One can estimate the total time required to solve a set of 30 linear equations with the ABC computer and it would be on the order of a day—very slow by modern standards. Still, by the standards of 1940 that would be very rapid.

World War II began, for the United States, in December 1941. I left for the Naval Ordnance Laboratory in June 1942. Cliff had married in May, and he left Iowa for mass-spectrometer work with Consolidated Engineering Corp. in Pasadena. JV and several of his graduate students left that Fall to join the Naval Ordnance Laboratory. I think we all fully expected to reassemble in Ames after a hiatus for the war.

A few bits and pieces of the ABC still remain in the Physics Department museum at Iowa State, along with some excellent photographs. In the postwar years the ABC was dismantled to make space for new academic activities required by the surge of returning veterans.

Much legal argument was made during the litigation of the 1970s about a visit of John Mauchly to Atanasoff in June 1941. I believe that Mauchly had support at that time from the Army's Aberdeen Proving Ground for computer research on computation of shell trajectories. JV also had some war research support for experimentation in a room adjacent to the computer space. Several students were employed in that research, many of us were guinea pigs part time. My impression was that the purpose of the war research was to work out and measure some of the human factors in the visual tracking of targets such as by a gunner. We spent our time as subjects chasing galvanometer spots across a screen using various types of tracking controls. It seems now that Mauchly's visit would have been natural, and there would have been an expectation that JV would be quite open about all of his work that might be useful in the war effort. I do recall a visitor to the computer in June 1941 whom I think must have been Mauchly, although I was not introduced to him. It is evident in retrospect that Mauchly was much more adept at business skill, with support from his university, than JV was.

Mauchly's computing machine later became widely known under the acronym ENIAC (Electronic Numerical Integrator and Computer), and portions of it have been on display at the Smithsonian's National Museum of American History in Washington, D.C. The ENIAC involved an effort probably 1,000 times larger than the ABC, so that in comparing the two projects one needs to be careful as to what aspects are being compared. Obviously the ENIAC benefited from a professional full-time staff, better quality control of components, longer-term support, and the blessings of adequate technical administration and management. In short, money. The ENIAC was a special-purpose machine primarily funded and designed to solve the differential equations of shell trajectories. The technical management allowed a versatility to be incorporated, however, which permitted it to work on other problems. The ENIAC had continuing applications from 1946 to 1955. This long period of demonstration by a single machine established the productivity of the electronic digital computer to US business managers. The preceding small academic machine, the ABC had made its contribution to the history of computing.

I always felt Cliff had the better understanding of the arts of electronics and had more patience with imperfect performance of both machines and people. Looking back, I know I must have been irritating at times in spite of my great eagerness to please, and yet I recall no time at which Cliff expressed irritation and he was very patient to search out my foibles and go through an explanation to get me back on track. I always left with the impression that he respected and trusted me. Cliff worked well with people.

Since the electronic punch-card memory was Cliff's master's thesis, no doubt that was largely his work from the start. I always thought that the reduction to practice for all parts of the machine was likely to have been due to Cliff. There were other technicians besides myself who had to be supervised and instructed, and that again was a contribution of Cliff. Cliff's contribution was a major one.

In the legal wrangling of the 1970s, there was some emphasis on whether the computer had ever actually demonstrated its capabilities. At the time I left the project, it had not, but I knew there was no permanent reason that it should not work. I remember a later brief conversation with Cliff in which he told me that he had actually solved a small set of linear equations using the machine before he had left for California. I assumed that there were still bugs that remained to be worked out and plenty of work for all of us should we ever return to Ames.

In summing up the six-year court case, Judge Earl R. Larson declared that Atanasoff's had been the first automatic electronic digital computer, and that the ENIAC patent was invalid, having derived much from the Atanasoff-Berry Computer.

Iowa State is proud of being the home of the first digital computer (though chagrined over its failure to patent the ABC). In October 1983, at a celebration of the 10-year anniversary of the completion of the ENIAC court case, ISU awarded its highest honor, the Distinguished Achievement Citation, to John V. Atanasoff. In June 1985, the same honor was awarded to Clifford Berry—the first time it had been given posthumously.

BIBLIOGRAPHY

Biographical

Atanasoff, J.V., "Computing Machine for the Solution of Large Systems of Linear Algebraic Equations," in B. Randell, ed., *The Origins of Digital Computers, Selected Papers,* New York, Springer-Verlag, New York, 1973, Chapter 7.2.

Atanasoff, John Vincent, "Advent of Electronic Digital Computing," *Ann. Hist. Comp.,* Vol. 6, No. 3, July 1984, pp. 229–282.

Berry, Jean R., "Clifford Edward Berry, 1918–1963: His Role in Early Computers," *Ann. Hist. Comp.,* Vol. 8, No. 4, Oct. 1986, pp. 361–369.

Ralston, Anthony, *A First Course in Numerical Analysis,* McGraw-Hill, New York, 1965.

Richards, R.K., *Electronic Digital Systems,* Wiley and Son, New York, 1966.

Significant Publications

Berry, Clifford E., Doyle E. Wilcox, Sibyl M. Rock, and H.W. Washburn, "A Computer for Solving Linear Simultaneous Equations," *J. of Applied Physics,* Vol. 17, No. 4, April 1946, pp. 262–272.

HEINZ BILLING

Born April 7, 1914, Salzwedel, Germany; an inventor[14] of magnetic drum storage and built the first working electronic computer in Germany; searched for gravity waves and became unsurpassed in not finding them.

Education: doctoral degree, University of Göttingen, 1938.

Professional Experience: Aerodynamic Test Centre, Göttingen (Aerodynamische Versuchsanstalt, AVA) 1938–1946; German Air Force, 1938–1941; Institute für Instrumentenkunde (Institute for Scientific Instruments), Kaiser-Wilhelm-Gesellschaft (later Max-Planck-Gesellschaft), 1946–1949, 1950–1972; Commonwealth Scientific and Industrial Organization, Sydney, Australia, 1949–1950; Max Planck Institute, Garching, Germany, 1972–1982.

Honors and Awards: honorary professorship in computing, Erlangen University, 1967; Konrad Zuse Prize, 1987.

Heinz Billing was born on April 7, 1914 in Salzwedel, a small town some 30 miles north of Wolfsburg, where Volkswagen automobiles are made. He went to school at Salzwedel, graduated from high school ("Abitur"—examination) at 18 and, after studies at Göttingen (a famous university town south of Hanover) and Munich, he received his doctorate in physics at the age of 24. His thesis under Walter Gerlach was on *Light Interference with Canal Rays.*

He began his career June 1, 1938, at the Aerodynamic Test Centre at Göttingen (*Aerodynamische Versuchsanstalt,* AVA) connected with Ludwig Prandtl, the famous director of the *Kaiser-Wilhelm-Institut für Strömungsforschung* (fluid mechanics). By October 1, 1938, he was drafted to the Air Force, where he worked in weather forecasting. He was released from these duties in May 1941 to do research in aeronautical acoustics.

Magnetic Sound Recording

In those days German engineering was well known for excellent results with magnetic sound recording, first on steel wire and then on tape. Telefunken's "Magnetophon" was introduced at the 1935 radio exhibition in Berlin (*Funkausstellung*) and remained a well known trademark until the Fifties.

The goal was to apply this technology to the problem of reducing propeller noise for better communications in the aircraft cockpit.

---

[14]See also Howard Aiken and Andrew Booth.

Billing tried to design a rotating magnetic audiotape which would neutralize the sound of the propeller by feeding the inverse signal into the headphones during its next rotation. The contraption didn't work, as the propellers were not inclined to sound the same each time around.

Göttingen was spared British bombardment, perhaps in order to capture its research centers and their scientists intact.

In 1945–1946 Billing wrote an AVA report on "Modern Aeronautical Acoustics" (in "Naturforschung und Medizin in Deutschland 1939–1946," the German edition of the "FIAT Review of German Science"). By November 1, 1946, he moved to the *Institut für Instrumentenkunde* (Institute for Scientific Instruments) of the Kaiser-Wilhelm-Gesellschaft, later Max-Planck-Gesellschaft, which was also housed on the site of the AVA. Billing did research in high-frequency engineering, in the amplification of brain currents, and with Geiger counters.

The First German Magnetic Drum Storage

But then his special knowledge of magnetic storage technology became very helpful to Billing.

At that time the earliest use of computers was strongly biased towards what we would call today "scientific applications." Newly invented, non-mechanical computation devices were used for mathematical algorithms and pure number crunching rather than for data storage. The processors were designed with electromagnetic relays, and decisions were made by switching electrical currents within the machine. Then fast and silent electronic vacuum tubes were used to do this task. But how could the machine be made to remember its digits, to freeze the electric current and store the results for later use? Even the ENIAC, the legendary first "Electronic Numerical Integrator and Computer," doing nearly one thousand operations per second back in 1945 (.001 MIPS in today's notation), had just a minimal data storage of only 20 figures; only some 2,000 tubes of the total 18,000 were for storage purposes.

In the summer of 1947 Heinz Billing and Konrad Zuse were present at a meeting of Alan Turing and J.R. Womersley from Britain with the German computer pioneer Alwin Walther from Darmstadt. Womersley spoke in vague terms about data storage by transmitting the data back to the sender, who then could choose to send it on another trip or to use it. In fact in England a mercury-delay line storage for 16 binary numbers had been built, keeping 30-digit binary figures "on the move" for 1 millisecond at a time—an expensive, insecure, and volatile system. Billing had no knowledge of this technology and misunderstood Womersley's remark, interpreting it along his own lines of thinking.

With his background in electro-acoustics he took a rotating cylinder and attached magnetic tape to it. Later the magnetic surface was directly sprayed on to it to avoid seams. This became the very first magnetic storage system for computers; rotating at 3,000 cycles per minute, it sounded like a whistling monster. The average access time from one half-rotation was a mere 10 milliseconds! On this first drum storage the read-and-write heads were firmly mounted about half a millimeter over the magnetic surface. Only later the heads were modified to ride on self-made air cushions and used new technologies that increased the storage density such as the non-return-zero system. A later version of Billing's drum can be seen today at the Deutsches Museum in Munich—although it is now mercifully silent.

Heinz Billing emphasizes that Joachim Lehmann, independently working in Dresden, had the same idea, but was a few months late—not too late, however, for a life-long friendship. Both Billing and Lehmann were of course unaware of similar developments of Andrew Donald Booth at Birkbeck College, London, and Howard Aiken on the Harvard Mark III computer, both of whom started in 1947 as well.

First Attempts

After Billing had started his work in December 1947 on an electronic adder with magnetic drum storage, it attracted the interest of Ludwig Biermann, the famous astrophysicist who had been brought to Göttingen by Werner Heisenberg. In July 1948, Billing reported on his plans in the annual GAMM[15] meeting. (See *Zeitschrift für angewandte Mathematik und Mechanik, Jahrgang,* No. 29, 1949, pp. 38–42). As an example of a practical application Billing chose the numerical solution of the Schrödinger differential equations, a problem that was tried with desk calculators by Biermann's computing group—and found out only later that the special method that they used was in fact due to Biermann.

In the spring of 1948, Biermann visited Billing's workshop and saw, as he later reported, a glimmer of hope that the calculation time for his astrophysical computations could be reduced to a reasonable level—from years perhaps to weeks.

---

[15]GAMM is the "Gesellschaft für angewandte Mathematik und Mechanik," the Society for Applied Mathematics and Mechanics.

Sidetracked to Australia
In those economically tough times Billing was called to work for half a year in 1949 at the Commonwealth Scientific and Industrial Organization at Sydney, Australia. He might even have stayed "down under," had it not been for its remoteness from the main technology centers in these early days before the advent of electronic mail systems.

Back to Germany
Back in Göttingen, Ludwig Biermann persuaded his senior colleague, Werner Heisenberg, to call Heinz Billing back to Germany with a plan to actually create the first German-built, fully electronic computer system. And Billing accepted for the relatively exorbitant salary of 9,660 DM—per year. He returned May 1, 1950, and found the physicists planning on having some sort of small machine quite soon.

Therefore, in the fall of 1950, the plan was to make a series of electronic calculators: first, as a start and to gain experience, a small model, G1, paper-tape controlled but with an arithmetic unit about ten times more powerful than the mechanical desk calculators of those days. This was to be followed shortly afterwards by model G2 with a drum storage of 2,048 binary numbers, and already equipped with stored program control. All these systems would be built with vacuum tubes and drum storage. A large model, to be called G3, would come later.

Billing finished the small G1 model in 1952, using his proven drum storage technology for 26 binary coded numbers of 32 bits each, giving 10 decimal digits of precision. This idea, to save elements by encoding the whole number in binary form rather than by each decimal digit (used by Stibitz, Aiken), was first used by Konrad Zuse with his relays. It cut the number of vacuum tubes to 83 percent while retaining the same precision. (Stibitz and Aiken needed 4 bits per decimal digit, Zuse needed $\log_{10}2$ or 3.322 bits per decimal digit. The ratio 3.322:4 is 0.83.) Billing's G1 had less than 500 tubes, which made it quite reliable and robust. History tells us that the G1 worked until early 1953, logging 2,100 hours of activity, 400 of which were for service and re-runs, giving an overall availability of 80 percent—well done for a vacuum tube system. Several modified copies of the G1, called G1a, were made. One is on display in the Deutsches Museum in Munich.

The first German electronic calculators were used for scientific calculations such as predicting the paths of electrically charged particles in magnetic fields, a problem in which Ludwig Biermann was particularly interested, by using ordinary differential equations of fifth order.

The G1 already managed about two operations per second. A round of calculating the orbit of a particle took 3 to 4 hours, while doing the same job by hand with the help of mechanical machines would have taken a week of full-time work.[16]

When the Konrad Zuse Prize was first awarded in 1987, Heinz Billing received it for his creation of Germany's first electronic universal computer with stored program control, the G2.

The later and larger model already had 2,000 storage locations, and was ten times faster than the G1. It was ready in 1954 and used in 1956 to calculate the exact time of the reappearance of the asteroid Amor, which comes into view every 8 years. It was not until the tedious manual prediction proved to be off by up to two angular minutes that the virtues of electronic calculation were retroactively acknowledged by the incredulous German Astronomical Society: "In calculations of the highest precision the machine is superior to manual calculation," they wrote in their next annual report. Little Amor had brought scientific acceptance to this new calculating wizard that silently glowed in the man-made vacuum of glass tubes.

In 1953 Billing started to build a really large machine. The model G3 was completed in 1960 and proved to be the most powerful vacuum tube computer ever built in Germany, perhaps even the most beautiful, as Heinz Billing remembers. Even in these early days it used a microprogram, had a ferrite core memory of 2,000 binary numbers of 43 bits each with a 10-microsecond access time. A new invention, Friedrich L. Bauer's patented hardware stack, appropriately called "cellar" in Germany, was implemented, as well as microinstructions for the display of color pictures: automatically red, green, and blue filters were moved over a cathode ray tube. The resulting photo could be a full-color graph of the mathematical results. The G3 was moved with the Max Planck Institute for Astrophysics to Munich, Bavaria. It was still in service as late as November 9, 1972.

In 1967 Heinz Billing received an honorary professorship in computing at Erlangen University.

Billing Leaves the Computer Field
After transistors had been firmly established, when microelectronics arrived, after scientific computers were slowly overshadowed by commercial applications and computers were mass-produced in factories, Heinz Billing left the computer field in which he had been a pioneer for nearly 30 years.

---

[16]As early as 1949 Dr. Walter Sprick had built an electronic multiplication unit connected to a Powers tabulating machine.

In 1972, Billing returned to his original field of physics, at the Max Planck Institute's new location at Garching near Munich. Beginning in 1972 he became known for building the world's most sensitive instruments to measure hypothetical gravity waves.

Today, after his retirement in 1982, Professor Billing is still connected with the Max Planck Institute and has his home in the same small village, Garching, north of Munich.[17]

JAMES BIRKENSTOCK

Born May 7, 1912, Burlington, Iowa; key motivator to IBM's entry into the electronic computer business.[18]

Education: BSc, University of Iowa, 1935.

Professional Experience: IBM Corp., 1935–1973.

Honors and Awards: member, President Johnson's Commission on the US Patent System; Distinguished Alumni Award, University of Iowa; Distinguished Service Award, Computer and Business Equipment Manufacturers Association (CBEMA); Distinguished Service Award, Electronic Industries Association; LLD, Fairfield University.

Birkenstock joined IBM Corporation in 1935. His combined work experience of almost 38 years with IBM plus 17 years as a management consultant totals 55 years. For more than 40 years he was engaged in all phases of technology asset management and technology transfer, primarily within the field of information processing.

His work experience with IBM was that of data processing salesman, branch manager, general sales manager, executive assistant to the president of IBM, executive director of market analysis and product planning, and vice president of commercial development. For more than 20 years prior to retirement from IBM in 1973, he was IBM's ranking senior officer/executive responsible for directing all phases of management of IBM's intellectual property rights, including IBM's relations with foreign governments pertaining thereto.

---

[17]Fritz Jörn, 1990.
[18]Cited by Watson, Jr., 1990.

In 1973 Birkenstock formed Intercal, Inc., a management consulting firm specializing in the field of technology asset management, and in this capacity served a number of high technology clients operating primarily in the field of electronics. He has been given recognition by IBM and others for his pioneering efforts in connection with IBM developments in the field of electronic data processing.

Thomas J. Watson, Jr., in his book *Father, Son & Co.*, describes Birkenstock as an indispensable member of IBM's "inner circle." He credits Birkenstock with being the key motivator in IBM's entry into the electronic computer business in 1950, and for conducting the tedious negotiations with the Japanese government, which led to the establishment of IBM Japan as a Japanese-validated, wholly-owned IBM subsidiary in 1960.

During 1965–1966 Birkenstock was appointed to and served on President Lyndon B. Johnson's commission on the US patent system. For more than 10 years, while with IBM, Birkenstock served as a director of the Computer and Business Equipment Manufacturers Association (CBEMA) and was for a 2-year period chairman of the board of the association. He was also cited for distinguished service to the Electronics Industries Association, and was awarded an honorary life membership in this organization.

Birkenstock served as a Director of the IBM World Trade Organization from 1966 until his retirement from IBM in 1973. He is a former member of the board of directors of Motorola, and is currently director of the Harris Bank of Florida. He is a trustee of the Charles Babbage Institute and Fairfield University.

BIBLIOGRAPHY

Biographical

Bashe, Charles J., Lyle R. Johnson, John H. Palmer, and Emerson W. Pugh, *IBM's Early Computers*, MIT Press, Cambridge, Mass., 1986.

Hurd, Cuthbert, "Early IBM Computers: Edited Testimony," *Ann. Hist. Comp.*, Vol. 3. No. 1, 1981, pp. 163–182.

Pugh, E.W., *Memories That Shaped an Industry—Decisions Leading to IBM System/360*, MIT Press, Cambridge, Mass., 1984.

Watson, Thomas J., Jr., and Peter Petre, *Father, Son & Co*, Bantam Books, New York, 1990.

GARRETT BIRKHOFF

Born January 10, 1911, Princeton, N.J.; noted for significant research in computational mathematics related to fluid mechanics and nuclear reactor theory.

Education: AB, Harvard University, 1932.

Professional Experience: Harvard University: junior fellow, Harvard Society of Fellows, 1933–1936, faculty member, 1936–1969, George Putnam Professor of Pure and Applied Mathematics, 1969–1981; professor emeritus, 1981–present, visiting lecturer, Universidad Nacional de Mexico, 1945, 1958; Walker-Ames Lecturer, University of Washington, 1947; Taft Lecturer, University of Cincinnati, 1947; Fairchild Distinguished Scholar, California Institute of Technology, 1981; ONR Visiting Research Professor, Naval Postgraduate School, 1984.

Society Positions: president, Society for Industrial and Applied Mathematics (SIAM); chairman, Conference Board of the Mathematical Sciences; vice president, American Mathematical Society (AMS); vice president, American Academy of Arts and Sciences; vice president, Mathematical Association of America (MAA); chairman, Section A, American Association for the Advancement of Science (AAAS), 1979.

Honors and Awards: member, American Philosophical Society; member, National Academy of Sciences; honorary degrees from Universidad Nacional de Mexico, University of Lille (France), Case Institute of Technology, Technische Universität of Munich, Technische Hochschule (Darmstadt, Germany); Guggenhiem Fellow, 1948; George D. Birkhoff Prize, American Mathematical Society, 1978; von Neumann Lecturer, SIAM, 1981.

BIBLIOGRAPHY

Biographical

Birkhoff, Garrett, "Computing Developments 1935–1955, as Seen from Cambridge, USA," in Metropolis, N., J. Howlett, and Gian-Carlo Rota, *A History of Computing in the Twentieth Century*, Academic Press, New York, 1980, pp. 21–30.

Birkhoff, Garrett, "Fluid Dynamics, Reactor Computations, and Surface Representation," in Nash, Stephen. G., *A History of Scientific Computing*, ACM Press History Series, 1990, pp. 63–87.

Significant Publications

Birkhoff, Garrett, "Mathematics and Psychology," *SIAM Rev.*, Vol. 10, 1969.

Birkhoff, Garrett, "Numerical Fluid Dynamics," *SIAM Rev.*, Vol. 25, 1983.

Birkhoff, Garrett, "Mathematics and Computer Science," *American Scientist*, Vol. 63, 1975.

Birkhoff, Garrett, "Applied Mathematics and Its Future," in Thomson, Robb W., ed., *Science and Technology in America*, National Bureau of Standards Publ. #465, 1977.

Birkhoff, Garrett, and Robert E. Lynch, *Numerical Solution of Elliptical Problems*, SIAM Publications, 1984.

ERICH BLOCH

Born January 9, 1925; headed the IBM development of the Solid Logic Technology program, which provided IBM with the microelectronics technology for its System/360 computer.

Education: BS, electrical engineering, University of Buffalo, 1952.

Professional Experience: IBM Corp., 1952–1984; director, National Science Foundation, 1984–1990; distinguished fellow, Council on Competitiveness, 1990–present.

Honors and Awards: IBM Patent Award, 1961; National Medal of Technology, 1985; IEEE United States Activities Board Award for Distinguished Public Service, 1989; IEEE Founders Medal, 1990; member, National Academy of Engineering; fellow, American Association for the Advancement of Science; fellow, IEEE.

Bloch, a native of Germany, moved to Switzerland at the age of 14. There he obtained his pre-college education and studied electrical engineering for 2 years at the Swiss Federal Institute of Technology before emigrating to the US in 1948. Taking courses at night and working days as a research assistant in an industrial laboratory, Bloch obtained a bachelor's degree in electrical engineering from the University of Buffalo. He joined IBM in January 1952 and soon developed the first ferrite-core storage units used in commercial products. Later he initiated development of the company's first ferrite-core memory with over 1 million bits.

Subsequently, while serving as engineering manager for the high-performance Stretch computer, he became involved in the development of the SMS circuit and packaging technology. In 1962, he headed development of the Solid Logic Technology program, which provided IBM with the microelectronics technology for its System/360 computer. Subsequently, Bloch was appointed a vice president of the company's Data Systems Division and general manager of the East Fishkill facility, which was responsible for the development and manufacture of semi-conductor components used in IBM's product line. He was elected as IBM vice president in 1981. From 1981 to 1984, Bloch served as chairman of the Semiconductor Research Cooperative, a group of leading computer and electronics firms that funded advanced research in universities. He was also the IBM representative on the board of the Semiconductor Industry Association. In 1985, B.O. "Bo" Evans, Fred Brooks, and Eric Bloch received the National Medal of Technology at a White House ceremony for their work in developing the IBM System/360, described as "revolutionizing the industry." After leaving IBM in 1984 he served as director of the National Science Foundation until 1990. In 1989 Bloch was the recipient of the IEEE United States Activities Board Award for Distinguished Public Service and the 1990 IEEE Founders Medal. He is a member of the National Academy of Engineering, a Fellow of the American Association for the Advancement of Science and of the Institute of Electrical and Electronics Engineers.[19]

BIBLIOGRAPHY

Significant Publications

Bloch, E., "The Engineering Design of the Stretch Computer," Proc. EJCC, Boston, 1959, pp. 48–58.

Bloch, E., "Magnetic Core Logic in a High Speed Card to Tape Converter," *IRE Transactions on Electronic Computers*, Vol. EC 8, No. 2, June 1959.

---

[19]From Pugh, Emerson W., Lyle R. Johnson and John H. Palmer, *IBM's 360 and Early 370 Systems*, MIT Press, Cambridge, Mass., 1991.

Bloch, E., "The Engineering Design of the STRETCH Computer," *Proc. of the EJCC,* pp. 48–58; revised as chapter, *Planning a Computer System,* by Buchholz, McGraw Hill, 1962; reprinted as Part 2, Section 1, Chapter 34, Bell/Newell, *Computer Structures,* McGraw-Hill, New York, 1971.

Bloch, E., "Advances in Circuit Technology and Their Impact on Computer Systems," *Proc. IFIP,* 1968.

Bloch, E., "Component Progress—Its Impact on Systems Architecture and Machine Organization," *High Speed Computer and Algorithm Organization J.,* Academic Press, New York, 1977, pp. 13–39.

Bloch, E., "High Performance, Large Scale Computers," *The Financial Analysts Federation and the Los Angeles Society of Financial Analysts,* March 7, 1978.

Bloch, E., "Component Progress: Its Effect on High-Speed Computer Architecture and Machine Organization," *Computer,* Vol. 11, No. 4, Apr. 1978, pp. 64–75.

Bloch, E., "VLSI and Computers: Challenge and Promise," *Computers,* 1980.

Bloch, E., "Semiconductor Research Cooperative," Chapter 10, *Global Stakes— The Future of High Technology in America,* by Botkin, Dimancescu, and Stata; Ballinger Press, 1982.

Bloch, E., "Semiconductor Research Cooperative," *IEEE Spectrum,* Nov. 1983.

Bloch, E., "Manufacturing Technologies," *The Bridge,* National Academy of Engineering, Vol. 15, No. 3, Fall 1985, pp. 10–15.

Bloch, E., "The NSF Role in Fostering University-Industry Research Relationships," *IEEE Trans. Eng. Education,* Fall/Winter 1985.

Bloch, E., "Managing for Challenging Times: A National Research Strategy," *Issues in Science and Technology,* Vol. 2, No. 2, 1986, pp. 20–29.

Bloch, E., "Basic Research in a Modern Society," *The Royal Society for the Encouragement of Arts Manufactures and Commerce J.,* Vol. 134, No. 5357, Apr. 1986, pp. 286–298.

Bloch, E., "Science: Not for Experts Only," syndicated by the National Academy Press Service, May 1986.

Bloch, E., "Basic Research and Economic Health: The Coming Challenge," *Science,* Vol. 232, May 1986, pp. 595–599.

Bloch, E., "Science, Technology, and Cultural Change," *Encyclopedia of Physical Science and Technology,* June 1986.

Bloch, E., "Supercomputing and the Growth of Computational Science in the National Science Foundation," *Int'l. J. Supercomputer Applications,* Vol. 1, No. 1, Spring 1987, pp. 5–8.

Bloch, E., "Meeting Our Need for Science and Engineering Talent: The Precollege Connection," *J. of College Science Teaching,* 1987.

Bloch, E., "Basic Research: The Key to Economic Competitiveness," *Interdisciplinary Science Reviews,* Vol. 12, No. 2, 1987.

Bloch, E., "The United States Technology Base: Erosion, or a Changing World?," *World Link,* Jan.–Feb. 1990.

GEORGE BOOLE

Born November 2, 1815, Lincoln, UK; died December 8, 1864, Cork, Ireland; British creator of a logic and a number system that bears his name.

Boole's father was a simple tradesman skilled in the construction of optical instruments, but extremely interested in mathematics and sciences, an interest which he passed on to his son. George Boole attended an elementary school in Lincoln, where he was described by one of his classmates as "being of a shy and retiring disposition,"[20] but it was from his father that he acquired his fundamental instruction in mathematics. At an early age he was more interested in classical languages and was tutored in the rudiments of Latin by William Brooke, a local bookseller. Boole and Brooke remained close throughout his life and maintained an uninterrupted correspondence. Independently Boole added Greek to his repertoire. At the age of 14 Boole's father sent his metric translation of an "Ode of Homer" to the local newspaper with an annotation regarding his age. A local schoolmaster challenged the entry, thereby sparking a controversy which lasted many weeks.

At the age of 16 Boole undertook employment as an assistant teacher at a school in Doncaster (Yorkshire). He returned to the Lincoln area by taking a similar position in Waddington, where he began studies of modern languages and religion. These studies were to be left unfinished, however, since his finances were becoming limited by the dependence of his parents on his support.

In his twentieth year, Boole opened a school of his own in Lincoln, only to return to Waddington shortly thereafter when the schoolmaster there died. Throughout this period he continued his independent

---

[20]Boole 1852.

studies and began to write his first memoirs on mathematics. His first paper was entitled "On Certain Theorems in the Calculus of Variations." From this start and based on subsequent studies, he developed what is now regarded as the foundation for modern higher algebra. The publication of his papers was significantly assisted by the work of D.F. Gregory, the editor of the *Cambridge Mathematical Journal*. Gregory and other friends, suggested that Boole take courses in mathematics at the University of Cambridge, but because of the paucity of his finances he was unable to take up this opportunity.

Boole was able to understand the separation of symbols and values, and based on this insight saw that relationships represented by symbols could be manipulated mathematically—thus founding the concept of symbolic logic. These finding were published in the *Transactions of the Royal Society of London*; in return the Society awarded him a medal.

As a result of his achievements, Boole was offered the chair of mathematics at Queen's University at Cork, Ireland in 1848, shortly after the publication of his book *Mathematical Analysis of Logic*. This opportunity allowed him to extend his studies and to produce a work, regarded as his most significant, entitled "An Investigation of the Laws of Thought," which had the subtitle "on which are founded the mathematical theories of logic and probabilities." Later he added *Differential Equations and Finite Differences* to his list of publications.

To make up for his lack of formal training and consequent paper qualifications, Boole was awarded honorary degrees from Dublin and Oxford Universities; the Royal Society elected him as a fellow, and in 1858 he was elected as an honorary member of the Cambridge Philosophical Society.

In late 1864 Boole walked to Queen's University from his home—a distance of just over 2 miles—in a rain storm, and then gave his lecture. Suffering from pneumonia, Boole died at the age of 50 on December 8, 1864.

BIBLIOGRAPHY

Biographical

MacFarlane, Alexander, *Ten British Mathematicians*, John Wiley and Sons, New York, 1916, pp. 50–53.

Significant Publications

Boole, George, *Mathematical Analysis of Thought*, 1847.

Boole, George, *Studies in Logic and Probability*, Open Court Pub. Co., 1852.

Boole, George, *An Investigation of the Laws of Thought,* 1854; reprinted Dover, 1951.

Boole, George, *Treatise on Differential Equations,* 1859.

Boole, George, *Calculus of Finite Differences,* Chelsea Pub. Co., 1860; reprinted 1970.

Boole, George, *Collected Logical Works,* Open Court Pub. Co., La Salle, Ill., 1952.

ANDREW DONALD BOOTH

Born February 11, 1918, East Molesy, Surrey, UK; early computer developer at the University of London who worked with John von Neumann; with Warren Weaver in 1946, first conceived of machine translations, and manufactured magnetic drum memories for many early computers.

Education: BSc (External), mathematical physics, University of London,1940; PhD, chemistry, University of Birmingham, 1944; DSc, physics, University of London, 1951.

Professional Experience: Actuarial Dept., Sun Life of Canada, 1947; graduate apprenticeship (mechanical engineering and administration), Rootes Securities Aircraft Factory, Coventry, 1938–1940; physicist, Armstrong Siddley Aircraft, Coventry, 1940–1941; research physicist, British Rubber Producers' Research Association, Welwyn Garden City, 1944–1945; Nuffield Fellow, Birkbeck College, University of London, 1946–1949; Rockefeller Fellow and member of the Institute for Advanced Studies, Princeton, 1946; visiting (full) professor of theoretical physics, University of Pittsburgh, 1949; director Birkbeck College Electronic Computer Project, 1950–1955; head, Department of Numerical Automation, Birkbeck College, 1955–1962; professor and head of Department of Electrical Engineering, University of Saskatchewan, 1962–1963; dean, College of Engineering and university professor, University of Saskatchewan 1963–1972; professor of autonetics (at large) Case-Western Reserve University, Cleveland 1963–1972; UNESCO visiting professor, University of Mexico, 1963, and Techniche Hohschule, Hanover, 1964; visiting professor Georgia Tech. 1967–1969; president, Lakehead University, Ontario, Canada, 1972–1978 (retired); chair, Autonetics Research Associates, B.C., Canada, 1978–present.

Honors and Awards: fellow, Institution of Electrical Engineers, 1951; fellow, Institute of Physics, 1951; honorary fellow, Institute of Linguists, 1961;

director of research, Birkbeck College, University of London, 1962; Centennial Medal, Canada, 1967; member of the board, National Research Council of Canada, 1975–present; honorary professor of physics, Lakehead University 1973.

Booth always considered himself to be a philosophical mathematician, yet his training and practice dealt with engineering and physics. During the World War II years, Booth did research in London on the crystallographic structure of explosives and had numerous persons under him doing tedious and mundane mathematical calculations. As a mathematician he had an "aversion" to trivial arithmetic and took pity on those under his management. He was able to rewrite some of the formulae into simpler forms to make the tasks easier but, still far from satisfied, he developed a small analog calculator to aid in the computations.

Post-war efforts centered around crystallographic problems research at Burbeck College; with a grant from the British Rubber Corporation, he was able to design and construct a digital Fourier Synthesis device. During this development he met Douglas Hartree, who introduced him to the work of Alan Turing and John von Neumann on logical automata. Based on this new information Booth began work on the design of the logical circuits for a digital binary arithmetic unit.

With funding from the University of London and the Rockefeller Foundation, Booth traveled to the US to study current American computer systems. His first stop was at Bell Telephone Laboratories where he studied Stibitz' Complex Number Machine. At the Institute for Advanced Studies at Princeton he met John von Neumann; at the Eckert-Mauchly Corporation he studied the Univac developments. Visiting Cambridge, Mass., he met Vannevar Bush and Samuel Caldwell, who were operating the Digital Differential Analyzer, and he crossed town to Harvard to meet Howard Aiken.

Returning to London, Booth continued his work on devising computational systems to solve crystallographic problems. He identified the major problem of computation to be the need for a storage system, and as a result constructed a magnetic drum storage device, 2 in. diameter, and 2 in. long, capable of storing 10 bits per inch. Meanwhile, he received an invitation from von Neumann to return to Princeton and join their research activities. On arrival Booth was introduced to the concepts of electronic binary circuits similar to those developed for the ENIAC and being extended to the EDVAC and eventually the IAS Machine. However, Booth decided to emphasize his work on magnetic storage systems, and to test his concepts developed the Automatic Relay Computer (ARC). This system matched the speed of the drum storage system, which was capable of a response time of only 0.002 seconds, far slower than the (then) capabilities of electronic circuits.

Booth returned to London to continue work on his relay computer and drum memory research. He next developed the SEC 6-bit computer, which was fully electronic with a two-address instruction word. The principal storage was the magnetic drum. The SEC was followed by the APEX, an all-purpose electronic X-ray calculator, which had significantly higher precision of 32 bits, and a 1-kiloword magnetic drum. Booth claimed that the major accomplishment of the APEX was the implementation of a non-restoring binary multiplication circuit which von Neumann had claimed to be impossible.[21]

Andrew Booth said in his personal autobiography: [22]

My father was descended from a long line of engineers and shipbuilders. He used to tell of his own young days when he and another youngster thought that they would try their hand at smoothing the deck of a liner which was under construction using an adze which they had seen in the hands of a skilled workman. The result was a disaster and resulted in my father being sent to sea for a period. Later, after graduating at Edinburgh University, he was again at sea during the first world war, this time as Commander of a "Q" boat; a sort of decoy which lured German submarines to surface and then unmasked its own armament and (hopefully) sunk the enemy. As a baby I was regaled with exciting stories of the loss of rudders and propellers and what to do about it.

My mother's family were quacks (i.e., medical doctors!) although mother herself was more interested in music and was an accomplished pianist and a soprano of some note. During the same war she was engaged in nursing.

I was born on 11 February 1918. My earliest recollection is of a visit to the theater on armistice night (November 11, 1918) where the brass band, the red plush curtains and the bright brass rail are still vivid memories. Many people have cast doubt on this early memory but I authenticated it with my parents who confirmed the accuracy of my description. Another early memory, about two years of age this time, was seeing my father mend a fuse which had blown and, next day when he was at work, performing the same service for my mother. Our "nannie," Rosie, was horrified and I well remember her screams, per-

---

[21] From an interview recorded by Christopher Evans in the Imperial College Collection.
[22] Personal communication.

haps justified by the fact that British electrical mains' power ran at 240 volts and was quite lethal.

In pre-kindergarten days I remember helping my father with the assembly of a mains charger for radio batteries which he had invented. Semi-conductor rectifiers had not yet reached England and his device used an assemblage of Nickel-Copper thermoelectric junctions which were heated over the gas stove grill. Surprisingly this device sold quite well! Shortly afterwards father invented what I believe to be the first automatic ignition advance for motor cars. I had no part in this but was fascinated to see how engineering drawings were made. Another enterprise, in which I played the part of laboratory assistant was in the production of "Anti-mist," an idea which father had for preventing the large plate glass mirrors in restaurants steaming up.

Like most children of professional families I was, in due course, sent to prep-school. Here I learned Latin, Greek, and French but almost no mathematics. I remember that when I sat for Public school entrance, I got 6 percent in mathematics. My father was livid and took my mathematical education in hand to such effect that when I resat the exam 3 months later I got 100 percent in this subject. Father continued his instruction and, by the age of 10 I was quite at home with differential and integral calculus.

School

My Public school days were not particularly happy ones, largely because, even then I suffered from "foot in mouth" disease. In particular I had no respect for the Gods of the school, the first 15 Rugby football team, and this led to numerous excursions to the prefect's room for a flogging. It may interest the modern generation of "do-gooders" to know that I have never had any ill feeling towards my tormentors, have had no mental problems, and have been happily married for nearly 40 years. So much for psychologists!

One happy thing at school was physics and another mathematics. In the event I was chosen to be the school entry for various Oxford and Cambridge scholarship examinations and had instruction from some wonderful Masters, H.C. Oliver, S.L. Baxter and W.L. Edge in particular. Another influence was W.L. Rawnsley, a Cambridge physicist.

University

In due course I went to Cambridge, as a Scholar, but found life there uncongenial. I was able to attend lectures by Eddington, Dirac, and Rutherford to the detriment of my mathematical studies. After an unpleasant interview with my tutor who seemed to think that I should be more interested in 'pure' mathematics, I decided to leave, much to the disgust of my parents. I entered for the next available University of London External Degree examination and was fortunate enough to get a "first" which placated my father to the extent that he let me do a graduate apprenticeship in his aero-engine factory in Coventry. As another early influence I worked for some months in the Actuarial department of the Sun Life of Canada, this gave me a taste for numerical mathematics and an appreciation of its difficulty.

I had several interesting jobs in industry, including metallurgy, setting up a department for X-ray inspection of components, design of search-lights. and designing motor car engines. These were only stop gaps; my mind was set on returning to a University and, in due course, I was lucky enough to obtain a graduate scholarship at the University of Birmingham to research in X-ray crystallography in which subject I eventually obtained a PhD. The team with which I was associated was heavily involved in computational work which, like Babbage at an earlier date, "I found no fit occupation for a gentleman." I therefore determined that, if I could get an academic job, I would attempt to use my engineering knowledge to produce a computer to do this kind of work. In fact, during my graduate student days I designed three small analog computers (Booth, 1945, 1947) which proved to be of considerable service to the crystallographers of that era.

My scholarship at Birmingham was donated by the British Rubber Producers' Association. Its Director, John Wilson, C.B.E., became a life-long friend and supported my later computing activities to the extent of funding the production of two of my machines. I spent a short time as a research physicist at the British Rubber Producers' Association laboratories at Welwyn Garden City, near to London. There I started on the design of the machine later to be called the ARC (Automatic Relay Computer). The first model was to use paper tape input and to be fairly special purpose, in fact a Fourier synthesizer. One innovative feature was the incorporation of a one-to-many function table which used selenium diodes. This was before I had even heard of John von Neumann, or of the electronic work going on in the USA. I was also involved in the design of a mechanical device for the same purpose (Booth, 1948) but, like Babbage, abandoned this in favor of the digital scheme.

In 1946 I was appointed to my first University post, at Birkbeck College London. There I taught third (fourth in North America) year theoretical Physics and spent my research time at the Davy-Faraday Laboratory of the Royal Institution. My "boss" was Prof. Desmond

Bernal, a distinguished but controversial physicist who really should have received the Nobel prize for helix work. He was a splendid person for a young man to work with, always ready for discussion and advice but never interfering. He was as interested in computing as I was and, having contacts in the US soon heard of the intense electronic computer activity there. As a result he arranged for me to visit the US in 1946 under the joint sponsorship of the Rockefeller and Nuffield Foundations.

America and After

After speaking at a conference at Lake George, I proceeded to New York for conversations with Warren Weaver, then Natural Sciences Director of the Rockefeller Foundation. This resulted in introductions to most of the known computer research establishments and, with the help of the late Prof. I. Fankuchen, "Fan" to his friends, to a lecture tour. The latter was a unique experience, it involved talking to Ladies Dining Clubs, something unknown in the UK. They seemed more interested in seeing a live Britisher and hearing his accent than in the science which I attempted to instill!

On the serious side, I visited MIT to see and talk to Bush and Caldwell of differential analyzer fame, project Whirlwind and Jay Forrester, the Harvard Computation Laboratory where I met Howard Aiken, Bell Telephone Laboratories in New Jersey, Moore School in Philadelphia with Morris Rubinoff, and von Neumann at Princeton. I also had a visit to California where I lectured to Linus Pauling and his colleague Corey. I still find it hard to understand that there is any major difference between the lock-and-key theory which they then had and the Watson, Crick, Kendrew (but really Rosalind Franklin) helix.

After the visits I returned to New York for discussions with Warren Weaver who suggested that I choose some group and come over on a visit on 1947. The choice which I had no difficulty in making was Princeton. The other contender was Aiken at Harvard but my feeling was that the thinking of his group was not very profound, in particular with respect to conditional transfer facilities.

England Again

The period between returning from the US and taking up my Rockefeller Fellowship at the Institute for Advanced Studies in March 1947 was one of intense activity. First I had to complete a book (Booth, 1948) and second I had to finish as much as possible of the BRPRA machine. In the latter activity I was greatly helped by two young lady assistants, Miss Kathleen Britten and Miss Zenia Sweeting. Between them they were responsible for most of the construction on work both at this stage and with the later machine. John Wilson decided to send Miss Britten to the Institute to assist in operations and, most generously paid both of our transatlantic fares, first class on the Queen Elizabeth.

Princeton

Despite a contrary report,[23] the computer laboratory at the Institute was in operation by the time we arrived although little progress seemed to have been made with the actual construction of the machine. I soon realized that the electronic technology to be used would be unavailable in England and, after reading the Burks-Goldstine-von Neumann reports,[24] determined that the central problem was that of storage. For this reason I designed a von Neumann type, parallel, machine (ARC) using Siemen's high-speed relays which were available in Europe. These devices had a switching time of less than 1 milli-second and, by devising an anticipatory carry mechanism, I was able to produce a device which would add two n-bit numbers in 1 milli-second. The design of the whole of the relay part of the machine was completed in about 2 months, the drawings were made by Miss Britten after which we wrote up the work in two reports (Booth and Britten, 1947, 1947a).

I was astonished when I looked at our first report (Booth and Britten, 1947) in preparation for writing this note that I had suggested the principle of the hologram as a means of data storage (ibid, p. 6. section 1.21). I even pointed out how optical interrogation would lead to an associative memory. This had slipped my memory for 40 years!

Meanwhile I devoted my attention to the problem of producing a reliable storage device. The Princeton group were proposing to use the RCA "SELECTRON." This did not appeal to me for two reasons, first I did not feel that it would work and second I knew that we could not afford it. In the event I was proved correct, from a design objective of 4096 bits/SELECTRON the final device stored only 16 bits (or so I was told). Many ideas were thought of and discarded: delay lines because of the NIH syndrome, capacitor storage because "discrete element stores were impracticable" (how wrong we were, see modern

---

[23]Regis, E. 1987. *Who got Einstein's office?* Penguin Books, London, p. 111.
[24]Burks, A. W., Goldstine, H. H. and von Neumann, J. 1947. *Preliminary discussion of the logical design of an electronic computing instrument,* Institute for Advanced Study, Princeton. Goldstine, H.H., and J. von Neumann, 1947–1948. *Planning and coding of problems for an electronic computing instrument,* Parts I-III, Institute for Advanced Study, Princeton.

RAM) and secondary emission, CRT storage because it seemed to me hopelessly unreliable (how right I was this time). In the event I decided that magnetism could provide the only practical solution, I devised a matrix device known to the boys in the laboratory as "the bed of nails" and abandoned it because the only really effective way of using this type of device was to use toroidal structures which were unavailable. Then I thought of magnetic recording, a well-known audio technique at that time. It transpired that paper coated with appropriate oxide was available in the Brush Mail-a-Voice recorder. I acquired a number of the 10 inch discs and a player to conduct tests. The latter were satisfactory so this matter was settled to await construction in England.

My recollections of Princeton are entirely pleasant. First a ripening friendship with Miss Britten, later to become Dr. Kathleen Booth, second contact with people like Johnny von Neumann and Hermann Weyl and last, but not least, the happy gang of young engineers involved with the project. Among these I must mention Dicky Schneider, Willis Ware, Jim Pomerene, and Ralph Slutz. Ralph was a wit and adept at limerick construction; a favorite one was:

> There was a computer named Booth,
> Who said by-gad and forsooth,
> To shorten the delay
> of the highest speed relay,
> Apply a spot of Vermouth.

I never realized that Johnny was a lightening calculator. He was certainly quick on the uptake and could make approximations in his head but not in a way which seemed particularly remarkable. Also he sometimes gave insufficient thought before answering a question; for example, I once asked him if his non-restoring method of binary division had a parallel for multiplication. He replied that no such algorithm was possible which deterred me from seeking one for some time. He was also incorrect over a question in Fourier series which later resulted in a paper which I had published in the Proceedings of the Royal Society (Booth and Britten, 1948). These are minor points as our visit was an unqualified success.

After leaving Princeton in August 1947 I traveled to New York to meet with Warren Weaver with the object of getting Rockefeller support for my project. Weaver reminded me that mere calculation would not attract money as the Americans were ahead in this field. During the discussion I raised the questions of Machine Translation and Medical Diagnosis. It seems that Weaver already had thoughts on the translation business and had discussed it with Norbert Weiner. His thought was that translation was simply a form of code and that, since codes could be broken, we should approach the problem that way. In the event this proved unworkable but the Machine Translation application provided us with major support.

Another interesting experience was with IBM. Weaver gave me an introduction to T.J. Watson, Sr. with the idea that IBM might provide funding. Far from it! T.J. informed me that there was no future in this new-fangled electronic business and that, if I came back in 5 years, the relay would still be paramount.

Return to England

After returning I immediately turned my attention to the construction of a memory whilst Miss Britten and Miss Sweeting set about building the relay portion of the ARC. My first thought was the floppy disc! I would spin the 10 inch Mail-a-Voice disc at about 3,000 rpm at which speed it would stay flat, and then move a rigidly mounted read-write head close to the surface. The theory was that the Bernoulli effect would draw the disc to a fixed distance from the head and maintain a very small air gap. Unhappily this did not occur, the attraction was perfect but the distortion of the disc surface resulted in unstable "flapping" which led to eventual disintegration. Thus, although I suppose I really invented the floppy disc, it was a real flop!

My second attempt was more successful. I had a 2 inch diameter brass cylinder plated with .0005 inch of Nickel. This metal is robust and is magnetically remanent. It stored data permanently and well. The original device is now on display in the Science Museum in London as is the larger drum actually used on our first machines. Our original, Nickel plated drum was a parallel device with 21 channels plus a clock channel. It stored 256 words of 21 bits and fed the ARC which was demonstrated to members of the Board of Directors of BRPRA on May 12, 1948. Warren Weaver and his colleague Gerard Pomerat also saw the machine in operation on May 25 of the same year.

T. Kilburn, from the F.C. Williams group at Manchester, visited the laboratory on November 2, 1948 and took away a sample of our read-write heads which we later found to have been copied by that group and by the Ferranti organization.

With the ARC in operation I set about the next phase which was to design an all-electronic control and arithmetic unit. The test bed was SEC, or Simple Electronic Computer; it formed the Master's thesis for Norbert Kitz. This led to the final machine of the series APE(X)C or

All Purpose Electronic (Sponsors name) Computer of which we built several to make money to support students (Booth, 1965).

It may be of interest to mention some of the achievements of my group in the period 1948–1962. First there was the Binary Multiplication procedure (usually called Booth's algorithm) (Booth, 1951). Then the binary partitioning technique applied to the solution of equations and to dictionary search (Booth, 1955, 1956). Finally the idea of binary trees (Booth, 1960). Major activity was devoted to Mechanical Translation with the support of the Nuffield Foundation and then led to numerous publications and a book (Booth et al., 1956).

By this time I was Director of the Computer Project and a senior faculty member. My father, who had retired by then, set up a small factory to produce our magnetic drums. This factory (Wharf Engineering Co.) probably made more drums than any other in the world, largely for export to the US. It continued in operation until I left England in 1962.

To support my laboratory I made various arrangements with industry. In particular we supplied details to the British Tabulating Machine Company in return for cash but with a non-publication agreement. This was an undoubted mistake in the light of the archaic technology deployed at that time, but the Company offered the University funds to endow a Chair in Computer Engineering for me in 1962 and I acknowledge with gratitude the efforts of Cyril Holland Martin their then Technical Director.

Unfortunately, because of the preoccupation of the then Master of Birkbeck College, Sir John Lockwood, with Colonial education, and the petty mindedness of F.C. Williams, T. Kilburn, and Herman Bondi (Bigmouth Bondi to most of his acquaintances) the proposal fell through. As a result I decided to depart from the hive of socialist mediocrity which England had become and go elsewhere. Within a few weeks I had offers of Chairs in the US, New Zealand, and Canada. As the latter had the prospect of advancement to the rank of Dean in one year I accepted it but, at the same time accepted a "professorship at large" of Autonetics at the then Western Reserve University. Autonetics, incidentally, is a neologism invented by Jack Millis then Chancellor of Western Reserve, from Greek roots meaning Self Control, otherwise "doing what you like." A happy thought which I have perpetuated in our present Company name.

Both Canada and Case Western Reserve proved good choices. At Saskatchewan I was able to raise a moribund College of Engineering into the 20th century. In fact, by the time I left in 1972 it had the third largest graduate school of engineering in Canada. At Saskatchewan, with the help of Ken Cameron, a bright graduate student we constructed the M3 computer (Booth, 1965) in less than 1 year. It was sponsored by the National Research Council of Canada and by the Defence Research Board. The machine worked well for a decade and is now honorably retired.

Into the Sere and Yellow

My tale is nearly told. In 1972 I was invited to the Presidency of Lakehead University in Ontario. Again the objective was to start graduate programs. This did not prove easy as there was an economy drive on the part of the Provincial Government during my term of office. However some things were achieved. The particular program of which I am most proud was the "bright kids" program. In this any youngster who had the ability could take courses, free, at Lakehead and if a pass was obtained, credit would be banked against the time when the student should enter the University. We had a number of these young people, amongst which were my own children, both of whom started full time studies at 12 and graduated at 16 with first class honours. I am pleased to say that they graduated after I had retired so that influence cannot be implied against their record. I feel very strongly that the present psychological rubbish about peer groups which prevails in the schools prevents our best young people from achieving their full potential. It is simply the Cancer of Socialism which seeks to make all men equal—of course to the lowest!

In conclusion it may be of interest and even amusement to remark that I was probably the only University President on record to have his political affiliation recorded in *Who's Who* as Anarchist (Philosophical of course).

BIBLIOGRAPHY

Biographical

Booth, Andrew D., "Computers in the University of London," in Metropolis, N., J. Howlett, and Gian-Carlo Rota, *A History of Computing in the Twentieth Century,* Academic Press, New York, 1980, pp. 551–561.

Lavington, Simon, *Early British Computers,* Digital Press, Bedford, Mass., 1980, see Chapter 12: "Pioneering Small Computers."

Significant Publications

Booth, A.D., "A method of calculating reciprocal spacings for X-ray reflections from a monoclinic crystal," *J. Sci. Instr.*, Vol. 22, 1945, p. 74.

Booth, A.D., "Two calculating machines for X-ray crystal structure analysis," *J. Appl. Phys.*, Vol. 18, 1947, p. 837.

Booth, A.D., *Fourier technique in X-ray organic structure analysis*, Cambridge University Press, 1948, pp. 76–81.

Booth, A.D., "A signed binary multiplication technique," *Q. J. Mech. and Appl. Math.* Vol. 4, No. 2, 1951, pp. 236–240.

Booth, A.D., "Use of a computing machine as a mechanical dictionary," *Nature*, Vol. 176, 1955, p. 565.

Booth, A.D., "A computer programme for finding roots," *Comp. and Auto.*, Vol. 5, 1956, p. 20.

Booth, A.D., and Booth, K.H.V., *Automatic Digital Calculators*, 3rd Ed., Butterworth-Heinemann (Academic Press) London, 1965, p. 22.

Booth, A.D., and Britten, K.H.V., *General considerations in the design of an all-purpose electronic digital computer*, Institute for Advanced Study, Princeton, 1947.

Booth, A.D., and Britten, K.H.V., *Coding for A.R.C.*, Institute for Advanced Study, Princeton, 1947a.

Booth, A.D., and Britten, K.H.V., "The accuracy of atomic coordinates derived from Fourier series in X-ray crystallography, Part V," *Proc. Roy. Soc.*, Vol. A 193, 1948, pp. 305–310.

Booth, A.D., and Cameron, K., "A small transistorized digital computer," *Electronic Eng.*, Vol. 37, 1965, pp. 368–374.

Booth, A.D., and Colin, A.J.T., "On the efficiency of a new method of dictionary construction," *Information and Control*, Vol. 3, No. 4, 1960, pp. 327–334.

Booth, A.D., Brandwood, L., and Cleave, J.P., *Mechanical resolution of linguistic problems*, Butterworth-Heinemann (Academic Press), London, 1956.

Booth, A.D., et al., "Principles and Progress in the Construction of High Speed Digital Computers," *Quart. Jour. Mechanical and Appl. Math.*, Vol. 2, 1949, pp. 182–197.

TAYLOR L. BOOTH

*Born September 22, 1933, Middletown, Conn.; died October 20, 1986,
Storrs, Conn.; computer science educator who established the computer department at University of Connecticut in 1959, well before most computer engineering or computer science departments, and who was the first president of
the Computer Sciences Accreditation Commission.*

Education: BS, electrical engineering, University of Connecticut, 1955; MS,
electrical engineering, University of Connecticut, 1956; PhD, electrical engineering, University of Connecticut, 1962.

Professional Experience: instrumentation engineer, United Aircraft, 1955-1956;
systems engineer, Westinghouse Electric Corporation, Baltimore, 1956–1959;
University of Connecticut: research assistant and instructor, 1959–1963, assistant professor, 1963–1969, professor, 1969–1986, chairman, Computer Science
and Engineering Department, 1971–1977 and 1979–1984, director, Computer
Applications Research Center, 1985–1986.

Honors and Awards: fellow, IEEE; Fortesque Fellowship, 1965; ASEE Frederick
E. Terman Award, 1972; IEEE Computer Society Centennial Award 1984;
IEEE Computer Society Distinguished Service Award, 1985.

Taylor Booth was a professor of computer science and engineering,
and head of the department, at the University of Connecticut, deeply
involved with improving computer science education through the
IEEE Computer Society, in cooperation with the Association for
Computing Machinery. At the time of his death he was a candidate for
the presidency of the IEEE Computer Society, having served as a member of the board of governors, secretary, and vice president in the early
1980s. After his untimely death, the board of governors of the IEEE
Computer Society voted to establish an annual education award in his
name.

BERTRAM VIVIAN BOWDEN

Born January 18, 1910, Chesterfield, UK; died July 28, 1989, Altrincham, UK; premiere, and possibly the first, computer salesman, and editor of the 1953 book Faster than Thought.

Education: BA, Cambridge, 1931, MA,[25] PhD, Cambridge, 1934, MSc (Tech).

Professional Experience: Cavendish Laboratory, Cambridge, 1931–1934; University of Amsterdam, 1934–1935; chief physics master, Collegiate School, Liverpool, UK, 1935–1937; chief physics master, Oundle School, 1937–1940; Telecommunications Research Establishment, UK, 1940–1946 (Radar research in UK, 1940–1943; in US, 1943–1946); UK Atomic Energy Authority, 1946–1947; Sir Robert Watson Watt & Partners, 1947–1950; Ferranti, Ltd. 1950–1953; dean of faculty of technology, Manchester University, and principal of the Manchester College of Science and Industry, 1953–1964; Minister of State, Department of Education and Science in 1964–1965 (on leave from Manchester College of Science and Technology).

Honors and Awards: Baron Bowden of Chesterfield, life peerage, 1963; fellow, Institute of Electrical Engineers (UK); fellow, Institute of Electrical and Electronics Engineers (US).

Bertram Vivian Bowden was born in Chesterfield, Staffordshire, England, son of a schoolmaster. After attending Chesterfield Grammar School, he went up to Emmanuel College, Cambridge, with an open scholarship and took successive firsts in the natural science Tripos. After graduating he joined the Cavendish Laboratory and worked with Rutherford from 1931 to 1934 on the measurement of radioactive levels, receiving a PhD in 1934. After Cambridge, Bowden took an ICI[26] fellowship at the University of Amsterdam, which he left after just 1 year in order to teach, first at the Collegiate School, Liverpool, and then at Oundle, where he was chief physics master.

During World War II, like many of the other British computer pioneers, he found employment at the Telecommunications Research Establishment (TRE) working on radar. At TRE he was appointed principal scientific officer and worked alongside other future computer pioneers including F.C. (Freddie) Williams, who was to figure prominently in Bowden's future career and in the development of the computer field.

In 1943 Bowden led a British team that collaborated with American scientists at the Naval Research Laboratory in Washington, D.C., to assist in the development of new equipment. He remained in the US until late 1946, including a year at MIT.

---

[25]It is the right of a graduate of Cambridge, after two years of experience, to apply for the granting of a master's degree without examination.

[26]Imperial Chemical Industries, Ltd.

On return to the United Kingdom, Bowden joined the Atomic Energy Authority for a period, before being recruited to join the Manchester-based electronics firm of Ferranti, Ltd. Here Bowden's wartime contacts, his electronics expertise, and his undoubted energy secured him a sales and marketing position in what was then an exotic field—computers. Ferranti was developing a commercial version of the Manchester University Mark I computer, which under William's direction had run the world's first stored program in June 1948. Bowden was charged with exploring the possibilities of selling these new machines, becoming, in effect, the sales manager, although as Bowden recalled, "it was all very informal," with no formal title. However, based on this appointment Bowden claimed to have been the first computer salesman in the world.

The potential market for computers was unknown; in the postwar depression, the idea of paying tens of thousands of pounds on machines for calculations seemed to place computers in the realm of science fiction. Clearly there was to be a shortage of computer operators, who were assumed, at that time, to be qualified mathematicians. Operating (programming) procedures were not yet codified, and there was a serious question of reliability. Bowden observed "at one time it looked as if we were going to spend more time mending them than using them!" Bowden found the process of selling machines unrewarding and slow; the time to decide to purchase after the decision to acquire could extend to 2 years.

Although his work brought Bowden into contact with Alan Turing and Christopher Strachey, Bowden never claimed any detailed knowledge of programming, instead describing himself as a "systems engineer." In 1952 his negotiations with the Royal Dutch Shell Laboratories (Amsterdam) led to the purchase of a machine in the face of competition from the US, Cambridge University, and the National Physical Laboratory (Teddington). That same year, the UK Ministry of Supply ordered two computers for "classified work." As perhaps the result of a prior agreement in the commercialization of the "Manchester machine," Ferranti provided a machine to the university for mathematical research.

Bowden regarded the sale of a Ferranti Mark I to the University of Toronto in 1951 as his greatest coup. The machine, codenamed FERUT, was used by the Canadian government in their part of the engineering design of the St. Lawrence Seaway.[27] The project served as

---

[27]See Williams, M.R., "History of Computing in Canada," Special Issue, *Ann. Hist. Comp.,* Vol. 16, No. 2, 1994.

a springboard for the programming talents of Christopher Strachey, who arrived in Canada in fall 1952 to develop a program for calculating the effects of the new seaway on the water flow past the Thousand Islands.[28] Bowden reported that the success of this work "gave the Americans the fright of their lives" and a "giant inferiority complex." However, the success still did not convince US industry to buy British machines.

Bowden left Ferranti in 1953 to become principal of the Manchester College of Science and Industry. Bowden drew the attention of industrialists and the public to the importance of science and technology to the needs of the country. Eventually his efforts were rewarded by a life peerage in 1963. The Labour government under prime minister Harold Wilson appointed Bowden as minister of state at the Department of Education and Science in 1964 through 1965. In 1968 Bowden agreed to chair an informal group of computer scientists, including Stanley Gill, for the discussion of data transmission networks. Subsequently known as the "Bowden Committee," it foresaw the need for adequate communications for the proper development of computing.

Bowden is perhaps best remembered for his 1953 book *Faster than Thought: A Symposium of Digital Computing Machines,* which initially began as a sales brochure and grew in scope as the work progressed with assistance from the British computing community. The result is a "Who's Who" of the industry at that time and gave a place of pride to Charles Babbage and Ada, Lady Lovelace, at a time when their achievements were not well known.

Bowden retired in 1976, and although troubled by increasing blindness, he remained active "listening to music, pottering about his home [Altrincham, Cheshire] and in the House of Lords."[29] He died at the age of 79 on 28 July 1989.[30]

QUOTATION

"It seems probable that we shall have a second Industrial Revolution on our hands before long."[31]

---

[28]Located at the eastern end of Lake Ontario at the head of the river between Ontario and New York state.

[29]Who's Who, 1987.

[30]Based on Tweedale 1990, with assistance by Geoffrey Tweedale.

[31]From the preface to *Faster than Thought.*

BIBLIOGRAPHY

Biographical

Swann, Bernard, *History of the Ferranti Computer Department,* unpublished manuscript, National Archive for the History of Computing, The University, Manchester, UK.

Tweedale, Geoffrey, "Bertram Vivian Bowden," *Ann. Hist. Comp.,* Vol. 12, No. 2, 1990, pp. 138–140.

Significant Publications

Bowden, Bertram V., ed., *Faster than Thought: A Symposium of Digital Computing Machines,* Sir Isaac Pitman & Sons, London, 1953.

CHARLES L. BRADSHAW

Born August 30, 1923, Powder Springs, Tenn.; early programmer who made contributions to the techniques of programming in support of nuclear engineering and space programs.

Education: BS, mathematics, Tennessee Tech, 1947; MA, mathematics, University of Tennessee, 1950.

Professional Experience: member, Mathematics Panel, Oak Ridge National Laboratory; Marshall Space Flight Center, Huntsville, Ala.: staff member, deputy director, Computation Laboratory, founder and chairman, General Computer Services; director of computing, Vanderbilt University, 1971–1988.

Honors and Awards: ACM Distinguished Service Award, 1988; associate fellow, AIAA.

As a member of the mathematics panel at Oak Ridge National Laboratory, Bradshaw worked with Alston Householder on the ORACLE computer, one of the first IAS machines developed as part of John von Neumann's plans for the AEC. After working on some of the first computer programs to determine the criticality of nuclear reactors, he joined the rocket team headed by Werner von Braun at the

Marshall Space Flight Center. He was responsible for the early orbit computations for Explorer 1, the first US artificial earth satellite.

BIBLIOGRAPHY

Significant Publications

Bradshaw, Charles L., "Improved Approximations to Numerical Solutions of Partial Differential Equations," *J. Mathematics and Physics*, 1956.

Bradshaw, Charles L., "Real Time Testing in the Saturn Program," *Control Engineering*, 1962.

JOHN GRIST BRAINERD

Born 1904; died February 1, 1988, Kennett Square, Pa.; dean at the Moore School and co-principal investigator for the ENIAC Project.

Education: BS, Moore School of Electrical Engineering, University of Pennsylvania, 1925; PhD, Moore School, 1929.

Professional Experience: Brainerd remained his whole life with the Moore School: instructor, 1925; administrative leader of the ENIAC project, 1943–1946; director, 1954–1970; retired Emeritus University Professor, 1975; established the first evening graduate school in electrical engineering, 1929; first academic program in systems engineering, 1953.

John Grist Brainerd, a life-long professor at the Moore School of Electrical Engineering of the University of Pennsylvania, and head of the team that created ENIAC from conception through construction to final operation, died on February 1, 1988, at the age of 83, at the Quaker retirement community of Crosslands in Kennett Square, Penn. He formerly lived in Exton, Penn. At the time of his death he was Emeritus University Professor.

Brainerd earned his BS, MS, and PhD degrees at the University of Pennsylvania and began teaching there in 1925. While working his way through college, he was at one time a part-time police reporter for the now-defunct *Philadelphia North American*. In 1927 he helped establish the first evening graduate program in electrical engineering. He initiated new electrical engineering courses and was co-author of two pioneering textbooks, *High Frequency Alternating Currents* (1931), and *Ultra-High Frequency Techniques* (1942). The latter was a major aid in training and upgrading engineers who were needed for radar development. In addition to his research, publication, and teaching (which was his lifetime love), he contributed to the work of technical committees and the organization of the IRE, AIEE, and its jointure, the IEEE. Even after retirement in 1975, he continued to commute from Crosslands to his Moore School office and served as president of the Society for the History of Technology, in which he had been active for many years.

He made his chief contribution to computing when he played a major management role in realizing the proposals of engineer J. Presper Eckert and the late physicist John W. Mauchly to build ENIAC. As a professor at the Moore School, he endorsed and took formal responsibility for the design and construction proposal to the Army, and was designated as the principal investigator. That is, if ENIAC had failed, it would have been his neck. Controversy about the relative roles and contributions to ENIAC has been constant since the importance of the computer was first recognized by others, but there is no question about Brainerd's support of the project when it was just a dream, declared to be wild, impractical, and impossible by some who have since forgotten their myopia. There is also no question that he was formally designated as project head or that he was responsible for getting and managing its $486,000 budget, of which he later said that "considering the magnitude of the result, it was one of the cheapest research and development projects the government ever invested in." Some of this controversy has been reported in *Annals* articles, most notably in "The ENIAC: First General Purpose Electronic Computer," by Arthur W. Burks and Alice R. Burks (Vol. 1, No. 4, October 1981), and "John Mauchly's Early Years," by Kathleen R. Mauchly, (Vol. 6, No. 2, April 1984), and the associated comments, queries, and debates.

When Eckert and Mauchly left the Moore School as a consequence of a disagreement about patent rights,[32] Brainerd remained at the University of Pennsylvania. It appears, that whereas they thought the patents should be theirs, Brainerd and others thought the benefits of the inventions should go to the University.

---

[32]See the biographies of J. Presper Eckert and John W. Mauchly.

Brainerd took no further part in later Moore School computer project work, but devoted himself to graduate teaching, administration as director of the Moore School, and curriculum revision. His tenure as professor encompassed the transition of the electrical engineering field from a near-exclusive emphasis on power, with a slight concern with telegraphy and telephony, to the vacuum tube era, and ended as the discipline actually developed into what is now called computer science and engineering. Brainerd handled the first part of the transition well, and was a leader in the introduction of the mathematics of electric and magnetic fields and the transmission of energy and information into the teaching of electrical engineering. Although he participated in the earliest development of computers (especially in regard to his specialty, electronic circuits), like some leading classical physicists who never really accepted quantum electrodynamics, he never became a full participant in the new world of computing. He always admitted its worth but he never felt that he understood the field sufficiently to contribute to it.

In the early days of computers, Brainerd's idea of the proper way to employ them was to set them to solving differential equations and publish the results in the form of highly precise tables of functions. Engineers could then use these new tables much as they did tables of Bessel Functions. At that time he did not see the possibility of solving problems directly, or conceive of the computer age.

Several generations of students learned the basic principles of electrical engineering and its related mathematics as a consequence of Dr. Brainerd's long and useful career as a teacher, textbook author, and hands-on department administrator. Although in public he may have presented a quiet and reserved personality, and to his students sometimes seemed overly rigorous and demanding, his friends and professional associates appreciated his sharp mind and enjoyed his quiet but quick sense of humor.[33]

BIBLIOGRAPHY

Biographical

Burks, Arthur W., and Alice R., "The ENIAC: First General Purpose Electronic Computer," *Ann. Hist. Comp.*, Vol. 3, No. 4, 1981, pp. 310–399.

---

[33]From Weiss 1988.

Fegley, Kenneth A., and S. Ried Warren, "Eloge: John Grist Brainerd," *Ann. Hist. Comp.*, Vol. 10, No. 4, 1989, pp. 361–365.

Weiss, E.A., "John Grist Brainerd: Obituary," *Ann. Hist. Comp.*, Vol. 10, No. 1, 1988, pp. 78–79.

Significant Publications

Brainerd, J.G., and T.K. Sharpless, "The ENIAC," *Electrical Engineering*, Vol. 67, No. 2, Feb. 1948, pp. 163–172.

Brainerd, J.G., "Genesis of the ENIAC," *Technology and Culture*, Vol. 17, No. 3, July 1976, pp. 482–488.

Eckert, J. Presper, Jr., John W. Mauchly, Herman H. Goldstine, J.G. Brainerd, *Description of the ENIAC and Comments on Electronic Digital Computing Machinery*, Contract W/670/ORD 4926, Moore School of Electrical Engineering, Univ. of Penn., Philadelphia, Nov. 30, 1945.

HERBERT S. BRIGHT

Born 1919; died November 28, 1986, Washington D.C.; developer of the first Fortran user program and consequently the recipient of the first error message; promoter of security through data encryption.

Education: BS, electrical engineering, University of Michigan, 1943; MS, electrical engineering, University of California, 1963.

Professional Experience: AT&T Laboratories, 1943–1945; research engineer, University of California, 1945–1950; head, instrumentation branch, US Navy Radiological Defense Laboratory, 1950–1954 [attended the hydrogen bomb tests at Eniwetok and Bikini Atolls in 1954]; computation planning section, Westinghouse-Bettis Atomic Power Laboratory, 1954–1960; director of engineering, Data Processing Group, Business and Equipment Manufacturers Association (BEMA), 1960–1961; Philco-Ford, 1961–1965; director, Systems Programming and senior staff consultant, Informatics, 1965–1966; president, Computation Planning Corp., 1966–1986.

Bright was president of Computation Planning, Inc., developer and vendor of cryptographic and related software, hardware, and processes, from 1966. He served ACM in several appointive offices and as Council member-at-large, secretary, and vice president. He was a principal member of the American Bankers Association/ANSI X9E9

Working Group on Financial Institution Cryptographic and Authentication Key Management. Bright published 34 technical papers, articles, and book chapters and held (as co-inventor) one US patent, "DP Security System."

BIBLIOGRAPHY

Biographical

Anon., "Herbert Samuel Bright," *Ann. Hist. Comp.*, Vol. 10, No. 3, 1988, pp. 217–218.

Bright, Herbert, "Fortran comes to Westinghouse-Bettis," *Ann. Hist. Comp.*, Vol. 1, No. 1, 1979, p. 72.

HOWARD BROMBERG

RCA representative on the committee that created Cobol; purchaser and deliverer of the Cobol tombstone to Charles Phillips.[34]

Professional Experience: US Department of Commerce, 1954–1955; Univac Division, Automatic Programming Department, Sperry-Rand Corp., 1956–1958; administrator, advanced programming languages, Radio Corporation of America, 1958–1963; senior staff consultant, C-E-I-R, Inc., 1963–1966; president, Information Management, Inc., 1966–1973; founder and president, International Technology Corp., 1973–1981; independent computer consultant, 1982–present.

Honors and Awards: fellow, British Computer Society.

Bromberg has been in the forefront of the development of software utilities, languages, and applications. In addition to leading the development of the world's first Cobol compiler, he worked on the earliest English language compilers, B-0 and FLOWMATIC, with Grace Murray Hopper, developed assemblers and interpreters for minicomputers and mainframes, and created a set of Cobol preprocessors to increase

---

[34]See *Ann. Hist. Comp.*, Vol. 7, No. 4, 1985, p. 309.

programmer productivity. He served as the chairman of the ANSI Cobol Standards subcommittee for the first 10 years, and established the concept of compatible standards. He also served as the first chairman of the ISO committee on Programming Languages Standardization.

BIBLIOGRAPHY

Biographical

Phillips, Charles A., "CODASYL: Reminiscences (Plus a Few Facts)," *Ann. Hist. Comp.,* Vol. 7, No. 4, 1985, pp. 304–316.

Significant Publications

Bromberg, Howard, "Cobol Makes its Debut," *J. of Machine Accounting,* Dec. 1960.

Bromberg, Howard, "Compilers—Where They are Today," *Business Automation,* Dec. 1962.

Bromberg, Howard, "The Real Effects of Standardization," *Datamation,* Nov. 1967.

Bromberg, Howard, "In Search of Productivity," *Datamation,* August 15, 1984.

RALPH ANTHONY (TONY) BROOKER

Born September 22, 1925; developer of "Autocode," an early formula-like code for the Ferranti Mark I and the Manchester Mercury.[35]

Education: BSc, first class honors, Imperial College, London, 1946.

Professional Experience: assistant lecturer, engineering mathematics, Imperial College, London, 1947–1949; assistant in research, University Mathematical Laboratory, Cambridge University, 1949–1951; staff, Computing Machine

---

[35]There is some confusion between the contributions of Brooker and the work of A.E. Glennie, but they never were collaborators. About the same time as Brooker's papers on Autocode, Glennie gave a talk at Carnegie Institute of Technology on "meta-compilers." Brooker suggests that it is possible, however, that Glennie coined the word "autocode."

Laboratory, Electrical Engineering Department, Manchester University, 1951–1967; consultant, Mathematical Sciences Department, IBM Research Laboratories, Yorktown Heights, N.Y., 1962–1963; Essex University, UK: professor, computing science, 1967–1988, chairman, Computer Science Department, 1967–1973, dean, School of Mathematical Studies, 1969–1972 and 1985–1988, pro-vice-chancellor (services), 1976–1980, professor emeritus, 1989–present; visiting scientist, Informatics Division, European Economic Community Joint Research Center, EURATOM, Ispra (Varese), Italy, 1984.

Honors and Awards: MA (Hon.), Cambridge University, 1951; doctor of the University of Essex, 1990; fellow, British Computer Society.

Brooker was responsible for the "Autocode" compilers written for the Manchester University computers (marketed as the Ferranti Mark I and Mercury). The autocode languages provided for arithmetic expressions and the use of two-level storage but did not allow the creation of functions and procedures with formal parameters. Nevertheless, these languages inspired similar developments for the Ferranti Pegasus and other British computers in the late 1950s and early 1960s.

Later Brooker, with Derrick Morris, was responsible for the concept of the "Compiler Compiler," one of the first programs in the early 1960s that could take the syntactic and semantic descriptions of a language and output a compiler for that language.

More recently Brooker has been developing a programming language named DATAFIX, which will integrate the procedures for database description, integrity constraints, data manipulation, updates, and queries. DATAFIX has its intellectual origin in SIMULA, but goes further in the use of type hierarchies; the language incorporates a hierarchical locking protocol based on that used in System R.

BIBLIOGRAPHY

Significant Publications

Brooker, R.A., "The Autocode Program Developed for the Manchester University Computers," *Computer Journal,* Vol. 1, 1958, pp. 15–21.

Brooker, R.A., "Some Technical Features of the Manchester Mercury AUTOCODE Programme," *Mech. of Thought Processes, Nat'l. Physical Lab. Symp.,* Vol. 10, 1958, pp. 201–229.

Brooker, R.A., I.R. MacCallam, Derrick Morris, and J.S. Rohl, "The Compiler Compiler," *Annual. Rev. Automatic Programming,* Vol. 3, 1963, pp. 229–275.

FREDERICK P. BROOKS, JR.

Born April 19, 1931, Durham, N.C.; discoverer of the bottomless software tar pit and debunker of the concept of the Mythical Man-Month in his book of the same title; developer of OS/360.

Education: AB, Duke University, 1953; SM, Harvard University, 1955; PhD, applied mathematics, Harvard University, 1956.

Professional Experience: IBM Corp., 1956–1965: associate engineer, Production Development Laboratory, 1956, staff engineer, 1956–1958, advanced systems planner, 1958–1959, member, research staff, 1959–1960, systems planning manager, 1960–1961, corporate processor manager and System/360 manager, 1961–1964, Operating System/360 manager, 1964–1965; University of North Carolina, 1964–present: professor, 1964–1980, Kenan Professor and chairman, Department of Computer Science, 1980–present.

Honors and Awards: IEEE W.W. McDowell Award, 1970; Computer Science Award, DPMA, 1970; IEEE Computer Society Pioneer Award, 1980; National Medal of Technology, 1985; ACM Distinguished Service Award, 1987; AFIPS Harry Goode Award, 1989; IEEE John von Neumann Medal, 1993.

From project inception in late 1961 to near announcement in April 1964, Fred Brooks was the project manager for the IBM System/360. After February 1964 he managed development of OS/360 during the first two years that were to ensue before delivery of that operating system's initial version. He then left IBM to accept a professorship in computer science at the University of North Carolina.[36] In 1985, B.O. "Bo" Evans, Fred Brooks, and Eric Bloch received the National Medal of Technology at a White House ceremony for their work in developing the IBM System/360, described as "revolutionizing the industry." The 1989 Harry Goode Award citation reveals Brook's versatility: "For lasting contributions to computer science education to interactive 3-D computer graphics, and to hardware and software architecture in the development of the IBM System/360 series."

QUOTATIONS

"I believe the hard part of building software to be the specification, design, and testing of this conceptual construct, not the labor of repre-

---

[36]From Pugh, Emerson W., Lyle R. Johnson, and John H. Palmer, *IBM's 360 and Early 370 Systems,* MIT Press, Cambridge, Mass., 1991.

senting it and testing the fidelity of the representation." (Brooks 1987)

"The tar pit of software engineering will continue to be sticky for a long time to come." (Brooks 1975)

BIBLIOGRAPHY

Biographical

Brooks, Frederick P., Jr., et al., "Discussion of the SPREAD Report," *Ann. Hist. Comp.*, Vol. 5, No. 1, 1983, pp. 27–44.

Significant Publications

Brooks, Frederick P., Jr., *The Mythical Man-Month: Essays on Software Engineering*, Addison-Wesley, Reading, Mass., 1975.

Brooks, Frederick P., Jr., "No Silver Bullet," *Computer*, Apr. 1987, p. 11.

George H. Brown

Born 1908; died December 11, 1987; chief engineer at RCA when the company entered the computer market with the RCA 501.

Education: BS, University of Wisconsin, 1930; MS, University of Wisconsin, 1933; EE, University of Wisconsin, 1942.

Professional Experience: 40 years an employee and executive of the Radio Corporation of America.

In 1934 Brown established the correct theory for the performance of vertical radio antennas, and in 1936 he published the fundamental principle for calculating the patterns of directional antenna arrays. In 1938 he developed the vestigial sideband filter for television transmitters. Later during World War II he developed radio frequency heating devices for the production of penicillin, and in 1948 he co-authored the definitive papers on the propagation of ultrahigh-frequency radio signals. He was named RCA's executive vice president for research and engineering in 1965, and before his retirement in 1972, he served in other corporate executive positions and on boards of directors.

In 1958 the RCA 501, the company's first large transistorized data processor, was produced under Brown's direction as the chief engineer of commercial electronic products. Brown believed that with proper management the firm could have succeeded with commercial computers. He ascribed RCA's failure to ill-advised decisions by president John J. Burns and board chairman David Sarnoff as to how to compete with and be compatible with IBM. As to David's son (Robert), Brown wrote, "I believe that all the elements for failure were in place when he [Burns] became president . . . he simply hastened the termination."[37]

QUOTATION

"It has been my good fortune to have had an exciting and pleasant life and a rewarding professional career. I have encountered some of the world's great people, the near-great, and the supposed-to-be great. Of course, most of the folks I would classify as 'great' never make the headlines."

BIBLIOGRAPHY

Biographical

Brown, George H., *A Part of Which I Was: Recollections of a Research Engineer,* Angus Cupar Publishers, Princeton, N.J., 1982.

---

[37]From Brown 1982.

GORDON S. BROWN

*Born August 30, 1907, Drummoyne, NSW, Australia; founder of the MIT
Servomechanisms Laboratory, which pioneered the development of
feedback-control theory and applications, digital computer technology, and
automatic numerical control of machine tools.*

Education: diploma, mechanical and electrical engineering, Royal Melbourne
Technical School, Australia, 1925; SB, electrical engineering, MIT, 1931; SM,
electrical engineering, MIT, 1934; ScD, electrical engineering, MIT, 1938.

Professional Experience: engineer, Electrical Supply Branch, State Electricity
Commission, Victoria, Australia, 1926–1929; MIT: research assistant, electrical
engineering, 1931–1932, instructor, electrical engineering, 1932–1939, assistant professor, electrical engineering, 1939–1941, associate professor, electrical engineering, 1941–1946, professor, electrical engineering, 1946–1973,
Dugald C. Jackson Professor of Engineering, 1968–1973, institute professor,
1973–1974, institute professor emeritus, 1974–present, founder and director,
Servomechanisms Laboratory, 1941–1952, chairman of the faculty, 1951–1952,
head, Department of Electrical Engineering, 1952–1959, dean, School of
Engineering, 1959–1968.

Honors and Awards: President's Certificate of Merit, 1948; Naval Ordnance
Development Award, 1948; George Westinghouse Award, American Society
for Engineering Education, 1952; Lamme Medal, American Society for
Engineering Education, 1959; Medal in Electrical Engineering Education,
American Institute of Electrical Engineers, 1959; Joseph Marie Jacquard
Annual Memorial Award, Numerical Control Society, 1970; Bronze Beaver
Award, Alumni Association, MIT, 1973; Robert Thayer Award, Thayer School,
Dartmouth College, 1976; Rufus Oldenburger Medal, Automatic Control
Division, American Society of Mechanical Engineers, 1977; Gordon Stanley
Brown Building, MIT, dedicated 1985; DSc, Purdue University, 1958; DSc,
Dartmouth College, 1964; DSc, Technical University of Denmark, 1965; DSc,
Southern Methodist University (SMU), 1967; DSc, Stevens Institute of
Technology, 1968.

Gordon S. Brown entered MIT from Australia in the junior year in
1929. With the BS degree in 1931, he was urged by Vannevar Bush to
pursue graduate study instead of joining the Westinghouse Company
test course as planned. He began his lifetime career at MIT as a
research assistant in 1931; he retired in 1973 as Institute Professor
Emeritus. His graduate study leading to the SM degree in 1934 and the
ScD degree in 1938 was influenced by Vannevar Bush, Norbert Wiener,
and Harold L. Hazen, whom he succeeded as head of the Department
of Electrical Engineering in 1952; he became dean of engineering in
1959. The subject of his doctoral thesis was the Cinema Integraph, one
of the precursors to the analog computer. He continued to work in the
field of computers and automation and made contributions in the

area of feedback controls, specifically for guns, radar, and industrial processes.

In 1941, Brown founded the Servomechanisms Laboratory, and served as its director until 1952. He and his laboratory colleagues undertook an extensive program of research and education in the field of servomechanisms and feedback control. The early work that led to the Whirlwind digital computer was done in his laboratory. Just prior to his retirement as director, the laboratory began a program that led to numerical control of machine tools and the development of the Automatically Programmed Tool System[38] (APT—automatic control of machine tools), which had a profound impact on industry. During World War II, Brown served as consultant to the fire control department of the Sperry Gyroscope Company, and from 1942 to 1944 he was War Department consultant to the fire control design section of the Frankford Arsenal, and participated in other ordnance activities. He was appointed associate head of the Department of Electrical Engineering in 1950 and was chairman of the faculty from 1951 to 1952. In 1952 he was appointed head of the Department of Electrical Engineering and his department embarked on a major program of educational innovation. Under his direction the curriculum of the department was revised, and new textbooks and laboratory equipment were developed. These changes initiated widespread reforms in the teaching of electrical engineering throughout the world. The work had important influence on the teaching of electrical engineering in most US engineering schools and many others abroad.

In 1959 Brown was appointed dean of the School of Engineering and his educational reforms were extended to other departments. He led a movement to enlarge the interdisciplinary nature of engineering and to strengthen its concern for societal issues.[39] A substantial grant that year from the Ford Foundation made possible a new emphasis on themes important to rapidly changing technology. Brown was a key figure in the establishment of the Center for Materials Science and Engineering, the Center for Advanced Engineering Study, the Information Processing Services Center, and Project Intrex.

Although many members of the engineering faculty had contacts with foreign universities prior to 1960, there was no concerted effort by the School of Engineering to sponsor such contacts. During the 1960s and 1970s MIT established more formal technology-transfer

---

[38]See biography of Douglas Ross.
[39]From Brown and Wiener 1955.

programs by assisting developing nations to establish technological education and research institutions. He advised these programs on administrative and educational issues. Included among these institutions were the Birla Institute of Technology and Science in India, the Technical University of Berlin, the Ayra-Mehr University of Technology in Iran, and the University of Singapore.

Brown's activities as an administrator and educator for more than three decades do not overshadow his important technological contributions.

From November 1968 through June 1973 Brown was the first occupant of the Jackson Chair, established to honor Dugald C. Jackson, head of the Department of Electrical Engineering from 1907 to 1935. As Jackson Professor, Brown contributed to the evolution of educational philosophy, giving attention to research and education in his own field and to the continued development of technology and engineering on a national and international scale. In March 1973 Brown was appointed Institute Professor, an honor bestowed by the faculty and administration of MIT. The Gordon Stanley Brown Building at MIT was dedicated December 6, 1985. Since the fall of 1986, Brown has served as a key participant in restructuring the Orange Grove Middle School in the Catalina Foothills School District in Tucson, Arizona. A new paradigm named Systems Thinking with Learner Directed Learning has been introduced and accepted district wide including a new high school that opened in 1993.

QUOTATION

"Too many people today begin to worry about qualifying for a new or different job only after their old one has disappeared. This is too late; they run and run and never catch up." (Private communication)

BIBLIOGRAPHY

Biographical

Brown, G.S., and Norbert Wiener, "Automation 1955: A Retrospective," reprinted in *Ann. Hist. Comp.,* Vol. 6, No. 4, 1955.

Significant Publications

Brown, G.S., and Donald P. Campbell, *Principles of Servomechanisms,* John Wiley & Sons, New York, 1948.

Brown, G.S., "Can Universities Fulfill the Challenge of Relevance," *Technology Review,* Oct./Nov. 1973.

Brown, G.S., "Improving Education in Public Schools: Innovative Teachers to the Rescue," *System Dynamics Review,* Vol. 8, No. 1, 1992.

James L. Buie

Born 1920; died September 1988; inventor of transistor-to-transistor logic circuits.

Education: BSEE, University of Southern California, 1950.

Professional Experience: Ramo-Woolridge Corp. (later to become TRW, Inc.), 1954–1983.

Honors and Awards: As a naval aviator in World War II, Buie rose to the rank of lieutenant commander, and was awarded the Distinguished Flying Cross.

While working for TRW, Inc., Los Angeles, in the early 1960s, Buie developed and patented TTL circuitry, which became the dominant IC technology in the 1970s and early 1980s. His other innovations in microelectronics included dielectrically isolated ICs, single-chip parallel multipliers, single-chip analog-to-digital converters, and triple-diffused bipolar devices. In 1963 he helped establish the company's Microelectronics Center, and in 1977 the LSI Products Division.[40]

---

[40]From the IEEE.

ALICE R. BURKS

Born August 20, 1920, East Cleveland, Ohio; with her husband, Arthur W. Burks, she wrote extensively about the early history of the electronic computer, especially on the original work of John Vincent Atanasoff.

Education: BA, mathematics, University of Pennsylvania, 1944; MS, educational psychology, University of Michigan, 1957.

Professional Experience: writer and author.

Honors and Awards: University of Michigan Press Award, 1989, for *The First Electronic Computer: The Atanasoff Story.*

Burks did her undergraduate work at Oberlin College, on a competitive mathematics scholarship, and at the University of Pennsylvania, where she received her BA in mathematics in 1944. She earned her MS in educational psychology at the University of Michigan in 1957. She has assisted her husband in the writing of his book, *Chance, Cause, Reason,* and several of his articles. Alice Burks is also the author of a young people's novel.

BIBLIOGRAPHY

Significant Publications

Burks, Alice Rowe, *Leela and the Leopard Hunt,* Methuen, London, 1983.

Burks, Alice Rowe, and Arthur W. Burks, *The First Electronic Computer: The Atanasoff Story,* Univ. Michigan Press, Ann Arbor, Mich., 1988.

Burks, Arthur W., and Alice R. Burks, "The ENIAC: First General-Purpose Electronic Computer," *Ann. Hist. Comp.,* Vol. 3, No. 4, 1981, pp. 310–399.

Arthur Walter Burks

*Born October 13. 1915, Duluth, Minn.; one of the principal designers of the
ENIAC, working with John Mauchly and J. Presper Eckert; with Herman H.
Goldstine, helped John von Neumann develop the logical design of the
Institute for Advanced Study (IAS) computer—the von Neumann architecture.*

Education: BA, mathematics and physics, DePauw University, 1936; PhD, philosophy and logic, University of Michigan, 1941.

Professional Experience: instructor, Moore School of Electrical Engineering, 1941–1946; Institute for Advanced Study, 1946, and summers 1947, 1948; University of Michigan, 1946–present, now professor emeritus of philosophy, and of electrical engineering and computer science.

Honors and Awards: DSc (Hon.), DePauw University, 1973; Russel Lecturer, University of Michigan, 1977–1978; IEEE Computer Pioneer Award, 1982.

Arthur W. Burks earned his BA in mathematics and physics from DePauw University in 1936, and his PhD in philosophy from the University of Michigan in 1941. He became an instructor at the Moore School of Electrical Engineering in the fall of that year and did war research on mine-sweeping, radar antennas, and the ENIAC. He left the Moore school after the ENIAC was dedicated and then worked at the Institute for Advanced Study with John von Neumann. There he joined with John von Neumann and Herman H. Goldstine to write one of the most influential reports in the field of computing, "Preliminary Discussion of the Logical Design of an Electronic Computing Instrument," which is mentioned in the biographies of many other pioneers.

Burks joined the philosophy department at Michigan in 1946. In 1949 he founded a research group in the logic of computers, which operated until his retirement in 1986. This group did research on programming, automata theory, neural net simulation, computer modeling, self-reproducing and cellular systems. He now does research on adaptive computation.

He co-founded a doctoral program in computer and communication sciences at Michigan in 1956, and when it became a department, he was its first chairman. He was named the Henry Russel Lecturer for 1977–1978, the highest honor his university can bestow on a faculty member. He has been a visiting Professor at the University of Chicago, University of Illinois, Indian Institute of Technology (Kanpur, India), Center for Advanced Study in Behavioral Sciences (Stanford University), and the Chinese Academy of Social Sciences (Beijing, People's Republic of China).

BIBLIOGRAPHY

Biographical

Bigelow, Julian, "Computer Development at the Institute for Advanced Study," in Metropolis, N., J. Howlett, and Gian-Carlo Rota, *A History of Computing in the Twentieth Century,* Academic Press, New York, 1980, pp. 291–310.

Salmon, Merrilee, ed., *The Philosophy of Logical Mechanism,* Kluwer Academic Publishers, Dordrecht, Holland, 1990.[41]

Significant Publications

Burks, Alice Rowe, and Arthur W. Burks, *The First Electronic Computer: The Atanasoff Story,* Univ. of Michigan Press, Ann Arbor, Mich., 1988.

Burks, Arthur W., "Super Electronic Computing Machine," *Electronics Industries,* July 1946, pp. 62–67, 96.

Burks, Arthur W., H.H. Goldstine, and John von Neumann, "Preliminary Discussion of the Logical Design of an Electronic Computing Instrument," reprinted in Randell, Brian, *Origins of Digital Computers: Selected Papers,* Springer-Verlag, Berlin Heidelberg, 1982, pp. 399–414.

Burks, Arthur W., *Chance, Cause, Reason—An Inquiry into the Nature of Scientific Evidence,* Univ. of Chicago Press, Chicago, 1977.

Burks, Arthur W., "From ENIAC to the Stored-Program Computer: Two Revolutions in Computers," in Metropolis, N., J. Howlett, and Gian-Carlo Rota, *A History of Computing in the Twentieth Century,* Academic Press, New York, 1980, pp. 311–344.

Burks, Arthur W., and Alice R. Burks, "The ENIAC: First General Purpose Electronic Computer," *Ann. Hist. Comp.,* Vol. 3, No. 4, 1981, pp. 310–399.

von Neumann, John, and Arthur W. Burks, *Theory of Self-Reproducing Automata,* Univ. of Illinois Press, Urbana, Ill., 1966.

Patents

Holland, John H., and Arthur W. Burks. 1987. "Adaptive Computing System Capable of Learning and Discovery," US Patent 4,697,242.

Holland, John H., and Arthur W. Burks. 1989. "Method of Controlling a Classifier System," US Patent 4,881,178.

---

[41]A *festschift* with comments by Burks.

VANNEVAR E. BUSH

Born March 11, 1890, Everett, Mass.; died June 28, 1974, Belmont, Mass.; inventor of the pre-World War II electromechanical differential analyzer, and wartime US scientific leader whose conception of "Memex" foreshadowed personal computers; instrumental in the development of the atomic bomb.

Education: BS, MS, Tufts College, 1913; DEng, electrical engineering, MIT and Harvard University, 1916.

Professional Experience: General Electric, 1913; electrical inspector, New York Navy Yard, 1919; MIT, associate professor of electric power transmission, 1919–1932, first vice president and dean of engineering, 1932–1939; president, Carnegie Institution, 1939–1955.

Honors and Awards: member, National Academy of Sciences, 1934; honorary Knight of the British Empire (KBE), 1948.

Between 1927 and 1943 Bush developed a series of electromechanical analog computers which greatly facilitated the solution of complex mathematical problems. Notably in 1931, with Frank D. Gage, Harold L. Hazen, King E. Gould, and Samuel H. Caldwell, Bush completed the Differential Analyzer. It could solve sixth-order differential equations and three simultaneous second-order differential equations.

Bush's 1936 paper, entitled "Instrumental Analysis," given as the American Mathematical Society's Gibbs Lecture that year, was an excellent survey of both analog and digital calculating devices. It included several references to Charles Babbage's work and in particular to the collection of papers published by Babbage's son (1889). The section on digital devices concluded with a discussion of how it might be possible to devise a programmable master controller that would turn a set of existing IBM punched-card machines into, effectively, what Bush described as "a close approach to Babbage's large conception."[42]

It turns out that Bush did not stop at speculation, but went on to set up a project, the Rapid Arithmetical Machine, of which astonishingly little is known. Bush himself in his later years had either forgotten, which seems unlikely, or consciously downplayed the significance of this work. Indeed, in his autobiography, *Pieces of the Action* (1970), he wrote, "Who invented the computer? I can write at once that I did not; in fact I had little to do with that whole development." In 1936 the Rockefeller Foundation awarded a major grant to MIT, which resulted in the famous Rockefeller differential analyzer of World War II.

---

[42] In many ways, of course, this is exactly what Aiken, starting in 1937, convinced IBM to do, thus starting a project that led to the successful completion in 1944 of the first US program-controlled calculator, the Harvard Mark I.

Immediately after he delivered his 1936 paper, Vannevar Bush apparently started to work on the design of an electronic digital computer. There is evidence that he documented these ideas in a series of memoranda written during 1937 and 1938 but, despite extensive searches, these have not been found.[43] What we know of them comes from later MIT reports by W.H. Radford (1938, 1939) and from some letters and one 1940 memorandum by Bush.

The proposed machine was to be completely automatic, able to read data on perforated paper tape, to store the data in internal registers, to perform any of the four basic arithmetic operations, and to print the results of its calculations. It was to be controlled by a program represented on perforated tape. Each row of holes would consist of several fields that together constituted one instruction. Each field could contain but a single punched hole, whose position indicated directly which operation was to be performed, say, or which storage reservoir was to provide the operand. There was apparently no thought of having numerically coded addresses, nor of providing means of conditional branching.

Support was obtained from the National Cash Register Co., and later resulted in the full-time employment of first Radford and then W. P. Overbeck on the project. Radford's work concentrated on the design of the basic electronic units. Various units were built and demonstrated successfully, including a scale-of-four counter and a stepping ring—the means proposed for storing each decimal digit. Bush's 1940 memorandum reviewing progress-to-date contains estimates that the machine would be able to multiply two six-decimal digit numbers in about 0.2 seconds, assuming a basic pulse rate of 10,000 per second.

Overbeck took over in late 1939 and spent the next year or so devising special-purpose tubes in an attempt to reduce the number of vacuum tubes needed. Work on the project came to an abrupt and premature end in early 1942, when Overbeck was claimed for work on the atomic bomb project. About the same time, Bush left MIT to become president of the Carnegie Institute.

During the war Bush headed the National Defense Research Committee (NDRC) and its successor, the Office of Scientific Research and Development (OSRD). This office directed the work of some 30,000 scientists and engineers, working on everything from radar, proximity fuses, and amphibious vehicles, to the atom bomb.

The shortened title "Diff. Analyzer," inferring the construction of a Bush-type machine, included in the proposal to the NRDC for the

---

[43]See Randell, Brian, "The Case of the Missing Memoranda," *Ann. Hist. Comp.*, Vol. 4, No. 1, 1982, pp. 66–67.

funding of ENIAC by Brainerd (for Mauchly and Eckert) has been attributed to sensitivity to potential opposition to the project by Bush's associates.[44] Outside the field of computation, Bush was probably best known for his leadership of the "Manhattan Project."

Yet the Rapid Arithmetical Machine project had been forgotten. It was rediscovered during the extensive historical investigations undertaken in connection with the patent litigation between Univac and Honeywell over the validity of the ENIAC patent—litigation that lasted six years and involved testimony by over 150 witnesses and 30,000 pieces of evidence, ranging from a single sheet of paper to a file cabinet-full. Bush's project played only a very small role in the evidence and the testimony, perhaps because none of the MIT people directly involved in the project testified at the trial. Indeed, the Rapid Arithmetical Machine project was not mentioned in the 319-page volume entitled *Findings of Fact, Conclusions of Law and Order for Judgment* that was the sole official publication resulting from the litigation.[45]

Bush had a long history of interest in the problem of information searching, and in 1945 wrote an article describing "Memex," composed of a desk which provided instant access to microphotographed books, periodicals, and documents.[46] To assist the researcher the Memex maintained a trail so that backtracking to earlier searches could be rapidly achieved.[47] This concept was basically achieved in the development of interactive computer systems at MIT in the mid-1960s.[48]

After the war Bush returned to his responsibilities at the Carnegie Institution. When he retired in 1955 he went home to Cambridge and took up duties as a member of the boards of several companies, including the MIT Corp.

When Bush died in 1974, papers such as the *New York Times* carried lengthy accounts of his most impressive career (see Reinhold, 1974). They detailed his many inventions, his illustrious academic career at MIT and the Carnegie Institute, and, perhaps most important, his vital wartime role as director of the National Defense Research and Development.[49]

---

[44]Stern, Nancy, *From ENIAC to UNIVAC*, Digital Press, Bedford, Mass., 1981.

[45]Larson, E. R., "Findings of Fact, Conclusions of Law and Order for Judgment," File No. 4–67, Civ. 138, US District Court, District of Minneapolis, Fourth Division (180 USPQ 673), Oct. 19, 1973.

[46]In the *Atlantic Monthly.*

[47]See esp. Nyce and Kahn, 1991.

[48]See biographies of Fernando Corbató and Robert Fano.

[49]Based primarily on Owens 1987 and Randell 1982.

QUOTATIONS

"On the occasion of the first experimental atomic bomb explosion in New Mexico, someone remarked '. . . if this thing goes off, the President will have to look for a new director of the OSRD.' Bush replied 'If it does not, he will too!'"

"Who invented the computer? I can write at once that I did not, in fact I had little to do with that whole development."

"Those damn digital computers!"[50]

BIBLIOGRAPHY

Biographical

Burks, Arthur W., and Alice R. Burks, "The ENIAC: First General Purpose Electronic Computer," *Ann. Hist. Comp.,* Vol. 3, No. 4, 1981, pp. 310–399.

Bush, Vannevar, *Pieces of Action,* Morrow, New York, 1970.

Nyce, James M., and Paul Kahn, eds., *From Memex to Hypertext: Vannevar Bush and the Mind's Machine,* Academic Press, Boston, 1991.

Owens, Larry, "V. Bush," in *Encycl. of World Biographies, 20th Century Suppl.,* Jack Heraty & Assoc., Palatine, Ill., Vol. 13, 1987, pp. 240–241.

Radford, W.H., "Notes on Arithmetical Machine Memoranda," MIT Press, Cambridge, Mass., 1938.

Radford W.H., *Report on and Investigation of the Practicality of Developing a Rapid Computing Machine,* MIT Press, Cambridge, Mass., 1939.

Randell, Brian, "From Analytical Engine to Electronic Digital Computer: The Contributions of Ludgate, Torres, and Bush," *Ann. Hist. Comp.,* Vol. 4, No. 4, 1982, pp. 327–341.

Reinhold, R., "Dr. Vannevar Bush . . . ," *New York Times,* June 30, 1974; pp. 1, 36.

Weisner, Jerome, "Vannevar Bush," *Biographical Memoirs,* National Academy of Science, Washington, D.C., Vol. 50, 1979.

---

[50]Quoted by Robert Fano in Lee, John A. N., "Time-Sharing and Interactive Computing at MIT: Part II—Project MAC," *Ann. Hist. Comp.,* Vol. 14, No. 2, 1992.

Significant Publications

Bush, Vannevar, "Arithmetical Machine," reprinted in Randell, Brian, ed., *Origins of Digital Computers: Selected Papers*, Springer-Verlag, Berlin Heidelberg, 1982, pp. 337–344.

Bush, Vannevar, "As We May Think," *Atlantic Monthly*, July 1945, pp. 101–108.

Bush, Vannevar, *Endless Horizons*, Public Affairs Press, Washington, D.C., 1946.

Bush, Vannevar, *Pieces of the Action*, Morrow, New York, 1970.

NOLAN BUSHNELL

Born 1943, Clearfield, Utah; created the video game industry in 1972 by founding Atari with $250, and was able to sell out to Warner Communications 4 years later for $25 million.

Education: BS, electrical engineering, University of Utah.

Bushnell is a consummate gamesman who wins, loses, and bounces back. "I like getting companies started, not running them," he says. His ventures include Atari, Pizza Time Theater, and Catalyst Technologies. The latter is an "incubator facility" with a dozen start-up companies in such diverse fields as robotics, advanced color television, toys, games, and electronic car navigation.

The P.T. Barnum of Silicon Valley made his debut in 1972 when he and Al Alcorn devised the table tennis-like game Pong, launching the national video game craze. Atari, the resulting company, became the pioneering giant in the field, with sales of nearly two billion dollars by 1982.

QUOTATION

"Business is the greatest game of all. Lots of complexity and a minimum of rules. And you can keep score with the money."

BIBLIOGRAPHY

Biographical

Caddes, Carolyn, *Portraits of Success: Impressions of Silicon Valley Pioneers,* Tioga Publishing Co., Palo Alto, Calif., 1986.

Slater, Robert, *Portraits in Silicon,* MIT Press, Cambridge, Mass., 1987, chapter 27.

WALTER M. CARLSON

Born September 18, 1916, Denver, Colo.; distinguished computer engineer who combined careers in chemical engineering and computing to concern himself and his society with the future of computing and the benefits of the computer.

Education: BS, Chemical Engineering, University of Colorado, 1938; MS, Chemical Engineering, University of Colorado, 1939.

Professional Experience: manager, Operations Analysis, Engineering Service Division, DuPont Co., 1939–1963; director of Technical Information, US Department of Defense, 1963–1967; IBM Corp.: technical consultant to chief scientist, 1967–1968, marketing consultant, corporate office, 1968–1985; director, Engineering Information, Inc., 1984–1990.

Honors and Awards: fellow, American Institute of Chemical Engineers; ACM Distinguished Service Award, 1991.

Walter Carlson joined DuPont's industrial engineering division in October 1939, and after 15 years in process improvement and planning assignments, he set up the organization to install, operate, and program Serial #12 Univac I in August 1954. The group also provided company-wide consultation in statistics, mathematical analysis, quality control, and operations research.

In 1963, he was employed by the US Department of Defense to create the office of director of technical information. At that time, he was chairman of the Engineering Information Committee of the Engineer's Joint Council, predecessor of the American Association of Engineering Societies.

In February 1967 he joined the IBM Corporation as technical consultant to the chief scientist, and in June 1968 he became a marketing consultant in IBM's corporate office. He retired from that position in 1985 while covering product development and marketing planning for storage products, printers, copiers, and application software on a world-wide basis.

John Weber Carr III

Born May 16, 1923, Durham, N.C.; numerical analyst; founder and first editor of ACM Computing Reviews.

Education: BS, Duke University, 1943; MS, MIT, 1949; PhD, mathematics, MIT, 1951.

Professional Experience: University of Michigan: research mathematician, 1952–1955; assistant and associate professor, 1955–1959; University of North Carolina: associate professor and director, Research Computing Center, 1959–1962, associate professor, 1962–1963, professor, 1963–1966, chairman graduate group, Computing and Information Sciences, 1966–1973; Moore School of Engineering, University of Pennsylvania: professor, 1966–present.

Honors and Awards: president ACM, 1957–1958; ACM Distinguished Service Award 1975.

W. W. Chandler

Born December 1, 1913, Bridport, Dorset, England; died September 11, 1989, London, England; a member of the General Post Office team that developed, installed, and maintained the Colossus machines for the Government Code and Cipher School at Bletchley Park during World War II.

Education: BSc, London University, 1938.

W.W. Chandler began his career as an apprentice telephone engineer with Siemens Bros. in 1930. He joined the British Post Office Research department in 1936 and obtained a BSc degree from London University in 1938 by private study. Prior to World War II he worked on long-distance signaling and dialing systems of the Post Office telephone network. During the war he was responsible for the installation and maintenance of the Colossus machines at Bletchley Park. After the war he helped develop and install the MOSAIC computer for the Radar Establishment at Malvern and later worked on optical character recognition for the Post Office.

BIBLIOGRAPHY

Biographical

Randell, Brian, "The Colossus," in Metropolis, N., J. Howlett, and Gian-Carlo Rota, eds., *A History of Computing in the Twentieth Century*, Academic Press, New York, 1980, pp. 47–92.

Significant Publications

Chandler, W.W., "The Installation and Maintenance of Colossus," *Ann. Hist. Comp.*, Vol. 5, No. 3, 1983.

JULE G. CHARNEY

Born January 1, 1917, California; died June 16, 1981, Boston, Mass.; with John von Neumann, first introduced the electronic computer into weather prediction in 1950.

Education: PhD 1946.

Professional Experience: leader, Meteorology Group, Princeton, 1948–1956; Alfred P. Sloan Professor of Meteorology at the Massachusetts Institute of Technology, 1956–1981.

Jule Gregory Charney, Alfred P. Sloan Professor of Meteorology at the Massachusetts Institute of Technology, died June 16, 1981, at the Sidney Farber Cancer Institute. He was the leading world figure in meteorology ever since he and John von Neumann first introduced the electronic computer into weather prediction in 1950.

Charney was born on January 1, 1917, in California, to Russian immigrants. His original graduate studies at UCLA were in mathematics, but he changed to meteorology in about 1942. The basic principle of numerical weather forecasting is to express the physical laws of atmospheric hydrodynamics and thermodynamics that can be numerically solved by the computer as a step-wise marching process in time. As a concept this was not new in 1950—it had been outlined in some detail 30 years earlier by the Englishman Lewis F. Richardson (1922). Richardson's test calculation—done "by hand," under difficult front-line conditions in World War I—gave very erroneous results, however.

As early as May 1946, von Neumann had envisaged meteorology as a major component of his newly formed Electronic Computer Project at the Institute for Advanced Study (Goldstine 1972; Platzman 1979). Charney's 1946 doctoral thesis had suggested to him that the large-scale circulations in the atmosphere could only be analyzed in a physically appealing and mathematically tractable way, if certain specific approximations were used to distinguish those circulations from sound waves and gravity waves of higher frequency (Charney 1947). After being exposed to von Neumann's hopes for numerical meteorology in an August 1946 meeting (Platzman 1979), Charney spent most of the following year in Oslo. There he extended his ideas and arrived at the "quasi-geostrophic prediction equations" (Charney 1948). These equations predicted only the slow large-scale motions and were free of the sensitivity to high-frequency motion that had plagued Richardson.

On Charney's return he joined von Neumann at Princeton as leader of the Meteorology Group. He then set about answering a series of critical technical questions such as: How important are friction and heating? From how large an atmospheric volume must one have data in order to make a 24-hour forecast for the US? What is the simplest formulation that might have some predictive skill?

The first computations were made in 1950 with the ENIAC and were gratifyingly successful (Charney, Fjörtoft, and von Neumann 1950; Platzman 1979). Similar research was quickly started in other countries, and more elaborate and accurate formulations were used at Princeton as soon as the new IAS computer was ready in 1952 (Goldstine 1972).

With Charney's help, the US Weather Bureau, Air Force, and Navy established in 1954 a Joint Numerical Weather Prediction Unit in Suitland, Maryland, for routine daily prediction of large-scale atmospheric flow patterns and weather. The Weather Bureau, also with intellectual encouragement from Charney, soon started a specifically research-oriented group, the Geophysical Fluid Dynamics Laboratory, to use computers for basic atmospheric and oceanic research. Nowadays, computers are used for weather prediction at the 1- to 4-day range in all of the larger industrial nations and many smaller countries. This success has revolutionized other types of meteorological research as well, by emphasizing both the possibility and the responsibility to see that the consequences of hypotheses about the atmosphere are examined quantitatively. The computer has to a marked extent become for meteorologists the equivalent of the laboratory for physicists and chemists.

It must be admitted that these developments would have occurred eventually in the absence of Charney's personal insight. After all, Princeton was not the only center of computer development in the late 1940s, and Charney's quasi-geostrophic equations were being developed independently at that time in England, Norway, and the Soviet Union. It is very doubtful, however, that the first meteorological use of electronic computers would have been as successful elsewhere as it was under Charney and von Neumann. Their immediate success was a profound stimulus to the postwar development of atmospheric science.

In 1956 Charney left IAS to become professor of meteorology at MIT. A stream of major contributions in dynamic meteorology and oceanography came from him in the ensuing 25 years, including studies of the generation of the Gulf Stream, vertical propagation of hydrodynamic energy in the atmosphere, large-scale wave instability, formation of hurricanes, and hydrodynamic effects on desert climate. In the mid-1960s his clear view of the atmosphere as a single physical system, expressed in a report of the National Academy of Sciences (Charney et al., 1966), led to the extraordinary international effort in 1979 known as the Global Weather Experiment. Charney communicated his infectious enthusiasm for understanding the atmosphere and ocean to many students and collaborators, but his inspiring insights will be difficult to match.[1]

BIBLIOGRAPHY

Biographical

Goldstine, H.H., *The Computer from Pascal to von Neumann,* Princeton University Press, Princeton, N.J., 1972.

Phillips, Norman A., "Eloge: Jule G. Charney, 1917–1981," *Ann. Hist. Comp.,* Vol. 3, No. 4, 1981, pp. 308–309.

Platzman, G., "The ENIAC Computations of 1950—Gateway to Numerical Weather Prediction," *Bull. Amer. Meteorol. Soc.,* Vol. 60, 1979, pp. 302–312.

Richardson, L., *Weather Prediction by Numerical Process,* Cambridge University Press, London, 1922 (reprinted, Dover, New York, 1965).

---

[1]From Phillips 1981.

Significant Publications

Charney, J., "Dynamics of Long Waves in a Baroclinic Westerly Current," *J. Meteor.*, Vol. 4, 1947, pp. 135–162.

Charney, J., "On the Scale of Atmospheric Motions," *Geofys. Publikasjoner*, Oslo, Vol. 17, 1948, pp. 1–17.

Charney, J.G., R. Fjörtoft, and John von Neumann, "Numerical Integration of the Barotropic Vorticity Equation," *Tellus*, Vol. 2, 1950, pp. 237–254.

Charney, J., R. Fleagle, V. Lally, H. Riehl, and D. Wark, "The Feasibility of a Global Observation and Analysis Experiment," report to the Committee on Atmospheric Science, Washington, National Research Council, *Tellus*, Vol. 2, 1966, pp. 237–254.

HAROLD CHESTNUT

Born November 25, 1917, Albany, N.Y.; first president of the International Federation of Automatic Control (IFAC).

Education: BSEE, MIT, 1939; MSEE, MIT, 1940.

Professional Experience: manager, Systems Engineering and Analysis, 1940–1966; Information Science Laboratory, 1966–1967; Systems Engineering and Analysis, 1967–1971; consulting systems engineer, Research and Development Center, General Electric Co., 1971–present.

Honors and Awards: DEE., Case Western Reserve University, 1966; D Eng., Villanova University, 1972; National Academy of Engineering; president, IFAC, 1957–1959; fellow, Instrument Society of America; president, American Automatic Control Council, 1962–1963; fellow, AAAS.

Dov Chevion

Born April 16, 1917, Lodz, Poland; died October 5, 1983, Jerusalem, Israel;
Israeli educator and pioneer computer scientist. Dov Chevion was a giant
among his fellow men and women. He was respected for his strength of leader-
ship, for his commitment toward worthy goals, and as the spokesman in the
computer field for Israel for over two decades. He was particularly concerned
with education, an area in which he made major contributions.

Dov was born on April 16, 1917, in Lodz, Poland. He was educated in
the gymnasium in Lodz and immigrated to Palestine in 1935. He
attended the Hebrew University in Jerusalem, where he studied philosophy, mathematics, and physics. His student days were interrupted by
World War II, after which he worked in the field of statistics for the
British government. He became active in the computer field in the late
1950s and, with Aaron Gertz, was responsible for teaching and training
hundreds of computer and communication systems designers, computer analysts, and programmers who now hold senior positions throughout Israel. He left his mark of accomplishment on the computer user
community of his country and those other countries that were privi-
leged to benefit from his teaching.

IPA Contribution
In the early 1960s Chevion, together with some professors of the
Weizmann Institute and Aaron Gertz, planned and founded the
Information Processing Association of Israel (IPA). He served as chair-
man of the board from 1966 to 1976 and president from 1976 to 1982.
Early in 1983 he was given the title of Honorable President of IPA for
life.

He helped create the first International Jerusalem Conference on
Information Technology (JCIT) in 1971 and was deeply involved in
those that followed in 1974 and 1978. He was an active advisor for JCIT
IV, held in May 1984, until his death in October 1983. Just before his
death, he was awarded the IPA Certificate for his lifelong efforts for
the development of computing in Israel. The Israeli government
awarded Chevion the Kaplan Prize in 1972 and 1973 for teaching the
blind to work with computers. He always employed blind people in his
computing center.

IFIP Participation
IPA became a member of the International Federation for
Information Processing (IFIP) in January 1964, and Chevion was
its first representative. He served until 1978, when he was elected an

individual member for a 3-year term. He was an IFIP trustee in the periods 1965–1967, 1970–1973, and 1973–1976, and a vice president from 1967–1970. As the chairman of the Future Policy Committee from 1967–1969 and a member of that committee from 1979–1981, he helped focus attention on the development of IFIP as the most important international federation in the computer field.

He served as a member of the following IFIP committees:

Tenth Anniversary Committee	1969–1970
Statutes and Bylaws Committee	1969–1981
IFIP Committee for International Liaison	1969–1983
Technical Committee 3 (Education)	1971–1979
Education Policy Committee	1973–1974
Activities Planning Committee	1975–1981
Committee for Liaison with SEARCC	1976–1981

Chevion was chairman of Working Group 3.1 (Informatics Education at the Secondary Education Level) from 1966–1968 and chairman of a Nominations Committee for IFIP trustees. In 1974 he received the Silver Core award for services rendered to IFIP.

Chevion was a personal contributor as well as an active IFIP proponent of each of the World Conferences on Computer Education and was chairman from 1973 of the steering committee for the Second World Conference on Computers in Education, which took place in 1975. In addition, he organized, participated in, and led Israeli lecture teams on computer education to many countries in Central and South America. In recognition of his singular contribution he was appointed honorary professor of computer science by the University of Sao Paulo in Brazil.

Obviously, Chevion was one of IFIP's most active contributors and an outstanding organizer of many important IFIP activities, reflecting, in particular, his devotion and dedication to education about computing and information processing. He was responsible for developing computer curricula for schools, teacher training, and information booklets. These efforts, plus his ability to get people to work together, will be acknowledged for a long time.

IPA Fellowship Program

In November 1965 Chevion suggested a joint fellowship program between one of the Auerbach corporations and IPA to increase the knowledge, experience, and productivity of the people working in the field of computer technology in Israel. Young computer professionals agreed to accept a position for one year in the US so they could gain technical experience, after which they would return to Israel to share their knowledge.

After providing the success of the fellowship program, IPA was able to expand the program to five other US companies in the data processing field. A total of 30 fellows have participated in the program to date.

Final Days

In 1977 Chevion stimulated the General Assembly's interest in governmental and municipal data processing to the extent that he was named chairman of an IFIP task group to investigate the topic. The first IFIP conference on the Impact of New Technologies on Information Systems in Public Administration in the 1980s was held in Vienna in February 1983. Chevion presented a paper entitled "International Cooperation as a Vehicle of Information Technology in Public Administration." He returned home from the conference and underwent major surgery in March. He died in Hadassah Hospital on October 5, 1983, with his family present.[2]

BIBLIOGRAPHY

Biographical

Auerbach, Isaac L., "Eloge: Dov Chevion, 1917–1983," *Ann. Hist. Comp.*, Vol. 7, No. 1, Jan. 1985, pp. 4–6.

NOAM CHOMSKY

Born December 7, 1928; mathematical linguist who is responsible for the hierarchy of grammars that bears his name; recipient of the 1988 Kyoto Prize in Basic Science.

Chomsky's work on the syntax of languages coincided neatly with the early development of programming languages and thus his work

---

[2]From Auerbach 1985.

found ready application to the more formal style of artificial language than those of his original interest—natural languages. The recognition of a hierarchy of syntactic forms each properly subsetted inside the next and each representing a particular language style also matched some of the lower levels of programming language elements. The Chomsky hierarchy places regular (or linear) languages as a subset of the context-free languages, which in turn are embedded within the set of context-sensitive languages also finally residing in the set of unrestricted or recursively enumerable languages. By defining syntax as the set of rules that define the spatial relationships between the symbols of a language, various levels of language can be also described as one-dimensional (regular or linear), two-dimensional (context-free), three-dimensional (context sensitive) and multi-dimensional (unrestricted) relationships. From these beginnings, Chomsky might well be described as the "father of formal languages."

Like Edmund Berkeley, Chomsky became embroiled in the peace movements of the 1960s and so divided his efforts between his linguistic studies and his social concerns. His publications since 1960 have been divided between the two subjects.

QUOTATIONS

"The fundamental aim in linguistic analysis of language L is to separate the *grammatical* sequences which are sentences of L from the *ungrammatical* sequences which are not sentences of L and to study the structure of grammatical sequences." (1957)

"The notion grammatical cannot be identified with meaningful or significant in any semantic sense. Sentences (1) and (2) are equally nonsensical, but any speaker of English will recognize that only the former is grammatical:

(1) Colorless green ideas sleep furiously.

(2) Furiously sleep ideas green colorless." (1957)

BIBLIOGRAPHY

Biographical

George, Alexander, ed., *Reflections on Chomsky,* B. Blackwell, Oxford, 1989.

Piattelli-Palmarini, Massimo, ed., *Language and Learning: the Debate Between Jean Piaget and Noam Chomsky,* Harvard University Press, Cambridge, Mass., 1980.

Significant Publications

Chomsky, Noam, *Syntactic Structures,* Mouton & Co., The Hague, 1957.

Chomsky, Noam, *Chomsky: Selected Readings,* Oxford University Press, Oxford, 1971.

Chomsky, Noam, *Language and Mind,* enl. ed., Harcourt Brace Jovanovich, New York, 1972.

Chomsky, Noam, *Topics in the Theory of Generative Grammar,* Mouton & Co. The Hague, 1975.

Chomsky, Noam, *The Logical Structure of Linguistic Theory,* Plenum Press, New York, 1975.

Chomsky, Noam, *Reflections on Language,* 1st ed., Pantheon Books, New York, 1975.

Chomsky, Noam, *Rules and Representations,* Columbia University Press, New York, 1980.

Chomsky, Noam, *Knowledge of Language: Its Nature, Origin, and Use,* Praeger, New York, 1986.

Chomsky, Noam, *Language and Problems of Knowledge: the Managua Lectures,* MIT Press, Cambridge, Mass., 1988.

ALONZO CHURCH

Born June 14, 1903, Washington, D.C.; mathematical logician, creator of the Lambda Calculus who contributed the Church-Rosser theorem to the study of computer science.

Education: AB, Princeton University, 1924; PhD, mathematics, Princeton University, 1927.

Professional Experience: national research fellow in mathematics, Harvard University, 1927–1928; University of Göttingen and University of Amsterdam, 1929; Princeton University, assistant professor, professor, 1929–1967; UCLA, professor, philosophy and mathematics, 1967–present.

Honors and Awards: DSc, Case Western Reserve University member, 1969; National Academy of Science.

QUOTATIONS

"Our subject is *logic*—or, as we may say more fully, in order to distinguish from certain topics and doctrines which have (unfortunately) been called by the same name, it is *formal logic*." (*Introduction to Formal Logic*, 1956)

BIBLIOGRAPHY

Biographical

Kleene, S.C., "Recursive Function Theory," *Ann. Hist. Comp.*, Vol. 3, No. 1, 1981, pp. 52–67.

Significant Publications

Church, Alonzo, "The Calculi of Lambda-Conversion," Kraus Reprint Corp., New York, 1965, reprint of the 1941 ed. published by Princeton University Press.

Church, Alonzo, "Introduction to Mathematical Logic." Princeton University Press, Princeton, 1956.

ARTHUR C. CLARKE

Born December 16, 1917, Minehead, Somerset, UK; science fiction writer who "invented" HAL in the movie 2001: A Space Odyssey. *Originator of the concept of communications satellites.[3]*

Education: Huish's Grammar School, Taunton, 1927–1936; BSc, first class honors, physics and mathematics, King's College, London, 1946–1948.

Professional Experience: Auditor, H.M. Exchequer and Audit Department, 1936–1941; Royal Air Force: Instructor, No. 9 Radio School, then Flight Lieutenant, Ground Controlled Approach Radar,[4] 1941–1946; assistant editor, *Physics Abstracts*, IEE, 1949–1950; self-employed author, 1950–present; chancellor, University of Moratuwa, Sri Lanka, 1979–present.

---

[3]See *Wireless World*, October 1945.
[4]Developed by MIT Radiation Laboratory.

Honors and Awards: honorary fellow, British Interplanetary Society; honorary fellow, American Astronomical Association; academician, World Academy of Art and Science; honorary fellow, International Academy of Astronautics, 1960; Stuart Ballantine Medal, Franklin Institute, 1963; fellow, Franklin Institute, 1971; DSc (Hon.), Beaver College, Pennsylvania, 1971; Aerospace Communications Award, American Institute of Aeronautics and Astronautics, 1974; honorary fellow, American Institute of Aeronautics and Astronautics, 1976; Bradford Washburn Award, Boston Museum of Science, 1977; fellow, King's College, 1977; DSc (Hon.), University of Moratuwa, 1979; Engineering Award, Academy of Television Arts and Sciences, 1981; fellow, Institute of Robotics, Carnegie Mellon University, 1981; Marconi International Fellowship, 1982; honorary fellow, Institute of Engineers, Sri Lanka, 1983; Centennial Medal, IEEE, 1984; foreign associate, National Academy of Engineering, 1986; Charles A. Lindbergh Award, 1987; associate fellow, Third World Academy of Sciences, 1987; Hall of Fame, Society of Satellite Professionals, 1987; DLitt, University of Bath, 1988; fellow, International Aerospace Hall of Fame, San Diego, 1989; fellow, International Space Hall of Fame, Alamagordo, N.M., 1989; R. A. Heinlein Memorial Award, National Space Society, 1990; honorary life president, UN Association of Sri Lanka, 1990; honorary fellow, Ceylon College of Physicians, 1991; International Science Policy Foundation Medal, 1992; freeman, Town of Minehead, 1992.

Arthur C. Clarke was born in the small Somerset town of Minehead, not far from Exmoor, the site of the story of *Lorna Doone,* in 1917. He was educated at Huish's Grammar School, Taunton. Clarke entered H.M. Exchequer & Audit Department in 1936, and served in the Royal Air Force during World War II. While operating the prototype Ground Control Approach radar system, he conceived the basic theory of communication satellites, and published the concept in 1945.

After demobilization, he took a first class honors degree in physics and mathematics at King's College, London, which later elected him as a fellow. From 1948 to 1950 he was assistant editor of *Physics Abstracts,* a publication of the Institution of Electrical Engineers. Twice he was chairman of the British Interplanetary Society—1946–1947, and 1950–1953.

Since 1954 his interest in underwater exploration has taken him to the Great Barrier Reef of Australia and the Indian Ocean; he is now a director of the Colombo-based "Underwater Safaris."

He has published more than 70 books and made many appearances on radio and television, most notably with Walter Cronkite on CBS during the NASA Apollo missions. His 13-part "Mysterious World" and "Strange Powers" television programs have been seen worldwide, and reappear frequently on PBS in the US.

He is a council member of the Society of Authors, a vice president of the H.G. Wells Society, and a member of many other scientific and literary organizations. He was nominated for an "Oscar" for the screenplay of *2001: A Space Odyssey.*

Clarke has lived in Sri Lanka for the past 30 years, and in 1979 was appointed Chancellor of the University of Moratuwa by President Jayewardene. The university, near Colombo, is the location of the government-established Arthur C. Clarke Centre for Modern Technologies, specializing in communications and computers. He is also chancellor of the International Space University.

In 1989 H.M. Queen Elizabeth awarded him a CBE for "services to British cultural interests in Sri Lanka." On returning to the UK in 1992 for his 75th birthday celebrations, he was made the first Freeman of his hometown, Minehead, Somerset.

BIBLIOGRAPHY

Biographical

Clarke, Arthur C., *Astounding Days—A Science Fictional Autobiography*, Bantam Books, New York, 1989.

McAleer, Neil, *Odyssey: The Authorized Biography*, Contemporary Books, Chicago, 1992.

Significant Publications

Clarke, Arthur C., "The Obsolescence of Man," in *Profiles of the Future*, Harper Press, London, 1958.

Clarke, Arthur C., "The Steam Powered Word Processor: A Forgotten Epic of Victorian Engineering," *Analog*, Vol. 106, No. 9, Sept. 1986, pp. 175–179.

JOSEPH CLEMENT

Born 1779, Great Ashby, Westmoreland, UK; died 1884; Babbage's chief mechanic for the Difference Engine.

Introduction[5]

When Charles Babbage began work on his famous Difference Engine, he was in need of a professional mechanic and draftsman. He managed to arrange for the majority of his work to be done in the work-

---
[5]From Williams 1992.

shop of Joseph Clement. This arrangement continued for a number of years, essentially during the entire time that the Difference Engine was under active construction. The arrangements between Babbage and Clement are reasonably well known (Hyman 1984) and the story of how the two of them came to part company has been part of almost every paper written about the project. However, very little information is available about Joseph Clement himself. Clement was not simply a run-of-the-mill machinist who happened to be fortunate enough to work for Babbage, and who was partly responsible for the failure of the construction of the Difference Engine (an impression easily obtained from reading the majority of accounts of the project). Rather he was a highly respected member of the mechanical engineering community when Babbage first contacted him and when Babbage actually delegated a large part of the responsibility of the actual design of the Difference Engine to Clement.

In 1990, while examining some letters in the Fitzwilliam Museum in Cambridge, I came across two letters from Charles Babbage (August 19, 1863 and August 26, 1863) to a certain George Clowes.[6] Clowes evidently was associated with a publishing venture because the content of the letters was Babbage's response to having been shown some proofs of an article written by a Samuel Smiles.[7] The article concerned the life of Babbage's chief mechanic and draftsman Joseph Clement. In the first letter (August 19, 1863) Babbage offers some corrections to the proofs and says "he is too busy to do more but will pass the proofs on to Mr. Wilmot Buxton, who fully comprehends the subject."[8] In the second (August 26, 1863) Babbage begins:

> I enclose a letter from Mr. Buxton which it may be interesting to Mr. Smiles to see. The substance of it or any extracts are at his service but I have not permission to publish the writer's name. I wish it to be returned to Dorset St.

and then continues to give a summary of his dealings with Mr. Clement. We conclude that these letters relate to a book called

---

[6]These letters once belonged to Douglas Hartree, the early British computer pioneer, and were evidently given by him to the Fitzwilliam Museum in 1947. The author does not know how they came into the possession of Hartree.

[7]George Clowes was likely associated with the London publishing firm of John Murray. It was this firm that published the first edition of Smiles' book.

[8]Mr. Wilmot Buxton was Babbage's friend and, after Babbage's death, produced a biography which has only recently been published. It was not unusual for Buxton to deal with matters relating to Babbage's engines; for example, he was the person who explained the working of the first Difference Engine when it was displayed in the Exhibition of 1862.

Industrial Biography written by Samuel Smiles in 1863 (Smiles 1882).[9] It contains not only a chapter on the life of Joseph Clement, quite evidently the one for which Babbage had been given the proofs, but also an appendix consisting of a lightly edited version of the letter (August 26, 1863) I had seen in the Fitzwilliam Museum. The book is typical of the Victorian writings designed to inspire the populace with successful tales of hard-working individuals who have made their own way in life, and, in what follows, I have attempted to eliminate the most obvious inspirational tales and concentrate on what I believe to be the more factual information.[10] Unfortunately, Smiles, who occasionally mentions the papers Clement left behind, does not give any information as to the location of any papers or relics.

Joseph Clement (1779–1844)

Joseph Clement was born in Great Ashby in Westmoreland (northern England) in 1779. He came from simple stock; his father was a weaver by profession, with a strong interest in nature. It is reported that his hobby was a beetle and insect collection and that he set up a number of bee hives near his loom so that he could watch their activities without leaving his work. Joseph appears to have inherited at least some of his mechanical ability from his father, as Old Clement was known to have a lathe that he used both for recreation and for turning items, such as bobbins, that he needed in his profession. While no portrait appears to exist of Joseph Clement, he is described as a heavy-browed man without any polish of manner or speech. He had a very heavy North Country accent, developed in his youth, which never left despite his living most of his adult life in other areas of Britain. Although he did attend the village school, it was only to master the rudiments of reading and writing, and he was almost illiterate as an adult. Indeed John Herschel (the son of the great astronomer and himself an astronomer of note), a friend of Babbage, actually comments on the impression that Clement gave in matters of business: while Babbage was away in Europe, Herschel was looking after the business side of the construction of the Difference Engine and wrote to Babbage saying (December 22, 1827):

> . . . C. told me he must have £150, which he (after much hesitation and what at first I took for reluctance, but which I fancy to be the mere consequence of his singular slowness of thought) put into writing in

---

[9]Smiles first wrote *Industrial Biography* in 1863. It subsequently had at least sixteen other editions published in both Britain and America. There also exist at least two editions in Spanish. Further information on Smiles can be obtained from examining his autobiography and the work of Timothy Travers.

[10]Unless otherwise noted, all personal information concerning Clement in this paper is based on the contents of the 1882 edition of *Industrial Biography* (Smiles 1882).

the following form which is a curiosity at least as great as the Engine will be when done.

This is to certify that eight men have been employed on Mr. Babbage's calculating machine this five weeks past. I have likewise got a man to assist me in the drawing. Joseph Clement December 5th 1827. I want £150 to enable me to go on.

After his short schooling, Clement worked with his father at the weaver's trade, but the increasing mechanization of that industry soon led to his seeking alternate employment. From age 18 to 23 he apparently worked as a thatcher and then a slater in the area around his village. As this trade did not occupy him full time, he became friends with the village blacksmith; together, they produced a lathe which Clement used to manufacture various instruments such as flutes, clarinets, and Northumberland bagpipes. Clement's cousin, a watch and clock maker who had spent some time in London, lent him some books on mechanics and he used these as a resource guide to construct a microscope for his father's use in his hobby of collecting insects, and a reflecting telescope. Anyone with this level of talent was not likely to stay as a part-time village thatcher and, sometime in 1805, he left to take a job in the nearby town of Kirby Stephen, where he was employed in the construction of looms at a wage of 3 shillings 6 pence per day. He apparently lived with his employer, a Mr. George Dickinson, to whom he sold the telescope for the sum of £12. In late 1805 he moved to Carlisle and, in 1807, to Glasgow. While in Glasgow he happened to meet a Mr. Peter Nicholson, a writer of popular woodworking books at the time. Mr. Nicholson lent Clement one of his drawings of a power loom and Clement, although he had no training, copied it so expertly that Nicholson had difficulty in telling the original from the copy. The writer was so impressed that he gave Clement a series of free lessons in technical drawing. After a year in Glasgow, Clement again moved, this time to Aberdeen, where he was employed by Leys, Masson & Co. in the construction of power looms. Clement evidently found the tools inappropriate, for he constructed a turning lathe with a sliding mandrill[11] and guide screw,[12] and a device for

---

[11]A mandril, now spelled 'mandrel' is the spindle running through the center of the headstock. It is turned by the driving pulley to which it is keyed and at one end holds the work with a faceplate or chuck. The meaning of 'sliding mandril' is not clear. It may imply a two-part spindle in which the inner cylinder, keyed to rotate with the outer cylinder, can be slid in and out, toward and away from the work. This might well be an example, as suggested by the editor of this Department, of Babbage simply making up terms to express his thoughts whereas Clement would have been in the habit of using the accepted terminology of the mechanical engineering practice of his day.

[12]The guide screw, also 'feed screw' or 'lead screw,' is a long screw with rectangular threads mounted parallel to the main axis of the lathe by which the tool holder on the slide rest is moved longitudinally. If used to cut screw threads, its pitch must be precise and uniform.

correcting errors in the guide screw. He also produced a special tool-holding device, the slide rest, which, although not unknown earlier, was one of the earliest in Britain. During this time his wages rose from one and a half guineas per week to three guineas (1 guinea = 21 shillings), showing that his employers were quite pleased with the quality of work he was able to produce. Not content with simply advancing his employers' stock of tools, he evidently enrolled in the Marischal College in Aberdeen where he attended at least one course in Natural Philosophy during the 1812–1813 term. Later in 1813 he took his savings, which had amounted to almost £100, and moved to London. After spending a few weeks in an ordinary machine shop, he moved to one of the most famous engineering firms of the day, that of Joseph Bramah, famous for engineering feats ranging from hydraulic presses that could lift 1,144, tons, to the construction of continuous-process papermaking machines. Clement was placed in charge of the tools in the shop and quickly distinguished himself in not only improving the tools, but in organizing and improving the flow of work. On April 1, 1814 Bramah and Clement signed an agreement in which Clement was to be the chief draftsman and superintendent of Bramah's main works at Pimlico. Unfortunately Bramah died on December 9, 1814, and his sons, who returned from college to take over the business, did not see Clement as indispensable as had, apparently, their father. The contract was broken and Clement joined the firm of Maudslay and Fields as their chief draftsman. Finally, in 1817, he struck out on his own and set up a small shop in Prospect Place, Newington Butts, where he advertised himself as a mechanical draftsman and manufacturer of small machinery requiring first class workmanship.

Some indication of Clement's talent can be taken from the fact that he often produced the illustrations of mechanical machinery in the Transactions of the Society for the Encouragement of Arts. Between 1817 and 1832 his tiny signature can be found in the corner of many of the best drawings of such complex items as theodolites, complicated drawing machines, and lathes. In the process of his technical drawing work, he often had to produce both paper drawings and copper engravings of perspective views of circles, ellipses, and other complex items.

In 1827 the Society of Arts again gave him their Gold Medal, and in 1828 their Silver Medal, for the invention of several improvements to lathes, the most important of which was a device to change the speed of rotation of the work as the tool came closer to the axis of rotation, as it might when turning the surface of a large flat disk. Another of his successes was the development of a very large and accurate planing machine by means of which the surfaces of metal plates of large dimension could be finished to a fine tolerance. Although he never attempted to patent this device, a full description was published (Varley 1832) but, perhaps because of his limited skill at writing, it was not done by Clement himself. Another of his inventions which, at the time, was highly regarded, resulted from his need to produce large accurate drawings for Babbage's projects. He therefore designed and constructed a special drawing table which, because of its size, required an intricate and adjustable set of supports.

His list of inventions and improvements is impressive, but none has had more impact than his attempt, started in 1828, to produce screws and bolts with standard diameters and with threads of a standard shape and pitch—essential elements for interchangeability. Although his campaign in this area did not immediately result in success, his best journeyman at the time, Mr. (later Sir) Joseph Whitworth, was the man who ultimately established the standard Whitworth thread, which dominated British machine practice for almost 175 years until replaced by the metric standard. Whitworth left Clement's shop when the demand for work on Babbage's Difference Engine came to an end. He moved to Manchester and within a few years became the foremost precision machinist in Britain. In later years, Charles Babbage even had some correspondence with Whitworth, who had offered to undertake the actual construction of his Analytical Engine, but this was never taken beyond the initial stages of discussion. As Hyman (1984) speculates, Whitworth, having seen the effects of the Difference Engine project upon the advancement of the tool-making industry, may well have thought it worth undertaking the construction of the Analytical Engine just because of the potential 'spin-offs' it might produce. When Clement died in 1844, the business was continued by his nephew. The new owner was evidently not as good a workman as his uncle had been and the business gradually faded away.

Clement-Babbage Relationship

In 1823, when the Government grant of £1500 made it feasible for Babbage to think seriously about constructing his Difference Engine, he needed a proper draftsman and mechanic. In one of the letters mentioned earlier (August 26, 1863) he states:

> At the commencement of the Diff. Engine I wanted a person to assist me in the drawings and afterwards if necessary to construct the Engine. The late Sir Isambard[13] Brunel recommended Mr. Clement as

---

[13]Note that this reference is to Sir Mark Isambard Brunel, not his son, Isambard Kingdom Brunel, although by the time this letter was written they were both dead.

likely to suit me. Mr. Clement then possessed one lathe small but very good having also an excellent screw. His workshop at that time was his front kitchen. The lathe had also a very valuable slide rest rather too large for it. His small stock of tools were all excellent of their kind. As soon as any part of the Diff. Engine was contrived and drawn, I proceeded to ask Clement what was the perceived mode of making it. The plans then in use were tedious and demanded the skill of the very best workmen. Now as I required an identity amongst hundreds and even thousands of similar parts the then existing methods were insufficient. I suggested special tools and by the aid of Clement's admirable skill and availing myself of his practical knowledge arranged the plan of several new machine tools. So far was the 1st Diff. Engine from not [sic] having a printing apparatus that I well remember the discussion I had with Clement on its first suggestion. I remarked that I required what I should call a coordinate machine which I explained to Clement. I then sketched two slides at right angles to each other and proposed to place these vertical slides at the back of a lathe having a cylindrical mandrel. This plan was adopted and at once gave us the command of the use of circular cutters, drills, and saws over every part of the plane. Copper plates were inscribed by steel figure punches on this machine. Again I required for making the bolts the vertical motion of an horizontal plane upon a slide rest. I proposed inclined planes as the simplest method but Clement preferred four screws driven by a central wheel which probably was the best of the two plans. Under the demands of the Diff. Engine the number of machine tools increased and Mr. Clement converted a large building at the back of his house into a workshop. The improvements in tools are mainly due to the stronger system of iron framing now employed; circular cutters, slides, slotting, and even planing machines, adapted to ornamental turning may be found drawn and described in several of the older authors in that subject.

It would appear that Babbage, either through the haze of years or because of a lasting feud, could not accurately remember his first dealing with Clement nor the state of Clement's establishment. This letter makes it look very much like Clement was a poor man who happened to have the luck of being recommended to Babbage. The fact that Clement possessed only one small lathe was not an indication that his business was not a success, but rather than he was in a specialized shop dedicated to high quality workmanship. We have seen how, in earlier years, he had actually made several lathes of very high quality and was fully used to constructing any tool that he needed. Again, Babbage's remark that his workshop was in his front kitchen would also imply a certain lack of success and sophistication. Clement was, as amply demonstrated by Herschel's remark above, not a sophisticated man, but he was certainly successful and well respected in his craft when Babbage first met him. The fact that he was good enough to have already won his Society's Gold Medal (an honor of which Babbage, who received the Gold Medal of the Astronomical Society in 1824, was always very proud) seems to have been overlooked in any consideration of Clement's contributions to the construction of the Difference Engine. The latter part of this letter seems to be, other than the first few sentences, in accordance with what must have been the actual working relationship. Babbage appears to give Clement credit for some of the advances in the machine tools and methods of construction and the description of their working relationship (essentially Babbage suggesting a special tool and Clement agreeing that one was needed but making it to his own design) rings true.

In fact Babbage completely abdicated the office of design engineer for the Difference Engine and, at least for a time, left entirely in Clement's hands the technical details of how it was to be implemented. During the time that Babbage went off on his trip to Europe, leaving Herschel in charge of the Difference Engine project, the two friends wrote several letters back and forth. The majority of the contents of these letters concern the changes that Clement had made to the detailed design of the Difference Engine. Herschel spends a lot of effort, including drawing diagrams, trying to explain to Babbage these modifications. Herschel, whatever his qualifications in other areas, was not good at explaining complex mechanical questions and, at the end of one letter (December 22, 1827) is forced to admit:

> On reading this description I see that it is unintelligible and what is worse that I can't mend it. I had it all there before my mind when I left Clement, and last night when he called here I rehearsed it to him, and now I am puzzled, but you will see the principles from this. . . .

Again, when describing some of the work that had taken place, Herschel tells Babbage about some new drawings containing (February 12, 1828):

> . . . in part a new scheme of Clement's who says you left it to him to plan as well as he could.

Babbage's reply shows that he had complete confidence in Clement (May 9, 1828):

> I left Clement so well acquainted with all the mechanical actions of the machine that I have not the least fear of his making such changes as he may think necessary.

Later, in the same letter, he again demonstrates the fact Clement had been given a free hand when he indicates that Clement had made very major changes to the mechanical motions:

The plan for locking the axes in their places until the wheels are ready to be bolted seems to me better than rollers which latter I never intended and know not how they got into the drawings.

Although not absolute proof, these quotations imply that Clement had a much larger hand in the actual detailed design of the Difference Engine than has previously been appreciated. The one other major factor in the Babbage-Clement relationship was the fact that, when the working relationship deteriorated to the point where they parted company, Clement took all the tools and drawings that he had made for the Difference Engine project and left Babbage without the means of continuing. There is no doubt that Clement had a legal right to take the tools, but the fact that he did so has caused him to have a lot of bad press. It would appear that both Babbage and Herschel were not unaware of this potential problem. In the letters between Herschel and Babbage, mentioned above, are a number of remarks which seem to indicate a growing unease with Clement's activities. Just prior to Christmas 1827, Herschel wrote to Babbage about the progress of the project (December 22, 1827):

I went over to him [Clement] to see how he gets on, at the early part of the week. He has been making a new drawing to show the effect of certain alterations he recommends (which I shall explain presently) I am so new to the scale of daily weekly and monthly progress that such work ought to make, that I will confess to you it seemed to me not to have got on too much since you left.

A few weeks later he again writes to Babbage (February 12, 1828) saying:

Clement . . . tells me he keeps 10 men constantly at work on the Engine. I saw 7 there in the workshop and one man working on the drawings when I last called. He seems to have been chiefly at work on the drawings . . . he has drawn upon me for £200 more making in all £350 since you left England. Verily it makes not much show, but I am a sad novice in matters of workmanship and I suppose the secret is that good work is not cheap.

Having received no answer from Babbage[14], Herschel, apparently getting more concerned about several aspects of the project, writes again (April 10–17, 1828):

---

[14]It is not surprising that Babbage had not yet answered as Herschel had simply sent the letters to Rome and Florence knowing that these cities were on Babbage's route. Babbage did receive the letters, but only after a delay.

Clement has drawn on me for £200:0:0 more making in all £550 since you left. It may be that £550 worth of work is done, but I confess it makes marvelous little show for the money.

Babbage eventually wrote back (May 9, 1828):

I have just received yours of the 10–17 April. The accounts you gave me of the progress of the machine are by no means discouraging as to the work done and the drawings. It is a species of work which makes but little show. As to the actual steel and brass cut up for my use I fear it is little and that Clement is spending much time in making tools. This is to a certain extent necessary and requires considerable supplies of money but I should wish you incidently [sic] if possible to find out whether it is not Clement's intention to make me pay for the construction of these tools and then to keep them as his own property. From the multitude he is making it looks so.

Babbage had obviously become more than just a little suspicious. Considering this early suspicion, and the fact that Babbage had access to the best of advice from very knowledgeable friends and associates, it is interesting that he let the problem develop to such an extent that it eventually put him out of business.

BIBLIOGRAPHY

Biographical

Babbage, C., Letter dated May 9, 1828 (4 quarto pages), Library of the Royal Society, London, UK, Herschel Papers, Babbage letter 226.

Babbage, C., Letter dated August 19, 1863 (2 quarto pages), Fitzwilliam Museum Library, Cambridge, UK, Mss 69/1947.

Babbage, C., Letter dated August 26, 1863 (3 quarto pages), Fitzwilliam Museum Library, Cambridge, UK, Mss 70/1947.

Buxton, W.H., *Memoir of the Life and Labours of the Late Charles Babbage Esq. F.R.S.*, Vol. 13, Charles Babbage Institute Reprint Series of the History of Computing, MIT Press, Cambridge, Mass., 1988.

Herschel, J.F.W., Letter dated December 22, 1827 (4 folio pages), Library of the Royal Society, London, UK, Herschel Papers, Babbage letter 218.

Herschel, J.F.W., Letter dated February 12, 1828 (4 folio pages), Library of the Royal Society, London, UK, Herschel Papers, Babbage letter 219.

Herschel, J.F.W., Letter dated April 10–17, 1828 (4 folio pages), Library of the Royal Society, London, UK, Herschel Papers, Babbage letter 225.

Hyman, Anthony, *Charles Babbage, Pioneer of the Computer,* Oxford University Press, Oxford, 1984.

Mackay, Thomas, ed., *The Autobiography of Samuel Smiles*, E.P. Dutton, New York, 1905.

Smiles, Samuel, *Industrial Biography: Iron Workers and Tool Makers,* John Murray, London, 1882.

Travers, Timothy, *Samuel Smiles and the Victorian Work Ethic,* Garland, New York, 1987.

Varley, Timothy, *The Transactions of the Society for the Encouragement of Arts,* London, 1832, p. 157.

Williams, Michael R., "Joseph Clement: The First Computer Engineer," *Ann. Hist. Comp.*, Vol. 14, No. 3, 1992.

RICHARD F. CLIPPINGER

Born 1913, East Liberty, Ohio; computing laboratory staff member, Aberdeen Proving Ground, who converted the ENIAC to a stored program computer using its read-only hand-set function tables.

Education: PhD, mathematics, Harvard University, 1940.

Professional Experience: ballistic research laboratory, Aberdeen Proving Ground, 1944–1952; Raytheon Computer Laboratory (later Datamatic Corporation, and later still EDP Division of Honeywell), 1952–1976.

Clippinger went to the Ballistic Research Laboratory at Aberdeen Proving Ground in 1944. There he invented and developed the closed-chamber firing range, which rivaled the wind tunnel for measuring forces on a supersonic model. At Aberdeen he also worked in the development of numeric methods for solving ordinary and partial differential equations on the ENIAC, EDVAC, and ORDVAC. In 1952 he joined the Raytheon Computer Laboratory, which became Datamatic Corporation in 1954 and the EDP division of Honeywell in 1956. He was in charge of software development for the Honeywell 800 family until 1959 when he supervised the development of the FACT business language compiler by Computer Sciences Corporation. He became Honeywell's representative to CODASYL when it was created.

He chaired the ANSI and ISO language-standardization committees, and retired from Honeywell in 1976. Currently he consults on doing color graphics on a Macintosh Quadra.

BIBLIOGRAPHY

Biographical

Clippinger, R.F., "Comments on the Meeting of October 14, 1959," Special Issue, Cobol: 25th Anniversary, *Ann. Hist. Comp.*, Vol. 7, No. 4, 1985, pp. 327–329.

Significant Publications

Clippinger, R.F., "FACT—A Business Compiler: Description and Comparison with COBOL and Commercial Translator," in Goodman, R., ed., *Ann. Rev. in Automatic Computing*, Pergamon Press, New York, Vol. 2, 1961, pp. 231–292.

JOHN COCKE

Born May 25, 1925, Charlotte, N.C.; computer scientist who specializes in compiler optimizations techniques.

Education: BS, mechanical engineering, Duke University, 1946; PhD, mathematics, Duke University, 1956.

Professional Experience: IBM research, 1956–1993; fellow, IBM, Yorktown Heights.

Honors and Awards: IEEE Computer Society Pioneer Award, 1989; ACM/IEEE Eckert-Mauchly Award, 1985; ACM Turing Award, 1987; National Medal of Technology, 1991; National Medal of Science, 1994.

Burnout has never bothered John Cocke, the inventor of reduced-instruction-set computer (RISC) technology. His interest in all parts of the computer business and his ability to "always find something a little different" to engage his attention have led to some 22 patents. Besides those for RISC technology, his patents cover logic simulation, coding theory, and compiler optimization. Inventing is something Cocke does with great enthusiasm. A self-motivator, he does not feel acceptance or acclaim are important for motivation. In fact, he enjoys discovering his mistakes because "that is when you learn something." But he recalls no major failures in his career.

Cocke's approach to solving problems is not guided by rules or any particular philosophy. He feels that solutions come through continuous work and does not remember ever having had dramatic flashes of inspiration. Claiming that he is clumsy at using a keyboard or a mouse, he prefers a pencil and paper or a blackboard. He also told *IEEE Spectrum* that he is more diagram- than word-oriented.

His most productive period, Cocke feels, was when he was about 35 and "wildly interested in computers." At that time, he had the opportunity to work in the laboratories of IBM Corp. with such luminaries as Frederick P. Brooks Jr., now Kenan Professor of Computer Science at the University of North Carolina, Chapel Hill. Cocke describes those days of freedom in thinking, when there were few known procedures at IBM, as energizing, but, ever self-effacing, said he was "just there to learn."

Cocke's keen intellect is combined with an avid curiosity and an ability to totally immerse himself in a technical challenge, according to colleagues. "The smartest man I ever met, " said Joel S. Birnbaum, vice president and general manager of the information architecture group at Hewlett-Packard Co., who was once interviewed for a job by Cocke at IBM and subsequently worked there. Lewis M. Branscomb, director of science technology and public policy at Harvard University, Cambridge, Mass., and a former IBM chief scientist, describes Cocke as "one of the very few people I know whose IQ is higher than his blood cholesterol level."

Cocke's interest in inventing was sparked at an early age by an uncle's comment that you could catch a bird by putting salt on its tail. But his attempts to develop an effective salt sprayer failed. He also experimented early on with a device to wash windows. This invention worked. By moving an electromagnet on the inside of a window, he was able to cause a piece of iron attached to a cloth to move in tandem on the outside. Another of his first experiences with "inventing" was a hydraulic pipe wrench. Its jaws were opened and closed by pressing a button each time. But he discovered that such a wrench had already been patented in 1890.

Born May 25, 1925, in Charlotte, N.C., Cocke was the youngest of three sons. His father was chairman of the board of a local power company. Because Cocke was not a good student in grammar school, his mother had to have him tutored. When he got to high school, he did a little better by studying general science and physics, courses he took to avoid taking Latin, a subject he considered "too difficult." The mathematics he felt he could handle without a lot of study, he told Spectrum.

He fared even better at Duke University, Durham, N.C., where he received a bachelor's degree in mechanical engineering in 1946. His courses in engineering and physics were selected because "they were easier" than art courses, which he felt would have been "too difficult memorizing hundreds of paintings and painters."

As a student at Duke, he had been in the US Navy's V-12 program and was called back into the Navy in 1952. In the interval from 1946 to 1952, he held several jobs, including one with a heating and air-conditioning company and another with General Electric Co.'s high-voltage laboratories.

Cocke returned to Duke in 1954. While there, he took a summer job at Patrick Air Force Base in Florida, where he designed a Monte Carlo program to determine the optimum number of aircraft required for delivering supplies to the Bahamas. After receiving a doctorate in mathematics from Duke, he joined IBM in 1956. The decision to go with IBM at that time, he said, was a lucky one: it put him where the action was in computer development.

Over the years his work habits have changed. When he was younger, he arrived at work late and stayed late, principally to have access to a computer, a scarce resource in those days. He often stayed up all night, he said, so satisfying was it to get a lot done. Now, because he needs "to sleep at night," his work hours are more routine.

In his younger years, too, Cocke used to ski, play golf, and unicycle. He has never been a game-playing type, he told us. He prefers, for example, to speculate on how to build a chess-playing machine, rather than to play chess itself.

Cocke's successes have been recognized at the highest levels. In September President Bush named him a recipient of the 1991 National Medal of Technology "for his development and implementation of Reduced Instruction Set Computer (RISC) architecture that significantly increased the speed and efficiency of computers, thereby enhancing US technological competitiveness."

In 1987 Cocke received the Turing Award from the Association for Computing Machinery—the group's highest honor—for technical contributions in computing. In 1990 he was the first to receive the US $100,000 IBM John E. Bertram Award for sustained technical excellence. In making the award, IBM chairman John F. Akers said, "John has that rare ability to understand and synthesize both hardware and software concepts, optimize the design of both, and produce a unique synergy."

In 1991, a group of Cocke's colleagues held an all-day symposium celebrating his 35th year with IBM. Some attendees also participated in a videotape, "John Cocke: a retrospective by friends." On the tape, Abraham Peled, now IBM's Research Division vice president and director of computer sciences, remembered being interviewed by Cocke. "John asked what my thesis topic was, " he said. "After I had talked for about 5 minutes on the topic—digital signal processing—he went to the blackboard and more or less wrote out a major part of my thesis. It was a rude awakening."[15]

In the announcement of the award of the National Medal of Science in 1994, the National Science Foundation attributed the award to "his contributions to computer science in the design and theory of compilers and for major advances in the theory and practice of high-performance computer systems. RISC machines are the essential building blocks for today's high-performance parallel machines. Cocke's thinking and technical leadership has been widely credited for setting the tone for these developments. The RISC concept is a stunning unification of hardware architecture and optimization compiler technology and John Cocke had the total mastery of both fields to have made the RISC breakthrough."

QUOTATIONS

In reflecting on his career, Cocke is self-critical: "Things have always taken too long," he said.

BIBLIOGRAPHY

Biographical

Jurgen, Ronald K., "John Cocke: Vision with Enthusiasm," *IEEE Spectrum,* Dec. 1991, pp. 33-34.

Significant Publications

Allen, F.E., and J. Cocke, "A Catalogue of Optimizing Transformations," *Courant Computer Science Symp. 5,* Prentice Hall, 1972, pp. 1–30.

Allen, F.E., and J. Cocke, "A Program Data Flow Analysis Procedure," *Comm. ACM,* Vol. 19, No. 3, Mar. 1976, pp. 137–147.

Cocke, J., "Global Common Subexpression Elimination," *Proc. Symposium of Compiler Optimization,* SIGPLAN Notices, July 1970.

Cocke, J., and R.E. Miller, "Some Analysis Techniques for Optimizing Computer Programs," IBM Research Center, Yorktown Heights, New York.

---

[15]From Jurgen 1991.

EDGAR FRANK CODD

Born August 19, 1923, Portland, UK; invented the first abstract model for database management, as a whole undertaking, including retrieval, manipulation, logical integrity constraints, views and view updatability, and the management of distributed databases with distribution independence; recipient of the 1981 ACM Turing Award.

Education: BA and MA, mathematics, Oxford University, 1948; PhD, communication sciences, University of Michigan, 1965.

Professional Experience: captain, Royal Air Force, 1942–1945; instructor, mathematics, University of Tennessee, 1949; IBM Corp.: mathematician/programmer, SSEC,[16] 1949–1951, designer, IBM-701 and IBM-702, 1951–1952, designer, STRETCH (IBM-7030), 1957–1959, creator, STEM, 1957–1961, developer, Relational Database Model, 1970–1981, retired, 1984; Computing Devices of Canada, 1953–1957.

Honors and Awards: fellow, British Computer Society, 1974; fellow for life, IBM, 1976; Turing Award, ACM, 1981; member, National Academy of Engineering, 1983; fellow, American Academy of Arts and Sciences, 1994.

Codd joined IBM in June 1949 after a short stint at the University of Tennessee, and began his professional career in the computer industry as a mathematician and programmer for the SSEC in New York City. As IBM moved into the computer field more solidly he worked on the logical designs of the IBM 701, initially named the "Defense Calculator," and the IBM 702, which was the first machine designed for business use rather than scientific computations. After four years in Canada he returned to IBM at the time of the development of the STRETCH system (IBM 7030) and created the first multiprogrammed control system capable of managing the interleaved and concurrent execution of programs designed independently of each other—STEM.

On leave from IBM for four years, he completed his PhD at the University of Michigan and presented a thesis on the topic of a self-reproducing computer consisting of a large number of simple identical cells, each of which interacts in a uniform manner with its four immediate neighbors. Codd reported this work in a book entitled *Cellular Automata* published by Academic Press in 1968.

Returning to IBM after the announcement of System/360, but at the beginning of the push for the development of a universal language which would match in software the basic concepts of the 360 line of hardware, he backed the IBM laboratory in Vienna (Zemanek, Lucas,

---

[16]Selective Sequence Electronic Computer.

et al. 1965) to create a formal definition of the language PL/I. This language became known as the Vienna Definition Language (VDL).

He began work in 1969 on the relational model for database management, a project which he continued to promulgate for the next 12 years within IBM, although the corporation was less than enthusiastic about the work. Eventually, in 1982, IBM announced the availability of SQL/DS, a database management system (DBMS) based on the relational model, intended for mid-size systems. The following year a system for large scale computer systems, DB2, also based on the relational model, was released.

Since retirement from IBM in 1984 at the age of 61, Codd has established two companies to provide world-wide lecturing and consulting services to vendors and users of database management systems, and continues to write technical papers in response to ill-conceived criticisms of the relational model.

In a private communication, Codd provided an outline of what he considered to be his 10 major technical contributions to the field:

- multiprogramming;
- self-reproducing computers;
- the relational model for database management, version 1;
- the Rendezvous project for the casual user of a Relational DBMS;
- the Tasmanian version of the Relational Model RM/T;
- a system for managing Bill-of-Materials applications;
- 12 rules for distinguishing RDBMS from non-relational DBMS;
- the relational model for database management, version 2;
- 12 rules for Repositories;
- developed the new model for DELTA for business specification and management.

BIBLIOGRAPHY

Significant Publications

Codd, E.F., "Multiprogramming STRETCH: Feasibility Considerations," *Comm. ACM*, Vol. 2, No. 11, Nov. 1959, pp. 13–17.

Codd, E.F., *Cellular Automata*, Academic Press, New York, 1968.

Codd, E.F., "A Relational Model of Data for Large Shared Data Banks," *Comm. ACM*, Vol. 13, 1970, No. 6.

Codd, E.F., "How about Recently?," *Proc. Int'l. Conf. Databases: Improving Useability and Responsiveness*, Haifa, Israel, August 2–3, 1978.

Codd, E.F., "Extending the Relational Model to Capture More Meaning," (RM/T), *ACM Trans. Database Systems*, Vol. 4, No. 4, 1979.

Codd, E.F., "Missing Information (Applicable and Inapplicable) in Relational Databases," *ACM SIGMOD Record*, Vol. 15, No. 4, 1986.

Codd, E.F., "Relational Database: A Practical Foundation for Productivity," *Comm. ACM*, Vol. 25, No. 2, 1982.

Codd, E.F., "More Commentary on Missing Information in Relational Databases," *ACM SIGMOD Record*, Vol. 16, No. 1, 1987.

Codd, E.F., *The Relational Model for Database Management: Version 2*, Addison-Wesley Publ. Co., Reading, Mass., 1990.

Codd, E.F., "DELTA: a Model for Business Specification and Management," available to software vendors from Codd under contract, 1991.

Arnold A. Cohen

Born August 1, 1914, Duluth, Minn.; an employee of Engineering Research Associates (ERA) from its inception in 1946, and a founder of AFIPS; his IEEE Fellow citation read: "For pioneering achievement on computers and storage devices, and sustained service to the profession in this field."

Education: BEE, University of Minnesota, 1935; MS, University of Minnesota, 1938; PhD, physics, University of Minnesota, 1947.

Professional Experience: development engineer, electron tubes, RCA Corp., 1942–1946; computer development engineer, technical director, Engineering Research Associates Inc., (ERA),[17] 1946–1971; assistant dean, Institute of Technology, University of Minnesota, 1971–1979; senior fellow, Charles Babbage Institute, 1980–present; member, board of directors, Charles Babbage Foundation, 1980–present.

---

[17]Cohen served in this position in several successor companies, through to Sperry Rand Corporation, St. Paul MN.

Honors and Awards: national chair, IRE Professional Group—Electronic Computers,[18] 1960–1962; member, board of directors, AFIPS, 1960–1965; member, scientific advisory board, National Security Agency, Ft. Meade, Md., 1960–1974; Valuable Invention Citation, Minnesota and American Patent Law Association, 1962; fellow, IEEE, 1964; member, advisory board, Chemical Abstracts Service, 1969–1972; IEEE Centennial Award, 1984.

Cohen joined RCA in 1942, working in gaseous electron tube development, largely for military use, later for other applications. His first contact with the computer field came when he joined ERA in 1946. He was first assigned to information storage problems, under ONR sponsorship, initially analyzing the feasibility of storing information on beams of charged particles. Then, he worked on the development of selectively alterable digital storage on magnetic drums; the patent that resulted turned out to be basic in the field. He then led system design of the ATLAS I magnetic drum computer for the National Security Agency (a later commercial version was called the ERA 1101). ATLAS I, which was delivered in December 1950, is believed to be the first stored-program electronic digital computer actually shipped to a customer site. Cohen was also responsible for the ATLAS II system design (commercialized as the Univac Scientific 1103 after the Remington-Rand merger in 1952). ATLAS II had both CRT and magnetic drum storage. Variations on these systems, including a magnetic core memory at an early date, were built and delivered for specific requirements, mostly military. The commercial 1103A which followed incorporated powerful new system features, in addition to core and drum storage.

An important aspect of ERA's business was to conduct digital systems work for outside customers, in response to requests for proposals, or as unsolicited proposals. Cohen had responsibility for much design and development in these areas. One early effort (1949–1950) led by him was a design study for IBM that called for a magnetic drum computer with punched-card input and output, for commercial applications. Although this work resulted in a massive system patent that was assigned to IBM, a parallel design program within IBM prevailed, ultimately producing the IBM 650.

ERA was acquired in 1952 by Remington-Rand, which had a development group of its own in Connecticut, and which had in addition

---

[18]Now IEEE Computer Society.

picked up Eckert-Mauchly Corporation in 1950. This brought together, as the Remington-Rand Univac division, three development and manufacturing locations, and an assortment of marketing groups. Cohen continued to be actively engaged in various phases of technical management, including system planning, government relations, and marketing support.

In 1971 Cohen joined the staff of the dean of the Institute of Technology at the University of Minnesota, as assistant dean for industry and professional relations. Upon retirement from the dean's staff in 1979, he became active in helping to form the Charles Babbage Institute for the History of Information Processing, which has since become a part of the University of Minnesota. He has been a senior fellow at CBI and is a member of the Charles Babbage Foundation's board of directors.

BIBLIOGRAPHY

Biographical

Armer, Paul, et al., "Reflections on a Quarter Century: AFIPS Founders," *Ann. Hist. Comp.*, Vol. 8, No. 3, July 1986, pp. 225–256.

Tomash, Erwin, and Arnold A. Cohen, "The Birth of an ERA: Engineering Research Associates, Inc., 1946–1955," *Ann. Hist. Comp.*, Vol. 1, No. 2, 1978, pp. 83–97.

Significant Publications

ERA Staff (Arnold A. Cohen, contributing author), *High Speed Computing Devices,* McGraw-Hill, 1950; reprinted in Charles Babbage Reprint Series, MIT Press, Boston, Mass., 1983, with introductory chapter by Cohen.

HARVEY COHN

Born December 27, 1923, New York City; mathematical researcher with innovative uses of computers in number theory, particularly for algebraic number theory and modular functions; specific computations involve class numbers, genus, and systems of modular equations (using computer algebra).

Education: BS, mathematics and physics, City College of New York, 1942; MS, applied mathematics, New York University, 1943; PhD, mathematics, Harvard University, 1948.

Professional Experience: Wayne State University (Detroit) 1948–1956; Washington University (St. Louis), 1956–1958, director of Computer Center, 1957–1958; University of Arizona, 1958–1971, head of Mathematics Department, 1958–1967; distinguished professor chair at City College of New York and the Graduate Center (CUNY), 1971; Stanford University, 1953–1954; member, Institute for Advanced Study, Princeton, 1970–1971; lektor, University of Copenhagen, 1976–1977.

Awards: Putnam Prize Fellowship at Harvard, 1946; Townsend Harris Alumni Award, 1972.

In my Townsend Harris high school years in New York, 1936–1939, I found myself honored as a mathematics prodigy but troubled by the idea that the honor might be of dubious value in earning a living. At the College of the City of New York, 1939–1942, my feelings were accentuated. The gospel of the purity of mathematics was echoed dogmatically but yet defensively by teachers whom I otherwise admired greatly. Their attitude seemed encapsulated in the famous "Mathematician's Apology" of G.H. Hardy, which they recommended to me to read.[19]

This book appalled me as the ultimate in snobbery for its theme that "if real mathematicians do no good they also do no harm." Indeed Hardy used "real" provocatively to mean "pure" as compared with "trivial" which meant "applied." He seemed to say that a gentleman never works with his hands, and felt this arrogance expressed the academic workings of the British class system, which Americans were sanctimoniously taught to disdain, particularly since they had not yet formalized their own academic class privileges.

At that time some of the best mathematical brains, nationally, were in the academic engineering departments, and they were effective rivals of the pure mathematicians. At City College, it was necessary to go to the Electrical Engineering Department to find a course in matri-

---

[19] Hardy, G.H., *A Mathematician's Apology*, Cambridge Univ. Press, Cambridge, UK, 1940, pp. 139–143.

ces or in applications of complex analysis, and to the Physics Department to learn of the applications of differential equations. This was not unusual; it was their purity, their avoidance of real applications, that gave mathematics departments their sense of class.

I never accepted the folklore of the mainstream mathematician "purists," who viewed nonappreciation of their calling as a form of ennoblement, as though it were some idealistic political cause. On the other hand, I did not believe the mathematical "crowd-pleasers," who said that everything abstract shall eventually be applied. (They proved to be largely correct, but I understood then they were making very uninformed guesses couched in generalities which can only be proved right, but never proved wrong). I ended up as an applied mathematician in spirit, specializing in number theory, which looked very "applied" since the interest created by a theorem concerning numbers at that time lay in its numerical examples.

The advent of computing still took time. First I had an exciting two-year adventure, 1942–1944, with Richard Courant, which included an MS in applied mathematics at New York University in 1943. Courant had only an embryonic "Applied Mathematics Group" (quickly renamed "Graduate Center of Mathematics"), which was unpretentiously housed in a corner of the Judson Women's Dormitory at Washington Square. It was the forerunner of the present lavish Courant Institute in Weaver Hall. The classrooms were in the main buildings, but the library was housed at the dormitory and furnished mainly with Courant's own books and reprints, one of many aspects of a "zero-budget" operation. He, with K.O. Friedrichs and J. J. Stoker, formed a triumvirate, but, also because of budget, they had to be supported in part, not as mathematicians but as engineering teachers. Also present was Donald A. Flanders, whom I was to later meet at the Argonne National Laboratory. Courant obviously was thinking ahead in terms of his world-renowned Institute at Göttingen, which he himself had largely created but had to abandon when the Nazis took power. Not surprisingly, he did have a computing center, consisting of a bank of desk calculators in search of users. To look busy, he employed his wife Nina and for director gave a start to the career of Eugene Isaacson, who stayed on to become a more meaningful director of the computing center for the Courant Institute.

The environment seemed mathematically felicitous, particularly to see a mathematician of Courant's stature so lacking in pretension of "purity." Courant reminded us continually that Gauss had always tested results numerically with extravagant precision (like 40 decimals), and indeed that Gauss gained fame by tracking asteroids numerically as they disappeared behind the sun and reemerged. This numerical work inspired some of Gauss's deepest research in number theory and function theory. Clearly there had to be a moral here for aspiring mathematicians. Numerical work was also an important aspect of Courant's public relations campaign to obtain government support from the Office of Scientific Research and Development (OSRD). He was not at all modest about the eternal relevance of his famous work[20] with K.O. Friedrichs and H. Lewy on *numerical solutions* of partial differential equations. He also made the ethnically generous point that the British mathematicians should not be put down as mere "problem solvers," compared with French and German "theorists," since the British had a special instinct for numerical answers, as he saw in such work as that of Rayleigh and Southwell. One of his favorite associates was a very cheerful self-styled "Scotsman" J.K.L. MacDonald, from Cooper Union, who carried asymptotics to a higher state of the art. He developed techniques to estimate Bessel functions for "medium-sized" values, not being content with the ordinary infinite behavior. MacDonald's proclivity for numerical tricks seemed to go well with his love of gadgets, which he collected and even built. When he died in a private airplane crash during World War II, I felt he had tried one gadget too many. Looking back, I must acknowledge Courant's prescience of the early hold the British would have on computation within the next five years because of their skill with numerical computations. I thought of Richard Courant's endeavor as a "shoe-string" operation and such efforts seemed to occur very often in academic computing. What was lacking by most entrepreneurs, including me, was an "irresistible force" to overcome the "immovable administration."

After service in the Navy (1944–1946) as an electronic (radar) technician's mate, I felt I had acquired an understanding of electronics of the future. Unquestionably the "Captain Eddy" (Navy) training program was the start for many of my generation who became attracted to computing. (The total effect of this program on American computer skills might prove comparable with the Fulbright Program if an accounting were made.)

The automation used even in the earliest tracking radar was like science fiction. Some of my immediate Navy classmates whose names I noticed later in programs of computing meetings include James Butler, Fernando Corbató, and Saul Padwo (and there must have been many others).

---

[20]Courant, R., K.O. Friedrichs, and H. Lewy, "Über die partiellen Differenzengleichungen der mathematischen Physik," *Math. Annalen* Vol. 100, 1928, pp. 32–74.

Even after I returned to "pure" number theory at Harvard for my PhD (in 1948 as a Putnam Fellow), I must have been influenced greatly by Norbert Wiener's doctrines of cybernetics and the Second Industrial Revolution.[21] In fact his work was talked about more by laymen than mathematicians, who tended to look instead to John von Neumann, who was writing in more technical terms on automata.[22] But for whatever motivation, I felt machines had to "think" at least in routine fashion. (Maybe it was negative of me to want machines to think; maybe I did not consider mathematicians to be doing as much creative thinking as they pretended.) At any rate, I was beginning to become obsessive on this matter of "thinking."

From the wonders of naval radar, I looked to fancy electronics. The only machines I knew of in any functional detail beyond desk calculators were "analogue computers," and some of Derrick H. Lehmer's "garage-made" models for number theory, which were used in prime factorization.[23] All I saw, however, were mathematicians "riding hobby horses." I had heard enough about the electronic ENIAC to be unimpressed by the Harvard Mark I, which gave itself away with its noise background as a mere relay machine.

Far from "thinking," Mark I was routinely calculating tables of Bessel functions, or something similar, when I saw it in operation.

Wayne State University, Detroit (1948–1956)

My first academic position was in the Mathematics Department at Wayne (now Wayne State) University in Detroit (1948–1956), which was upgrading the curriculum to a PhD program by getting research-oriented faculty even from as far away as Harvard. In view of the many recalcitrant nonresearch faculty members in all departments, I soon realized that Wayne was an unfortunate choice for me, except that computing unexpectedly happened to me in the form of two unlikely persons for Wayne. One was Arvid Jacobson, who pursued applied mathematics with literally religious zeal for what he called "industrial community service." His career was extraordinary. He spoke with an accent acquired from a Finnish-speaking community in northern Michigan. He became involved with, but later renounced, Communism, after a disastrous imprisonment in Finland. He then

---

[21]Wiener, N., *Cybernetics,* John Wiley and Son, New York, 1948.

[22]von Neumann, J., *Collected Works,* Vol. 5, *General and Logical Theory of Automata* (1948), Macmillan, New York, 1963, pp. 288–328.

[23]Lehmer, D.H., "A Photo-Electric Number Sieve," *Amer. Math. Mo.,* Vol. 40, 1933, pp. 401–406.

returned to Christianity with messianic zeal, always speaking of "spiritual leadership and community service" with a combination of religious and secular meanings. Since he was known to (and cited as a Communist by) Whittaker Chambers, his past came back to haunt him in the McCarthy era, but his many friends (including me) were adamant in vouching for him. His outlook was scarred by his past suffering. He saw his enemies in Detroit as an "Anglo-Saxon clique," and carried this paranoia to the point of explaining his vote for Eisenhower over Stevenson in 1952.

Jacobson worked in the automobile industry before obtaining his PhD at the University of Michigan in his forties. He knew most of the industrial research people in Detroit. Then came his calling. I must say I had to believe in him after I saw his miracles. He got a completely indifferent university whose administration feared progress to accept the largess of Detroit industries which feared mathematics (two characteristic fears). He formed his Industrial Mathematics Society (IMS) somewhat before the (now) better-known SIAM. Arvid soon became ready for computing. He first got Vannevar Bush's original Differential Analyzer, scrapped by MIT, to Wayne as a preliminary but ineffective start. Ultimately, however, he brought the Burroughs UDEC (Universal Digital Electronic Computer) to Wayne University. This was the first stored program machine I saw (1953). It had 1,000 ten-digit words of drum storage, did about 30 multiplications per second, and had all of 10 instructions (one per digit). The UDEC was loaded by paper tape with punched holes, sensed mechanically not optically. The machine was so slow that even the small problems I had in mind were not practical for it because of normal down times of vacuum tube computers, possibly every half hour.

Also, coincidentally with UDEC, Wayne University acquired Joe Weizenbaum. His friendship was very valuable to me. From him I learned what a stored program was, and I soon learned what a Turing Machine was. Now I felt that I knew the meaning of a "giant brain." Joe Weizenbaum was a psychologist with an amazing fondness for mathematics. He went on to fame at MIT (with ELIZA).

Arvid Jacobson stayed on at Wayne to perform the further miracle of attracting rather prominent persons to serve as director of the computing program (through industrial donations). They served in succession, all leaving dissatisfied.

Among the names I can recall are Harry Huskey (who had been associated with Derrick H. Lehmer at Berkeley), Elbert Little (who was an industrial consultant), and, after I left (1956), Wallace Givens, who had been at the Oak Ridge National Laboratory, but who did not want to continue living in the South as a matter of political choice. In the long run, sadly, Arvid Jacobson quit in despair, and went into private consulting in 1959. He summed up his career as "pushing a great big sponge." The last straw, I am told, was a donnybrook involving what should have been a routine but predictably unpleasant problem, choosing a new machine to replace the IBM-650, which followed the UDEC. (The IBM-650 remains the great performer in this memoir.) At the same time as the UDEC was set up at Wayne University, in 1953, John Carr set up the MIDAC at the University of Michigan, and got it operating very quickly. (It was a faster machine by a factor of ten; it was a miniaturized version of the National Bureau of Standards SEAC, and was also better supported, by the Air Force). The MIDAC even had an *optical* tape reader. I had the distinction in 1953 of being the first one to run a "real" program (not an exercise) successfully on that machine. The program was in pure mathematics, on cubic units, and I was ecstatic to find that Derrick H. Lehmer (whom I had not yet met) encouraged me to publish it in 1954 in *Mathematical Tables and Aids to Computation (MTAC)* (Cohn, 1954), the forerunner of today's *Mathematics of Computation.*

Thus in 1953 I began my career as a professional parasite, using anybody else's machine, which was always better and bigger. This was easier then than now, since most managers of machine installations were easily flattered and very obliging, and bureaucracy then was not as intimidating as today (with batches, accounts, and priorities). I used many machines unknown today, such as MIDAC, UDEC, ORDVAC, EDVAC, SEAC, Univac, CDC-3600, and George (the Argonne Laboratory machine). Ironically, for my first 18 years of research using computers, the "home" facilities were not adequate until in 1971, when I achieved my current position.

I also learned of the potentially seductive appeal of computing. In 1955 I was not alone in wanting to leave Wayne University, nor was I averse to taking a nonacademic job (although my wife, Bernice, who claimed telepathic foresight, insisted I never could!). The three papers I wrote about using computers seemed to have had more weight than my ten papers in pure mathematics. I was interviewed by several computation laboratories, including the Ballistic Research Laboratories (Aberdeen, Md.), Argonne National Laboratory, Burroughs Research Laboratory (Philadelphia), IBM (Columbia), and Oak Ridge National Laboratory, but the MIT interview stands out in my mind. That was the job I really wanted. Philip Morse was a man whose work (including textbooks) at MIT in mathematical physics and operations research (in World War II) was legendary, and I was overwhelmed that he and

Jay Forrester wanted to arrange a joint appointment for me with his laboratory and the MIT Mathematics Department. In the interview, he made me aware of the current interest in speeding up Monte Carlo and simulation computations; he felt number theory was important for randomness research.

When the Mathematics Department would not come up with its share, Morse discussed a job, using "soft" money, which was outside grants and would not lead to tenure. This still interested me, but clearly he would not offer it because he knew that I had achieved tenure at Wayne University and was becoming "established" in mathematics (despite my obvious dissatisfaction).

The most active period of my involvement with computers was about to begin. In 1953 I had a small US Army Ordnance grant to do algebraic number theory. It was not large enough to cover computing, so I obtained access to the computing facility at the US Army's Ballistic Research Laboratories at Aberdeen, Maryland. In 1949 I had corresponded with John Giese, one of the mathematicians at Aberdeen, on a problem in aerodynamics using numerical methods I had learned while taking my master's degree with Courant much earlier. Giese's connection with the laboratories seemed a logical lead to me, and it led me to his colleague Saul Gorn. Saul had a PhD from Columbia in algebra, and quickly took an interest in the problem which led me there. It was the discovery of integral solutions in *a, b, c* to the equation

$$n(a^3+b^3+c^3) + m(a^2b+b^2c+c^2a) + k(ab^2+bc^2+ca^2) + labc = 1$$

with specially selected integral parameters *n, m, k, l* chosen so as to make the cubic polynomial factorable in the real domain. If the problem looked messy and limited in appeal, the method of solution involved an even messier three-dimensional version of continued fractions. The details later appeared in a paper jointly with Saul Gorn (Cohn and Gorn, 1957).

It was this unlikely problem which made me appreciate Saul Gorn's vision of computing beyond number crunching.

He was looking to create a machine-independent programming system. His logistics were very simple. Since our problem in number theory was approved by the Army, he could obtain the time to work on his "universal code" using our problem as the pretext. It became his *cause célèbre* as well as mine. In the summer of 1954, he programmed ORDVAC at Aberdeen's Ballistic Research Laboratories to translate this program from universal code to internal code and to run it successfully. These were heady days of self-realization. We were not upset to find that Peter Swinnerton-Dyer had done a similar calculation simultaneously at Cambridge University, England, by a different method, because he wrote his program only in more direct code and he had a less automated program. His work was never published. Saul had now shown new potentialities for mathematics to evolve its own *language*.

During that same summer (1954) I worked at the AEC computing facility of the Courant Institute (NYU). This was sponsored by Remington-Rand with personal support of its honorary president, former General Douglas MacArthur, for whom Courant had great praise and with whom he claimed to have had very profitable discussions. (Since Courant was famous for speaking tentatively and mumbling subliminally, we in the laboratory amused ourselves trying to reconstruct the dialogue and imagining the strain on the dignified and redoubtable general.) The installation was built around the Univac and very much influenced by Grace M. Hopper. I now became aware of a larger movement to regard computers as thinking machines and accordingly to regard "thinking" as a concept with different degrees of depth.

Grace Hopper set the moral tone with such maxims as: *If you do it once, it is permissible to do it by hand; if you do it twice, it is questionable as to whether or not to do it by hand; but if you do it more than twice, it had best be done by machine.* Her Univac B-2 Compiler, indeed, meant that translation to machine (assembly) code and the assignment of memory would never again have to be done by hand. She even refined the compiler to sense systematic typographical errors and correct them (with the author's permission each time). She was also one of Saul Gorn's spiritual leaders. Some of the speakers at the Courant Institute that summer told of efforts at MIT to produce automated algebra (not yet called MACSYMA). I was delighted to find computing beginning to mean something "cybernetic." This computing group at the Courant Institute was independent of Courant (I saw him only once) but it clearly was part of his master plan. Yet I knew the computer would not be permitted to be the tail that wags the dog. Courant was determined to keep numerical analysis dominant over machine usage. Combinatoric Computing was represented by George Dantzig and David Fulkerson, who were summer visitors. The only other guest I recall from the summer of 1954 was Wallace Givens. I had first met him at the Oak Ridge National Laboratory in 1953 and I was destined to keep running into him. He had just finished his famous work on the computation of eigenvalues.[24]

---

[24]Givens, W., "Numerical Computation of the Characteristic Values of a Real Symmetric Matrix," *Oak Ridge Nat. Lab. Report 1574*, 1974.

He had a sobering thought on it later on. He said that aside from its mathematical value, his method has demonstrably saved so much in machine time that if he does nothing else, he will still have deserved whatever salary he is paid. This idea was vicariously comforting to me too, and it was also symbolic of the new age, representing the capacity of the machine to amplify man.

In the summer of 1956, preparatory to leaving Wayne University, I worked at the National Bureau of Standards in Washington, D.C. It was my great opportunity to learn what computing people thought, particularly about one another. Having been influenced by both Saul Gorn and Grace Hopper, I felt my interest would have a cutting edge. I was even more fortunate in having the sponsorship of John Todd and Olga Taussky (who shared my interests in algebraic number theory). John Todd was the guru of traditional numerical analysts, who were looking only to make their well-established skills more effective by enlisting the computer. More than that, he was aware of the special groups of computer abstractionists. Although he was distant from them, he did not disparage ideas which he did not share. That was not true of everyone on the NBS staff, however.

The bureau had inherited an active group of famous Works Project Administration (WPA) table-makers from the 1930s who seemed to set the tone. I remember Irene Stegun, Ida Rhodes, and Henry Antosiewicz particularly. Phrases were bandied about which were largely derogatory to computing machines and were too numerous to recount. A small sample would include: "programming is garbage," "a machine is just a big slide rule," "we don't teach flowcharts," "programmers just don't understand error estimates," or best of all, "don't trust a subroutine you didn't write." Obviously "computer science" was oxymoronic there. I was disappointed but not surprised to also find that Saul Gorn and Grace Hopper were not considered relevant either. The members of John Todd's and Olga Taussky's crew included mathematicians who functioned independently of computing, such as Philip Davis, Everett Dade, and Morris Newman. They tried to be "political centrists" on computing but they must have felt themselves caught in the middle when I argued and sometimes harangued about computer progress.

I was still gratified enormously that John and Olga appreciated me sufficiently to have me represented in both the theorist's and user's side of computing in one of John's handbook-type books (Cohn 1962, 1962a). John also wanted me to join his group permanently later on despite my offbeat attitudes toward the role of computers. I could not accept his offer because of my growing instinctive fear of the nonacademic world. Although computing was no more secure in the academic world, I felt more comfortable with its irrationalities, and the university did have an irrational love-hate relationship with the computer!

The pattern seemed to be nationwide, maybe worldwide. Computer science did not exist the way mathematics did (with a 2,500-year history) and had no obvious home academically. Even more so, the computer scientist, whether in mathematics or engineering, was regarded as a *nouveau riche* technician whose pay unfortunately came out to be insufferably high compared with the prevailing salary scales.

Washington University, St. Louis (1956–1958)

My next permanent job began September 1956 at Washington University in St. Louis in the Mathematics Department.

The chairman, Holbrook MacNeille, was a capable administrator and a former executive director of the American Mathematical Society. He was intent on helping to prepare the university for computing. The then current Computer Center consisted of a leased IBM-650 housed in an old shack (formerly a student theater) and run by the Industrial Engineering (IE) Department. This arrangement was based on a promise to run it "efficiently" in terms of producing some university income (which was just about forbidden under the "noncommercial" terms of the IBM academic discount). The IE Department members were known, however, to be using the machine only to produce unrecorded consulting income for themselves. This was doubly bad news because they usually took program decks and manuals away with them on house calls, leaving the laboratory denuded. The provost had known of this, too, and had made those IE Department members promise to resign from the center as soon as a better arrangement could be made. He then asked me if I would take over the Computer Center to make it academically responsible. Although I felt Washington University was a respectable institution, the Computer Center was not then an attractive proposition. (Among other things, the building was like a barn with an unfinished interior and wooden partitions which made the occupants feel like cows, and there was no washroom.)

Before I could give an answer, a climactic incident in my life occurred in February 1957, the last one linking me to my mentor Saul Gorn. He was now at the Moore School of the University of Pennsylvania, trying to form a Computer and Information Sciences Department, the first of its kind. He recommended me for the position of head of the department; this time the appointment was to be supported by Mathematics. I went to Philadelphia for an interview, which seemed like a triumphal entry as I knew many members of the Mathematics Department, chiefly Hans Rademacher's number theory group at the University of Pennsylvania, who were involved in related research interests and would welcome my presence. Clearly I was to be made the offer, but a lingering doubt arose somehow in my mind. Likewise Saul also had doubts about the adequacy of the support. In fact, he pointed out to me that the only support available was a one-year grant from NSF, with no supporting funds promised by the university. I verified that the administration would promise nothing more to me, even as an outside candidate, than to Saul. We were both used to computing centers not having the respect of colleagues in more established disciplines. We naturally wondered if nonacademics such as the administration would respect us as little.

The answer to our fears came a day after I returned to St. Louis, when I received a call from the telephone operator in Philadelphia asking me to accept a *collect call* from the vice president of the University of Pennsylvania! I sensed the usual disrespect for computing personnel and declined to accept charges until the VP offered not one but three improbable reasons why he had no phone credit. The phone call continued with a discussion of salary, starting lower than my salary at Washington University and working its way up to parity with very little effort on my part. I suppose I disappointed Saul Gorn by declining the offer. He took it himself, mainly to get the program started, and tried to get me to come as a visitor, but I had changed jobs too recently to accept something temporary. He stepped down as head after a year, and I saw him only a few times afterwards for pleasant reminiscences.

The result was that I could now accept the position of director of the Computer Center at Washington University rather honorably, since Brook MacNeille would support me as much as possible and accept me back in Mathematics if I later wanted to quit. (The administration still would not install a minimal $300 washroom!) I served as director from May 1957 to July 1958 but with no previous illusions. I accepted the fact that the position was for image rather than development. Ominously, the center remained administratively in Engineering.

Things started badly for my directorship. Right off, IBM (which was silent when the Computer Center was mismanaged) now started to enforce its rule against nonacademic income for the university. This led to an ugly incident.

The Bemis Bag Company of St. Louis was starting to work with IBM on computing, and one of their staff formally invited our laboratory to set up a demonstration with a practical problem in linear programming. It was a classic allocation of differently priced paper stocks to various end products subject to supply restrictions. The problem was so classic that we even happened to have the right program deck for the IBM-650. We were already rejoicing over the prospect of outside money for the laboratory when IBM intervened with Bemis, telling them we were not allowed to do it because the problem was "commercial" not "academic." The IBM staff high-handedly brought the Bemis group to their headquarters to do the demonstration without telling us.

Thus ended our first and only outside job.

The lack of income was not alleviated even by meager "legitimate" income from grants; most grants that used the laboratory were tiny and seldom in sciences, so big money was clearly absent.

The provost and his advisers soon reacted in shock at the failure of income. Everyone was very "forgiving" of me, although they announced that the Computer Center had incurred a loss of $80,000 and would have to be discontinued. (This figure involved "creative bookkeeping" since that was more than twice the budget!) Moreover, they came up with the desperate idea of replacing the IBM-650 Computer Center with some cheaper (short-lived) IBM desk machine with an external paper tape for programs but no internal memory. The machine and center would then go back into obscurity in the Industrial Engineering Department. It seemed I had no say.

At this point, however, the Russians came charging to the rescue like the Red Army Cavalry. They sent up not one but two Sputniks, the second one with a dog. I quickly tried (with no success) to find a relevant scientific program to run, but had to resort to an exercise program to keep the lights flashing for the many visitors.

Nevertheless, our IBM-650 became a prime newspaper, television, radio, and newsreel photo opportunity of St. Louis. One of our programmers, Pat Zwillinger, even brought along Athena, her racing greyhound, to pose standing with her paws on the console of the machine, looking at the flashing lights and eagerly panting for a message from the Russian canine in space. The St. Louis *Post Dispatch* failed to use that picture, preferring some serious ones with us humans. There were also laudatory newspaper editorials, which now served to make the center impregnable. Some of my more political friends solicited statements of support from Sen. Stuart Symington of Missouri and Rep. Melvin Price of Illinois, both with influential congressional committee memberships. We also received unsolicited offers from some of the financial angels of Washington University to put up a building to replace our shack (I assume with a washroom). This was dangerous in itself since the financial angels are not supposed to talk directly with faculty. Edward U. Condon, of Bureau of Standards fame, was chairman of Physics, and he insisted on lending his professional weight to the cause of having a scientifically competent laboratory. (His influence was considerably augmented by his public stand against McCarthyism.)

I was not surprised to be asked finally to continue as center director but was more than disappointed at the *reduced budget*. I kept thinking that my idol, Courant, could sell ice to Eskimos, while I could not sell computing, with two Sputniks raging overhead. I now knew that I was not enough of a promoter to deal with the situation. MacNeille did attempt to rescue the situation by trying to get the Computer Center moved administratively into Mathematics, where it would have a larger budgetary base, but this idea was premature, and the Mathematics Department was not impressed. Also, the National Science Foundation could not help much because the Sputniks had created demands far beyond their budget for the present year. I must have appeared unsportsmanlike, but I asked to be relieved of the position of director in April 1958.

I also resigned from Washington University at that time, taking solace in the fact that no one wished me to leave, but that a better position was awaiting me at the University of Arizona in the fall of 1958.

I left for my next job with very fond memories of my colleagues and my staff at Washington University, which also included programmers Alan V. Lemmon, Joe Paull, David Tinney (all part-time students), and one full-time technical supervisor, Robert Carty. It is to my eternal regret that I did not keep up with my enthusiastic staff, whom I also regarded as cherished friends. Those on my staff in a sense were typical of the coming generation of computing. At the age of 35, I knew only the mathematical stereotypes for the younger generation, so I was still in for an education on what species of man was evolving under the influence of computer science. Fortunately the more distinctive species of hackers and nerds were not fully evolved at the time. Alan V. Lemmon was an undergraduate mathematical prodigy who came to the Computer Center to inquire about computers reluctantly, and only because one of his professors sent him. He timidly confessed ignorance about machines and programs. I gave him an IBM-650 Programming Manual to look at. The manuals in those days were written in real English prose, so I felt it was not unfair to ask him to read it through (it was only about 50 pages) and to come back when he understood the program on the last page.

That program was depicted on an IBM card which clears the memory except for the zero-cell and the accumulators. He came back the next day with several cards, one of which cleared *all memory* and accumulators and others which did special tricks like labeling the memory so that in a memory dump, the unused cells could be identified. He now works for the GTE (General Telephone and Electronics) Laboratories in Waltham, Mass. Not all neophytes were that startling, but the cases of "genetic computer readiness" in the younger generation are so common today that I can believe in Lamarck's adaptive theory of evolution. Bob Carty was a much different stereotype. He was a totally rigid personality, a strict observing Catholic, who saw in machines a kind of model of law and order. He had been a Marine and an FBI agent, and even then was an auxiliary sheriff; also, he believed in the rights of gun owners and had his own arsenal, including many types of handcuffs. He was a very serious and effective worker with no special compulsion for polemics or evangelism. Yet he was very social and made a large number of political contacts in our behalf. Bob left when I did, in 1958, to work in a supervisory capacity at the Wright Air Force Computing Center in Dayton, Ohio, but I lost track of him subsequently. I often think of him today when I observe that programming and software systems are very attractive as exercises in logic to a variety of rigid religious groups, who would feel considerably less comfortable with the humanistic scientific culture which both motivated computing and made it technically possible.

Joe Paull was originally a chemical engineer, and I must remark that there were a remarkable number of chemical engineers who switched to computing in the early stages (maybe second only to mathematics). The flood tide of physicists as machine users with money was yet to come. Patricia Zwillinger had been an honors student of mathematics at Wellesley, and her motivation for continuing in mathematics was largely due to computing. She and her husband had an overriding interest in animals, however, which caused them to move west. David Tinney had little motivation for any career. He was raised in comparative luxury (his father was Calvin Tinney, the humorist). His motivation for that brief period of the Computer Center also came from computing.

It was hard to resist the attraction of consulting. I worked for the IBM SBC (Service Bureau Corporation) in St. Louis for about six months from October 1956 to April 1957 as part of my enthusiastic search for what "real people" do in everyday computing. Surprisingly, it had some very interesting moments. It gave me the opportunity to visit large commercial and industrial computing installations, which only whetted my appetite for "more and more." I learned that most businesses claimed to have an "inventory routine," which did not function, owing to the noncooperation of their accounting departments. (This was not unlike the behavior of pure mathematicians, who feared a similar degradation of their role.) The most delightful moment was an official house call that a group of us from SBC made on Oscar Johnson, a shoe tycoon in St. Louis. He greeted us at the door of an impressive mansion in a private enclave with two sports cars and two Afghan hounds the size of ponies sitting on his driveway. He invited us in for drinks in a dining room with Queen Anne chairs, which he boasted were still safe to sit on.

He had been using the SBC to gather data for his "programmed trading" in the stock market. His method was (typically) the following: He had the SBC gather data daily on each of hundreds of favorite issues and print out to *four-decimal accuracy* results of computations in four-column format.

$$\text{NAME OF ISSUE} \qquad \frac{a}{b} \qquad \frac{b}{a} \qquad \frac{a}{b} \times \qquad \frac{b}{a}$$

Here *a* and *b* were data taken from the financial pages. If I recall, *a* was *balance shares* (shares bought minus shares sold) and *b* was total shares traded, all arranged in order of *current yield*. He noticed, of course, that for some mysterious reason the last column was close to 1.0000, undoubtedly proving the stability of the market, but seldom *precisely* 1.0000. For high figures like 1.0002 he would buy and for low figures like 0.9997 he would sell, but (I give him credit) he did use some additional judgment. I suppose it was my duty to tell him politely that he was starting with a random criterion, but I held back because of the rejoinder he would surely be too polite to make: "How many sports cars, Afghan hounds, and Queen Anne chairs do *you* have?" The problem for the men from SBC was far from mathematical, although I believe they knew enough algebra. The problem was to keep him from getting his own IBM-650 and giving up their service. I believe they succeeded by stressing that his basement, however attractive, would require remodeling with a possible change of decor for the heavier air-conditioning.

One other SBC problem, which stands out in my mind for its pioneering value, was an on-line use of the IBM-650 for scheduling the ecological use of water power for generating electricity. The idea was to use power during the dead hours of the night to pump water uphill into reservoirs so as to ensure availability during the heavy usage of the day. This very successful program was written first in flowchart form by an enthusiast in the power company named Estil Mabuse. The SBC easily wrote a program for him facilitated by his clear thinking. He apparently just learned about programming *ad hoc*. He told me later that he put in so much overtime playing with the program that it threatened his marriage.

I also acquired a more professional consulting arrangement with the AEC Laboratory at Argonne, Illinois. It lasted from 1956 to 1969 and it permitted me to see the evolution of computing at a very dedicated and active organization. The original director of the mathematics division who initiated the arrangement was Donald A. Flanders. Later directors were William Miller and Wallace Givens (again), who symbolized the evolving discipline. "Moll" Flanders was a member of Courant's original crew before going to the Oak Ridge National Laboratory. He had an old-fashioned gentle character, which seemed to make him find automation menacing.

He lived in the world of hand computation. We used George, which happened to be Argonne's proprietary (binary) machine. The normal usage was to enter data in decimal form (called "binary coded decimal"), which the machine converted to binary for internal purposes. But Moll converted input and output from decimal to binary and back by hand, using tables, obviously suspicious of an untraditional operation. Nevertheless, he gave the laboratory the high-level mathematical character which served as an asset later on. He had his own problems of depression and erratic behavior, which endangered his clearance from time to time. The fact that his brother, Sen. Ralph Flanders of Vermont, was a leading and outspoken opponent of McCarthyism made the concerns of security look somewhat political. Yet his personal problems were real, culminating in suicide in 1956.

Bill Miller, his successor, was a computational nuclear physicist from Purdue. He was a supreme administrator, with a healthy agenda for all kinds of growth, service, and expansion. His professional input was important, with the emerging role of physics in computing, but there were many users in physics who were lacking in "cybernetic" instincts and overly endowed with money for machine time. Several times the machines were tied up overnight by physicists who looked for errors by running their program in "single-cycles," one instruction at a time, or otherwise expressed, at less than one-millionth its running speed. Bill ultimately left in 1962 to become a vice president of Stanford University. I felt he should have eventually become president of Stanford University, but he became the target of student anger over the Vietnam War. This was an especially cruel blow for him because he was honestly sympathetic and liberal-minded. He did become president of the Stanford Research Institute.

Wallace Givens took over as next director of the mathematics division. He had a full-time appointment now at Northwestern University in Evanston, Illinois, but he had a flexible leave arrangement which lasted indefinitely. His work in numerical analysis and his knowledge of hardware made him the director the most in tune with the functioning of the mathematics division of the laboratory.

The bread-and-butter work was with other science divisions at the Argonne National Laboratory but the mathematical program was not restricted to servicing. There was a large number of inspiring visitors in pure and applied mathematics sometimes only distantly related to computing, but all computer-progressive. My work in number theory led to at least one research paper a year, always using the computers. All in all, I was able to enjoy an environment with a broad, healthy vision of computing to offset the usual narrow academic vision. Some of my closer associates were James Butler, Joe Cook, Bert Garbow, and Bob Buchal. I knew them less well than my crew at Washington University, but I recall things that again are somewhat characteristic of the personnel at computing laboratories. Jim Butler and Burt Garbow had not gotten their BS degrees, but were "redeemed" through their ability at computing. Joe Cook, on the other hand, was a very sophisticated mathematical physicist with a PhD at the University of Chicago under Irving Segal. He had an aversion toward academic stereotypes, which prevented him from obtaining a university position for which he would have been uniquely qualified and, I believe, in great demand.

All of these associates (and others at the Argonne National Laboratory) were involved in imaginative research projects going beyond what usually arises in purely academic context. The most imaginative work I did there, however, would be trivial for a PC today, namely the representation of the three-dimensional boundaries of a four-dimensional object in two-dimensional cross section, all printed by character pixels (like '*') on an unsophisticated line-printer (Cohn 1965). I only wish that the university computing centers I knew personally were that well supported and could deal in ideas as visionary as the Argonne National Laboratory. My impatience was undoubtedly reflected in a talk I gave at a meeting of the American Mathematical Society in June 1963 on computing. The invitation came from John Todd, who chaired the meeting. From sentiments expressed at the NBS in 1956, he knew I looked upon computing as more than the sum of individual tricks.

Instead of simply boasting of the wonders, I asked for a more sober distribution of effort toward new areas which could stimulate development. The title, "Purposeful and Unpurposeful Computing," conveyed the message (Cohn 1963). This was my last public venture at influencing computing. From that point on, it would all be private, through my own research, or through my influence as a mathematician.

Later Positions (after 1958)

By the time I took my next job as head of mathematics at the University of Arizona, Tucson, in August 1958, I knew I was not a good promoter. My moment was past. I could serve the cause of computing only as an outsider doing mathematics and building up a compatible PhD department. Happily, I did not appreciate the main difficulty immediately, namely the low salaries. I tended to discount this because the Southwest was so beautiful (and cheap) as a place to live. I did not count on the major difficulties in recruiting created by the ego of most professional mathematicians expressed in the appeal of the "established" departments with which I had to compete.

Nevertheless, the creation of the new Mathematics Department in Tucson, Arizona, was my only great administrative glory. Of course, one factor was working in my favor, which would not have been present in computing. This was the major university in Arizona and, whether the administration liked it or not, they needed a Mathematics Department. It soon became the largest department in the university.

The location was no hindrance in getting money. Our senator Carl Hayden was chairman of the Senate Finance Committee. With or without his influence, one never knows, we obtained many departmental grants from the government.

Also, Arizona was fortunately notoriously behind in its social thinking; a department head was a boss, not a chairman of the board, so he could act decisively when necessary. The problems with the administration arose only when computing entered, because it was an innovative budget concept and involved equipment.

I did like the idea that the West was known for healthy, independent thinking, but unfortunately this meant I had to contend with skeptical administrators who did not think anything called "Mathematics" could be trusted to do anything useful; in fact to them "Applied Mathematics" was a type of engineering (if it existed at all).

Although I had the largest departmental budget in the university, I could not get permission from the administration for even the smallest computer. In fact, we did get a free Teletype connection to the GE BASIC Mainframe in Phoenix in 1965.

It was installed without university funds; only the phone bill was charged. The administration would not let the Mathematics Department pay the phone bill, but Southwest Bell assumed the money *had* to be there, so they let us run up some $3,000 over two years before the service was terminated. Computing was officially a small activity of the Engineering College. The engineering dean was very mathematically oriented and had made no objections to the participation of the Mathematics Department in computing. The reluctance came from my own dean of Liberal Arts, who possibly also thought Mathematics was too big a department for his comfort. My attempts to play up the future destiny of computers were stagnant for a while, but suddenly they became counterproductive. The engineering dean was replaced in 1965 by a fortunately short-tenured one who had experience only in physics laboratory supervision. He got the novel idea to counter the engineers' (and his own) fear of mathematics by removing the source of fear.

This involved a catalogue proposal to reduce the Engineering mathematics requirements to advanced placement calculus (in high school) supplemented in college by a short calculus course taught not in the Mathematics Department but in the Computing Center (taught by engineers). My skepticism, of course, was predictable.

To show mathematics courses were superfluous, the engineering dean gave a demonstration to an "impartial committee" appointed by the Faculty Senate, purporting to show how calculus problems were "solved" by computer *without* mathematics courses. I had the privilege of observing with the committee. This demonstration was a procedure more reminiscent of convention centers than universities.

It included signs in large letters on tripods explaining even to the most ignorant exactly what problem was being solved at each time, and even signs announcing when each problem had been solved. The only things missing were the models in miniskirts carrying the signs. The main operation was a charade of students looking on a shelf for the appropriate deck of IBM cards for each problem and loading them into, you guessed it, the IBM-650.

In today's world of terminals, interactive demonstrations are quite legitimate and very much in vogue, but they are scarcely advertised as freeing engineers from the study of college mathematics.

I politely sat through this sideshow, trying to look dignified, and interrupting only to remark that obviously somebody has to do mathematics for the programs. This was so silly to say that I could scarcely refrain from laughing, but this select committee voted that a "new method had just been unveiled which will make the University of

Arizona famous." The few votes favorable to mathematics came from such unlikely sources as deans of agricultural engineering and architecture, not from the heavy mathematics users and surely not from the nonscience departments. Of course I had to react. I quickly gathered data from colleagues who were on national engineering evaluation committees and I sent word to the university president privately that we might become famous by having the Engineering College disaccredited. The president (who was experienced enough to consider the source of his advice as well as the rhetoric) assured me it was never necessary for me to have worried. He soon made a statement to the faculty senate that "an engineer has to have a lot of mathematics to do his arithmetic," and he summarily canceled out the calculus-without-mathematics notion before its popularity could swell to even more gigantic proportions. This did not improve my political popularity with my bewildered colleagues. After I stepped down as head of the department (in 1967) and was no longer a public figure, the Mathematics Department was quietly permitted to start what later became a decent computation laboratory in mathematics. In fact there was a simultaneously created university computer laboratory in its own building.

Over and over again, I saw that the fruits of the innovators were enjoyed, unappreciatively, by the succeeding generations. *The dream is not for the dreamer.*

I spent a delightful summer vacation in 1963 teaching at John Green's Institute for Numerical Analysts at UCLA. Considering that the University of California at Los Angeles was central to the development of computers (SWAC) as well as curricula in numerical analysis, I expected computing to be treated better than at the National Bureau of Standards. Again, however, the emphasis was on using computers to make numerical analysts look better, not to inspire any new attitudes in mathematics. My only cybernetic soulmate turned out to be Charles Coleman, whom I had briefly met at the National Bureau of Standards in 1956. He had also become so engrossed in computing that he did not complete his bachelor's degree at the University of Virginia. He worked later for IBM at Yorktown Heights. I did not engage in polemics at UCLA, as I had experience with the intransigence of numerical analysts, but I thought to myself that computing might have been better respected by American academics if it were not so "American" looking. To be a great scientist even in 1963, it was not necessary to have an "accent," but it helped.

I came to my present chair appointment at my alma mater City College, now part of CUNY, in 1971. My main purpose is to supervise doctoral students and to teach computing as numerical methods in analysis for undergraduates and as number theory or cryptography for graduates, including computer scientists. In any case, I am now on the sidelines enjoying the achievements of others, with more time to write papers using computers.

I am involved with many computing laboratories, owing to the multiple bureaucratic structure enjoyed by the City University, but when "bad things" happen to the laboratories, they are not my problem. I have no longer any input into sources of computer power and destiny. My encounters with computing still continue but in increasingly satisfactory form from the scientific viewpoint. Machines are faster and programming aids (and even programming assistants) are available. The NSF (National Science Foundation) also helps to make computing relatively easy for me now.

Epilog

Looking back, probably I am pretending to have had a mutual relationship to computing like that of James Boswell to Samuel Johnson. In fact it may have been more like the rooster to the sunrise. I am not modest, however, about having pioneered in the intensive use of computers in an innovative way in a large number of classical mathematical problems. Therefore my presentation is that of a mathematician who uses computing rather than who serves as a creator of hardware, software, or systems. There are many such, but I also claim to have been an early "true believer" who felt that computers are more than devices to aid mathematicians, but rather devices which *must* change the nature of mathematics. To use the classical analogy, when rational mechanics was introduced in the seventeenth century to an environment of scientists using geometry, this was not just another application of geometry, but the entrance cue for *calculus*. In retrospect it may be said that the introduction of computers has been an entrance cue for many fields which seem to vary with fashion, like *information* theory, *complexity* theory, *knowledge* theory, and so on, and others which surely shall follow. I am not advocating any one of these viewpoints. To the contrary, I make no choice because my involvement was a search for the future which I did not fully understand, nor do I now. I must count on others to find it.[25]

---

[25]An enlarged version of Cohn 1994.

BIBLIOGRAPHY

Biographical

Cohn, H., "Reminiscences of a True Believer," *Ann. Hist. Comp.*, Vol. 16, No. 1, 1994, pp. 71–76.

Significant Publications

Cohn, H., "Numerical Study of Signature Rank of Cubic Cyclotomic Units," *Math. Tables Aids to Comput.*, Vol. 8, 1954, pp. 186–188.

Cohn, H., "Use and Limitations of Computers," in John Todd, ed., *Surveys in Numerical Analysis,* McGraw-Hill, New York, 1962, pp. 208–221.

Cohn, H., "Some Illustrative Computations in Algebraic Number Theory," in John Todd, ed., *Surveys in Numerical Analysis,* McGraw-Hill, New York, 1962, pp. 543–549.

Cohn, H., "Numerical Survey of the Floors of Various Hilbert Fundamental Domains," *Math. of Comp.*, Vol. 33, 1965, pp. 594–605.

Cohn, H., and Gorn, S., "Computation of Cyclic Cubic Units," *NBS J. Res.*, Vol. 59, 1957, pp. 155–168.

LESLIE JOHN COMRIE

Born August 15, 1893, Pukekohe, New Zealand; died December 11, 1950, London, England; developer in 1930 of mathematical tables for the British Nautical Almanac Office using punched-card bookkeeping machines and who, in that decade, established the first commercial calculating service in Great Britain.[26]

Education: BA, chemistry, University College, Auckland, New Zealand, 1915; MA, chemistry, University College, Auckland, New Zealand, 1916.

Professional Experience: assistant professor, mathematics and astronomy, Swarthmore College, Swarthmore, Pa., 1923–1924; assistant professor, astronomy, Northwestern University, Evanston, Ill., 1924–1925; deputy director,

---

[26]See Wilkes' comments on Comrie's contributions to the construction of tables in his biography of Charles Babbage: Wilkes, M.V., "Babbage's Expectations for His Engines," *Ann. Hist. Comp.*, Vol. 1B, No. 2, pp. 141–146.

Nautical Almanac Office, 1925–1931, superintendent, 1931–1936; founder and director, Scientific Computing Service, 1936–1950.

Leslie Comrie had begun his professional life as a chemist in Pukekohe and Auckland, New Zealand, when World War I broke out, during which he served in France in the New Zealand Expeditionary Force. He was invalided out of the force, having lost a leg; he turned to a past interest in astronomy, and became a research student at St. John's College, Cambridge, in 1918 with a University Expeditionary Force scholarship. While there he developed a means for the application of new computational techniques to the problems of spherical astronomy, which he carried forward into his later appointment as the deputy superintendent of the *Nautical Almanac,* for the British Navy (the Admiralty) in London. Later as superintendent he modified the almost one-hundred-year-old *Almanac* and introduced the concept of a "standard equinox" (Comrie 1926 and 1929).

He left the Admiralty in 1934 to found the Scientific Computing Service, where he was able to better apply his ideas of mechanical computation for the preparation of mathematical tables. Using card processing systems he prepared the way for the electronic computer, which he would observe shortly before his death in 1950.

In May 1946 Leslie Comrie returned from a visit to the US with a copy of von Neumann's *First Draft of a Report on the EDVAC.* Maurice V. Wilkes, later developer of the EDSAC at the University of Cambridge, was given the opportunity of one night in which to read and digest the document which described the stored-program computer concept. Wilkes "recognized this at once as the real thing, and from that time on never had any real doubt as to the way computer development would go."[27]

Wilkes has credited Comrie with providing some of the enthusiasm for mechanical computational techniques which would affect the Cambridge Mathematics Laboratory and later the Computer Laboratory.

In 1982 the *Annals of the History of Computing* provided the following anecdote about Leslie Comrie:

> Comrie, who has lost a foot [sic] during World War I, was in the habit of unscrewing his artificial limb when he came home in the evening to relax and listen to the BBC. On one of those evenings he heard an announcement on the radio that the Works Project Administration (WPA) was to be ended; with it, he realized, would come the demise of the Mathematical Tables Project (MTP). Without stopping to put on

---

[27] See also the biography of Maurice Wilkes.

his artificial limb, he hopped to the nearest telegraph office and wired President Roosevelt to save the MTP.

There was no way to verify the story, Ira Rhodes said, but a few days later their loft in New York City was visited by a group of government people who gave the appearance of not really knowing what they were doing there. Shortly thereafter, the MTP, instead of ceasing to exist, was made part of the National Bureau of Standards of the US Department of Commerce.[28]

QUOTATION

Sadler (1980) said: "Comrie, with no claim to be a mathematician, had the clarity of mind, tenacity of purpose, scientific courage, and immense energy that enabled him, by using essentially simple and direct methods, to obtain practical solutions to many problems that defied theoretical analysis. But he was inclined to impatience with those who did not share his devotion to perfectionism, and this led to some difficult personal relationships."

BIBLIOGRAPHY

Biographical

Greaves, W.M.H., "Leslie John Comrie," *Monthly Notices of the Royal Astronomical Society,* Vol. 113, 1953, pp. 294–304.

Massey, H.S.W., "Leslie John Comrie," *Obituary Notices of Fellows of the Royal Society,* Vol. 8, 1952, pp. 97–107.

Sadler, D.H., "Comrie, Leslie John," in Gillispie, C.G., ed., *Dictionary of Scientific Biography,* Vol. 3, Charles Scribner's Sons, New York, 1980, pp. 373–374.

Tropp, Henry. S., "Leslie John Comrie," Anecdotes Dept., *Ann. Hist. Comp.,* Vol. 4, No. 4, Oct. 1982, pp. 371–372.

Significant Publications

Comrie, Leslie John, "The Use of a Standard Equinox in Astronomy," *Monthly Notices of the Royal Astronomical Society,* Vol. 86, 1926, pp. 618–631.

Comrie, Leslie John, "Explanation," *The Nautical Almanac and Astronomical Ephemeris for 1931,* London, 1929.

Comrie, Leslie John, "Interpolation and Allied Tables," *The Nautical Almanac and Astronomical Ephemeris for 1937,* London, 1936.

---

[28] Tropp 1982.

Comrie, Leslie John, *Barlow's Tables of Squares etc. of Integral Numbers up to 12,000,* London, 1947.

Comrie, Leslie John, *Chamber's Six-figure Mathematical Tables,* London, 1950.

LARRY L. CONSTANTINE

Born February 14, 1943, Minneapolis, Minn.; 1960s pioneer of disciplined, structured software design methodologies.

Education: SB, management, Massachusetts Institute of Technology, 1967 (plus graduate study); certificate, Family Therapy, Boston Family Institute, 1973.

Professional Experience: staff consultant, programmer/analyst, CEIR, Inc., 1963–1966; president, Information & Systems Institute, Inc., 1966–1968; faculty member, IBM Systems Research Inst., 1968–1972; independent consultant, information system design, 1969–1976; assistant clinical professor of psychiatry, Tufts University, School of Medicine, 1973–1980; independent consultant, organization development, 1975–1978; assistant professor of human development and family studies, University of Connecticut, 1983–1987; clinical supervisor, adolescent and family intervention, LUK, Inc., Fitchburg, Mass., 1984–1986; consulting supervisor and family therapist, private practice, 1973–1991; independent consultant, software development, 1987–1992; principal consultant, Constantine & Lockwood, Ltd., 1993–present.

Honors and Awards: Research Award, Society for Family Therapy and Research, 1984.

Constantine began his work on the "invention" of structure charts, first used in essentially their modern form in 1966 and "published" in course material most of which later appeared in Yourdon and Constantine (1975). The direct precursor was Jim Emery's hierarchy charts of 1962.[29]

A year later (1967) Constantine introduced data flow diagrams based on Martin and Estrin's "data flow graphs." This was first used, in its modern form, as an analysis and design tool by Constantine and his company later that year and first made widely accessible in the *IBM Systems Journal* piece (1974).

The concept of coupling and cohesion developed by Constantine in the mid-1960s was first published in 1968 and repeated in the 1974

---

[29]Emery, J., "Modular Data Processing Systems Written in COBOL," *Comm. ACM,* Vol. 5, No. 5, 1962.

publication. These two measures have been the subject of more than 100 studies and are at the heart of a number of software quality and complexity metrics (including Card and Aggresti's intrinsic complexity metric). They have also demonstrated their resilience as fundamental intellectual constructs in that they have carried over into metrics for object-oriented software.

A significant event in the structural revolution, a sort of "coming out" for what would become structured analysis and design, was the first (and only) National Symposium on Modular Programming, sponsored by the Information and Systems Institute in July 1968. This conference gathered such luminaries as Mealy, Morenoff and McLean, Yourdon, Vincent, Aron, and Constantine, to discuss issues in modular system architecture and development methods long before these were *au courant*. This conference saw the first more or less complete summary of structured design.

It was also at this conference that Conway's Law (*"the structure of a system resembles the structure of the organization that developed it"*) was named by George Mealy.[30] Also named at the conference was Mealy's Law: *"There is an incremental programmer who, when added to a project, consumes more resources than are made available."*

The first publication using the term "structured design" appeared in May 1974 (Stevens, Myers, and Constantine 1974) and generated more reprint requests than any other in the journal's history. It has been widely cited and reprinted as one of the seminal works of software engineering. In a more widely accessible forum it gave a more complete explanation of coupling and cohesion and presented structure charts and data flow diagrams in modern form.

The concept was further expounded in a pair of editions of books entitled *Structured Design: Fundamentals of a Discipline of Program and Systems Design,* published successively by Yourdon Press and Prentice-Hall in 1975 and 1979.

QUOTATION

Constantine has laid his claim to pioneer status by stating:

"I know there is an understandable ACM and academic bias in this, but if you are going to include publication of Knuth, "Art of Computer Programming," [in a listing of landmark articles on software

---

[30]Mealy, George, "How to Design Modular (Software) Systems," *Proc. Nat'l. Symp. Modular Programming,* Information & Systems Institute, July 1968.

A recent Internet thread on the history of computing reported that Conway's article appeared in *Datamation* in April 1968 but didn't refer to the "law" by name.

engineering] how can you ignore a landmark like *Structured Design*, one of the most successful books in the history of computing, still in print in original form some 17 years after first publication? I may never have the academic legitimacy to even be considered for a Turing Award, but the methodology is the most widely practiced today and the book is used in colleges and universities around the world.

"You should also consult Paul Ward's series on the history of structured analysis in *American Programmer*. He documents Ross's role with SADT and the advent of SA by DeMarco, Gane, and Sarson. These should be represented in the chart also.

"It seems to me a disservice to reduce the entire thread of structured methods and the structural revolution to one letter to the editor (even though it did appear in the *Comm. ACM*). As a footnote to history, although I have been cited dozens of times in *Comm. ACM*, I was never able to get published there."

BIBLIOGRAPHY

Significant Publications

Constantine, Larry L., "Segmentation and Design Strategies for Modular Programming," in Barnett and Constantine, L.L., eds., *Modular Programming: Proceedings of a National Symposium,* Information & Systems Press, Cambridge, Mass., 1968.

Stevens, Myers, and Larry L. Constantine, "Structured Design," *IBM Systems J.*, Vol. 13, No. 2, May 1974.

Yourdon, Edward, and Larry L. Constantine, *Structured Design: Fundamentals of a Discipline of Program and Systems Design*, Yourdon Press, 1975.

Yourdon, Edward, and Larry L. Constantine, *Structured Design: Fundamentals of a Discipline of Program and Systems Design*, Prentice-Hall, Englewood Cliffs, N.J., 1979.

Lynn Conway

Born January 2, 1938, Mt. Vernon, N.Y.; Xerox Parc (Palo Alto Research Center) researcher who with Carver Mead created a radically new way of designing chips.

Education: BS, Columbia University, 1962; MSEE, Columbia University, 1963.

Professional Experience: member, research staff, computer architecture, IBM Corp., 1964–1969; senior staff engineer, Memorex Corp., 1969–1973; Xerox Palo Alto Research Center: member, research staff, Digital Systems Architecture, 1973–1977; manager, LSI Systems Area, 1977–1980; research fellow and manager, VLSI System Design Area, 1980–present

Stephen A. Cook

Recipient of the 1982 ACM Turing Award for "contributions to the Theory of Computational Complexity, including the concept of nondeterministic, polynomial-time completeness."

James William Cooley

Born September 18, 1926; with John Tukey, creator of the fast Fourier transform.

Education: BA, arts, Manhattan College, 1949; MA, mathematics, Columbia University, 1951; PhD, applied mathematics, Columbia University, 1961.

Professional Experience: programmer, Institute for Advanced Study, Princeton University, 1953–1956; research assistant, mathematics, Courant Institute, New York University, 1956–1962; research staff, IBM Watson Research Center, 1962–1991; professor, electrical engineering, University of Rhode Island, 1991–present.

Honors and Awards: Contribution Award, Audio and Acoustics Society, 1976; Meritorious Service Award, ASSP Society, 1980; Society Award, Acoustics Speech and Signal Processing, 1984; IEEE Centennial Award, 1984; fellow, IEEE

James W. Cooley started his career in applied mathematics and computing when he worked and studied under Professor F.J. Murray at Columbia University. He then became a programmer in the numerical weather prediction group at John von Neumann's computer project at the Institute for Advanced Study in Princeton, New Jersey.[31] In 1956, he started working as a research assistant at the Courant Institute at New York University, New York. Here he worked on numerical methods and programming of quantum mechanical calculations (Cooley 1961). This led to his thesis for his PhD degree from Columbia University.

In 1962 he obtained a position as a research staff member at the IBM Watson Research Center in Yorktown Heights, New York. Here he worked on numerical methods for solving ordinary and partial differential equations, solutions of hole-electron diffusion equations for semiconductors, and numerous other research projects. He collaborated with Fred Dodge, a neurophysiologist, in research in neurophysiology including modeling of electrical activity in nerve membranes and in heart muscle (Cooley and Dodge 1966).

With John Tukey, he wrote the fast Fourier transform (FFT) paper (Cooley and Tukey 1965) that has been credited with introducing the algorithm to the digital signal processing and scientific community in general.

Cooley spent the academic year 1973–1974 on a sabbatical at the Royal Institute of Technology, Stockholm, Sweden. He gave courses on the FFT and its applications there and in several other locations in Europe and worked on new versions of the FFT and on number-theoretic Fourier transforms.

In 1974 Cooley started collaboration with S. Winograd and R. Agarwal on applications of computational complexity theory to convolution and Fourier transform algorithms (Agarwal and Cooley 1977).

Around 1985 he worked with a group that programmed the elementary functions for the new IBM 3090 Vector Facility. He and the same group also produced the Digital Signal Processing subroutines for the Engineering and Scientific Subroutine Library (ESSL) for the IBM 3090 Vector Facility and, later, for the new IBM RS6000 computer (Agarwal and Cooley 1987).

---

[31]See the biography of Jule Charney.

Cooley retired from IBM in 1991 and joined the faculty of the Electrical Engineering Department of the University of Rhode Island as director of the computer engineering program.

BIBLIOGRAPHY

Significant Publications

Agarwal, R.C., and J.W. Cooley, "New Algorithms for Digital Convolution," *IEEE Trans. Acoust., Speech, Signal Processing*, Vol. ASSP-25, No. 5, Oct. 1977, pp. 392–410.

Agarwal, R.C., and J.W. Cooley, "Vectorized Mixed Radix Fourier Transform Algorithms," *IEEE Proc.*, Sept. 1987, pp. 1283-1292.

Cooley, J.W., "An Improved Eigenvalue Corrector Formula for Solving the Schrodinger Equation for Central Fields," *Mathematics of Computation*, Vol. 15, No. 7, Oct. 1961, pp. 363–374.

Cooley, J.W., and F.A. Dodge, Jr., "Digital Computer Solutions for Excitation and Propagation of the Nerve Impulse," *Biophysical J.*, Vol. 6, No. 5, 1966.

Cooley, J.W., and J.W. Tukey, "An Algorithm for the Machine Calculation of Complex Fourier Series," *Mathematics of Computation*, Vol. 19, Apr. 1965, p. 297.

ALLEN W. M. COOMBS

Born October 23, 1911, Bristol, Gloucestershire, UK; early computer engineer responsible for the construction of the Colossus computer system designed by Alan M. Turing and others.

Education: BSc, Glasgow University, 1932; ARTC,[32] Strathclyde University, 1932; PhD, Glasgow University, 1936.

Professional Experience: engineer, research branch, British Post Office (now British Telecom), 1936–1973.

From 1936 to 1973, Coombs was employed by the British Post Office (now British Telecom) on various projects in its research branch, most

---

[32]Later designated ARCST (Associate of the Royal College of Science and Technology).

of them still classified. He spent some of the World War II years in association with the project to design and implement the Colossus computer for Bletchley Park for the government code and cipher school together with Thomas Flowers.

BIBLIOGRAPHY

Biographical

Coombs, Allen W.M., "Colossus, and the History of Computing: Dollis Hill's Important Contribution," *Post Office Electrical Engineer's J.*, Vol. 70, Pt. 2, July 1977.

Coombs, Allen W.M., "The Making of Colossus," *Ann. Hist. Comp.*, Vol. 5, No. 3, July 1983.

Lavington, Simon, *Early British Computers,* Digital Press, Bedford, Mass. 1980; see Chapter 5: "The ACE, The 'British National Computer.'"

Randell, Brian, "The Colossus," in Metropolis, N., J. Howlett, and Gian-Carlo Rota, *A History of Computing in the Twentieth Century,* Academic Press, New York, 1980, pp. 47–92.

Significant Publications

Coombs, Allen W.M., "Mosaic, an Electronic Digital Computer," *Post Office Electrical Engineer's J.*, Vol. 48, Pts. 1–4, Vol. 49, Pts. 1, 2, 1955–1956.

Coombs, Allen W.M., "On the Construction of an Efficient Feature Space for Optical Character Recognition," in Meltzer, Bernard, and Donald Michie, eds., *Machine Intelligence,* Vol. 4, Edinburgh Univ. Press, 1969.

Fernando Jose Corbató

Born July 1, 1926, Oakland, Calif.; creator of the Compatible Time-Sharing System (CTSS), the first general-purpose interactive system.

Education: BS, physics, California Institute of Technology, 1950; PhD, physics, Massachusetts Institute of Technology, 1956.

Professional Experience: US Navy, electronics technician, 1943–1945; research associate, MIT Computation Center, 1956–1959; assistant director for programming research, 1959–1960; associate director, 1960–1963; deputy director, 1963–1966; group leader in the computing systems research group, Laboratory for Computer Science, 1963–1972; co-head, systems research division, 1972–1974; co-head, automatic programming division, 1972–1974; associate head, Department of Computer Science and Engineering, 1974–1978, 1983–present; Cecil H. Green Professorship, 1978–1980.

Honors and Awards: W.W. McDowell Award, IEEE, 1966; Harry Goode Memorial Award, American Federation of Information Processing Societies, 1980; IEEE Computer Society Pioneer Award, 1980; ACM Turing Award, 1990.

When the war broke out in 1941 (for the US) Corbató's high school went into long hours and he saw a chance to get out in a hurry. He went to UCLA as a student, with the threat of the draft looming over his head. People came by the school who were concerned about the ability of the Navy to maintain and repair the incredible amount of electronic equipment they were getting. There was a program called the Eddy Program, and they gave Corbató the opportunity to join the program and get an education as an electronic technician. One of the benefits, of course, was one did not get drafted, or get assigned to be a cook, or something worse. So Corbató enlisted at the age of 17 in the Navy and went through a year-long program as an electronic technician. He got exposed to some of the earliest and largest electronic systems then deployed in the Navy—mostly radar, loran, and sonar systems—both on land and on ship. He did not realize until later how important that was.

After the war he got a chance to go back to college, this time at Cal Tech. Since everyone wanted to be a physicist in those days, Corbató read to be a physicist following his undergraduate studies with graduate work at MIT, still with the intention of undertaking a career as a physicist. He got his doctorate in physics, but along the way got exposed to digital computers by the late Philip M. Morse [later to be director of the MIT Computation Center]. In 1951 Morse recruited Corbató to take on a new research assistantship in the use of digital computers. The people who signed on with this initial ONR-sponsored research assistantship program were exposed to punched cards in the spring, and in the summer they were introduced to Whirlwind. The Whirlwind was just barely operational; it had approximately 1,000 words of 16-bit custom-built electrostatic memory that had a mean time between failures (on a good day) of about 20 minutes. Jay Forrester was very prescient in recognizing that the Williams tubes (Manchester University) were flaky in design, and he had actually gone back basically to first principles to design a very elaborate mosaic storage tube. Somewhat similar in storage retention (charge retention) to Williams tubes, it was a tour de force in electronics to make it work. A group headed by Patrick Youtz built them in a basement at MIT.[33]

The people who operated Whirlwind recognized the need to have unclassified work and be able to use it in an open way. So the deal they worked out was that approximately three to four hours a day were made available for that purpose. In the morning were the times when the nonclassified personnel were permitted to use the machine. This meant that general users worked all day and all evening preparing Flexowriter tapes, which were the input medium, and then took a quick shot at the machine the next morning. If one were really fast, the user might get two shots in during each two-hour period. Most times it was one shot a day, which could be very frustrating, but on the other hand, the machine was not that big, and the programs were not that huge.

It was a personal computer; there were many things about it that got lost in the next few years, such as graphical display output and even audio output—there was a probe put on the circuit of the accumulator which gave the users a "signature" of each program they were running. The users actually could hear where the program was, could sense the loops, and could even get the tempo of how the program was running. Occasionally people recognized from the audio that they had a program that was misbehaving, because it did not sound as they thought it should at that point.

After Corbató got his doctorate in physics in 1956, Phil Morse recruited him into the newly formed Computation Center, which he

---

[33]Wildes and Lingren 1986.

had established that year. The focal point of the new center was an IBM-704; Morse had worked out a package deal with IBM, where in return for the use of the machine on campus for one shift, MIT would also make it available to a cooperative group of New England colleges for the second shift. The third shift would be retained to be used by IBM's own local scientific office. Time was also provided for a group in Cambridge, formed and directed by Martin Greenberger, that computed the orbits for the first USSR Sputnik.

Corbató played various roles in the center, ranging from initially supervising a research assistantship program to later becoming an assistant director, associate director, and finally deputy director of the Computation Center.

In the spring of 1961 when the IBM-704 had been replaced by an IBM-709, Corbató started up a project which eventually developed the Compatible Time-Sharing System (CTSS) with just a couple of the key staff people—Marjorie Daggett (who was then Margaret Merwin) and Bob Daley. By November 1961 they were able to demonstrate a really crude prototype of the system. They had eked out 5K words of the user address space from the standard operating system and inserted a tiny operating system that managed four typewriters. Backup storage was achieved by assigning one magnetic tape drive per typewriter.

This system could operate effectively as long as no other user wanted an "all-the-core-memory" type job to run under the Fortran (FAP) monitor system. This system could coexist with that kind of an operating system and could run jobs. So it could run *compatibly*; it could run while ordinary batch work was being run on the IBM-709. It used the same language systems as the batch system; thus, using CTSS meant not having to start programming over again, as had happened in most system and machine changes up to that time. Even early versions of LISP ran under CTSS.

The IBM-7090 replacement hardware arrived in the early spring of 1962, supporting the necessary interrupt capabilities which had not been available in the earlier machine. Corbató et al. presented a paper at the 1962 Spring Joint Computer Conference (Corbató et al. 1962), which suggested that they were running CTSS on IBM-7090 hardware on the basis that this would be fact by the time the paper was presented. In fact, it was not operational until the fall of that year.[34]

That paper was the first description of a working time-sharing system. It stated:

---

[34]Editor's note: A prime example of why historians cannot even always trust the primary sources of information on an event.

. . . it is best to give a . . . precise interpretation to time-sharing. One can mean using different parts of the hardware at the same time for different tasks, or one can mean several persons making use of the computer at the same time. The first meaning, often called multiprogramming, is oriented toward hardware efficiency in the sense of attempting to attain complete utilization of all components. The second meaning of time-sharing, which is meant here, is primarily concerned with the efficiency of persons trying to use a computer. Computer efficiency should still be considered, but only in the perspective of the total system utility.

An experimental time-sharing system has been developed. This system was originally written for the IBM-709 but has been converted for use with the 7090 computer.

The 7090 of the MIT Computation Center has, in addition to three channels with 19 tape units, a fourth channel with the standard Direct Data Connection. Attached to the Direct Data Connection is a real-time equipment buffer and control rack designed and built under the direction of H. Teager and his group. This rack has a variety of devices attached but the only ones required by the present systems are three Flexowriter typewriters. Also installed on the 7090 are two special modifications (i.e., RPQ's): a standard 60-cycle accounting and interrupt clock, and a special mode which allows memory protection, dynamic relocation and trapping of all user attempts to initiate input-output instructions.

In the present system, the time-sharing occurs between four users, three of whom are on-line each at a typewriter in a foreground system, and a fourth passive user of the background FAP-MAD-MADTRAN-BSS Monitor System (FMS) used by most of the Center programmers and by many other 7090 installations.

Significant design features of the foreground system [for the user] are [that he can]:

1. Develop programs in languages compatible with the background system,
2. Develop a private file of programs,
3. Start debugging sessions at the state of the previous session, and
4. Set his own pace with little waste of computer time.

The foreground system is organized around commands that each user can give on his typewriter and the user's private program files which presently (for want of a disk [sic] unit) are kept on a separate magnetic tape for each user.

The commands are typed by the user to the time-sharing supervisor (not to his own program) and thus can be initiated at any time regardless of the particular user program in memory. For similar coordination reasons, the supervisor handles all input/output of the foreground system typewriters. Commands are composed of segments separated by vertical strokes; the first segment is the command name and the remaining segments are parameters pertinent to the command. Each segment consists of the last six characters typed (starting with an implicit six blanks) so that spacing is an easy way to correct a typing mistake. A carriage return is the signal which initiates action on the command. Whenever a command is received by the supervisor, "WAIT" is typed back followed by "READY" when the command is completed. (The computer responses are always in the opposite color from the user's typing.) While typing, an incomplete command line may be ignored by the "quit" sequence of a code delete signal followed by a carriage return. Similarly after a command is initiated, it may be abandoned if a "quit" sequence is given. In addition, during unwanted command type-outs, the command and output may be terminated by pushing a special "stop output" button.

Although experience with the system to date is quite limited, first indications are that programmers would readily use such a system if it were generally available. It is useful to ask, now that there is some operating experience with the IBM-7090 system, what observations can be made. An immediate comment is that once a user gets accustomed to [immediate] computer response, delays of even a fraction of a minute are exasperatingly long, an effect analogous to conversing with a slow speaking person. Similarly, the requirement that a complete typewritten line rather than each character be the minimum unit of man-computer communication is an inhibiting factor in the sense that a press-to-talk radio-telephone conversation is more stilted than that of an ordinary telephone. Since maintaining a rapid computer response on a character-by-character basis requires at least a vestigial response program in core memory at all times, the straightforward solution within the present system is to have more core memory available. At the very least, an extra bank of memory for the time-sharing supervisor would ease compatibility problems with programs already written for 32,000-word IBM-7090's.

In conclusion, it is clear that contemporary computers and hardware are sufficient to allow moderate performance time-sharing for a limited number of users. There are several problems which can be solved by careful hardware design, but there are also a large number of intricate system programs that must be written before one has an adequate time-sharing system. An important aspect of any future time-shared computer is that until the system programming is completed, especially the critical time-sharing supervisor, the computer is completely worthless. Thus, it is essential for future system design and implementation that all aspects of time-sharing system problems be explored and understood in prototype form on present computers so that major advances in computer organization and usage can be made.

After the success of CTSS Corbató continued the development of time-sharing systems under Project MAC, which was headed by Robert Fano. While Project MAC initially used CTSS as its basic system, it was superseded by Multics operating on GE computers in the late 1960s, and Multics was marketed by Honeywell Information Systems for many years after GE sold its Computer Division in 1968.

In 1991 Corbató received the ACM Turing Award: "For his work in organizing the concepts and leading the development of the general purpose large-scale time-sharing system and resource-sharing computer systems CTSS and MULTICS." His major research interests continue to be in time-sharing systems, automatic programming, and knowledge-based application systems.

QUOTATION

Regarding the November 1961 primitive CTTS: ". . . we were just trying to get a demonstration system going to convince people that it was a good idea. A lot of people did not understand what it meant to interact. [That] was amazing." (Lee and Rosin 1992)

BIBLIOGRAPHY

Biographical

Corbató, Fernando J., "On Building Systems That Will Fail," 1991 Turing Award Lecture, *Comm. ACM,* Vol. 34, No. 9, Sept. 1991, pp. 73–81.

Frenkel, Karen A., "An Interview with Fernando Jose Corbató," *Comm. ACM,* Vol. 34, No. 9, Sept. 1991, pp. 83–90.

Lee, J.A.N., and Robert Rosin, "Time-Sharing and Interactive Computing at MIT," Special Issue, *Ann. Hist. Comp.,* Vol. 14, Nos. 1 & 2, 1992.

Significant Publications

Corbató, Fernando J., et al., *The Compatible Time-Sharing System. A Programmer's Guide,* MIT Press, Cambridge, Mass., 1963.

Corbató, Fernando J., et al., "Multics—The First Seven Years," *Proc. Spring Joint Computer Conf.,* Vol. 40, AFIPS Press, Montvale, N.J., 1972, pp. 571–583.

Corbató, Fernando J., "Time-sharing," in Ralston, Anthony, and Edwin D. Reilly, Jr., eds., *Encyclopedia of Computer Science and Engineering,* 2nd ed., Van Nostrand Reinhold Co., New York, 1983, pp. 1520–1526.

Corbató, Fernando J., Marjorie Merwin-Daggett, and Robert C. Daley, "An Experimental Time-Sharing System," *Proc. Spring Joint Computer Conf.,* AFIPS, Vol. 21, The National Press, Palo Alto, Calif., 1962, pp. 335–344.

Corbató, Fernando J., and V.A. Vyssotsky, "Introduction and Overview of the Multics System," *Proc. Fall Joint Computer Conf.,* AFIPS, Vol. 27, Spartan Books Inc., Washington, D.C., 1965, pp. 185–196.

LOUIS COUFFIGNAL

Born 1902; died 1966; French computer pioneer who designed and attempted to construct an early innovative system.

Education: DSc, mathematical sciences, University of Paris, 1938.

Couffignal's career began in secondary school education, teaching mathematics and mechanics at the Ecole des Élèves Ingenieurs Mecaniciens, belonging to the Ecole Navale de Brest. At that time the wisdom of providing schools with calculating machines was being debated in the French scientific journals; the arguments for and against put forward by the opposing sides remind one of those used more recently concerning the place of computer science in secondary education. Interested in the problems of calculation, Couffignal decided to write a thesis on the subject, under M. d'Ocagne's supervision. This was the first time that the theory of calculating machines had been proposed as the subject of a doctorate thesis in mathematical sciences in the University of Paris; the thesis was submitted in March 1938 and was greeted by d'Ocagne as the start of a new line of research that promised "consequences with a breadth of scope one could not yet assess."

After d'Ocagne's death in September 1938, Couffignal, an established expert in numerical calculation, was to take on greater responsibilities. He had applied for the chair of applied mathematics at the Conservatoire National des Arts et Metiers, but had been ranked second, after A. Saint-Lague, by the Academie des Sciences.

However, the course of events was to favor Couffignal. After the Munich agreement, it became steadily clearer that war was approaching; mobilization of scientific, technical, and industrial resources was begun and the plans of the Centre National de la Recherche Scientifique Appliquée (CNRSA) started to be put into effect in October 1938.[35] Henri Laugier, director of CNRSA, asked a number of leading individuals to draw up a report on the state of research and the resources available in various fields. Couffignal was asked to report on the application of mathematics to scientific and technical research, and this marked the beginning of his administrative career.

One of Couffignal's hopes was that he would be able to build a calculating machine of his own design. He had become secretary of CNRSA's specialist committees, secretary general of the CNRSA com-

---

[35]The CNRSA was established in 1938 to consolidate all sources of funding for scientific research. In October 1939 the name of the organization was changed to Centre National de la Recherche Scientifique (CNRS), and it took on a wide range of objectives in fostering pure and applied sciences.

mittee dealing with inventions, and was appointed director of the laboratory for calculation and mechanics in the Institut Poincaré, where he found himself alongside laboratories in which there was a certain amount of calculating machinery and some computing staff. He had the task of organizing his laboratory.

Couffignal was to find his plans held up by the events of the start of the war and the occupation of France, especially as it seemed for a time that the survival of the CNRS, which had replaced CNRSA in 1939, was threatened by the attitude of the Vichy government. Couffignal collaborated with the new director of CNRS, suggesting that the Inventions Committee should be disbanded as it had failed to achieve its objectives—in his view, because of the opposition of the ministers for the various armed services and boycotting by the CNRS directorate. This committee was later replaced by the Inventions and Patents Committee, of which Couffignal became and remained secretary general. His involvement in many of the CNRS committees made it possible for him to observe what was being done in France in scientific research. He was appointed inspector general for technical education, and found time to write a book, *Histoire de la machine à Calculer*, which had the distinction of being awarded the Binoux Prize of the Academie des Sciences, usually reserved for works on the history and philosophy of science.

Building his own machine remained his ambition and thanks to his position at the heart of CNRS, he now saw a possibility of achieving it. In 1938 the Institut Poincaré's Statistical Laboratory, directed by Borel and Frechet, had obtained a grant of FF 100,000 for the construction of a calculating machine that was to work in binary, and had gone as far as signing a contract with the Outillage R.B.V. Company to produce an electromechanical device comprising an Ellis-type adder and two converters, binary/decimal and decimal/binary. In December 1939 General Desmazieres, who had recently assumed responsibility for artillery tables, suggested to Couffignal that he should turn his laboratory into a center for artillery calculations and should equip it with a powerful machine. At that time Couffignal had arranged a contract, also with Outillage R.B.V., worth FF 80,000, for the construction of an electromechanical linking of a Sanders-Octoplex 10-column accounting machine to a Monroe A-1–213 calculating machine. This link was to enable any number produced by either machine to be transferred to the keyboard of the other, and all operations would be controlled automatically by means of a perforated tape.

The events of the war delayed the fulfilling of these contracts; further, the board of Outillage R.B.V., most of whom were Jewish, was disbanded and it was not until the beginning of 1942 that a new board was constituted. With the advance of the German armies some of the company's machines were scattered and some were seized by the occupying forces. The new management told Couffignal that they would not be able to fulfill the 1938 and 1939 contracts because there was no possibility of acquiring a Monroe machine, and in the course of these discussions an idea developed: why not combine the two projects into a single new one? For the same total sum, FF 180,000, the company would build a machine of the Sanders type and add to it a "calculating mechanism" working in binary. To make this possible, the statistical laboratory would have to give up its grant and Couffignal set about persuading its director, Frechet, of the virtue of this idea. After some procrastination Frechet agreed, subject to certain conditions that he presented to Jacob, the director of CNRS: he would transfer his grant of FF 100,000 to Couffignal provided that the latter guaranteed him two-thirds of the time to be under the sole control of the statistical laboratory. Frechet insisted on a rigorous accounting of the machine's working time.

Couffignal was a member of the committee for Mechanics and Applied Mathematics; in the autumn of 1944, at the suggestion of Dautry, the Minister of Reconstruction, this committee began discussion of the formation within CNRS of a foundation to be called the Centre d'Etudes Superieures en Mecanique (CEMA) whose capital would be in the form of government stock and shares in national industries, SNCF for example. The latter would be able to call on the foundation to undertake various investigations or to provide training for young recruits. In November 1944 the view was formed that computing services should form the kernel of CEMA and accordingly Couffignal was asked by the Mathematics Committee to make a survey of the tables of numerical functions available in France. At the same time he kept in touch with the activities of a scientific mission to Germany in so far as these concerned bringing back machinery for calculation. Awareness of this mission's activities led many laboratories to put in requests for calculating machines, and also for slide rules that could not be bought in France; CNRS was swamped with demands and was unable to satisfy all of them.

Couffignal again saw a possibility of building his own machine; these aspirations led to the regrouping which was to give birth to the Institut Blaise Pascal. Couffignal obtained the grants he needed for the building of his machine, and at a meeting of the CNRS board on May 6, 1947, Peres proposed that a contract should be drawn up with the Logabax Company for the design and construction of a universal computing machine.

The sequel is well known in France: the machine was never finished. Meanwhile the mechanical computing section of the Institut Blaise Pascal performed calculations for scientists, using the classical methods of the interwar years. When the first commercially produced computers appeared, priorities began to change, the emphasis going to training in programming electronic computers. In 1957 a decision of the director of CNRS abolished the post occupied by Couffignal at the Institut Blaise Pascal; the man who in 1938 had been heralded as the one who would revolutionize the subject of automatic computation was removed from the field unnoticed.

Couffignal's unvarying aim was to reorganize, on rational scientific lines, the computing bureaus that were operating up to the start of World War II. He felt that one of the first uses of his machine should be to automate the accounting processes for postal checks. He always envisioned a computer center as a laboratory for constructing tables, nomograms, and charts to be used as aids for rapid approximate calculation, "useful calculations" in his definition. Conditioned by this outlook, he always believed that the real problem was interconnecting classical machines: he never understood that the speeds made possible by the new electronic machines changed the problem of automatic calculation completely.

Might this be attributed to a certain French insularity? It is difficult to answer that question. Certainly in Couffignal's case there were gaps in his mathematical awareness. In 1938, he published a note in *Comptes-Rendus* claiming that he had designed a machine for proving theorems in logic; the consequences of the famous Gödel Theorem (1931) seem never to have crossed his mind, and he made no reference to the "Turing Machine" of 1936. This contrasts strongly with his usual practice of claiming priority, that he had had the same idea earlier, without giving any details of his work.

The seriousness of the decision to entrust Couffignal with the task of building an electronic computer is shown by its consequences. As scientific activities expanded, the need for computers became ever more pressing; in the face of this rising demand the decision taken was to wait for Couffignal's machine, and when the failure of that project became evident those with the needs turned to commercial products, and especially to foreign manufacturers. Precious time for training and education in computer techniques had been lost.

A last point needs to be mentioned. The decision to build the machine seems to have been based more on Couffignal's reputation than on any rational evaluation of his project. Further, there was no regular monitoring of progress, which would have shown that it was running into the sands, and consequently the decision to halt it in time to minimize the damage was not taken. This problem of project evaluation is still with us. Whoever is entrusted with the decision must pronounce equally on the skills needed for carrying out the project. As we have noted, the necessary expertise in electronics was, effectively, available in France at this time; should not the first course have been to approach those who held this expertise? The point to make here is that the history of this project raises the question, "to what extent did its failure give rise to a kind of mutual distrust between research workers and engineers, between research and industrial laboratories?" No doubt those who lived through the events will have an answer to the question.[36]

BIBLIOGRAPHY

Biographical

Ramunni, Girolamo, "Louis Couffignal, 1902–1966: Informatics Pioneer in France," *Ann. Hist. Comp.*, Vol. 11, No. 4, 1989, pp. 247–256.

Significant Publications

Couffignal L., *Les machines à calculer. Leur principes, leur evolution*, Gauthier-Villars, Paris, 1933.

Couffignal, L., "Calculating Engines: Their Principles and Evolution," reprinted in Randell, Brian, *Origins of Digital Computers: Selected Papers*, Springer-Verlag, Berlin, 1982, pp. 145–154.

Couffignal, L., "Scheme of Assembly of a Machine Suitable for the Calculations of Celestial Mechanics," reprinted in Randell, Brian, *Origins of Digital Computers: Selected Papers*, Springer-Verlag, Berlin, 1982, pp. 121–126.

Couffignal, L., "Les grandes machines mathematiques. Introduction," *Annales des Telecommunications*, Vol. 2, 1947, pp. 376–387.

Couffignal, L., "La Machine de l'Institut Blaise Pascal," *Report Conf. High Speed Automatic Calculating Machines, 22–25 June 1949*, Univ. Math. Lab., Cambridge, UK, 1950, pp. 56–66.

Couffignal L., *Resolution numerique des systemes d'equations*, Paris, 1956.

---

[36]Extracted from Ramunni 1989.

PERRY O. CRAWFORD

Engineer who worked on Whirlwind and other early military computers.

In his oral interview with Christopher Evans, J. Presper Eckert mentions that he had considered building a memory device which was composed of a magnetic disk—"I had gotten the idea of using disks for memory, digital memory, from a master's thesis written by Perry Crawford at MIT. He had not built any such disks; it was just speculation."

BIBLIOGRAPHY

Biographical

Burks, Arthur W., and Alice R. Burks, "The ENIAC: First General Purpose Electronic Computer," *Ann. Hist. Comp.*, Vol. 3, No. 4, 1981, pp. 310–399.

Evans, Christopher, "J. Presper Eckert," Oral History of Computing, Science Museum, London and National Physical Laboratory, Teddington, No. 3, Audiotape, 1975.

SEYMOUR R. CRAY

Control Data Corporation (CDC) designer responsible for the CDC 6600, which was perhaps the first modern supercomputer, and subsequently leading designer of supercomputers for his own corporation.

Honors and Awards: IEEE Computer Society Pioneer Award, 1980; ACM/IEEE Eckert-Mauchly Award, 1989.

BIBLIOGRAPHY

Biographical

MacKenzie, Donald, "The Influence of the Los Alamos and Livermore National Laboratories on the Development of Computing," *Ann. Hist. Comp.*, Vol. 13, No. 2, 1991.

Slater, Robert, *Portraits in Silicon*, MIT Press, Cambridge, Mass., 1987.

Thorton, James E., "The CDC 6600 Project," *Ann. Hist. Comp.*, Vol. 2, No. 4, 1980, pp. 338–348.

KENT K. CURTIS

NSF director who got the foundation going in the field of computer science, who got researchers going and founded (and expanded) many university computing centers through innovative funding opportunities.

Curtis studied mathematics, physics, and music at Yale, Dartmouth, and Berkeley. He did scientific programming for the Lawrence Berkeley Laboratory of the University of California, where he was head of the Division of Mathematics and Computing from 1957 until 1967. He joined the National Science Foundation in 1967 and became head of the Computer Research Section of the Division of Mathematical and Computer Sciences at a time when the foundation was to be very influential in the development of university and college computing centers. He took leaves at the Atomic Energy Commission and the Courant Institute of Mathematical Sciences at New York University, and served as a consultant to the Department of Energy, other federal agencies, and the Swedish Technical Development Union. He was one of the founders and first president of VIM, the user's group for CDC-6600 computers.

BIBLIOGRAPHY

Significant Publications

Curtis, Kent K., et al., "John R. Pasta, 1918–1981: An Unusual Path Toward Computer Science," *Ann. Hist. Comp.*, Vol. 5, No. 3, July 1983.

JOHN H. CURTISS

Born December 23, 1909; died August 13, 1977, Port Angeles, Wash.; man of many talents; first and always a mathematician, but also a highly able administrator, musician, and tennis player; during the years 1946–1953 he was at the National Bureau of Standards (NBS) and played a vital role in the development, procurement, and widespread application of computers in the US.

Education: MS, statistics, Northwestern University, 1930; MS, statistics, University of Iowa, PhD, Harvard University, 1935.

Professional Experience: instructor, mathematics, Johns Hopkins University, 1935–1936; mathematics faculty, Cornell University, 1936–1943; Lt. Commander, Bureau of Ships, US Navy, 1943–1946; National Bureau of Standards: assistant to the director, E.U. Condon, 1946–1947; chief, National Applied Mathematics Laboratories (later the Applied Mathematics Division), 1947–1953; visiting lecturer, Harvard University, 1952; executive director, American Mathematical Society (AMS), 1954–1959; professor of mathematics, University of Miami, Coral Gables, 1959–1977.

John Curtiss was born on December 23, 1909, into an academic environment. His father, D.R. Curtiss (1878–1953), was professor of mathematics at Northwestern University, and president of the Mathematical Association of America in 1935–1936; he wrote a standard introduction to complex variable theory (1926), still in print. His uncle, Ralph H. Curtiss, was professor of astronomy at the University of Michigan.

After graduating with highest honors from Northwestern University in 1930, John Curtiss obtained an MS degree in statistics under H.L. Rietz at the University of Iowa, then one of the leading centers in the Midwest for mathematical training. Two of Curtiss' fellow graduate students there were S.S. Wilks and Deane Montgomery, who went on to distinguished mathematical careers at Princeton University and the Institute for Advanced Study, respectively.

John Curtiss then went to Harvard University, where he earned his PhD in 1935 under Professor J.L. Walsh. His first job after obtaining the doctorate was an instructorship in mathematics at Johns Hopkins University in 1935–1936. In 1936 he joined the mathematics faculty at Cornell University, where he taught until entering the US Navy in January 1943. He was stationed in Washington, D.C., with the quality control section of the Bureau of Ships until April 1946, when he was discharged with the rank of Lt. Commander.

He immediately joined the NBS as an assistant to the director, E. U. Condon, and was initially responsible for statistical matters. On July 1, 1947, he was appointed chief of a new division of the NBS initially called the National Applied Mathematics Laboratories; later the designation Applied Mathematics Division (AMD) was used. John Curtiss remained at the NBS until mid-1953, except for a semester as visiting lecturer at Harvard University in 1952. He spent a year at the Courant Institute of New York University, and was executive director of the American Mathematical Society (AMS) in Providence, R.I., from 1954 to 1959. In 1959 he became professor of mathematics at the University of Miami, Coral Gables, where he worked intensively on one of his first areas of interest: approximation theory in the complex domain. One by-product of this period was a graduate text on complex variable theory (1978). He died of heart failure at Port Angeles, Wash., on August 13, 1977, while en route to the AMS summer meeting in Seattle.

While no one can recall ever seeing John Curtiss at the console of a computer—he always said that "I was involved in the salt mines of computing"—his interest in numerical analysis was considerable. He wrote one paper on numerical algebra (1954b) and edited the proceeding of an important symposium (1956). Although the main body of his work on approximation theory is peripheral to practical computation, as a statistician he was deeply interested in "Monte Carlo" methods. One paper on this subject (1950), delivered at an IBM conference in 1949, was much acclaimed, and another (1954a) was translated into Russian. He gave courses on numerical algebra at NYU in 1953–1954 and on numerical analysis at the University of Miami. During his time in Providence he made a careful analysis of the book-sales policies of the AMS.

John Curtiss was quite sure that the nascent computing fraternity had to become a national society with publications of its own if it were to develop appropriately and be able to exert influence. Thus, he helped enthusiastically in the organization of the Eastern Association of Computing Machinery (ACM), which dropped the regional adjective from its title in 1948. He was the first president in 1947 and always encouraged his staff to participate in the work of this and other professional organizations. Of these, Franz L. Alt, Harry D. Huskey, and George E. Forsythe later became presidents of ACM and Thomas H. Southard was president of SIAM. Curtiss also saw that publications were supported, in particular *Mathematical Tables and Other Aids to Computation* and *The Pacific Journal of Mathematics*.

It is appropriate to point out here that John Curtiss' contributions to the development of modern numerical mathematics cannot be overestimated. He realized that any experienced pure mathematician could find attractive, challenging, and important problems in numerical mathematics, if the person chose to do so. From the death of Gauss in 1855 to 1947, the field of numerical mathematics was, with a few exceptions, cultivated by nonprofessional mathematicians whose real interests lay elsewhere. Accordingly Curtiss recruited professionals from far and near to take part in the programs he had envisaged. Indeed, nearly all of his recruits contributed significantly to his program.

John Curtiss once documented the remarkable success of the operation he planned by counting the papers presented at the 1952 International Congress of Mathematicians by various organizations. NBS was in the middle of the top seven; the others were the University of California at Berkeley, the University of Michigan, the University of Chicago, the Institute for Advanced Study, Harvard University, and the University of Pennsylvania—all organizations founded long before the Applied Mathematics Division of NBS.

For further details of the numerical mathematics programs at the NBS see Lowan (1949), Blanch and Rhodes (1974), and Todd (1975).

The Prospects

NBS was no stranger to computing equipment. It had been responsible for the Mathematical Tables Project of the Works Progress Administration in New York since 1938. This group was supported during World War II by the Applied Mathematics Panel of the Office of Scientific Research Development and from 1946 by the organization that later developed into the Office of Naval Research (ONR). Led by Arnold N. Lowan, the group included Milton Abramowitz (later chief of the Computation Laboratory), Ida Rhodes, Gertrude Blanch, Herbert E. Salzer, and Irene A. Stegun.

While John Curtiss was first concerned with statistical matters within NBS, he soon had a national responsibility. Several incidents led to this. In 1945, Eckert and Mauchly, who were largely responsible for the ENIAC, approached the Census Bureau (which, like NBS, was part of the US Department of Commerce) with the suggestion that a computer could facilitate its work—in the coming 1950 census, for example. This suggestion was discussed by the Science Committee of the Department of Commerce, which asked NBS for technical advice. The final agreement (April 1946) was that the Census Bureau would transfer funds to NBS, which would select a suitable computer and purchase it. The Army Ordnance Department also transferred funds to the electronics division of NBS for the development of computer components.

At this time Condon instructed Curtiss to survey the federal needs for computers and for a national computing center. This investigation had its source in ONR, and Rear Admiral H.G. Bown suggested that NBS and ONR should jointly establish such a center, to develop as well as use computers. Funds for this purpose were transferred in September 1946. In other countries, similar plans were being considered (see Todd 1975, p. 362).

Curtiss' investigation led to a broadening of the program. He realized very early, for example, that the mathematics needed to exploit the new computers had also to be developed, an opinion shared by Mina Rees of ONR (1977). The program he formulated was described in the prospectus issued in February 1947. The AMD was to have four sections:

1. Institute for Numerical Analysis (INA)—to be a field station at UCLA.

2. Computation Laboratory (CL).

3. Statistical Engineering Laboratory (SEL)

4. Machine Development Laboratory (MDL)

The last three were to be in Washington, D.C. The nucleus of the CL was to be the Lowan group. The program of the AMD was to be guided, within NBS operations, by the Applied Mathematics Executive Council, consisting of representatives of various federal agencies and some outside experts. Later the title of this group was changed to Applied Mathematics Advisory Council (AMAC). A total staff of about 100 was contemplated, and of that only about 30 were on the NBS payroll when the AMD was founded.

The AMD came into being on July 1, 1947. The prospectus had been a remarkable document insofar as there was little need to change its contents as time passed. Curtiss undertook a massive recruitment program to implement the aims of the AMD. He was highly qualified for this activity, with his outgoing personality and many academic contacts. Fortunately, too, the time was opportune for such an expansion, because many mathematicians were being demobilized from their World War II activities—a number of them fresh from some experience with applied mathematics.

The soundness of the original structure of AMD is clear from the fact that despite a succession of NBS directors and several reorganizations, the organization was essentially unchanged for 25 years, apart from the transfer of the MDL activities elsewhere.

Procurement Problems

By late 1946, once certain legal situations were resolved, NBS had funds available for two computers. The first was the Univac for the

Census Bureau, contracted for with the Eckert-Mauchly organization in 1946, and the second was the NBS computer (financed by ONR), contracted for with the Raytheon Company early in 1947.

The terms of these contracts were discussed by various committees, by advisers (notably, G. Stibitz), and by the AMAC. There were many complications, both administrative and technical. During these discussions the one Univac became three: one for the Air Comptroller and another for the Army Map Service were added.

It is appropriate to mention here the division of responsibilities between the Applied Mathematics Division and the Electronics Division of NBS. The AMD was responsible for the logic design of the computers and their suitability for the jobs envisaged, and for initial liaison with the contractors. The Electronics Division was responsible for the soundness of the design of components and for all engineering matters. Once the development was complete, the divisions were to share the liaison and documentation duties.

The chief of the MDL from 1946 was E.W. Cannon, who succeeded John Curtiss as chief of the AMD in 1953. Ida Rhodes, originally with the Mathematics Tables Project, was active in ensuring the suitability of proposed designs and later in educating the coders and programmers.

Early in 1948, as it became clear that none of these machines would be completed on schedule, two enormously significant events took place. The Air Comptroller, while awaiting the delivery of the Univac, realized that a small "interim" computer to be developed at NBS would provide useful experience. This led to SEAC, discussed below. The Air Materiel Command wanted two computers, one for Wright Field and one for INA, but no supplier could be found. Consequently, it accepted a proposal for a modest machine to be developed at INA by Harry D. Huskey. This led to SWAC.

To end this historical sketch, the Census Univac was completed early in 1951 and was dedicated on June 16, 1951. The Univac for the Air Comptroller was completed in February 1952, and the one for the Army Map Service was completed in April 1952. The Raytheon machine for NBS was never completed, but a related machine was delivered to the Naval Air Missile Test Center at Point Mugu, Calif., in 1952.

SEAC

The NBS Interim Computer, later called SEAC (Standards Eastern Automatic Computer), was constructed for the Air Comptroller by a group in the NBS Electronics Division (led by S.N. Alexander), beginning in the fall of 1948. The MDL collaborated in the design, and it was agreed that as soon as the computer became operational it would be moved to the CL. At that time John Todd was the chief of the CL, and they had a considerable group (led by Alan J. Hoffman) working for the Air Comptroller on linear programming, a subject just being developed by G.B. Dantzig and his associates.

In about 15 months SEAC became productive. On April 7, 1950, with help from R.J. Slutz, Todd ran his first program: solving the Diophantine equation $ax + by = 1$. Actually a and b were originally taken to be the largest pair of consecutive Fibonacci numbers that fitted into the machine (<244); this was chosen to give the slowest Euclidean algorithm. The day before, Franz Alt had run a factorization program using a small sieve.

SEAC was dedicated on June 20, 1950. Originally it had a 512-word delay-line memory, but 512 words of electrostatic memory were added. The original Teletype input/output was supplemented by magnetic wire.[37]

On a visit to Los Alamos in 1951, after Todd had described (perhaps too enthusiastically) the current state of CL operations, the laboratory authorities there decided that SEAC was just the thing they needed for their weapon-related computations. Accordingly they preempted SEAC, providing their own crew (for security reasons and to educate them in the use of computers). Even less time was then available for developmental work, and pleas to move the machine to the CL, where they now realized how odd minutes could be used effectively, were rejected on the grounds that the delicate equipment might not survive the trip. John Curtiss finally negotiated with the AEC for the construction of a cinderblock building abutting the SEAC building, and those in direct contact with the machine moved into the new structure. A few years later the machine was moved to the CL, where it operated until it was retired on April 23, 1964.

SWAC

Earlier, we noted the origin of the Air Materiel Command machine, later called SWAC (Standards Western Automatic Computer). This project began from scratch in January 1949, and the first Williams tube machine to be completed in the US was dedicated on April 7, 1950. Just as the British ACE was designed by a mathematician (A.M. Turing), the SWAC was designed by Harry D. Huskey, who was trained as a mathematician. It was built among and for mathematicians.

There was a rather long period of debugging but in due course all troubles were overcome and SWAC became a reliable machine with

---

[37]For more technical information, see NBS (1947, 1950, 1951, 1955), Greenwald et al. (1953), Shupe and Kirsch (1953), and Leiner et al. (1954).

many significant accomplishments. When the INA operation closed in 1954, SWAC was transferred to UCLA and remained in operation until 1967.

Conclusion

John Curtiss, with the full support of NBS director E.U. Condon, and with modest encouragement from various federal agencies, accelerated the progress of the US toward a preeminent position in the construction of computers and their exploitation for scientific computations. We have already mentioned the use of SEAC by the AEC; rocket and comet orbits were computed on commercial equipment at INA (Herrick 1973), and perhaps the first automatically computed earth-moon trajectory was done on SEAC (Froberg and Goldstein 1952).

Had Curtiss been able to stay at NBS and had support for INA been continued, there is no doubt that the mathematical development would have kept up with the enormous achievements of the engineers. Those who remained did what they could to carry on the work for which Curtiss laid solid foundations. Those who were with him at NBS enjoy getting together and recalling the exciting times of 1946 to 1953 and were grateful to have had the privilege of working with a fine American mathematician.

Postscript—Some Personal Reminiscences—John Todd

My own first contact with John Curtiss was a letter dated early in 1947, enclosing the prospectus and inviting me to consider joining INA. During World War II, I had been active in organizing an Admiralty Computing Service in Great Britain. Later, with my colleagues A. Erdelyi and D.H. Sadler, I suggested the formation of a National Mathematical Laboratory, later established as a division of the National Physical Laboratory. During that time my wife, Olga Taussky, and I had many contacts with American mathematicians stationed in or visiting Europe, especially H.P. Roberston, H.M. MacNeille, G. Baley Price, R. Courant, and J. von Neumann. They were aware of my activities, and I was in correspondence with members of the Applied Mathematics Panel. Some of these people probably suggested my name to John Curtiss. We arrived in New York on a troop ship late in September 1947. Our first contact with the computer world outside Washington was at the Aberdeen Meeting of ACM on December 11–12, 1947.

John Curtiss was a bachelor who enjoyed fast cars and plenty of good food and drink. In introducing us to Washington society he asked me to arrange a sherry party in his apartment. I provided sherries of varying quality and served them according to his evaluation of the guests, reserving the Bristol Cream for the director. For the benefit of many of the visitors to INA he compiled a list of restaurants labeled according to the civil service gradings P1 to P8.

He did not find the civil service regime too convenient, and much of his activity was spent maintaining contacts with other agencies, often after regular hours. He dictated a diary late at night; a transcription was circulated to his staff the next day so that we were aware of what commitments he had made.

He was not happy on planes and did not travel to Europe until 1976. A letter from him dated May 11, 1976, from the Mathematical Research Institute at Oberwolfach, is addressed to me as "The Savior of Oberwolfach." (A British naval officer, G.E.H. Reuter, and I were able in 1945 to prevent the dissolution of an institution that has since made great contributions to mathematics, including formal languages, complexity theory, many aspects of numerical analysis, and for instance computerized tomography.) He complained about staying in "magnificent old fire traps" and characterized one of the famous London clubs as "the awfullest fire trap of all, but interesting." He indicated two remembrances of England, the first "an infinite series of near-head-on collisions," and the second musical: "I recently got a record of Elgar's organ music at Colston Hall, Bristol, which we inspected amid chaotic preparation for a Salvation Army Choral concert. Then we heard the Sonata itself, included by coincidence in a noon recital in Hertford Chapel in Oxford (and played too slowly)."

My last meeting with John Curtiss was at the 1976 Los Alamos Research Conference on the History of Computing. He said then that he thought that historians, so far, had not fully appreciated the contribution of the National Bureau of Standards in the field. I hope this essay will begin to put things in balance.[38]

BIBLIOGRAPHY

Biographical

Blanch, Gertrude, and Ida Rhodes, "Table-Making at the National Bureau of Standards," *Studies in Numerical Analysis, Papers in Honor of Cornelius Lanczos*, B. K.P. Scaife, ed., Academic Press, New York, 1974, pp. 1–6.

Curtiss, D.R., "Analytic Functions of a Complex Variable." *Carus Mathematical Monographs*, No. 2, Math. Assoc. of America, 1926.

---

[38]Based on Todd, 1980.

Froberg, C.E., and A.A. Goldstein, "A collision path from the earth to the moon in the restricted problem of three bodies," *Kung. Fysiografisha Sallskapets i Lund Forhandlingar,* Vol. 22, No. 14, 1952.

Greenwald, S., R.C. Hunter, and S.N. Alexander, "SEAC," *Proc. IRE,* Vol. 41, 1953, pp. 1300–1313.

Herrick, S., "Rocket and Comet Orbits," *Applied Math Series #20,* Government Printing Office, Washington, D.C., 1953.

Huskey, H.D., "Characteristics of the Institute for Numerical Analysis Computer," *Mathematical Tables and Other Aids to Computation,* Vol. 4, No. 30, 1950, pp. 103–108.

Huskey, H.D., R. Thorensen, B.F. Ambrosio, and E.C. Yowell, "The SWAC-Design Features and Operating Experience," *Proc. IRE,* Vol. 41, No. 10, 1953, pp. 1294–1299.

Leiner, A.L., W.A. Notz, J.L. Smith, and A. Weinberger, "System Design of the SEAC and DYSEAC," *IRE Trans. Electronic Computers,* 1954, pp. 8–23.

Lowan, A.N., "The Computation Laboratory of the National Bureau of Standards," *Scripta Math,* Vol. 15, 1949, pp. 33–63.

NBS, Technical News Bulletin, Feb. 1947.

NBS, Technical News Bulletin, Sept. 1950.

NBS, Technical News Bulletin, May 1951.

NBS, "Computer Development (SEAC and DYSEAC) at the National Bureau of Standards," *NBS Circular 551,* Government Printing Office, Washington, D.C., 1955. (This volume contains reprints of several of the more hardware-oriented papers in this list of references.)

Rees, Mina S., "Mathematics and the Government: The Post-War Years as Augury of the Future," in D. Tarwater, ed., *The Bicentennial Tribute to American Mathematics 1776–1976,* Math. Assoc. of America, Washington, D.C., 1977, pp. 101–116.

Shupe, P.D., Jr., and R.A. Kirsch, "SEAC—Review of Three Years of Operation," *Proc. East. Joint Computer Conf.,* 1953, pp. 83–90.

Todd, John, "Numerical Analysis at the National Bureau of Standards," *SIAM Review,* Vol. 17, 1975, pp. 361–370.

Todd, John, "John Hamilton Curtiss, 1909–1977," *Ann. Hist. Comp.,* Vol. 2, No. 2, 1980, pp. 104–110.

Significant Publications

Administrative Papers

Curtiss, John H., "A Review of Government Requirements and Activities in the Field of Automatic Digital Computing Machinery," in C.C. Chambers, ed..

Theory and Techniques for Design of Electronic Digital Computers, lectures delivered July 8 to August 31, 1946, Moore School of Electrical Engineering, Univ. of Pennsylvania, Philadelphia, 1948, pp. 29.1–29.32.

Curtiss, John H., "The National Applied Mathematics Laboratories—A Prospectus," Feb. 1947, 46 pp.

Curtiss, John H., "A Federal Program in Applied Mathematics," *Science,* Vol. 107, 1948, pp. 257–262.

Curtiss, John H., "Some Recent Trends in Applied Mathematics," *Amer. Scientist,* Vol. 37, 1949, pp. 1–5.

Curtiss, John H., "The Program of a Large Computation Center," unpublished address, ACM, Washington, D.C., Sept. 9, 1950.

Curtiss, John H., "The Institute for Numerical Analysis of the NBS," *Monthly Research Report, Office of Naval Research,* May 1951, pp. 8–17; another version of this appeared in *Amer. Math. Monthly,* Vol. 58, 1951, pp. 372–379.

Curtiss, John H., "The National Applied Mathematics Laboratories of the NBS," unpublished progress report covering the first five years of its existence, Apr. 1, 1953.

Books
Curtiss, John H., *Introduction to Functions of a Complex Variable,* Dekker, New York, 1978.

Curtiss, John H., *Numerical Analysis,* Proc. Symp. Applied Math Vol. 6, McGraw-Hill, New York, 1956.

Technical Papers
Curtiss, John H., "Interpolation in Regularly Distributed Points," *Trans. Amer. Math. Soc.,* Vol. 38, 1935, pp. 458–473.

Curtiss, John H., "A Note on the Degree of Polynomial Approximation," *Bull. Amer. Math. Soc..* Vol. 43, 1936, pp. 703–708.

Curtiss, John H., "On Extending the Definition of a Harmonic Function," *Amer. Math. Monthly,* Vol. 47, 1940, pp. 225–228.

Curtiss, John H., "Generating Functions in the Theory of Interpolation in the Complex Domain," *Ann. of Math.,* Ser. 2, No. 42, 1941, pp. 634–646.

Curtiss, John H., "Sampling Methods Applied to Differential and Difference Equations," *Proc. Seminar on Scientific Computation,* Nov. 1949, IBM, New York, 1950, pp. 87–109.

Curtiss, John H., "Monte Carlo—Methods for the Iteration of Linear Operators," *J. Math. Physics,* Vol. 32, 1954a, pp. 209–232. [Russian translation in: Uspephi Mat Nauk (N.S.) 12, 5(77) (1957), 149–174.]

Curtiss, John H., "A Generalization of the Method of Conjugate Gradients for Solving Systems of Linear Algebraic Equations," *Mathematical Tables and Other Aids to Computation*, Vol. 8, 1954, pp. 189–193.

Curtiss, John H., "Interpolation with Harmonic and Complex Polynomials to Boundary Values," *J. Math. Mech.*, Vol. 9, 1960, pp. 167–192.

Curtiss, John H., "Solution of the Dirichlet Problem by Interpolating Harmonic Polynomials," *Bull. Amer. Math. Soc.*, Vol. 68, 1962, pp. 333–337.

Curtiss, John H., "Solutions of the Dirichlet Problem in the Plane by Approximation with Faber Polynomials," *SIAM J. Numer.*, Anal. 3, 1966, pp. 204–228.

Curtiss, John H., "Transfinite Diameter and Harmonic Polynomial Interpolation," *J. Analyse Math.*, Vol. 22, 1969, pp. 371–389.

Curtiss, John H., "Faber Polynomials and the Faber Series," *Amer. Math. Monthly*, Vol. 78, 1971, pp. 577–596.

Curtiss, John H., "Over Determined Harmonic Polynomial Interpolation," *J. Approx. Theory*, Vol. 5, 1972, pp. 149–175.

OLE-JOHAN DAHL

Born October 12, 1931, Mandal, Norway; with Kristen Nygaard, developer of the SIMULA programming language, which introduced classes and inheritance into the field of programming languages.

Education: MS, numerical mathematics, University of Oslo, 1957.

Professional Experience: Norwegian Defense Research Establishment (NDRE), 1952–1963; Norwegian Computing Center, 1963–1968; professor, computer science, University of Oslo, 1968–present.

Dahl worked with the Norwegian Defense Research Establishment (NDRE) from 1952 to 1963 in computing and programming under Jan V. Garwick. From 1956 onwards his main activity was software development. His master's thesis ("Numerical Mathematics," 1957, University of Oslo) addressed the representation and manipulation of multidimensional arrays on a two-level store computer. His main contribution at the NDRE was a high-level programming language, MAC, used locally during the 1960s (first specification was dated 1957; the implemented version was modified as a result of the Algol effort). In 1963 he joined the Norwegian Computing Center for full-time work on SIMULA, and in 1968 he became a professor of computer science, then a new discipline at the University of Oslo. His main research during recent years has been in the areas of program architecture, specification tools, and verification techniques.

From 1964 to 1976 he was the Norwegian delegate to IFIP Technical Committee 2 (Programming Languages), and from 1970 to 1977 he was a working member of IFIP Working Group 2.2 (Language Definition). He has been a member of IFIP Working Group 2.3 (Programming Methodology) since its founding in Oslo in 1969.[1]

---

[1]Adapted from the biography in Wexelblat, Richard L., ed., *History of Programming Languages,* Academic Press, New York, 1981, Chapter 9.

BIBLIOGRAPHY

Biographical

Nygaard, Kristen, and Ole-Johan Dahl, "The Development of the SIMULA Languages," in Wexelblat, Richard L., ed., *History of Programming Languages*, Academic Press, New York, 1981.

Significant Publications

Dahl, O.-J., and K. Nygaard, "SIMULA—An Algol Based Simulation Language," *Comm. ACM*, Vol. 9, No. 9, Sept. 1966, pp. 671–682.

Dahl, O.-J., and K. Nygaard, "Classes and Subclasses," in Buxton, J., ed., *Simulation Programming Languages*, North-Holland, Amsterdam, 1967.

Dahl, O.-J., and C.A.R. Hoare, "Hierarchical Program Structures," in Dahl, O.-J., E. Dijkstra, and C.A.R. Hoare, *Structured Programming*, Academic Press, New York, 1972.

Dahl, O.J., *Verifiable Programming*, Prentice-Hall, Englewood Cliffs, N.J., 1992.

GEORGE BERNARD DANTZIG

Born November 8, 1914, Portland, Ore.; inventor of the Simplex method of linear programming.

Education: AB, University of Maryland, 1936; MA, University of Michigan, 1937; PhD, mathematics, University of California, Berkeley, 1946.

Professional Experience: junior statistician, US Bureau of Labor Statistics, 1937–1939; statistician, US Air Force, 1941–1945; chief mathematician, US Air Force Hq. Comptroller, 1945–1952; research mathematician, Rand Corp., 1952–1960; professor of engineering science and chairman, Operations Research Center, University of California, Berkeley, 1960–1966; professor of operations research and computer science, Stanford University, 1966–present.

Honors and Awards: DSc (Hon.): Israel Institute of Technology, 1973; University Linkoping, Sweden, 1975; University of Maryland, 1976; Yale University, 1978; Exceptional Meritorious Service Medal, War Dept., 1944; National Medal of Science, 1975; Von Neumann Theory Prize, Operations

Research Society and Materials Science Society, 1975; Applied Mathematics and Numerical Analysis Prize, National Academy of Science, 1976; member, National Academy of Science; fellow, American Academy of Arts and Science; fellow, Operations Research Society; fellow, Institute for Management Science (president, 1966).

QUOTATION

"For a short period of time Dantzig almost deliberately tried to avoid discovering the simplex method that made him famous. But logic triumphed over doubt. In a few months of brilliant, concentrated effort in the latter half of 1947, Dantzig conceived the inclusive framework into which the scattered pieces fitted and added a critical missing piece, the simplex method of solution. With that, linear programming was born." (Dorfman 1984)

BIBLIOGRAPHY

Biographical

Dantzig, George B., "Reminiscences About the Origin of Linear Programming," in Schlissel, Arthur, ed., *Essays in the History of Mathematics, Memoirs of the American Math. Soc.,* No. 298, AMS, Providence, R.I., 1984, pp. 1–11.

Dantzig, George B., "Origins of the Simplex Method," in Nash, Stephen G., ed., *A History of Scientific Computing,* ACM Press History Series, 1990, pp. 141–151.

Dorfman, Robert, "The Discovery of Linear Programming," *Ann. Hist. Comp.,* Vol. 6, No. 3, 1984.

Orchard-Hays, William, "History of Mathematical Programming Systems," *Ann. Hist. Comp.,* Vol. 6, No. 3, 1984.

Charles H. Davidson

Early user's group leader who created one of the earliest "load-and-go" compilers for Fortran.

Davidson did his undergraduate work at the American University in Washington, D.C., and received both his MS and his PhD from the University of Wisconsin-Madison, all in physics. His thesis in 1952 involved the design and programming of a digital computer being built in the Department of Electrical Engineering there. In 1961 he organized the Engineering Computing Laboratory in the College of Engineering, and served as its director until 1981. Davidson played an active role in the early days of the 1620 Users Group, serving as chairman of the Midwest Region, and as the representative of its successor organization, Common, to the ASA Fortran standardization committees. In 1961 he supervised the design and development of FORGO, the first load-and-go Fortran compiler. He has participated in many activities within ACM, including serving two terms on the council, and as chairman of SIGCAS for four years. He recently retired as professor of electrical and computer engineering, professor of computer sciences, and assistant to the director of the Madison Academic Computing Center for Instructional Computing.

BIBLIOGRAPHY

Biographical

Davidson, Charles, "The Emergence of Load-and-Go Systems for Fortran," *Ann. Hist. Comp.,* Vol. 6, No. 1, Jan. 1984, pp. 19–20.

Donald W. Davies

Born June 7, 1924, Treorchy, Wales; worked on the Pilot ACE, one of the first operational stored-program computers, and later was responsible for the concept of packets in network communication.

Education: BS (Honors), physics, Imperial College, London University, 1943; BS (Honors), mathematics, Imperial College, London University, 1946.

Professional Experience: National Physical Laboratory, 1947–1984; private consultant, 1984–present.

Honors and Awards: John Player Award, British Computer Society, 1974; distinguished fellow, British Computer Society, 1975; John von Neumann Award, John von Neumann Society, Budapest, 1983; DSc (Hon.), Salford University, 1983; Commander of the British Empire (CBE), 1983; fellow, Royal Society, 1987.

Donald Davies graduated in physics with first-class honors from Imperial College, University of London, 1943, at the age of 19. Thereafter his wartime work was mainly related to the application of numerical mathematics to fluid flow and diffusion problems on an industrial scale. In 1947 he graduated from Imperial College with a second first-class honors degree in mathematics.

After his second graduation he joined the team of scientists at the National Physical Laboratory, which built the ACE Pilot Model, then the fastest of the three pioneer digital computers in the UK. He designed the input/output equipment, and the arithmetic and logic units. He used the computer, among other applications, to simulate road traffic control and to optimize the settings of controllers, and to simulate warning and escape systems in coal mines.

From 1955 to 1965 he was a project leader for a number of research projects at NPL. He played a leading role in the design of the full-scale ACE computer. His projects included such diverse topics as machine translation from Russian into English, and the development of the Cryotron, an early superconducting logic and storage device. His interest and involvement with the commercial application of computers began during this period when he led a group investigating the choice of magnetic characters for checks for the London Clearing Banks.

Davies was the first project leader of the Advanced Computer Technology Project for the UK Ministry of Technology—a precursor of the 1980s Alvey Project. Among its successes were the ICL Distributed Array Processor (DAP) and the Context Addressable File Store (CAFS).

In 1965 Davies pioneered new concepts for computer communications in a form to which he gave the name "packet switching." He introduced this concept to the UK Post Office (at that time the equivalent of a PTT) in 1966, and to the CCITT and the US Advanced Research Projects Agency (ARPA) in 1967. The design of the ARPA network (ArpaNet) was entirely changed to adopt this technique.

In 1966 Davies became head of the computer science division of NPL. He initiated research in data communications at NPL including the building of a packet switched local network (completed in 1971), and simulation studies of flow control, congestion, and routing in networks. He wrote and lectured widely to promote the concept of a data communication system with well-defined interfaces and protocols. At CCITT, on behalf of the UK Post Office, he helped to formulate some of the X recommendations for data communication services.

Other research of the computer science division at this time was in pattern and speech recognition, CAD in architecture, human factors, and office systems that used the local network.

In 1978 he was given an "individual merit" post as deputy chief scientific officer, allowing him to lead a research group without the management tasks of a division. He chose as his specialty the security of data in networks. The group developed the application of cryptographic methods to the practical needs of network security, especially the use of asymmetric (public key) cryptography. Consulting work under contract to financial institutions and others provided the practical experience.

Since leaving NPL in 1984, Davies has provided consultancy to financial institutions on high value payment systems (SWIFT and CHAPS), ATMs, and EFT/POS. He has advised suppliers and users of secure systems of many kinds, including mobile telephone and direct broadcast satellites.

BIBLIOGRAPHY

Biographical

Campbell-Kelly, Martin, "Data Communications at the National Physical Laboratory (1965–1975)," *Ann. Hist. Comp.,* Vol. 9, No. 3/4, 1988, pp. 221–248.

Significant Publications

Davies, D.W., "A Theory of Chess and Noughts and Crosses,"[2] *Penguin Science News,* Vol. 16, 1950, pp. 40–64.

[2]Known in the US as "Tic Tac Toe."

Davies, D.W., "Sorting Data on an Electronic Computer," *Proc. Inst. Elect. Eng.,* Vol. 103, No. 1, 1956, pp. 87–93.

Davies, D.W., "Switching Functions of Three Variables," *Trans. Inst. Radio Eng.,* Vol. 6, No. 4, 1957, pp. 265–275.

Davies, D.W., "A Communication Network for Computers and Their Remote Peripheral Devices," *Proc. Post Office/Industry Joint Symp. on Pulse Code Modulation Transmission and Switching Systems,* Brighton, UK, 1967.

Davies, D.W., and D.L.A. Barber, *Communication Networks for Computers,* John Wiley, London, 1973.

Davies, D.W., K.A. Bartlett, R.A. Scantlebury, and P.T. Wilkinson, "A Digital Communication Network for Computers Giving Rapid Response at Remote Terminals," *Proc. ACM Symp. Operating System Principles,* ACM, New York, 1967.

Davies, D.W., and W.L. Price, *Security for Computer Networks,* John Wiley, Chichester, UK, 1984.

ROBERT H. DENNARD

Born 1932, Terrell, Texas; National Medal of Technology winner for IBM invention of the basic, one-transistor dynamic memory cell used in virtually all modern computers.

Education: BS, electrical engineering, Southern Methodist University, 1954; MS, electrical engineering, Southern Methodist University, 1956; PhD, Carnegie Institute of Technology, 1958.

Professional Experience: IBM: Research Division, 1958–present; Thomas J. Watson Research Center, Yorktown Heights, 1963–present.

Honors and Awards: member, National Academy of Engineering, 1984; IBM fellow, 1979; fellow, IEEE, 1980; National Medal of Technology, 1988; IEEE Cledo Brunetti Award, 1982; Industrial Research Institute Achievement Award, 1989; Harvey Prize, Technion, Haifa, Israel, 1990; DSc (Hon.), State University of New York, Farmingdale, 1990; six IBM Outstanding Invention and Outstanding Contribution Awards; two IBM Corporate Awards.

Robert Dennard joined the IBM Research Division in 1958, where his early work included the study of new devices and circuits for logic and memory applications, and the development of advanced data communication techniques. Since 1963 he has been at the IBM Thomas J. Watson Research Center, Yorktown Heights, New York, where he has been involved in research and development of microelectronics from its inception.

Starting in the mid-1960s, he was a leader in the development of IBM's N-channel MOSFET[3] devices and technology. This work led to the first IBM MOSFET memory products in the early 1970s, and a number of his circuit and device innovations were in the products. In 1967, he invented the one-transistor DRAM memory cell and obtained a basic patent for IBM. In the early 1970s, he led a group working on scaling MOSFET devices to smaller dimensions, and in 1974 published, with his colleagues, the historic paper on MOSFET device scaling theory. In the 1970s he also worked on yield models for integrated circuits, which led to development of the theoretical base for word and bit line redundancy in DRAMs. In recognition of his contributions, he was appointed an IBM fellow in 1979. Through the 1980s to the present, he has continued to be a leader in the IBM efforts to miniaturize devices and integrated circuits. This work has culminated in the demonstration of sub-0.1-micron MOS devices. He has also been a leader in setting directions for IBM technology research and development.

Dr. Dennard has received six IBM Outstanding Invention and Outstanding Contribution Awards, and two IBM Corporate Awards. The invention and contribution awards were for:

1. MOSFET device design,
2. the MOSFET technology and device design manual used throughout the company in the early days of MOSFET development,
3. the one-transistor DRAM memory cell,
4. word and bit line redundancy,
5. MOSFET scaling theory, and
6. 1-micron latch-up-free CMOS technology development.

The corporate awards were for the 1-transistor memory cell and for the MOSFET scaling theory.

---

[3]MOSFET—metal-oxide-semiconductor field effect transistor.

PETER J. DENNING

Born January 6, 1942, New York City; computer scientist whose work on virtual memory systems helped make virtual memory a permanent part of modern operating systems.

Education: BEE, Manhattan College, 1964; SM, electrical engineering, MIT, 1965; PhD, electrical engineering, MIT, 1968.

Professional Experience: assistant professor, electrical engineering, Princeton University 1968–1972; Purdue University: associate professor, 1972–1975; professor of computer sciences, 1975–1984, head, Computer Sciences Department, 1979–1983; Research Institute for Advanced Computer Science (RIACS), NASA Ames Research Center, Mountain View, Calif.: founding director, 1983–1990, research fellow, 1990–1991; associate dean for computing and chair of the Computer Science Department, School of Information Technology and Engineering, George Mason University, 1991–present.

Honors and Awards: teaching award, Princeton University, 1971; ACM Service Award, 1974; two best paper awards: "The Working Set Model for Program Behavior," *Comm. ACM,* May 1968; and "Operating Systems Principles and Undergraduate Computer Science Curricula," *Proc. Spring Joint Computer Conference,* 1972; fellow, IEEE, 1981, for "contributions to the understanding of virtual memory systems and the development of the working set concept"; fellow, American Association for the Advancement of Science, 1984, "for outstanding contributions to computer systems development and computer security, and for service to the profession and to his professional society"; doctor of law, Concordia University, 1984; doctor of science, Manhattan College, 1985; ACM Distinguished Service Award, 1989; Centennial Engineering Award, Manhattan College, 1992.

Peter J. Denning is associate dean for computing and chair of the Computer Science Department in the School of Information Technology and Engineering at George Mason University. He took up this appointment in August 1991.

Denning was the founding director of the Research Institute for Advanced Computer Science (RIACS) at the NASA Ames Research Center in Mountain View, Calif. He served in that capacity from 1983 to 1990, when he stepped down and became research fellow until August 1991.

Before accepting the RIACS assignment, Denning was head of the Computer Sciences Department at Purdue University, where he was a professor of computer sciences (1975–1984) and an associate professor (1972–1975). He was an assistant professor of electrical engineering at Princeton University (1968–1972). Denning was one of the four cofounders of the CSNET, which began with NSF support and evolved into the first fully self-supporting community network; CSNET is a predecessor of the NSFNET and the NREN. He has worked closely with

NASA on computational science and on the high-performance computing and communications program.

Denning's primary research interests are computer systems architecture, parallel computation, operating systems, performance modeling, and organizational informatics. He has published over 230 papers and articles since 1967. His work on virtual memory systems helped make virtual memory a permanent part of modern operating systems. His book with E.G. Coffman, Jr., *Operating Systems Theory*, was published by Prentice-Hall in 1973 and is still widely used today. His book with Jack Dennis and Joseph Qualitz, *Machines, Languages, and Computation*, was published by Prentice-Hall in 1978. His edited collection, *Computers Under Attack: Intruders, Worms, and Viruses*, published by Addison-Wesley in fall 1990, is a best-seller.

Denning was the president of the Association for Computing Machinery (1980–1982). He has participated actively in the ACM since 1968, where he has served as chairman of the Special Interest Group on Operating Systems (SIGOPS) (1969), chairman of the Board on Special Interest Groups (1970–1974), member-at-large of Council (1974–1978), and vice president (1978–1980). In June 1984 he retired from Council after 14 years of service. He served as chairman of the Task Force on the Core of Computer Science (1986–1988), as chair of the ACM Editorial Committee, and member of the Publications Board (1986–1992). He was elected chair of the Publications Board in 1992.

Denning served as editor-in-chief of the *Communications of the ACM* (1983–1992), which under his guidance has become the leading technical magazine in computing. During this period, he radically altered the character of the journal from a research publication to an up-to-date communication for practitioners. He continues as a contributing editor of the *Communications*. He is an associate editor of *Acta Informatica*. He was consulting editor for computer science for the MIT Press, editor-in-chief of ACM's *Computing Surveys*, and editor of the Elsevier/North-Holland Series on Operating and Programming Systems. He was writer of the column, "The Science of Computing," in each issue of *American Scientist* from January 1985 through October 1993.

BIBLIOGRAPHY

Significant Publications

Denning, Peter J., "The Working Set Model for Program Behavior," *Comm. ACM*, Vol. 11, No. 5, May 1968, pp. 323–333.

Denning, Peter J., "Operating Systems Principles and Undergraduate Computer Science Curricula," *Proc. Spring Joint Computer Conference*, Vol. 40, 1972, pp. 849–855.

Denning, Peter J., and E.G. Coffman, Jr., *Operating Systems Theory*, Prentice-Hall, Englewood Cliffs, N.J., 1973.

Denning, Peter J., Jack Dennis, and Joseph Qualitz, *Machines, Languages, and Computation*, Prentice-Hall, Englewood Cliffs, N.J., 1978.

Denning, Peter J., *Computers Under Attack: Intruders, Worms, and Viruses*, Addison-Wesley, Reading, Mass., 1990.

JOHN H. DESSAUER

Born May 13, 1905, Aschaffenburg, Germany; died August 12, 1993, Rochester, N.Y.; directed research and engineering at Xerox Corporation for 33 years, having been the major influence in persuading the tiny Haloid Company to acquire Chester Carlson's electrostatic photographic reproduction process and develop it into the technology which was the basis of xerography and the Xerox success.

Education: BS, Institute of Technology, Munich; MS, Institute of Technology, Aachen; PhD, Institute of Technology, Aachen.

Professional Experience: Agfa Ansco, Binghamton, N.Y., 1929–1935; director of research, director of research and engineering, director of research and advanced engineering, executive vice president, member and vice chairman of the board of directors, Xerox Corp.,[4] 1935–1970; retired, 1970.

Dessauer was born in Aschaffenburg, Germany, on May 13, 1905. He first studied liberal arts at the Albertus Magnus University in Freiburg and then chemical engineering at the Institute of Technology in Munich, where he obtained the equivalent of a bachelor of science degree. He received his master's and doctoral degrees in engineering sciences at the Institute of Technology in Aachen, both magna cum laude. He emigrated to the US in 1929, and first joined the research department, and later the photographic paper manufacturing depart-

---

[4]Rectigraph Co., Rochester, N.Y., acquired by Haloid Co., which became Xerox.

ment, of Agfa Ansco in Binghamton, N.Y. In 1935 Dessauer joined the Rectigraph Company in Rochester, which shortly afterwards was acquired by the Haloid Company, a small manufacturer of copying cameras and silver-halide photographic papers. It was one of several firms that in the World War II era offered wet-process machines and material to make photocopies of documents. Dessauer established Haloid's research department.

Early in 1945 Dessauer, looking for new product opportunities, came upon an article from the July 1944 issue of *Radio News* which described Chester F. Carlson's electrophotography process. He later recalled, "It was as if lightning struck when I read that article. What came to mind first was that it could be used for reproducing documents and letters." After some preliminary investigation, Dessauer and the new young vice president of Haloid, Joseph C. Wilson, visited the Battelle Memorial Institute in Ohio where Carlson gave a manual and very messy demonstration of his novel copying process. The two Haloid executives were impressed, saw the problems and the possibilities, and as of January 1, 1947, took a limited license. It was an offer that had been turned down by dozens of others, including GE, RCA, IBM, and Remington-Rand, which later became major computer companies.

Carlson's copier concept was embryonic and far from commercial viability. It took Dessauer's fervent conviction of its potential value, which he demonstrated in enthusiastic leadership, to resolutely and persistently attack the thousands of problems in the poorly understood technologies of photoconductivity and electrostatics that had to be overcome.

A corporate obituary had this to say of him [Bickmore et al. 1993]:

> The uncertainties of pioneering the unproven technology required great faith, perseverance, and courage. "JD," as he was affectionately known to the technical community, embodied all of those qualities in abundance.
>
> He skillfully assembled and managed a team of young, creative engineers and scientists, and guided the multi-functional efforts needed to solve problems ranging from solid state physics, to optics, to the chemistry of polymers and pigments, and to mechanical design. He instilled a spirit of teamwork in R&D groups by recognizing the individual skills within the groups, thus avoiding intra-team rivalries. Dessauer's conduct at staff meetings was formal and somewhat authoritarian in approach; yet he showed a ready smile and a personal warmth that inspired trust.
>
> Dr. Dessauer also maintained effective interactions with the business staff. He viewed himself as a "transducer" between the technical

and business communities, and, as he wryly noted, at times this required him to act as a "filter." On the one hand, he shielded the technical staff from unrealistic business pressures; on the other hand, he reassured the business staff that seemingly insurmountable technical problems could be solved. His overall appreciation of both technical and business issues allowed him to plan and direct the R&D work in a manner consistent with business realities—the needs of customers were foremost objectives in all technical activities.

In 1949 Haloid made its first abortive attempt to market a product based on xerography, a Haloid-invented name. The Xerox (with a capital "X") Model A Copier (also called the "Ox Box"), was really three machines with one operator who had to execute 39 manual steps in three minutes and transfer a flat, dirty, heavy metal plate from each machine to the next for every single copy to be made. It worked, but nobody wanted to lease it.

This market failure shook even Dessauer's confidence, but although the Model A failed as an office copier, a redesigned version found success producing paper master plates for high volume offset duplicating. This fortuitous application supplied cash for further development. The Model A also showed that a successful office copier had to be child-simple in use.

In 1955 the Xerox Copyflow was tried out on the public. It was semiautomatic and made continuous copies on ordinary paper. It lacked the necessary simplicity. It was not what was needed.

Finally, in 1959, almost 14 years and $75 million after Dessauer first looked at Carlson's process, Haloid Xerox Inc., as it had now become, offered the revolutionary 914 copier, so named because it could copy sheets as large as 9 by 14 inches) This, the first automatic plain-paper office copier, swept all other copiers from the market, including Mimeograph, Photostat, ThermoFax, and Verifax. The 914 and its many successors, copies, and clones, foreign and domestic, became as indispensable as the telephone and changed office life and office practices forever. "Xerox" became a household term and, in spite of the corporation's protests, is now a lowercase addition to the languages of the world as a generic noun and verb.

In that same year Dessauer became executive vice president. In this role he directed an explosive expansion in R&D personnel and facilities. He gave thought to the nurturing and management of creative scientists. Appreciating that peer recognition could be a powerful motivator, he made sure that key contributors had opportunities to present their findings at technical seminars. He was also willing to let creative scientists fail occasionally, for in his view, the only unacceptable behavior was *inaction*. Recognizing that creative people may not be managers, he instituted a "dual ladder" promotion policy to reward valuable technical and scientific employees without requiring that they become administrators.

He, as well as Wilson, always felt deeply about the social responsibilities of corporations, and turned this concern into social awareness supported by action that became a mark of identity for Xerox.

Dessauer continued as executive vice president of Xerox until 1968, when he relinquished the office to an executive from outside Xerox. His replacement, Jack Goldman of Ford, was said to have been surprised to find that the concentration of Xerox's management and research and development, under Dessauer's direction, had been so narrowly focused on xerography that they had very little understanding of the world of digital technology [Bickmore et al. 1993] except, perhaps, that involved in digital imaging.

A member of the board of directors from 1946, Dessauer was vice chairman of the board and executive vice president in charge of the Research and Advanced Engineering Division from 1966 to 1970, when he retired. He participated in the corporate decision process that led to the 1969 purchase of "$900 million in stock of the computer vendor" Scientific Data Systems (SDS), and in the next year to the creation of the Xerox Palo Alto Research Center (PARC). The purchase of SDS is now seen as the first of several ill-advised and abortive efforts by Xerox to buy its way into computing, while PARC, which pioneered in digital imaging, is now recognized as having essentially invented the personal computer, "windows," Ethernet, and the laser printer, all of which were largely ignored by Xerox but accepted and exploited with great success by its competitors.

After retirement, Dessauer set up an office near his home in Pittsford, N.Y., from which he gave financial assistance to charities. He was a trustee, board member, and adviser to several charitable and educational institutions. He was a fellow of the New York Academy of Sciences and of the American Institute of Chemists, a member of the National Academy of Engineering, and in the last year of his life, was made an honorary member of the Society for Imaging Science and Technology. Dessauer held eleven patents. He coedited *Xerography and Related Processes*, published in 1965, the first technical textbook about the subject. In 1971 Doubleday published his now out-of-print autobiography, *My Years with Xerox: The Billions Nobody Wanted.*[5]

---

[5]By Eric Weiss.

QUOTATIONS

At the time of Dessauer's death, as part of a brief press release, Paul A. Allaire, Xerox chairman and chief executive officer, eulogized, "No history of the commercial development of the xerographic process or Xerox Corporation would be complete without early and prominent tribute to the many contributions made by John Dessauer. All of us at Xerox owe a great deal to him for our jobs, our company, and our industry. The world is a different place because of the part he played in making the office copier a vital element in propelling all of us into the information age."

BIBLIOGRAPHY

Biographical

Bickmore, John, Robert Gundlach, and Eric Pell, "In Memoriam: John H. Dessauer, 1905–1993," Xerox Corporation, 1993.

Smith, D.K., and R.C. Alexander, *Fumbling the Future, How Xerox Invented, Then Ignored, the First Personal Computer,* William Morrow & Co., New York, 1988.

Significant Publications

Dessauer, John H., *Xerography and Related Processes,* 1965.

Dessauer, John H., *My Years with Xerox: The Billions Nobody Wanted,* Doubleday, New York, 1971.

Edsger W. Dijkstra

Born 1930, Rotterdam, The Netherlands; leading critic of programming without a mathematical proof of correctness and condemner of the infamous GOTO; recipient of the 1972 ACM Turing Award.

Education: MS, mathematics and theoretical physics, University of Leiden, 1956; PhD, computing science, Municipal University of Amsterdam, 1959.

Professional Experience: professional programmer, Mathematisch Centrum, 1952–1962; professor of mathematics, Eindhoven University of Technology, 1962–1984; research fellow, Burroughs Corp., 1973–1984; Schlumberger Centennial chair, computer sciences, University of Texas at Austin, 1984–present.

Honors and Awards: fellow, Netherlands Royal Academy of Sciences; distinguished fellow, British Computer Society, 1972; ACM Turing Award, 1972; IEEE Computer Society Pioneer Award, 1980.

Dijkstra, recipient of the 1972 ACM Turing Award, is known for early graph-theoretical algorithms, the first implementation of Algol 60, and the first operating system composed of explicitly synchronized sequential processes. He is also credited with the invention of guarded commands and of predicate transformers as a means for defining semantics, and programming methodology in the broadest sense of the term. In recent years he has been deeply involved in the applications of mathematical proof techniques to programming and the development of programs from mathematical axioms.

At the 1972 ACM Turing Award ceremony M. Doug McIlroy read the following citation:

> The working vocabulary of programmers everywhere is studded with words originated or forcefully promulgated by E.W. Dijkstra: "display," "deadly embrace," "semaphore," "go-to-less programming," "structured programming." But his imprint on programming is more pervasive than any catalog of jargon can indicate. The precious gift that this Turing Award acknowledges is nothing less than Dijkstra's *style*—his approach to programming as a high intellectual challenge; his eloquent insistence and practical demonstration that programs should be composed correctly, not just debugged into correctness; and his illuminating perception of problems at the foundations of program design. He has published about a dozen papers, both technical and reflective, among which are especially to be noted his philosophical addresses at IFIP (1962, 1965a), his already classic papers on cooperating sequential processes (1965b, 1968a), and his memorable indictment of the *go to* statement (1968b). An influential series of underground letters by Dijkstra have recently been published in monograph on the art of composing programs (1971).
>
> We have come to value good programs in much the same way as good literature. And right at the center of this literary movement, creating, and reflecting patterns no less beautiful than useful, stands E.W. Dijkstra.

His interests focus on the formal derivation of programs and the streamlining of the mathematical argument. His publications represent only a minor fraction of his writings—he writes, in fact, so much that he cannot afford the use of time-saving devices such as word processors. He owns, however, several fountain pens, three of which are Mont Blancs, for which he mixes his own ink. His writings, which include technical papers, trip reports, and essays on various topics, are distributed in an informal distribution tree to many colleagues. The latest is "numbered" EWD1070, which is an indication of how prolific he has been.

In 1964 at a WG 2.3 meeting in Baden bei Wein, van Wijngaarden was showing how to get rid of GOTOs by replacing them with recursive procedure calls that never return. Dijkstra's reaction to this academic result was to spend the evening deriving programs that had no GOTOs in the first place. On the terrace during next morning's coffee break, and throughout the day, he peddled his new style, pointing out that many programs became simpler in the process and that none got harder. He invented a LOOP-EXIT statement to solve some structural problems. In less than 24 hours, Dijkstra had converted a sterile academic exercise into a movement that would shake the field when the eruption came later in 1968 with his famous letter on "the GOTO considered harmful."[6] Most people regard his 1968 letter as the start of the eliminate-the-GOTO movement; few realize that it began as a reaction to an academic talk in 1964.

Perhaps the measure of this man is best expressed by those he has influenced, and who more influenced and better placed than his students? This influence has been caused by his particularly perceptive and brilliant mind, his intense desire to be professionally honest, a discipline that is unequaled, and a way with the pen (in both form and content) that others would kill to attain. His ability to make a decision on technical grounds and then to put it into practice is unrivaled. He seems to have been endowed with all the good qualities one would like to see in a scientist, and he has taken care to sharpen them. On the occasion of his 60th birthday, the University of Texas organized a celebratory symposium on the "Frontiers of Computing" primarily staffed by his disciples. This was an occasion to provide insights of the person behind the facade of the "professor." Even Dr. W.S. Livingston, vice president and dean of graduate studies of the University of Texas at Austin, could not resist relating his "Dijkstra experience":

> In 1983 Dr. Dijkstra was being interviewed by the University of Texas at Austin to determine his suitability for appointment to the distinguished position. Someone decided that it was my task as vice president (even though I am by trade a political scientist) to conduct an

---

[6]Dijkstra, Aug. 1968.

interview on behalf of the University administration. I was not quite certain just what topics we might discuss, but Professor Dijkstra soon solved that problem. After some very short preliminaries he stood up and provided me with a lecture on his thoughts on the subject, striding up and down in my office. It is not at all clear to me just who interviewed whom.

Tony Hoare, himself a Turing Award winner and pioneer (but not a student of Dijkstra's), told of their first meeting, which exemplifies the discipline of programming that Dijkstra espoused (see Dijkstra 1976):

The first time I visited Edsger in Eindhoven was in the early Seventies. My purpose was to find out more about the THE operating system,[7] which Edsger had designed. In the computing center at which the system was running I asked whether there was really no possibility of deadlock. *"Let's see"* was the answer. They then input a program with an infinite recursion. After a while, a request appeared at the operator's console for more storage to be allocated to the program, and this was granted. At the same time they put a circular paper tape loop into one of the tape readers, and this was immediately read into buffer file by the spooling demon. After a while the reader stopped; but the operator typed a message forcing the spooler to continue reading. At the same time even more storage was allocated to the recursive program. After an interval in which the operator repeatedly forced further foolish storage allocations, the system finally ground to a complete halt, and a brief message explained that storage was exhausted and requested the operator to restart operations.

So the answer was YES; the system did have a possibility of deadlock. But what interested me was that the restart message and the program that printed it were permanently resident in expensive core storage, so that it would be available even when the paging store and input/output utilities were inoperative. And secondly, that this was the very first time it had happened. I concluded that the THE operating system had been designed by a practical engineer of high genius. Having conducted the most fundamental and far-reaching research into deadlock and its avoidance, he nevertheless allocated scarce resources to ensure that if anything went wrong, it would be recognized and rectified. And finally, of course, nothing actually ever did go wrong, except as a demonstration to an inquisitive visitor.

David Gries remembered that Dijkstra's main contributions have been in programming methodology, and that he was one of the founders of IFIP Working Group 2.3 in 1970. On the other hand the remembrance indicated that Dijkstra is not infallible:

---

[7]Dijkstra, May 1968.

WG 2.3 met in a log hotel overlooking Oslo during the week that man landed on the moon. During that summer week, Edsger, slightly short of breath while climbing a steep hill during an outing, said he did not believe that programming as a field of research would last another ten years—fifteen at the outside. Wlad Turski says it is a pity that he did not challenge Edsger with a bet at the time, for he would have won. Turski was hesitant to bet because he had just lost a case of cognac: almost a decade earlier, at a New Year's party in Moscow, Turski bet a Russian scientist that man would not set foot on the moon before December 31, 1969, so Wlad had just lost that bet by five months!

An unsubstantiated anecdote illustrates to what lengths people go to get the upper hand on Edsger:

After Carel Scholten had built one of the early computers at the Mathematical Centre [Mathematisch Centrum, Amsterdam], Edsger claimed that nobody could write a shorter routine than his for some problem, and he offered a free meal to whoever could beat his routine (quite a bold bet for a Dutchman). He lost his bet, because Carel Scholten secretly added an instruction to the machine just so that he could write a shorter program! Thus, Edsger lost his one and only bet!

Dijkstra watchers, be they students of his lectures, or lecturers who have had him in the audience, are often perturbed by his lecturing and listening activities. Students are irritated by his habit of pausing between sentences to think about what he is to say next. Asked about it on one occasion he pointed out that English is not his native language and he picked up the habit early in his using the language. Doug McIlroy (Bell Telephone Laboratories) recalled the penury of a speaker who finds Dijkstra in his audience:

As the speaker drones on, Edsger will become displeased at something, or begin thinking about something the speaker said. The body will rise, the sandals will come off, and the walking at the back of the room will begin. The unsuspecting new lecturer will continue blithely on. A more experienced lecturer will suspect and begin to worry. If he can contain himself, Edsger will wait until the end of the lecture, but sometimes he just has to interrupt. A snort will erupt, the nostrils will flare, the chin will elevate, and out will come an inspired, amazingly logical and eloquent, commentary. Both parties will emerge pleased, one for having vanquished stupidity, the other for having evoked the commentary and for the understanding they have gained. In the long run, this supreme effort of abrasion has polished the understanding of both.

McIlroy recalls only once that an eruption went supercritical. Unfortunately, the verbal outburst was saved for the end, and when it came, it lacked all divine inspiration: *"This stuff makes me sick!"* he thundered. Understanding was nonetheless polished, and two years later Dijkstra had taken up the topic himself.

David Gries (Cornell University) was one of the recipients of "on-line" coaching during a lecture:

> My own experience with lecturing before Edsger took place in Marktoberdorf. It rests on the fact that in some languages (notably Fortran), the equality symbol and the assignment symbol are the same, and many people say:
>
> *"x equals e"*
>
> when they mean
>
> *"store the value of e in x," or "x becomes e."*[8]
>
> I was lecturing along, when I said *"x equals e,"* meaning an assignment of e to x. From the back of the room came a loud *"becomes,"* and then a stunned silence. Finally, I gathered my wits and said, "Thank you, Edsger, for correcting me. If I make the same mistake again, stop me." Twenty minutes later, I made the same mistake, and again from the back of the room came *"becomes." "Thanks, I won't make the mistake again,"* I said, and to this day I haven't!

Without doubt Edsger Dijkstra, for all his technological contributions, epitomized by many to be the "GOTO" letter in the *Communications of the ACM,* is one of the "characters" of the field. He is difficult to predict. The titles of the two lectures he gave on accepting the ACM Turing Award and the SIGCSE Education Award are typical of this proclivity: "The Humble Programmer" and "On the Cruelty of Really Teaching Computer Science."

QUOTATIONS

"The question of whether computers can think is just like the question of whether submarines can swim." (Attrib.; posted on the CMU Board, December 1986)

"I would require of a programming language that it should facilitate the work of the programmer as much as possible, especially in the most difficult aspects of his task, such as creating confidence in the correctness of his program. This is already difficult in the case of a spe-

---

[8]More precisely one should say "store the representation of the value e in the memory location associated with the name x." Ed.

cific program that must produce a finite set of results. But then the programmer only has the duty to show (afterwards) that if there were any flaws in his program they apparently didn't matter . . .' ("On the Design of Machine Independent Programming Languages," *Ann. Rev. in Auto. Prog.,* Vol. 3)

"For the absence of a bibliography I offer neither explanation nor apology." (*A Discipline of Programming*)

"Program testing can be used to show the presence of bugs, but never to show their absence." (*Structured Programming,* 1969 NATO Conference)

"Suffering as I am from the sequential nature of human communication, . . ."

BIBLIOGRAPHY

Biographical

Dijkstra, E.W., "The Humble Programmer," Turing Award Lecture, *Comm. ACM,* Vol. 15, No. 10, Oct. 1972, pp. 859–866.

Dijkstra, Edsger W., "A Programmer's Early Memories," in Metropolis, N., J. Howlett, and Gian-Carlo Rota, *A History of Computing in the Twentieth Century,* Academic Press, New York, 1980, pp. 563–573.

Lee, J.A.N., ed., "Frontiers of Computing: A Tribute to Edsger W. Dijkstra on the Occasion of his 60th Birthday," *Ann. Hist. Comp.,* Vol. 13, No. 1, 1991, pp. 91–96.

Significant Publications

Dijkstra, E.W., "Some Meditations on Advanced Programming," *Proc. IFIP Congress,* North-Holland, Amsterdam, 1962, pp. 535–538.

Dijkstra, E.W., "Programming Considered as a Human Activity," *Proc. IFIP Congress,* 1965, pp. 213–217.

Dijkstra, E.W., "Solution to a Problem in Concurrent Programming Control," *Comm. ACM,* 1965, Vol. 8, 1965, p. 569.

Dijkstra, E.W., "The Structure of the 'THE'—Multiprogramming System," ACM Symp. on Operating Systems, *Comm. ACM,* Vol. 11, No. 5, May 1968, pp. 341–346.

Dijkstra, E.W., "GO TO Statement Considered Harmful," letter to the editor, *Comm. ACM,* Vol. 11, No. 8, Aug. 1968, p. 538.

Dijkstra, E.W., *A Short Introduction to the Art of Computer Programming,* Technische Hogeschool, Eindhoven, 1971.

Dijkstra, E.W., "The Humble Programmer," Turing Award Lecture, *Comm. ACM,* Vol. 15, No. 10, Oct. 1972, pp. 859–866.

Dijkstra, Edsger, *A Discipline of Programming,* Prentice-Hall, Englewood Cliffs, N.J., 1976.

Dijkstra, E.W., "On the Cruelty of Really Teaching Computer Science," *Comm. ACM,* Vol. 32, No. 12, Dec.1989, pp. 1398ff.

PHILIP HENRY DORN

Born August 14, 1930, New York City; died June 8, 1993, New York City; software pioneer, champion of computing, skilled industry analyst, respected consultant, gifted writer and speaker, and friend and supporter of people in the world of computing and beyond.

Education: BA, political science, Princeton University, 1952.

Professional Experience: US Army, 1953–1956; Personnel Laboratory, Inc., 1956–1958; System Development Corp. (SDC), 1958–1961; General Motors Research Laboratories (GMR), Warren, Michigan, 1961–1965; Computer Applications, Inc., New York City, 1965–1966; Technical Services Group, Union Carbide Corp., New York City, 1966–1972; The Equitable Life Assurance Society, 1972; Dorn Computer Consultants, Inc. 1972–1993.

Philip Henry Dorn, software pioneer, champion of computing, skilled industry analyst, respected consultant, gifted writer and speaker, and friend and supporter of people in the world of computing and beyond, died suddenly while returning by taxi to his New York City home from a ballet performance on June 8, 1993. He was 62 years old.[9]

---

[9]Rosin 1994.

Dorn was born on August 14, 1930, and brought up in New York City, in Manhattan. He attended the Lawrenceville School in New Jersey, from which he graduated in 1948. Discouraged by his parents from pursuing studies in engineering, he earned a BA in political science from Princeton University in 1952. He then entered the law school at Stanford University. At Stanford he met Sue Bricker, a native of the Pacific Northwest, who became his wife in 1955 and was at his side when he died.

Dorn was drafted out of law school in 1953, and, while serving in the Army, he decided that law was not for him. In 1956, following his discharge and marriage, he took a customer-liaison position with a firm, Personnel Laboratory, Inc., that specialized in testing candidates for employment. This enabled him to support his family, but he became restless and intellectually dissatisfied.

In 1958, with his wife's encouragement, he answered an employment advertisement placed by System Development Corporation (SDC). In those days, when most people had no concept of computers, SDC would simply seek people who were intelligent and intellectually curious—which described Dorn perfectly. He told the interviewer that he had no background in mathematics or engineering, but his score on a screening examination was off the top of the scale, and he was offered a position.

SDC had major responsibilities for programming the SAGE air defense system on AN/FSQ-32 computers. [See the Special Issue on SAGE, *Ann. Hist. Comp.*, Vol. 5, No. 4, Oct. 1983.] There was no ready supply of programmers; computer science departments did not exist, and few universities even offered serious courses in programming. So SDC ran its own school, offering its employees introductory courses in "bits, bytes, ones, and zeros" and advanced courses in air defense applications.

Dorn excelled in both the introductory and advanced courses and, upon completing the latter, became one of SDC's instructors. His teaching colleagues found him delightful to work with. But he also had very high standards. If Dorn respected a colleague intellectually, their relationship could be very positive; but woe to a lesser person who let Dorn get the upper hand.

Although he enjoyed his work and the opportunity to play tennis year-round, Dorn was not cut out for Southern California—in particular, he did not drive a car—so in 1961 he joined the staff at General Motors Research Laboratories (GMR) in Warren, Michigan.

At this time, an IBM-7090 computer was installed at GMR to support development of a system for vehicle body design. The resulting system,

DAC-1, was the first industrial computer-aided design system and the system that pioneered the use of computer graphics in industry. [See Krull, F., "The Origin of Computer Graphics within General Motors" *IEEE Annals of the History of Computing*, Vol. 16, No. 3, 1994, pp. 40–56.]

Along with a colleague, Phyllis Cole, Dorn's role in the DAC-1 project was to develop the disk-based memory system, including the design of a storage access method. The work began before any disk drive was available for the IBM-7090, so Dorn and Cole simulated the storage system they were designing, first using tape drives, and then with an IBM-1401 that had a very early disk drive. Dorn wrote and checked out the first customer-developed programs for the IBM-1301 disk drive at IBM prior to delivery of that hardware to GM.

Dorn's professional relationship with Cole was typical of the way he interacted with women throughout his career; he treated them equally with men. Women whom he respected intellectually, and there were many, became trusted colleagues and friends. He also encouraged women, telling one who expressed doubts, "You are not a woman manager—you are a manager!"

While DAC-1 was the most exciting experience in his entire career—and Michigan was closer to home than California—Dorn was an inveterate Manhattanite. So in 1965 he joined Computer Applications, Inc., in New York City, where he codirected implementation of the Indexed Sequential Access Method (ISAM) for OS/360 under a contract with IBM.

In 1966 Union Carbide Corporation formed a corporate-level Technical Services Group in New York City, and Dorn was one of four people selected to staff it. This group established policies and plans for third-generation computing in Union Carbide, and its members served on related committees and projects in data centers throughout the corporation. Here Dorn honed his skills as a technical consultant. He had a reputation for offering an opinion on everything, but that opinion was formed on the basis of what he heard and read—and he always knew everyone else's opinion. When the Technical Services Group was broken up a few years later, its members were assigned to various Union Carbide data centers. Dorn, of course, stayed in New York.

While at GM, Dorn had become involved in SHARE, then known as the "IBM user group for large, scientific computers."[10] During his 12-year formal relationship with SHARE, he managed the SHARE

---

[10]See Armer, Paul, "SHARE—A Eulogy to Cooperative Effort," *Ann. Hist. Comp.*, Vol. 2, No. 2, Apr. 1980, pp. 122–129.

PL/I Project and its Systems Division, served as SHARE vice president and, in 1969–1970, as president. After his presidency, he served another term on the SHARE Board as past president, and he continued to consult for the SHARE management long after he was affiliated with a SHARE member corporation.

The 1960s were years of significant turmoil in SHARE. Among other major issues, IBM announced and delivered its System/360 and OS/360, and in 1969 IBM announced its decision to "unbundle" its software and sell it separately from its hardware products. Dorn took a leading role in developing SHARE's response to this announcement, which resulted in vendors other than IBM participating in SHARE and SHARE's incorporation as a tax-exempt organization. An attorney retained by SHARE during this period credits Dorn with teaching him to write with a precision that, he says, still distinguishes him from most other lawyers.

Dorn left Union Carbide in late 1972 and, after a short stint with the Equitable Life Assurance Society, began independent consulting under the rubric Dorn Computer Consultants, Inc. He set up an office in his Manhattan cooperative apartment, and began to serve clients in the US and abroad. In addition to his areas of technical expertise, he offered services in organizational studies, installation audits, product planning and marketing, and evaluation and selection of hardware and software.

As a consultant Dorn also capitalized on his talents as a writer and editor. He was a member of the *Datamation* editorial advisory board and contributed regularly to that publication. He was a regular columnist for data processing publications in Denmark, Finland, Iceland, Japan, New Zealand, and Australia. He was a reviewer for the *Annals* and *ACM Computing Reviews,* a referee for *Communications of the ACM,* and, for a while, edited the News and Notices Section of the *Annals.*

Dorn was also an effective speaker. In his first lecture in Iceland, which filled the largest room in the university, he introduced his audience of data processing managers to spreadsheets. He warned them to "embrace the coming personal computer revolution or lose control. . . . Departments will find ways to buy personal computers even if not budgeted to do so." This prediction was made in 1979, well before introduction of the IBM PC. Dorn was the most frequent speaker at the annual Scandinavian Norddata Conference, at which he addressed overflow audiences for 15 consecutive years.

One of Dorn's more recent activities was to serve as a charter member of the Harvard Business School History of MIS Project, which is led by James L. McKenney, a colleague from their days at SDC. This project, some of whose reports appear periodically in the *Annals,* has as its goal to show how information technology, especially software, has transformed industries. [See Carlson, Walter M., "Transforming an Industry Through Information Technology," *Ann. Hist. Comp.,* Vol. 15, No. 1, 1993, pp. 39–43.] Dorn was a strong force in the project and was an extraordinary and most critical editor—making English mean what it says.

Dorn's relationship with New York City was an abiding one. He was a regular attendee at the ballet, concerts, and New York Ranger hockey games—and he never did drive an automobile. His other interests included the history of the Civil War and the art of the Inuit people. He was also a frequent visitor to the Museum of Modern Art, where his wife Sue has been deputy director for development and public affairs since 1987.

Dorn's public image was as an outspoken, opinionated pragmatist, but those who knew him well benefited from a very different, private personality. To his many friends, he was warm, loyal, and caring. He was a source of personal support to those who needed it—phoning daily to friends suffering the death of a spouse, serving as surrogate father to children whose fathers had died, sending personal notes of praise for work well done, and generously providing free advice and counsel to professional colleagues in difficulty. This aspect of his character is also reflected in obituaries that have appeared in computer industry publications throughout the world, for example, *ComputerWorld Denmark,* June 11, 1993, *Information Week* (USA), June 14, 1993, and *ComputerWorld Australia,* July 16, 1993.

BIBLIOGRAPHY

Biographical

Rosin, Robert F., "Philip Dorn," *Ann. Hist. Comp.,* Vol. 15, No. 4, 1994, pp. 84–85.

Stephen W. Dunwell

Born April 3, 1913, Kalamazoo, Mich.; died March 21, 1994, Poughkeepsie, N.Y.; IBM engineer primarily responsible for the development of the first super-computer—STRETCH, IBM-7030.

Education: BS, electrical engineering, Antioch College, Ohio.

Professional Experience: IBM Corp., 1933–1976; Lt. Colonel, Army Security Agency, 1941–1945.

Honors and Awards: Legion of Merit, 1945; IBM Outstanding Invention Award; IBM fellow, 1966; Computer Pioneer Award, IEEE Computer Society, 1992.

Stephen W. Dunwell was born April 3, 1913 in Kalamazoo, Mich. His first contact with electronics came in 1928, when, while in high school, he designed, built, and operated an amateur radio station. He later attended Antioch College, Ohio, where he majored in electrical engineering. As part of a cooperative program with IBM, he entered the IBM student engineering program for graduate engineers in 1933 in Endicott, N.Y., and joined the company on a full-time basis the following year.

As a demonstration to IBM management of the possibilities for use of electronics in punched-card machines, he designed and built a machine which sorted marked cards. Also during that period, he designed and built the switching device used by Dr. Wallace Eckert of Columbia University for his experiments in the use of punched-card machines for the computation of the lunar orbit. In 1938, Dunwell was transferred to the IBM world headquarters in New York City, where he worked on the specification and design of future IBM products. During World War II he received a direct commission to the Army Security Agency, whose mission was cryptography and code-breaking, using IBM machines with attached relay calculators. He received the Legion of Merit for this work, and returned to IBM at the end of World War II with the rank of Lt. Colonel.

At IBM Poughkeepsie he was involved in the specification and design of a number of calculators, including the IBM-502-A, the 603 and the 604, and the Card-Programmed Calculator, known as the CPC. This was followed by work on the stored-program computers including the IBM-650, the Tape Processing Machine, and the IBM-702 and 705 (commercial data processing machines). Then, in 1958, he became the director of Project STRETCH, the stretching of transistor technology for both commercial and scientific applications. The project had three objectives: (1) provide components for commercial transistorized computers, (2) combine in one machine both scientific and commercial capabilities, and (3) establish the ground rules for the design of future IBM computers. Among the 22 ground rules so established were the 8-bit byte, a standard interface to peripheral equipment, and automatic error correction.

While the IBM-7030 (the actual "STRETCH" Machine) never became a commercial success, the transistors, the circuits, the packaging, the cooling, the design automation system, the diagnostic techniques, and the design ground rules that were developed for the project became the model on which IBM's successful 7080 and 7090 lines were based. Dunwell received an IBM Outstanding Invention Award for patents relating to STRETCH. In 1966 he was made an IBM fellow, giving him the freedom for pursuing any topic of research or development that he was interested in.

Between 1966 and 1976, when he retired from IBM, Dunwell had produced COURSEWRITER, the first time-sharing software marketed by IBM, and led a program which put in place a worldwide computer time-sharing network offering computer-assisted instruction for the education of IBM field engineering. This network was the basis for the current RETAIN network, which provides for the exchange of engineering information, and the HONE network, which provides for the exchange of sales information.

After retirement, Dunwell and his wife, Julia McClure Dunwell, rescued and, for three years, operated Poughkeepsie's historic Bardavon 1869 Opera House, until it could be turned over to a professional management team. In 1980 they established a computer time-sharing company and laboratory to search for a universal computer language capable of replacing all computer languages now in use. This kept them busy until his death.[11]

---

[11] From the press release for the presentation of the IEEE Computer Society Computer Pioneer Award, 1992.

J. (JOHN) PRESPER ECKERT

Born April 9, 1919, Philadelphia; with John Mauchly, the inventor of the ENIAC, created the EDVAC, BINAC, and Univac computers.

Education: BS, Moore School, University of Pennsylvania, 1941; MS, Moore School, University of Pennsylvania, 1943.

Professional Experience: chief engineer, ENIAC Project, Moore School, University of Pennsylvania, 1943–1946; founder (with John Mauchly), Electronic Control Corporation (1947, named Eckert-Mauchly Computer Corp.), 1946–1950; director of engineering, Eckert-Mauchly Division, Remington-Rand Corp., 1950–1955; vice president and director of commercial engineering, Remington-Rand Corp.,  1955–1959; vice president and executive assistant to the general manager, Remington-Rand Corp., 1959–1963; vice president and technical adviser to the president, Univac Division, Sperry-Rand Corp., 1963–1982.

Honors and Awards: IEEE Computer Society Pioneer Award, 1980; member, Information Processing Hall of Fame, Infomart, Dallas, Texas, 1985.

J. Presper Eckert was attending the University of Pennsylvania in the Moore School of Electrical Engineering when, as an undergraduate, he became interested in computing. Like so many other students, he was bothered by the fact that his statistics homework required hours of time-consuming use of a calculator to answer his professor's questions. He observed that the school had a copy of the Vannevar Bush differential analyzer and, besides desiring its use, began to think of ways to overcome its limitations. His adviser, Dr. Wygant, proposed to the governmental sponsors that these improvements be implemented, and received a grant which enabled Wygant, Eckert, and a fellow graduate student, Bill Cook, to improve the machine's accuracy and efficiency by an order of magnitude.

During this time, John Mauchly[1] became interested in the work but decided that there were not many improvements that could be made so long as the calculator was analog. They replaced the gears by installing electronic devices, and devised a mechanism which counted pulses, thus replacing the integrators. However, they felt that even with these improvements the system was still too limited in its applicability. The pulse counter used a monadic representation for numbers and so they decided that they needed a place value system, such as binary or

---

[1]See Mauchly's biography for a discussion of his background and prior interests in digital computing devices.

decimal. About this time, the war in North Africa required that all the firing tables be recomputed as a result of the local climatic differences. From this grew their concept of a new machine and with help from John Brainerd, dean of the school, and Herman H. Goldstine, liaison to the school on behalf of the Aberdeen Proving Ground, they presented a proposal for the construction of a digital calculator.

On April 9, 1943 (Eckert's 24th birthday) the university received the authority to commence the ENIAC (Electronic Numerical Integrator and Calculator) project with an initial budget of approximately $150,000—an amount which was slowly increased to approximately $400,000 as new requirements were added. World War II had created the need for improved computing power. Bell Telephone Laboratories had already developed relay-based fire control calculators for ground-to-air use,[2] but the military sought airborne systems. Further, the use of radar required sophisticated computation techniques to identify moving targets, a problem which was not being solved by analog means or by women "computers" with calculators.

There were two main criticisms of the work: mathematicians criticized the use of primitive integration methods in their calculations of the trajectories of ordnance devices, and the engineers predicted that the low reliability of the vacuum tubes would undermine the project. Eckert countered the mathematical objections by pointing out that the intervals were much less than had been used in hand calculations. In any case the flexibility of the system, as a result of the ability to "program" the calculator, permitted the use of more sophisticated methods. There was some concern regarding the cumulative effect of round-off or truncation errors, but this too was overcome. These problems were primarily solved by John Mauchly, who concentrated on the "software" and "programming" problems, while Eckert dealt with the hardware problems, including the tube reliability difficulty. The primary problem that Eckert and Mauchly encountered in this project was the need to use a large number of vacuum tubes (eventually over 18,000), which were notoriously unreliable.[3] No one had built any machine with so many tubes. Eckert went for assistance to RCA in Harrison, N.J. They provided much useful advice on this problem— mainly to keep the heaters of the tubes under power, rather than turning them on and off continually. They also received help from the

---

[2] See the biography of George Stibitz.

[3] Eckert noted that Fermi heard about their problems and, based on his experiences with equipment including 2–300 tubes, estimated that the mean time to failure of their proposed machine would be 2–3 minutes. Fermi's prediction was off by two orders of magnitude.

International Resistance Company, of which Brainerd was a primary stockholder, for the supply of reliable, accurate resistors.

Once the first two panels of the ENIAC had been completed, Eckert was convinced of the team's ability to complete the machine. The telltale lamps, which they had installed to indicate the operation of the panels, intrigued everyone on the project; Eckert believed that this innovation was the basis for the inclusion of flashing lights in every science fiction film thereafter.

Besides the development of the first general-purpose calculator, there were two major contributions which were not part of prior conceptions of calculators—hierarchical memory and "subroutines."[4] The concept of a hierarchical storage system derived from the inability to create and afford an efficient single-level memory. Rather than a single cheap and fast memory, they developed a hierarchy of memories, some cheap and some fast. The concept of subroutines was derived from the need to repeat groups of instructions iteratively, and the need to re-use clusters of instructions. Since the ENIAC was not a stored-program machine, subprograms could be stored on cards and tapes, but the concept was extended in later machines.[5]

In 1946 a dispute broke out at the university when Dean Brainerd asked the ENIAC project participants to sign documents which would assign their intellectual property rights to the university. Rather than agree to give up their rights, Eckert and Mauchly chose to found the Electronic Control Corporation, which was renamed the Eckert-Mauchly Computer Corporation in 1947. While the EDVAC (Electronic Discrete Variable Computer) was still a dream at the university, Eckert and Mauchly had the concept of a commercial system, but with limited financial backing they needed a contract in order to provide the funding for further developments. With the design of the Univac system, they sold their promises to Northrop Aircraft Company, to the US Air Force, and to the Bureau of the Census. The Northrop contract was initially fulfilled with the delivery of their first stored-program machine—the BINAC. This small machine never operated effectively after delivery to Northrop, but instead of persevering, Northrop allowed it to grow dusty in a corner. The Univac machine was completed and worked successfully for several clients, although not to the profit of the company. In the meantime the corporation was bought out by Remington-Rand, and Eckert was appointed as the director of engineering, Eckert-

---

[4] Eckert ascribes the invention of the term "hierarchical memory" to John von Neumann.

[5] The prior paragraphs are based on the interview by Christopher Evans for the Science Museum and the National Physical Laboratory, 1975.

Mauchly Division, Remington-Rand Corporation in 1950. The line of machines created by Eckert and Mauchly was continued through a sequence of reorganizations with Eckert serving successively as vice president and director of Commercial Engineering, Remington-Rand Corporation (1955–1959), vice president and executive assistant to the general manager, Remington-Rand Corporation (1959–1963), and vice president and technical adviser to the president, Univac Division, Sperry-Rand Corporation (1963–1982). Eckert retired the same year as the Univac name was finally dropped from the product line of the company.

In the 1970s, Eckert was unfortunate to find himself put on the sidelines by counterclaims to the technology which he and Mauchly developed. During the final stages of the construction of the ENIAC, John von Neumann was inserted into the environment as a consultant and mentor (and perhaps possible user). Eckert and Mauchly had already recognized (in 1944, at a time when their project was still classified) that the hierarchy of memory, in which different memories were associated with different elements of the "program"—data, constants, functions, instructions—was unnecessary. A homogeneous memory would allow for interchangeability—a conclusion which implied the insertion of instructions into a modifiable, internal memory. The design of the successor to ENIAC, named the EDVAC, was described in a report[6] which identifies only von Neumann as the author. The report is clearly entitled "Draft" and there is a belief that the final copy would have had the names of other contributors. However, this report is the primary source of the concept of the stored program, sometimes named the "von Neumann concept." Apparently, von Neumann never denied this assignation, and thus Eckert and Mauchly found it difficult to lay claim to their far-reaching, quite possibly most important invention.[7] In 1968 the patents to the invention of the computer (by then in the possession of Sperry-Rand) were challenged by Honeywell. In the process of the trial the source of John Mauchly's ideas for the electronic devices was in question. Honeywell supported the claim that Mauchly had acquired the basic concepts from John Vincent Atanasoff during a 1941 visit to the latter's home in

---

[6]von Neumann, John, *First Draft of a Report on the EDVAC*, Contract No. W-670-ORD-492, Moore School of Electrical Engineering, Univ. of Pennsylvania, Philadelphia, June 30, 1945. Reprinted in Randell, Brian, *Origins of Digital Computers: Selected Papers*, Springer-Verlag, Berlin, 1982, pp. 383–392. Corrected and reprinted in *IEEE Ann. Hist. Comp.*, Vol. 15, No. 4, 1993, pp. 27–45.

[7]Aspray, W.F., "History of the Stored Program Concept," Meetings in Retrospect, *Ann. Hist. Comp.*, Vol. 4, No. 4, 1982, pp. 358–361.

[8]See biographies of John V. Atanasoff and Clifford Berry.

Iowa. Judge Earl Larson found in favor of the Honeywell claim and invalidated the Eckert-Mauchly patents.[8] Eckert has never accepted this judgment, but rather than fighting it has quietly reaffirmed his own belief in the integrity of his colleague and the uniqueness of his own contributions.

BIBLIOGRAPHY

Biographical

Berkeley, Edmund C., *Giant Brains or Machines That Think,* John Wiley, New York, 1949.

Burks, A.W., and A.R. Burks, "The ENIAC: First General-Purpose Electronic Computer," *Ann. Hist. Comp.,* Vol. 3, No. 4, Oct. 1981, pp. 310–399.

Eckert, J. Presper, "The ENIAC," in Metropolis, N., J. Howlett, and Gian-Carlo Rota, *A History of Computing in the Twentieth Century,* Academic Press, New York, 1980, pp. 525–539.

Evans, Christopher, "J. Presper Eckert," Oral History of Computing, Science Museum, London and National Physical Laboratory, Teddington, No. 3, Audiotape, 1975.

Mauchly, John W., "The ENIAC," in Metropolis, N., J. Howlett, and Gian-Carlo Rota, *A History of Computing in the Twentieth Century,* Academic Press, New York, 1980, pp. 541–550.

Maynard, M.M., "Eckert, J. Presper," in Ralston, Anthony, and Edwin D. Reilly, Jr., *Encyclopedia of Computer Science and Engineering,* Van Nostrand Reinhold Co., New York, 1983.

Ritchie, David, *The Computer Pioneers,* Simon and Shuster, New York, 1986, Chapter 8.

Slater, Robert, *Portraits in Silicon,* MIT Press, Cambridge, Mass., 1987, Chapter 7.

Stern, Nancy, *From ENIAC to Univac: An Appraisal of the Eckert-Mauchly Computers,* Digital Press, Bedford, Mass., 1981.

Significant Publications

Eckert, J. Presper, Jr., John W. Mauchly, Herman H. Goldstine, and J.G. Brainerd, *Description of the ENIAC and Comments on Electronic Digital Computing Machinery,* Contract W/670/ORD 4926, Moore School of Electrical Engineering, Univ. of Pennsylvania, Philadelphia, Nov. 30, 1945.

WALLACE J. ECKERT

Born June 19, 1902, Pittsburgh, Pa.; died August 24, 1971, Englewood, N.J.; prewar pioneer with his "Punched-card Methods in Scientific Computation" who was instrumental in the postwar construction of IBM's SSEC and the NORC for the Navy.

Education: AB, Oberlin College, 1925; MA, Amherst College, 1926; PhD, astronomy, Yale University, 1931.

Professional Experience: assistant instructor, Department of Astronomy, Columbia University, 1926–1940; director, US Nautical Almanac Office, 1940–1945; head, IBM Pure Science Department, and director, Watson Scientific Computing Laboratory, 1945–1967; professor, celestial mechanics, Columbia University, 1967–1970.

The Columbia University Statistical Bureau was founded in 1928 with punched-card equipment donated by T. J. Watson, Sr. Here Eckert had his first encounter with large calculating devices to complete his own work in astronomy. Eckert's success in convincing Watson to contribute further equipment led to the establishment of the T. J. Watson Astronomical Computing Bureau at Columbia, a unit which was jointly sponsored by the university, IBM, and the American Astronomical Society. During World War II, Eckert headed the US Nautical Almanac Office in Washington, D.C., and introduced mechanical methods of computation to the Office and to the Naval Observatory. This work led to his being appointed to the directorship of the Astronomical Computing Bureau at Columbia, and the concurrent appointment as head of the Pure Science Division of IBM. In the latter capacity Eckert was extremely influential in the development of the Selective Sequence Electronic Calculator (SSEC) in 1949, which was IBM's response to their rejection from recognition for the coinvention of the Harvard Mark I.[9] The NORC (Naval Ordnance Research Calculator) was also developed under Eckert's auspices.

Eckert continued to work in astronomy, and in the early days of US space flight provided many of the coordinates and orbital parameters of heavenly bodies for use by NASA.

---

[9] See biography of Howard Aiken.

Tropp (1976) has described Eckert's computer contributions to astronomy as being as important as the introduction of the telescope and the use of photography.

BIBLIOGRAPHY

Biographical

Bashe, Charles J., "The SSEC in Historical Perspective," *Ann. Hist. Comp.*, Vol. 3, No. 4, 1982, pp. 296–312.

Tropp, H.S., "Wallace J. Eckert," in Ralston, Anthony, and Edwin D. Reilly, Jr., eds., *Encyclopedia of Computer Science and Engineering*, Van Nostrand Reinhold Co., New York, 1983.

Tropp, H.S., "Eckert, Wallace John," in Gillispie, C.G., ed., *Dictionary of Scientific Biography*, Vol. 15, Supplement I, Charles Scribner's Sons, New York, 1976, pp. 128–130.

Significant Publications[10]

Eckert, W. J., "Electrons and Computation," *The Scientific Monthly*, Vol. 67, No. 5, Nov. 1948, pp. 315–323. Reprinted in Randell, Brian, ed., *The Origins of Digital Computers: Selected Papers*, Springer-Verlag, Berlin, 1982, pp. 223–232.

Eckert, W.J., and Rebecca Jones, *Faster, Faster, Simple Description of a Giant Electronic Calculator*[11] *and the Problems It Solves*, IBM, New York, 1955.

---

[10]See Tropp 1976 for a list of publications including those in the field of astronomy.
[11]The NORC.

Doug Engelbart

Born January 25, 1925, Portland, Ore.; inventor of the mouse and strong proponent of the potential for high-performance human augmentation.

Education BS, electrical engineering, Oregon State University, 1948; PhD, electrical engineering and computer science, University of California, Berkeley, 1957.

Professional Experience: Ames Laboratory, Mountain View, 1948–1951; assistant professor, University of California, Berkeley, 1951–1956; Stanford Research Institute (now SRI International), 1957–1977; senior scientist, Tymshare, Inc., 1977–1984; senior scientist, McDonnell Douglas Corporation, 1984–1989; director, Bootstrap Institute, 1989–present.

Honors and Awards: Computer Pioneer Award, IEEE Computer Society, 1992.

Douglas C. Engelbart serves as the director of the Bootstrap Institute, a California corporation which is committed to launching the "bootstrap initiative," a consortium supporting the bootstrap strategy for continuous improvement of organizational capability.

Engelbart was born in Portland, Oregon, on January 25, 1925. He served in the US Navy as an electronics technician during World War II, and received his BS in electrical engineering from Oregon State University in 1948. He worked at the NACA (before it became "NASA") Ames Laboratory until 1951 before going on to earn his PhD in electrical engineering (with a computer specialty) at the University of California, Berkeley. His thesis was on applying plasma phenomena to digital devices. This work resulted in the issuance of a dozen patents.

He stayed on at Berkeley as assistant professor until 1956, when he left for the Stanford Research Institute (now SRI International) where he worked on magnetic computer components, and studied digital device phenomena and miniaturization scaling potential. This work produced another dozen patents.

In 1959 Dr. Engelbart launched the SRI Augmentation Research Center, which he directed until 1977. This center provided him with the opportunity to pioneer the modern interactive working environment, for which he was honored by the presentation of the IEEE Pioneer Award.[12] He used NLS (On-Line System) as an exploratory vehicle for research into the "knowledge worker/organization." Results included the basic patent for the "mouse," development of two-

---

[12]From the press release on the occasion of the presentation of the IEEE Computer Society Computer Pioneer Award, 1992.

dimensional editing, the concept of windows, cross-file editing, uniform command syntax, remote procedure-call protocol, mixed text-graphic files, structured document files, idea processing, and hypertext, among many more developments. When he left the center, it had some 47 members.

Tymshare bought SRI's commercial rights to NLS, renamed it "Augment," and set it up as a principal line of business of its Office Automation Division. Engelbart became senior scientist of Tymshare until McDonnell Douglas Corp. acquired Tymshare in 1984. He then joined McDonnell in the same position, but working on integrated information-systems architectures and associated evolutionary strategies in its aerospace program. He retired from MDC in 1989, but continued his pursuit of "the augmented knowledge organization," which found a home at Stanford University in the "Bootstrap Project." In 1990 this became the Bootstrap Institute and was incorporated as a separate entity from the university.

ANDREI PETROVICH ERSHOV

Born 1931, Soviet Union; died December 8, 1988, Moscow, USSR; internationalist and humanist, he was a true scholar in the field of computation science and the first, foremost, and perhaps only computation science academician in the entire USSR Academy of Information Sciences.

Education: diplomat of Lomonosov University, Moscow, 1954; candidate, physical and mathematical sciences, Scientific Council, Siberian Division, USSR Academy of Sciences, 1962; doctor, physical and mathematical sciences, Supreme Qualification Commission, USSR Ministry of Higher Education.

Professional Experience: staff member, department head, Computing Centre, USSR Academy of Sciences (Moscow), 1957–1960; laboratory head, Institute of Mathematics, Siberian Division, USSR Academy of Sciences (Novosibirsk), 1960–1963; laboratory head, Informatics Department head, Computing Centre, Siberian Division, USSR Academy of Sciences (Novosibirsk), 1963; assistant, Moscow University, 1958–1960; lecturer,

Novosibirsk University, 1961–1967; professor, Novosibirsk University, 1968–1988.

Honors and Awards: corresponding member, Academy of Sciences, USSR (Mathematical Sciences).

Andrei Petrovich Ershov (Yershov), one of the best-known computer scientists of the world, like many of his generation, got involved in computing almost by accident.

Born in 1931, in the autumn of 1949 at the age of 18, he enrolled in the Physico-Technical Department of Lomonsov University in Moscow. Incidentally, "enrolled" is far too bland a verb. To register as a student in this very prestigious department, one had to pass a three-stage entrance examination, designed and implemented to select the brightest and most gifted applicants. Years later Ershov was known to comment that, more than a keen interest in nuclear physics, it was the challenge of these incredibly tough examinations which made him apply. Soon, however, fate, in the particularly unattractive guise of Stalinist paranoia, intervened: the department was to become an extra-university Physico-Technical Institute, whose students were to be not only very talented, but also totally reliable. In those days, someone, who—like Ershov—as a child lived in Soviet territories overrun by Germany in World War II, and thus found themselves, however briefly, under Nazi occupation, could not be considered entirely reliable. In 1950 Ershov was transferred to the Mathematics Department in the university, where the maverick mathematician S. Sobolev was setting up a new chair of computational mathematics, to which Ershov was attracted.

Sobolev, who worked also for the Institute of Atomic Energy, was heavily involved in the design of the first Soviet electronic computers, but most of his work was at that time classified and very little of it was known in the much freer university environment. Computational mathematics was still primarily about numeric schemata, mathematical tables, and clanking electro-mechanical adding machines. Things had changed a little when in 1952 a young professor, A.A. Lyapunov, joined Sobolev's group and started teaching the fundamentals of programming for automatic computers. To Ershov, with his penchant for intellectual challenges, Lyapunov's brand of programming, full of forbidding symbols and tortured conventions, must have appeared a paradise. A close collaboration between Lyapunov and Ershov lasted for more than a decade and survived their migration to the Science City in Siberia (in the vicinity of Novosibirsk), where their paths eventually diverged: Lyapunov established a chair in the university, Ershov chose to work in the Computing Centre of the Siberian Branch of the

Soviet Academy of Sciences, led by a brilliant numerical analyst G.I. Marchuk (a future deputy prime minister of the USSR and the president of the Soviet Academy). In the Computing Centre Ershov was the head of the Software Division.

Another important source of early inputs to Ershov's computing education and development was S. Lebedyev's design of "civilian" computers, first in Kiev, where he was frequently visited by Lyapunov, then in a specially established Institute for Computing Machines in Moscow. It was for Lebedyev's machines, BESM and STRELA, that toward the end of the 1950s Ershov started developing his "programming programmes"—as language/compiler combinations were then known in Soviet terminology.

Ershov graduated in 1954 with a diploma of the Lomonsov University (the class of 1954 was the very first crop of Soviet university-educated programmers), and until 1960 continued his research in Moscow. In 1958 he was sent to England to attend the Teddington Conference on the Mechanisation of Thought Processes. It was his first trip abroad. It was there that he met another newcomer on the international computing scene, John McCarthy, a meeting that some years later developed into friendship and collaboration almost unthinkable in the Cold War. To generations born after Garry Powers' U2 plane was shot down over the Russian heartland it may seem quite commonplace that McCarthy visited Ershov in Novosibirsk in 1965; in fact, he was the first Westerner to be allowed to. Three years later, McCarthy spent two months there, teaching and interacting with students and faculty. Ershov, however, was not allowed to accept a return invitation to spend a semester at Stanford University.

Even though Ershov traveled to the West quite often and struck friendships with many eminent scientists, almost to the end of his days he had to apply for the Soviet exit visa for each trip, and never could be quite sure that one would be granted. He was never allowed to take up a visiting position in a foreign university; all his trips abroad were short, and thus incredibly packed with talks, seminars, conversations, and the greedy sight-seeing that was special to people who never know if this isn't their last chance.

Ershov keenly supported international scientific exchanges and cooperation. He was very active in various IFIP committees and conferences, served as an editor of the international journals *Acta Informatica* and *Information Processing Letters*, and organized numerous international conferences in Novosibirsk and other regions of the Soviet Union. Acting as an adviser to several Soviet publishing houses, Ershov initiated (and often edited) a large number of Russian translations of important Western books on computing. Establishing and developing personal and professional links between foreign computer scientists and their Soviet colleagues were goals to which Ershov devoted a good deal of his enviable energy.

In his homeland, Ershov established his reputation as a leading software expert with two major compiler projects: ALPHA and BETA. ALPHA was an optimizing compiler for an Algol-like language (its final version, ALPHA-6, is still being used). BETA is a multilanguage environment of Gargantuan scope and surprisingly elegant internal design. Ershov was also very active in the design of a multiaccess operating system AIST-0, and in a host of other practical programming projects, including a very comprehensive desktop publishing system MRAMOR, commissioned by the largest Soviet daily newspaper, *Pravda*.

Ershov was also a prolific research scientist, whose interests ranged from artificial intelligence to mixed computing (partial evaluation and transformational programming); for the latter he gained a truly international recognition. His pioneering work on minimal-memory compilation and on the theory of programming (Yanov-Ershov schemata) is somewhat less well known in the Western countries but equally important and highly regarded by the experts. In 1985 he launched a novel approach to program semantics, according to which the fundamental notions of a program would be defined by a program lexicon, a growing, structured collection of nontrivial facts about the program domain (objects), expressed in a formal notation.

Ershov was a recognized leader in the field of computer programming in the Soviet Union. He was the first ever programmer to receive the coveted Krylov Prize in mathematics, a corresponding member of the Soviet Academy of Sciences since 1970, and its full member since 1980. Ershov was finally elected the chairman of the Academy's Scientific Committee on Cybernetics—the supreme Soviet authority on computing. He used his influential positions well.

Back in 1972, Professor F.L. Bauer of Munich wrote *Andrei und das Untier*, a children's introduction to computers, charmingly illustrated with graffiti-like drawings based on original sketches by Ershov's son, Vassilyi. The choice of the first name of the book's main character and the setting of the story in a town "half way between Tomsk and Omsk," two Siberian cities, proved to be prophetic.

Fully aware of the social consequences of the ability to use computers, and of the cultural importance of programming (he called it "the second literacy"), Ershov was a tireless champion of school informatics—introduction of computers and information processing into pre-university education. He himself wrote (and coauthored) school curricula and textbooks, sponsored computer holiday camps for children, hosted an educational-TV series on information processing, begged for computers for schools, lectured on the dangers of computer illiteracy to the public and to the government of his country, and carried his crusade to an apparently successful meeting with the then Soviet president, Gorbachev.

Ershov fully appreciated the liberating power of a personal computer. His passionate pursuit of school computing embraced a dual purpose: to enrich young people with the intellectual gift of programming, and to put the power of information processing at their disposal. To see his campaign for school informatics in a proper perspective, one should remember that it was initiated in a country where access to ordinary copying machines was severely restricted and strictly controlled.

Ershov's views on programming, expressed in a series of essays started in 1972 by an article entitled "Aesthetic and Human Factors in Programming," attracted worldwide attention. Describing the profession, he wrote: "A programmer has to have the ability of a first-class mathematician for abstraction and logical thinking combined with an Edisonian talent for making anything in the world from a zero and unity. He must combine the accuracy of a bank clerk with the foresight of a scout, the imagination of a writer of detective stories with the sober practicality of a businessman, and, in addition to all this, he has to have a taste for teamwork, be loyal to its organizer, and possess many other qualities. Since a program-equipped machine behaves rationally and the programmer is the first to notice it, then, to use the idea of trinity, at this moment he feels like the father—the creator of the program—the son—the spiritual brother of the machine—and the bearer of the holy spirit—the intellect put into it."

As a typical member of the Russian intelligentsia, Ershov was the very opposite of a technocrat. He was a book-lover and read voraciously in his native Russian and in English; he could quote at length from Pushkin and Shakespeare, Evtushenko and Kipling. At the age of 50, Ershov turned to active poetry, first as a translator of English poems into Russian, then as an author. His poems, of classical form and rich in ornamental detail, are disturbingly intimate in their concentration on inner disquietudes and anxieties of a scientist's creative mind. "From hidden places, I obtained knowledge for people not to live by bread alone, and bear my cross without knowing if I shall be merely crucified or also sent to heaven" and "Which is the better: to ask myself a million questions, or to answer a single one asked by another man?" are two (roughly translated) samples from Ershov's poems.

In the last years of his life, Ershov was fighting an unwinnable battle against a terminal cancer. Scientifically and politically active to the end, Andrei Petrovich Ershov died on December, 8, 1988. East and West, many miss him.[13]

QUOTATIONS

"Programmers constitute the first large group of men whose work brings them to those limits of human knowledge which are marked by algorithmically unsolvable problems and which touch upon deeply secret aspects of the human brain." (From keynote speech, 1972 SJCC, reprinted in the *Honeywell Comp. J.*, Vol. 6, No. 1, 1972)

BIBLIOGRAPHY

Biographical

Ershov, Andrei P., and Mikhail R. Shura-Bura, "The Early Development of Programming in the USSR," in Metropolis, N., J. Howlett, and Gian-Carlo Rota, *A History of Computing in the Twentieth Century*, Academic Press, New York, 1980, pp. 137–196.

Gries, David, "International Pioneer Dies," *Ann. Hist. Comp.*, Vol. 12, No. 1, 1990, p. 62.

Turski, Wladylaw, "Obituary: Andrei Ershov," *Ann. Hist. Comp.*, Vol. 15, No. 2, 1993, pp. 55ff.

Significant Publications

Ershov, A.P., "On Programming of Arithmetic Operations," *Comm. ACM*, Vol. 1, No. 8, 1958, pp. 3–6.

Ershov, A.P., *Input Language for Automatic Programming Systems*, Academic Press, New York, 1963.

Ershov, A.P., "ALPHA—An Automatic Programming System of High Efficiency," *Proc. IFIP 1965*, Vol. 2, 1965, pp. 622–623, and *J. ACM*, Vol. 13, 1966, pp. 17–24.

Ershov, A.P., "An Experimental Automatic Information Station AIST-O," *Proc. Spring Joint Computer Conf.*, Spartan Books, N.Y., 1967, pp. 577–582.

---

[13]From Turski 1993.

Ershov, A.P., "Theory of Program Schemata," *Proc. IFIP 1971,* North-Holland, Amsterdam, pp. 144–163.

Ershov, A.P., "Aesthetic and Human Factors in Programming," *Comm. ACM,* Vol. 15, 1972, pp. 501–505.

Ershov, A.P., "A History of Computing in USSR," *Datamation,* Vol. 21, No. 9, 1975, pp. 80–88.

Ershov, A.P., "Axiomatics for Memory Allocation," *Acta Inform.,* Vol. 6, 1976, pp. 61–75.

Ershov, A.P., "An Implementation-Oriented Method for Describing Algorithmic Languages," *Proc. IFIP 1977,* North-Holland, Amsterdam, pp. 117–122.

Ershov, A.P., "On the Partial Computation Principle," *Inf. Proc. Letters,* Vol. 6, 1977, pp. 38–41.

Ershov, A.P., "Mixed Computation in the Class of Recursive Program Schemata," *Acta Cybernetica,* Vol. 4, 1978, pp. 19–23.

Ershov, A.P., *Origins of Programming: Discourses on Methodology,* trans. by Robert H. Silverman, Springer-Verlag, New York, 1990.

BOB OVERTON (BO) EVANS

Born August 19, 1927, Grand Island, Neb.; influential manager within IBM committed to compatibility, a concept which led to the IBM System/360 family of machines.

Education: BEE, Iowa State University, 1949.

Professional Experience: electrical operating engineer, Northern Indiana Public Service Co., Hammond, Ind., 1949–1951; IBM Corp.: staff member, 1951–1962, vice president, Data Systems Division, 1962–1964, president, Federal Systems Division, 1965–1969, Systems Development Division, 1970–1974, Systems Communications Division, 1975–1977, IBM vice president, engineering, programming and technology, 1977–1984; general partner, Hambrecht and Quist Venture Partners, 1984–1988; senior vice president, managing partner, Technology Strategies & Alliances, 1988–present.

Honors and Awards: Distinguished Public Service Award, NASA, 1969; Meritorious Service Award, Armed Forces Communication and Electrical Association, 1969; member, National Academy of Engineering, 1970; fellow, IEEE, 1971; Professional Achievement Citation in Engineering, Iowa State University, 1973; National Security Agency Citation, 1975; Edwin H. Armstrong Medal, IEEE Communications Society, 1984; National Medal of Technology, 1985; Distinguished Achievement Citation, Iowa State University, 1991; Computer Pioneer, IEEE Computer Society, 1992.

"Bo" joined IBM in 1951 as a junior engineer working on the IBM-701 (Defense Calculator), and had various responsibilities through 1962 when he was appointed vice president for the Data Systems Division, developing the System/360. In 1961, only 10 years after joining IBM, he almost single-handedly persuaded management to abandon a less ambitious product plan for one that resulted in the IBM System/360. He demonstrated a model of the IBM System/360 on April 7, 1964, the day the system was announced. In 1985, Bo Evans, Fred Brooks, and Eric Bloch received the National Medal of Technology at a White House ceremony for their work in developing the IBM System/360, described as "revolutionizing the industry."[14]

QUOTATION

"I am the luckiest person in the world to have worked at IBM during the time of its entry into electronic computing, and to be part of the computer industry in those most exciting years."

BIBLIOGRAPHY

Biographical

Evans, B.O., et al., "Discussion of the SPREAD Report," *Ann. Hist. Comp.*, Vol. 5, No. 4, 1983, pp. 27–44.

Evans, B.O., "System/360: A Retrospective View," *Ann. Hist. Comp.*, Vol. 8, No. 2, 1986, pp. 155–179.

[14]Based on Pugh, Emerson W., Lyle R. Johnson, and John H. Palmer, *IBM's 360 and Early 370 Systems*, MIT Press, Cambridge, Mass., 1991.

ROBERT RIVERS EVERETT

Born June 26, 1921, Yonkers, N.Y.; designer of Whirlwind under Jay Forrester, and later president of the MITRE Corporation.

Education: BSEE, Duke University, 1942; MSEE, MIT, 1943; DEng, Northeastern University, 1985.

Professional Experience: research and development engineer, Servomechanism Laboratory, MIT, 1942–1951; associate director, computation laboratory, MIT, 1951–1956; associate head, Digital Computing Division, Lincoln Laboratory, 1951–1956; head, Digital Computing Division, 1956–1958, technical director, Command and Control Systems, 1958–1959, vice president, Technical Operations, 1959–1969, executive vice president, 1969; president, MITRE Corporation, 1969–present.

Honors and Awards: member, National Academy of Engineering; fellow, IEEE, 1969; IEEE Computer Society Pioneer Award, 1987.

Everett joined the MIT Servomechanisms Laboratory in 1942 as a graduate student and in 1943 as a staff member. He was Jay W. Forrester's assistant and became associate director of the Digital Computer Laboratory. Everett and Forrester had little or no experience working out the precise sequences of controlled electrical states required. In lieu of the knowledge of experience, Everett had at his disposal the theoretical insights of the pioneering investigators, among whom were Aiken, Babbage, Bush, Eckert, Goldstine, Mauchly, Stibitz, and von Neumann. Everett was compelled to undertake highly complicated system-building of his own, which had no precedent, especially in the realms of reliability of performance and rapidity demanded by Whirlwind. One never knew when Everett or Forrester would stop by a workbench or a test rig to see what was going on; there was no question they were keeping in touch, nor was there any reason to doubt their ability to grasp the essentials of problems and see avenues of attack. "Forrester would come into the lab and tear everything apart," recalled [an engineer], "and Bob would come along and put it back together again."[15]

When the Lincoln Laboratory was formed by MIT in 1951, Everett became associate head of Division 6, of which he became head in 1956. Division 6 was responsible for overall systems design and testing of the SAGE system and its direction centers; it developed the first magnetic-core memories developed by Forrester. The SAGE-design parts of Lincoln were spun off into the nonprofit MITRE Corporation

---

[15]From Redmond, Kent C., and Thomas M. Smith, 1980.

in 1958, and Everett was technical director. In 1959 he was appointed vice president and chief executive officer; ten years later he was appointed executive vice president and then president. He is a fellow of IEEE and is an adviser to several federal defense organizations.

BIBLIOGRAPHY

Biographical

Everett, Robert R., "Whirlwind," in Metropolis, N., J. Howlett, and Gian-Carlo Rota, *A History of Computing in the Twentieth Century,* Academic Press, New York, 1980, pp. 365–384.

Redmond, Kent C., and Thomas M. Smith, *Project Whirlwind: The History of a Pioneer Computer,* Digital Press, Bedford, Mass., 1980.

Ritchie, David, *The Computer Pioneers,* Simon and Shuster, New York, 1986, Chapter 10.

Significant Publications

Everett, R.R., *Digital Computing Machine Logic,* Mem. M-63, MIT Servomechanisms Lab., Cambridge, Mass., 1947.

Everett, R.R., et al., "SAGE—A Data-Processing System for Air Defense," *Proc. EJCC,* Washington, D.C., pp. 148–155, reprinted in *Ann. Hist. Comp.,* Vol. 5, No. 4, Oct. 1983, pp. 330–339.

FREDERICO FAGGIN

Born December 1, 1941, Vicenza, Italy; with Ted Hoff, the developer of the silicon gate process and the microprocessor.

Education: Dottore in Fisica, summa cum laude, University of Padua, Italy, 1965.

Professional Experience: Olivetti R&D Labs, Borgolombardo (Milan), Italy, 1960–1961; assistant professor, University of Padua, Italy, 1965–1966; senior engineer, CERES, Cornaredo (Milan), Italy, 1966–1967; group leader, SGS-Fairchild, Agrate (Milan), Italy, 1967–1968; group leader, Fairchild Semiconductor R&D Laboratories, Palo Alto, Calif., 1968–1970; Intel Corp., Santa Clara, Calif., 1970–1974; cofounder, president, and CEO, Zilog, Inc., Cupertino, Calif., 1974–1980; Computer Systems Group vice president, Exxon Enterprises, Inc., New York, 1981; cofounder, president, and CEO, Cygnet Technologies, Inc., Sunnyvale, Calif., 1982–86; cofounder, president, and CEO, Synaptics, Inc., San Jose, Calif., 1986–Present.

Honors and Awards: International Marconi Fellowship Award, 1988; Gold Medal for Science and Technology from the President of the Italian Government, 1988; Grande Ufficiale, (the highest title given by the Italian Republic), the President of Italy, 1992.

Frederico Faggin commenced his career at the Olivetti R&D Labs, Borgolombardo (Milan), in 1970 where he codesigned and built a small electronic digital computer. Following a one-year stint as an assistant professor at the University of Padua (1965–1966), he joined CERES, Cornaredo (Milan), as a senior engineer, working on various aspects of thin-film circuit technology. One year later he was employed as a Group Leader with SGS-Fairchild, Agrate (Milan), where he developed SGS's first MOS fabrication process technology and two commercial MOS integrated circuits.

In 1968 he transferred to the Fairchild Semiconductor R&D Laboratories, Palo Alto, Calif., where he led the development of the MOS Silicon Gate Technology process. Working with Thomas Klein, he developed the first viable process for the fabrication of high-density and high-speed MOS integrated circuits using a doped polycrystalline gate electrode, instead of an aluminum gate currently used at the time. He also designed, in 1968, the first commercial circuit using the silicon gate technology—the Fairchild 3708, an 8-bit analog multiplexer. The MOS silicon gate technology was a major stepping-stone making possible the early development of semiconductor memories and microprocessors and formed the basis of today's IOS/VLSI technology.

In 1970, he joined Intel Corp. and led the design of the first microprocessor family. The basic architecture of what was to become the MCS-4 had already been outlined by Ted Hoff, working in conjunction with Busicom, the exclusive customer of the MCS-4. This chip set was to be used for a series of electronic calculators. Faggin took over the project and, in 11 months, single-handedly developed the four-chip set that included the first single-chip microprocessor. His work involved the refining of the architecture, doing the logic design, the circuit design, and the layout, and also bringing the MCS-4 into production. Faggin then demonstrated noncalculator applications for the MCS-4 and convinced Intel's management to offer the MCS-4 for sale as a general-purpose chip set.

In the spring of 1971, Faggin led the development of the "8008," the first 8-bit microprocessor, and brought it to market one year later. Faggin conceived the 8080 in 1972, development took place in 1973, and he led the design of the product in early 1974.

During his almost five years at Intel, Faggin developed or directed the development of approximately 30 integrated circuits and provided the key leadership role in all of Intel's microprocessor direction.

At the end of October 1974, Faggin left Intel to start a new company—Zilog, Inc. His idea was to create a company dedicated to the emerging microprocessor and microcomputer market. The first product that Faggin conceived was the "Z80." Introduced in 1976, the Z80 was the most successful 8-bit microprocessor ever produced and was still in high volume production in 1992. He led the company that for several years was at the forefront of microprocessor technology.

After some years with Exxon Enterprises, Inc., in New York, and founding Cygnet Technologies, Inc., in Sunnyvale, Calif. (1982–1986), Faggin cofounded Synaptics, Inc., a company with the purpose of developing integrated circuits for information sensing and processing, using some of the working principles of animal nervous systems. Such artificial neural networks are expected to enable the creation of autonomous intelligent machines. Synaptics has developed the world's first Optical Character Recognizer Integrated Circuit, combining an area imager and two neural networks on the same chip. Synaptics is the leading company in the development and application of neural network technology for the solution of practical problems. Synaptics has created a new implementation technology, Adaptive Analog VLSI, for sensory, sensory preprocessing, and pattern recognition tasks.

Faggin is currently (1993) president of Synaptics.

BIBLIOGRAPHY

Significant Publications

Allen, T., C. Mead, F. Faggin, and G. Gribble, "Orientation Selective VLSI Retina," *Proc. Visual Communications and Image Processing*, 1988, pp. 1040–1046.

Faggin, F., "Microelectronics in the Eighties," *Microprocessing and Microprogramming*, Vol. 9, 1982, pp. 1–6.

Faggin, F., "The Challenge of Bringing New Ideas to Market," *High Technology*, Feb. 1985.

Faggin, F., "Trends in Microprocessors," *IEEE Circuit and Systems J.*, Mar. 1975.

Faggin, F., "The Birth of the Microprocessor," *Byte*, Mar. 1992, pp. 145–150.

Faggin, F., "How VLSI Impacts Computer Architecture," *IEEE Spectrum*, May 1978.

Faggin, F., and F. Capocaccia, "A New Integrated MOS Shift Register," *Atti del Convegno Elettronico Internazionale di Roma*, Rome, Italy, Apr. 1968.

Faggin, F., and F. Capocaccia, "An Integrated High Noise Immunity MOS Logic Circuit with Hysteresis," *Atti del Convegno Elettronico Internazionale di Roma*, Rome, Italy, Apr. 1968.

Faggin, F., et al., "The MCS-4—An LSI Microcomputer System," *IEEE Region Six Conference*, San Diego, Calif., Apr. 1972.

Faggin, F., D. Forsyth, and T. Klein, "Room Temperature Instability of Silicon-Gate Devices," *Reliability Conference*, Las Vegas, Nev., Apr. 1970.

Faggin, F., and T. Hoff, "Standard Parts and Custom Design Merge in Four-Chip Processor Kit," *Electronics*, Apr. 1972.

Faggin, F., and T. Klein, "Silicon Gate Technology," *Solid State Electronics*, Vol. 13, 1970, pp. 1125–1144.

Faggin, F., and T. Klein, "A Faster Generation of MOS Devices with Low Threshold Is Riding the Crest of the New Wave, Silicon-Gate ICs," *Electronics*, Sept. 1969.

Faggin, F., and C. Mead, "VLSI Implementations of Neural Networks," *An Introduction to Neural and Electronic Networks*, Academic Press, New York, 1990, pp. 275–292.

Platt, J.C., and F. Faggin, "Network for the Separation of Sources That Are Superimposed and Delayed," *Advances in Neural Information Processing Systems 4*, Morgan-Kaufmann, San Mateo, Calif., 1992, pp. 730–737.

Shima, M., F. Faggin, and R. Ungermann, "Z80: Chip Set Heralds Third Microprocessor Generation," *Electronics*, Aug. 1976.

Patents:

Klein, Thomas; Faggin, Federico: To Fairchild Camera and Instrument. *Doped Semiconductor Electrodes for MOS Type Devices*. Patent No. 3,673,471. June 27, 1972.

Faggin, Federico: To Intel Corp. *Power Supply Settable Bi-Stable Circuit*. Patent No. 3,753,011. Aug. 14, 1973.

Hoff, Marcian; Mazor, Stanley; Faggin, Federico: To Intel Corp. *Memory System For Multi-Chip Digital Computer.* Patent No. 3,821,715. June 28, 1974.

Faggin, Federico; Shima, Masatoshi; Mazor, Stanley: To Intel Corp. *MOS Computer Employing A Plurality of Separate Chips.* Patent No. 4,010, 499. Mar. 1, 1977.

Shima, Masatoshi; Faggin, Federico; Ungermann, Ralph K.: To Zilog, Inc. *Microprocessor Apparatus and Method.* Patent No. 4,332,008. May 25, 1982.

Faggin, Federico; et al.: To Cygnet Technologies, Inc. *Digital and Voice Telecommunication Apparatus.* Patent No. 4,524,244. June 18, 1985.

Faggin, Federico; Lynch, Gary S.; Sukonick, Josef S.: To Synaptics, Inc. *Brain Emulation Circuit with Reduced Confusion.* Patent No. 4,773,024. Sept. 20, 1988.

Faggin, Federico; Lynch, Gary S.: To Synaptics, Inc. *Brain Learning and Recognition Emulation Circuitry and Method of Recognizing Events.* Patent No. 4,802,103. Jan. 31, 1989.

Mead, Carver; Allen, Timothy; Faggin, Federico: To Synaptics, Inc. *Dynamic Synapse for Neural Network.* Patent No. 4,962, 928. Oct. 9, 1990.

Mead, Carver; Allen, Timothy; Faggin, Federico; Anderson, Janeen: To Synaptics, Inc. *Synaptics Element and Array.* Patent No. 5,083, 044. Jan. 21, 1992.

Mead, Carver; Faggin Federico: To Synaptics, Inc. *Integrating Photosensors and Imaging System Having Wide Dynamic Range.* Patent No. 5,097,305. Mar. 17, 1992.

Mead, Carver; Faggin, Federico; Allen, Timothy; Anderson, Janeen: To Synaptics, Inc. *Synaptic Element and Array.* Patent No. 5,120,996. June 9, 1992.

JOHN W. FAIRCLOUGH

Born August 23, 1930, Thirsk, Yorkshire, UK; Fairclough managed the development of IBM System/360 Model 40 at IBM's laboratory in Hursley, England;[1] development manager for SNA and CICS.

Education: BSc (Tech.), electrical engineering, Manchester University, 1954.

Professional Experience: Ferranti Ltd. (UK) and Ferranti Electric (US), 1954–1957; IBM Corp.: project engineer, Poughkeepsie, 1957–1959, project manager, UK Laboratories, Ltd., 1959–1964, laboratory director, UK

---

[1]According to Pugh, Emerson W., Lyle R. Johnson, and John H. Palmer, *IBM's 360 and Early 370 Systems,* MIT Press, Cambridge, Mass., 1991.

Laboratories, Ltd., 1964–1968, director of data processing, marketing, 1969–1970, laboratory director, IBM Laboratory, Raleigh, N.C., 1970–1972, vice president, Communications Systems, 1972–1974, chairman, UK Laboratories, Ltd., 1974–1986, chairman, manufacturing and development, 1982–1986; chief scientific adviser, Cabinet Office, UK, 1986–1990; chairman, Rothschild Ventures, Ltd., 1990–present.

Honors and Awards: fellow, Institute of Electrical Engineering, 1975; fellow, British Computer Society, 1975; fellow, Fellowship of Engineering, 1987; fellow, National Academy of Engineering, 1989; DSc (Hon.), University of Southampton, 1983; DSc (Hon.), University of Cranfield, 1987; DSc (Hon.), University of Manchester, 1988; freeman, City of London, 1989; Gold Medal, Institution of Production Engineers, 1989; DSc (Hon.), University of Aston, 1990; DTech (Hon.), University of Loughborough, 1990; knight bachelor, 1990; honorary fellow, Portsmouth Polytechnic, 1991; DSc (Hon.), Central London Polytechnic, 1991; DSc (Hon.), City University, 1992.

After a spell with Ferranti Ltd., John Fairclough moved to the US and the IBM Corporation in 1957 to work on the project which created the STRETCH computer (IBM-7030). He then returned to the UK to manage the development of the IBM System/360 Model 40 at IBM's laboratory in Hursley, England. Earlier he had managed Hursley's SCAMP project, which led to an important IBM System/360 technological feature: the control store and the use of microprogramming. In April 1965, the Model 40 was the first System/360 model tested and the first shipped to a customer.

In 1968 Fairclough was given responsibility for IBM's marketing and service activities in the UK, where he was a prime mover in the development of on-line, terminal-based, banking systems, including the first on-line automatic cash dispensers (ATMs).

In 1970 Fairclough was appointed director of IBM's laboratory in Raleigh, N.C., where he identified the need for a unified communication architecture to support IBM systems. In partnership with Earl Wheeler, the director of IBM Kingston Laboratory, he set up the effort to define and develop the System Network Architecture (SNA).

In 1974 he returned to the UK as chairman of IBM's laboratory at Hursley, England. He reshaped the mission of the laboratory to make significant contributions to display technology with the development of the first production high-resolution color display, the IBM-3279, and in graphics systems with the IBM-3250 system. He also introduced the development responsibility to the Hursley Laboratory for IBM's Customer Information Communication System (CICS), which has become IBM's most valuable programming product.

In 1986 Fairclough was appointed chief scientific adviser to Prime Minister Thatcher's government, a post he held until 1990. In this position he played a pivotal role in reshaping national science policy.

In 1992 Fairclough was engaged in a number of national activities: chairman of the UK Engineering Council, chairman of the Centre for the Exploitation of Science and Technology, and chairman of the Prince of Wales Innovation Initiative. He was chairman of Rothschild Ventures Limited, and a director of the N.M. Rothschild Bank.

ADIN D. FALKOFF

Born December 19, 1921, New Jersey; with Ken Iverson, coauthor, implementer and promoter of the programming language APL.

Education: BChE, chemical engineering, City College of New York, 1941; MA, mathematics, Yale University, 1963 (under the IBM Resident Scholarship Program).

Professional Experience: joined IBM, 1955; staff member (part-time), IBM Systems Research Institute, 1963–1967; visiting lecturer, Yale University, 1968–1970; established and managed IBM Philadelphia Scientific Center, 1970–1974; manager, APL Design Group, T.J. Watson Research Center, 1977–1987; research staff member, Computer Science Department, T. J. Watson Research Center, 1987–present.

Honors and Awards: IBM Outstanding Contribution Awards for development of APL and APL/360; first recipient, ACM Award for "outstanding contribution to the development and application of APL," 1983.

BIBLIOGRAPHY

Biographical

Falkoff, Adin D., and Kenneth E. Iverson, "The Evolution of APL," in Wexelblat, Richard L., ed., *History of Programming Languages,* Academic Press, New York, 1981, Chapter 14.

Significant Publications

Falkoff, A.D., "Algorithms for Parallel Search Memories," *J. ACM,* Vol. 9, No. 4, 1962, pp. 488–511.

Falkoff, A.D., K.E. Iverson, and E.H. Sussenguth, "A Formal Description of System/360," *IBM Systems J.*, Vol. 3, No. 4, 1964, pp. 198–262.

Falkoff, A.D., and K.E. Iverson, "The Design of APL," *IBM J. Research and Development*, Vol. 17, No. 4, 1973, pp. 324–334.

Falkoff, A.D., "A Note on Pattern Matching," *APL79 Proceedings, APL Quote Quad*, Vol. 9, No. 4, Part 1, 1979, pp. 119–122.

Falkoff, A.D., and D.L. Orth, "Development of an APL Standard," *APL79 Proceedings, APL Quote Quad*, Vol. 9, No. 4, Part 2, 1979, pp. 409–453.

Falkoff, A.D., "The IBM Family of APL Systems," *IBM Systems J.*, Vol. 30, No. 4, 1991, pp. 416–432.

ROBERT M. FANO

Born November 11, 1917, Torino, Italy; leader of Project MAC, which established interactive computing through time-sharing as a common part of modern computer systems.

Education: SB, electrical engineering, MIT, 1941; ScD, electrical engineering, MIT, 1947.

Professional Experience: student engineer, General Motors Corp., 1941; MIT: Radiation Laboratory, 1944–1946, Research Laboratory of Electronics, 1946–1963, research associate, Department of Electrical Engineering, 1946–1947, assistant professor, Department of Electrical Engineering, 1947–1951, associate professor, Department of Electrical Engineering, 1951–1956, group leader, Radar Techniques Group, Lincoln Laboratory, 1950–1953, professor, Department of Electrical Engineering, 1956–1984, director, Project MAC (now Laboratory for Computer Science), 1963–1968, associate head, Department of Electrical Engineering and Computer Science, 1971–1974, Ford Professor of Engineering, Department of Electrical Engineering and Computer Science, 1962–1984, professor emeritus, Department of Electrical Engineering, 1984–present; visiting scientist, IBM Zurich Research Laboratory, 1974–1975; member, board of trustees, Bentley College, Waltham, Mass., 1973–present.

Honors and Awards: member, National Academy of Sciences; member, National Academy of Engineering; fellow, American Academy of Arts and Sciences; fellow, IEEE; Shannon Lecturer, IEEE Information Theory Group, 1976; IEEE Education Medal, 1977; International Institute of Communications "City of

Columbus, Ohio" Prize, 1969; International Institute of Communications Columbian Gold Medal of the city of Genova, Italy, 1986.

Robert Fano did most of his undergraduate work at the School of Engineering of Torino before moving to the US in 1939. He received the bachelor of science degree in 1941 and the doctor of science degree in 1947, both in electrical engineering, from MIT. He has been a member of the MIT staff since 1941 and a member of its faculty since 1947.

During World War II, Professor Fano was on the staff of the MIT Radiation Laboratory, working on microwave components and filters. He was also group leader of the Radar Techniques Group of Lincoln Laboratory from 1950 to 1953. He has worked and published at various times in the fields of network theory, microwaves, electromagnetism, information theory, computers, and engineering education. He was author of the book entitled *Transmission of Information* and coauthor of *Electromagnetic Fields, Energy and Forces* and *Electromagnetic Energy Transmission and Radiation*. He was also coauthor of Volume 9 of the Radiation Laboratory Series.

Professor Fano was Ford Professor of Engineering, in the Department of Electrical Engineering and Computer Science at MIT, until his retirement in June 1984. He organized MIT's Project MAC (now Laboratory for Computer Science) in 1963 and was its director until September 1968. He also served as associate head of the Department of Electrical Engineering and Computer Science from 1971 to 1974.

Professor Fano is a member of the National Academy of Sciences and of the National Academy of Engineering, and a fellow of the American Academy of Arts and Sciences, and of the Institute of Electrical and Electronic Engineers (IEEE). He was the 1976 Shannon Lecturer of the IEEE Information Theory Group, and the recipient of the 1977 Education Medal of the IEEE. He was also the recipient of the 1969 prize "City of Columbus, Ohio" and of the 1986 Columbian Gold Medal of the city of Genova, Italy, both awarded by the International Institute of Communications. He has served on the board of trustees of Bentley College, Waltham, Mass., since 1973, and is presently (1991) a member of its Executive Committee.

QUOTATION

In discussing his background of electrical engineering during the 1988 *Annals of the History of Computing* interviews associated with the 25th anniversary of the MIT Laboratory of Computer Science, he said of himself in 1963 that he "learned enough about computers to become the leader of Project MAC."

BIBLIOGRAPHY

Biographical

Fano, Robert M., "Project MAC," in Belzer, Jack, et al., eds., *Encyclopedia of Computer Science and Technology,* Marcel Dekker, New York, 1979, pp. 339–360.

Significant Publications

Fano, R.M., "The MAC System: The Computer Utility Approach," *IEEE Spectrum,* Jan. 1965, pp. 56–64.

Fano, R.M., "The MAC System: A Progress Report," in Sass, M.A., and W.D. Wilkinson, eds., *Computer Augmentation of Human Reasoning,* Spartan Books, 1965, pp. 131–150.

Fano, R.M., and Fernando J. Corbató, "The Time-Sharing of Computers," *Scientific American,* Vol. 215, No. 3, Sept. 1966, pp. 128–140.

Fano, R.M., "The Computer Utility and the Community," *1967 IEEE Int'l Conv. Record,* Part 12, 1967, pp. 30–34.

Fano, Robert M., "Proposal for a Research and Development Program on Computer Systems," proposal submitted to the Advanced Projects Agency, MIT, Cambridge, Mass., 1963.

Fano, Robert M., "On the Social Role of Computer Communications," *Proc. IEEE,* Vol. 60, No. 11, Nov. 1972, pp. 1249–1253.

EDWARD E. FEIGENBAUM

Born January 20, 1936, Weehawken, N.J.; originator and promoter of the Fifth Generation and father of expert systems.

Education: BS, electrical engineering, Carnegie Institute of Technology, 1956; PhD, industrial administration, Carnegie Institute of Technology, 1960.

Professional Experience: Fulbright research scholar, Great Britain, 1959–1960; assistant professor, business administration, University of California at Berkeley, 1960–1964, associate professor, computer science, and director,

Computing Center, 1965–1969, professor of computer science, 1969–present, chairman, Department of Computer science, 1969–present; founded two start-up companies—Technowledge and IntelliCorp.

Honors and Awards: member, National Academy of Engineering, 1986 (for pioneering contributions to knowledge engineering and expert systems technology).

QUOTATION

"[Knowledge] is power, and computers that amplify that knowledge will amplify every dimension of power."

BIBLIOGRAPHY

Biographical

Caddes, Carolyn, *Portraits of Success: Impressions of Silicon Valley Pioneers,* Tioga Publishing Co., Palo Alto, Calif., 1986.

Significant Publications

Feigenbaum, E.A., and Julian Feldman, *Computers and Thought,* McGraw-Hill, New York, 1963.

SIDNEY FERNBACH

Born August 4, 1917, Philadelphia, Pa.; died February 15, 1991, Almo, Calif.; first (1952) head of the computing group at Lawrence Livermore National Laboratory, which used the very Univac I that predicted Eisenhower's landslide election; presented with the IEEE Computer Society W. Wallace McDowell Award "for continuously challenging, inspiring, and supporting American designers and industry to produce many successive generations of supercomputers."

Education: AM, Temple University, 1940; PhD, theoretical physics, University of California at Berkeley, 1952.

Professional Experience: physicist, Frankford Arsenal, 1940–1943; assistant instructor, University of Pennsylvania, 1943–1944; assistant professor, University of California, 1946–1948; member, staff, Stanford University, 1951–1952; physicist, 1948–1951 and 1952–1955, head, Computation Department, 1955–1979, head, Theoretical Division, 1958–1968, deputy associate director for scientific support, 1975–1979, Lawrence Livermore National Laboratory.

Honors and Awards: fellow, American Physical Society; fellow, American Association for the Advancement of Science; IEEE Computer Society Richard E. Merwin Award; IEEE Computer Society W. Wallace McDowell Award.

Trained as a physicist, Fernbach received the PhD in theoretical physics from the University of California, Berkeley, in 1952. After receiving his PhD he began his long and productive career as a physicist at the Lawrence Livermore National Laboratory. Immediately he began work with Edward Teller and Herb York to acquire the world's largest computer, the Univac I. It was that machine, while still at Philadelphia, which was used to support the CBS television reports on the 1952 presidential election. In 1955 he was appointed head of the Computation Department, a position he was to hold for the next 20 years. He was internationally recognized as one of the most influential scientists affecting the designs of high-performance computers during the period that the modern electronic computer grew from embryo to adolescence. From the first supercomputer systems, such as the Univac I and the IBM-704, to today's supercomputers, almost one million times faster, Sid Fernbach played a pivotal role.

Early on, he recognized that the "Livermore Lab" required ever-increasing power for its weapons designs. Fernbach developed important relationships with the primary computer vendors, but especially with Cray Research. Additionally, Fernbach's deep understanding of science, and his ability to abstract and generalize its needs, influenced the designs of the machines conceived in and built by one of the world's most innovative industries. Early on, he was able to convince his own laboratory management and the Atomic Energy Commission (later to become the Department of Energy) to support these multi-million-dollar acquisitions. No other individual at any of the other national laboratories has dominated the scene as strongly or for as long as did Sid, in a most complex position.

For the 10-year period between 1958 and 1968, Fernbach was also head of the theoretical division at Livermore. In 1975, until his retirement in 1979, he was deputy associate director for scientific support at the laboratory. He then became an independent consultant and maintained a long-term consultant relationship with Control Data Corporation.

He was involved in a broad array of committees for the Departments of Energy, Commerce, and Defense, and played important roles in the export control of high-performance computers. He was also in demand as a member of the board of directors of numerous high-performance computer start-ups. For a number of years he was a member of the Computer Science and Engineering Board of the National Academy of Sciences and of the NSF Computer Activities Advisory Board.

During his last eight years he founded and chaired the IEEE subcommittee on scientific supercomputing. In that role, he used his experience and understanding of the problems involved in high-performance computing to help mold US government policy to take cognizance of the importance of supercomputing to the economic and national security health of the country. Fernbach also founded the IEEE Computer Society Compcon Spring meeting in San Francisco and served for many years as an organizer and catalyst for that meeting. He organized the highly successful tutorial week preceding the conference.

He was a member of a number of professional societies and, driven by his broad interests, gave time and energy to many of them unstintingly. Although he eschewed them, he received many honors, including the Computer Society Richard E. Merwin Award and the McDowell Award, the latter "for continuously challenging, inspiring, and supporting American designers and industry to produce many successive generations of supercomputers."

He also edited a number of books relating to computing and physics. He was the originating editor of the *Journal of Computational Physics*. From their founding in 1985, he was subject area editor for applications for *The Journal of Supercomputing* and a member of the advisory board of the *International Journal of Supercomputer Applications*.

Perhaps Sid's most lovable attribute was an independent and a no-nonsense attitude toward getting the job done. He would not tolerate bureaucracy, and when discussing an issue, he would quickly get down to the core of the problem. This characteristic earned him the reputation of a no-nonsense sage who got things done. For these reasons, he was also an extremely effective member of visiting or oversight committees, often challenging the organization to perform at high levels. On a more personal level, he influenced many young colleagues by inspiring them to stretch and achieve higher goals.

He had close professional and personal relationships with leaders of supercomputing throughout the world. Those who worked closely with him developed great affection for him as well as enormous respect for him as an individual and as a scientist; we enjoyed his company enormously. He will be sorely missed.[2]

BIBLIOGRAPHY

Biographical

MacKenzie, Donald, "The Influence of the Los Alamos and Livermore National Laboratories on the Development of Computing," *Ann. Hist. Comp.*, Vol. 13, No. 2, 1991.

Williams, Michael R., "Pioneer Day 1984: Lawrence Livermore National Laboratory," *Ann. Hist. Comp.*, Vol. 7, No. 2, 1985, pp. 179–183.

Significant Publications

Fernbach, Sidney, "Scientific Uses of Computers," in Dertouzos, Michael, and Joel Moses, eds., *The Computer Age: A Twenty Year View*, MIT Press, Cambridge, Mass., 1979, pp. 146–160.

RICHARD P. FEYNMAN

Born May 11, 1918, Far Rockaway, N.Y.; died February 15, 1988, Los Angeles, Calif.; Nobel Laureate, who, in the late 1940s, first identified computer addiction as a disease.

Education: BS, theoretical physics, MIT, 1939; PhD, theoretical physics, Princeton University, 1942.

Professional Experience: physicist, Princeton University, 1941–1942; physicist, Los Alamos Project (Manhattan Project), 1941–1945; associate professor, physics, Cornell University, 1945–1951; Tolman Professor of Physics, California Institute of Technology, 1951–1988.

Honors and Awards: Nobel Prize in Physics, 1965; Einstein Award, 1954.

Feynman, one of the most influential scientific thinkers and calculators of the post-World War II era, cowinner of the Nobel Prize for his

---

[2]By the staff of the LLNL.

reconstruction of quantum mechanics and electrodynamics, best-selling author, and whistle-blowing commissioner-investigator of the Challenger space-shuttle disaster, died February 15, 1988, at the age of 69, of abdominal cancer. He is survived by a generation of students who learned quantum physics from the three volumes of his lectures published in 1963 and called by *The Economist* "one of the best physics texts, as well as the most readable."

Feynman was born in 1918 in Far Rockaway, N.Y., and graduated with a BS from MIT in 1935. At Princeton, where he received his PhD in 1942, he started working on the Manhattan Project. This kept him at Los Alamos from 1943 to 1946, where he was put in charge of the group using IBM punched card machines for implosion calculations. There he identified the now well-known computer disease, describing it in these terms: "It's a very serious disease and it interferes completely with the work. The trouble with computers is you *play* with them. They are so wonderful. You have these switches—if it's an even number you do this, if it's an odd number you do that—and pretty soon you can do more and more elaborate things if you are clever enough, on one machine. . . . If you've ever worked with computers you understand the disease—the *delight* in being able to see how much you can do."

After Los Alamos, Feynman never contracted that disease and he never worked with the military again.

Hans Bethe took him to Cornell where he did the work that led to his Nobel Prize, reconstructing and restating quantum mechanics and electrodynamics in terms of particles. This work resulted in his famous diagrams of their interaction trajectories and his simplified rules of calculation, which became standard tools of theoretical analysis.

In 1951 he went to Cal Tech where he remained until his death.

His autobiography, described by him as a collection of stories, was published in 1985 as told to Ralph Leighton with the title, *'Surely You're Joking, Mr. Feynman!' Adventures of a Curious Character.* Reissued in softcover, it has been for several years one of the top sellers in college bookstores. The stories describe an outrageous, provocative, mischievous, compulsive smart-aleck puzzle solver who is indignantly impatient with the pretension and hypocrisy encountered in academia, government, and real life, and with a talent and determination to put down and one-up those who would do the same to him.

Although the stories tell much about Feynman the warm human, they say little about the central focus of his life, his attitude toward the science of physics. In the autobiography's introduction, Albert R. Hibbs tells how Feynman's feelings about physics came across to his Cal Tech students:

I remember when I was his student how it was when you walked into one of his lectures. He would be standing in front of the hall smiling at us all as we came in, his fingers tapping out a complicated rhythm on the black top of the demonstration bench that crossed the front of the lecture hall. As latecomers took their seats, he picked up chalk and began spinning it rapidly through his fingers in a manner of a professional gambler playing with a poker chip, still smiling happily as if at some secret joke. And then—still smiling—he talked to us about physics, his diagrams and equations helping us to share his understanding. It was no secret joke that brought the smile and the sparkle in his eye, it was physics. The joy of physics. The joy was contagious. We are fortunate who caught that infection. . . .

His fame in the scientific and academic worlds as a teacher, theoretician, and author broadened to all the world when in 1986 he was appointed to the President's Commission on the Space Shuttle Challenger Accident. When the appointment was announced an old friend asked the pertinent question, "Do they realize that Feynman asks questions—and that he keeps asking them until he gets answers?" Feynman believed that NASA and its contractors were overrun by zealotry, self-delusion, and complacency, said so, and called out specific details in his independently issued report, "Personal Observations on the Reliability of the Shuttle." His demonstration that the shuttle's O-ring material hardened when cold, which he made by dipping a piece in his glass of ice water while listening to testimony with the commission in front of the TV cameras, was typical of his iconoclastic, elegant, but simple approach to the realities of technology.[3]

QUOTATION

"[There is a] computer disease that anybody who works with computers knows about. It's a very serious disease and it interferes completely with the work. The trouble with computers is that you *play* with them!" (*Reminiscences of Los Alamos, 1943–1945*)

BIBLIOGRAPHY

Biographical

Feynman, Richard P., *Surely You're Joking, Mr. Feynman: Adventures of a Curious Character*, W.W. Norton & Co., New York, 1985.

---

[3]From Weiss 1988.

Feynman, Richard P., "Los Alamos from Below," *Ann. Hist. Comp.*, Vol. 10, No. 4, 1989, pp. 343–345.

Weiss, E.A., "Richard P. Feynman: Obituary," *Ann. Hist. Comp.*, Vol. 10, No. 2, 1988, pp. 141–142.

LEONARDO OF PISA, AKA FIBONACCI

An early proponent of the Hindu-Arabic number system and developer of "Fibonacci Numbers," which model many natural progressions.

AARON FINERMAN

Born April 1, 1925, Bronx, N.Y., died April 5, 1994, Boca Raton, Fla.; 1950s computer scientist who has been recognized for his outstanding service to professional societies, to computer science education, and to computer center management.

Education: BS, civil engineering, College of the City of New York, 1948; SM, civil engineering, MIT, 1951; ScD, civil engineering, MIT, 1956.

Professional Experience: US Army, 1944–1946; Republic Aviation Corporation: Scientific Computing Group, 1956–1957, manager, Digital Computing and Data Processing Division, 1957–1961; State University of New York at Stony Brook: professor of engineering, director of the Computing Center, 1961–1969, professor of computer science, 1969–1977, chairman, Computer Science Department, 1975–1977; Jet Propulsion Laboratory, California Institute of Technology: National Academy of Science senior post-doctoral fellow, 1968–1969, manager, Office of Computing and Information Services, 1971–1973, distinguished visiting scientist, 1990–1994; University of Michigan: director, Computing Center, 1978–1986, professor, Computer and

Communications Sciences, 1978–1984, professor, electrical and computer engineering, 1979–1984, professor, electrical engineering and computer science, 1984–1990, special adviser on information technology, 1986–1990, professor emeritus, EECS, 1990–1994, director emeritus, Computing Center, 1990–1994; distinguished visiting professor, Computer Science and Engineering, Florida Atlantic University, 1989–1994; editor-in-chief, *ACM Computing Reviews,* 1987–1994; chairman, implementation committee, Software Patent Institute, 1992–1994.

Honors and Awards: president, SHARE, 1961; ACM Distinguished Service Award, 1981; fellow, American Association for the Advancement of Science, 1983; fellow, ACM, 1994.

Aaron Finerman entered the field of computing in 1954 while a graduate student at MIT, by using the Whirlwind computer. Finerman was active in the Association for Computing Machinery (ACM) from 1957, and during that time served as the chairman of the editorial board, association treasurer, and council member. He also served as chairman of the Long Island Chapter, and chair of the Special Interest Group on Computer Science Education (SIGCSE). He served as the editor-in-chief of *Computing Reviews* from 1963 to 1967 and again from 1987 to 1994.

As the representative of ACM, Finerman was active in the American Federation of Information Processing Societies (AFIPS) for 10 years commencing in 1974, serving as a board member, member of the executive committee, and chair of the AFIPS publications committee. During this period he proposed, and was instrumental in obtaining approval of the AFIPS Board for the establishment of, the *Annals of the History of Computing.*

By invitation he visited over 30 countries in North America, Central and South America, Europe, Southeast Asia, and the Middle East, speaking on the management of computing, software practices, education and training programs in computer science, the history of computing, and trends in computing.

BIBLIOGRAPHY

Significant Publications

Finerman, A., ed., *University Education in Computing Science,* Academic Press, New York, Jan. 1968.

Finerman, A., "Thoughts on Managing the Computing Organization," *INFOPOL-76 International Conference on Data Processing,* 1976.

Finerman, A., "Computing Capabilities at United States Universities," *Informatic,* Vol. 11, No. 9, Sept. 1969, pp. 360–367.

Finerman, A., "Computing Capabilities at Western European Universities," *Comm. ACM*, Vol. 9, No. 12, Dec. 1966, pp. 840–844.

Finerman, A., "Professionalism in the Computing Field," *Comm. ACM*, Vol. 18, No. 1, Jan. 1975, pp. 4–9.

Finerman, A., and E. Koffman, "Education in Computer Science," *Encyclopedia of Computer Science*, 3rd ed., Van Nostrand Reinhold, New York, 1993, pp. 493–501.

Finerman, A., and A. Ralston, "Undergraduate Programs in Computing Science in the Tradition of Liberal Education," *IFIP World Conference on Computer Education*, Vol. 2, Aug. 1970, pp. 195–199.

THOMAS H. (TOMMY) FLOWERS

Builder of Colossus, the cryptanalytical machine designed by Alan Turing and others at Bletchley Park, England; perhaps the first electronic computer in the UK.

Education: BSc, London University, 1933; Honorary DSc, University of Newcastle upon Tyne, 1977.

Professional Experience: Post Office Communications Laboratories, 1930–1950; ITT-England, 1950–1970.

For its time Colossus was a notable innovation, different from its predecessors in many dramatic aspects. Flowers made the following claims for Colossus:

1. It was electronic. Other machines, such as Heath Robinson, had had electronic subsystems, but they were of minor size. Colossus had 2,400 vacuum tubes—big bottles. Ah, the warmth at 2 a.m. on a damp, cold English winter!

2. It was digital, and experience with digital circuits was then very limited. The vacuum tubes of the day were mainly intended as amplifiers; manufacturers strove for linear response. Fortunately for Colossus they were successful over only a limited range.

3. It was programmable by means of a switchboard. Toggle switches enabled one to choose among binary functions of the

input, which was a long string of cipher text, and then the out-puts of these functions were counted. At the end of each pass of the input string, the counts were used to control the printer, suppressing those counts of lesser interest.

Colossus was not sequence-controlled, nor was its program stored. Nor did any of us see that possibility.

Parameters of the cipher were entered by means of the bottle plugs on the remote back of Colossus—to keep leads short. The cipher text was on very long Teletype punched tapes pasted into a loop and then run at 5,000 characters per second. When a paper tape parted it caused some excitement.

The tapes were prepared and mounted by women of the Women's Royal Naval Service (WRNS)—called "Wrens"—who were very skilled and adroit. Others tried but invariably caused trouble. Without the Wrens they were helpless.

Colossus was useful in more than one way, and there were even demonstrations applying it to number theory. But these demonstrations were more notable for their ingenuity than their effectiveness.

A successful result from Colossus was not plaintext, but an intermediate product that was completed by hand by skillful specialists.

The cipher system under attack was on-line, an integral part of the communications links; a typist at one end ran a typewriter at the other. Once synchronization had been established, the typist fed in message after message until the backlog had been exhausted. A cryptanalytical solution would reveal an avalanche of plaintext.

This cryptanalysis was a superb technical achievement, and the cryptanalysts were very proud of it. At the same time they were painful-ly aware that their dominance was precarious, and were fearful that a change by the Germans might deprive them of their sustenance. When I was scheduled by the US Navy to join the "Newmanry" as a working member and observer, my plans were unsettled by a dispatch that the Germans had begun to use new wheel patterns each day instead of once a month, and that there was little chance that the system would ever be read again. But two months later the effort had been doubled and redoubled, and more was being read than ever before. Part of the redoubling was to build more Colossi; earlier there had been one, now there were to be twelve.[4]

---

[4]Campaigne, Howard. From the foreword to Flowers, Thomas H., "The Design of Colossus," *Ann. Hist. Comp.*, Vol. 5, No. 3, July 1983. Howard Campaigne joined the newly formed National Security Agency after the war, where he eventually became chief of research. After serving as professor and chairman of the Mathematics Department at Slippery Rock State College from 1970 to 1976, he retired to Portales, N.M.

BIBLIOGRAPHY

Biographical

Flowers, Thomas H., "The Design of Colossus," *Ann. Hist. Comp.*, Vol. 5, No. 3, July 1983, pp. 239–252.

Lavington, Simon, *Early British Computers,* Digital Press, Bedford, Mass., 1980. See Chapter 5: "The ACE, The 'British National Computer.'"

Randell, Brian, "The Colossus," in Metropolis, N., J. Howlett, and Gian-Carlo Rota, *A History of Computing in the Twentieth Century,* Academic Press, New York, 1980, pp. 47–92.

ROBERT W. FLOYD

Born June 8, 1936, New York, N.Y.; substantial contributor to understanding the meaning of programs, predating the seminal work of Antony Hoare; recipient of the 1978 ACM Turing Award.

Education: BA, University of Chicago, 1955; BS, University of Chicago, 1958.

Professional Experience: electrical engineer, Westinghouse Electrical, 1955–1956; computer operator, programmer, and analyst, Armour Research Foundation, 1956–1962; senior project scientist, Computer Associates, 1962–1965; associate professor of computer science, Carnegie-Mellon University, 1965–1968; Stanford University: associate professor, 1968–1970, chairman, 1973–1976, professor of computer science, 1970–present.

Honors and Awards: ACM Turing Award, 1978; fellow, American Academy of Arts and Sciences; IEEE Computer Society Pioneer Award, 1991.

JAY WRIGHT FORRESTER

Born July 14, 1918, Climax, Neb.; Massachusetts Institute of Technology leader of the Whirlwind Project and inventor of the random-access magnetic-core memory matrices.[5]

Education: BSc, University of Nebraska, 1939; SM, MIT, 1945.

Professional Experience: MIT: member, staff, Servomechanisms Laboratory, 1940–1946, director, Digital Computer Laboratory, 1946–1951, head, Digital Computer Division, Lincoln Laboratory, 1951–1956, professor of management, 1956–1972, Germeshausen professor, 1972–1989, Germeshausen professor emeritus and senior lecturer, 1989–present.

Honors and Awards: DEng, University of Nebraska, 1954; National Academy of Engineering, 1967; DSc, Boston University, 1969; Valdemar Poulsen Gold Medal, Danish Academy of Technical Sciences, 1969; DEng, Newark College of Engineering, 1971; Medal of Honor, Institute of Electrical and Electronics Engineers, 1972; System, Man, and Cybernetics Award for Outstanding Accomplishment, IEEE, 1972; Benjamin Franklin Fellow, Royal Society of Arts, London, 1972; DEng, Union College, 1973; DEng, University of Notre Dame, 1974; Howard N. Potts Award, Franklin Institute, 1974; honorary member, Society of Manufacturing Engineers,[6] 1976; Harry Goode Memorial Award, American Federation of Information Processing Societies, 1977; Doctor of Political Science, University of Mannheim, Germany, 1979; Inventors Hall of Fame, 1979; Computer Pioneer Award, IEEE Computer Society, 1982; Jay W. Forrester Chair in Computer Studies at MIT, endowed by Thomas J. Watson, Jr., 1986; James R. Killian, Jr., Faculty Achievement Award, MIT, 1987; honorary professor, Shanghai Institute of Technology, China, 1987; Information Storage Award, IEEE Magnetics Society, 1988; Doctor of Humane Letters, State University of New York, 1988; US National Medal of Technology (with Robert R. Everett), 1989; Pioneer Award, IEEE Aerospace and Electronic Systems Society (with Robert R. Everett), 1990; DPhil, University of Bergen, Norway, 1990; fellow, IEEE; fellow, Academy of Management; fellow, American Academy of Arts and Sciences; fellow, American Association for the Advancement of Science.

Forrester became interested in digital computing when a project to develop a Navy aircraft stability analyzer was determined to be too difficult for an analog computer. The characteristics of the system

---

[5]The "invention" of the magnetic core as a memory device is claimed by An Wang. Forrester developed the addressing mechanism which made it a practical random-access system.

[6]For contributions to the digital control of machine tools.

required a fast, accurate, general-purpose machine. Perry Crawford, then with the Special Devices Center of the US Navy, suggested the use of a digital system. Forrester took charge of the design and construction of Whirlwind I, but discovered that the delay line and electrostatic memory systems being used in other digital machines of the time would not permit the construction of a machine which met the reliability and speed requirements. From this need Forrester developed the basic concept of random-access storage in 1947 based on glow-discharge cells, and later recast the concept in 1949 as toroidal, random-access, coincident-current magnetic storage that became the standard internal memory for computers for nearly 30 years. By 1951, the Whirlwind computer was in operation, but by then the purpose of the machine had been changed to support the planning and design of the SAGE (Semi-Automatic Ground Environment) Air Defense System.

In 1956 Forrester became professor of management at MIT's Alfred P. Sloan School of Management, where he established the field of system dynamics for determining how the structure and policies of physical, social, and environmental systems determine growth, oscillation, and stability. He has developed the System Dynamics National Model for understanding economic fluctuations. The model demonstrates the underlying theory of the economic long wave (or Kondratieff cycle) that has created the great depressions of the 1830s, 1890s, 1930s, and probably of the 1990s. From his work in understanding complex systems has come the international System Dynamics Society and applications to corporate management, economic behavior, medicine, urban growth and decay, and world population and environmental forces. Most recently, system dynamics is becoming a foundation for an integrated educational framework in junior and senior high schools.

QUOTATIONS

"The pioneering days in digital computers were exciting times. Computer development was part of the last hundred years of technological discovery. However, the major challenges facing society will not be solved by still more technology. The next hundred years will be the age of social and economic discovery. The field of system dynamics, with which I have been associated since 1956, has pioneered in understanding how organizational structures and decision-making policies interact to produce desirable and undesirable behavior in physical, biological, environmental, business, and social systems. I see this next frontier in social systems as far more exciting and important than was the technological frontier."

"There is now promise of reversing the trend of the last century toward ever greater fragmentation in education. There is real hope of moving back toward the 'Renaissance man' idea of a common teachable core of broadly applicable concepts. We can now visualize an integrated, systemic, educational process that is more efficient, more appropriate to a world of increasing complexity, and more supportive of unity in life. Several high schools, curriculum-development projects, and colleges are using a system dynamics core to build study units in mathematics, science, social studies, and history."

BIBLIOGRAPHY

Biographical

Evans, Christopher, "Conversation: Jay W. Forrester," *Ann. Hist. Comp.*, Vol. 5, No. 3, 1983, pp. 297–301; also available as an audiotape, "Pioneers of Computing," Tape 4, Science Museum, London, 1975.

Everett, Robert R., "Whirlwind," in Metropolis, N., J. Howlett, and Gian-Carlo Rota, eds., *A History of Computing in the Twentieth Century*, Academic Press, New York, 1980, pp. 365–384.

Forrester, Jay W., "From the Ranch to System Dynamics: An Autobiography," in Bedeian, Arthur G., ed., *Management Laureates: A Collection of Autobiographical Essays*, Vol. 1 of 3, JAI Press, Greenwich, Conn., 1992; also available as D-4197, System Dynamics Group, Sloan School of Management, MIT, Cambridge, Mass.

Redmond, Kent C., and Thomas M. Smith, *Project Whirlwind: The History of a Pioneer Computer*, Digital Press, Bedford, Mass., 1980, 280 pp.

Ritchie, David, *The Computer Pioneers*, Simon and Shuster, New York, 1986, Chapter 10.

Slater, Robert, *Portraits in Silicon*, MIT Press, Cambridge, Mass., 1987, Chapter 9.

Significant Publications

Forrester, Jay W., "Digital Information Storage in Three Dimensions Using Magnetic Cores," *J. Applied Physics*, Vol. 22, No. 1, 1951, pp. 44–48.

Forrester, Jay W., "Digital Computers: Present and Future Trends," in *Review of Electronic Digital Computers, Joint AIEE-IRE Computer Conference, Philadelphia, December 10–12, 1951*, American Institute of Electrical Engineers, New York, 1952, pp. 109–113.

Forrester, Jay W., *Industrial Dynamics,* Productivity Press, Cambridge, Mass., 1961, 464 pp.

Forrester, Jay W., 1968. *Principles of Systems,* 2d ed., Productivity Press, Cambridge, Mass., 1961, 391 pp.

Forrester, Jay W., *Urban Dynamics,* Productivity Press, Cambridge, Mass., 1969, 285 pp.

Forrester, Jay W., *World Dynamics,* Productivity Press, Cambridge, Mass., 1971, 144 pp.; second edition (1973) has an added chapter on physical vs. social limits.

Forrester, Jay W., *Collected Papers of Jay W. Forrester,* Productivity Press, Cambridge, Mass., 1975, 284 pp.

Forrester, Jay W., "World Models: The System-Dynamics Approach," in Marois, M., ed., *Volume 4: Proceedings of the World Conference: Towards a Plan of Actions for Mankind,* Pergamon Press, Oxford, UK, 1977, pp. 107–112.

Forrester, Jay W., "Global Modelling Revisited," *Futures,* Vol. 14, No. 2, 1982, pp. 95–110; from a lecture at the IIASA Global Modelling Conference, Laxenburg, Austria, Sept. 1981.

Forrester, Jay W., "The Economy: Where is it Headed?," *Los Angeles Daily News,* Los Angeles, Oct. 25, 1987; also available as Report D-3937, System Dynamics Group, Sloan School of Management, MIT, Cambridge, Mass.

Forrester, Jay W., "Policies, Decisions, and Information Sources for Modeling," *European Journal of Operational Research,* Vol. 59, No. 1, 1992, pp. 42–63.

Patents

Forrester, Jay W., 1956. *Multicoordinate Digital Information Storage Device, US Patent No. 2,736,880.* Washington, D.C.: US Patent Office, 11 pp. Patent for the memory system used during most of the first 30 years of digital computers.

Forrester, Jay W., William M. Pease, James O. McDonough, and Alfred K. Susskind. 1962. *Numerical Control Servo-System, US Patent No. 3,069,608.* Washington, D.C.: US Patent Office, 37 pp.

GEORGE ELMER FORSYTHE

Born January 8, 1917, State College, Pa.; died April 9, 1972, Stanford, Calif.; numerical analyst and early inspiring teacher of computing who transformed Hamming's famous aphorism into "The Purpose of Computing Numbers Is Not Yet in Sight."

Education: BS, mathematics, Swarthmore College, 1937; PhD, mathematics, Brown University, 1941.

Professional Experience: Stanford Junior University: instructor, mathematics, 1941, professor, mathematics, 1957–1972; meteorologist, US Air Force, 1941–1946; Boeing Aircraft Company, 1947; Institute for Numerical Analysis, University of California at Los Angeles, 1948–1957.

Honors and Awards: president, ACM, 1964–1966; ACM Distinguished Service Award, 1972; fellow, British Computer Society; ACM named its own award for student papers in memoriam to Forsythe.

Forsythe was born on January 8, 1917, in State College, Pa., and moved as a small boy with his family to Ann Arbor, Mich. His undergraduate work was at Swarthmore College, where he majored in mathematics. His experience there had a strong influence on his life. An even earlier interest in computing is described in a biographical note in *The Mathematical Sciences* (MIT Press, 1969), p. 152:

> His interest in computing began early, when as a seventh-grader he tried using a hand-cranked desk calculator to find the decimal expansion of 10000/7699. He wanted to see how the digits repeated.

In 1941 Forsythe's first year as a Stanford mathematics instructor was interrupted by service in the Air Force, in which he became a meteorologist and coauthor of an outstanding book on meteorology. His interest in his students and in education had manifested itself very early. After his service in the Air Force, his interest in numerical mathematics and computation developed rapidly. He spent a year at Boeing Aircraft Corp., where he introduced what may have been the first use of automatic computing in that company: inspired by W.J. Eckert's book, *Punched Card Methods in Scientific Computation,* he had a tabulating machine set up for scientific data processing. Then he spent several years in the Institute for Numerical Analysis of the National Bureau of Standards, a special section located on the campus of the University of California, Los Angeles. He joined the institute because he wanted to watch the development of the Standards Western Automatic Computer (SWAC), one of the first of the digital computers. He had many interesting tales to tell of these early days in computing.

When I (John Herriot) thought about getting involved with numerical mathematics and computers at the time that Stanford was acquiring its first computer, it was only natural that I should consult Forsythe, who was already a leading figure in the field. His advice, or rather his analysis of the pros and cons, demonstrated his great vision. The only chance I have had to lay claim to similar astuteness was when, as chairman of a search committee, I recommended that we invite Forsythe to join the Stanford Mathematics Department. He accepted our invitation, rejoining our department, this time as professor, in 1957. Forsythe and I worked together during these years developing the nucleus of courses in computer science. He quickly saw the need for more activity in numerical mathematics and computing. His leadership was inspiring and persuasive. He saw the computer revolution developing, and recognized the need for more study, research, and teaching in the computer area. He conceived of it as related to but still different from the traditional emphasis in mathematics; thus, he was convinced of the need for adding to the faculty scholars well versed in this area. Under his leadership, the Computer Science Division of the Mathematics Department was formed in 1961, and we began the slow process of gathering an outstanding group of colleagues.

The culmination of this effort was the founding of the Computer Science Department, one of the first such departments in the US, on January 1, 1965. As the result of his dynamic leadership and foresight, the department developed into one of the nation's outstanding computer science departments. Forsythe was very skillful in bringing together our many diverse points of view. He captured the loyalty of all of his colleagues. He had a sense of responsibility to others and to the institutions he chose to serve. It was a principle of his life that people were not instruments to be manipulated toward some end. In each of his positions of leadership, but particularly in his position as department chairman, he felt that the threads of many people's lives, and of their productive work and aspirations, ran through his hands, and that each of these must be worried about and cared for in the proper way. Carefulness, thoughtfulness, energy, attention to detail, a determination not to pass the buck—these give some of the dimensions of his sense of responsibility. He was a master at resolving differences between people with opposing views. In the closing days of his life he passed the remaining threads of responsibility, not in a tangle but in good order, to his colleagues, with thought for the lives and careers of others.

He had high standards and delighted in excellence. He expected everyone to do his best. He did not seek acclaim for his own work, but he sought it for the deserving work of others. Students' progress and development were his constant concern; perhaps the most visible and enduring evidence of his influence on other people is to be seen in the significant contributions that have been made and are being made by the students whose research he guided. He chose problems wisely and was never too busy to see and encourage his students. He instilled in them such a fine feeling for the techniques of research that most of them have continued work in important areas. The influence of his students on the direction of research in numerical analysis and on the development of computer science has been remarkable.

He was especially concerned with the welfare of students. In any discussion with his colleagues, he was a strong advocate of what he felt would most benefit students. Forsythe's rapport with our students has perhaps been best described by one of them, Mark Smith, in his tribute at the memorial service for Forsythe. Among other things, he said:

> Forsythe and I got to know each other when I was a graduate student in the department. It was two years ago during the student strike on the Stanford campus. I was active in the protests, and Forsythe, as chairman, was very concerned about what was going on. We used to meet together every afternoon to discuss the campus situation. And if someone had wandered by and peeked through the window he would have seen me with my arms flailing, pacing back and forth, and he would have seen Forsythe sitting back in his chair, calm and alert. Forsythe brought his clear mind to bear on everything we talked about, and always found some new and reasonable way to see problems that I had thought were insoluble. But what most impressed me was not so much the clarity of Forsythe's thinking, but the feelings that lay in back of that thinking. Forsythe cared. Every day I would leave our meeting a little more amazed by the gentleness and humanity of this man.

Besides his untiring service to many organizations in various capacities, Forsythe served a term as president of the Association for Computing Machinery from 1964 to 1966. His letters to the members published in *Communications of the ACM* during those two years discuss many of his views on computer science as well as ACM business.

He always enjoyed an active life, continuing to play tennis until a few weeks before his death. He was also a jogger and a hiker and he loved the out-of-doors. His wife Sandra shared his interest in computation and his early experiences in using SWAC. While Forsythe was developing computer science education at the college level, Sandra was actively pioneering this area at the high school level. Together they enjoyed traveling in many countries and hiking in the High Sierras.

All of the lives which have been touched by Forsythe have been affected in a meaningful way. We are all in his debt for his wise counsel, his friendly encouragement, and his inspiring leadership. We will continue to build on the foundation he so carefully constructed.[7]

QUOTATIONS

"The Purpose of Computing Numbers Is Not Yet in Sight."[8]

"In the past 15 years, many numerical analysts have progressed from being queer people in mathematics departments to being queer people in computer science departments!" (Knuth 1972)

About Forsythe: "One might almost regard him as the Martin Luther of the Computer Revolution." (Knuth 1972)

BIBLIOGRAPHY

Biographical

Herriot, John G., "In Memory of George E. Forsythe," *Comm. ACM*, Vol. 15, No. 8, Aug. 1972, pp. 719–720.

Knuth, Donald E., "George Forsythe and the Development of Computer Science," *Comm. ACM*, Vol. 15, No. 8, Aug. 1972, pp. 721–726.

Varah, J., "The Influence of George Forsythe and His Students," in Nash, Stephen G., *A History of Scientific Computing*, ACM Press History Series, ACM, New York, 1990.

Significant Publications

A complete list of Forsythe's publications—four books and 83 articles—is contained in Knuth 1972.

---

[7]Based on Herriot 1972.

[8]A parody of Richard Hamming's dedication to his book—"The purpose of computing is insight, not numbers."

LESLIE FOX

Born September 30, 1918, Dewsbury, Yorkshire, England; died August 1, 1992, Oxford, England; British Post-World War II numerical analyst who established the clear needs for a careful balance between the academic rigor of the field and its practical utility.

Education: BA (first-class), Oxford University; DPhil, Numerical Techniques in Engineering (under R.V. Southwell).

Professional Experience: Nautical Almanac Office, 1943–1945; mathematics division, National Physical Laboratory, Teddington, Middlesex, 1945–1957; director of the Computing Laboratory, Oxford University, 1957–1990.

Leslie Fox exerted a profound influence on the development of numerical mathematics in Great Britain in the post-World War II period, bringing discipline to an increasingly vigorous but initially disordered field of research.

During and after World War II, the demand for the numerical solution of mathematical problems grew explosively, accelerated by wartime advances in physics and engineering. The end of the war also heralded the rapid development of the electronic computer. The situation was potentially chaotic, with well-tried methods of computation being ousted in favor of new techniques designed to exploit the speed of the new machines. Fox argued consistently for adherence to basic principles; in particular he argued that all computed results should be assumed *wrong* until proved otherwise.

From this time the emerging discipline of numerical analysis became dominated in Britain by two men, Leslie Fox and his close friend Jim Wilkinson, FRS, with whom he shared many interests, including a love of music and cricket. Wilkinson was the brilliant academic, eager to exploit the potential of the computer. Fox was the intuitive mathematician with a vision of his goal and an unerring sense of direction. Together they inspired two generations of numerical analysts.

The most eminent of a remarkable set of mathematicians to emerge from the Wheelwright Grammar School in Dewsbury, Yorkshire, Fox took a first-class degree at Oxford University before studying numerical techniques in engineering (under R.V. Southwell) for his DPhil. There followed an influential spell of two years (1943–1945) at the Nautical Almanac Office under D.H. Sadler (also from the Wheelwright Grammar School).

At the end of the war, Fox joined the newly formed Mathematics Division of the National Physical Laboratory (NPL), Teddington, Middlesex, in a section led by E.T. Goodwin. The division also recruited Wilkinson and, for two years, Alan M. Turing. Dealing with the flow of problems into the division did much to convince Fox that numerical analysis had to maintain a careful balance between academic rigor and practical utility.

After returning to Oxford in 1957 as the first director of the computing laboratory, Fox introduced numerical analysis there as a branch of university mathematics. He also gave his active support to the forging of links between academics and industrial mathematicians, to ensure that his subject remained close to its roots. Equally importantly, he and his colleagues passed on his philosophy to a stream of research students, many of whom now occupy influential positions in British universities. Above all, Fox was a great communicator. The lucid simplicity is evident in eight books and 86 papers, while the easy elegance of his public speaking entertained and informed audiences in Great Britain and overseas. In later years academic honors rained upon him.

Fox was a keen and able all-round sportsman. He played soccer for Oxford against Cambridge during the war, and later for Oxford City. At NPL he played soccer, became a champion in tennis, represented the laboratory in the Civil Service Athletics Championships as a sprinter, and was captain of the cricket team. He graduated from the seam bowling of his youth into the subtle craft of spin bowling before his return to Oxford, and there he played regularly for the Barnacles Cricket Club. He later took up golf and inevitably became proficient.

While achieving so much in diverse spheres of activity, Leslie Fox retained his innate modesty with quiet dignity. He was a private man of equable temperament, strong-minded and fair. With his wide interests, his wit, and his erudition, he was always worth listening to, and always ready to listen.[9]

BIBLIOGRAPHY

Biographical

Clenshaw, Charles, "Professor Leslie Fox," *The Independent*, Aug. 11, 1992, p. 25.

Fox, L., "Early Numerical Analysis in the United Kingdom," in Nash, Stephen G., *A History of Scientific Computing*, ACM Press History Series, New York, 1990, pp. 280–300.

---

[9]Drawn from Clenshaw 1992.

BERNARD AARON GALLER

Born 1928, Chicago, Ill.; significant contributor to early programming language development and, as key leader in computer organizations, provided direction to the academic and industrial field; with Bruce Arden and Robert Graham, developed the programming language MAD—Michigan Algorithm Decoder—a "take-off" on the international language Algol.

Education: BS, University of Chicago, 1947; MA, University of California at Los Angeles, 1949; PhD, mathematical logic, University of Chicago, 1955.

Professional Experience: faculty member, University of Michigan, 1955–present; president, ACM, 1968–1970; founding editor-in-chief, *AFIPS Annals of the History of Computing*, 1979; CSNET Executive Committee, 1988–1989.

Honors and Awards: ACM Distinguished Service Award, 1980; AFIPS Distinguished Service Award, 1984.

Early computer scientist responsible for the Michigan Algorithmic Decoder (MAD) which, for a period, was the most commonly used language system on IBM large-scale machines.

QUOTATION

Regarding contents of theses: "Don't evaluate your own work, other people will do that!"

BIBLIOGRAPHY

Significant Publications

Galler, B.A., *The Language of Computers*, McGraw-Hill, New York, 1962.

Galler, B.A., and A.J. Perlis, *A View of Programming Languages*, Addison-Wesley, Reading, Mass., 1970.

Saul I. Gass

Born February 28, 1926, Chelsea, Mass.; operations research scientist who helped pioneer in applications of linear programming and their computer-based solution, who wrote the first text on linear programming, and who had a major role in the development and operation of the first US manned space project's real-time computational system.

Education: BS, education, Boston University, 1949; MA, mathematics, Boston University, 1949; PhD, engineering science, University of California, Berkeley, 1965.

Professional Experience: mathematician, US Air Force, 1949–1955; IBM Corp.: applied science representative, project manager, Project Mercury, 1955–1959, and 1960–1963, manager, civil programs, 1965–1969; director, operations research, CEIR, 1959; vice president, MATHEMATICA, 1970–1975; professor, College of Business and Management, University of Maryland, 1975–present; Westinghouse Professor, University of Maryland, 1983–1992; council member, ACM, 1960–1962; secretary, AFIPS, 1962–1965; president, Operations Research Society of America, 1976–1977; director, Winter Simulation Conference, 1978–1982; president, Omega Rho International Honor Society, 1986–1988.

Honors and Awards: George E. Kimball Medal for Distinguished Service, Operations Research Society of America, 1991; Outstanding Faculty Award, University of Maryland Alumni Association, 1980.

From 1949 to 1955 Dr. Gass was employed as a mathematician by the US Air Force and worked for the Aberdeen Bombing Mission, Los Angeles, Calif., and the Directorate of Management Analysis, Washington, D.C. (headquarters USAF). In the latter position, he was a member of the Air Force's Project SCOOP, the group that first developed the basic concepts and early applications of linear programming. Gass helped formulate new approaches to solving military planning and programming problems and developed new computational procedures for solving such problems on the Univac I.

Gass joined IBM as an applied science representative and was assigned to the Washington Commercial and Federal Offices from 1955 to 1958. In this position he assisted a wide variety of customers, both civilian and federal, in the solution of their computational problems. In 1959 he joined CEIR, Inc., as director of the Operations Research Branch. Gass rejoined IBM in 1960 as manager of the Simulation Group of the Project Mercury Man-in-Space Program. Here he was responsible for the development of a full range of real-time simulation procedures used to validate the IBM-developed Project Mercury Computational and Data Flow Equipment System, and to train NASA flight controllers. In May 1961, he was appointed project manager of IBM's total efforts on Project Mercury. The IBM group developed and operated Project Mercury's real-time computational and data-flow system that included a duplexed computing center at the Goddard Space Flight Center, Greenbelt, Md.; an engineering and communications subsystem between Cape Canaveral and Goddard; and a computational subsystem for analysis of lift-off and orbital data that enabled flight controllers to monitor all phases of a Project Mercury mission. In 1963, he received an IBM resident graduate fellowship and completed his doctoral studies in operations research at the University of California, Berkeley, in 1965. For his dissertation, Gass developed the dualplex method for the solution of large-scale linear-programming problems under the supervision of George B. Dantzig.

In 1966 Gass was a full-time member of the Science and Technology Task Force of the President's Commission on Law Enforcement. He was responsible for developing the Task Force's approach to how science and technology can best serve law enforcement agencies. For the IBM Federal Systems Division (1966–1970), he was manager of federal civil programs and was responsible for applying information retrieval and other data procedures, advanced graphic techniques, and operations research to urban problems.

Gass joined MATHEMATICA, Inc., in 1970, and managed the operations research projects being conducted in the Washington, D.C., area. He joined the University of Maryland as professor and chairman (1975–1979) in Management Science and Statistics of the College of Business and Management. Gass has served as a consultant to the US General Accounting Office, the National Institute of Standards and Technology, and other federal and private operations research and systems analysis organizations.

BIBLIOGRAPHY

Significant Publications

Gass, Saul I., *Linear Programming*, McGraw-Hill, New York, 1958 (5th edition published in 1985).

Gass, Saul I., *An Illustrated Guide to Linear Programming*, McGraw-Hill, New York, 1970.

Gass, Saul I., *Decision Making, Models, and Algorithms,* John Wiley and Sons, New York, 1985.

Gass, Saul I., and R. Sisson, *A Guide to Models in Government Planning and Operations,* Sauger Books, Potomac, Md., 1975.

STANLEY GILL

Sometime professor of computing at Imperial College, London; a former fellow of St. John's College, Cambridge; a past president of the British Computer Society; former trustee of IFIP; member of the Pilot ACE team who with Maurice Wilkes and David Wheeler developed the concepts of subroutines and subroutine libraries.

BIBLIOGRAPHY

Biographical

Campbell-Kelly, Martin, "Programming the Pilot ACE: Early Programming Activity at the National Physical Laboratory," *Ann. Hist. Comp.,* Vol. 3, No. 2, 1981, p. 136.

Douglas, Sandy, "Some Memories of EDSAC I: 1950–1952," *Ann. Hist. Comp.,* Vol. 1, No. 2, 1980, pp. 98–99, 208.

Wilkes, M.V., "Early Programming Developments in Cambridge," in Metropolis, N., J. Howlett, and Gian-Carlo Rota, *A History of Computing in the Twentieth Century,* Academic Press, New York, 1980, pp. 497–501.

Significant Publications

Wilkes, M.V., D.J. Wheeler, and Stanley Gill, *The Preparation of Programs for an Electronic Digital Computer,* Addison-Wesley, New York, 1951.

Victor Mikhaylovich Glushkov

*Born August 24, 1923, in Rostov, Ukraine; died January 30, 1982; USSR
computer scientist with a great influence on automata and cybernetics.*

Academician Victor M. Glushkov, vice president of the Ukrainian
Academy of Sciences, director of the Institute for Cybernetics in Kiev,
and holder of the IFIP Silver-Core, died on January 30, 1982, after a
long and severe illness.

Glushkov was born on August 24, 1923, in Rostov on the river Don.
After graduating from Rostov University he began his career as an
assistant at the Ural Timber Institute. His first scientific contributions
were in the field of modern algebra, where he obtained some fundamental results in the theory of graphs; they provided the basis for his
doctoral dissertation (1955).

In 1956 he went to Kiev. From that moment all his activities were
closely connected with the Ukrainian Academy of Sciences. In the
same year, a computing center was established within the academy, in
whose organization Glushkov played an essential role and of which he
was appointed director. Under his leadership the scientific developments of the computing center progressed at an amazing pace, and its
excellent international reputation was established.

In 1962 the computing center was transformed into the Institute
of Cybernetics of the Ukranian Academy of Sciences. Glushkov
became its director, a position he held until his death. The institute
was of primary importance for the development of the theory and
application of computers and informatics in the Soviet Union. Many
well-known scientists have worked and are still working there—among
others N.M. Amosov (medicine and biology) and V.A. Kovalevsky (pattern recognition).

Glushkov was a scientist with a very broad range of interests.
Beginning with abstract algebra, he went on to the theory of automata
and still further to the theory of computers and programming languages. In addition to the theoretical aspects, he also dealt with the
practical design of computers and, during the last years of his life, of
computing networks. It is difficult to find any branch of computer science to which Glushkov did not make new and original contributions.
His books, *Synthesis of Computing Automata* (1962) and *Introduction to
Cybernetics* (really: Automata Theory) (1964), are classics even beyond
the socialist countries. He designed several special programming languages such as ANALYTIC, similar to but much more comprehensive

than FORMAC, for the analytical transformation of algebraic expressions on the computer. The application of computers for process control was the first practical achievement of the Institute of Cybernetics making use of the new technology, and many participants of the IFAC Congress of 1960 in Moscow will remember Glushkov and will possibly have visited the Kiev Institute.

The first step toward international cooperation in the field of computer science was followed by many more. Glushkov contributed, in particular, significantly to the activities of IFIP. He was a member of the Program Committee for the 1968 and 1974 congresses and was chairman in 1971. He participated as an IFIP representative in the preparation of the UN report, "Computers for Development." The IFIP Silver-Core award was only a modest token of gratitude for his work in IFIP.

It is not only the computer community of the Soviet Union and of the socialist countries that has lost one of its most prominent and active members—it is the computer community of the whole world. V.M. Glushkov's scientific work and the results he achieved in science and practice will for a long time to come influence the development of computer science throughout the whole world.[1]

BIBLIOGRAPHY

Biographical

Zemanek, Heinz, "Eloge: Victor Mikhaylovich Glushkov, 1923–1982," *Ann. Hist. Comp.*, Vol. 4, No. 2, 1982, pp. 100–101.

---

[1] From Zemanek 1982.

RICHARD GOLDBERG

Born May 22, 1924, Philadelphia, Pa.; member, Fortran development group, who helped to develop the earliest method of register allocation.

Education: BA, Swarthmore College, 1948; PhD, mathematics, New York University, 1954.

Professional Experience: postgraduate fellow, NYU's Courant Institute, 1954–1955; member, research staff, IBM Thomas J. Watson Research Center, 1955–present.

Honors and Awards: Several IBM awards for the work on Fortran.

Participant in the Fortran development project with John Backus, Goldberg was involved in working on the code optimization routines and especially register allocation. The method, when used on straight line code, was later shown to be optimum.

BIBLIOGRAPHY

Biographical

Backus, John W., "The History of Fortran I, II, and III," in Wexelblat, R.L., ed., *History of Programming Languages,* Academic Press, New York, 1981, pp. 25–74.

Goldberg, Richard, "Register Allocation in Fortran I," *Ann. Hist. Comp.,* Vol. 6, No. 1, Jan. 1984, pp. 19–20.

Significant Publications

Goldberg, Richard, "On the Solvability of a Subclass of the Suronyi Reduction Class," *J. Symbolic Logic,* Vol. 28, No. 3, Sept. 1963, pp. 237–244.

HERMAN HEINE GOLDSTINE

Born September 13, 1913, Chicago, Ill.; Army representative to the ENIAC Project, who later worked with John von Neumann on the logical design of the IAS computer which became the prototype for many early computers—ILLIAC, JOHNNIAC, MANIAC; author of The Computer from Pascal to von Neumann, *one of the earliest textbooks on the history of computing.*

Education: BS, mathematics, University of Chicago, 1933; MS, mathematics, University of Chicago, 1934; PhD, mathematics, University of Chicago, 1936.

Professional Experience: University of Chicago: research assistant, 1936–1937, instructor, 1937–1939; assistant professor, University of Michigan, 1939–1941; US Army, Ballistic Research Laboratory, Aberdeen, Md., 1941–1946; Institute for Advanced Study, Princeton University, 1946–1957; IBM: director, Mathematics Sciences Department, 1958–1965, IBM fellow, 1969.

Honors and Awards: IEEE Computer Society Pioneer Award, 1980; National Medal of Science, 1985; member, Information Processing Hall of Fame, Infomart, Dallas, Texas, 1985.

Herman H. Goldstine began his scientific career as a mathematician and had a life-long interest in the interaction of mathematical ideas and technology. He received his PhD in mathematics from the University of Chicago in 1936 and was an assistant professor at the University of Michigan when he entered the Army in 1941. After participating in the development of the first electronic computer (ENIAC), he left the Army in 1945, and from 1946 to 1957 he was a member of the Institute for Advanced Study (IAS), where he collaborated with John von Neumann in a series of scientific papers on subjects related to their work on the Institute computer. In 1958 he joined IBM Corporation as a member of the research planning staff. He was director of mathematical sciences at the Thomas J. Watson Research Center, 1958–1965; director of scientific development of the data processing division, 1965–1967; and consultant to the director of research, 1967–1969. In 1969 he was appointed as an IBM fellow. He wrote his book on the history of computing in 1972, primarily to highlight John von Neumann's contributions. Goldstine claimed that he introduced John von Neumann to the existence of the ENIAC in a chance meeting which took place on the railroad station platform in Philadelphia in the summer of 1944, although as a member of the Scientific Advisory Committee of the Ballistics Research Laboratories, von Neumann probably should have known of the contract with the University of Pennsylvania. Goldstine has been highly supportive of the claims attributed to von Neumann of the invention of the "stored program concept."

At the founding of Hampshire College in Amherst, Mass., Goldstine contributed his archives to the school. This is said to include a handwritten copy of the *First Draft of a Report on the EDVAC* by von Neumann.

BIBLIOGRAPHY

Biographical

Bigelow, Julian, "Computer Development at the Institute for Advanced Study," in Metropolis, N., J. Howlett, and Gian-Carlo Rota, *A History of Computing in the Twentieth Century*, Academic Press, New York, 1980, pp. 291–310.

Burks, Arthur W., and Alice R. Burks, "The ENIAC: First General Purpose Electronic Computer," *Ann. Hist. Comp.*, Vol. 3, No. 4, 1981, pp. 310–399.

Goldstine, H.H., "Remembrances of Things Past," in Nash, Stephen G., *A History of Scientific Computing*, ACM Press History Series, ACM, New York, 1990, pp. 5–16.

Significant Publications

Eckert, J. Presper, Jr., John W. Mauchly, Herman H. Goldstine, and J.G. Brainerd, *Description of the ENIAC and Comments on Electronic Digital Computing Machinery*, Contract W/670/ORD 4926, Moore School of Electrical Engineering, Univ. of Pennsylvania, Philadelphia, Nov. 30, 1945.

Goldstine, Herman H., *The Computer from Pascal to von Neumann*, Princeton Univ. Press, Princeton, N.J., 1972, 378 pp.

Goldstine, Herman H., and Adele Goldstine, "The Electronic Numerical Integrator and Computer (ENIAC)," *Math. Tables and Other Aids to Comp.*, Vol. 2, No. 15, 1946, pp. 97–110; reprinted in Randell, Brian, *Origins of Digital Computers: Selected Papers*, Springer-Verlag, Berlin, 1982, pp. 359–374.

RALPH E. GOMERY

Born May 7, 1929, Brooklyn Heights, N.Y.; IBM executive vice president and director of research; National Medal of Science; president of the Sloan Foundation.

Education: BA, Williams College, 1950; PhD, mathematics, Princeton University, 1954.

Professional Experience: US Navy, 1954–1957; Higgins lecturer and assistant professor, Princeton University, 1957–1959; IBM: Research Division, 1959–1989, director of the Mathematical Sciences Department, 1965–1970, IBM director of research, 1970–1986, vice president, 1973–1985, senior vice president, 1985–1986, senior vice president for science and technology, 1986–1989; president, Alfred P. Sloan Foundation, 1989–present.

Honors and Awards: Lanchester Prize, 1963; IBM fellow, 1964; John von Neumann Theory Prize, 1984; IEEE Engineering Leadership Award, 1988; National Medal of Science, 1988; member, President's Council of Advisors on Science and Technology, 1990; member, National Academy of Science; member, National Academy of Engineering.

Dr. Gomory's scientific research interests have included integer and linear programming, network flow theory, nonlinear differential equations, and computers. In recent years he has written on the nature of technology and product development, on research in industry, and on industrial competitiveness.

IRVING JOHN (JACK) GOOD

Born Isidore Jacob Gudak December 9, 1916, London, England; cryptologist, statistician, and early worker on Colossus at Bletchley Park and the University of Manchester Mark I; major contributor, if not promulgator, of Bayesian Statistics.

Education: major scholar of Jesus College, Cambridge, 1934; state scholar, 1934; BA, Cambridge, 1938; PhD, mathematics, Cambridge, 1941 (supervisor: G.H. Hardy, FRS.); MA, Cambridge, 1943; ScD,[2] Cambridge, 1963; DSc, Oxford, 1964.

---

[2]"Doctor of science" is an advanced "postdoctoral" degree in the UK.

Professional Experience: Foreign Office, 1941–1945; worked at Bletchley Park, Government Code and Cypher School, on Ultra (both the Enigma and a teleprinter encrypting machine) as the main statistician under A.M. Turing, FRS, C.H.O.D. Alexander (British chess champion), and M.H.A. Newman, FRS, in turn; lecturer in mathematics and electronic computing, Manchester University, 1945–1948; Government Communications Headquarters, UK, 1948–1959; visiting research associate professor, Princeton, 1955 (summer); consultant to IBM for a few weeks, 1958/59 (information retrieval and evalu-

ation of the Perceptron); Admiralty Research Laboratory, 1959–1962; consultant, Communications Research Division of the Institute for Defense Analysis, 1962–1964; senior research fellow, Trinity College, Oxford, and Atlas Computer Laboratory, Science Research Council, Great Britain, 1964–1967; Virginia Polytechnic Institute and State University: professor (research) of statistics since July 1967, University Distinguished Professor since November 1969, adjunct professor of the Center for the Study of Science in Society since 1983, adjunct professor of philosophy since 1984.

Honors and Awards: Cambridgeshire Chess Champion, 1939; Smith's Prize, Cambridge (one or two Smith's Prizes are awarded each year for mathematical essays by graduate students), 1940 (supervisor: A.S. Besicovitch, FRS); fellow, Institute of Mathematical Statistics, 1958; one of the original six people designated the title "University Professor," 1969; title changed to "University Distinguished Professor," without change of meaning, in 1975; Horsley Prize, Virginia Academy of Science (shared with R.A. Gaskins), 1972, for the best scientific paper presented that year at the annual meetings; fellow, American Statistical Association, 1973; member, New York Academy of Sciences, 1974; fellow, American Academy of Arts and Sciences, 1985; honorary member of the International Statistical Institute, 1990.

Good rediscovered irrational numbers and the infinity of solutions of $2x^2 = y^2 \pm 1$ at the age of 9. He rediscovered mathematical induction and, in a sense, integration, at the age of 13.[3] In 1943, Good was one of seven people who helped design Mark II of a large-scale (classified) binary electronic digital computer called Colossus (which was not entirely general purpose).[4]

Jack Good is probably one of the most highly multifaceted persons I have ever met. If we refer to Charles Babbage as a "polymath," a

---

[3] Good states "I cannot legally prove these two statements but they are true."

[4] The two principal designers were M.H.A. Newman and T.H. Flowers. Flowers headed the engineering group among whom the next most influential were S.W. Broadhurst, W.W. Chandler, and A.W.M. Coombs. The main users were Max Newman, Donald Michie, and Good, and later about 20 mathematicians. Good was the best user and produced more than half the theory for its use.

person of great or varied learning, then surely we must refer to Good as a "multimath." If we refer to John Vincent Atanasoff as the "Forgotten Father of Computing," then we must refer to Good as the "Overlooked Father of Computation." With over 900 papers to his credit, Good has used his learning and writing skills to give deep insights into not only the present state of science, mathematics, statistics, computing, and philosophy, but also into their future. Arthur C. Clarke used Good's name in 1968, along with that of Marvin Minsky, to explain the thinking capabilities of HAL 9000, his science fiction machine of the book and film *2001: A Space Odyssey*. Good himself made some remarkable predictions of the future, including the 1962 speculation that by 1978 "a pulse repetition frequency of 10^9 per second [i.e., a nanosecond] will be attained . . . and a machine of a million units might well be large enough [to model the cerebral cortex], especially if it had an additional 10^{10} binary digits [about a gigabyte] of comparatively slow subsidiary storage. . . ."

Good's career can be divided into four periods:

- His early prewar years when he developed his self-learning abilities.
- The wartime years with Max Newman, Donald Michie, and Alan Turing.
- The immediate postwar years at the University of Manchester, the Government Communications Headquarters (GCHQ), and Oxford University, and his early visits to the US.
- His years at Virginia Tech, the longest period in which he remained in one spot.

In each of these periods he achieved significant advances in philosophy and sciences. Two things have prevented him from being given the recognition he really deserves—the still-classified nature of his wartime work on cryptanalysis and the application of statistical methodology to code breaking, and his own reticence for showmanship. Within limits Good will talk about what happened around him at Bletchley Park and the University of Manchester. But one really has to "pry" about Good's own contributions.

Born of an immigrant London shopkeeper, Good discovered mathematics independently at the age of 9 and, through readings of library books, extended his knowledge and interest of mathematics and probability. During his adolescent years Good learned about cyphers and substitution codes, and amused himself creating and breaking simple codes. Good entered Jesus College, Cambridge, well equipped for advanced studies and eventually completed a doctorate degree under the direction of the well-known mathematician G.H. Hardy. Having completed his studies he was put on the "reserve list," rather than being called directly into the military. Good was interviewed by Hugh Alexander, British chess champion, for a job with the civil service, and after a background check, was recruited to join a band of Cambridge dons and graduates at the Government Code and Cypher School (GCCS) at Bletchley Park.[5] Alexander and Good were acquainted through their interest in chess, though Good was not of the caliber of Alexander, except when playing "five minute" chess. While the interview did not reveal directly the type of work which Good was to undertake, Bernard Scott, a friend of Good's, who was interviewed at the same time, had guessed the reason for the interest in their mathematical backgrounds. Scott had gone so far as to suggest that Good downplay his student style of dress by putting his collegiate scarf inside his coat instead of wearing it in the common nonchalant style.

Alexander met Good at the railroad station on the day he reported to Bletchley Park, and while walking across the fields to the main building, told Good of the work of the "school." Coincidentally that was the day (May 27, 1941) that the Royal Navy sank the German battleship *Bismarck*. The Enigma was a cipher machine which was being used for encipherment by each of the German Armed Forces. The German Air Force (Luftwaffe) and Army Enigma codes had already been broken, but the Naval Enigma was still a major problem—and a problem of significant proportions during the Battle of the Atlantic, when Britain's supply lines from North America were being strangled by the U-boat war.

Initially Good was assigned to Hut 8 in the grounds of Bletchley Park working with Alan M. Turing, Hugh Alexander, Peter Twinn, Joan Clarke, and others. Hut 8 was already using the machines known as "Bombes" to discover the Enigma wheel settings.[6] Turing had come up with the method of disproving the validity of conjectures by contradiction, instead of merely searching for the one elusive solution. Using "cribs," conjectures of the contents of elements (usually the header) of messages, the techniques and methods of determining the wheel settings became algorithmic. During this early period, Max Newman, another Cambridge don, working in another hut, had become disenchanted with the hand methods of code breaking and had established a program to use electronic methods of decipherment. He had

---

[5] Also known as the "Golf Club and Chess Society."
[6] Good 1979.

recruited Donald Michie, an undergraduate classics student from Balliol College, Oxford, to examine linguistic methods of solution. Good joined this group about the time that a new line of machines, named the "Robinsons," were introduced to Bletchley Park.[7] Good and Michie began to use their joint backgrounds in statistics and linguistics to further the code-breaking technologies that eventually led to the development of the Colossus machines and the breaking of a family of codes known as "fish." These machines were, arguably, the first working, special-purpose, electronic computers, developed just in time to have an impact on the invasion of "Fortress Europe" in June 1944.

Following the war, the staff of the GCCS dispersed to various locations, but still restricted by the official secrets act. It was not until 1974 that their code-breaking work, the development of their machines, and the impact of their endeavors were revealed to some extent.

In 1945 Good accepted the invitation of Max Newman to join him at the University of Manchester where Newman planned to build a computer based on Turing's designs, but with the intention of using it primarily in the exploration of "pure" mathematical notions, rather than numeric computations. Along with Tom Kilburn and Fred Williams, Good took his place in the computer development that created the Manchester Mark I, which is credited as the first computer in the world to be controlled from an internally stored program. During this period Good suggested his idea of "Machine Building," which may have been an early form of microprogramming. At the same time Good was developing ideas that resulted in his first book, *Probability and the Weighing of Evidence,* which expanded on the concept of Turing's unit "deciban," which measured the smallest weight of evidence perceptible to the intuition.

In 1948 Good returned to government service within the Government Communications Headquarters (GCHQ) and in 1959 he joined the Admiralty Research Laboratory. After several other sojourns, including a visit to the Institute for Defense Analyses in Princeton, N.J., Good returned to the academic life at Trinity College, Oxford, and was associated with the Atlas Computer Laboratory, sponsored by the Science Research Council of Great Britain, and directed by Jack Howlett. In 1967 Good chose to move his base of operations to the US: "I found [Oxford] a bit stiff actually, taking meals and all that stuff. You couldn't easily converse at the high table. The table was rather wide and the students were noisy, so it was difficult to talk to people on the other side. You could only really talk with the people to

---

[7]The various machines were called the "Heath Robinson" (after the cartoonist in Great Britain who parallels the American Rube Goldberg), "Peter Robinson," and "Robinson and Cleaver" (a restaurant in London).

your left and right; also it was somewhat taboo to talk shop at dinner-time. One could talk about cricket, and things like that. That was all right. I wasn't sorry to leave to come to America." As a University Distinguished Professor at Virginia Polytechnic Institute and State University (Virginia Tech), Good has continued his prolific writing habits and slowly, as permitted, revealed more and more of his wartime exploits. His "vanity" car license plate is 007 IJG.

QUOTATIONS

"All 'analogue' (= continuous) records gradually deteriorate. The only form of storage of unlimited life is discrete (e.g., digital): when it begins to deteriorate it can be regenerated in a mint copy. I suggest that the greatest works of art should be stored discretely in order that they should have a chance of literal immortality. This suggestion would already be practical for all musical performances (by means of pulse code modulation). It will become practical for films and painting in due course, and ultimately even for the legitimate theatre."

(Good 1962)

As important as are quotations *by* Good, quotations *about* Good are equally illuminating:

"When I first met Jack, he held out his hand and said 'I'm Good.' And he has been getting better ever since."(Donald Michie)

"In the 1980s, [Marvin] Minsky and [Jack] Good had shown how neural networks could be generated automatically—self replicated—in accordance with any arbitrary learning program. Artificial brains could be grown by a process strikingly analogous to the development of a human brain."(Arthur C. Clarke, in *2001: A Space Odyssey*, 1968, p. 92.[8])

Of the people at Bletchley Park, Winston Churchill complimented them as "the geese who laid the golden eggs but never cackled."

BIBLIOGRAPHY

Biographical

Good, I.J., "Early Work on Computers at Bletchley," *Ann. Hist. Comp.*, Vol. 1, No. 1, 1979, pp. 38–48.

---

[8]Good has since wished that Clarke had said the "1990s" but then the Space Odyssey may have had to have been postponed for 10 years to become "2011!"

Good, I.J., "Pioneering Work on Computers at Bletchley," in Metropolis, N., J. Howlett, and Gian-Carlo Rota, *A History of Computing in the Twentieth Century,* Academic Press, New York, 1980, pp. 31–45.

Good, I.J., "Enigma and Fish," in Hinsley, Sir Harry H., and Alan Stripp, *Code Breakers: The Inside Story of Bletchley Park,* Oxford Univ. Press, Oxford, 1993, pp. 149–66.

Significant Publications

Good's published writings run to about two million words and receive many citations in the *Science Citation Index.* He numbers his publications, but skipped numbers 1901–2000, so as to not cause confusion with year numbers!

Good, I.J., *Probability and the Weighing of Evidence,* Charles Griffin, London, 1950. The first book on subjective (personal) probability.

Good, I.J., *The Scientist Speculates,* Heinemann & Basic Books, New York, 1962. (There were French and German translations, and a paperback in 1965.)

Good, I.J., *The Estimation of Probabilities,* MIT Press, Cambridge, Mass., 1965.

Osteyee, D.B., and I.J. Good, *Information, Weight of Evidence, the Singularity between Probability Measures and Signal Detection,* Lecture Notes in Mathematics, Springer-Verlag, New York, 1974.

Good, I.J., *Good Thinking: The Foundations of Probability and Its Applications,* Univ. of Minn. Press., Minneapolis, 1983.

HARRY H. GOODE

Born June 30, 1909; New York City; died October 30, 1960; early leader of simulation computers Whirlwind, Cyclone, Hurricane, Typhoon, and (at Michigan) MIDAC and MIDSAC. Chairman of the National Joint Computer Committee (NJCC) and the principal architect of what was to become AFIPS (American Federation of Information Processing Societies).

Education: BA, history, New York University, 1931; BS, chemical engineering, Cooper Union, 1941; MS, mathematics, Columbia University, 1945.

Professional Experience: statistician, New York City Department of Health, 1940–1946; US Navy's Special Devices Section of the Training Division of the Bureau of Aeronautics, Tufts College, 1942–1945; Special Devices Center in

Sands Point, Long Island, 1946–1949; Willow Run Research Center of the University of Michigan, 1950–1954; University of Michigan: professor of electrical engineering, 1954–1960, professor of industrial engineering, 1956–1958; technical director, Systems Division of the Bendix Corporation, 1958–1959.

At his untimely death on October 30, 1960, Harry H. Goode was chairman of the National Joint Computer Committee (NJCC) and the principal architect of what was to become AFIPS (American Federation of Information Processing Societies). Had he lived, Goode undoubtedly would have become the first president of AFIPS, for he was the prime mover in organizing into one federation the three American constituent societies that were members of NJCC.

Early Training[9]

Harry Goode was born in New York City on June 30, 1909. He received his BA in history from New York University in 1931, when the country was in the depths of the Depression. While studying chemical engineering at Cooper Union, Goode earned his living playing the clarinet and saxophone in New York jazz bands. He received his second bachelor's degree in 1940, and in 1941 became a statistician for the New York City Department of Health. During the war years, Goode and Leonard Gillman worked on a special project for Tufts College for the US Navy's Special Devices Section of the Training Division of the Bureau of Aeronautics. At the same time, Goode attended Columbia University and received a master's degree in mathematics in 1945.

From 1946 to 1949, Goode was on the staff of the Special Devices Center in Sands Point, Long Island, and worked with Perry Crawford. Goode progressed through successive responsibilities to become the head of the Special Projects Branch, where he contributed to flight-control-simulation training, aircraft instrumentation, antisubmarine warfare, weapons systems design, and computer research. He and Crawford were responsible for initiating such pioneering computer-based simulation projects as Whirlwind at MIT, Cyclone at Reeves Instrument Company, Hurricane at Raytheon, and Typhoon at RCA Laboratories.

Willow Run

In 1950 Goode joined the Willow Run Research Center of the University of Michigan, serving first as head of the Systems Analysis and Simulation Group, then as chief project engineer, and finally as

---

[9]This biography is taken from Auerbach 1986.

director of the center. Under his stewardship, the center carried forward a broad program of research for the US Army, especially the concept and development of the Air Defense Integrated Systems Project, over-the-hill radar used in battlefield surveillance;[10] the computerized ground control system for the BOMARC missile; the MIDAC (Michigan Automatic Computer), which was similar to the SEAC; and the MIDSAC (Michigan Digital Special-Purpose Automatic Computer), which used electrostatic storage.

Goode's work in the field of air defense was of profound importance. He believed that his understanding of system reliability and the value of a decentralized defense system had never been fully appreciated; years after his death the country abandoned the centralized system it had built (SAGE—the Semi-Automatic Ground Environment system) and returned to Goode's concept of decentralization.

I (Isaac Auerbach) met Harry Goode at Willow Run in late 1953. One of my section chiefs at Burroughs wanted me to meet this man who had accomplished so much. Goode gave me a tour of the laboratory, where they were just completing MIDAC and MIDSAC. He was involved in every aspect of the laboratory's activities; his comprehension of systems design and computer design was extraordinary, and he could explain concepts simply and clearly. Harry would be an asset to any organization, and so I recommended him for membership on the administration committee of the Professional Group on Electronic Computers (PGEC) of the Institute of Radio Engineers (IRE). He was later chairman of PGEC, and we became the closest of friends.

Teaching

Goode's ability to break complicated concepts down to simpler essentials made him a brilliant teacher. In 1954 he was appointed professor of electrical engineering at the University of Michigan, and in 1956 he was also appointed professor of industrial engineering. During the summers of 1955 and 1956, he became a consultant to me at the Burroughs Research Laboratory, and we spent a great deal of working and leisure time together.

Goode's passion for the pursuit of his profession was always evident. One evening we were enjoying an outdoor concert at the Robin Hood Dell in Philadelphia, when I noticed that Harry was distracted by the traffic on the adjacent Schuylkill Expressway. He explained that he was studying the traffic patterns; he was involved in developing sim-

---

[10]The code name for the system was RAWOL, an acronym for radar without line of sight, but everyone knew that it meant radar over the hill—AWOL, of course, meaning over the hill.

ulation models having to do with traffic control in large cities. He developed the theory of bunching in automobile traffic, similar to the effect that one got from electrons in a traveling-wave tube. This interest later led him to a study of the optimum speed for maximum traffic movement through the New York-New Jersey Holland Tunnel.

Goode spent 1958 as technical director of the systems division of the Bendix Corporation, maintaining a fractional appointment at the University of Michigan so he could continue to teach his newly introduced course on systems engineering. In 1959 he decided that he was happier teaching and conducting his own research, so he left Bendix and returned to Michigan as a professor of electrical engineering.

Publishing and Consulting

Harry Goode published many papers touching on statistics, simulation modeling, vehicular traffic control, and systems engineering (see bibliography). He and an associate, R.E. Machol, wrote *Systems Engineering*, the first book on the subject, which was a direct outgrowth of Goode's course at Michigan: Large-Scale Systems Design. The book was a milestone in the concepts of systems engineering and systems analysis, and helped the development of weapons systems as well as commercial ones.

Goode's advice was highly valued and widely sought. His service to industry included consultation with United Aircraft Corporation, Bendix Corporation, Burroughs Corporation, Auerbach Corporation for Science and Technology, Du Pont Company, Ford Motor Company, Texas Instruments, and the Franklin Institute. He served the government as a consultant to the National Bureau of Standards, the Post Office Department, the Air Force, and the House of Representatives Appropriations Committee. He was the chairman of the Committee on Advanced Reconnaissance for the Air Force, and he was a member of the study group on missile reliability for the House committee. He was a key member of the US delegation of computer experts to the Soviet Union in 1959 in the first East-West technical exchange; his presence helped to ensure an effective in-depth study on the Russian state of the art in computer hardware, software, and system design.

Genesis of AFIPS

When Harry Goode was chairman of the National Joint Computer Conference, I served as chairman of the NJCC International Relations Committee and was the NJCC representative on the Committee of Experts organizing the 1959 UNESCO (United Nations Educational, Scientific, and Cultural Organization) conference on information processing in Geneva. The conference led to the formation of IFIP (the International Federation for Information Processing) in 1960. [See Auerbach, Isaac L., "The Start of IFIP Personal Recollections," *Ann. Hist. Comp.*, Vol. 8, No. 2, Apr. 1986.]

A single organization was needed to appoint a US representative to IFIP. At that time the NJCC consisted of four representatives from three member societies: the PGEC of the Institute of Radio Engineers (IRE), the Committee on Computing Devices of the American Institute of Electrical Engineers (AIEE), and the Association for Computing Machinery (ACM). The relationship between the NJCC and the three societies was cumbersome and had no legal standing. Each society had to approve NJCC as being the designated representative to IFIP because NJCC was not a legal entity. Clearly, a federation of information processing societies was needed in the US to be the representative to IFIP.

With uncanny perception, great perseverance, and the ability to forge diverse points of view into a common understanding, Harry Goode did the creative work that would bring AFIPS to fruition. As chairman of NJCC, he was aware that the issue of control was highly sensitive. He asked me to sound out ideas with representatives from the societies, so that he would avoid conflict at formal meetings. If an idea seemed acceptable, he proposed it as a statute for the organization of AFIPS. In his clear and low-key manner, he used these ideas to convince the leaders of the groups that the time had come for such a central organization and, through them, got agreement from their parent societies.

Harry Goode was killed in an automobile accident in October 1960, just a few months before the AFIPS constitution was signed in May 1961. As Morris Rubinoff remarked at the meeting of the founders of AFIPS in 1984, "Without Harry Goode, AFIPS wouldn't have happened." In 1964, AFIPS established the Harry Goode Memorial Award in recognition of his pursuit of excellence; the first award was presented to Howard H. Aiken, professor emeritus at Harvard, in October 1964 at the Western Joint Computer Conference in San Francisco.

Harry Goode was a man of rare versatility and energy. He was a distinguished lecturer, brilliant teacher, outstanding researcher, and capable administrator. He was also a devoted family man and a true friend. He had an ebullient personality and was endowed with a manner disarming in its directness. His sudden death cut short his accomplishments; one can scarcely imagine where his talents might have led him had he lived. Even so, he left behind a rich legacy and friends who will remember him as a man of rare talent, vigor, and vision.

The Harry Goode Memorial Award
At the urging of a number of people, the AFIPS Awards Committee made recommendations which were approved for the establishment of an award for highly significant and meritorious work in the field falling within the scope of AFIPS on June 7, 1962. This award, which may be granted annually to an individual chosen by a group of eminent scientists, was established in memory of Professor Harry Goode, whose efforts were instrumental in the formation of AFIPS.

The Harry Goode Memorial Award was initiated by AFIPS in 1964 in recognition and appreciation of Mr. Goode's invaluable contributions to the information-processing sciences. The annual award was established to encourage further development of the field and to acknowledge and honor outstanding contributions to the information processing sciences.

Harry Goode Memorial Award Recipients
1964	Howard Hathaway Aiken
1965	George Robert Stibitz and Konrad Zuse
1966	J. Presper Eckert and John William Mauchly
1967	Samuel Nathan Alexander
1968	Maurice Vincent Wilkes
1969	Alston Scott Householder
1970	Grace Murray Hopper
1971	Allen Newell
1972	Seymour R. Cray
1974	Edsger W. Dijkstra
1975	Kenneth E. Iverson
1976	Lawrence G. Roberts
1977	Jay W. Forrester
1978	Gordon E. Moore and Robert N. Noyce
1979	Herman H. Goldstine
1980	Fernando J. Corbató
1981	C.A.R. Hoare
1982	Kingsun Fu
1983	Gene M. Amdahl
1984	Ralph E. Gomory
1985	Carver A. Mead
1986	Robert E. Kahn
1992	Edward S. Davidson
1994	Azriel Rosenfeld

BIBLIOGRAPHY

Biographical

Auerbach, Isaac, "Harry H. Goode, June 30, 1909–October, 1960," *Ann. Hist. Comp.*, Vol. 8, No. 3, July 1986, pp. 257–260.

Significant Publications

Goode, Harry H., "The Crippled Child in New York City," 1940.

Goode, Harry H., "Health Center Districts, New York City" (with Bellows and Drolet), New York TB and Health Association, 1944.

Goode, Harry H., "Mathematical Analysis of Ordinary and Deviated Pursuit Curves" (with Leonard Gillman), NAVAER, 1944.

Goode, Harry H., "Service Records and Their Administrative Uses," (with Kantrow and Baumgartner), *American J. Public Health*, Oct. 1945.

Goode, Harry H., "An Estimate of the Correlation Coefficient of a Bivariate Normal Population when X is Truncated and Y is Dichotomized" (with Leonard Gillman), *Harvard Education Review*, Jan. 1946.

Goode, Harry H., "Summary of German Results on Pursuit Curves," Tufts College Mathematical Research Project NAVEXOSP425, June 15, 1946.

Goode, Harry H., "The Tufts College Mathematical Research Project NAVEX-OSP528," Tufts College, Apr. 30,1948.

Goode, Harry H., "Generation of a N-Dimensional Normal Distribution by Means of Analog Equipment," (with G.G. den Broeder and William A. Wheatley), *Symposium on REAC*, New York City, Feb. 1951.

Goode, Harry H., "Simulation: Its Place in System Design," *Proc. IRE*, Vol. 39, No. 12, Dec. 1951.

Goode, Harry H., "Complexity of Research and Industry," *Proc. Third Annual Int'l Methods Time Measurement Conf.*, Oct. 1954.

Goode, Harry H., "The Use of a Digital Computer to Model a Signalized Intersection" (with C. Pollmar and J. Wright), *Proc. Highway Research Board*, Vol. 35, No. 3600, 1956.

Goode, Harry H., "Preparatory Work in Connection with the Installation of an Automatic Data Processing System," *Proc. Society for the Advancement of Management*, Nov. 30, 1956.

Goode, Harry H., "The Application of a Digital Computer to the Definition and Solution of the Vehicular Traffic Problem," *J. Operations Research Society of America*, Jan. 1957.

Goode, Harry H., "The Application of the System Design Process to the Problems of a Large Business," *Proc. Symp. Case Institute of Technology,* Feb. 1, 1957.

Goode, Harry H., *Systems Engineering,* McGraw-Hill, New York, 1957.

Goode, Harry H., "Survey of Operations Research and Systems Engineering," paper presented at *Conf. Engineering Deans on Science and Technology,* Purdue Univ., W. Lafayette, Ind., Sept. 10, 1957.

Goode, Harry H., "Greenhouses of Science for Management," keynote address, Institute for Management Sciences, Detroit, Oct. 15, 1957.

Goode, Harry H., "Qualification and Training of System Engineers," Special Report No. 24, *Problems and Practices in Engineering Management,* American Management Association, 1957.

Goode, Harry H., Review of Shannon and McCarthy, "Automata Studies," *Econometrica,* Vol. 26, No. 1, Jan. 1958.

GEOFFREY GORDON

Originator of the simulation language GPSS.

When the GPSS language first appeared, Geoffrey Gordon was manager of Simulation Development in the Advanced Systems Development Division of IBM, soon after joining the corporation from the Bell Telephone Laboratories. The division had been formed principally to investigate the design and application of information processing systems using telecommunications. Simulation was an essential tool for studying these complex systems,  both for the design of the systems themselves and for understanding the impact of the systems on the organizations that were to use them.[11]

---

[11]From Wexelblat 1981.

BIBLIOGRAPHY

Biographical

Gordon, Geoffrey, "The Development of the General Purpose Simulation System (GPSS)," in Wexelblat, Richard L., ed., *History of Programming Languages,* Academic Press, New York, 1981, Chapter 8.

Significant Publications

Gordon G., "A General Purpose Systems Simulation Program," *Proc. EJCC,* Vol. 20, 1961, pp. 87–104.

SAUL GORN

Born November 10, 1912, Boston, Mass.; died February 22, 1992, Philadelphia, Pa.; educator, mathematician, computing pioneer, philosopher of computer development, and central figure in the philosophy of computer language design.

Education: BS, cum laude, mathematics, Columbia College, 1931; diploma of higher studies in mathematics, University of Bordeaux, France, 1932; PhD, Columbia University, 1942.

Honors and Awards: ACM Distinguished Service Award, 1974.

Gorn was born November 10, 1912, in Boston. His family moved to New York City where his father was an editor of the *Jewish Daily Forward* and where Gorn attended a high school of science. He graduated cum laude in mathematics from Columbia College in 1931 and into the depth of the Depression. An exchange fellowship allowed him to study newer areas of geometry at the Institute of International Education at the University of Bordeaux, from which he received the diploma of higher studies in mathematics in 1932, returning to the US with hundreds of mathematics books in French, purchased by skimping on his living expenses. He was a reader and instructor at Columbia until 1938 and then taught as an instructor in the evening session at Brooklyn College until 1942. In that year he received his PhD from Columbia and entered the Army as a private in the Air

Force. His first duty was teaching illiterate recruits to read. His mathematics doctorate led to a commission as a first lieutenant in Wright Field's radar laboratory in Dayton, Ohio. At that time he married short story writer and novelist Frances Schlesinger.

He participated in the Army's computational development at Wright Field, first as an officer and then, following the war, from 1946 to 1951, as a civilian staff mathematician in the Aircraft Radiation Laboratory. He then served as mathematics adviser for the computing laboratory at the Ballistic Research Laboratory, Aberdeen Proving Ground, which had just received from the Moore School of Electrical Engineering of the University of Pennsylvania the first and only ENIAC and EDVAC computers. Here he developed computer procedures for calculating firing tables and methods of automatic error control, and made the first experiments in devising universal coding systems that could be used for more than one variety of computer.

In 1955 he joined the faculty at the Moore School as an associate professor. In 1957 he became the first director of the University of Pennsylvania Computer Center, which used a very early UNIVAC I. In 1960 he was named director of the Office of Computer Research and Education, a post which he held for one year before returning to full-time teaching and research at the Moore School. In 1964 he became professor of computer and information science.

While he was chair of the university's Graduate Group in Computer and Information Science, the university, under his guidance, granted the first named PhD in computer science ever given anywhere.[12] In the decade just before this milestone event, in the late 1950s and early 1960s, the academic world was struggling with the question of where computing was to be fitted into its often hidebound structure. Was it a subdivision of mathematics or electrical engineering? Would it last or would it fade away? Did it have enough philosophical and intellectual content to be considered in any way a science in its own right?

Gorn argued that computer science was a worthy addition to the academic potpourri. His 1963 paper, "The Computer and Information Sciences: A New Basic Discipline," is considered to be the first formal mention of computer science as a discipline. Gorn improved on the concept in his 1967 paper, "The Computer and Information Sciences and the Community of Disciplines," which went from its first publication in *Behavioral Sciences* into a 1970 French translation in *Analyse et Prevision,* and thence, in reviews and quotations into social science journals everywhere. His arguments gave the needed aura of

---

[12]To Richard L. Wexelblat.

respectability to this novel discipline, allowing the formation of hundreds of computer science (and equivalent) departments throughout the world. In essence, Gorn applied his broad educational and life experience to convince his academic contemporaries, within and without the computer field, that the computer was of more than mere practical importance; it had philosophical importance and the discipline associated with it had intellectual content even beyond that of electrical engineering. This was a political and intellectual coup that only someone of Gorn's character could have accomplished.

He was an international figure, serving as a leading philosopher of computer development, a central figure in computer language design, and a prophet of the future impact of the computer on society. His theory of mechanical languages, based on the work of modern philosophers, has become a central guideline for both theorists and practical computer language developers. His work on standards with the American National Standards Institute led his colleagues to agree to move toward a single set of rules for computer hardware and software, a consummation not yet reached but devoutly to be wished.

In 1974 the Association for Computing Machinery (ACM), which he helped to found and whose journals he helped to edit, awarded him its Distinguished Service Award. The citation praised his contribution to the standardization of computer languages.

Gorn's contributions to actual working computer technology paralleled his philosophical concepts. Many basic ideas, later developed commercially, stemmed from experiments tried out with his students and coworkers on such early machines as ENIAC, EDVAC, Univac I, and the Burroughs computers, all developed in the Philadelphia area. Present-day language and programming techniques involve innovations out of these contributions. He passed many of these ideas on into commercial computers while serving as a consultant to Burroughs, IBM, Sperry-Rand, RCA, and Electricité de France, and gave them to the world through public lectures and his writings, which include 30 articles in technical journals and more than a dozen reports to the Air Force and the Army. Some of the earliest efforts on the validation, or proof of the correctness, of programs are found in his 1973 paper on proving computer symbol manipulation.

His associates knew him as a man of gentleness and gentility of whom it was said, "He has no enemies." Knowledgeable in music and the dance, he produced many original ideas as to how computers might aid these arts, including investigations into the use of choreographic languages with computers. He was admired and loved by his colleagues for his humorous open critique of communication styles.

His mechanical languages theory involved the consideration of paradoxes. As practical ordinary-life examples of linguistic paradoxes, which were always part of his theory of mechanical languages, he collected, and often used in conversation and in his writings, simple self-contradictory sentences, often comedians' oneliners. In 1985 he published a list of several hundred of them as "Self-Annihilating Sentences: Saul Gorn's Compendium of Rarely Used Clichés," starting with "This book fills a much needed gap" and ending with "Things are more like they used to be than they are now," and including "Down deep, he's shallow," as well as "Reality is an illusion."

Always interested in students, his last position before retirement to emeritus status in 1983 was as undergraduate curriculum chairman of the department he developed. He was a member of Phi Beta Kappa, Sigma Xi, the Franklin Institute, the Society for Industrial and Applied Mathematics (SIAM), and ACM, and a fellow of the American Association for the Advancement of Science and the American Mathematical Society.[13]

Immediately following the announcement on the Internet of Saul's death, the following messages were broadcast:

> Saul Gorn, a pioneer of Computer Science died last weekend. A response to my posting (to a smaller mailing list) of the NYT death notice leads me to believe that Saul was not very well known, or at least not well known to the younger generation. I guess that's not surprising. Although he was very active in earlier years—founding member and early officer of ACM, I believe—he didn't publish very much and some of his publications were in very obscure (from the CS mainstream) places. Since I don't have sources to check, the following should be considered reminiscence, not history.
>
> Saul was a mathematician at Aberdeen when ENIAC came along. He learned how to program it and (I don't know what, if anything came in between) ended up at the Moore School. If programmers got serial numbers—perhaps Lady Lovelace would have number 1—Saul's number was certainly below 25. I knew him as a Professor at Penn when I was a grad student there. He taught numerical math, strictly from the classical point of view: splines and isoclines. He taught the basic programming languages courses and he taught a course called compilers, but it was strictly theoretical (and the theory was pretty sparse in those days). He felt that we should be able to prove program correctness, and developed a process he called command recursion. Those who have studied Denotational Semantics would see some of the invariant and lattice theory in his papers. I don't know if Saul had contacts with Chris Strachey, but that wouldn't surprise me. He was

---

[13]From *Ann. Hist. Comp.*, Vol. 14, No. 3, 1992.

certainly influential in getting several important CS researchers to join the Moore School.

Long before "what's-his-name" (from Ohio State and the *Scientific American*), Saul was interested in ambiguity and self-referencing. This particular bent of his cost me close to a full extra year in finishing my dissertation. Self-referencing (which he called unstratified control) meant that a machine language was in some sense more powerful (read: more virtuous) than a "stratified" language like Fortran. Therefore, clearly, an operating system *must* be written in assembly language. It was only a couple of years later that I realized I could have implemented 95% of my system in Fortran taking 6 rather than 18 months. Oh, well.

During my time in and around Penn, no one ever finished a PhD for Saul, but several did master's degrees. Despite this, he was very influential, having a hand in virtually every aspect of graduate studies, from counseling to curriculum development to preliminary exams to defenses. He chaired my defense committee. I'll never forget my defense: I had a yelling, screaming argument with my advisor with Saul as chair, trying to mediate. Bob McNaughton was trying to keep from laughing, and John Carr, new to the Moore School, was trying to figure out what was going on. Saul did eventually restore order. I never saw him afterwards but he reminded me of that absurd day.

He was always writing a book with Al Perlis but I think nothing came of it. Nothing in book form, I mean. Perlis' periodic visits were gala affairs at the Moore School as Al and Saul would gather up a party of faculty and grad students and we'd go to the South China Restaurant and hog out. Perlis would order and we'd eat whatever we were given. I suspect Al and Saul picked up more than their share of the tab.

During the early 1980s when my son was at the Moore School, Saul was retired and mostly doing undergraduate advising. He told me that he knew he had achieved one of his major goals in life when the undergraduate computer science degree was established.

Richard L. Wexelblat, Editor, ACM/SIGPLAN Notices

How sad! Yes, I did know him. He was still an active professor when I was at Penn (and seemed ancient to me at the time). He taught undergrad theory and was undergraduate program director, both jobs I suspect no one else in the department was willing to take on. My funniest memory of him is that his theory class was back-to-back with another course that most of us took (I can't remember now what it was), but he would always run over the period, making us late for the next class. Finally one day someone planted an alarm clock in the wastebasket right next to the lectern which went off promptly at the end of class. I think he jumped a few feet when the thing went off to gales of laughter in the class. Of course we were all extremely late for our next class that day as we had to suffer through an extra long lecture, first about the material and then about the seriousness of it. Still

I guess it was worth it as it really is one of the few things I remember from the class.

My memory of him that showed how much he did care about the undergraduate curriculum is the hard time he gave me about approving mine. At the time (maybe still, I don't know) we were required to have our entire 4 years of courses approved as "meeting the requirements of the major." Technically we were supposed to do it sometime in late sophomore, early junior year, but due to changing availability of courses and general procrastination, we all put it off until our senior years. As far as I could tell I had fulfilled all the requirements and my advisor had been cheerfully signing off each semester's worth of courses without ever looking at them, so I figured getting the 4 years worth approved would be a piece of cake. No dice—Prof. Gorn looked over my courses and began to lecture me on my lack of classical studies, no philosophy, no literature, no history (I studiously avoided them for several reasons, one being that I enjoyed them as hobbies and didn't want to make them work, and the other that writing papers while taking an engineering load at Penn was nearly impossible). Anyway, I managed to convince him that I was still fairly literate and had worked hard and "done good." Despite the haranguing, he convinced me that someone in the department was vigilant for the cause of undergraduate education.

Probably more than you expected to get in response, but as I've recently been thinking a lot about what kind of faculty member I might make, you triggered a few memories. Thanks for forwarding the mail.

Adele Howe, University of Massachusetts

Dick [Wexelblat] did a nice job of paying tribute to Saul Gorn and I echo everything he noted (including the PhD dissertation defense when once again the faculty member had to be led from the room—I guess Saul was getting good practice at diplomacy . . .).

> Saul was the first person I had met who always had a new twist on how to approach a problem, on how to evaluate a situation that you thought was straightforward, and to show how many different ways of looking at it there were if you were being careful. He was the ultimate "spin doctor," in the intellectual sense. Talking to him was for me always a high-intensity affair, where I had to be on my toes all the time to follow the argument. He was an inspired teacher, and gave lovely lectures, and in his own peculiar way, deeply cared about the people around him—he was a mensch.
>
> One personal anecdote. He hammered home some of his favorite points perhaps a bit much. So when Dick and I approached him on what to study for prelims, and he started in on some of his favorites, I beat him to one punch, by blurting out without checking myself "digi-

tal computer: common storage of data and instructions . . . awk." Saul at most raised an eyelid at this parrot imitation and calmly went on with the catechism, ignoring my impertinence in a good-humored way.
    In pace requiescat!

Andy van Dam, Brown University

BIBLIOGRAPHY

Biographical

Weiss, Eric, "Saul Gorn: Obituary," *Ann. Hist. Comp.*, Vol. 14, No. 3, 1993, pp. 76–77.

Significant Publications

Gorn, Saul, "The Computer and Information Sciences; A New Basic Discipline," *SIAM Review*, Vol. 5, No. 2, 1963, pp. 150–155.

Gorn, Saul, "The Computer and Information Sciences and the Community of Disciplines," *Behavioral Sciences*, Vol. 12, No. 6, 1967, pp. 433–452; French translation, *Analyse et Prevision*, Vol. 10, No. 5, 1970, pp. 687–706.

Gorn, Saul, "How Do You Know It Has to Work?, On the Conclusive Validation of Symbol Manipulative Processes," *J. Franklin Institute*, Vol. 296, No. 6, Dec. 1973.

Gorn, Saul, "Self-Annihilating Sentences: Saul Gorn's Compendium of Rarely Used Cliches," Moore School Tech. Report MS-CIS-85-03, Univ. of Pennsylvania, Philadelphia, 1985.

RALPH GRISWOLD

Born May 19, 1934, Modesto, Calif.; inventor and creator of the SNOBOL programming language in the 1960s, and the Icon language in the 1980s.

Education: BS, physics, Stanford University, 1956; MS, electrical engineering, Stanford University, 1960; PhD, electrical engineering, Stanford University, 1962.

Professional Experience: Bell Telephone Laboratories: member, technical staff, Programming Research Department, 1962–1967, supervisor, Computer Languages Research Group, 1967–1969, head, Programming Research and Development Department, 1969–1971; University of Arizona: professor, Department of Computer Science, 1971–1990, head, Department of Computer Science, 1971–1981, Regent's Professor, 1990–present.

Honors and Awards: Top-10 Award Winner, Westinghouse National Science Talent Search, 1952; Distinguished Teaching Award, Faculty of Science, University of Arizona, 1988.

Following the completion of his doctoral work at Stanford, Griswold joined the Bell Telephone Laboratories in New Jersey with an initial assignment in the Programming Research Studies Department, where he worked on developing programs for the manipulation of symbolic expressions. This work led to the development of the SNOBOL programming language with Ivan Polonsky and Dave Farber in 1963. In 1967 Griswold was made supervisor of the Computer Languages Research Group, and in 1969 he was appointed head of the Programming Research and Development Department with a variety of responsibilities ranging from programming language research to the operation of a time-sharing system for document preparation. In 1971 Griswold left the Laboratories to head the computer science program at the University of Arizona, where he continued his work on programming languages and eventually developed the Icon language.

QUOTATION

"The relative lame humor exhibited in choice of SNOBOL was not limited to the name of the language itself. Dave [Farber]'s error messages such as "ALL OUT OF SPACE, YELL FOR HELP" and "NO END STATEMENT, WHISPER FOR HELP" and the cryptic "RECOMPILE NOT ENABLED" quickly became wearisome to users." (Griswold 1981)

BIBLIOGRAPHY

Biographical

Griswold, Ralph E., "A History of the SNOBOL Programming Languages," in Wexelblat, Richard L., ed., *History of Programming Languages*, Academic Press, New York, 1981, Chapter 13.

Significant Publications

Griswold, Ralph E., David J. Farber, and Ivan P. Polonsky, "SNOBOL, a String Manipulation Language," *J. ACM*, Vol. 11, No. 1, 1964, pp. 21–30.

Griswold, Ralph E., and Madge T. Griswold, *A SNOBOL4 Primer*, Prentice-Hall, Englewood Cliffs, N.J., 1973.

Griswold, Ralph E., and Madge T. Griswold, *The Icon Programming Language*, Prentice-Hall, Englewood Cliffs, N.J., 1983.

Griswold, Ralph E., and Madge T. Griswold, "History of the Icon Programming Language," *J. ACM*, Vol. 28, No. 3, 1993, pp. 53–68.

HERBERT REUBEN JOHN GROSCH

Born September 13, 1918, Saskatoon, Sask., Canada; discoverer of the computer price/performance law that bears his name.

Education: BS, astronomy, University of Michigan, 1938; PhD, astronomy, University of Michigan, 1942.

Professional Experience: astronomer, US Naval Observatory, 1941–1942; physicist, Navy Ordnance, 1942; optical engineer, Sperry Gyroscope Co., 1943; designer, Farrand Optical Co., 1944–1945; computer scientist,[14] IBM Corporation, 1945–1951; head, logical design research, Digital Computer Laboratory, MIT, 1951–1952; manager, investigations, Aircraft Gas Turbine Division, General Electric Company, Evendale, Ohio, and Lynn, Mass., 1952–1956; man-

---

[14]Obviously in 1945 the title "computer scientist" had not been invented; in his autobiography Grosch refers to himself simply as "scientist"—the second to be hired by IBM. Grosch's autobiography does note that he was "made into a computer" in 1936, so perhaps the combination of words is not totally inappropriate. In his autobiography, Grosch explains this move to IBM by writing "Drafted into IBM by the Manhattan Project" and "Helps establish the Watson Laboratory at Columbia."

ager, applications, Computer Department, General Electric Company, Phoenix, Ariz., 1956–1958; manager, space programs, IBM Corp., 1958–1959; consultant, computer manufacturing, New York City, 1959–1962, Monte Carlo and Lausanne, 1962–1965; director, Deacon Project, Center for Advanced Studies, General Electric Company, Santa Barbara, Calif., 1965–1967; National Bureau of Standards, Washington, D.C.: director, Center for Computer Science and Technology, 1967–1970, senior research fellow, 1970–1973; editorial director, *Computerworld*, Boston, Mass., 1973–1976; consultant, International Computer Manufacturing, Sunnyvale, Calif., 1976–1980, Netherlands, 1980–1983, Switzerland, 1980–present; president, AIAA, 1951; Association for Computing Machinery: council member, 1968–1987, vice president, 1974–1976, president, 1976–1978.

Honors and Awards: fellow, AIAA; fellow, British Computer Society.

The computer fraternity has characters, notables, and pioneers; Herb Grosch is an all-in-one of these. Originally trained as an astronomer, with the credits of the discovery of several satellites of Jupiter, and having served as the president of the Rocket Society, he transmogrified into a computer attendee (as contrasted with *being* a computer) through the Watson Scientific Computing Laboratory at Columbia University under the tutelage of Wallace Eckert. Grosch has been a compulsive documenter throughout his career, appearing as a curmudgeon with the trademark of a black hat in *Computerworld* and as a extender of the truth as a regular contributor to the "Comments, Queries, and Debate" department of *The Annals of the History of Computing*. Grosch discovered the relationship between the speed and cost of computer systems in 1950, a concept which was only overtaken in the mid-1980s by radical changes in computer architecture. He has worked twice for IBM (and on many occasion has claimed to be the only person *fired* twice by IBM), twice for General Electric Company, and twice for the federal government. He was a charter member, in 1947, of the Association for Computing Machinery (ACM), eventually being elected as president in 1976 after a membership petition placed him on the ballot alongside those selected by the nominations committee. His autobiography, *Computer: Bit Slices from a Life,* is a mixture of corporate, professional, personal, and interpersonal relationships, which is well worth reading if one wants to learn about many of his associates. If anything, Herb gets overlooked because he has been in on the birth of many, many projects and endeavors, has had his fingers in many, many aspects of the history of computing, but has rarely stayed around long enough to be in on the culminating celebrations—at the time it got uninteresting to Herb, he moved on to another challenge.

QUOTATION

"Mini[computer]s are the methadone by which users hope to get unhooked from the heroin of time-sharing."

BIBLIOGRAPHY

Biographical

Grosch, Herbert R. J., "The 701 at General Electric," *Ann. Hist. Comp.*, Vol. 5, No. 2, Apr. 1983, pp. 195–197.

Grosch, Herbert R. J., *Computer: Bit Slices from a Life,* Third Millennium Books, Lancaster, Pa., 1991.

Significant Publications

Grosch, Herbert R. J., "In von Braun Country," *Ann. Hist. Comp.*, Vol. 11, No. 1, 1989, pp. 44–48.

A. Nico Habermann

Born June 26, 1932, Amsterdam, Holland; died August 8, 1993, Pittsburgh, Pa.; a well-respected leader in the fields of programming languages and software engineering environments; he was instrumental in founding the Software Engineering Institute and served as acting director until the first permanent director could be appointed.

Education: BS, mathematics, Free University, Amsterdam, 1958; MS, mathematics, Free University, Amsterdam, 1963; doctorate, applied mathematics, Technological University, Eindhoven, Netherlands, 1967; first doctoral student of Edsger Dijkstra.

Professional Experience: Carnegie Mellon University: visiting research scientist, 1968–1969, associate professor, 1969–1973, full professor 1973–1993, acting department head, 1979; department head, 1980–1988, dean of the School of Computer Science, 1988–1991; adjunct professor, computer science, Jiao Tong University, Shanghai, People's Republic of China, 1986–1993.

Honors and Awards: member, New York Academy of Sciences.

A. Nico Habermann, the Alan J. Perlis professor of computer science at Carnegie Mellon University and a founder of the Software Engineering Institute, suffered a heart attack after a morning run and died on the porch of his Squirrel Hill (Pittsburgh) home on August 8, 1993. He was 61.

Since 1991, Habermann had been on leave from CMU to be assistant director for computer and information science and engineering at the National Science Foundation. He commuted regularly from Washington, D.C., to Pittsburgh.

An internationally renowned computer scientist, Habermann was known for his work in programming languages, operating systems, software engineering, and packages.

He worked on language design and implementation for Algol 60, Bliss, Pascal, Ada, and other special-purpose computer languages. Habermann's contributions to the field include a critique of the Pascal programming language and research on deadlock prevention, path expressions, and integrated software development as exemplified in the Gandalf project he started at CMU in the early 1980s.

A native of Amsterdam, Habermann received a doctorate in applied mathematics from Technological University, Eindhoven, Netherlands, in 1967. He earned his bachelor's and master's degrees in mathematics in 1958 and 1963, respectively, from the Free University in Amsterdam.

In 1968, Habermann went to CMU as a visiting research scientist in the Computer Science Department. He became associate professor in 1969, full professor in 1973, and acting department head in 1979. He led the department from 1980 to 1988, a period during which it became first a department independent of any college within the university, and then a school. He then was first dean from 1988 to 1991. By that time the School of Computer Science represented one third of Carnegie Mellon's research income and was consistently ranked among the top two or three computer science research schools in the US.

Since 1986, he had been an adjunct professor of computer science at Jiao Tong University, Shanghai, People's Republic of China.

Habermann was a member of the Computer Science and Telecommunications Board of the National Academy of Science. He was an adviser to the Max Planck Institute in Germany and a member of the New York Academy of Sciences. He was an editor of the *IEEE Transactions on Software Engineering.*

Nico exercised regularly and usually walked to work. He jogged shortly before suffering the attack on the porch of his home. He also was an avid wind surfer.[1]

QUOTATION

"The original dream of a general purpose language used by all programmers will never materialize, primarily for two reasons. First, our collective understanding of computing keeps evolving and leads to new or enhanced concepts which we want to see reflected in our programming languages. Second, programming tasks can often be served better by specialized tools which directly support the specific nature of these tasks. But giving up the dream . . . implies that we should be willing to live with a possibly large number of special purpose languages. This is acceptable provided we pay serious attention not only to the art but also to the engineering of programming languages. In addition, it will be necessary to use a common implementation language for making programs portable. . . . An ideal language allows us to express easily what is useful for the programming task and at the same time makes it difficult to write what leads to incomprehensible or incorrect programs."

---

[1]This biography is based on *The Pittsburgh Post-Gazette*, Monday, August 9, 1993.

BIBLIOGRAPHY

Significant Publications

Habermann, A.N., "Prevention of System Deadlocks," *Comm. ACM,* 1973.

Habermann, A.N., "Critical Comments on the Programming Language Pascal," *Acta Informatica,* Vol. 3, 1973.

Habermann, A.N., and D.E. Perry, *Ada for Experienced Programmers,* Addison-Wesley, New York, 1984.

Habermann, A.N., "Technological Advances in Software Engineering," *Proc. ACM Computer Conf.,* Cincinnati, Ohio, 1986.

Habermann, A.N., and D. Notkin, "Gandalf: Software Development Environments," *IEEE Trans. Software Engineering,* Vol. 12, 1986.

JERRIER A. HADDAD

Born July 17, 1922, New York, N.Y.; manager of the development project which resulted in the IBM-701 (Defense Calculator).

Education: BEE, Cornell University, 1945.

Professional Experience: IBM: member, IBM Engineering Laboratory, Endicott, N.Y., 1945–1946, member, IBM Engineering Laboratory, Pough-keepsie, N.Y., 1946–1953, engineering manager, IBM-701, 1951–1953, manager, Component Development, 1953, manager, IBM Endicott Engineering Laboratory, 1953–1954, director, advanced machine development, IBM Headquarters, New York, 1954–1956, general manager, Special Engineering Products Division, 1956–1958, general  manager, Advanced System Development Division, 1959–1962, vice president of development, Data Systems Division, 1962–1963, vice president of system engineering, Data Processing Division, 1963–1964, director of engineering, programming and technology, IBM Headquarters, 1964–1970, IBM vice president, 1967–1981, director, Poughkeepsie Laboratory, 1971–1972, vice president of development, Systems Products Division, 1972–1975, vice president, engineering, programming and technology, 1975–1977, vice president, technical personnel development, 1978–1981, retired 1981.

Honors and Awards: member, National Academy of Engineering, 1968; Order of the Cedar, Lebanese Republic, 1970; DSc, Union College, 1971, DSc, Clarkson College, 1978; IEEE Computer Society Pioneer Award, 1984; fellow, IEEE.

"Jerry" Haddad joined IBM's Endicott, N.Y., engineering laboratory in 1945. He served in a number of technical capacities within IBM. He was a member of the IBM-604 development team and headed the IBM-701 engineering team. He has been general manager of the Special Engineering Products and Advanced Systems Development Divisions; a vice president of the Data Processing Division, the Data Systems Division, and the Systems Products Division; and manager of the Endicott Laboratory and the Poughkeepsie Laboratory. In 1963, he became director of technology and engineering in Corporate Headquarters, and in 1967 was elected IBM vice president, engineering, programming and technology, a position he held until 1977. At the time of his retirement in September 1981, he was IBM vice president, technical personnel development.

Haddad received the BEE degree from Cornell University's College of Engineering, where he was awarded a McMullen Industrial Scholarship and was an undergraduate teaching assistant. He has served Cornell as a member of its Engineering College Advisory Council, and presently is chairman emeritus. He is a trustee of Clarkson University, a trustee of the Webb Institute of Naval Architecture, and a former chairman of the board of the Engineering Foundation.

Haddad is a member of the National Academy of Engineering (NAE), and has served on its Committee on Technology and International Economic and Trade Issues. He was chairman of the National Research Council (NRC) Committee on Education and Utilization of the Engineer and was a member of the NRC Board on Army Science and Technology, the NRC Committee on Engineering Personnel Data Needs, and the NAE Education Advisory Board.

He is a fellow of both the American Association for the Advancement of Science (AAAS) and the IEEE. He was a member of the IEEE Education Activities Board and the IEEE Academy Committee. He was a member of the IEEE Committee on Continuing Education and the IEEE Publications Board. He is an IEEE appointed member and secretary of the Board of Directors of the Accreditation Board for Engineering and Technology (ABET).

He has received honorary doctor of science degrees from Union College (1971) and Clarkson University (1978). In 1970, he received the Order of the Cedars Medal from the Republic of Lebanon for his scientific and technical achievements. He is the holder of 18 patents for inventions in the computer and electronics field, and has written and lectured extensively on engineering, scientific, and educational topics.

BIBLIOGRAPHY

Biographical

Haddad, J.A., "701 Recollections," *Ann. Hist. Comp.*, Vol. 5, No. 2, Apr. 1983, pp. 118–123.

MAURICE HOWARD HALSTEAD

Purdue University professor and originator of the concepts of software science, which led to the development of software metrics.

FRANK E. HAMILTON

IBM inventor of punched card and computing machinery who made significant contributions to the Harvard Mark I (ASCC) and the IBM SSEC.

CARL HAMMER

Born May 10, 1914, Chicago, Ill.; educator and lecturer who conveyed the exciting message of computers and their mind-boggling future applications early on to audiences worldwide; long-time seeker of the solution to the Beale Cypher.

Education: PhD, magna cum laude, University of Munich, 1938.

Professional Experience: mathematician and statistician, Texas Company Research Laboratories, Beacon, N.Y., 1938–1943; statistician, Pillsbury Mills, Inc., New York, N.Y., 1944–1947; chairman, Division of Technical Education, Walter Hervey Junior College, New York, N.Y., 1947–1951; senior staff engineer, Franklin Institute of the State of Pennsylvania, Philadelphia, Pa., 1951–1955; director, Univac European Computing Center (Univac I), Frankfurt/Main, Germany, 1955–1957; staff consultant and acting manager, Programming and Analysis Department (UDOFT, ELECOM 125, IBM-709), Sylvania Electronic Products, Inc., Needham, Mass., 1957–1959; senior engineering scientist, Surface Communications Division, Radio Corporation of America, New York, N.Y., 1959–1961; manager, Scientific Computer Applications, RCA Computer Division, Washington, D.C., 1961–1963; director, Computer Sciences, Sperry Univac, Washington, D.C., 1963–1981; retired October 1981.

Honors and Awards: member, Scientific Research Society of America, 1954; National Defense Executive Reserve, 1970; member, New York Academy of Sciences, 1955, fellow, 1976; fellow, American Association for the Advancement of Science, 1969; fellow, Institute of Electrical and Electronic Engineers, 1986; Chester Morrill Memorial Award, Association for Systems Management, 1972; lifetime member and Computer Sciences Man-of-the-Year Award, Data Processing Management Association, 1973; fellow, World Organization of General Systems and Cybernetics, 1978; ACM Distinguished Service Award, 1979; Distinguished Service Award, American Federation of Information Processing Societies, 1981; Lifetime Achievement Award, Federation of Government Information Processing Councils, 1986.

During his years, Hammer has given talks and made presentations in Argentina, Australia, Austria, Belgium, Brazil, Canada, Czechoslovakia, Colombia, France, Germany, Great Britain, Greece, India, Italy, Korea, Malaysia, Mexico, The Netherlands, New Zealand, Norway, Peru, The Philippines, Puerto Rico, Russia (the Soviet Union), Singapore, South Africa, Sweden, Switzerland, Yugoslavia, in addition to all of the United States.

QUOTATION

"Government is as guilty as industry in the retention of old systems."

BIBLIOGRAPHY

Biographical

Donlan, Hugh, "At the Top," *INSIDE DPMA,* Vol. 29, No. 9, Dec. 1991, p. 5.

McGraw, Tim, "Computer Expert Stresses ADP Role in the Office," *Government ComputerNews,* Vol. 7, No. 1, Jan. 1988, p. 7.

Meyers, Robert, "Spotlight on Dr. Carl Hammer," *Government ComputerNews,* Vol. 3, No. 1, Jan. 1984, pp. 1, 41–42.

Ross, James, "An Interview with Carl Hammer," Charles Babbage Institute, University of Minnesota, Minneapolis, Minn., Apr. 15, 1983.

Significant Publications

Hammer, Carl, "Univac Programming with Compilers," *Proc. First Int'l Congress on Cybernetics,* Namur, Belgium, 1956.

Hammer, Carl, and F. Ikle, "Intercity Telephone and Airline Traffic Related to Distance and the Propensity to Interact," *Sociometry,* Dec. 1957.

Hammer, Carl, "Computers and Simulation," *Cybernetica,* Vol. 4, No, 4, 1961, pp. 204–209.

Hammer, Carl, "Detection of Synchronization in Pulse Trains," *Symposium on Time Series and Sequence Analysis, Society for Industrial and Applied Mathematics,* Stanford Research Institute, Menlo Park, Calif., April 26, 1963.

Hammer, Carl, "Autoregressive Data Analysis, Fortran IV, Univac 1107— Statistical Programs for High Speed Computers," *Technometrics,* Vol. 6, No. 2, May 1964, p. 235.

Hammer, Carl, "Statistical Validation of Mathematical Computer Routines," *AFIPS Conf. Proc.,* Vol. 30, Apr. 1967, pp. 331–333.

Hammer, Carl, "Signature Simulation and Certain Cryptographic Codes," *Comm. ACM,* Vol. 14, No. 1, Jan. 1971, pp. 3–14.

Hammer, Carl, "Second Order Homophonic Ciphers," *Cryptologia,* Vol. 12, No. 1, Jan. 1988, pp. 11–20.

Hammer, Carl, "Is Today's Office Receiving Full Value from Its Computers?" *Information & Management,* Vol. 15, No. 1, Aug. 1988, pp. 15–24.

RICHARD WESLEY HAMMING

Born February 11, 1915, Chicago, Ill.; inventor of error-correcting codes which bear his name, and of the aphorism "The purpose of computing is insight not numbers," and many others.

Education: BS, mathematics, University of Chicago, 1937; MA, mathematics, University of Nebraska, 1938; PhD, mathematics, University of Illinois, 1942.

Professional Experience: Bell Telephone Laboratories; Naval Postgraduate School.

Honors and Awards: IEEE Computer Society Pioneer Award, 1980; fellow, IEEE.[2]

Richard W. Hamming's invention of error-correcting codes for computers was the result of fortune favoring the prepared mind—and of frustration.

Richard W. Hamming was having a bad day. It was 1947, and Hamming was the Bell Telephone Laboratory computer evangelist. He was the one to whom the other Bell Labs researchers would turn when they found themselves mired in problems they were unable to solve with their then-current, hand-driven desk calculators. Hamming would show them how computers could get them going again.

On this Monday, Hamming was expecting a number of useful results from a large-scale relay computer[3] that had been running unattended since Friday evening at Bell Telephone Laboratory's New York City site. But the machine had had a failure early on, and Hamming had no results to give to his colleagues in Murray Hill, N.J.

"Dammit," he thought, "if a machine can find out that there is an error, why can't it locate where it is and change the setting of the relay from one to zero or zero to one?"

A mathematician by training, Hamming set out to find an efficient means by which computers could correct themselves. He puzzled over the problem at odd moments, soon finding a solution based on parity checking. Adding extra bits to a block of data would allow not only the detection of bad bits, but their position within the block as well. He found an even better method several months later, as he was riding in the BTL mail delivery car from New Jersey to New York City.

---

[2]IEEE named their medal for exceptional contributions to the information sciences and systems after Richard Hamming.

[3]See biography of George Stibitz.

Hamming concentrated on the problem during the entire ride, since, he said, "New Jersey isn't worth looking at." He thought of more and more efficient arrangements of data, realizing that the real question was, What is the best possible solution? Within a matter of weeks, success was his. His techniques for finding and correcting a single error in a stretch of data, as well as finding two errors and correcting one of them, were to become known as the Hamming Codes. His solution was used by BTL in computer systems and in telephone switching systems.

Hamming moved on to other projects, and error correction moved on, too, being developed by other scientists into a scientific discipline used in everything from extracting data transmitted from space probes, to recovering jammed communications, to guaranteeing high quality music from a compact disc.

Computer Janitor

Hamming's first involvement with the large-scale computing of his day was as the computing maintenance man—a computer janitor, he called it—for the Manhattan Project, whose members built the atomic bomb during World War II.

Becoming interested in mathematics in high school where, during freshman algebra, he realized he was a better mathematician than the teacher, Hamming had intended to study engineering. But his only scholarship offer came from the University of Chicago, which did not have an engineering school. So he majored in mathematics, going on for a master's degree at the University of Nebraska and a PhD at the University of Illinois, both in mathematics. With those credentials, he expected to have a teaching career, and began one. But that smooth career path shifted after Hamming received a letter from an old friend.

The friend told him: "I'm in Los Alamos, and there is something interesting going on down here. Come down and work." With not much more to go on except that he was needed for war work, Hamming took the train to New Mexico, and his wife followed a month later. They both began work on the Manhattan Project.

Hamming's wife was hired to run a desk calculator, eventually working for Enrico Fermi and Edward Teller. Hamming was taken to a large room where a group of IBM relay computers were clacking away. At night they cast eerie shadows in the dim light. It was science fiction come true, "the mad scientist's laboratory," Hamming recalled, telling *IEEE Spectrum* that his avid interest in science fiction ended that day.

Hamming's job was to keep the computers running so the physicists who had set up the elaborate computations could get back to their work on the atomic bomb. Although Hamming knew nothing about computing on such large machines, he learned quickly.

"And when I had time to think about it, I realized that it meant that science was going to be changed," he said. Experiments that were impossible in the laboratory were going to be possible with computers.

When the Manhattan Project ended after the war, Hamming accepted a job at Bell Telephone Laboratories, but delayed his move to New Jersey. Instead, he stayed in Los Alamos for six more months, even though most of the other scientists had left. "I wanted to figure out what had happened there, and why it had happened that way," he said. And he wanted to create a written record of what had been computed, because he believed that part of the job of a scientist is to write and teach, to enable others to carry on his work.

One thing that puzzled him was why the bomb worked so well. Why, when so many of the numbers used in the calculations were of questionable accuracy, were the final computations so accurate? He concluded that it was due to the feedback loops of large-scale computations. Years later this experience served him well as he searched for clues as to why certain failures of early Nike missile test vehicles could also be accurately simulated. He also asked himself why designing the bomb—an engineering job if he ever saw one—was done by a group of young scientists, not engineers. He concluded that engineering schools do not prepare students to work at the frontier of knowledge. Rather, he said, "they prepare them to do run-of-the-mill work," and he thanked his good luck that his original ambition to study engineering had been thwarted. "As an engineer," he said, "I would have been the guy going down manholes instead of having the excitement of frontier research work."

Young Turks

When Hamming finally left Los Alamos for Bell Telephone Laboratories in 1946, he joined a mathematics department that had recently hired Claude E. Shannon, Donald P. Ling, and Brockway McMillan. The four called themselves the Young Turks. All around 30 years of age, they shared a baptism in scientific research that had started with the war, and they were much alike.

"We grew up in the Great Depression," Hamming said, "so we believed we owed the world a living. During the war we all had to learn things we didn't want to learn to get the war won, so we were all cross-fertilized. We were impatient with conventions, and had often had responsible jobs very early." The situation was right for great achievements, Hamming said, and the four went on to fulfill their promise, although not in the way BTL expected. "We were first-class trouble-makers," Hamming said. "We did unconventional things in unconventional ways and still got valuable results. Thus management had to tolerate us and let us alone a lot of the time." Hamming, for one, was hired to work on elasticity theory. But the presence of computers required him to devote more and more time to them, and his career became centered on the computer revolution, with his key advances being made in error-correcting codes and in digital filter theory.

Hamming's contribution to digital filters arose out of his concern for teaching the analog computing specialists the new digital ways of thinking before they became ossified. He was encouraged to write a text for them, learning the field from such digital experts as John W. Tukey and James F. Kaiser.

His work on that text also led to a patent on a new filter design method, and to a certain "window" being named after him. The Hamming window is a statistical tool that lets users look at a small region of a signal, often a spectrum, with the least amount of leakage from any other part of the signal. These developments illustrated a maxim that Hamming adopted from Louis Pasteur: "Luck favors the prepared mind." They also fit in with another one of his oft-repeated axioms: "If you don't work on important problems, it's not likely that you'll do important work." The moments of such discoveries are the high points of Hamming's life. He said, "The emotion at the point of technical breakthrough is better than wine, women, and song put together."

But being a first-class troublemaker does not make one universally popular. Some former colleagues from BTL recall Hamming as egotistical, and comment that he occasionally went off "half-cocked, after some half-baked idea," and he was slow to pick up on his misdirection. "He is very hard to work with," one former BTL scientist said, "because he does a lot of broadcasting and not a lot of listening."

Hamming appears to be aware of such feelings. He said, "To reform the system, you have to be willing not to be liked."

Manager—Not

While Hamming believes that he did a lot of good for BTL by bringing in computers, he suspects that he could have contributed more if he had been willing to be a manager. He was not. Several times Hamming found himself promoted to the head of a department of researchers. As fast as he could, he found those scientists other jobs in the laboratories and transferred them out. "I was so busy doing what I wanted that I couldn't give them the attention they deserved," Hamming said. "I knew in a sense that by avoiding management, I was not doing my duty by the organization," he said. "That is one of my biggest failures."

Frustrated at several points in his career by aging scientists who were taking up space and resources that, he believes, could have been put to better use by Young Turks like himself, Hamming resolved while still young to retire early and get out of the way. So he ended his career at Bell Telephone Laboratories after 30 years, at age 61.

He still believes his decision was the right one—that mathematicians are most productive early in their careers and their productivity drops off rapidly as they age.

That he believes he is right, however, does not seem to make him happy. On an anniversary of BTL, he recalled receiving a commemorative poster listing year-by-year contributions BTL had made to research. Partially unrolling the poster, Hamming scanned the listing for his early years at BTL and noted complacently that he had worked on, or been somehow associated with, most of the chief contributions listed.

He then hung the poster on a door, where it unrolled. Glancing at it again a few days later, Hamming realized that all his valued contributions came in the first 15 years of his tenure—he had not been associated with any of the subsequent projects listed. He tore up the poster and threw it away.

The Professor

Hamming knew that the day he left BTL, his research career would be over. But he thought he had another career or two left in him—those of an author and a teacher. He had already written a number of books on computing theory and went on to produce more, continuing his writing for many years. His teaching included various evening classes while at BTL, and he decided to expand that experience into a full-time teaching career at the Naval Postgraduate School in Monterey, Calif., because, he said, he wanted to live in California (to escape harsh New Jersey winters) and his wife suggested Monterey.

Life after research has mixed appeal for Hamming, now 78. He finds the students at the Naval Postgraduate School, where he is an adjunct professor, to be "marvelous." "There is no school I know of in which the students are better selected and more likely to be worth the trouble," he said. And he likes the idea that he is teaching people who in 30 years or so will be very important in the military organizations of this and other nations. But he misses the intellectual climate of BTL.

Hamming's philosophy of teaching is simple. Since he is preparing students for the year 2020, and he has no clue as to what technology they will be dealing with at that date, whatever subject he is teaching is really a class on learning to learn.

In a basic undergraduate-level circuit theory class, Hamming, who never studied circuit theory, goes through the text with the students, line by line. "I tell them that I will do very little writing on the blackboard. We will learn to read this book and learn how you go about following a book full of formulas."

During the class attended by *Spectrum*, Hamming reminded the students that "this is not an exciting class, it is routine and boring. And much of engineering is like that. But I'm teaching you how to learn."

Hamming occasionally digresses to a story about his days at Los Alamos or BTL. The students find the digressions interesting. As for reading the book page by page, well, some say there are more effective ways for them to be taught, particularly in an undergraduate class. "You want the fundamentals drilled into you," one student told *Spectrum*, "so you can do them in your sleep. This is more like a self-taught course." Hamming still spends a lot of time reading journals to stay technically current on a range of scientific topics. But, he said, annoyed: "I don't keep up as well as I used to. I'm falling slowly behind. There is no way out of it. Frustrating? It's worse than frustrating!"

Hamming expects to retire from teaching in the next few years. With few outside interests, he does not know what he will do with himself. "A friend told me recently," he recounted, "'Hamming, the day you quit teaching, you are going to fall apart.' He's probably right. When I left BTL, I knew that that was the end of my scientific career. When I retire from here, in another sense, it's really the end."[4]

QUOTATIONS

"The purpose of computing is insight, not numbers."

Regarding the teaching of mathematics: "You should know enough mathematics to protect yourself against it!"

"Anything a faculty member can learn, a student can easily."

"Once, when Sir Isaac Newton was asked how he made all of his discoveries, he replied 'If I have seen further than others, it is by standing on the shoulders of giants.' Today, in the programming field, we mostly stand on each other's feet."

---

[4]From Perry 1993.

BIBLIOGRAPHY

Biographical

Hamming, R.W., "We Would Know What They Thought When They Did It," in Metropolis, N., J. Howlett, and Gian-Carlo Rota, *A History of Computing in the Twentieth Century,* Academic Press, New York, 1980, pp. 3–9.

Perry, Tekla S., "Richard W. Hamming," IEEE *Spectrum,* May 1993, pp. 80–82.

Significant Publications

Hamming, Richard W., *Calculus and the Computer Revolution,* Houghton Mifflin, New York, 1968.

Hamming, Richard W., *Introduction to Applied Numerical Analysis,* McGraw-Hill, New York, 1971.

Hamming, Richard W., *Numerical Methods for Scientists and Engineers,* McGraw-Hill, New York, 1973.

Hamming, Richard W., *Coding and Information Theory,* Prentice-Hall, Englewood Cliffs, N.J., 1980.

Hamming, Richard W., *Digital Filters,* Prentice-Hall, Englewood Cliffs, N.J., 1983.

Hamming, Richard W., *Coding and Information Theory,* Prentice-Hall, Englewood Cliffs, N.J., 1986.

Hamming, Richard W., *Introduction to Applied Numerical Analysis,* Hemisphere Pub. Corp., New York, 1989.

Hamming, Richard W., *The Art of Probability—for Scientists and Engineers,* Addison-Wesley, Reading, Mass., 1991.

JOHN V. HARRINGTON

Responsible for developing radar data-processing and transmission equipment for the SAGE system, as well as the first telephone-line modems.

Education: BEE, Cooper Union Institute of Technology, 1940; MEE, Polytechnic Institute of Brooklyn, 1948; ScD, MIT, 1957.

Honors and Awards: fellow, IEEE; fellow, AIAA; fellow, AAAS; Air Force Medal for exceptional civilian service; Gano Dunn Award of the Cooper Union.

Harrington served with the US Navy during World War II, and then worked with the US Air Force Cambridge Research Laboratory as leader of the Data Transmission Group of Division 2, and was responsible for developing radar data-processing and transmission equipment for the SAGE system, as well as the first telephone-line modems. He served as head of Lincoln Laboratory's Radio Physics Division 3 from 1958 to 1963, when he joined MIT's faculty and became the first director of MIT's Center for Space Research. In 1973 he went to the Communications Satellite Corporation, where he is now senior vice president of research and development and director of COMSAT Laboratories.

DOUGLAS HARTREE

Born March 27, 1897, Cambridge, UK; died February 12, 1958; designer, with A. Porter, of the Manchester Meccano differential analyzer; very influential early British computer user at both Manchester and Cambridge, and originator of the method of self-consistent field.

Education: BA, University of Cambridge; MA, University of Cambridge; PhD, University of Cambridge; MSc, University of Manchester.

Professional Experience: Antiaircraft Experimental Group, Inventions Department, Ministry of Munitions, 1916–1919; research fellow, St. John's College, Cambridge, 1924–1927; research fellow, Christ's College, Cambridge, 1928–1929; University of Manchester: professor of applied mathematics, 1929–1937, professor of theoretical physics, 1937–1945; professor of mathematical physics, University of Cambridge, 1946–1958; on leave, acting chief,

Institute of Numerical Analysis (INA), National Bureau of Standards (at UCLA)

In 1933 Hartree visited MIT to use the Vannevar Bush Differential Analyzer. As a result of this work he received a copy of the design, which he then used to create his own model using Meccano parts, and costing about £20, a tiny fraction of the expenditures at MIT. This machine was so successful that several copies were made and used throughout the country. Hartree used his influence to promote the mechanical solution of differential equations as related to a wide range of applications from ballistics to atomic energy.

BIBLIOGRAPHY

Biographical

Douglas, Sandy, "Some Memories of EDSAC I: 1950–1952," *Ann. Hist. Comp.*, Vol. 1, No. 2, 1980, pp. 98–99, 208.

Medwick, Paul A., "Douglas Hartree and Early Computations in Quantum Mechanics," *Ann. Hist. Comp.*, Vol. 10, No. 2, 1988, pp. 105–112.

Significant Publications

Hartree, D.R., *Calculating Machines—Recent and Prospective Developments*, Cambridge Univ. Press, Cambridge, UK, 1947.

Hartree, D.R., "Automatic Calculating Machines," *Mathematical Gazette*, Vol. 34, Dec. 1950, pp. 241–252.

HAROLD LOCKE HAZEN

Born August 1, 1901, Philo, Ill.; died February 21, 1980, Belmont, Mass.; early pioneer in the field of machine computation and automatic control; developer of the Hazen servo.

Education: SB, electrical engineering, MIT, 1924; SM, electrical engineering, MIT, 1929; PhD, electrical engineering, MIT, 1931.

Professional Experience: General Electric Company, Schenectady, 1924–1925; MIT: research assistant, 1925–1926, instructor, 1926–1931, assistant professor, 1931; head, Department of Electrical Engineering, 1938–1942; head, Fire Control, NRDC, 1942–1945; dean, Graduate School, 1945–1967; Robert College, Istanbul, interim president, 1961.

Honors and Awards: Levy Medal, Franklin Institute, 1935; President's Certificate of Merit, 1948.

A student of Vannevar Bush, Hazen's career followed Bush's closely in interests and positions at MIT. His contributions to the development and use of the differential analyzer earned him numerous awards, and his concern for the welfare of his students as a teacher and administrator gained him the admiration and abiding respect of his disciples.

BIBLIOGRAPHY

Biographical

Brown, Gordon, "Eloge: Harold Locke Hazen, 1901–1980," *Ann. Hist. Comp.*, Vol. 3, No. 1, 1981, pp. 4–12.

Significant Publications

Bush, V., and H.L. Hazen, "Integraph Solutions of Differential Equations," *J. Franklin Inst.*, Vol. 204, Nov. 1927, pp. 575–615.

Hazen, H.L., "Theory of Servomechanisms," *J. Franklin Inst.*, Vol. 218, Sept. 1934, pp. 209–331.

Hazen, H.L., "Design and Test of a High Performance Servomechanism," *J. Franklin Inst.*, Vol. 218, Nov. 1934, pp. 543–580.

Hazen, H.L., J.J. Jaeger, and G.S. Brown, "An Automatic Curve Follower," *Rev. Scientific Instruments*, Vol. 7, Sept. 1936, pp. 354–357.

Hazen, H.L., O.R. Schurig, and M.F. Gardner, "The MIT Network Analyzer, Design and Application to Power System Problems," *AIEE Trans.*, Vol. 49, July 1930, pp. 1102–1113.

Spencer, H.H., and H.L. Hazen, "Artificial Representation of Power Systems," *AIEE Trans.*, Vol. 44, 1925, pp. 42–79.

ROBERT A. HENLE

Born 1923; died January 27, 1989, New York City; the chief IBM designer of the complimentary npn-pnp circuits used in the experimental, transistorized 604 calculator in 1964 known as the 608. He was also a major contributor to the circuits used in STRETCH and the 7000 series of computers in the 1960s; appointed as an IBM fellow in 1964 and spearheaded the IBM entry into monolithic memory technology.[5]

Education: University of Minnesota, 1951.

Professional Experience: IBM, 1951–1988.

Honors and Awards: Department of Defense Citation, 1974; member, National Academy of Engineering, 1982; fellow, IEEE; IEEE Edison Medal, 1987.

Following his graduation from the University of Minnesota in 1951, Henle joined an IBM group studying the application of transistor technology to computers. This work resulted in the development of the IBM-608, the company's first transistorized system. He then worked on the high-speed circuits for the IBM-7030 (STRETCH) computer and eventually the 7090. In the mid-1960s he began to concentrate on the development of monolithic memory technology, the first application of which was a storage-protect memory in System/370 Models 91 and 95. His work led in 1970 to the first 128-bit chip memory, which was used in the Model 145. He was appointed manager of Advanced Technology for the IBM Components Laboratory in 1975, and director of the Advanced Silicon Technology Laboratory in 1981. In April 1988, a symposium was held at the T.J. Watson Research Laboratory in honor of his 35th year of service to the corporation. He held 48 patents in computer technology.

BIBLIOGRAPHY

Biographical

Weiss, Eric A., "Obituary," *Ann. Hist. Comp.*, Vol. 11, No. 3, 1989, p. 225.

---

[5]This biography is based on Pugh, Emerson W., Lyle R. Johnson, and John H. Palmer, *IBM's 360 and Early 370 Systems*, MIT Press, Cambridge, Mass., 1991.

MAGNUS R. HESTENES

Born 1906, Bricelyn, Minn.; died May 31, 1991, Los Angeles, Calif.; best known for his work on the "Problem of Bolza,"[6] for his 1951 paper on quadratic forms in Hilbert space, and for the development of the conjugate gradient method.

Education: BS, St. Olaf College, 1927; MA, University of Wisconsin, 1928; PhD, University of Chicago, 1932.

Professional Experience: postdoctoral scholar, University of Chicago, 1932–1933; national research fellow, Harvard University, 1933–1937; assistant (and later associate) professor, University of Chicago, 1937–1947[7]; UCLA: professor, 1947–1973, part-time member, INA, 1949–1954, chair, Mathematics Department, 1950–1958, director, Computing Facility, 1961–1963.

In the late 1940s the introduction of "high-speed" computers was raising questions about the usefulness and accuracy of such methods as Gaussian elimination for the solution of linear systems. During this time, the Institute for Numerical Analysis (INA), National Bureau of Standards, organized a seminar to study computational methods, and from this interaction many fruitful ideas arose, including the method of conjugate gradients. Hestenes and Eduard Stiefel (of Zurich) devised the method independently, but merged their ideas into a single paper in 1952. It took almost 20 years for computer technology to catch up with Hestenes' ideas, making possible the storage and solution through conjugate gradients of large sparse linear systems for which elimination methods were impractical.[8]

BIBLIOGRAPHY

Biographical

Berkovitz, Len, Tony Chan, Alfred Hayes, Dianne O'Leary, and Richard Tapia, "Obituary," *SIAM News,* Vol. 24, No. 5, Sept. 1991.

Hestenes, Magnus, "Conjugacy and Gradients," in Nash, Stephen, *A History of Scientific Computing,* ACM Press, New York, 1990, pp. 167–179.

---

[6]Also known as the Problem of Lagrange or the Problem of Mayer.

[7]During the latter years of World War II, Hestenes was a member of the Applied Mathematics Group at Columbia University concerned with the mathematics of aerial gunnery.

[8]From Berkovitz et al. 1991.

Significant Publications

Hestenes, Magnus, and E. Stiefel, "Methods of Conjugate Gradients for Solving Linear Systems," *J. Research*, National Bureau of Standards, Vol. 49, 1952, pp. 409–438.

WILLIAM HEWLETT

Born May 20, 1913, Ann Arbor, Mich.; with David Packard, founder of the computer company which bears their names; holders of patents on resistor-capacitance oscillators and other electronic devices.

Education: BA, Stanford University, 1934; MS, electrical engineering, MIT, 1936; BS, electrical engineering, Stanford University, 1939.

Professional Experience: Hewlett-Packard Corp.: co-founder and partner, 1939–1947, vice president and director, 1947–1957, executive vice president and director, 1957–1964, president and director, 1964–1968, president, chief executive officer and director, 1969–1977, chairman of executive committee, chief executive officer and director, 1977–1978, chairman of executive committee and director, 1978–1983, vice chairman, board of directors, 1983–1987, director emeritus, board of directors, 1987–present.

Honors and Awards: life fellow, Institute of Radio Engineers (now IEEE), 1948; honorary lifetime membership, Instrument Society of America, 1963; member, National Academy of Engineering, 1965; life fellow membership, the Franklin Institute, Philadelphia, 1976; member, National Academy of Sciences, 1977; fellow, American Academy of Arts and Sciences, 1970; member, American Philosophical Society, Philadelphia, 1981; member, National Academy of Sciences, the President's Circle, 1989; director, Institute of Radio Engineers (now IEEE), 1950–1957, president, 1954; California Manufacturer of the Year, California Manufacturers' Association, 1969; Business Statesman of the Year, Harvard Business School of Northern California, 1970; Medal of Achievement, WEMA (Western Electronic Manufacturers Assn.), 1971; Founders Medal, the Institute of Electrical and Electronics Engineers (IEEE), to Hewlett and Packard, 1973; Industrialist of the Year, to Hewlett and Packard, California Museum of Science and Industry and California Museum

Foundation, 1973; SAMA (Scientific Apparatus Makers Association) Award, to Hewlett and Packard, 1975; Vermilye Medal, to Hewlett and Packard, the Franklin Institute, Philadelphia, 1976; Corporate Leadership Award, Massachusetts Institute of Technology, 1976; Medal of Honor, City of Böblingen, West Germany, 1977; Herbert Hoover Medal for Distinguished Service, Stanford University Alumni Association, 1977; Henry Heald Award, Illinois Institute of Technology, 1984; National Medal of Science, 1985; Santa Clara County Business Hall of Fame Laureate Award, Junior Achievement, 1987; World Affairs Council Award, World Affairs Council of Northern California, 1987; Degree of Uncommon Man, Stanford University, 1987; Commander's Cross of the Order of Merit of the Federal Republic of Germany, 1987; National Business Hall of Fame Laureate Award, Junior Achievement, 1988; John M. Fluke, Sr., Memorial Pioneer Award, *Electronics Test Magazine*, 1990; Silicon Valley Engineering Hall of Fame Award, Silicon Valley Engineering Council, 1991; Exemplary Leader Award, American Leadership Forum, Silicon Valley Chapter, 1992; Alexis de Tocqueville Society Award, United Way of Santa Clara County, 1991; National Inventors Hall of Fame Award, National Inventors Hall of Fame Foundation, Akron, Ohio, 1992; LLD, University of California (Berkeley), 1966; LLD, Yale University, 1976; DSc, Kenyon College, 1978; DSc, Polytechnic Institute of New York, 1978; EngD, University of Notre Dame, 1980; EngD, Utah State University, Logan, Utah, 1980; EngD, Dartmouth College, 1983; LLD, Mills College, 1983; LHD, Johns Hopkins University, 1985; Doctor of Public Policy, Rand Graduate Institute, 1985; Doctor of Electronic Science, University of Bologna, Italy, 1989; Doctor of Humanities, Santa Clara University, 1991; National Medal of Science, 1985.

Hewlett was born May 20, 1913, in Ann Arbor, Mich. He attended Stanford University, and received a bachelor of arts degree in 1934 and a bachelor of science degree in electrical engineering in 1939. He also received a master's degree in electrical engineering from the Massachusetts Institute of Technology in 1936.

Hewlett met David Packard during their undergraduate days at Stanford. The two engineering classmates became friends and formed a partnership known as Hewlett-Packard Company (HP) in 1939. HP's first product was a resistance-capacitance audio oscillator based on a design developed by Hewlett when he was in graduate school. The company's first "plant" was a small garage in Palo Alto, and the initial capital amounted to $538. Walt Disney's purchase of eight of the audio oscillators for the film *Fantasia* put the small company in business (Caddes 1986).

Hewlett was involved actively in management of the company until 1987, with the exception of the years he served as an Army officer during World War II. He was on the staff of the Army's Chief Signal Officer and then headed the electronics section of the New Development

Division of the War Department Special Staff. During this latter tour of duty, he was on a special US team that inspected Japanese industry immediately after the war.

In 1947, shortly after he returned to Palo Alto, Hewlett was named vice president. He was elected executive vice president in 1957, president in 1964, and chief executive officer in 1969.

Hewlett resigned as president in 1977 and retired as chief executive officer in 1978 in accordance with his previously announced plans for management succession within HP. He then served as chairman of HP's executive committee until 1983, when he became vice chairman of the HP board of directors. In 1987, he was named director emeritus.

Over the years, Hewlett has contributed to the advancement of various organizations within the electronics industry. From 1950 to 1957 he was on the board of directors of the Institute of Radio Engineers—now the Institute of Electrical and Electronics Engineers (IEEE)—and served as president of the institute in 1954. He also has played an important role in the development of the former Western Electronic Manufacturers Association, now called the American Electronics Association. In 1985, President Ronald Reagan awarded him the National Medal of Science, the nation's highest scientific honor.

Hewlett has a keen interest in education and medicine. He was a trustee of Mills College in Oakland, Calif., from 1958 to 1968 and Stanford University from 1963 to 1974, and was a member of the San Francisco regional panel of the Commission on White House Fellows from 1969 to 1970.

He served as board president and later director of the Palo Alto-Stanford Hospital Center from 1958 to 1962 (now Stanford Medical Center). He was director of the Kaiser Foundation Hospital and Health Plan Board from 1972 to 1978, and the Drug Abuse Council in Washington, D.C., from 1972 to 1974.

Hewlett is an honorary trustee of the California Academy of Sciences, a member of the National Academy of Engineering and the National Academy of Sciences, and a fellow of the American Academy of Arts and Sciences.

Hewlett currently is director of the National Academies Corporation and the Monterey Bay Aquarium Research Institute. Since 1966, he has served as chairman of the William and Flora Hewlett Foundation, which he established with his late wife Flora. He is trustee emeritus of the Carnegie Institution of Washington.

Hewlett holds 11 honorary degrees from American colleges and universities: honorary doctor of law degrees from the University of California in Berkeley, Yale University, and Mills College in Oakland, Calif.; honorary doctor of science degrees from Polytechnic Institute of New York and Kenyon College in Ohio; honorary doctor of engineering degrees from the University of Notre Dame, Dartmouth College, and Utah State University; an honorary doctor of humane letters from Johns Hopkins University; an honorary doctor of public policy degree from the Rand Graduate Institute; and an honorary doctor of humanities degree from Santa Clara University in California. He also holds an honorary doctor of electronic science degree from the University of Bologna in Italy.

Hewlett has a wide range of outside interests and hobbies, most of them based on his love for the outdoors. He is a part-time botanist and an accomplished mountain climber, skier, and fisherman. He also maintains various ranching and cattle-raising operations with Packard in California and Idaho.

BIBLIOGRAPHY

Biographical

Caddes, Carolyn, *Portraits of Success: Impressions of Silicon Valley Pioneers,* Tioga Publishing Co., Palo Alto, Calif., 1986.

CHARLES ANTONY RICHARD (TONY) HOARE

Born January 11, 1934; major contributor to the understanding of the logic of programs, developer of the Axiomatic Approach to program description, and recipient of the 1980 ACM Turing Award.

Education: scholar and senior scholar, the King's School, Canterbury, 1948–1952; exhibitioner, Merton College, Oxford, 1952–1956; first-class honors, moderations, second-class honors, Lit. Hum., Oxford University, 1956; civil service interpreter's qualification, Russian; certificate in statistics (with distinction), 1958–1959.

Professional Experience: National Service, Royal Navy, 1956–1958; British Council Visiting Student, Moscow State, 1959–1960; Elliott Bros. (London) Ltd.: programmer, senior programmer, chief engineer, technical manager, chief scientist, 1960–1968, project leader in the implementation of Algol 60, 1960–1962, chief engineer, responsible for design and implementation of all general-purpose hardware and software products, 1963–1966; chief scientist, Computing Research Laboratory, 1966–1968; chief consultant, National Computing Centre, 1968; Queen's University of Belfast: professor of computing science, 1968–1977, director of the University Computer Laboratory, 1968–1970; visiting professor, Stanford University, 1973; SERC senior fellow, 1976–1977; Oxford University: professor of computation, fellow of Wolfson College, 1977–present, director of the University Computing Laboratory, 1984–1986, 1991–present; Admiral R. Inman Centennial Chair in Computing Theory, University of Texas, Austin, 1986–1987.

Honors and Awards: distinguished fellow of British Computer Society, 1978; DSc (Hon.), University of Southern Carolina, 1979; ACM Turing Award, 1980; AFIP Harry Goode Memorial Award, 1981; elected fellow of the Royal Society, 1982; IEE Faraday Medal, 1985; DSc (Hon.), Warwick University, 1985; honorary doctor of science, University of Pennsylvania, 1986; DSc (Hon.), Queen's University of Belfast, 1987; foreign member, Accademia dei Lincei, 1988; honorary doctor of the University of York, 1989; member, Academia Europaea, 1989; IEEE Computer Society Pioneer Award, 1990; honorary doctor of the University of Essex, 1991; IEEE Computer Society Pioneer Award, 1991; Lee Kuan Yew Distinguished Visitor, Singapore, 1992.

QUOTATIONS

"In the interest of increased quality of software products, we may be well advised to get rid of many facilities of modern, baroque programming languages that are widely advertised in the name of "user-orientation," "scientific sophistication," and "progress." (Hoare 1975)

"I don't know what the programming language of the year 2000 will look like, but I know it will be called Fortran."

BIBLIOGRAPHY

Significant Publications[9]

Hoare, C.A.R., E-W. Dijkstra, and O-J. Dahl, *Structured Programming*, Academic Press, New York, 1972.

---

[9]A publication list up to 1987 may be found in Hoare 1989.

Hoare, C.A.R., and N. Wirth, "An Axiomatic Definition of the Programming Language Pascal," *ACTA Informatica*, Vol. 2, 1973, pp. 335–355.

Hoare, C.A.R., "An Assessment of the Programming Language Pascal," *IEEE Trans. Software Eng.*, June 1975.

Hoare, C.A.R., "The Emperor's Old Clothes," *Comm. ACM.*, Vol. 24, No. 2, Feb. 1981, pp. 75–83.

Hoare, C.A.R., *Communicating Sequential Processes,* Prentice-Hall International, New York, 1985.

Hoare, C.A.R., and C.B. Jones, eds., *Essays in Computing Science,* Prentice-Hall International, New York, 1989.

FRANCES ELIZABETH (BETTY) SNYDER HOLBERTON

In 1951–1952, Betty devised the first sort-merge generator for the Univac I from which Grace Murray Hopper claimed to have derived the first ideas about compilation.

Professional Experience: mathematician, Aberdeen Proving Ground, 1945–1947; logic design engineer, Eckert-Mauchly Corporation, 1947–1950; programmer, Remington-Rand Corp., 1950–1953; member, Applied Mathematics Laboratory, David Taylor Basin, 1953–1956; staff member, Institute for Computer Science and Technology (ICST), National Bureau of Standards, 1956–1983.

Herman H. Hollerith

*Born February 20, 1860, Buffalo, N.Y.; died November 17, 1929,
Washington, D.C.; inventor of the punched card which bears his name and
the associated machinery for use in the 1890 US census; founder of the company (Hollerith Tabulating Company) that eventually became IBM.*

Education: graduate, School of Mines, Columbia University, 1879; PhD,
Columbia University, 1890.

Professional Experience: statistician, US Bureau of the Census, 1879–1882;
instructor, MIT, 1882–1883; US Patent Office, 1883–1886; self-employed,
1886–1929.

Herman Hollerith was born in 1860 in Buffalo, N.Y., and graduated at
the age of 19 from the Columbia School of Mines. His supervisor,
William P. Trowbridge, who was a consultant to the US Bureau of the
Census, introduced Hollerith to John Shaw Billings, who employed
him as an assistant in his work on the statistical analysis of the 1880
census. Billings remarked that there ought to some way to mechanize
the tabulating process. Following this early involvement with the
bureau, Hollerith moved to MIT[10] in 1882 with Francis Walker, who
had served as the director of the bureau, and where Hollerith developed a flair for invention. A year later he returned to Washington to
become an examiner for the Patent Office. During this period at MIT
he developed the basic ideas of the tabulating machine, using rolls of
perforated paper tape as the means of input. Replacing the continuous tape by cards, Hollerith also developed a pantograph punch for
preparing the data on the cards, and a "reader" in which spring loaded
pins completed electrical circuits to increment selected counters in
the tabulator. In response to a request for bids to automate the tabulation of the data collected during the 1890 census with the hope of
completing the analysis of the data before the 1900 census even in the
face of an increased number of questions, Hollerith proposed his card
processing system. The new system proved to be a success, and the
time to completion of the data analysis was reduced to one third of
that for the hand-counted 1880 census. A repeat performance in 1900
confirmed the efficacy of the system by reducing the time to process to
one quarter of the previous census and cutting labor costs considerably.

In the meantime, Hollerith's system was purchased for use in several European census activities, and he formed a company, the

---

[10]Then called the *Boston* Institute of Technology and not yet moved across the river to Cambridge.

Tabulating Machine Company, to service these opportunities. The company eventually merged with others and, under the direction of T. J. Watson, in 1924, became "International Business Machines Corporation," or IBM.

BIBLIOGRAPHY

Biographical

Austrian, G.D., *Herman Hollerith: The Forgotten Giant of Information Processing,* Columbia Univ. Press, New York, 1982.

Chase, George C., "History of Mechanical Computing Machinery," *Ann. Hist. Comp.,* Vol. 2, No. 3, 1980, pp. 198–226.

Luebbert, W.F., "Hollerith, Herman," in Ralston, Anthony, and Edwin D. Reilly, Jr., *Encyclopedia of Computer Science and Engineering,* Van Nostrand Reinhold Co., New York, 1983.

Reid-Green, Keith S., "The History of Census Tabulation," *Scientific American,* Vol. 260, No. 2, Feb. 1989, pp. 98–103.

Trueswell, L.E., *Punch Card Tabulator in the Bureau of the Census, 1890–1940,* US Dept. of Commerce, US Printing Office, Washington, D.C., 1965. Chapter 3, pp. 35–56.

Significant Publications

Hollerith, H., "An Electric Tabulating System," reprinted in Randell, Brian, *Origins of Digital Computers: Selected Papers,* Springer-Verlag, Berlin, 1982, pp. 133–144.

GRACE BREWSTER MURRAY HOPPER

Born December 17, 1906, New York City; died January 1, 1992, Arlington, Va.; Rear Admiral, US Navy; developer of programming technology for the Harvard Mark I[11] and the Univac I, early protagonist of high-level languages, and leader in the development of compilers for, and the use of, Cobol.

Education: Hartridge School, Plainfield, N.J., 1924; BA, Phi Beta Kappa, Vassar College, 1928; MA, Yale University, 1930; PhD, Yale University, 1934; Sigma Xi, 1934; Vassar faculty fellow, New York University, 1941–1942.

Military Record: apprentice seaman and midshipman USNR, midshipman, School-W, Northampton, Mass., 1944; Lieutenant (junior grade), 1944; Lieutenant, 1946; Lieutenant Commander, 1952; Commander, 1957; retired with rank of Commander, 1966; recalled to active duty, 1967; Captain, 1973; Commodore, 1983; Rank of Commodore renamed as Rear Admiral, 1985.

Professional Experience: instructor to associate professor, Department of Mathematics, Vassar College, 1931–1943; assistant professor of mathematics, Barnard College, 1943; mathematical officer, US Navy, Bureau of Ordnance, 1944–1946; research fellow in engineering sciences and applied physics, Computation Laboratory, Harvard University, 1946–1949; senior mathematician, Eckert-Mauchly Computer Corp., 1949–1952; systems engineer, director of Automatic Programming Development, Univac Division of the Sperry Corp., 1952–1964; visiting lecturer to adjunct professor, Moore School of Electrical Engineering, University of Pennsylvania, 1959; staff scientist, systems programming, Univac Division of Sperry Corp. (on military leave 1967–1971), 1964–1971; active duty, US Navy, serving in the Information Systems Division as OP-911F, 1967–1977; professorial lecturer in management sciences, George Washington University, 1971–1978; active duty, US Navy, serving as NAVDAC-OOH, 1977–1986; senior consultant, Digital Equipment Corporation, 1986–1991.

Honors and Awards: Naval Ordnance Development Award, 1946; fellow, Institute of Electrical and Electronics Engineers, 1962; fellow, American Association for the Advancement of Science, 1963; Society of Women Engineers, SWE Achievement Award, 1964; Institute of Electrical and Electronics Engineers, Philadelphia Section Achievement Award, 1968; Connelly Memorial Award, Miami Valley Computer Association, 1968; Data Processing Management Association, Computer Science "Man of the Year" Award, 1969; Upsilon Pi Epsilon, honorary member, Texas A&M, Alpha Chapter, 1970; American Mothers Committee, Science Achievement Award, 1970; Harry Goode Memorial Award, American Federation of Information

---

[11]Known within IBM as the Automatic Sequence Controlled Calculator (ASCC).

Processing Societies, 1970; honorary doctor of engineering, Newark College of Engineering, Newark, New Jersey, 1972; Wilbur Lucius Cross Medal, Yale University, New Haven, Conn., 1972; fellow, Association of Computer Programmers and Analysts, 1972; Epsilon Delta Pi, honorary member, SUNY Potsdam Chapter, Potsdam, N.Y., 1973; honorary doctor of science, C. W. Post College of Long Island University, Greenvale, N.Y., 1973; member, National Academy of Engineering, 1973; Legion of Merit, 1973; distinguished fellow, British Computer Society, 1973; honorary doctor of laws, University of Pennsylvania, Philadelphia, 1974; Distinguished Member Award, Washington, D.C., Chapter, Association for Computing Machinery, 1976; honorary doctor of science, Pratt Institute, 1976; W. Wallace McDowell Award, Institute of Electrical and Electronic Engineers Computer Society, 1976; honorary doctor of science, Linkoping University, Sweden, 1980; IEEE Computer Society Pioneer Award, 1980; honorary doctor of science, Bucknell University, Lewisburg, Pennsylvania, 1980; honorary doctor of science, Acadia University, Wolfville, Nova Scotia, 1980; Navy Meritorious Service Medal, 1980; honorary doctor of science, Loyola University, Chicago, 1981; honorary doctor of science, University of Chicago, 1981; honorary doctor of science, Southern Illinois University, Carbondale, Ill., 1981; fellow, Institute for the Certification of Computer Professionals, 1981; honorary doctor of public service, George Washington University, Washington, D.C., 1981; honorary doctor of humane letters, Seton Hill College, Greensburg, Pa., 1982; Gold Medal, Armed Forces Communications and Electronics Association, 1982; honorary doctor of science, Marquette University, Milwaukee, 1982; dedication of the Grace Murray Hopper Center for Computer Learning, Brewster Academy, Wolfeboro, N.H., 1983; Ada August Lovelace Award, Association of Women in Computing, 1983; honorary doctor of business administration, Lake Forest College, Lake Forest, Ill., 1983; honorary doctor of science, Clarkson University, Potsdam, N.Y., 1983; Computer Pioneer Medal, Institute of Electrical and Electronic Engineers, 1983; honorary doctor of science, Hood College, Frederick, Maryland, 1983; honorary doctor of science, Russell Sage College, Troy, N.Y., 1983; Golden Plate Award, American Academy of Achievement, Coronado, Calif., 1983; honorary doctor of science, Villa Julia College, Baltimore, Md., 1983; Achievement Award, American Association of University Women, 1983; Federally Employed Women Achievement Award, 1983; Distinguished Service Award, Association of Computing Machinery, 1983; Living Legacy Award, Women's International Center, San Diego, Calif., 1984; Jane Addams Award, Rockford College, Rockford, Ill., 1984; Woman of the Year Award, Young Women's Christian Association of the National Capital Area, 1984; Andrus Award, American Association of Retired Persons Annual Award, 1984; Centennial Award, Institute of Electrical and Electronics Engineers, 1984; Engineering and Science Hall of Fame, Dayton, Ohio, 1984; Samuel Eliot Morison Award for Distinguished Service, USS Constitution Museum, Boston, 1984; honorary doctor of science, University of Maryland, College Park, 1984; honorary doctor of laws, Smith College, Northampton, Mass., 1984; honorary doctor of science, St. Peter's College, Jersey City, N.J., 1984; honorary doctor of science, Worcester State College, Worcester, Mass., 1984; honorary doctor of science, Hartwick College, Oneonta, N.Y., 1984; honorary doctor of business administration, Providence College, Providence, R.I., 1984; honorary doctor of science, City College of Morris, Morristown, N.J., 1984; honorary doctor of science, Bloomsburg College, Bloomsburg, Pa., 1984; honorary doctor of science, Aurora College, Aurora, Ohio, 1985; honorary doctor of science, Wright State University, Dayton, Ohio, 1985; honorary doctor of letters, Western New England College, Springfield, Mass., 1985; INFOMART Information Processing Hall of Fame, Dallas, Texas, 1985; Award of Merit, American Consulting Engineer Council, Colorado Springs, Colo., 1985; Honorary Navy Recruiters, United States Navy Recruiting Command, 1985; Henry T. Heald Award, Illinois Institute of Technology, Chicago, 1985; honorary doctor of laws, College of William and Mary, Williamsburg, Va., 1985; honorary doctor of science, Rivier College, Nashua, N.H., 1985; honorary doctor of science, Marist College, Poughkeepsie, N.Y., 1985; honorary doctor of science, Saint John Fisher College, Rochester, N.Y., 1985; honorary doctor of science, Syracuse University, Syracuse, N.Y., 1986; honorary doctor of humane letters, Caldwell College, Caldwell, N.J., 1986; honorary doctor of science, University of Massachusetts at Amherst, 1986; honorary doctor of military science, Northeastern University, Boston, 1986; Lifetime Achievement Award, Federation of Government Information Processing Councils, 1986; Unsung Heroine Award, Ladies Auxiliary to the Veterans of Foreign Wars, 1986; Distinguished Achievement Award, American Aging Association, 1986; Meritorious Citation, Navy Relief Society, 1986; Navy Distinguished Service Medal, 1986; honorary doctor of letters, Drexel University, Drexel, Pa., 1987; Charles Holmes Pette Medal, University of New Hampshire, Durham, 1988; The Emanuel R. Piore Award, Institute of Electrical and Electronics Engineers, 1988; National Medal of Technology, 1991; National Women's Hall of Fame, 1994 (posthumously).

Rear Admiral Grace Brewster Murray Hopper, first lady of software and first mother-teacher of all computer programmers, died in her sleep in her Arlington, Va., home on January 1, 1992. She was 85.

Born in New York City on December 9, 1906, she received a BA in mathematics and physics from Vassar College in 1928, where she was elected to Phi Beta Kappa. Her graduate studies in mathematics at Yale University earned her an MA in 1930 and a PhD in 1934. She returned to Vassar where she taught mathematics from 1933 to 1943. In December of that year she joined the US Naval Reserve, attended Midshipmen's School at Northampton, Mass., and on graduation in July 1944, was commissioned a lieutenant, junior grade. She was at once assigned to the Bureau of Ordnance's Computation Project at Harvard University, where she was greeted by Naval Reserve Commander Howard Hathaway Aiken with the words, "Where the hell have you been?"

He pointed to the Harvard Mark I, said it was a computing machine, and told Lieutenant Hopper to compute the coefficients of the arc tangent series by Thursday. Thus it was that she, who later said,

"I had never met a digit and I wanted nothing to do with digits," came into the computer business, becoming, in her words, "the third programmer on the world's first large-scale digital computer." (The two who preceded her, then called "coders," were Ensigns Robert Campbell and Richard Bloch.)

In addition to using the Mark I for mathematical calculations she was assigned the task of drawing together all the mimeographed notes concerning the machine into a Manual of Operation for the Automatic Sequence Controlled Calculator. This became a 500-page volume that both explained how to set up the machine and outlined the operating principles of computing machines. It was published in the spring of 1946 as Volume 1 of the *Annals of the Harvard Computation Laboratory* and has since been reprinted by the Charles Babbage Institute as Volume 8 of its *Reprint Series on the History of Computing*. Although no title page credit is given, Hopper was both the editor and a major contributor to the volume, writing both the first chapter on history and the two chapters of machine description and electromechanical circuit operation.[12]

It was while working with the successor to the Mark I, the Mark II, in the summer of 1945, that the incident of what has come to be called the First Bug occurred. A large moth had caused a relay to fail. Hopper entered the moth, with Scotch tape, in the log book with the note, "First actual case of bug being found."(The log book and the moth are in the National Museum of American History, Smithsonian Institution.) It is clear from her note that she did not believe she had invented the term, which has since been traced back to at least the time of Edison, but was humorously pleased to have found a real bug that had caused a bug in the machine.[13]

At the end of World War II she resigned from Vassar and was appointed to the Harvard faculty as a research fellow in the Computation Laboratory. In 1949 she joined, as senior mathematician, the newly formed Eckert-Mauchly Corporation where BINAC and Univac were under construction and stayed with that firm and its successors (Remington-Rand and Sperry-Rand) until her retirement in 1971. It was in these years that her major contributions to programming were made. Inspired by John Mauchly's "Short Order Code"[14] of

---

[12]Extracts from the manual were published in 1946 under the authorship of both Aiken and Hopper in the AIEE magazine, *Electrical Engineering*, and are reprinted in *The Origins of Digital Computers, Selected Papers*, edited by Brian Randell.

[13]The story appears, with a photograph of the bug, in *Ann. Hist. Comp.*, Vol. 10, No. 4, 1989, pp. 340–342. A letter in Vol. 13, No. 4, 1991, pp. 360–361, raises a question about the date of the event.

[14]Schmitt, William F. ,"The UNIVAC Short Code," *Ann. Hist. Comp.*, Vol. 10, No. 1, 1988, pp. 7–18.

1949 and Betty Holberton's first Sort-Merge Generator of 1951, she developed the first compiler,[15] A-0 (1952), and later modified it to produce A-2 (1953). This work, and her view of what programming languages ought to be like, led her to the development of the first English-language data processing compiler, B-0 (FLOW-MATIC), completed in 1957.

Her views on programming and computing were expressed in "The Education of a Computer" first published in the *Proceedings of the ACM Conference,* May 1952.[16] In it she expressed the hope that "the programmer may return to being a mathematician." In this paper she anticipated artificial intelligence saying, "it is the current aim to replace, as far as possible, the human brain by an electronic digital computer." She recognized that the software would turn out to be more expensive than the hardware and foresaw that there would be the same kinds of applications in commercial programming as there were then in mathematics. The paper includes glimmerings of many tools and techniques concerning compilers that are now commonplace, including subroutines, translation of a formula, relative addressing, the linking loader, and code optimization. In it she also anticipated symbolic manipulation.

In the opinion of some who were there at the time, had Remington-Rand supported Hopper's efforts more vigorously and exploited her programming developments with the skill and force that IBM was then exploiting Fortran, she might have saved her employer from being overtaken by others in the industry.

Grace Hopper's involvement with Cobol was indirect, through her subordinates who served on the committee which developed the Cobol specifications, and through FLOW-MATIC. The influence of FLOW-MATIC on Cobol was enormous since it was the only English-language business data processing language in use at the time that the Cobol effort started. As such, FLOW-MATIC served as a model on which to build and augment with inputs from other sources.

She was an early member of the Association for Computing Machinery and served on its council. In 1957 she edited its first *Glossary of Computing Terms,* the discipline's first authoritative dictionary. For several decades she was the most requested speaker of all those on the ACM lecture circuit. Her talks, which were both educational and highly entertaining, are still remembered for the physical representations she would give to abstract concepts, such as the short

---

[15]Hopper's concept of a compiler was slightly different from that of today. In many ways her compiler would more qualify as a macro-assembler and was closer to the English dictionary description referring to library activities.

[16]Reprinted with an introduction by David Gries, in *Ann. Hist. of Comp.,* Vol. 9, No. 3/4, 1988, pp. 271–281.

piece of wire she would hold up to represent a nanosecond.[17] In speaking of the future she early expressed her hope that she would one day have a computer the size of a shoe box, this at a time when computers occupied several rooms.

Throughout her life she was active in the US Naval Reserve. In 1946 she was put on inactive status only to be recalled to active duty in August 1967 to help the Navy with its manifold computing problems. She was promoted successively through the ranks and after the regular retirement age of 62 was given repeated year-to-year extensions to stay on active duty until her final retirement as Rear Admiral, the rank she received as a special presidential appointment in 1983. The August 14, 1986, ceremony for the retirement of the oldest serving officer of the US Navy was held aboard the USS *Constitution*,[18] "Old Ironsides," the oldest warship still in commission in the US Navy. The ceremony took place not far from the location at Harvard University of the Mark I computer on which she first worked. At her retirement she was given the Navy Distinguished Service Medal. She had honorary degrees from more than 40 colleges and universities. She received the first Computer Sciences "Man of the Year" award from the Data Processing Management Association (1969); the Harry Goode Memorial Award from AFIPS (1970); and the Wilbur Lucius Cross Medal from Yale (1972). In September 1991 she was awarded the National Medal of Technology "for her pioneering accomplishments in the development of computer programming languages that simplified computer technology and opened the door to a significantly larger universe of users." She was the first woman to receive the award as an individual.

She always wanted to help young people and she took great pride in the fact that, in 1971, Sperry-Rand created the Grace Murray Hopper Award, which is presented annually by the ACM to a distinguished young computer professional. She considered her best biography to be *Grace Hopper, Navy Admiral & Computer Pioneer*, by Charlene W. Billings, which she hoped would encourage girls to look to careers in computing and in the Navy.

Her talent, vision, dedication, and persistence laid the foundation for computing as we know it and helped to guide it in its explosive growth. She was always a teacher, battling the entrenched attitudes of what she always called "the establishment." She could always give a humorous twist to the presentation of her ideas. For example, she hated the phrase, "but it's never been done that way," and, to remind

---

[17] I have met many people who remember Grace Hopper for her gift of a "nano-second," but no one can find a sample!

[18] The *Constitution* is actually a frigate, and thus its proper designation is USF, but this is rarely used today.

visitors of this dictum, kept a ship's clock on the office wall behind her desk—it ran backwards.

At the time of her death she was employed as a senior consultant at Digital Equipment Corporation, and until 18 months before her death was actively representing the company at industry forums, making presentations that focused on government issues and participating in corporate educational programs.

Admiral Hopper was sometimes called "Amazing Grace" because she recorded successful careers in academia, business, and the US Navy while making history in the computer field. Just as Admiral Hyman Rickover is considered the father of the nuclear navy, Admiral Hopper was the mother of computerized data automation in the naval service.

Grace Hopper was buried at Arlington Cemetery, Washington D.C., on January 7, 1992, in a full naval ceremony.[19]

QUOTATION

"If you ask me what accomplishment I'm most proud of, the answer would be all the young people I've trained over the years; that's more important than writing the first compiler."

BIBLIOGRAPHY

Biographical

Billings, Charlene W., *Grace Hopper, Navy Admiral & Computer Pioneer,* Enslow Publishers, Hillfield, N.J., 1989.

Classe, Alison, "An Appreciation: Grace Murray Hopper," *Computer Bulletin,* Mar. 1992, pp. 26–27.

Hopper, Grace M., "Keynote Address," in Wexelblat, Richard L., ed., *History of Programming Languages,* Academic Press, New York, 1981, Chapter 1.

Hopper, Grace Murray, "The First Bug," *Ann. Hist. Comp.,* Vol. 3, No. 3, 1981, pp. 285–286.

Lee, J.A.N., "Unforgettable Grace Hopper," *Reader's Digest,* Oct. 1994, pp. 181ff.

Sammet, Jean E., "Farewell to Grace Hopper—End of an Era!" *Comm. ACM,* Vol. 35, No. 4, Apr. 1992, pp. 128–131.

Slater, Robert, *Portraits in Silicon,* MIT Press, Cambridge, Mass., 1987, Chapter 20.

---

[19]Edited from Weiss 1992.

Tropp, Henry S., "Hopper, Grace Murray," in Ralston, Anthony, and Edwin D. Reilly, Jr., *Encyclopedia of Computer Science and Engineering*, Van Nostrand Reinhold Co., New York, 1983.

Tropp, Henry S., "Grace Hopper: The Youthful Teacher of Us All," *Abacus*, Vol. 2, No. 1, 1984, pp. 7–18.

Weiss, Eric A., "Grace Brewster Murray Hopper," *Ann. Hist. Comp.*, Vol. 14, No. 2, 1992, pp. 56–58.

Wetzstein, Cheryl, and Linda Forrestal, "Grace Murray Hopper," *The World & I*, Aug. 1987, pp. 198–205.

Significant Publications

Aiken, H.H., and Grace M. Hopper, "The Automatic Sequence Controlled Calculator," reprinted in Randell, Brian, *Origins of Digital Computers: Selected Papers*, Springer-Verlag, Berlin, 1982, pp. 203–222.

Hopper, Grace Murray, "The Education of a Computer," *Proc. ACM Conf.*, reprinted *Ann. Hist. Comp.*, Vol. 9, No. 3–4, 1952, pp. 271–281.[20]

ROBERT A. HUGHES

Later member of the IBM team that developed Fortran.

Hughes, a mathematical programmer/computer scientist at Lawrence Livermore National Laboratory (LLNL) since early 1954, was born in Hilltop, West Virginia. On leaving military service at the end of World War II, he studied mathematics and physics at three universities: Duquesne (Pittsburgh), Western Reserve (Cleveland), and Michigan (Ann Arbor). He was introduced to computing through work assignments on LLNL's large-scale application programs in mathematical physics set up to run on the early Univac, IBM-701, and IBM-704 computers. He gained an intimate knowledge of the first Fortran compiler while on a work assignment in New York with the Fortran development team in the summer of 1956, and has participated in various compiler

---

[20]The reprint of this paper states that it was presented in Pittsburgh, Pa.; however, other references to the 1952 ACM conference also list Toronto as the venue.

designs and implementations as a member of LLNL's Computer Language Group.

BIBLIOGRAPHY

Biographical

Hughes, Robert A., "Early Fortran at Livermore," *Ann. Hist. Comp.*, Vol. 6, No. 1, Jan. 1984, pp. 30–31.

Cuthbert C. Hurd

Born April 5, 1911, Estherville, Iowa; key leader within IBM in the introduction of computers to the corporation, and, later, a remarkable computer entrepreneur.

Education: BA, mathematics, Drake University, 1932; MS, mathematics, Iowa State College, 1934; PhD, mathematics, University of Illinois, 1936; postdoctoral work at Columbia University and MIT.

Professional Experience: assistant professor of mathematics, Michigan State College, 1936–1942; Lieutenant Commander, US Coast Guard Academy—Educational Officer, 1942–1945; dean, Allegheny College, chairman of curriculum committee, 1945–1947; technical research head, Union Carbide & Carbon Corp., Oak Ridge Tennessee (applied existing computational methods to the design of diffusion processes and commercial reactors), 1947–1949; IBM Corp. (1949–1962): director, Applied Science Department (led the development of System/701, IBM's first computer), 1949–1953; director, Applied Science Division (managed the development of System/650 and 704. Also directed the production of IBM's first software for customers, which included Bootstrap, Assembler, Utilities, SpeedCode, and Fortran), 1953–1955; director, electronic data-processing machines (responsible for developing IBM's first high-speed printer), 1955–1956; director, Automation Research (initiated the STRETCH project, IBM's first transistorized supercomputer), 1956–1961; director, Control Systems (participated in the design and manufacture of the System/1701),

1961–1962; consultant, IBM Corp. (advised on projects and participated in product decisions on the System/360 and System/370), 1962–1985; chairman of the board, Computer Usage Corporation (built to $15,000,000 in five years. Supervised software products for companies such as IBM and Texas Instruments), 1962–1974; Cuthbert C. Hurd Associates (consulted for companies including American Express and Rockwell), 1974–1978; chairman, Picodyne Corp. (oversaw operations of this microcomputer-based company that specializes in educational courseware and networking for educational projects), 1978–1986; founder, president, and chairman, Quintus Corp. (directed company until it was acquired by Intergraph Corporation), 1984–1989; chairman, Nu Thena (advises on the strategic direction and operation of Nu Thena, a company that produces CASE products), 1990–present.

Honors and Awards: university fellow, University of Illinois, 1934–1936; fellow, American Association for the Advancement of Science, 1960; LLD, Drake University, 1967; life fellow, MIT, 1975; IEEE Computer Society Pioneer Award, 1986.

After teaching and serving as a technical research head at the atomic energy facility in Oak Ridge, Tennessee, he joined IBM in 1949. He formed the Applied Science Department, which was responsible for introducing the 701, the 650, the 704, and Fortran. As the first IBM Applied Science leader, he pushed his reluctant management into using the IBM-701 to enter the world of computing. He created the environment and served as the manager of the group containing John Backus which developed the programming language Fortran. He also was involved in the development of the IBM-7030 (STRETCH) and the IBM-1710. From 1962 to 1974 he was chairman of Computer Usage Company. He is now chairman of Cuthbert Hurd Associates, the Holistic Construction Company, Quintus Computer Systems, and Picodyne Corporation. In addition, he consults with corporations and venture capitalists.

BIBLIOGRAPHY

Biographical

Hurd, Cuthbert C., *Computer Development at IBM,* Academic Press, New York, 1980.

Hurd, Cuthbert C., "Early IBM Computers: Edited Testimony," *Ann. Hist. Comp.,* Vol. 3, No. 2, Apr. 1981, p. 163ff.

Hurd, Cuthbert C., ed., "IBM 701 Thirtieth Anniversary 1953–1983," Special Issue, *Ann. Hist. Comp.,* Vol. 5, No. 2, Apr. 1983.

Hurd, Cuthbert C., "A Note on Early Monte Carlo Computations and Scientific Meetings," *Ann. Hist. Comp.,* Vol. 7, No. 2, Apr. 1985, p. 141ff.

Significant Publications

Hurd, Cuthbert C., "Asymptotic Theory of Linear Differential Equations Singular in the Variable of Differentiation and in a Parameter," *Tohoku Mathematical Journal*, Vol. 44, 1938.

Hurd, Cuthbert C., "Asymptotic Theory of Linear Differential Equations Singular in Several Parameters," *Tohoku Mathematical Journal*, Vol. 46, 1940.

Hurd, Cuthbert C., ed., *Seminar on Scientific Computation*, IBM Applied Science Department, Armonk, N.Y., 1949.

Hurd, Cuthbert C., "The IBM Card Programmed Calculator," *Proc. Seminar on Scientific Computation*, IBM, New York, Nov. 1949, pp. 37–41.

Hurd, Cuthbert C., "Automatic Digital Computing in Engineering," *Applied Mechanical Review*, July 1955.

HARRY DOUGLAS HUSKEY

Born 1916, Bryson City, N.C.; multifaceted computer designer responsible for the NBS SWAC and the Bendix G-15.

Education: BS, mathematics and physics, University of Idaho, 1937; MA, mathematics, Ohio University, 1941; PhD, mathematics, Ohio State University, 1943.

Professional Experience: teaching assistant, mathematics, Ohio University, 1938–1939; Ohio State University: teaching assistant, 1939–1942, instructor, 1942–1943; instructor, mathematics, University of Pennsylvania, 1943–1946; National Physical Laboratory, Teddington, England, 1947; National Bureau of Standards: National Applied Mathematical Laboratory (NAML), Washington, D.C., 1948, Institute for Numerical Analysis (INA), Los Angeles, Calif., 1948–1953; on leave, Wayne State University, 1952–1953; University of California, Berkeley, 1953–1967; on leave, MIT and University of California, Santa Cruz, 1966–1967; University of California, Santa Cruz: professor, 1967–1986, professor emeritus, 1986–present.

Honors and Awards: IEEE Computer Society Pioneer Award, 1980.

Huskey was an instructor at the University of Pennsylvania during the later stages of the development of ENIAC, where he wrote a technical manual for the ENIAC and worked on the early logical designs for the EDVAC. Following the departure of Eckert and Mauchly from the university in 1946, Huskey accepted a visiting position with the National Physical Laboratory in England contemporaneously with Alan M. Turing, who was working on his design of the ACE (Automatic Computing Engine). Based on his US experience, Huskey created the basic design of the Pilot ACE, which was the prototype of Turing's concept. After returning to the National Bureau of Standards in the US where he helped start the Standards Eastern Automatic Computer (SEAC) project in Washington, D.C., he moved on to the Institute for Numerical Analysis, Los Angeles, Calif., where he built the Standards Western Automatic Computer (SWAC). While on leave from INA at Wayne State University in 1952–1953, Huskey designed the Bendix G-15 drum computer and commenced a long-term association with the company. As a faculty member at the University of California, first at Berkeley and then at Santa Cruz, Huskey served as a consultant to many organizations and countries in computer education and the establishment of computing centers. The G-15, which the Bendix corporation gave to Huskey, and which was used by him for many years as his personal computer, was presented to the Smithsonian Institution for inclusion in the Information Age exhibit in the National Museum of American History in 1990.

See also the biography of Velma Huskey.

QUOTATION

"In all my relations with Turing, I found him helpful. I think Turing was reluctant to see effort diverted from the "big" ACE, but he did not "boycott" the development of the ACE Test Assembly, nor did I feel that he resented my part in its beginnings."

BIBLIOGRAPHY

Biographical

Campbell-Kelly, Martin, "Programming the Pilot ACE: Early Programming Activity at the National Physical Laboratory," *Ann. Hist. Comp.*, Vol. 3, No. 1, 1981, pp. 133–162.

Huskey, Harry D., "The SWAC: The National Bureau of Standards Western Automatic Computer," in Metropolis, N., J. Howlett, and Gian-Carlo Rota, *A History of Computing in the Twentieth Century,* Academic Press, New York, 1980. pp. 419–431.

Huskey, Harry D., "From ACE to the G-15," *Ann. Hist. Comp.,* Vol. 6, No. 4, 1984, p. 350ff.

Huskey, Harry D., "The National Bureau of Standards Western Automatic Computer (SWAC)," *Ann. Hist. Comp.,* Vol. 2, No. 2, 1991, pp. 111–121.

Huskey, Harry D., "Memoirs," *Ann. Hist. Comp.,* Vol. 13, No. 3, 1991, pp. 290–305.

Significant Publications

Huskey, Harry D., "Characteristics of the Institute for Numerical Analysis Computer," *Math. Tables and Other Aids to Computation,* Vol. 4, No. 30, Apr. 1950, pp. 103–108.

Huskey, Harry D., and Velma Huskey, "Lady Lovelace and Charles Babbage," *Ann. Hist. Comp.,* Vol. 2, No. 4, 1980, pp. 299–329.

VELMA ELIZABETH ROETH HUSKEY

Born October 8, 1917, Houston, Ohio; died January 2, 1991, Santa Cruz, Calif.; wife and collaborator of Harry Huskey, who worked behind the scenes with her husband, coauthoring several papers with him; paper on "Lady Lovelace and Charles Babbage," coauthored with her husband, appeared in Vol. 2, No. 4 of the Annals of the History of Computing *and is widely regarded as one of the keystone papers recording the life and work of Ada, Lady Lovelace.*

Education: BA, English, Ohio State University, 1939.

Professional Experience: information specialist, National Bureau of Standards, 1948–1952.

Honors and Awards: member, Phi Beta Kappa.

In 1938 Velma was attending Ohio University where she was the "best student and beautiful girl who sat in the front row"[21] of Harry Huskey's class in plane geometry. They were married on January 2, 1939, and moved to Columbus, Ohio, where they completed their education at Ohio State University (Velma graduated Phi Beta Kappa).

---

[21]See Huskey 1991.

With the start of World War II, they moved to Philadelphia where Harry taught Navy students and serendipitously became involved in the development of ENIAC. For the rest of her life she was directly or indirectly involved with computers, seeing them change from million-dollar to $200 devices.

After three years in Philadelphia, they spent a year in postwar England coping with the rationing system with their two girls, who were 3 and 5 years old. This was followed by a year in Washington, D.C., after which they moved to their beloved West, landing at the Institute for Numerical Analysis at UCLA in West Los Angeles. There she became a technical writer preparing reports about the computers that were being constructed. Meanwhile, in 1954 Harry became a professor at the University of California at Berkeley.

For some years she helped her husband edit reviews and articles for the *IEEE Transactions on Computers* for the Computer Society. She was a member of the official computer delegation visiting the USSR in 1959, and in 1980 she was a member of the IEEE computer delegation to China. During leaves from the university, Harry and Velma spent time in Amsterdam, Munich, and Cambridge, England. They became interested in applying computers to the solution of problems in developing countries, and assisted in developing computer activities at universities in India, Burma, China, Mexico, Brazil, Nigeria, Jordan, and Pakistan.

In later years Velma became interested in the life of Ada Byron, Countess of Lovelace, only daughter of poet Lord Byron, and confidant of Charles Babbage. Summer vacations were spent in Oxford reading letters in the Lovelace-Byron collection. As a result she wrote several articles for the *Annals of the History of Computing*.

See also the biography of her husband, Harry Douglas Huskey.

BIBLIOGRAPHY

Biographical

Huskey, Harry D., "Memoirs," *Ann. Hist. Comp.*, Vol. 13, No. 3, 1991, pp. 290–305.

Anon., "Velma E.R. Huskey," Obituary, *Ann. Hist. Comp.*, Vol. 13, No. 2, 1991, p. 230.

Significant Publications

Huskey, Harry D., and Velma Huskey, "Lady Lovelace and Charles Babbage," *Ann. Hist. Comp.*, Vol. 2, No. 4, 1980, pp. 299–329.

HADASSAH ITZKOWITZ, *SEE* IDA RHODES

KENNETH E. IVERSON

Born December 17, 1920, Camrose, Alberta, Canada; with Adin Falkoff, inventor and implementer of the programming language APL.

Education: BA, mathematics, Queen's University at Kingston, Ont., 1950; MA, mathematics, Harvard University, 1951; PhD, applied mathematics, Harvard University, 1954.

Professional Experience: assistant professor, Harvard University, 1955–1960; research division, IBM Corp., 1960–1980; I.P. Sharp Associates, 1980–1987.

Honors and Awards: IBM Fellow, 1970; AFIPS Harry Goode Award, 1975; ACM Turing Award, 1979; IEEE Computer Pioneer Award, 1982; National Medal of Technology, 1991; member, National Academy of Engineering.

Iverson has been one of those lucky individuals who has been able to start his career with a success and for over 35 years build on that success by adding to it, enhancing it, and seeing it develop into a successful commercial property. His book *A Programming Language* set the stage for a concept whose peculiar character set would have appeared to eliminate it from consideration for implementation on any computer. Adin Falkoff is credited by Iverson for picking the name APL for the programming language implementation, and the introduction of the IBM "golf-ball" typewriter, with the replacement typehead, which provided the character set to represent programs. The programming language became the language of enthusiasts (some would say fanatics) and the challenge of minimalists to contain as much processing as possible within one line of code. APL has outlived many other languages and its enthusiasts range from elementary school students to research scientists.

BIBLIOGRAPHY

Biographical

Falkoff, Adin D., and Kenneth E. Iverson, "The Evolution of APL," in Wexelblat, Richard L., ed., *History of Programming Languages,* Academic Press, New York, 1981, Chapter 14.

Iverson, K.E., "A Personal View of APL," *IBM Systems J.,* Vol. 30, No. 4, 1991, pp. 582–593.

Significant Publications

Falkoff, A.D., and K.E. Iverson, "The Design of APL," *IBM J. Research and Development,* Vol. 17, No. 4, 1973, pp. 324–334.

Iverson, Kenneth E., *Machine Solutions of Linear Differential Equations: Applications to a Dynamic Economic Model,* PhD thesis, Harvard Univ. , 1954.

Iverson, Kenneth E., *A Programming Language,* John Wiley, New York, 1962.

Iverson, Kenneth E., *Elementary Functions,* Science Research Associates, Chicago, 1966.

JOHN F. JACOBS

Born February 22, 1923, Golva, N.D.; responsibility for the SAGE computer program and weapons system integration.

Education: BSEE, Illinois Institute of Technology, 1950; MSEE, MIT, 1952.

Professional Experience: staff member, Digital Computer Laboratory, MIT, 1950–1952; associate head, Division Six, Lincoln Laboratory, 1952–1958; vice president for corporate planning and development, MITRE Corp., 1958–1977.

Jacobs joined the Whirlwind project at the Digital Computer Laboratory as an MIT graduate student and then as a staff member. From 1952 to 1958 at Lincoln Laboratory he worked on logical design for Whirlwind II/FSQ-7, established the Systems Office for design control, and held responsibility for the SAGE computer program and weapons system integration. He was associate head of Lincoln's Division 6 at the time he joined the MITRE Corporation in 1958 as associate technical director. He was senior vice president for corporate planning and development when he retired in 1977. He is currently special consultant to MITRE.

WALTER W. JACOBS

Born September 26, 1914, Newark, N.J.; died February 11, 1982; mathematician, cryptologist, and statistician who provided the environment in which George Dantzig and others created linear programming.

Education: BS, mathematics, City College of New York, 1934; MA, mathematical statistics, George Washington University, 1940; PhD, mathematical statistics, George Washington University, 1951.

Professional Experience: actuarial mathematician, Railroad Retirement Board,[1] 1937–1941; Army Security Agency, 1941–1947; Arlington Hall Station, US Army, 1941–1945; Government Code and Cypher School (GCCS), Bletchley Park (England), 1944–1945; chief, Production and Markets Section, US Dept. of Commerce, 1947–1951; deputy chief, Computation Division, US Air Force, 1951–1957; National Security Agency, Fort Meade, Md.: deputy, Office of Mathematical Research, deputy chief, Office of Research, chief, Office of Machine Processing, 1961–1963, 1964–1966, commandant, National Cryptologic School, 1966–1969; visiting staff member, Institute for Defense Analysis, 1963–1964; American University: faculty member, 1969–1981, chairman, Department of Mathematics, 1969–1972.

Honors and Awards: Beldan Medal, CCNY, 1934; Legion of Merit, War Department, 1945; Air Force Medal for Exceptional Civilian Service, 1956; Exceptional Civilian Service Award, 1968.

Jacobs, like others who were involved in intelligence work during World War II, will probably never be adequately credited with his contributions to the field of computation and its usage in special problems. He was given several awards by branches of the US government for his service. Jacobs' wartime activities saw him spend a short period at Bletchley Park in England, although the major recorded activity of that period was his playing chess on board six in a challenge of the Oxford University chess club by the Bletchley Park regulars, including I. Jack Good and Hugh Alexander. Following the war, Jacobs took on a series of administrative positions at the US Department of Commerce, the US Air Force, and the National Security Agency. While with the Air Force, he installed their first Univac I, and pioneered the application of the computer to management problems. Later while at the National Security Agency he oversaw the development of software for the IBM-developed Harvest system, including the large-scale operating system, a high-level language, and an assembly-language system. After retiring from the NSA, Jacobs undertook an academic career at American University. With his brother, Morton Jacobs, Walter was instrumental in establishing the patentability of embedded software systems in 1975 before the US Supreme Court.

---

[1]Jacobs' activities between 1934 and 1937 are unknown. It was the height of the depression and it is possible that he either was unemployed or worked a series of less professional jobs.

BIBLIOGRAPHY

Biographical

Blum, Joseph, Robert L. Kirby, and Jack Minker, "Eloge: Walter W. Jacobs, 1914–1982." *Ann. Hist. Comp.*, Vol. 6, No. 2, 1984, pp. 100–101.

SIGNIFICANT PUBLICATIONS

Jacobs, Walter W., *Random Matrices*, PhD thesis, George Washington University, 1951.

JOSEPH-MARIE JACQUARD

Born July 7, 1752, Lyons, France; died August 7, 1834, Ouillins, France; in the late eighteenth century Jacquard developed a practical automatic loom which wove patterns controlled by a linked sequence of punched cards; Jacquard looms are still in use today throughout the world.

Jacquard's father was a silk weaver and his mother a pattern maker, but he pursued careers as a plasterer, cutler, type founder, and soldier, before he found an interest in his father's loom and began weaving fabric experimentally. His early career was during the period of the French Revolution and so he did not begin seriously to weave until the early years of Napoleon's reign. In 1803 Jacquard traveled to England to construct a loom to fabricate fish nets for the London Society of Arts. In February 1804 he completed the loom and was presented with the society's gold medal for his services, and 3000 FF for his efforts. Napoleon heard of Jacquard's achievements in England and summoned him to Paris to join the Conservatoire des Arts to work on looms for the Republic. Jacquard took the opportunity to study the automatic loom created by Jacques de Vaucanson in 1745, which, in turn, was based on the design of Falcon (1728), and used punched tape.[2] Jacquard improved on Vaucanson's design by using punched cards to control the patterns which were to be woven. The cards were interconnected into a "program" and, as the weaving progressed, the cards passed over a perforated four-sided drum against which a set of needles, connected by wires to the warp threads, moved. The movement of the needles through the holes in the cards lifted the warp threads, allowing the filling threads to be passed over or under the warp, thus creating the pattern.

In 1806 Napoleon, pleased with Jacquard's progress, granted him a pension of 3000 FF on condition that he move his operations to the city of Lyons. However, the fear of automation preceded Jacquard and he was forced to flee for his life from the anger of weavers who believed that they were about to lose their livelihood. Against these odds Jacquard persevered and eventually Lyons became the major center of weaving using the Jacquard loom. By the time that Jacquard died in 1834, over 30,000 looms existed in Lyons alone. Jacquard looms, only slightly modified, are still in use today and are the source of exquisite fabrics for furniture.

Charles Babbage is believed to have obtained his ideas for the use of punched cards in the control of the Analytical Engine from his knowledge of the Jacquard loom, but it was Herman Hollerith who put cards to the most diverse use in his tabulators.[3] However, it is important to note that both Jacquard and Babbage intended to use the cards to store programs; Hollerith used the cards for data.

BIBLIOGRAPHY

Biographical

Posselt, E.A., *The Jacquard Machine Analyzed and Explained: With an Appendix on the Preparation of Jacquard Cards, and Practical Hints to Learners of Jacquard Designing*, Pennsylvania Museum and School of Ind. Art., Philadelphia, 1887.

---

[2]Vaucanson is perhaps most noted for his construction of a mechanical duck in 1738. The duck quacked, bathed, drank water, ate grain, digested it, and voided. It was described in detail by Voltaire.

[3]Babbage owned a self-portrait of Jacquard, created on a loom, which had all the appearance of an engraving. See Wilkes, M.V., *Automatic Digital Computers*, John Wiley & Sons, New York, 1956. Additionally, it may be noted that Ada Augusta, in describing the Analytical Engine, likened the action of the machine to "weaving patterns."

W. Stanley Jevons

Born 1835, Liverpool, England; drowned while swimming, 1882, Bulverhythe (near Hastings), England; inventor of an early logic machine, and a pioneer in the application of statistical techniques to economic questions.

Education: MA, University College, London, 1859.

Professional Experience: British Mint, Sydney, Australia, 1854–1859; Owens College, Manchester: tutor, 1859–1861, professor of logic and mental and moral philosophy, 1861–1876; professor of political economy, University of London, 1876–1880.

Honors and Awards: LLD, University of Edinburgh; fellow of the Royal Society.

As an economist, Jevons is regarded as one of the pioneers in the rigorous applications of statistical techniques to the study of economic issues. His *Theory of Political Economy* (1871) is the most important of his many books and papers on economic and political issues. Unfortunately his valuable contributions to economic theory (especially his trenchant analysis of marginal utility) are less well remembered today than his speculations on the relation of sunspots to business cycles. In the light of present-day knowledge and statistical sophistication, such a theory can only be regarded as eccentric, but we must remember that in Jevons' time it was far from a "crank" notion. The view that sunspots might influence weather and crops, which in turn would affect the business cycle, then had a plausibility that deserved careful exploration.

In a somewhat similar fashion, Jevons' fame as the inventor of a logic machine has tended to obscure the important role he played in the history of both deductive and inductive logic. He was one of the pioneers of modern symbolic logic, and his *Principles of Science,* first issued in 1874, deserves far more recognition than it has today, as an important treatise on the philosophy and methods of science. At a time when most British logicians ignored or damned with faint praise the remarkable achievements of George Boole, Jevons was quick to see the importance of Boole's work as well as many of its defects. Jevons believed that Boole had been led astray by efforts to make his logical notation resemble algebraic notation. He also saw clearly the weakness in Boole's preference for the exclusive rather than the inclusive interpretation of "or." Jevons devised a method of his own that he called the "method of indirect inference." The system is very similar to Venn's diagrammatic method as well as a primitive form of a truth table.

Jevons' "logical abacus" was a labor-saving device that required only the addition of keys, levers, and pulleys to become a logic machine. The abacus consisted of small rectangular wooden boards, all the same size and each bearing a different combination of true and false terms. The boards were lined up in a rack. An arrangement of pegs on the side of each board was such that one could insert a ruler under the pegs and quickly peg out whatever group of boards one wished to remove from the rack.

Jevons' "logical piano" was built in 1869. In appearance the machine resembles a miniature upright piano. On the face of the piano are openings through which one can see letters representing the 16 possible combinations of four logical terms and their negatives. The keys at the bottom are used to introduce the terms of a logical equation. This action automatically eliminates from the face of the machine all combinations of terms which are inconsistent with the proposition just fed to the machine. After all premises have been fed to the device, its face is then examined to determine what conclusions can be drawn.[4]

QUOTATION

"I am quite convinced that Boole's forms . . . have no real analogy to the similar mathematical expressions."

BIBLIOGRAPHY

Biographical

Gardner, Martin, *Logic Machines and Diagram,* McGraw-Hill Book Co., New York, 1958, Chapter 5.

Significant Publications

Jevons, W. Stanley, *Pure Logic and Other Minor Works,* MacMillan and Co., London, 1890.[5]

[4]Drawn from Gardner 1958.

[5]Published posthumously; edited by Robert Adamson, professor of logic at Owens College, and Harriet A. Jevons.

STEVEN PAUL JOBS

Born 1955, Los Altos, Calif.; evangelic bad boy who, with Steve Wozniak, co-founded Apple Computer Corporation and became a multimillionaire before the age of 30; subsequently started the NeXT Corporation to provide an educational system at a reasonable price.

Education: ungraduate, physics, literature, and poetry, Reed College, Ore.
Professional Experience: Atari Corp.; Apple Corp.; NeXT Corp.

Going to work for Atari after leaving Reed College, Jobs renewed his friendship with Steve Wozniak. The two designed computer games for Atari and a telephone "blue box," getting much of their impetus from the Homebrew Computer Club. Beginning work in the Jobs' family garage, they managed to make their first "killing" when the Byte Shop in Mountain View bought their first 50 fully assembled computers. On this basis the Apple Corporation was founded, the name based on Job's favorite fruit and the logo (initially used as the unregistered logo of the ACM APL Conference in San Francisco) chosen to play on both the company name and the word *byte.* Through the early 1980s Jobs controlled the business side of the corporation, successively hiring presidents who would take the organization to a higher level. With the layoffs of 1985 Jobs lost a power struggle with John Sculley, and after a short hiatus reappeared with new funding to create the NeXT Corporation.

QUOTATIONS

"Woz[niak] was the first person I met who knew more about electronics than I did."

About Jobs: "Like the Bhagwan, driving around Rancho Rajneesh each day in another Rolls-Royce, Jobs kept his troops fascinated and productive. The joke going around said that Jobs had a 'reality distortion field' surrounding him. He'd say something, and the kids in the Macintosh division would find themselves replying 'Drink poison Kool-Aid? Yeah, that makes sense.'" (Cringely 1992)

BIBLIOGRAPHY

Biographical

Caddes, Carolyn, *Portraits of Success: Impressions of Silicon Valley Pioneers,* Tioga Publishing Co., Palo Alto, Calif., 1986.

Cringely, Robert X., *Accidental Empires*, Williams Patrick/Addison Wesley, Reading, Mass., 1992.

Denning, Peter J., and Karen A. Frenkel, "A Conversation with Steve Jobs," *Comm. ACM*, Vol. 32, No. 4, Apr. 1989, pp. 437–443.

Levy, Steven, *Hackers: Heroes of the Computer Revolution*, Anchor Press/Doubleday, Garden City, N.Y., 1984.

Slater, Robert, *Portraits in Silicon*, MIT Press, Cambridge, Mass., 1987, Chapter 28.

Young, Jeffrey S., *Steve Jobs: The Journey is the Reward*, Scott, Foresman and Co., Glenview, Ill., 1988.

REYNOLD (REY) B. JOHNSON

Born 1906, Minnesota; Johnson devised a method for scoring multiple-choice tests by sensing conductive pencil marks on answer sheets, and initiated work leading to the first disk storage device.

Education: University of Minnesota.

Professional Experience: high school teacher; IBM Corp., 1934–1971; founder, Education Engineering Associates Laboratory, Palo Alto, Calif., 1971–present.

Honors and Awards: IEEE Computer Society Pioneer Award, 1980; National Medal of Technology, 1986.

While a high school teacher in Michigan in 1931, Johnson devised a novel method for scoring multiple-choice tests by sensing conductive pencil marks on answer sheets; his method was subsequently purchased by IBM. He joined IBM as an engineer and was first head (1952) of the IBM San Jose Laboratory.[6] He created the IBM 805 Test Scoring Machine in 1937. After opening the San Jose Laboratory, Johnson initiated work leading to the first disk storage device in 1955, first used with the IBM RAMAC[7] computer. The storage device had a 24-inch-diameter magnetic-oxide-coated disk on a vertical spindle.

---

[6]Based on Pugh, Emerson W., Lyle R. Johnson, and John H. Palmer, *IBM's 360 and Early 370 Systems*, MIT Press, Cambridge, Mass., 1991.

[7]Random Access Method of Accounting and Control.

QUOTATION

About Johnson: "Rey Johnson had some sort of magical combination of personal creativity and unorthodox management techniques." (Louis D. Stevens)

BIBLIOGRAPHY

Biographical

Caddes, Carolyn, *Portraits of Success: Impressions of Silicon Valley Pioneers*, Tioga Publishing Co., Palo Alto, Calif., 1986.

BRIAN DAVID JOSEPHSON

Born January 4, 1940; discoverer of the electronic effect that bears his name, intrinsic to the development of transistors.

MITCHELL (MITCH) KAPOR

Founder of Lotus Development Corporation.

Kapor is founder of Lotus Development Corporation, the world's largest developer of personal computer software. Kapor in 1981 created a program with Jonathon Sachs that became Lotus 1-2-3, today's standard spreadsheet. In 1982, he formed Lotus Development Corporation to sell software. In 1986, he designed Agenda, which helps people sort and order tasks. In 1987, Kapor launched ON Technology to try to design programs that will make computers easier to use. Graduating from Yale in cybernetics in 1971, he also has a master's degree in psychology. Featured on the PBS *NOVA* series, he recently studied linguistics and philosophy at MIT.

QUOTATION

About Kapor: "Mitch is a guy who was in the right place at the right time and saw clearly what had to be done to get very, very rich in record time. Sure enough, the Brooklyn-born former graduate student, disk jockey, . . . Transcendental Meditation teacher, mental ward counselor, and so-so computer programmer today has a $6 million house on 22 acres in Brookline, Massachusetts, a $12 million jet, and probably the world's foremost collection of vintage Hawaiian shirts. (Cringely 1992)

BIBLIOGRAPHY

Biographical

Cringely, Robert X., *Accidental Empires,* Williams Patrick/Addison Wesley, Reading, Mass., 1992.

KARL KARLSTOM

Early computer science textbook editor who put Prentice-Hall in the forefront, but who lost heart when he learned that the best textbook criteria are short words, big type, wide margins, and colored illustrations. ACM named its education award after him.

CHARLES KATZ

Born 1927, Philadelphia, Pa.; early developer of compilers from A-2, MATH-MATIC, to GECOM.

Education: BS, mathematics, Temple University, 1950; MS, mathematics, University of Pennsylvania, 1953.

Professional Experience: mathematician, Univac Division, Remington-Rand, 1953–1959; manager, Systems Software, Computer Department, General Electric Co., 1959–1966; Burroughs Corporation Xerox Corporation.

Katz joined Grace Murray Hopper at Remington-Rand and immediately became involved in the development of the compiler for the A-2 programming language that operated on the Univac-I. Continuing to work with Dr. Hopper, Katz then developed the compiler for MATH-MATIC, a language with free-form algebraic and English-like statements, which was followed by FLOW-MATIC. The latter was a business-oriented language which had a considerable influence on the development of the programming language Cobol. In 1957 Katz was appointed by John Carr III, president of ACM, to a committee to study the technical specifications of a universal programming language. The committee later accepted the invitation of the GAMM subcommittee for programming languages to create an international activity. Katz was one of four US members of the international committee, which included John Backus, Alan J. Perlis, and Joe Wegstein. The European committee members were F. L. Bauer, H. Bottenbruch, H. Rutishauser, and K. Samelson. Katz continued to develop compilers for GE, including support for Fortran, Cobol, WIZ (a dialect of Algol), and GECOM (a cross between Cobol and Algol). Later while with the Burroughs

Corporation, Katz directed the work on the TWA Airline Reservation System, and several software systems for the US Post Office.

BIBLIOGRAPHY

Biographical

Stern, Nancy, *From ENIAC to Univac: An Appraisal of the Eckert-Mauchly Computers,* Digital Press, Bedford, Mass., 1981.

Significant Publications

Katz, Charles, "GECOM: The General Compiler," in *Symbolic Languages in Data Processing,* Gordon and Breach, New York, 1962, pp. 495–500.

Alan C. Kay

Leader of the group at Xerox PARC which originated many of the concepts now common in personal computing, including the Alto workstation and the basic concepts of object-oriented programming which led to the programming language Smalltalk; sometimes referred to as the "father of the personal computer."

Education: BS, mathematics and molecular biology, University of Colorado, 1966; PhD, computer science, University of Utah, 1969.

Professional Experience: AI Project (SAIL), Stanford Junior University, 1969–present.

Honors and Awards: Apple Fellow; ACM Software Award, 1987.

Kay got his start through a "blank-check" project organized by Xerox Corporation at the Xerox Palo Alto Research Center (Xerox PARC), where he conceived of the Dynabook, a powerful notebook-sized personal computer, which in turn inspired the "Alto." Xerox did not take advantage of this development, and the concept appeared next in the Apple Macintosh system. Concurrently Kay conceived of a high-level, object-oriented programming language, named Smalltalk, and pioneered the use of icons as keys to actions that might be chosen by a user.

QUOTATIONS

"Computers are to computing as instruments are to music. Software is the score whose interpretation amplifies our reach and lifts our spirits. Leonardo da Vinci called music "the shaping of the invisible," and his phrase is even more apt as a description of software. " (Kay 1984)

"I think that since children appear to have to construct the world inside their heads in order to become human beings, then people must be natural constructors. Computers are the best construction material we have ever come up with outside of our brains."

"Some people worry that artificial intelligence will make us feel inferior, but then, anybody in his right mind should have an inferiority complex every time he looks at a flower."

BIBLIOGRAPHY

Biographical

Caddes, Carolyn, *Portraits of Success: Impressions of Silicon Valley Pioneers*, Tioga Publishing Co., Palo Alto, Calif., 1986.

Significant Publications

Kay, Alan, "Computer Software," *Scientific American*, Sept. 1984.

Kay, Alan, "The Early History of Smalltalk," *ACM SIGPLAN Notices*, Vol. 28, No. 3, Mar. 1993, pp. 69–96.

John George Kemeny

Born May 31, 1926, Budapest, Hungary; died December 26, 1992, Lebanon, N.H.; president of Dartmouth College, mathematician who was an assistant to Albert Einstein, chair of the Three Mile Island investigative committee; with Thomas Kurtz, invented the programming language BASIC.

Education: BA, mathematics, Princeton University, 1947; PhD, mathematics, Princeton University, 1949.

Professional Experience: assistant, Theoretical Division, Los Alamos Project, 1945–1948; Princeton University: research assistant,[1] Institute for Advanced Study, 1948–1949, Fine Instructor and ONR fellow, 1949–1951, assistant professor of philosophy, 1951–1953; Dartmouth College: professor of mathematics, 1953–1990, chairman, Department of Mathematics, 1955–1967, Albert Bradley Third Century Professor, 1969, president, 1970–1981; vice chairman, National Science Foundation Advisory Committee; member, National Research Council,

Honors and Awards: Between 1965 and 1989 he received honorary degrees from 20 universities, including Princeton University; Priestley Award, Dickinson College, 1976; IEEE Computer Society Pioneer Award, 1985; AFIPS Education Award, 1983; New York Academy of Sciences Award, 1984; fellow, American Academy of Arts and Sciences; First Louis Robinson Lifetime Achievement Award, EDUCOM, 1990.

John Kemeny came to the US in 1940 and was naturalized in 1945. He worked on the Los Alamos Project during World War II, and then completed his bachelor's and doctorate degrees at Princeton University, working with Albert Einstein. After several years as a faculty member at Princeton and Dartmouth College, he was elected president of Dartmouth College, serving 11 years. Kemeny and Thomas Kurtz coinvented and developed the Dartmouth Time-Sharing System (DTSS) and created the programming language BASIC to provide computing access to a broad spectrum of undergraduate students. The language has continued to develop and is perhaps the most widely used language, at least among younger and nonprofessional users; for many it is the first programming language learned. His citation for the first 1983 AFIPS Education Award recognized Kemeny for "his visionary efforts at making computing universal for students of all disciplines."

John Kemeny was born in Budapest on May 31, 1926.[2] His education and intellectual development in Hungary must have been very

---

[1] Assistant to Albert Einstein.

[2] Edited with permission from Internet posting by Jay Robert Hauben (bm665@cleveland.Freenet.Edu) on Newsgroups: alt.amateur-comp, comp.lang.misc, alt.lang.basic, sci.misc, and comp.misc. May 31, 1993. Also reprinted with permission from *The Amateur Computerist*, Vol. 5, No. 1–2, May 1, 1993.

impressive, but in 1940, to escape the Nazi tide, his family emigrated to New York City. Kemeny entered high school knowing virtually no English. He graduated three years later, first in his class, and was accepted at Princeton University to study mathematics.

By the time Kemeny turned 18, he had finished his first year at Princeton. He was immediately drafted and sent to Los Alamos to be a "computer," one of 20 operators who used 17 IBM bookkeeping calculators to get numerical solutions to differential equations connected with the design of the atom bomb. It took two or three weeks, working three 8-hour shifts, six days per week, to get one result. The calculators were fed punched cards, which were moved manually from machine to machine. Between calculations, the plug boards had to be rewired by hand. At the end of a cycle, the calculation was summarized on a print-out which had to be checked by eye for "catastrophes." If any were found, the cycle had to be repeated. Years later, Kemeny was to note that one undergraduate working one afternoon, using a 1970 time-sharing computer, could solve as many differential equations as the whole Los Alamos team did in a whole year. And there could be 100 other users on the computer at the same time.

While at Los Alamos, Kemeny heard a lecture by fellow Hungarian-born John von Neumann, who was a consultant to the "computer operation." Von Neumann proposed a fully electronic computer based on a binary number system, with internal memory for both data and a stored program. To Kemeny and the other "computers," von Neumann's machine sounded like a dream. Kemeny wondered if he would live long enough to ever use one.

After the war, Kemeny returned to Princeton. In 1948–1949, while finishing his dissertation, Kemeny served as Albert Einstein's research assistant at the Institute for Advanced Study. Von Neumann was at the institute also, working on the machine he had described in his lecture two years earlier. Einstein and Kemeny crossed paths with von Neumann occasionally and had some long conversations concerning symbol-handling (as opposed to number-handling) computers.

Kemeny finished his PhD and stayed at Princeton, teaching mathematics and philosophy until 1953. During his time at Princeton, his contact with von Neumann and his computer had a deep effect on Kemeny. Here was the brilliant mathematician playing around with the nuts and bolts of a computing machine and raising profound philosophical questions about the relation between humans and machines. In a *Scientific American* article, "Man Viewed as a Machine," Kemeny summarized lectures von Neumann had given just before Kemeny left Princeton. Kemeny framed the question of these lectures, "What could a machine do as well as or better than a man?" The conclusion in 1955 was that computers calculate faster than the human brain, may eventually match the human brain in memory capacity, but have a long way to go to exceed the compactness of the human brain or the complexity the human brain is capable of dealing with. Next, based on the work of the English logician Alan Turing, Kemeny argued that a universal machine can be designed. That universal machine would need a simple code designed for it that would describe any simple machine humans could devise. Then the universal machine could do anything every simple machine could do by converting the descriptions of the simple machines into programs for its own operation. It occurred to Kemeny that "a normal human being is like the universal machine. Given enough time he can learn to do anything." Kemeny carried this understanding with him throughout his career of encouraging universal teaching of computer programming.

In the summer of 1953, while a consultant at the Rand Corporation, Kemeny had a chance to use the JOHNNIAC, a copy of von Neumann's Princeton computer. He had great fun, he wrote, "learning to program a computer, even though the language used at that time was designed for machines and not for human beings" (Kemeny 1972, p. 7).

Kemeny joined the faculty of Dartmouth College in 1953 to teach mathematics and philosophy. For six years after he got there, Dartmouth had no computer. Kemeny could, however, commute 135 miles each way to use the computer at MIT in Cambridge, Mass. He did and therefore witnessed the coming, in 1957, of the Fortran programming language. Kemeny welcomed the language because it made much more sense to him to teach a machine a language than to force every human to learn the machine's own language. "All of a sudden access to computers by thousands of users became not only possible but reasonable" (Kemeny 1972, p. 8).

Dartmouth acquired its first computer in 1959, a Royal McBee LGP-30. Kemeny facilitated the use of the LGP-30 by undergraduate students. The ingenuity and creativeness of some of the students who had been given hands-on experience amazed the Dartmouth faculty. Kemeny and Thomas Kurtz, also of the Dartmouth Mathematics Department, were thus encouraged to "set in motion the then revolutionary concept of making computers as freely available to college students as library books" (Slater 1987, p. 22). The aim was to make accessible to all students the wonderful research environment that computers could provide.

The work of Kemeny and Kurtz in the early 1960s took two directions. Influenced by the work of J.C.R. Licklider and John McCarthy at MIT, Kemeny understood that a time-sharing system would make possible the universal access they aimed for. A team of the two faculty members and a group of undergraduate research assistants developed a prototype system. It allowed multiple users short spurts of access to the central computer from remote terminals in such a way that each user enjoyed the illusion that he was the sole user. This Dartmouth Time-Sharing System (DTSS) became operational in the fall of 1964. The value of a time-sharing system is that it ended the hardship of batch processing, which often required hours or even days of waiting between runs of a program while it was being developed and debugged. Time-sharing utilizes the great speed of computers compared to humans to greatly enhance the efficiency of computing from the point of view of the human users.

Today's packet switching networks (for example, the Internet) owe a great deal to the development of this time-sharing system, conceptually and technically. But earlier, DTSS almost got derailed. Kemeny had worked closely with General Electric during the time DTSS was being worked on. In 1966, GE and Dartmouth agreed to work on a joint development of the time-sharing operating system. However, GE's commercial purposes conflicted with Dartmouth's educational purposes. The story is told that GE tried to "stop the Dartmouth experiment" and the development of the time-sharing system called Phase I. (See Nelson 1974, p. 45.) But Kemeny and Kurtz, determined not to let DTSS disappear, encouraged the development of DTSS Phase II by 1969.

In addition to time-sharing, Kemeny and Kurtz realized that a new computer language was needed that could be easily learned and was accessible to typical college students. Kemeny noted, "We at Dartmouth envisaged the possibility of millions of people writing their own computer programs" (Kemeny 1972, p. 30). They designed their language with plain English and high school algebra-like commands so that the lay user could learn a very few commands and then be able to write interesting programs. Kemeny started to work on a draft version in September 1963. The result was BASIC, Beginners All-Purpose Symbolic Instruction Code. The first BASIC program ran on May 1, 1964, at 4:00 a.m. Kemeny and Kurtz made an effort to get as many students as possible using BASIC, and they were available to hear about problems and bugs and to come up with bug fixes. Kemeny and Kurtz wanted BASIC to be in the public domain; Dartmouth copyrighted BASIC but made it available without charge.

The careful work of Kemeny and Kurtz to make an easy-to-learn but powerful computer language bore tremendous fruit. After its introduction at Dartmouth in 1964, BASIC spread, as did DTSS, to other campuses and government and military situations. BASIC made personal computers possible. Beginning in 1975 with the success of Bill Gates and Paul Allen to write an interpreter for a subset of BASIC commands for the Altair computer, one form or another of BASIC spread to and accelerated the personal computer revolution.

For a while the great appeal of personal computers and their falling costs and general availability eclipsed Kemeny and Kurtz' seminal work on DTSS and the original BASIC. By the late 1980s, 10 to 12 million school children had learned BASIC, more people than speak, for example, Norwegian. The personal computer helped "distribute" computing, which Kemeny thought was crucial to the progress of society. But it also diminished in importance the centralized computing power and the interconnectivity of users that time-sharing made possible. Only recently, with the spread of computer networks, is the value of both developments being realized. Now the power of personal computer workstations, instead of dumb terminals, coupled with the connectivity and remote resource availability, is making possible the human-computer and human-human interfacing that Kemeny predicted.

From 1971 to 1980, Kemeny was the thirteenth president of Dartmouth College, presiding over (including other things) the transition there to coeducation. He continued his efforts to support a crucial role for computers in education but was unable to be a major contributor to developments like the personal computer and the various versions of BASIC. In 1979, Kemeny served as the chair of President Carter's Commission on the Accident at Three Mile Island. Kemeny "very much regretted" that the commission did not recommend a temporary halt on construction permits for nuclear reactors. The investigation had found that the government regulators were too lax in their regulation. The commission concluded, "the evidence suggests that the NRC (Nuclear Regulatory Commission) has sometimes erred on the side of the industry's convenience rather than carrying out its primary mission of insuring safety" and that the industry took inadequate safety precautions and failed to respond to known unsafe conditions (*The Report of the President's Commission on the Accident at Three Mile Island,* pp. 43, 51, 188).

After Kemeny stepped down from the presidency of Dartmouth and chair of the Three Mile Island Accident Commission, he took stock of the use of computers, especially in education. He was furious and frustrated by the slow progress of education in computer programming. Between 1983 and 1985, Kemeny and Kurtz went back to work and produced a portable and more powerful version of their original BASIC. They called it True BASIC and it is still marketed today with the intention of introducing "students to the very important art of computer programming and analytic thinking."

Kemeny had a very broad vision of the role computers would play in society. He foresaw a man-machine symbiosis that would help both to evolve rapidly. In the early 1970s he predicted that within 20 years there would be a national computer network with terminals in millions of homes, so every home would be a mini-university. He also predicted there would be a National Automated Reference Library, a national personalized computer-delivered news service, and, especially, greatly enhanced education via time-sharing and simple programming languages. Kemeny worked hard to implement his visions and felt by the late 1980s great disappointment in the slow progress. He died just as the great computer networking structures, which have developed in some large measure because of his pioneering work and vision, have begun to fulfill more of his expectations, but also just as a fight is being waged by those who want to commercialize these networking structures and those who want to keep them in the public domain.

Kemeny recognized that the social problems that have yet to be solved are immense. He wrote, "While computers alone cannot solve the problems of society, these problems are too complex to be solved without highly sophisticated use of computers" (Kemeny 1972, p. 80). He believed it is imperative that computers be freely available. "Only if we manage to bring up a computer-educated generation will society have modern computers fully available to solve its serious problems" (Kemeny 1972). He saw the computer revolution as a possible asset for society but felt "it is a major mistake to make plans for the solution of social problems on the assumption that society will in the future be organized in exactly the same way as today. For the first time in human history we have an opportunity for significant social planning. We cannot afford to waste it" (Kemeny 1972, p. 143).

John Kemeny was part of many of the seminal events of the computer revolution. He made major contributions to its foundation and he thought deeply into this revolution. His death was untimely but he has left the value of his work to help us take on the challenges that confront the progress to which he contributed.

QUOTATION

In his final address to Dartmouth College as president, Kemeny warned against the growing right-wing element on campus: "[This] voice, heard in many guises, is the most dangerous voice you will ever hear. It appeals to the basest of instincts in all of us. It appeals to human prejudice. It tries to divide us by setting whites against blacks, by setting Christians against Jews, by setting men against women. And if it succeeds in dividing us from fellow beings, it will impose its evil upon a fragmented society."

BIBLIOGRAPHY

Biographical

Anon., "John Kemeny," Obituary, *The Times,* London, Jan. 6, 1993.

Kurtz, Thomas E., "BASIC," in Wexelblat, Richard L., ed., *History of Programming Languages,* Academic Press, New York, 1981, Chapter 11.

Kemeny, John G., and Thomas E. Kurtz, *Back to BASIC. The History, Corruption and Future of the Language,* Addison-Wesley, Reading, Mass., 1985.

Slater, Robert, *Portraits in Silicon,* MIT Press, Cambridge, Mass., 1987, Chapter 22.

Weiss, Eric, 1993. "John George Kemeny," Obituary, *Ann. Hist. Comp.,* Vol. 15, No. 2, 1987.

Significant Publications

Kemeny, John G., "Man Viewed as a Machine," *Scientific American,* Vol. 192, Apr. 1955, pp. 58–67.

Kemeny, John G., and T.E. Kurtz, "Dartmouth Time Sharing," *Science,* Vol. 162, 1968, pp. 223–228.

Kemeny, John G., *Man and the Computer,* Charles Scribner's, New York, 1972.

TOM KILBURN

Born August 11, 1921, Dewsbury, Yorkshire, England; early worker on the Manchester Mark I who collaborated with Frederick Williams to develop the CRT memory and the first truly multiprocessor system—ATLAS.

Education: BA and MA, mathematics, Cambridge University, 1940–1942; PhD, computer research, Manchester University, 1948; DSc, computer research, Manchester University, 1953.

Professional Experience: scientific officer, Telecommunications Research Establishment, Malvern, 1942–1946; outside duty at Manchester University—computer research, 1946–1948; University of Manchester: lecturer, 1948–1951, senior lecturer, 1951–1955, reader in electronics, 1955, professor of computer engineering (first chair in computers in UK), 1960–1964; professor of computer science (first university computer department in UK), 1964–1981; professor emeritus, 1981–present.

Honors and Awards: fellow, IEEE, 1954; fellow, Royal Society, 1965; DV (Hon.), Essex University, 1968; McDowell Award, IEEE, 1971; CBE, 1973; first recipient of the John Player Award, British Computer Society, 1973; distinguished fellow of the British Computer Society, 1974; FEng, founder member of the Fellowship of Engineering, 1976; DUniv (Hon.), Brunel University, 1977; Royal Medal of the Royal Society, 1978; DSc (Hon.), Bath University, 1979; foreign associate, US National Academy of Engineering, 1980; DTech (Hon.), Council for National Academic Awards, 1981; Computer Pioneer Award, IEEE Computer Society, 1982; Mancunian of the Year, Manchester Junior Chamber of Commerce, 1983; Eckert-Mauchly Award, ACM/IEEE Computer Society, 1983; honorary fellowship, University of Manchester Institute of Science and Technology, 1984.

Kilburn was involved in the field of computing since the mid-1940s, and built the first machine (the Manchester Mark I) that put programs and data in the same store (1948). He developed the cathode ray store in the early 1940s with Frederick Williams. Later he was central in the development of the ATLAS system, which was designed from the outset as a multiprogrammed system based on virtual memory (paging) which exploited programmed operators (extracodes) residing either in read-only or alterable main store for extensibility, and which was expressly intended to run under control of a monitor system. The ATLAS was significant in influencing later thinking regarding computer systems throughout the world.

MARK I, 1946–1951
September 1942–December 1946: Kilburn worked on electronic circuits for radar in F.C. Williams' group at Telecommunications Research Establishment, Malvern. Towards the end of 1946, one binary digit

was stored on a cathode ray tube by the "anticipation pulse" method.

December 1946–December 1947: Williams and Kilburn moved to Manchester University, the former to the chair of electrotechnics, and work continued on the cathode ray tube store. This work resulted in the "anticipation pulse" method being abandoned to be replaced by the dot-dash, defocus-focus, and so on, methods, and later formed the substance of Kilburn's PhD thesis. By autumn 1947, 2046 digits had been stored on a cathode ray tube by the preferred defocus-focus method, and this was the first electronic immediate access alterable store.

December 1947–June 1948: In December 1947, Kilburn wrote a report on the store which was circulated in the UK and the US. With the primary aim of testing the store as thoroughly as possible, a small computer was designed and built. The program that first ran on this machine on June 21, 1948, was the first computer program to run on the world's first alterable stored-program computer.

June 1948–April 1948: The small computer was enhanced to create a large machine by the spring of 1949. It had two especially interesting features—the inclusion of index registers (a Manchester invention) and a synchronized magnetic drum as a backing store for the cathode ray tube store.

April 1949–July 1951: The large machine was copied by Ferranti Ltd. and marketed as the Ferranti Mark I. The first of these machines was delivered to Manchester University in about February 1951, and vies with the Univac for consideration as the first commercial machine. An inaugural conference was held at the university in July 1951.

MEG, 1951–May 1954, and MERCURY, 1957–1962
MEG was a megacycle computer and Kilburn's design aim was an increase in speed of 30 over MARK I, with greater reliability. It used semiconductor diodes and miniature pentodes, and distributed electromagnetic delay lines for the internal registers. Floating point hardware was provided. It ran its first program in May 1954, and was perhaps the first floating point machine. Again, Ferranti produced a commercial machine, renaming the MEG as MERCURY. MERCURY differed from MEG only in its use of ferrite core instead of cathode ray tube store. Ferranti delivered a MERCURY to the university at the end of 1957.

The Transistorized Computer, November 1953–April 1955
In parallel with the MEG project, Kilburn started a transistor computer project, using the transistors then available, namely germanium point-

contact devices. These were more unreliable than valves, but semiconductors held out a promise of great reliability in the future, and experience of their use would therefore prove useful. The machine was to be economic and had only a magnetic drum store. Registers were made by placing read-write heads at suitable distances along the drum surface. A pseudo two-address instruction format was used. A small transistor computer ran its first program in November 1953, and is believed to be the first transistor computer. A larger version using 200 point-contact transistors and 1300 point-contact diodes, with a power consumption of 150 watts, was completed in April 1955. This design was adopted by Metropolitan Vickers (later AEI and now GEC) and produced in 1956 using function transistors.

MUSE and ATLAS, December 1962–September 1971
It was apparent to Kilburn in 1956 that it would be possible to build a function transistor computer 80 times more powerful than MEG/MERCURY (2400 × MARK I), thus approaching 1 µsec per order. Responsibility for the computing service to the university and industry on Mark I had also made Kilburn realize that the use of the computer was inefficient, and that, if suitably designed, the computer could itself make its own use more efficient. Simultaneous operation of large numbers of input and output equipments would be arranged, and (apparently) simultaneous running of many programs would also occur. The irritation and cost to users of different levels of storage would be removed. Everything would be controlled by an internal program. To make these and other improvements, a number of inventions were required and these were made over the period 1956–1959. They resulted in techniques now known as multiprogramming, job scheduling, spooling, the supervisor or operating system, virtual storage, paging and the one-level store, read-only memory, interrupts, and so on. The learning program in the one-level store program was the first use of AI in a conventional computer. In 1959 Ferranti joined the project, which hitherto was known as MUSE, and it was rechristened ATLAS. Kilburn's team increased from 20 to 40, large compared with two on the prototype Mark I. The Atlas was inaugurated in December 1962 and provided computing service to many universities and industry until September 1971.

Department of Computer Science
In 1964 the computer group within Electrical Engineering became the Department of Computer Science—a separate department, and

undergraduates were accepted into a three-year honors degree course in October 1965 for the first time in a UK university.

MU5, 1966–1979

In 1966 work was started on a multicomputer system MU5. The principal design aims were a speed approaching 20 times that of ATLAS, and an architecture capable of running high-level language programs efficiently, extendable to a family of machines. A segmented virtual store with variable-sized pages would facilitate a multiprogramming environment. Associative storage would hold "names." The Ferranti computer department had been taken over by ICL, which now collaborated with the computer group in providing the hardware for the university. The university team of 16 staff and 25 research students was increased by 19 engineers from ICL in 1971. By October 1974 the MU5 multicomputer system was available for use by the department and remained so until 1979. The architectural concepts of the ICL 2900 series were derived in large measure from those of MU5.

QUOTATION

"I obviously overcoached him since he got his FRS[3] two years before I did." (James Wilkinson, Kilburn's supervisor at Cambridge University)

BIBLIOGRAPHY

Biographical

Evans, Christopher, *Pioneers of Computing* (audiocassettes), Tape No. 5, Science Museum, London, 1970.

Lavington, S.H., "Computer Development at Manchester University," in Metropolis, N., J. Howlett, and Gian-Carlo Rota, *A History of Computing in the Twentieth Century,* Academic Press, New York, 1980, pp. 433–443.

Lavington, Simon, *Early British Computers,* Digital Press, Bedford, Mass., 1980. See Chapter 4: "The Technology of Early Computers," and Chapter 7: "The Manchester Mark I."

---

[3]Fellow of the Royal Society.

Significant Publications

Kilburn, T., *A Storage System for Use with Binary Digital Computing Machines,* Univ. of Manchester, Manchester, UK, 1947, reprinted 1978.

Williams, F.C., and T. Kilburn, "Electronic Digital Computers," reprinted in Randell, Brian, *Origins of Digital Computers: Selected Papers,* Springer-Verlag, Berlin, 1982, pp. 415–416.

JACK ST. CLAIR KILBY

Born November 8, 1923, Jefferson City, Mo.; coinventor in 1958 of the integrated computer chip (the "IC").

Education: BS, University of Illinois, 1947; MS, University of Wisconsin, 1950.

Professional Experience: engineer, Globe-Union, Inc., Wis., 1947–1958; Texas Instruments, Inc.: engineer, assistant vice president, 1958–1970; consultant, 1970–present; distinguished professor, Texas A&M, 1977–present.

Honors and Awards: Outstanding Electrical Engineer Award, Dallas Section, IEEE, 1965; David Sarnoff Award, IEEE, 1966; fellow, IEEE, 1966[4]; National Inventors Hall of Fame, Sarnoff Award, IEEE, 1966; Ballantine Medal, Franklin Institute, 1966; Hall Minuteman Trophy, Order of Daedalians, 1966; member, National Academy of Engineering, 1967; National Medal of Science, 1969; Zworykwin Medal, National Academy of Engineering, 1975; Alumni Achievement Award, University of Illinois, 1975; member, National Academy of Engineering; Cledo Brunetti Award, IEEE, 1979; IEEE Consumer Electronics Award, 1980; Holley Award, American Society of Mechanical Engineers (ASME), 1982; National Inventors Hall of Fame, 1982; DEng (Hon.), University of Miami, 1982; member, Information Processing Hall of Fame, Infomart, Dallas, Texas, 1985; DEng (Hon.), Rochester Institute of Technology, 1986; IEEE Medal of Honor, 1986; DSci (Hon.), University of Illinois, 1988; US Department of Commerce, Medal of Technology, 1990; Kyoto Prize, Advanced Technology, 1993; IEEE Pioneer Award, 1993.

Kilby was the first person in the world to propose and corroborate the fundamental concept of the monolithic semiconductor integrated circuit (IC) that laid the foundation for today's leading-edge technology of LSI and VLSI chips. Further, he contributed greatly to the early

---

[4] "For contributions to the field of integrated circuits through basic concepts, inventions, and development."

state of monolithic IC development and its practical application. His pioneering contribution was a great asset to the development of micro-electronics.

Following a seminar at Bell Telephone Laboratories which he attended in 1952, Kilby turned his attention to the development of hearing aids for the deaf, based on germanium transistor technology. He soon found that silicon would be an improved base for the construction of transistors, but that his employer, Globe-Union, Inc., was committed to germanium. He found employment at Texas Instruments, Inc., and under their imprimatur was able to develop a new evolutionary progression beyond the solid-state technology. Kilby conceived and proved his idea of integrating a transistor with resistors and capacitors on a single semiconductor chip, which is a monolithic IC. His idea of a monolithic IC, together with the planar technology of Jean Hoerni and the late Robert Noyce's idea of "junction isolation" for planar interconnections, underpins the great progress of today's semiconductor IC and the microelectronics based upon it. Texas Instruments filed a patent application and filed a lawsuit against Robert Noyce and Fairchild Industries for infringement. In 1969 the courts ruled in favor of Noyce. It is generally agreed, in hindsight, that Kilby built the first integrated circuit, while Noyce provided a practical implementation that could be commercialized.

Kilby's achievements can be summarized as follows:

Original Concept and Corroboration of the Monolithic Semiconductor Integrated Circuit

In 1958, during the development of miniature packaging technology for electronic circuits, Kilby conceived the idea of fabricating all electronic components on the same piece of semiconductor material. He developed and operated the first hybrid IC prototype in which the electric circuit components, other than the inductor, consisted of semiconductor components connecting resistors made of semiconductor bulk and capacitors of *pn* junctions with a transistor. Next, using a mesa transistor, Kilby succeeded in building a prototype semiconductor IC in which all circuit elements were incorporated into a single semiconductor chip. This was the world's first proven monolithic IC and served to establish the basic concept of today's semiconductor integrated circuits.

Promotion of Integrated Circuit Applications

In 1959, Kilby designed a flip-flop IC using a mesa transistor, bulk resistors, and diffused capacitors. He then fabricated and tested a prototype successfully. Kilby also took the lead in promoting the practical application of this IC technology. His team developed the world's first ICs for a calculator and completed an epoch-making special computing system. He also invented and developed a compact calculator in order to apply the developed technology. This was the pilot model of present-day electronic calculators. In this way, Kilby demonstrated with numerous practical examples that the semiconductor IC had a wide range of applications.

BIBLIOGRAPHY

Biographical

Reid, T.R., *The Chip: How Two Americans Invented the Microchip and Launched a Revolution,* Simon and Schuster, New York, 1984.

Slater, Robert, *Portraits in Silicon,* MIT Press, Cambridge, Mass., 1987, Chapter 15.

Significant Publications

Kilby, J. St. C., and R.R. Roup, "Transister Amplifier Packaged in Steatite," *Electronics,* 1956.

Kilby, J. St. C., "Invention of the Integrated Circuit," *IEEE Trans. Electronic Devices,* ED-23, 1976.

Patents

Kilby, J. St. C., W.R. McKee, and W.A. Porter, Patent #4,188,177: System for Fabrication of Semiconductor Bodies, 1980.

Kilby, J. St. C., W.R. McKee, and W.A. Porter, Patent #4,322,379: Fabrication Process for Semiconductor Bodies, 1982.

Augusta Ada King (née Byron), Lady Lovelace

Born December 15, 1815, London, England; died November 1852, London, England; student, friend, confidante, and interpreter of the work of Charles Babbage, and the first conceptual programmer of his Analytical Engine.

Ada was a gift from the gods to so rigorous a subject as the history of mathematics (or computer science). Beautiful, charming, temperamental, her own life a minor tragedy, as Byron's daughter she acquired the romance that attaches to everyone associated with that magnificent *poéte maudit.*

Ada's mathematical work does not provide her with a position in the history of mathematics, except for her association with Charles Babbage. Ada's mother, the odious Lady Noel Byron, took her to Babbage's house in 1833, but it was only some years after Ada married Lord King (later Earl of Lovelace) that she began to see a great deal of Babbage. He was addicted to the company of beautiful and intelligent women, and for more than a decade she played an important part in his life.

Ada was an enthusiastic student of mathematics, becoming proficient at a time when it was exceedingly rare for a women to do so. She was an aristocratic hostess; the mathematicians of the day were fascinated. There is no evidence that she ever did any original work in mathematics; all that remains are her student exercises. If she did attempt anything it was probably developed in the "Book," her mathematical scrapbook, long since disappeared, which passed back and forth between her and Babbage. But she translated and made extensive notes to Count Menabrea's famous paper on Babbage's calculating engines.[5] These notes were made under Babbage's careful supervision, and Babbage himself carried out the calculation of the Bernoulli numbers contained therein. Thus her notes are by far the most important statement we possess of Babbage's views on the general powers of the Analytical Engines.[6]

---

[5] General Luigi F. Manabrea learned of Babbage's machines during the latter's visit to Italy; he published his report in Italian in 1842. Manabrea was later prime minister of Italy.

[6] Based on Anthony Hyman's review of Moore 1977, which appeared in *Ann. Hist. Comp.,* Vol. 1, No. 1, 1977, p. 75.

It has been suggested that Ada was interested in using the Analytical Engine to derive some advantage in betting on horse races, but this has been refuted.[7] She died of cancer at the same age as that of her father when he died; although she had never met him she requested to be buried alongside him.

QUOTATION

"We may say most aptly that the [Babbage's] analytical engine weaves algebraic patterns just as the Jacquard loom weaves flowers and leaves."

BIBLIOGRAPHY

Biographical

Elwin, Malcolm, *Lord Byron's Family: Annabella, Ada and Augusta, 1816–1824,* John Murray (Publishers), London, 1975.

Huskey, Harry D., and Velma Huskey, "Lady Lovelace and Charles Babbage," *Ann. Hist. Comp.*, Vol. 2, No. 4, 1980, pp. 299–329.

Huskey, Velma R., "Lovelace, Countess of," in Ralston, Anthony, and Edwin D. Reilly, Jr., *Encyclopedia of Computer Science and Engineering,* Van Nostrand Reinhold Co., New York, 1983.

Moore, Doris Langley, *Ada, Countess of Lovelace: Byron's Legitimate Daughter,* Harper and Row, New York, 1977.

Significant Publications

King, Augusta Ada, "Addition to the Memoir of M. Menabrea On the Analitical [sic] Engine," *Philosophical Magazine*, Vol. 23, Sept. 1843, pp. 235–239.

---

[7]See biography of Charles Babbage.

STEPHEN COLE KLEENE

Born 1909, Hartford, Conn.; logician and linguist, most remembered for his introduction of "Kleene closure," a mechanism for describing the repetition of phrases in a regular language.

Education: Amherst College, 1930; PhD, Princeton University, 1930.

Professional Experience: professor of mathematics, University of Wisconsin, since 1935; president Association for Symbolic Logic, 1956–1958; editor, *Journal of Symbolic Logic,* 1950–1962.

Honors and Awards: member, National Academy of Sciences, 1969.

QUOTATION

"Logic has the important function of saying what follows from what."

BIBLIOGRAPHY

Biographical

Kleene, Stephen C., "Origins of Recursive Function Theory," *Ann. Hist. Comp.,* Vol. 3, No. 1, 1981, pp. 52–67.

Significant Publications

Kleene, Stephen C., *Foundations of Intuitionistic Mathematics,* North-Holland, Amsterdam, 1965.

Kleene, Stephen C., *Introduction to Mathematics,* American Elsevier, N.Y., 1971.

DONALD ERVIN KNUTH

Born January 10, 1938, Milwaukee, Wis.; writer and teacher of the Art of Programming, *three of seven promised volumes having been completed; developer of the text language TEX.*

Education: BA and MS,[8] summa cum laude, physics, Case Institute of Technology, 1960; PhD, mathematics, California Institute of Technology, 1963.

Professional Experience: faculty member, California Institute of Technology, 1963–1968; mathematician, Institute for Defense Analysis, Princeton, N.J., 1968–1969; Fletcher Jones Professor of Computer Science, Stanford Junior University, 1969–1989; professor of the Art of Programming, 1990–present.

Honors and Awards: ACM Grace Murray Hopper Award, 1971; ACM Turing Award, 1974; Lester R. Ford Award, Mathematical Association of America, 1975; National Medal of Science, 1979; IEEE McDowell Award, 1980; IEEE Computer Society Pioneer Award, 1982; Computer Science Education Award, 1986; ACM Systems Software Award, 1986; Steele Prize, Association for Management Systems, 1986; New York Academy of Sciences Award, 1987; Franklin Medal, 1988; J.D. Warnier Prize, 1989; member, National Academy of Sciences, 1975; member, National Academy of Engineering, 1981; foreign associate, l'Academie des Sciences, Paris, 1992.

Donald Knuth cannot easily be summed up in a single sentence; he is like the elephant being described by six blind men, each with a restricted "view" of the whole beast. While Knuth is most cited for his work in computer software, ranging from compilers to word processing and algorithms, each biographer will find a pinnacle of excellence to emphasize. This author would credit Knuth with the development of the concept of LR-parsing, although it took others, notably Franklin DeRemer (1971), to provide a practical methodology for implementation. Computer science educators look at Knuth's *Art of Programming* series of books and give him tremendous credit for enhancing the study of algorithms and data structures. The word-processing community would look to Knuth's TEX system as a prime example of the application of user needs and programming language principles to the development of a word processor which, like Unix, transcends machine boundaries. Humanists would see an organist and prolific writer.

---

[8]The work for Knuth's bachelor's degree was so distinguished that the faculty of the Case Institute of Technology voted to award simultaneous bachelor's and master's degrees.

QUOTATIONS

"I sometimes consider myself a pure mathematician, but usually I'm a pure computer scientist who has found connections between computers and mathematics."

"Science is what we understand well enough to explain to a computer; Art is everything else." (*Reader's Digest,* July 1987, p. 24)

"Instead of imagining that our main task is to instruct a *computer* what to do, let us concentrate rather on explaining to *human beings* what we want a computer to do." (*Computer Journal,* Vol. 27, 1984, p. 97)

BIBLIOGRAPHY

Biographical

Albers, Donald J., and Lynn Arthur Steen, "A Conversation with Don Knuth," *Ann. Hist. Comp.,* Vol. 4, No. 3, July 1982, pp. 257–273.

Caddes, Carolyn, *Portraits of Success: Impressions of Silicon Valley Pioneers,* Tioga Publishing Co., Palo Alto, Calif., 1986.

Frenkel, Karen A., "Donald E. Knuth: Scholar with a Passion for the Particular," Profiles in Computing, *Comm. ACM,* Vol. 30, No. 10, Oct. 1987, pp. 816–819.

Slater, Robert, *Portraits in Silicon,* MIT Press, Cambridge, Mass., 1987, Chapter 31.

Significant Publications

Knuth, Donald E., "The Potrzebie System of Weights and Measures," *MAD Magazine,* E.C. Publications, Inc., June 1957; reprinted in Reidelbach, Maria, *Completely MAD,* Little, Brown, Boston, 1991, p. 191.

Knuth, Donald E., "On the Translation of Languages from Left to Right," *Information and Control,* Vol. 8, 1965, pp. 607–639.

Knuth, Donald E., "Von Neumann's First Computer Program," *Computing Surveys,* Vol. 2, 1970, pp. 247–260.

Knuth, Donald E., "Fortran: An Empirical Study of Fortran Programs," *Software: Practice and Experience,* Vol. 1, 1971, pp. 105–133.

Knuth, Donald E., "Ancient Babylonian Algorithms," *Comm. ACM,* Vol. 15, No. 7, July 1972, pp. 671–677 (errata Vol. 19, No. 2, 1976, p. 108).

Knuth, Donald E., "The Early Development of Programming Languages," in Metropolis, N., J. Howlett, and Gian-Carlo Rota, *A History of Computing in the Twentieth Century,* Academic Press, New York, 1980, pp. 197–273.

Knuth, Donald E., *The Art of Computer Programming*, 3 Vols., Addison-Wesley, Reading, Mass., 1968.

Knuth, Donald E., *Computers and Typesetting*, 5 Vols., Addison-Wesley, Reading, Mass., 1986.

THOMAS E. KURTZ

Born February 22, 1928, Oak Park, Ill.; with John Kemeny, developer of the programming language and system BASIC.

Education: BA, Knox College, 1950; PhD, mathematics/statistics, Princeton University, 1956.

Professional Experience: Dartmouth College: instructor, mathematics, 1956–1958, assistant professor, 1958–1963, associate professor, 1963–1966; professor, 1966–1993, director, Computing Center, 1959–1975, director, Kiewit Computation Center, 1966–1975, director, Office of Academic Computing, 1975–1978, vice chair and chair, Program in Computing and Information Science, 1979–1988; member, Pierce Panel, President's Science Advisory Council in Higher Education, 1965–1967; chairman, Council, EDUCOM, 1973–1974.

Honors and Awards: AFIPS Pioneer Award, 1974; DSc (Hon.), Knox College, 1987; IEEE Computer Science Pioneer Award, 1991.

Kurtz received his PhD in statistics from Princeton in 1956, his first contact with computing having occurred in 1951 at the summer session of the Institute for Numerical Analysis (INA) at UCLA in the summer of 1951. He joined the Dartmouth College Mathematics Department (chaired by John G. Kemeny) in 1956 as an instructor. Besides teaching statistics and numerical analysis, he served as the Dartmouth contact to the New England Regional Computer Center

(NERComP), which was supported in part by IBM at MIT. In 1959 Dartmouth obtained an LGP-30 computer, and Kurtz became the first director of Dartmouth's computing center.

Around 1962, Kurtz and John G. Kemeny began jointly to supervise the design and development of a time-sharing system for university use. The idea to use time-sharing to reach *all* Dartmouth students came from John McCarthy who, around 1961, advised, "you guys ought to do time-sharing." This effort culminated in 1964 in the first Dartmouth Time-Sharing System (DTSS). Although other languages such as Fortran and Algol were provided, the principal language was BASIC, which was deliberately designed to be easy to learn and easy to use.

Subsequently, Kurtz served as the director of the Kiewit Computation Center from 1966 to 1975, and as director of the Office of Academic Computing from 1975 to 1978. In 1979 he and Stephen J. Garland organized a professional master's program in Computer and Information Systems, funded in part with a grant from IBM. Upon termination of the CIS program in 1988, Kurtz returned to teaching. He retired from Dartmouth College in 1993.

Outside of Dartmouth, Kurtz served as council chairman and trustee of EDUCOM, as trustee and chairman of NERcomP, and on the so-called Pierce Panel of the President's Advisory Committee. He also served on the steering committee for two NSF- and ARPA-supported activities, and was the chair of the first CCUC conference on instructional computing. He helped form the American National Standards committee X3J2, which developed the ANSI standard for BASIC, serving as chair from 1974 to 1985, and as secretary from 1990 to the present. He is a member of the ISO committee SC22/WG8, concerned with the international standard for BASIC, and served as its convenor from 1987 to 1993.

In 1983, he joined John Kemeny and three former Dartmouth students in forming True BASIC, Inc., whose purpose was to develop quality educational software and a platform-independent BASIC compiler based on the ANSI standard. He continues to be associated with this company, and serves as its secretary/treasurer.

QUOTATION

"If Fortran is the lingua franca, then certainly it must be true that BASIC is the lingua playpen."

BIBLIOGRAPHY

Biographical

Kemeny, John G., and Thomas E. Kurtz, *Back to BASIC. The History, Corruption and Future of the Language,* Addison-Wesley, Reading, Mass., 1985. (Note: True BASIC Inc. is now the copyright holder and sole distributor of this book.)

Kurtz, Thomas E., "BASIC," in Wexelblat, Richard L., ed., *History of Programming Languages,* Academic Press, New York, 1981, Chapter 11.

Slater, Robert, *Portraits in Silicon,* MIT Press, Cambridge, Mass., 1987, Chapter 22.

Significant Publications

Kurtz, Thomas E., *Basic Statistics,*[9] Prentice-Hall, Englewood Cliffs, N.J., 1963.

Kemeny, J.G., and T.E. Kurtz, "Dartmouth Time Sharing," *Science,* Vol. 162, 1968, pp. 223–228.

Kemeny, J.G., and T.E. Kurtz, *BASIC Programming,* John Wiley & Sons, New York, 1967, 1971, 1980.

Kemeny, J.G., and T.E. Kurtz, *Structured BASIC Programming,* John Wiley & Sons, New York, 1987.

---

[9]Kurtz notes this to be his first use of the word BASIC.

CLAIR D. LAKE

Born 1888; died 1958; early IBM computer inventor and patentee of the rectangular hole in a punched card, who made significant contributions to the construction of the Harvard Mark I (ASCC).

Lake was hired by T. J. Watson, Sr., without prior calculator-like experience, to build printing tabulators for the predecessor to IBM, the CTR Corporation. Lake was highly successful at this venture; Watson rewarded him by making him head of the tabulator activities in Endicott, N.Y. When Howard Aiken approached IBM with the concept of building a mechanical calculator in the late 1930s, Lake was chosen to complete the assignment. At the time of the unveiling of the Harvard Mark I (ASCC), Aiken took the credit for the design *and* construction, but it would be fairer to give credit for the implementation to IBM and particularly to Clair Lake.

BIBLIOGRAPHY

Biographical

Bashe, Charles, et al., *IBM's Early Computers,* MIT Press, Cambridge, Mass., 1986.

EARL R. LARSON

US District Court judge who in 1973 invalidated the ENIAC patent and declared John Vincent Atanasoff to be the first inventor of the electronic computer.

QUOTATION

"Eckert and Mauchly did not themselves first invent the automatic electronic computer, but instead derived that subject matter from one Dr. John Vincent Atanasoff."

BIBLIOGRAPHY

Biographical

Mollenhoff, Clark R., *Atanasoff: The Forgotten Father of the Computer,* Iowa State Univ. Press, Ames, Iowa, 1988.

Significant Publications

Larson, US District Court Judge Earl R., Findings of Fact, Conclusions of Law and Order of Judgment, US District Court, District of Minnesota, Fourth Division, *Honeywell, Inc. v. Sperry-Rand Corp. et al.,* No. 4–67, Civ. 138. Decision printed in *US Patent Quarterly,* Vol. 180, 1974, pp. 673–773.

DERRICK HENRY LEHMER

Born February 23, 1905, Berkeley, Calif.; died May 22, 1991, Berkeley, Calif.; pre-WWII inventor of a mechanical method of solving congruence relations and finding prime numbers.

Education: AB, University of California, Berkeley, 1927; ScM, mathematics, Brown University, 1929; PhD, mathematics, Brown University, 1930.

Professional Experience: assistant, Brown University, 1928; National Research Council Fellow, California Institute of Technology, 1930–1932; researcher, Institute for Advanced Study, Princeton, N.J., 1933–1934; instructor, Lehigh University, 1934–1938; assistant professor, Lehigh University, 1938–1940; professor, University of California, Berkeley, 1940–1972, professor emeritus, 1972–1991; mathematician, Aberdeen Proving Ground, 1945–1946; director, Institute for Numerical Analysis (INA), National Bureau of Standards and University of California, Los Angeles, 1951–1953.

Honors and Awards: Guggenheim Fellow, Cambridge University, 1938–1939; Fullbright Lectureship in Australia, 1959; vice president, American Mathematical Society, 1953; vice president, Association for Computing Machinery, 1954–1957, research professor, Miller Institute for Basic Research in Science at Berkeley, 1962–1963.

Part I. Sieve Computers[1]

Mechanical Sieve Computers

While an undergraduate at the University of California at Berkeley, Dick became interested in mechanizing the solution of linear congruence relations such as $x = y(m)$. The problem is to find those integer values of x (y or m) such that $x - y$ is a multiple of m. For example, if one can find an m different from 1 which satisfies $2^{257} = 1(m)$, then the Mersenne[2] conjecture that $2^{257} - 1$ (a number of over 77 decimal digits) is prime is false. While still a graduate student (1928 to 1930) Dick and his wife, Emma, spent many hundreds of hours manually showing that $2^{257} - 1$ was not prime. They worked independently, comparing numbers at each step, so as to be confident in their results. Such congruence relations are useful in the problem of representing a number as the sum or difference of two squares. Obviously, if a number can be represented in the form $a^2 - b^2$ then $a - b$ and $a + b$ are factors. A machine (a special-purpose computer) which scans numbers in sequence searching for those that satisfy such congruence relations is called a sieve. Dick gives a more general definition in *A History of Computing in the Twentieth Century* (Metropolis et al. p. 445).

Dick's first sieve, constructed in the students' workshop at the University of California, Berkeley, in 1926, while he was an undergraduate, used 19 separately looped bicycle chains whose number of links were the primes up to 67. Actually, very short chains were not practical, so the small primes were handled by "composite" chains of non-prime lengths 22, 25, 26, 27, 49, and 64 links representing the primes 11, 5, 13, 3, 7, and 2. These chains hung in loops from 10-tooth sprockets on a common shaft which was driven by a motor. A counter indicated how many teeth or links had passed the top position. Each chain (both of prime and composite length) had a zero position or link (painted red). Suppose each chain had a "pin" attached at the zero link. The composite chains had several pins, one at each multiple of each prime which divided the length of that chain. For example, the chain of length 22 had pins on all the even numbered links as well as on link 11. If for some (large) number of teeth N, a pin of one of the chains was at the top, then that corresponding prime divided N.

---

[1] [Harry Huskey] I have divided this somewhat informal obituary of my friend, Dick, into two parts. First I describe his unique mechanical and electronic sieve computers, and then I tell the story of his life.

[2] Marin Mersenne (1588–1648) was a monk, a French mathematician, natural philosopher, and theologian. He studied numbers of the form $2p$-1 where p is prime, and now such numbers are called Mersenne numbers.

Conversely, if for N no pin was at the top, then any prime divisors must be greater than 67.

Dick described (Lehmer 1928, p. 115) the pin arrangement as follows: "Whenever a link provided with a pin arrives at the top of the shaft a small spring with a tungsten point is lifted by the projecting pin. This breaks for the moment the electric contact between the spring and a brass bar running parallel to the shaft. By means of a relay in the circuit, the motor is shut off and the machine stops itself. When several chains are provided with springs the machine will not stop unless all the springs are lifted, so that every time the machine stops it means that a number satisfying all the imposed conditions has appeared. This number can be read directly by means of a revolution counter connected to the shaft. The shaft revolves at 300 rpm so that the machine canvases 3,000 numbers per minute. When all chains are provided with springs a "solution" occurs once in several hours, during which time the machine runs without any attention." The machine scanned about 4.3 million numbers per day, so the Mersenne number $2^{256} - 1$ would require more than 1,070 years! This difficulty is overcome by applying number theory techniques too complicated for us to consider here.

To explain the use of the machine Dick gave (Lehmer 1928, p. 115) the following example: Consider the representation of the beautiful number

$$N = 9999000099990001$$

(which happens to be $(10^{20} + 1)/(10^4 + 1)$) as a difference of two squares, $a^2 - b^2$. After nearly two pages of analysis (Lehmer 1928, p, 118) he concluded that a must be congruent to

2,3,9,16,23,30,37, and 44 modulo 49 (i.e., $a = 2(49)$, $a = 3(49)$, etc.).

These are called quadratic residues since $49 = 7^2$. Now if pins are placed on links 2, 3, 9, 16, 23, 30, 37, and 44 on the 49-chain, then electrical contact will be broken for numbers satisfying the above relations. Similar relations are worked out for the other chains, pins are placed, and the machine started. After about two hours the machine stops, giving

$$a = 2983262201$$
$$\text{and}$$
$$N = (a - b) * (a + b) = 1676321 * 5964848081.$$

A model of this bicycle chain sieve has been constructed at the Computer Museum in Boston but in 1992 it was not on exhibit. In

1932 Dick constructed a much faster sieve using gears with different numbers of teeth (as above) driven from a common pinion.

He described it as follows (Lehmer 1934, p. 663): "There are 30 driven gears, all driven at the same linear speed of about 1700 meters per minute by a single driving gear. The 30 driven gears correspond to 30 moduli and have for numbers of teeth convenient multiples of every prime less than 127. The largest gear has 128 teeth and the smallest 67 teeth. At the base of each tooth on each driven gear, holes are drilled at a constant distance from the periphery of the gear, this distance being the same for all gears. These holes are about 2 millimeters in diameter and correspond to the numbers 0, 1, 2, . . . , p − 1 modulo p. If x is to be restricted to a set of s numbers modulo p the holes corresponding to these numbers are left open, while other holes are stopped with wooden pins. The gears are mounted parallel to one another and a common line of tangency so that if a beam of light from an incandescent lamp shines through a hole in any gear it is transmitted or blotted out by the next gear. If the driving gear is rotated (from some zero position) until x teeth have turned past and if x satisfies the conditions imposed by all the moduli, then there will be an alignment of open holes and the beam of light will traverse the system of gears." A photocell detected whether a beam of light could pass through all the holes. At speed, the device processed 5,000 numbers per second and coasted many thousands past a "hit." Dick exhibited this "photoelectric sieve" and ran the Mathematics Exhibit at the Chicago World's Fair during the summer of 1932.

Laura Gould, his daughter, describes a sieve "built sometime in the Thirties I suppose, which operated on loops of movie film—8 mm or 16 mm, I don't know which—of various lengths.[3,4]

"The frames of these film loops were either punched (with a streetcar conductor's punch) or not, depending on the characteristics of the problem being run. These loops ran over a row of parallel pulley heads while an electric eye watched along these heads to detect either no punches or all punches, I'm not sure which. This machine was stored in my closet when I was a child. At home it was called the "baby 'chine" because the celluloid would run smoothly over the wooden heads only if it was well dusted with baby powder. This fragrance lingered in my closet for many years."

---

[3]Laura Gould, private communication.

[4]According to Lehmer (1980) it was built in 1936 and was 16 mm.

General-Purpose Computers as Sieves

After describing the three kinds of sieves Dick said (1980): "Our next date is 1946 and this, of course, is the ENIAC. Can we use the high-speed computer to do the sieve process? This was a highly parallel machine, before von Neumann spoiled it. We were able to build a sieve into it. I remember the occasion very clearly. We had a Fourth of July weekend situation when the Lehmer family was allowed to come in and pull everything off the machine and reset the ENIAC for our particular problem. The Lehmer family consisted of myself, my wife, and two teenage kids [Donald and Laura]. We marched in on the Friday about 5 p.m. and started setting it up with an entirely different kind of problem not concerned with interior or exterior ballistics. There was one other person there, *a meteorologist named John Mauchly* (emphasis added). He was the one who suggested that we ought to use some of the arithmetic units to make a kind of sieve, and I remember that we worked it out in a restaurant just before we went to work." There were a long series of sieve programs written for various general-purpose computers such as the SWAC and the IBM-7094. Perhaps the best of these was a 7094 program written by John Brillhart that accomplished 100,000 counts per second. "The technique," Dick said, "to get the high speed was to combine many moduli into five or six very long chains which filled most of memory."

Electronic Sieves

In the early 1950s Dick, in cooperation with Paul Morton of the Electrical Engineering Department at Berkeley, had worked on a general-purpose magnetic drum computer (CALDIC—California Digital Computer). Thus, it was natural that they would cooperate in building electronic sieves. After a first abortive effort using electronic counters, which had reliability problems, they built a delay line version using Navy surplus electrical delay lines (Dick was "leery" of mercury delay lines). There were a number of recirculating delay lines of various lengths like the bicycle chains, movie film, or wheels of the earlier sieves. The system operated in two modes, serial (or idle) mode and parallel mode. In the idle mode all lines were connected in series, and bits were inserted one at a time using counting circuits; then the system was switched to parallel where each delay line recirculated independently. When a coincidence occurred the system automatically switched back to serial. I can remember stopping at the room in Cory Hall at UCB and if the sieve was in serial mode there was a flurry of activity as Emma or Dick copied down the "hit" number and did some auxiliary computation to see if this was a number of interest or a spurious result. In 1980 Dick said: "That's the way the delay line sieve has been operating for ten years now, 24 hours per day. We have no maintenance and since the whole system is just a long piece of wire, nothing ever went wrong to speak of except for occasional counter printer trouble." This system did 1 million counts per second. The above machine was followed by a shift register version that ran at 20 million counts per second. Dick mentioned (1980) that a Russian publication in 1970 said there was "one of Lehmer's sieves in the Institute for Mathematics in Leningrad," but claimed, "I don't know anything about it. All I can say is that none of my sieves is missing."

Part II. His Life

Early Life

Derrick H. Lehmer was born on February 23, 1905 in Berkeley, California. His father, Derrick N. Lehmer, was professor of mathematics and his mother, Eunice Mitchell, was a poet. He was one of five children; only an older sister survives. His father's interest in number theory and computation started Dick on a long and distinguished career in that field. He was educated in the Berkeley public schools and entered the University of California at Berkeley (UCB) in 1923. He graduated with an AB degree in mathematics in 1927 and spent 1927–1928 at the University of Chicago taking mathematics courses from Dickson, Bliss, Lane, and Graves. In 1928–1929 he was a graduate assistant at Brown University, where he received his MSc degree in mathematics in 1929 and his PhD in 1930, his thesis being titled, "An Extended Theory of Lucas' Functions." Lucas had published a well-known book on number theory in Paris in 1891 entitled "Theorie des Nombres." Dick's thesis was essentially unsupervised since no one at Brown was interested in number theory, but he did have weekly discussions with Tamarkin. His thesis was sent to E.T. Bell at the California Institute of Technology for review. In 1928 he married Emma Trotskaya, who was also a mathematician and number theorist and was one of his father's students. He was appointed to the Henry D. Sharpe Fellowship in 1929 at Brown University.

1930–1945

Dick had a National Research Fellowship from 1930 to 1932 working with E. T. Bell at the California Institute of Technology (1930–1931) and with Uspenski at Stanford (1931–1932). He then received a Princeton Institute Fellowship [the Institute for Advanced Study was just being formed] for 1933–1934. He taught at the Stanford Summer School in 1934, and then taught mathematics at Lehigh University from 1934 to 1940. He was on leave from Lehigh for 1938–1939 on a Guggenheim Fellowship at Cambridge and Manchester Universities in

England. In 1940 he joined the Mathematics Department at UCB as an assistant professor.

World War II
In 1945 Dick took a temporary appointment at the Ballistic Research Laboratory of Aberdeen Proving Ground. They were financing the construction of the ENIAC (the first electronic general-purpose computer) at the University of Pennsylvania. He observed the completion of the ENIAC and participated in its testing. It was while working on the ENIAC that I first met Dick. At the end of the war (1946) he returned to the Mathematics Department at UCB as an associate professor.

The Institute for Numerical Analysis
In 1950, taking exception to the loyalty oath requirements of UCB (a result of the McCarthy era), he left, taking leave without pay, and joined the Institute for Numerical Analysis of the National Bureau of Standards at the University of California at Los Angeles. He was director of the Institute for two years, 1951 to 1953. The SWAC (National Bureau of Standards Western Automatic Computer, the first stored-program computer on the West Coast) was just becoming operational at the institute. About this time, Raphael Robinson at the UCB Department of Mathematics, using the SWAC instruction documentation, programmed the Lucas test for primality to search for Mersenne primes. This was mailed from Berkeley to Los Angeles, the program was punched, and it ran on the SWAC without error. It quickly verified the known results and that evening found two new primes, $2^{521} - 1$ and $2^{607} - 1$.

Back to Berkeley
Dick returned to Mathematics at UCB in 1954, when the signing of the loyalty oath was no longer required. He was chairman of the Mathematics Department from 1954 to 1957, where he was instrumental in my joining UCB in 1954. He was vice chairman of the Letters and Science Computer Science Department from 1969 to 1970. He retired in 1972, becoming professor emeritus.

Publications, Awards, and Honors
He published over 181 research papers and received a number of awards, invitations, honors, and elective offices in professional societies. Among these were: Guggenheim Fellowship (Cambridge University, 1938), Fulbright Lectureship (Australia, 1959), Research Professorship (Miller Institute for Basic Research in Science, Berkeley, 1962–1963), invited address at the 1958 International Congress of Mathematicians, Gibbs Lecturer (American Mathematical Society,

1964), vice president of the American Mathematical Society (1953–1954) and of the American Association for the Advancement of Science (1955–1956), and Council Member at Large of the Association for Computing Machinery (1953–1954) and a Governor of the Mathematical Association of America (1953–1954).

Reprise

Dick excelled in using computers to solve problems in number theory. Typically, he used computers to prove conjectures wrong, to reduce the number of cases to be investigated, or to show that additional assumptions were required. Dick was a popular lecturer, spoke in a relaxed manner, and always provided opportunities for dialogue with students. His informal methods and droll humor were very effective. For example, he might start some pronouncement with the words "the other day . . ." and later you would discover that the event being described happened 20 years ago! Dick was a very considerate person. Many Saturday mornings he and Emma invited graduate students and young faculty to accompany them on walks in the Berkeley Hills.[5]

BIBLIOGRAPHY

Biographical

Brillhart, John, "Derrick H. Lehmer," *Mathematics of Computation*, to be published.

Kelley, J.L., Raphael M. Robinson, Abraham H. Taub, and P. Emery Thomas, "In Memoriam," University of California, Berkeley, 1991, pp. 112–115.

Lehmer, D.H., "A History of the Sieve Process," in Metropolis, N., J. Howlett, and Gian-Carlo Rota, *A History of Computing in the Twentieth Century*, Academic Press, New York, 1980, pp. 445–456.

Significant Publications

Lehmer, D.H., "The Mechanical Combination of Linear Forms," *American Mathematical Monthly*, Vol. 35, 1928, pp. 114–121.

Lehmer, D.H., "A Machine for Combining Sets of Linear Congruences," *Mathematische Annalen*, 1934, pp. 661–667.

---

[5]Harry D. Huskey.

GOTTFRIED WILHELM VON LEIBNIZ

*Born 1646, Saxony; died 1716, Berlin, Germany; inventor in the late 1600s
of the first machine to directly perform all four basic arithmetic operations.*

Leibniz was aware of Pascal's calculator, which had the capability of
adding and subtracting, like many previous machines, but had the
added ability to carry (or borrow) between unit positions. He designed
a special cylinder with a set of varying length teeth, such that when
rotated, the longitudinal position of the corresponding gear con-
formed to the multiplicand. Leibniz also studied "universal combina-
torics," which appears to have been the first attempt to symbolize logic.
His work was used later by Boole and others in their own developments of symbolic logic. Leibniz also was the first to note that integration and differentiation were complementary.

BIBLIOGRAPHY

Biographical

Chase, George C., "History of Mechanical Computing Machinery," *Ann. Hist.
Comp.*, Vol. 2, No. 3, 1980, pp. 198–226.

Jones, C.V., "Leibniz, Gottfried Wilhelm von," in Ralston, Anthony, and Edwin
D. Reilly, Jr., *Encyclopedia of Computer Science and Engineering*, Van Nostrand
Reinhold Co., New York, 1983.

Locke, L.L., "The Contributions of Leibniz to the Art of Mechanical
Calculation," *Scripta Mathematica*, Vol. 1, 1933, pp. 315–321.

Joseph C. R. Licklider

Born March 11, 1915, St. Louis, Mo.; died June 26, 1990, Arlington, Mass.; a principal contributor to the advent of interactive computing and computer networks.

Education: BA, Washington University, 1937; MA, Washington University, 1938; PhD, University of Rochester, 1942.

Professional Experience: Harvard University: faculty member, Psycho-Acoustics Laboratory, 1941–1946, lecturer, Psychology Laboratories, 1946–1949; MIT: faculty member, 1949–1957, professor, Electrical Engineering (later Computer Science), 1964–1985, professor emeritus, 1985–1990, director, Project MAC, 1968–1970; vice president, Psycho-acoustics, Engineering Psychology, and Information Systems, Bolt Beranek and Newman, 1957–1962; director, Behavioral Sciences and Information Processing Research, Advanced Research Projects Agency (ARPA), US Department of Defense, 1962–1964; consultant, IBM, 1964–1967.

Honors and Awards: Franklin V. Taylor Award, Society of Engineering Psychologists, 1957; member, National Academy of Sciences; fellow, Acoustic Society of America; fellow, Academy of Arts and Sciences.

Joseph C.R. Licklider, a principal contributor to the advent of interactive computing and computer networks, studied psychology, earning bachelor's and master's degrees from Washington University (1937 and 1938 respectively) and a doctorate at the University of Rochester in 1942.[6] He was a member of the Harvard University faculty and a researcher in its Psycho-Acoustics Laboratory beginning in 1941 until 1946, and lecturer at the Psychology Laboratories until 1949, when he joined the MIT faculty. In 1957 he was named vice president in the area of psycho-acoustics, engineering psychology, and information systems at Bolt Beranek and Newman (BBN), and in 1962 he was appointed director of behavioral sciences and information processing research at the Advanced Research Projects Agency (ARPA) of the US Department of Defense.

After a three-year stint as a research consultant for IBM commencing in 1964, Licklider returned to MIT as professor of electrical engineering (later computer science) and was named professor emeritus in 1985. He served concurrently as director of MIT's Project MAC from 1968 to 1970.

He was honored with the Franklin V. Taylor Award of the Society of Engineering Psychologists in 1957; member, National Academy of

---

[6]Based on the *New York Times* Obituary by Glenn Fowler, July 3, 1990, p. B6; and Licklider, 1960.

Sciences; fellow, Acoustic Society of America; fellow, Academy of Arts and Sciences; and member, Association for Computing Machinery.

Licklider is widely recognized for his fundamental impact on three aspects of computing:

- His paper "Man-Computer Symbiosis"[7] was seminal in bringing to the attention of large numbers of researchers in many fields the essential differences between traditional "batch" computing and interactive computing in terms of human perception and effectiveness.

- As an ARPA director, he formulated and put into place the program that funded Project MAC and led ultimately to computer networking.

- As teacher, researcher, and manager he identified, nurtured, and supported literally dozens of people who have become leaders in computing research and practice.

Remembrances of "Lick"

Licklider was universally called "Lick" by his friends, colleagues, and students. He was described as follows by former colleague Robert W. Taylor: "He was the most unlikely 'great man' you could ever encounter. His favorite kind of joke was at his own expense. He was gentle, curious, and outgoing."[8]

His widow, Louise, says that Licklider was totally dedicated to his work, spending evenings and weekends at his desk. "For recreation, he would be on the computer." She reports that he was "wonderfully happy" in his work. Had he been independently wealthy, "he would have paid to have worked in the field."

His enthusiasm and dedication are evident in comments he made during the Project MAC interview.[9] His statements abound with phrases such as, "The next summer projects were so wonderful . . . fantastically exciting. . . . that gave me access to the most marvelous electronics there was. . . . we'd all gotten really excited about interactive computing."

He used similar language when he expressed his attitudes about people. "The people who could turn me on and off easily were very bright people." ". . . along side each door [in an MIT hallway] is the name of whose office that was. . . . It was for me a very religious experience to walk slowly down those halls and look at the names."

---

[7]Licklider 1960.
[8]Taylor 1990.
[9]Lee, ed., 1992.

Given that his training was in psychology, Licklider got along surprisingly well with electrical engineers and (emerging) computer scientists. Perhaps this stems from the fact that his early work on the perception of speech complemented contemporaneous work in speech transmission.

Licklider's approach to technical problems was different from that of his engineering colleagues, and his point of view often provided the raison d'etre behind a technical project. For example, in an era when time-sharing research concerned scheduling algorithms, file system design, and new I/O devices, Lick was focusing on other issues. To quote again from the interview: "From my point of view, a lot hinged on a little study I had made on how I would spend my time. It showed that almost all my time was spent on algorithmic things that were no fun, but they were all necessary for the few heuristic things that seemed so important. I had this little picture in my mind about how we were going to get people and computers really thinking together."

A Personal Note[10]

In the fall of 1956, my senior year at MIT, I was a student in Lick's course in experimental psychology. Although I went in with no prior knowledge of the subject, he made those of us taking the course feel at home (almost like junior colleagues) in his pursuit of understanding about behavior in a laboratory setting. I also worked for a semester in his psycho-acoustics lab, as an assistant/technician, adjusting the phases of distinct signals at various frequencies and measuring the apparent audible level of the combined signal. The experience in Lick's laboratory made good use of my three previous years of interdisciplinary study at MIT, particularly in psychology and electrical engineering.

The fall of 1956 was also the semester in which I took my first two courses in computers. No computer equipment was present in Lick's laboratory, nor was there any evidence that a computer was used for data reduction or any other aspect of his research.

Although I did not see him again for many years, Lick still had an influence over me. In 1962, a graduate school colleague at the University of Michigan left to work on time-sharing system development at MIT Project MAC. I visited him in January 1963, and, after spending half an hour at a CTSS "console" (actually a model 33 teletypewriter), I came away convinced that interactive computing was going to replace "batch," and that to compute any other way was a

---

[10]Robert F. Rosin.

waste of human time and effort. I didn't know it at the time, but of course it was Lick who funded Project MAC through ARPA.

Just about that same time, I read "Man-Computer Symbiosis." For the life of me, I could not imagine how a psychologist who, in 1956, had no apparent knowledge of computers, could have written such a profound and insightful paper about "my field" in 1960. Lick's paper made a deep impression on me and refined my own realization that a new age of computing was upon us.

The next contact I had with Lick was as a moderator at the interview recorded in the *Annals*.[11] Of course, Lick didn't recall who I was, but I recognized him instantly, both by sight and from his spirit, which seemed not to have changed at all. I enjoyed that afternoon immensely.

J.C.R. Licklider's work affected many people, most of whom will never be aware of him. But his spirit endures in the people who knew him and who were affected by him. Few people who knew Lick will forget him.

BIBLIOGRAPHY

Biographical

Lee, John A.N., ed., "MIT Time-Sharing and Interactive Computing," Special Issue, *Ann. Hist. Comp.*, Vol. 14, No. 1, 1992.

Additional details about his life and work can be found in *The Boston Herald* (6/30/90), *The New York Times* (7/3/90), *The Boston Globe* (7/3/90), and *MIT Tech Talk* (7/18/90).

Significant Publications

Licklider, J.C.R., "Man-Computer Symbiosis," *IRE Trans. Human Factors in Electronics*, Vol. HFE-1, Mar. 1960, pages 4–11; reprinted in Pylyshyn, Z. W., ed., *Perspectives on the Computer Revolution*, Prentice Hall, Englewood Cliffs, N.J., 1970, pp. 306–318; reprinted in *Conversational Computers*, Orr, W. D., ed., John Wiley & Sons, New York, 1968, pp. 3–5; and Taylor, Robert W., "In Memoriam: J.C.R. Licklider 1915–1990," Research Report 61, System Research Center, Digital Equipment Corporation, Palo Alto, Calif., August 7, 1990.

---

[11]Lee, ed., 1992.

MARCEL LINSMAN

Born June 22, 1912, Liege, Belgium; died April 19, 1989, Belgium; early promoter of IFIP, computer scientist and computer developer.

Education: BS, mathematical sciences, Univ. Liege, 1934; PhD, Univ. Liege, 1937.

Professional Experience: Univ. Liege: assistant professor, 1938–1964, professor, 1964–1989.

Honors and Awards: IFIP Silver Core Award, 1974.

In 1943, Linsman became interested in numerical calculation and recognized immediately the electronic possibilities. A grant by the Belgian research organization I.R.S.I.A. gave him an opportunity to work at Harvard University during the school year 1947–1948, where he became a member of Howard Aiken's development group.[12] From 1951 to 1955, he managed the development of one of the earliest European electronic computers, known as Machine I.R.S.I.A. His interest then took him into nonnumerical applications of the computer. Starting with automatic language translation, he initiated many projects, including teaching informatics and medical applications. Throughout his career he was a recipient of many awards.

Within IFIP, he was present from the first Council meeting in Rome in 1971, representing the Belgium member society. He was also active in the Technical Committee on Education (TC-3). During the time IFIP was based in Belgium, 1962 through 1967, he served as IFIP assistant secretary and handled all legal matters for the federation. In 1974 he was among the first group to receive the IFIP Silver Core Award.

BIBLIOGRAPHY

Biographical

Zemanek, Heinz, "Marcel Linsman, 1912–1989," *IFIP Newsletter*, Vol. 6, No. 3, 1989, p. 8.

---

[12]During this period the Harvard laboratory was building the Mark III, which eventually was installed at the Naval Surface Weapons Center at Dahlgren, Va.

O. Scott Locken

Managed development of OS/360's control program under Fred Brooks; less than a year after it was released he took the challenging assignment of managing development of TSS/360 at a time when it was beset with delivery schedule and performance problems[13]; TSS was IBM's response to the rejection by MIT of IBM System/360 as a basis for Project MAC.

Locken was an electrical engineering graduate of the University of Denver; he joined IBM in Denver as a service representative. Later he managed machine installation and made his mark in the corporation when he supervised the development of the IBM 1410/7010 operating system which was delivered ahead of schedule.

Percy E. Ludgate

Born 1883, died 1922; Irish designer of a mechanical analytical engine in about 1900.

Ludgate described a general-purpose program-controlled computer in 1909, mechanical in operation, although perhaps powered by an electric motor. It was to be capable of storing 192 numbers, each of 20 decimal digits, and would perform all the basic arithmetic operations. It was to work automatically under the control of a perforated tape, or could be controlled manually from a keyboard. What is most impressive is that although Ludgate had, at least during the later stages of his work, known of Babbage's machine, much of his work was clearly entirely original, and indeed with respect to program control, a distinct advance on Babbage's ideas. In fact, all three main components of Ludgate's analytical machine—the store, the arithmetic unit, and the sequencing mechanism—show evidence of considerable ingenuity and originality.

Babbage had planned to use columns of coaxial toothed wheels to represent numbers, with the angular position of each wheel represent-

---

[13]Based on Pugh, Emerson W., Lyle R. Johnson, and John H. Palmer, *IBM's 360 and Early 370 Systems*, MIT Press, Cambridge, Mass., 1991.

ing the value of a particular digit.[14] His arrangements for transferring the contents of a particular storage location (that is, set of wheels) to and from the arithmetic unit involved a wondrous collection of gear wheels and racks. In contrast, Ludgate planned to represent each multidigit number by a set of sliding rods in a shuttle and to arrange such shuttles around a cylindrical shuttle box, which merely had to be rotated to bring the right number to the arithmetic unit.

Ludgate's planned arithmetic unit was even more novel. Most calculating machines of his day allowed the operator to perform multiplication using repeated addition, although some direct multiplication machines incorporated what was effectively a set of mechanical multiplication tables for single decimal digits. Ludgate, who may or may not have known of such machines, went for a novel—indeed, unique— scheme for multiplication, based on what a contemporary delightfully termed "Irish Logarithms."[15] Multiplication involved converting all the digits of the multiplicand and a single digit of the multiplier to index numbers; the index number corresponding to the multiplier digit was added to each of the index numbers corresponding to multiplicand digits (by additive linear motion); the results were then converted back to give a set of two-digit partial products. Ludgate's scheme for division was entirely different and equally novel. Instead of using either a conventional trial-and-error scheme of repeated subtraction and shifting, or a logarithmic scheme, he proposed a direct method, based on a series approximation. Moreover, he proposed organizing this as a built-in subroutine, using a form of read-only memory: the perforated surface of a rotating metal cylinder.

The final aspect of Ludgate's machine was the method of sequence control, or the means by which a program determined the machine's behavior. Each row of perforations across the control tape (or formula paper, as he called it) specified an instruction consisting of an operation code, two operations and addresses, and one or two result addresses. As such, the scheme was a definite advance and simplification of that proposed by Babbage and indeed has more in common with that used nearly 40 years later in the Harvard Mark I. Ludgate obviously agreed with Babbage's assessment of the crucial importance of providing a general means of conditional branching, presumably involving having a number of rows of the formula paper skipped, either forward or backward.

---

[14]The use of toothed wheels for such a purpose was already well established; it went back to at least the seventeenth century and Pascal's calculator.

[15]Boys, C.V., "A New Analytical Engine," *Nature*, Vol. 81, No. 2070, July 1, 1904, pp. 14–15.

In dramatic contrast to Babbage's Analytical Engine, Ludgate's machine was to be portable, occupying approximately 8 cubic feet. It was to be capable of multiplying two 20-decimal digit numbers in about 6 seconds. Apparently, he had made detailed drawings of the machine, but had not attempted to construct it.[16]

Highly respected by his colleagues, he was otherwise little known, and the only other significant achievement that was remembered was the major role he played in helping to organize the national provision of animal food supplies during World War I. He died in 1922 at the age of 39. No trace of his papers and drawings has been found.[17]

BIBLIOGRAPHY

Biographical

Randell, Brian, "From Analytical Engine to Electronic Digital Computer: The Contributions of Ludgate, Torres, and Bush," *Ann. Hist. Comp.*, Vol. 4, No. 4, 1982, pp. 327–341.

Significant Publications

Ludgate, P.E., "On a Proposed Analytical Machine," reprinted in Randell, Brian, *Origins of Digital Computers: Selected Papers,* Springer-Verlag, Berlin, 1982, pp. 73–88.

---

[16]Based on Randell 1982.

[17]This is a summary of the information that can be gleaned from the 1909 paper. But who was Ludgate, what was his environment, and what else had he done? My efforts to obtain answers to these questions soon had what seemed to me nearly all the librarians and archivists in Ireland working on my behalf. One initial report I received from an archivist stated that by all normal criteria, it was clear that Ludgate had never existed. Eventually, however, the heroic efforts of the librarian of the Royal Dublin Society, who telephoned all the Ludgates in the Dublin telephone directory, traced Ludgate's niece, who enabled me to obtain his picture and to start assembling an account of his life. It turns out that he had been an accountant, who had, it is believed, done all his work on his machines in his spare time, and on his own.

Brian Randell 1982

J. Lukasiewicz

Developer of the parenthesis-free notation for expressions which is generally known as "Polish notation."

BIBLIOGRAPHY

Biographical

Lukasiewicz, J., *Aristotle's Syllogistic from the Standpoint of Modern Formal Logic*, 2nd ed., Clarendon Press, Oxford, 1957.

Herman Lukoff

Born May 2, 1923, Philadelphia, Pa.; died September 24, 1979, Philadelphia, Pa.; ENIAC, EDVAC, and LARC design engineer.

Education: BS, University of Pennsylvania, 1943.

Professional Experience: Moore School, University of Pennsylvania: junior engineer, ENIAC Computer Project, 1943–1944; research associate, EDVAC Computer Project, 1946–1947; Eckert-Mauchly Computer Corp.: junior engineer, 1947–1948, senior engineer, Univac I, 1948–1950; Remington-Rand Univac: project engineer, 1950–1955, chief engineer, LARC Computer, 1955–1960, manager, computers, Univac Division, 1960–1964, director, engineering, 1966–1968, director, research and advanced technology, 1968–1970; director, technical operations, Univac Division, Sperry-Rand Corp., 1970–1979.

Honors and Awards: IEEE W.W. McDowell Award, 1969; Sperry Univac Presidential Excellence Award, 1976; IEEE Computer Society Pioneer Award, 1980; fellow, IEEE.

Herman Lukoff began his career on the ENIAC project at the Moore School of the University of Pennsylvania. When J. Presper Eckert and John Mauchly left the school to form the Electronic Control Company, Herman went with them and remained with the company through its name change to the Eckert-Mauchly Computer Corporation, its purchase by Remington-Rand, and the merger into the Sperry-Rand Corporation. Herman worked for the same people and the same company—at the time of his death, the Sperry Univac Division of the Sperry Corporation—for 35 years; he participated in and witnessed the entire metamorphosis of the company, and he worked long and hard at whatever job he was asked to perform. He always did the best he could, and he asked for the best and got it from the people working under him.

While still a student at the Moore School he built equipment to test the electronics of ENIAC. Later he helped design the circuits for both delay line memories and electrostatic memories, and showed that in the long run electrostatic memories were unreliable. When work on the Univac I began, Herman designed its input/output control (what would now be called the I/O channel and the magnetic tape-control unit). He supervised the manufacture, testing, and installation of the first dozen Univac Is, thus ensuring that the mass production of such complex electronic gear was feasible. Lukoff was in charge of the design team for the Univac LARC (operational in 1960), which implemented many features of present-day data processing systems, and he headed the Engineering Department from 1960 to 1968, overseeing the design of later systems such as Univac III, Univac 1050, and Univac 9200. Herman initiated the effort to build a semiconductor facility within Sperry Univac to design logic chips, coordinated the computer-aided design project, and was responsible for company standards and internal technical symposia.

In 1969 he was the fourth recipient of the IEEE McDowell Award, presented annually by the IEEE Computer Society. His membership status in IEEE was elevated to the rank of fellow in 1970.

Herman Lukoff helped to design many of the modern features in the LARC system, such as the following:

1. *Multicomputer operation.* A special mailbox was reserved in the memory for each pair of computers that were to communicate with each other. The address of a message was put into the mailbox. A hardware flip-flop ensured that no other message would interfere with this message until it was accepted, and the flip-flop would alert the receiver that a message was present.

2. *Lockout mechanism.* Different parts of the memory could not be altered by the unassigned computer.

3. *Input/output processor.* A vertically microprogrammed machine handled the details of executing many I/O commands in parallel.[18]

BIBLIOGRAPHY

Biographical

Lukoff, Herman, *From Dits to Bits,* Robotics Press, Portland, Ore., 1979.

Tonik, Albert B., "Eloge: Herman Lukoff: 1923–1979," *Ann. Hist. Comp.*, Vol. 2, No. 3, 1980, pp. 196–197.

---

[18]From Tonik 1980.

Neil D. Macdonald

Born March 21, 1909, New York City; died March 7, 1988, Newton, Mass.; longtime contributor to Computers and People, *and alter ego of Edmund Berkeley.*

Lifelong literary collaborator, close associate, and alter ego of the late Edmund C. Berkeley, died March 7, 1988, at the same instant as Ed. Macdonald, although known to many through his writings and editing, was personally known to almost no one.

In addition to being the permanent second editorial banana on Berkeley's magazine, *Computers and People,* he was as prolific a writer as was the proprietor himself. Every issue had contributions from them both, although Macdonald's were usually less serious or abstract than Ed's, running more to puzzles, problems for the reader, and lists of subjects to aid in clear and comprehensive thinking.

Not until Berkeley's death, when Eric Weiss asked his colleague for obituary material, was it discovered that Neil D. Macdonald was an alias Ed used to avoid the appearance that he produced his magazine almost single-handedly. In many ways this trick was characteristic of Ed. It was a gentle, sly, and entertaining joke that harmed no one.

This use of a pseudonymous associate editor and the inward chuckle that surely it gave Ed may be what will be remembered best and longest about the late, great Edmund C. Berkeley.

BIBLIOGRAPHY

Biographical

Weiss, Eric, "Obituary: Neil Macdonald," *Ann. Hist. Comp.,* Vol. 10, No. 3, 1988, p. 217.

JOHN WILLIAM MAUCHLY

Born August 30, 1907, Cincinnati, Ohio; died January 8, 1980, Abington, Pa.; the New York Times *obituary (Smolowe 1980) described Mauchly as a "co-inventor of the first electronic computer," but his accomplishments went far beyond that simple description.*

Education: physics, Johns Hopkins University, 1929; PhD, physics, Johns Hopkins University, 1932.

Professional Experience: research assistant, Johns Hopkins University, 1932–1933; professor of physics, Ursinus College, 1933–1941; Moore School of Electrical Engineering, 1941–1946; member, Electronic Control Company, 1946–1948; president, Eckert-Mauchly Computer Company, 1948–1950; Remington-Rand, 1950–1955; director, Univac Applications Research, Sperry-Rand 1955–1959; Mauchly Associates, 1959–1980; Dynatrend Consulting Company, 1967–1980.

Honors and Awards: president, ACM, 1948–1949; Howard N. Potts Medal, Franklin Institute, 1949; John Scott Award, 1961; Modern Pioneer Award, NAM, 1965; AFIPS Harry Goode Memorial Award for Excellence, 1968; IEEE Emanual R. Piore Award, 1978; IEEE Computer Society Pioneer Award, 1980; member, Information Processing Hall of Fame, Infomart, Dallas, Texas, 1985.

Mauchly was born in Cincinnati, Ohio, on August 30, 1907. He attended Johns Hopkins University initially as an engineering student but later transferred into physics. He received his PhD degree in physics in 1932 and the following year became a professor of physics at Ursinus College in Collegeville, Pennsylvania.

At Ursinus he was well known for his excellent and dynamic teaching, and for his research in meteorology. Because his meteorological work required extensive calculations, he began to experiment with alternatives to mechanical tabulating equipment in an effort to reduce the time required to solve meteorological equations. During the course of that experimentation, he conceived of the idea for an electronic version of tabulating equipment—one that would utilize vacuum tubes.[1]

Mauchly was not proficient in the field of electronics at the time, so he went to the Moore School of Electrical Engineering at the University of Pennsylvania for a summer course in 1941 to enhance his knowledge of electronic devices. He made a very favorable impression on the staff and was asked to stay as an instructor, which he did.

During his first few months at the Moore School, he learned of the institution's contractual work for the Ballistics Research Laboratory

---

[1]Mauchly, J.W., interview with Nancy Stern, May 6, 1977.

(BRL) and of BRL's great need for computational equipment to solve ballistics problems. During World War II, BRL was responsible for producing range tables for new artillery that would furnish gunners with the information they needed to aim and fire the weapons appropriately. The calculations required to prepare these tables were extensive. Because new artillery was being built to meet the needs of the war, the ability of BRL to provide the necessary tables was becoming a matter of increasing concern (Goldstine 1972).

Mauchly suggested to J. Grist Brainerd, the Moore School's liaison with BRL, and to Herman Goldstine, BRL's liaison with the Moore School, that his idea for a vacuum tube computer would resolve some of BRL's problems. In 1942 he wrote a memorandum, "The Use of High Speed Vacuum Tube Devices for Calculating," outlining the features of such a machine (Randell 1975).

Thus, Mauchly not only conceived of the idea for this machine, but also understood how it might be applied to problems in ballistics as well as meteorology.[2] Indeed, this vision was in large part responsible for the Moore School contract to build ENIAC, the first electronic digital computer. ENIAC, an acronym for Electronic Numerical Integrator and Computer,[3] was begun in April 1943 and completed in 1946. It had 18,000 vacuum tubes, 70,000 resistors, 6,000 switches, and 10,000 capacitors. The arithmetic unit consisted of 20 accumulators that could operate on 20 numbers and that functioned as high-speed registers, a high-speed multiplier, and a divider-square-root-er. The total cost to the government was $400,000.[4]

Mauchly was principal consultant for the ENIAC project, and J. Presper Eckert, Jr., the man who became Mauchly's close associate, was chief engineer. Eckert was a consummate engineer who, along with other first-rate engineers at the Moore School such as Arthur W. Burks (who was actually a mathematician), T. Kite Sharpless, and Robert Shaw, was able to develop and construct a reliable electronic computer. The principal investigator was John Brainerd.

When ENIAC was completed in 1946, it received widespread publicity.[5] It was, after all, capable of performing 5000 additions per second; this was considerably faster than any existing device or any

---

[2]The source of Mauchly's concepts has been questioned and the patents taken out by Eckert and Mauchly were invalidated. See biographies of J.V. Atanasoff, Clifford Berry, and Earl Larson.

[3]There has been some discussion whether this latter word was originally "Calculator" or "Computer."

[4]Burks, A.W., "Electronic Computing Circuits of the ENIAC," *Proc. IRE*, 1947, p. 756.

[5]US War Department Press Release, Bureau of Public Relations, Press Branch, University of Pennsylvania Archives, 1946.

machine that was even under development elsewhere. It is no over-statement, then, to suggest that without Mauchly's ideas and his under-standing of how the wartime need could be satisfied by this new inven-tion—and without the engineering expertise of Eckert and his associates—the development of electronic digital computers would have been delayed many years.

During the course of development work on ENIAC, Eckert and Mauchly and their associates recognized many deficiencies in this device that, because of wartime exigencies, could not be modified. The machine was extremely large; it consisted of 30 panels occupying an entire room. It could store only 20 ten-digit numbers. And most critically, it could only receive instructions by the external setting of switches.

In October 1944, the Moore School obtained a supplement to the ENIAC contract for the development of EDVAC, an acronym for Electronic Discrete Variable Automatic Computer, which was to be a stored-program computer with a 1,000-word capacity that would use mercury delay lines for storing data.

During the next 18 months, Mauchly and Eckert and their associates completed ENIAC and began development of EDVAC. John von Neumann became a consultant to the Moore School and assisted the staff in formalizing the stored-program concept for this computer.[6]

In addition to developing the US's first general-purpose electronic digital computer, therefore, Mauchly and Eckert and their associates were also responsible for developing the first machine with stored-program capability. The two inventors left the Moore School in 1946 because of a controversy over the school's new patent policy. At this point, EDVAC was still under development. Their departure seriously inhibited progress on this machine, and it was not actually completed until 1951.[7]

Mauchly was the key figure in developing these machines, and he, perhaps more than anyone else, had a keen awareness of their potential for both scientific and commercial applications. He convinced Eckert in 1946 that the time was ripe for marketing electronic digital computers. Even before commercial and government organizations were aware of the potential of computers, Mauchly was certain that he could apply this equipment to the needs of many users. As a result of his vision, Mauchly was singularly important in effecting the transfer of technology from the academic to the private sector.

---

[6]University of Pennsylvania Archives, March 14, 1945, Notes on meeting with Dr. von Neumann.

[7]Engineering Research Associates, *High Speed Computing Devices*, McGraw Hill, New York, 1950, p. 215.

Mauchly and Eckert were eager to disseminate information about electronic digital computers. The Moore School asked them to give several lectures during a summer course entitled "The Theory and Techniques for Design of Electronic Digital Computers," jointly sponsored by the Office of Naval Research and the Army Ordnance Department.[8] The two inventors were important contributors to this course, which was another critical step in the transfer of technology to other organizations in the US and Great Britain.

In June 1946, Mauchly and Eckert formed a partnership for the purpose of designing and marketing a Universal Automatic Computer, called Univac. This computer was to be used for a wide variety of commercial applications. The Census Bureau, with the National Bureau of Standards as its agent, was the first organization to contract for a Univac.[9]

Eckert supervised the design and construction of the machine. Mauchly was successful at convincing not only the Census Bureau but also several other government agencies, including the Army Map Service and the Air Comptroller's Office, of the feasibility, significance, and great potential of Univac. The government's computers were delivered during the years 1951 to 1953, when Univac became the world's first commercially produced electronic digital computer.[10]

In December 1948, Eckert and Mauchly incorporated, forming the Eckert-Mauchly Computer Corporation. Eckert became vice president, preferring to remain behind the scenes as chief engineer. Mauchly became president and was responsible for contributing to the logic design of the computer, for disseminating information on the company's progress, for contracts with the A.C. Nielsen Company and the Prudential Insurance Company, and for obtaining additional financial backing from the American Totalisator Company.

In general, Mauchly's main objective was to demonstrate the applicability of electronic digital computers for a wide range of problems. He was also interested in providing a forum where people in the computing field could discuss their respective projects. To this end, he was active in founding and organizing the Eastern Association for Computing Machinery in 1947, which later became the Association for Computing Machinery. Mauchly was this organization's first vice presi-

---

[8]University of Pennsylvania Archives, "The Theory and Techniques for Design of Electronic Digital Computers," 3 vols., 1948.

[9]NBS, National Bureau of Standards Contract DA-2, University of Pennsylvania Archives, October 24, 1946.

[10]NBS, "History of NBS Programs for the Development and Construction of Large-Scale Electronic Computing Machines," National Bureau of Standards Archives, n.d.

dent in 1947 and its second president in 1948. He was also a founder and president of the Society for Industrial and Applied Mathematics (SIAM).

Because Eckert and Mauchly were trying to sustain themselves in a high-technology field, they were continually in need of additional capital. In an effort to alleviate some of their financial problems, they undertook a second computer project in 1947 for the Northrop Aircraft Company for design of a small-scale binary computer. BINAC, an acronym for Binary Automatic Computer, was completed in 1949 and became the first US operational stored-program electronic digital computer (Stern 1981). In short, then, Mauchly and Eckert were responsible for four significant "firsts" in the computing field: ENIAC, EDVAC, BINAC, and Univac.

During the late 1940s, American Totalisator had agreed to finance Eckert and Mauchly's research and development work. But in October 1949 the key man responsible for the support, Henry Straus, vice president of Totalisator, was killed in an airplane crash. This put the Eckert-Mauchly Computer Corporation into very serious financial straits. Having exhausted all efforts to obtain additional support, the two inventors sold their company to the Remington-Rand Corporation in February 1950. Remington-Rand then merged with the Sperry Corporation in 1955 to form Sperry-Rand.

Both Mauchly and Eckert continued to work for Remington-Rand. Even after Univac 1 was completed, Eckert remained in his capacity as engineer. Mauchly became directly involved with the logic design and software for Univac, an area that had interested him since his ENIAC days. He made significant contributions to the programming of Univac and was responsible for developing the C-10 programming code.

Mauchly continued to work for the Univac division of Sperry-Rand as director of Univac Applications Research until 1959, when he formed Mauchly Associates, an organization that developed computers for scheduling purposes and introduced the critical path method (CPM) for scheduling by computers. He also formed a consulting company called Dynatrend in 1967.

During his prolific career, Mauchly received many honors. He was the recipient of the Howard N. Potts Medal of the Franklin Institute in 1949, the John Scott Award in 1961, the Modern Pioneer Award of NAM in 1965, the Harry Goode Memorial Award for Excellence in 1968, and the Emanual R. Piore Award of IEEE in 1978.

But like many other pioneers who played an important role in effecting a technological revolution, Mauchly never really received his share of recognition. Despite the tremendous impact computers have had in less than 40 years of development, pioneers in this field are not, in general, well known outside the computing area. Whereas Samuel Morse and Alexander Graham Bell, just to name two inventors, achieved significant fame, Mauchly and his colleagues never received very much publicity. As the *New York Times* stated in a 1971 editorial (Smolowe 1980), it was a "gross injustice" that the names of Mauchly and Eckert were "not likely ever to become household words on a par with the Wright Brothers or Thomas A. Edison, let alone the Beatles." Part of this lack of recognition is a result of litigation that in many instances attempted to minimize the contributions of specific inventors in an effort to invalidate patents. In addition, the fact that the computer field is so new means that historians have not, for the most part, had the opportunity to evaluate the history and the specific contributions of key pioneers. Moreover, in Mauchly's case, his contributions tended to be more intangible than those of engineers and hence more difficult to evaluate.

He was devoted to his family and is survived by his wife, the former Kathleen McNulty, who was a programmer for ENIAC, seven children, 17 grandchildren, and two great grandchildren. It is impossible to mention all his wide-ranging interests and contributions in areas not related to computers, like his invention of snap caps for bottletops and his formation of the Bach Society in Pennsylvania, to name just two.

For most of his life, John Mauchly sought to guide, advise, and educate. He was a person with interesting and even exciting ideas, but he can best be described as highly intelligent, very warm, gentle, and honest. He was always eager to explain the vast potential of computers—especially microcomputers in recent years. His interest in the younger generation was inspiring; indeed, his rapport with young people was truly remarkable.[11]

QUOTATION

Kathleen Mauchly, regarding the challenges to Mauchly's originality of thought with regard to the "invention" of the computer: "In the file were carbons of letters showing that Mauchly had been actively working on a computer at Ursinus—something he had claimed all along." (Mauchly 1984)

---

[11]From Stern 1980.

BIBLIOGRAPHY

Biographical

Anon., "John Mauchly Dies," *Charles Babbage Institute Newsletter*, Vol. 2, No. 1, Jan. 31, 1980, pp. 1, 4.

Berkeley, Edmund C., *Giant Brains or Machines That Think*, John Wiley & Sons, New York, 1949.

Burks, Arthur W., and Alice R. Burks, "The ENIAC: First General Purpose Electronic Computer," *Ann. Hist. Comp.*, Vol. 3, No. 4, 1981, pp. 310–399.

Costello, John, "He Changed the World," *The Washingtonian*, Dec. 1983, pp. 82–100.

Eckert, J. Presper, "The ENIAC," in Metropolis, N., J. Howlett, and Gian-Carlo Rota, *A History of Computing in the Twentieth Century*, Academic Press, New York, 1980, pp. 525–539.

Goldstine, H.H., *The Computer from Pascal to von Neumann*, Princeton Univ. Press, Princeton, N.J., 1972, p. 138.

Larson, E.R., *Findings of Fact, Conclusions of Law and Order for Judgment*, File No. 4–67 Civ. 138, *Honeywell Inc. vs. Sperry-Rand Corporation and Illinois Scientific Developments, Inc.*, US District Court, District of Minnesota, Fourth Division, Oct. 19, 1973.

Mauchly, John W., "The ENIAC," in Metropolis, N., J. Howlett, and Gian-Carlo Rota, *A History of Computing in the Twentieth Century*, Academic Press, New York, 1980, pp. 541–550.

Mauchly, Kathleen, "John Mauchly's Early Years," *Ann. Hist. Comp.*, Vol. 6, No. 2, 1984.

Randell, B., ed., *The Origins of Digital Computers*, Springer-Verlag, New York, 1975, pp. 329–332.

Ritchie, David, *The Computer Pioneers*, Simon and Schuster, New York, 1986.

Slater, Robert, *Portraits in Silicon*, MIT Press, Cambridge, Mass., 1987.

Smolowe, J., "John W. Mauchly, a Co-inventor of the First Electronic Computer," *The New York Times*, Jan. 9, 1980, D21.

Stern, Nancy, "The BINAC: A Case Study in the History of Technology," *Ann. Hist. Comp.*, Vol. 1, No. 1, July 1979, pp. 9–20.

Stern, Nancy, "John William Mauchly: 1907–1980," *Ann. Hist. Comp.*, Vol. 2, No. 2, 1980, pp. 100–103.

Stern, Nancy, *From ENIAC to Univac: An Appraisal of the Eckert-Mauchly Computers*, Digital Press, Bedford, Mass., 1981.

Tropp, Henry S., "John W. Mauchly," in Ralston, A., and C.L. Meeks, eds., *Encyclopedia of Computer Science*, Pertrocelli/Charter, New York, 1976, pp. 871–873.

Tropp, Henry S., ed., "Mauchly: Unpublished Remarks," *Ann. Hist. Comp.*, Vol. 4, No. 3, July 1982, pp. 245ff.

Tropp, Henry S., "Mauchly, John William," in Ralston, Anthony, and Edwin D. Reilly, Jr., *Encyclopedia of Computer Science and Engineering*, Van Nostrand Reinhold Co., New York, 1983.

Significant Publications

Eckert, J. Presper, Jr., John W. Mauchly, Herman H. Goldstine, and J.G. Brainerd, *Description of the ENIAC and Comments on Electronic Digital Computing Machinery*, Contract W/670/ORD 4926, Moore School of Electrical Engineering, Univ. of Penn., Philadelphia, Nov. 30, 1945.

Mauchly, J.W., "The Use of High Speed Vacuum Tube Devices for Calculating," reprinted in Randell, Brian, *Origins of Digital Computers: Selected Papers*, Springer-Verlag, Berlin, 1982, pp. 355–358.

Mauchly, J.W., "Preparation of Problems for EDVAC-type Machines," reprinted in Randell, Brian, *Origins of Digital Computers: Selected Papers*, Springer-Verlag, Berlin, 1982, pp. 393–398.

JOHN MCCARTHY

Born September 4, 1927, Boston, Mass.; one of the fathers of artificial intelligence and creator of the programming language LISP.

Education: BS, mathematics, California Institute of Technology, 1948; PhD, mathematics, Princeton University, 1951.

Professional Experience: Princeton University: Procter Fellow, 1950–1951, Higgins Research Instructor, 1951–1953; Stanford University: acting assistant professor, mathematics, 1953–1955, professor, computer science, 1962–present, director, Stanford Artificial Intelligence Laboratory (SAIL), 1965–1980, Charles M. Pigott Professor of Computer Science, 1987–present; assistant professor, Dartmouth College, 1955–1958; MIT: assistant professor, communications science, 1958–1961, associate professor, communications science, 1961–1962; Bobby R. Inman Professor of Computer Science, University of Texas, Fall 1987; fellow, ACM, 1994.

Honors and Awards: member, American Academy of Arts and Sciences; ACM Turing Award, 1971; president, American Association for Artificial

Intelligence (AAAI), 1983–1984; First Research Excellence Award, International Joint Conference on Artificial Intelligence, 1985; IEEE Computer Society Pioneer Award, 1985; member, National Academy of Engineering, 1987; Kyoto Prize, Inamori Foundation, 1988; member, National Academy of Sciences, 1989; National Medal of Science, 1990; fellow, American Association for Artificial Intelligence (AAAI), 1990; member, American Academy of Arts and Sciences.

At Princeton University, John McCarthy was a Proctor Fellow and later Higgins Research Instructor in mathematics. He was associated with the faculty of Dartmouth College and MIT, and more recently has been Charles M. Pigott Professor of Computer Science at Stanford University.

McCarthy has been interested in artificial intelligence since 1949, and coined the term in 1955 in connection with a proposed summer workshop at Dartmouth College. His main artificial intelligence research area has been the formalization of common sense knowledge. He invented the programming language LISP in 1958, developed the concept of time-sharing in the late 1950s and early 1960s, and has worked on proving that computer programs meet their specifications since the early 1960s. Since 1978, his most recent theoretical development is the circumscription method of nonmonotonic reasoning.

He was chosen as the 1971 ACM Turing Award recipient and awarded the 1988 Kyoto Prize for outstanding accomplishments in advanced technology. He has proposed the design of a new language entitled "Elephant 2000" which will never forget any event in its history, and which would probably not be implemented before the year 2000. Most recently he has been working on formalization in context.

QUOTATIONS

"There's no reason we can't build machines that think." (*National Geographic,* 1982)

"We should try to make AI systems as good as children." (Network posting, July 16, 1987)

Discussing the absence of parentheses in his proposed language "Elephant 2000": "Having invented the language LISP, I decided that I had used up my fair share of parentheses." (Keynote speech, ACM Computer Science Conference, San Antonio, Texas, March 1991)

BIBLIOGRAPHY

Biographical

McCarthy, John, "History of LISP," in Wexelblat, Richard L., ed., *History of Programming Languages,* Academic Press, New York, 1981, Chapter 4.

Significant Publications

McCarthy, John, "A Time-Sharing Operator Program for Our Projected IBM 709," unpublished memorandum, MIT, Cambridge, Mass., reprinted in *Ann. Hist. Comp.,* Vol. 14, No. 1, 1992, pp. 20–21.

McCarthy, John, Paul Abrahams, Daniel Edwards, Timothy Hart, and Michael Levin, *LISP 1.5 Programmer's Manual,* MIT Press, Cambridge, Mass., 1962.

McCarthy, John, S. Boilen, E. Fredkin, and J.C.R. Licklider, "A Time-Sharing Debugging System for a Small Computer," *Proc. Spring Joint Computer Conf.,* Vol. 23, Spartan Books, Washington, D.C., 1963, pp. 51–57.

McCarthy, John, "A Basis for a Mathematical Theory of Computation," in Braffort, P., and D. Hischberg, eds., *Computer Programming and Formal Systems,* North-Holland, Amsterdam, 1963, pp. 33–70.

McCarthy, John, "Programs with Common Sense," in Minsky, M., ed., *Semantic Information Processing,* MIT Press, Cambridge, Mass., 1968.

McCarthy, John, and P.J. Hayes, "Some Philosophical Problems from the Standpoint of Artificial Intelligence," in Michie, D., ed., *Machine Intelligence 4,* American Elsevier, New York, 1969.

McCarthy, John, "Ascribing Mental Qualities to Machines," in Ringle, Martin, ed., *Philosophical Perspectives in Artificial Intelligence,* Harvester Press, July 1979.

McCarthy, John, "Applications of Circumscription to Formalizing Common Sense Knowledge," *Artificial Intelligence,* Apr. 1986.

McCarthy, John, "Generality in Artificial Intelligence," *Comm. ACM,* Vol. 30, No. 12, 1987, pp. 1030–1035; reprinted in *ACM Turing Award Lectures: The First Twenty Years,* ACM Press, New York.

WILLIAM F. MCCLELLAND

Born December 16, 1925, Bronxville, N.Y.; programmed the SSEC for John von Neumann and later a member of the IBM-701 (Defense Calculator) design team from 1950 through 1952.

Education: BS, MIT, 1947.
Professional Experience: staff member, IBM Corp., 1947–1982

McClelland held various management positions in IBM, including serving as the IBM representative to national and international standards organizations. He retired in 1982.

BIBLIOGRAPHY

Biographical

McClelland, William F., "Remarks on Assemblers," *Ann. Hist. Comp.*, Vol. 5, No. 2, Apr. 1983, pp. 117–118.

McClelland, William F., "Activities of the Applied Science Mathematical Committee on the 701," *Ann. Hist. Comp.*, Vol. 5, No. 2, Apr. 1983, pp. 125–127.

McClelland, William F., "A Tracing Program Subordinate to the Given Program," *Ann. Hist. Comp.*, Vol. 5, No. 2, Apr. 1983, pp. 127–131.

McClelland, William F., "Further Developments in Assembly Program," *Ann. Hist. Comp.*, Vol. 5, No. 2, Apr. 1983, pp. 132–133.

DANIEL DELBERT MCCRACKEN

Born July 23, 1930, Hughsville, Minn.; pioneer prolific author of model computing and programming textbooks, including the first[12] textbook on Fortran.

Education: BA, mathematics, Central Washington University, 1950; BA, chemistry, Central Washington University, 1951; MDiv, Union Theological Seminary, 1970.

Professional Experience: General Electric Company, 1951–1958; New York University AEC Computing Center, 1958–1960; self-employed consultant and

---

[12] . . . and probably the most successful (editor).

author, 1959–1981; chairman, Computer Sciences, City College, City University of New York, 1989–1991.

Honors and Awards: president, ACM, 1978–1980; fellow, American Association for the Advancement of Science, 1985; Norbert Wiener Award for Social and Professional Responsibility, 1989; ACM SIGCSE Award for Outstanding Contributions to Computer Science Education, 1992; fellow, ACM, 1994.

Daniel D. McCracken is an author, a former president of the Association for Computing Machinery, and professor of computer sciences at the City College, City University of New York.

His *Digital Computer Programming* (1957) was the first textbook on the subject. Among his 26 titles are works on Fortran (1961, 1965, 1972, 1974, 1984, and 1988), Algol (1962), Cobol (1963, 1970, 1976, 1988, and 1990), and numerical methods (1964 and 1972), all published by John Wiley & Sons. He has also published on PL/M (1978) and Nomad (1981) with Addison Wesley Publishing Co. He is the editor, with Margaret Mead, of *To Love or to Perish: The Technological Crisis and the Churches* (1972). His books have been translated into 15 languages.

McCracken graduated in 1951 from Central Washington University with degrees in mathematics and chemistry, and earned the MDiv degree from Union Theological Seminary (New York) in 1970. After seven years with the General Electric Company in a variety of assignments in computer applications and programmer training, he spent a year at the New York University AEC Computing Center, then (1959) went into full-time consulting and writing on computer subjects. He joined the City College Computer Sciences Department in 1981. He was the chairman of the department from 1989 to 1991, and has served on a wide variety of committees of the College and of the School of Engineering.

McCracken was ACM vice president from 1976 to 1978 and president from 1978 to 1980. He was chairman of the History of Computing Committee of the American Federation of Information Processing Societies (AFIPS), chairman of the ACM Committee on Computers and Public Policy, and a four-time ACM National Lecturer. He has lectured in 49 states, Europe, and Japan. He is the 1989 recipient of the Norbert Wiener Award for Social and Professional Responsibility from Computer Professionals for Social Responsibility. The ACM Special Interest Group on Computer Science Education gave him their 1992 Award for Outstanding Contributions to Computer Science Education.

Other volunteer activities include: president of the Board of Education, Ossining, New York, 1965–1966; member of the board of the Institute for Certification of Computer Professionals, while ACM president; team member or chair for four accreditation visits under auspices of the Computer Sciences Accreditation Board, 1985–1988; and reader for the ACM/IEEE-CS joint task force on computer science curriculum.

QUOTATION

"Don't make predictions about computing that can be checked in your lifetime."

BIBLIOGRAPHY

Biographical

McCracken, D.D., "The Early History of FORTRAN Publications," *Ann. Hist. Comp.*, Vol. 6, No. 1, Jan. 1984, pp. 33–34.

Significant Publications

McCracken, D.D., *Digital Computer Programming*, John Wiley & Sons, New York, 1957.

McCracken, D.D., *A Guide to FORTRAN Programming*, John Wiley & Sons, New York, 1961.

JOHN C. MCPHERSON

Born April 5, 1911; IBM vice president who was very influential in the development of software systems for the 700 series machines.

Education: BS, electrical engineering, Princeton University, 1929.

Professional Experience: IBM Corp.: engineer, 1930–1943; director of engineering, 1943–1946, IBM vice president, 1948, first director, Systems Research Institute, 1960–1965; retired, 1971.

Graduating from Princeton University in 1929 with an electrical engineering degree, McPherson joined IBM in 1930 and began his lifelong interest in novel applications of punched-card machines and computers. He was a pioneer in the use of electromechanical machines for scientific computing. During World War II he was instrumental in the establishment of a punched-card computing facility at the Ballistic Research Laboratory at Aberdeen Proving Ground. As director of engineering at IBM from 1943 to 1946, he participated in the early planning of the SSEC. He was elected an IBM vice president in 1948. He was the first director of IBM's graduate-level Systems Research Institute, from 1960 to 1965. He retired in 1971.

BIBLIOGRAPHY

Biographical

Hurd, Cuthbert, "Early IBM Computers: Edited Testimony," *Ann. Hist. Comp.*, Vol. 3. No. 1, 1981, pp. 163–182.

McPherson, John C., "Early Computers and Computing Institutions," *Ann. Hist. Comp.*, Vol. 6, No. 1, Jan. 1984, pp. 15–16.

Significant Publications

McPherson, John C., et al., "A Large-Scale, General-Purpose Electronic Digital Calculator—the SSEC," originally unpublished 1948; printed *Ann. Hist. Comp.*, Vol. 4. No. 4, Oct. 1984, pp. 313–326.

RICHARD E. (DICK) MERWIN

Born October 2, 1922, East Palestine, Ohio; died August 28, 1981, Washington, D.C.; outstanding pioneer computer engineer who was a contributor to the concepts and implementation of microprogramming.

Education: BSEE, Moore School of Electrical Engineering, University of Pennsylvania, 1943; PhD, University of Pennsylvania, 1965.

Professional Experience: ENIAC Project, Moore School of Electrical Engineering, University of Pennsylvania; MANIAC computer project, Los Alamos National Laboratory; IBM Corp., 1951–1965; deputy director of data processing, US Army Ballistic Missile Defense Program Office, 1965–1977; research professor of computer science, George Washington University, 1977–1981.

Honors and Awards: IBM Academic Fellow, 1961–1965; fellow, IEEE, 1975; ACM SIGMicro Award, 1978.

Richard Merwin was a pioneer in the field of digital computer engineering, and, at the time of his death, was president of the IEEE Computer Society. A 1943 graduate of the Moore School of Electrical Engineering at the University of Pennsylvania, he participated in the development of the ENIAC computer. He then organized the engineering effort for the MANIAC computer built at Los Alamos National Laboratory. He was elected a fellow of the IEEE in 1975 for "development of ferrite core memories and computer hardware and software programs." In 1978, he received the second ACM SIGMicro Award for outstanding contributions to microprogramming.

After participating in the initial development of digital computing, he contributed to the commercial development of digital computers at IBM from 1951 to 1965. He worked on the IBM-702 and 705 computer systems, and was engineering manager of STRETCH, the computer which pushed the technology of the 1950s to its limit, and was a major influence on the design of computers for many years thereafter.

An IBM academic fellow from 1961 to 1965, Dick Merwin earned a doctorate from the University of Pennsylvania. He was deputy director of data processing of the US Army Ballistic Missile Defense Program Office until 1977. Merwin then joined George Washington University in Washington, D.C., as a research professor of computer science, working on microprogramming, software management, and distributed data processing.

Despite a busy and productive career, Dick Merwin found time to become a leader in professional societies. His generosity of spirit and genuine helpfulness were important in the progress of the computer profession. After his untimely death, the IEEE Computer Society established an award for distinguished service in his name.

BIBLIOGRAPHY

Significant Publications

Merwin, R.E., "The IBM 705 EDPM Memory System," *IRE Trans. Electronic Computers,* Vol. EC-5, 1956, pp. 219–223.

ROBERT M. METCALFE

Born 1946, Brooklyn, N.Y.; principal inventor of Ethernet, the local-area networking technology for which he shares four patents.

Education: BS, electrical engineering and management, MIT, 1969; MS, applied mathematics, Harvard University, 1970; PhD, computer science, MIT, 1973.

Professional Experience: Xerox Palo Alto Research Center: Computer Science Laboratory, 1972–1976, manager, Microprocessor and Communication Developments, 1976–1979; founder, 3Com Corporation, 1979–1990.

Honors and Awards: ACM Grace Murray Hopper Award, 1980; IEEE Alexander Graham Bell Medal, 1988.

Robert M. Metcalfe was born in 1946 in Brooklyn, New York. He graduated in 1969 after five years at the Massachusetts Institute of Technology, receiving bachelor's degrees in electrical engineering and in management. From Harvard University in 1970 he received a master's degree in applied mathematics, and in 1973 he received a PhD in computer science for work at MIT Project MAC on packet-switching in the Arpanet and Alohanet, and for his thesis, *Packet Communication.*

Metcalfe joined the Xerox Palo Alto Research Center's Computer Science Laboratory in 1972. In 1973 he was the principal inventor of Ethernet, the local-area networking technology for which he shares four patents. While at PARC he taught part-time at Stanford University for seven years, ending in 1982 as consulting associate professor of electrical engineering with a new course on distributed computing.

In 1976 Bob moved to manage microprocessor and communication developments leading to the Xerox Star workstation. He left Xerox in 1979 to promote local-area networks and especially Ethernet, which has become an international standard, and is today by far the world's most widely installed LAN. Also in 1979, Bob founded 3Com Corporation, which has grown past $400M in annual sales, with more than 2,000,000 of its Ethernet personal computer LAN adapters installed worldwide, and now more than 100,000 being added each month. During his 11 years at 3Com, from inception until retirement in June 1990, Bob held various positions including chairman of the board of directors, chief executive officer, president, vice president of engineering, vice president of sales and marketing, chief technical officer, and general manager consecutively of the software, workstation, and hardware divisions.

In 1980 Metcalfe received the ACM Grace Murray Hopper Award, and in 1988 the IEEE Alexander Graham Bell Medal, both for his invention, standardization, and commercialization of local-area networks. His publications include "Ethernet: Distributed Packet Switching for Local Computer Networks," with David Boggs in *Communications of the ACM* (July 1976), and an invited paper, "Local Networks of Personal Commuters," at the IFIP 9th World Computer Congress, Paris, 1983.

Metcalfe served for a year with the Executive Office of the President's Advisory Committee on Information Networks, and then for two years on the National Research Council's Computer Science and Technology Board. For two years he was chairman of the Corporation for Open Systems, promoting worldwide computer and telephone networking standards.

BIBLIOGRAPHY

Biographical Publications

Metcalfe, R.M., "How Ethernet was Invented," *Ann. Hist. Comp.*, Vol. 16, No. 4, 1994, pp. 81–88.

NICHOLAS (NICK) METROPOLIS

Born June 11, 1915, Chicago, Ill.;developer and implementer of the MANIAC system at Los Alamos Scientific Laboratory.

Education: BS, University of Chicago, 1937; PhD, physics, University of Chicago, 1941.

Professional Experience: research associate, University of Chicago, 1941; research associate, Metallurgy Laboratory, and instructor, Columbia University, 1942; Los Alamos Scientific Laboratory: research associate and group leader, 1943–1946, consultant, 1946–1948, member, staff, and group leader, 1948–1957; University of Chicago and Enrico Fermi Institute of Nuclear Studies: professor of physics, 1957–1965, director, Institutional Computer Research, 1958–1965; Los Alamos National Laboratory: member, staff, 1965–1980, senior fellow, 1981–1985; senior fellow emeritus, 1985–present.

Honors and Awards: Computer Pioneer Award, IEEE Computer Society, 1984; fellow, American Physics Society; fellow, American Academy of Arts and Sciences.

Nick was a staff member of the atomic-bomb project at Columbia University in 1942 and returned to Chicago during 1942–1943 to work on the university's metallurgy project. He was at Los Alamos on the Manhattan Project in 1943. After World War II he taught at the University of Chicago in the Physics Department as an assistant professor of physics, and also at the Enrico Fermi Institute of Nuclear Sciences at Chicago, returning to the Los Alamos Scientific Laboratory (LASL) in 1948 as group leader. During this second visit to Los Alamos he directed the construction of the MANIAC computer, a variant of the IAS machine designed by John von Neumann. From 1957 to 1965 he once again returned to Chicago, where he served as professor of physics and director of the Institute for Computer Research at the University of Chicago. He returned to LASL in 1965 and was appointed a senior fellow in 1980. He became a senior fellow emeritus in 1985, and was the 1992 Oppenheimer Memorial Lecturer.

BIBLIOGRAPHY

Biographical

MacKenzie, Donald, "The Influence of the Los Alamos and Livermore National Laboratories on the Development of Computing," *Ann. Hist. Comp.*, Vol. 13, No. 2, 1991, pp. 179–202.

Metropolis, Nicholas, and E.C. Nelson, "Early Computing at Los Alamos," *Ann. Hist. Comp.*, Vol. 4, No. 4, Oct. 1982, pp. 348–357.

Metropolis, Nicholas, "The Los Alamos Experience, 1943–1954," in Nash, Stephen G., *A History of Scientific Computing*, ACM Press History Series, New York, 1990, pp. 237–250.

Significant Publications

Metropolis, N., and J. Worlton, "A Trilogy of Errors in the History of Computing," *Proc. USA-Japan Computing Conference, First, Tokyo, October 3–5, 1972*, AFIPS, Montvale, N.J., 1972, pp. 683–691; reprinted in *Ann. Hist. Comp.*, Vol. 2, No. 1, Jan. 1980, pp. 49–59.

Metropolis, N., J. Howlett, and Gian-Carlo Rota, *A History of Computing in the Twentieth Century*, Academic Press, New York, 1980.

Metropolis, N., "The MANIAC," in Metropolis, N., J. Howlett, and Gian-Carlo Rota, *A History of Computing in the Twentieth Century*, Academic Press, New York, 1980, pp. 457–464.

Metropolis, N., "The Age of Computing: A Personal Memoir," *Daedalus, American Academy of Arts and Sciences*, 1991, pp. 119–130.

SIDNEY MICHAELSON

Born May 12, 1925, London; died February 21, 1991, Edinburgh, Scotland;
British computer scientist who first applied computers to the identification of
the authorship of manuscripts—and in particular books of the Bible.

Education: BSc (1st class hons.), mathematics, Imperial College, London, 1946.

Professional Experience: associate of Royal College of Science, Imperial College, London, 1945; research assistant, applied physical chemistry, Imperial College, 1945–1947; senior mathematician, Electrical Research Association Laboratories, Perivale, Middlesex, 1947–1949; lecturer, mathematics, Imperial College, 1949–1963; director of computer unit, University of Edinburgh, 1963; head, Department of Computer Science, University of Edinburgh, 1966–1975; professor of computer science, University of Edinburgh, 1966–1991.

Honors and Awards: Royal Scholar, Manchester, 1943; fellow, Royal Society of Edinburgh, 1969; fellow, Royal Society of Arts (London), 1979; fellow, British Computer Society, 1980.

Born and brought up in the East End of London, Sidney Michaelson gained his university education by winning a scholarship to Imperial College, London. He graduated in 1946 with a first-class honors degree in mathematics, and planned to work as a mathematician in the aircraft industry. When this plan was thwarted, he undertook a series of research jobs at Imperial College and at the Electrical Research Association Laboratories before taking up a lectureship in mathematics at Imperial College in 1949. There he worked with K.D. Tocher on the design and construction of digital computers. Although the only technology available to them was very elementary (telephone relays and uniselectors), they built a working machine (ICCE1) based on a principle, subsequently known as microprogramming, which has become the cornerstone of the design of almost all digital computers.[13] His natural modesty led to this work being largely unrecognized.

After a number of productive years pursuing the use of computers in numerical analysis, he was invited in 1963 to establish a Computer Unit at the University of Edinburgh. This became the Computer Science Department in 1966, and he was given the chair of computer science. His attention then turned to the development of systems software for computers. His vision of polymorphic computer systems was

---

[13]The general credit for the creation of microprogramming is given to Maurice Wilkes (see biography herein); there are three other pioneers who had similar ideas—William Tocher, Michaelson, and I. J. Good. As with so many other creations, the time was right, the need was present, and the supporting science was in place to develop an additional step forward in technology.

many years ahead of the available technology and has only recently been achieved in full with the development of networks of workstations. Nevertheless, he and H. Whitfield initiated significant research activity jointly with English Electric Computers to develop a multiuser operating system, common now but breaking new ground then. This system, EMAS, remained in use within Edinburgh University for an unprecedented 20 years.

Michaelson's personal and enduring passion was stylometry, in which his seminal work with Andrew Morton was particularly exciting and rewarding. Stylometry has been defined as the scientific study of the usage of words in an attempt to resolve literary problems of authorship and chronology. Morton and Michaelson used stylometry to cast light on the authorship of texts ranging from the Bible and the *Iliad*, through Elizabethan and Jacobean drama, to modern criminal "confessions."

Nationally, Michaelson played a leading role in establishing and maintaining professionalism within the British Computer Society. He always believed that computing was essentially a practical subject, and he was one of the dedicated band of computing professionals who worked hard to ensure that the society became a recognized institution within the Engineering Council.

Sidney Michaelson was never a dull character; he had a wicked sense of humor and it was sometimes difficult even in the most impassioned of arguments to know whether he was serious or not.

BIBLIOGRAPHY

Significant Publications

Michaelson, S., A.Q. Morton, and N. Hamilton-Smith, "Fingerprinting the Mind," *Endeavour*, 1979.

Michaelson, S., A.Q. Morton, and J. David Thompson, "A Critical Concordance to the Letter of Paul to the Galations," *The Computer Bible*, Vol. 21, Biblical Research Associates, Inc., 1981.

Morton, A.Q., S. Michaelson, and J. David Thompson, "A Critical Concordance to the Acts of the Apostles," *The Computer Bible*, Vol. 7, Biblical Research Associates, Inc., 1976.

Morton, A.Q., S. Michaelson, and J. David Thompson, "A Critical Concordance to I and II Corinthians," *The Computer Bible*, Vol. 19, Biblical Research Associates, Inc., 1979.

Donald Michie

Born November 11, 1923, Rangoon, Burma; code breaker at Bletchley Park and a foremost British pioneer in artificial intelligence.

Education: MA, human anatomy and physiology, Oxford University, 1949; DPhil, mammalian genetics, Oxford University, 1953; DSc, biological sciences, Oxford University, 1971.

Professional Experience: Foreign Office, Bletchley Park, 1942–1945; research associate, University of London, 1952–1958; University of Edinburgh: senior lecturer in surgical science 1958; reader in surgical science, 1962; director, Experimental Programming Unit, 1965; chairman, Department of Machine Intelligence and Perception, 1967; director, Machine Intelligence Research Unit, 1974–1984; Personal Chair of Machine Intelligence 1967–1984; cofounder and first board chairman, University Centre for Industrial Consultancy and Liaison, 1969; chairman of the board of trustees, A.M. Turing Trust, 1975–1984; professor emeritus of machine intelligence, University of Edinburgh, 1984–present; Turing Institute: founder and first executive director, 1983, executive director, 1983–1984, director of research and advanced study, 1984–1986, chief scientist, 1986, senior fellow, 1992.

Honors and Awards: Open Classical Scholarship, Balliol College, Oxford, 1942; Balliol College War Memorial Studentship, 1949; scientific fellow, Zoological Society of London, 1953; fellow, Royal Society of Edinburgh, 1969; fellow, British Computer Society, 1971; Pioneer Award, International Embryo Transfer Society, 1988; fellow, American Association for Artificial Intelligence, 1990; DSc (Hon.), National Council for Academic Awards, UK, 1991; DSc (Hon.), University of Salford, 1992.

Even before he had attended college, Michie joined Britain's brilliant minds at the Government Code and Cipher School at Bletchley Park to work on the breaking of German High Command codes. His contact there with Alan Turing, who laid the basis for the breaking of the Enigma code, implanted an interest in AI and particularly in machine learning, which stayed with him throughout his subsequent career. He was recruited by Max Newman for a mechanized attack on the top-level family of strategic cyphers known as "Fish." With I. Jack Good, he was to have a radical impact on the scope and powers of the new high-speed electronic machines engendered by the collaboration of Newman's group with the British Post Office research team headed by Tommy Flowers. The result of this work was the special-purpose computer known as Colossus.

Donald Michie completed his studies after the war in human anatomy and physiology, and earned a doctorate in mammalian genetics in 1953. Later he returned to the study of the inter-relationships between human intelligence and computers, founded the center for Machine Intelligence at the University of Edinburgh, and later the Turing Institute in Glasgow, Scotland. Dr. Michie is perhaps best known for his farsighted work in artificial intelligence, and for his being on the losing side of a bet with David Levy, the chess master, regarding the date by which a computer program would beat a world master at the game. The rate of improvement of chess playing programs would have caused many of the field to join Michie in his conjecture; in fact, although he lost, he was off by only a few months.

Michie is currently working on the development of software "clones" of real-time human skills. In computer-based flight-simulator tests, the machine learning method employed delivers autopilots that are found to fly complete missions in a more fail-safe style than that of their trained human counterparts.

Michie's work with Alan Turing and his early contributions in artificial intelligence were recently highlighted in the joint BBC/PBS television series entitled "The Machine that Changed the World."

QUOTATION

"Expert knowledge is intuitive; it is not necessarily accessible to the expert himself."

BIBLIOGRAPHY

Biographical

Hinsley, Sir Harry H., and Alan Stripp, *Code Breakers: The Inside Story of Bletchley Park*, Oxford Univ. Press, Oxford, 1993.

Michie, Donald, "Machines that Play and Plan," *Science J.*, Oct. 1968, pp. 83–88.

Michie, D., "The Bletchley Machines," in Randell, Brian, ed., *Origins of Digital Computers*, Springer-Verlag, Berlin, 1973, pp. 327–328.

Michie, D., "The Disaster of Alan Turing's Buried Treasure," letter to the editor, *Computer Weekly*, Mar. 3, 1977, p. 10.

Significant Publications

Barrow, H.G., D. Michie, R.J. Popplestone, and S.H. Salter, "Tokyo-Edinburgh Dialogue on Robots in Artificial Intelligence Research," *Computer J.*, Vol. 14, 1971, pp. 91–95.

Michie, D., "Future for Integrated Cognitive Systems," *Nature*, Vol. 228, 1970, pp. 717–722.

Michie, D., "Machines and the Theory of Intelligence," *Nature*, Vol. 241, 1973, pp. 507–511.

Michie, D., *On Machine Intelligence*, 2nd edition, Edinburgh Univ. Press, Edinburgh, 1986.

Michie, D., "Turing and the Origins of the Computer," *New Scientist*, Vol. 85, No. 1195, 1980, pp. 580–583.

Michie, D., "Turing's Test and Conscious Thought," *Artificial Intelligence*, Vol. 60, No. 1, 1993, pp. 1–22.

HARLAN D. MILLS

IBM innovator and documenter of software productivity techniques, such as the "clean room" concept; leader of the Time/Life project for IBM in which he tested his software development techniques, and which had an extremely low error rate after years of installation.

MARVIN LEE MINSKY

Born August 9, 1927, New York; with John McCarthy, established the basic concepts of artificial intelligence; with Seymour Papert in 1969, solidified the computational limits of Rosenblatt's Perceptron.

Education: BA, physics, Harvard University, 1950; PhD, Princeton University, 1954.

Professional Experience: Lincoln Laboratory, 1957–1958; MIT: professor, mathematics, 1958–1961; professor, electrical engineering, 1958–present; director,

Project MAC AI group, 1968–1970; director, Artificial Intelligence Laboratory, 1970–present.

Honors and Awards: ACM Turing Award, 1969.

Marvin Minsky has probably had more influence, or been a colleague of more people who have had influence, on the development of the concepts of artificial intelligence than any other single person. Over a period of 35 years he has probed most of the classic conjectures of the means to implement or model artificial intelligence. The Perceptron, conceived by Frank Rosenblatt in the mid-1950s, consisted of a set of photocells and random wiring which was capable of "learning" to recognize specific shapes, such as letters of the alphabet, possibly resembling the brain. Minsky and Papert wrote a book on Perceptrons and were able to define their mathematical properties, thereby allowing them to define the limits of the concept. Minsky gave up this field of study; however, in the form of neural nets, the concept is receiving attention again in the 1990s.

In the 1960s Minsky developed new mathematical ideas about artificial intelligence and applied his efforts towards pattern recognition and, eventually, vision. This led to the concept of "frames of information" and to the emergence of the ideas of "knowledge engineering." Throughout this period he worked on robotic devices endowed with vision in the early 1970s. These ideas were put into practical use as a means of inhabiting hostile environments.

QUOTATIONS

"The brain happens to be a meat machine."

"It is unreasonable . . . to think that machines could become *nearly* as intelligent as we are and then stop, or to suppose that we will always be able to compete with them in wit or wisdom. Whether or not we could retain some sort of control of the machines, assuming that we would want to, the nature of our activities or aspirations would be changed utterly by the presence on earth of intellectually superior beings."

BIBLIOGRAPHY

Significant Publications

Minsky, Marvin, "Steps Toward Artificial Intelligence," *Proc. IRE*, Vol. 49, 1961, pp. 8–30.

Minsky, Marvin, *Computation: Finite and Infinite Machines,* Prentice-Hall, Englewood Cliffs, N.J., 1979.

Minsky, Marvin, and Seymour Papert, *Perceptrons,* MIT Press, Cambridge, Mass., 1968.

Clark R. Mollenhoff

Born 1922, Burnside, Iowa; died March 2, 1991, Lexington, Va.; Pulitzer Prize-winning author who in later years championed the cause of John Vincent Atanasoff and who claimed loudly that John Mauchly had perjured himself at the Honeywell vs. Sperry-Rand trial.

Education: BA, Webster City Junior College, 1941; LLB, Drake University Law School, 1944.

Professional Experience: reporter, *Des Moines Register,* 1941–1978; professor, journalism, Washington and Lee University, 1976–1991.

Honors and Awards: Sigma Delta Chi Awards, 1952 and 1954; Pulitzer Prize for national reporting for "persistent inquiry into labor racketeering," 1958; Raymond Clapper Award, 1955; Heywood Broun Memorial Award, 1955; National Headliner Award for Magazine Writing (*Atlantic*), 1960; Society for Professional Journalists' Washington Correspondents' Hall of Fame, 1979; fellow, Society for Professional Journalists, 1980; George Mason Award, Richmond, Virginia Society for Professional Journalists, 1987; University of Missouri's Honor Medal and Award for lifetime contributions in the field of journalism, 1989; six honorary degrees.

Clark R. Mollenhoff, 69, Pulitzer Prize-winning journalist, author, syndicated columnist, and professor of journalism at Washington and Lee University since 1976, died Saturday, March 2, 1991, in Lexington, Va.[14] Mollenhoff was considered by many journalists to be one of the first and best practitioners of investigative reporting. Among the stories he helped uncover were those involving Jimmy Hoffa and Bobby Baker.

---

[14]From Washington and Lee University Press Release, March 1991.

A native of Burnside, Iowa, Mollenhoff graduated from Webster City Junior College in 1941. He received his LLB degree from Drake University Law School in 1944. He was also the recipient of numerous honorary degrees and fellowships.

Mollenhoff began his career in 1941 as a reporter for the *Des Moines Register,* where he covered the operations of city, county, and state governments and the operations of the field offices of federal agencies and courts. Except for service in the Navy, two brief leaves of absence, one of which was in 1949–1950 as a Nieman Fellow at Harvard, and a brief period early in the first Nixon administration when he was the deputy counsel to the president, or "presidential ombudsman," Mollenhoff remained with the *Des Moines Register and Tribune* until 1978. He went to Washington and Lee as a professor of journalism in 1976, a position he held until his death.

In 1946, after two years in the naval reserve including service in the South Pacific as a boat group commander, Mollenhoff returned to the *Des Moines Register* as an investigative reporter and political writer. He continued to spearhead exposure of mismanagement and corruption in city, county, and state government operations.

From 1950 to 1960 Mollenhoff was Washington correspondent for Cowles Publications, covering the national government for the *Des Moines Register and Tribune, Minneapolis Star and Tribune,* and *Look* magazine. His work included in-depth investigations of the operations of nearly every government department and agency.

Mollenhoff took a year's leave of absence in 1960 as an Eisenhower Exchange Fellow. He traveled in Europe, Africa, the Middle East, and Russia on a study of the administration and organization of government and the relations of government and labor organizations in those areas.

Mollenhoff returned to Washington as bureau chief for the Des Moines papers, focusing much of his energy on in-depth investigations of the Defense, State, and Agriculture departments. He eventually became Washington bureau chief in 1970.

Mollenhoff was the author of 11 books, including *Tentacles of Power* (1965), a history of labor racket investigations with particular emphasis on the influence of Jimmy Hoffa's corrupt Teamsters on city, county, state, and federal governments; *The Man Who Pardoned Nixon* (1976), on Gerald Ford's presidency; the best-selling *The President Who Failed—Carter Out of Control* (1980), an analysis of scandals and failures of the Carter presidency; and his last work of investigative journalism, *Atanasoff: Forgotten Father of the Computer* (1988), about the Iowa State College professor who invented the digital computer and fought to earn patent rights. He completed work on a book of poetry, published by Iowa State University Press in fall 1991.

QUOTATION

After 30 years as an indefatigable investigative reporter, Mollenhoff began a second career as a professor of journalism at Washington and Lee. He said of his second career: "Teaching at the undergraduate level . . . is enjoyable to me because of the opportunity for close personal contact with the younger students . . . to have the opportunity to guide, encourage, and, I hope, inspire them as they mature intellectually."

BIBLIOGRAPHY

Significant Publications

Mollenhoff, Clark R., *Atanasoff: The Forgotten Father of the Computer,* Iowa State University Press, Ames, Iowa, 1988.

GORDON MOORE

Born January 3, 1929, San Francisco, Calif.; with Robert Noyce, developer of the semiconductor chip; cofounder and chairman, Intel Corporation.

Education: BS, chemistry, 1950; PhD, chemistry and physics, California Institute of Technology, 1954.

Professional Experience: technical staff, Applied Physics Laboratory, Johns Hopkins University, 1953–1956; staff member, Shockley Semiconductor Laboratory, 1956–1957; Fairchild Semiconductor Incorporated: founder, director of engineering, 1957–1959, director of research and development, 1959–1968; Intel Corporation: founder, executive vice president, 1968–1975, president and chief executive officer, 1975–1987, chairman of the board, 1987–present.

Honors and Awards: fellow, IEEE, 1968;[15] member, National Academy of Engineering, 1976; AFIPS Harry Goode Award, 1978; W.W. MacDowell Award, IEEE Computer Society, 1978; IEEE Frederick Philips Award, 1979; IEEE Computer Society Pioneer Medal, 1984; Medal for the Advancement of Research, American Society of Metals, 1985; Founders Award, National Academy of Engineering, 1988; National Medal of Technology, US Department of Commerce, 1990.

Moore developed his research interest in extending the capabilities of transistors while at Johns Hopkins University, and extended that by working closely with Robert Noyce after they departed Shockley Semiconductor Laboratory to found Fairchild Semiconductor Incorporated. This was a period when Moore was able to implement the concepts and ideas of Noyce to create "wireless clusters" of transistors which formed the basic idea of the "chip." They applied for a patent contemporaneously with Texas Instruments, and were able to convince the court to find in their favor.[16] The biggest boost to the chip and to Fairchild was the announcement in 1964 by IBM of System/360. In 1968 Noyce and Moore left Fairchild to found Intel Corporation and to manufacture memory and processor chips, and thereby created "Silicon Valley."

QUOTATION

Moore's Law (1965 prediction): "The number of transistors on a chip seems to double every year."

BIBLIOGRAPHY

Biographical

Bylinsky, Gene, *The Innovative Millionaires,* Charles Scribner's, New York, 1976.

---

[15]"For contributions and leadership in research, development, and production of silicon transistors, and mono-lithic integrated circuits."

[16]See the biography of Jack St. Clair Kilby.

JOHN NAPIER, LAIRD OF MERCHISTON

Born 1550, Merchiston Castle, Edinburgh, Scotland; died April 3, 1617, Edinburgh, Scotland; developer of logarithms, the "bones" which bear his name, a (binary) chessboard computer, and the promptuary.

Little is known of Napier's younger years, although the Bishop of Orkney encouraged his parents to "send your son Jhone to the schuyllis; oyer to France or Flanderis; for he can leyr na guid at hame, nor get na proffeitt in this maidst perullous worlde." By 1563 (at 8 years of age) he matriculated at St. Salvatore's College, St. Andrews, although there is no evidence of his having graduated afterwards. Perhaps Napier studied on the continent, as was the tradition among the gentry, but he returned to Scotland in 1571, when plans were commenced for him to marry Elizabeth Stirling and to construct a castle at Gartness, where he and his wife took up residence in 1574. Apparently this was a period when Napier was most involved in religious matters and after some involvement with the Protestant movement, he published his first book, *A Plaine Discovery of the Whole Revelation of Saint John,* in 1593. In true Protestant tradition, the treatise interpreted St. John's writings to show that the Pope was also the anti-Christ. During these years Napier had also been working on his other avocation—mathematics—and had commenced writing a book on the art of reckoning, but had abandoned it in favor of his discovery of logarithms, although the latter did not appear in print until 1614. His work on logarithms is all the more astounding when one realizes the restrictions under which he worked—the lack of a notation for a power series, the absence of the decimal point notation, and the only recent introduction of the concept of decimal fractions. The impact of logarithms on the scientific world was immense, and led to the invention of the slide rule, a device which was predominant in calculations for three and a half centuries.

Napier was not satisfied with his invention of logarithms but needed to produce tables of logarithmic values, a task which was not substantially assisted by the existence of logarithms themselves. Napier needed assistance in the computation of logarithmic values, especially in the process of multiplication. He developed the *Rabdologia,* otherwise known as "Napier's bones," to solve this problem. His book on this subject contained the first printed reference to the decimal point and descriptions of two other devices which have not been the subject of extensive review—the "promptuary," an extension of the bones which permitted the multiplication of two multidigit numbers, and the "chess-board computer" for location (positional) arithmetic. The latter is unique in its use of binary notation, although it is not clear that Napier based the design on that notation. With respect to each of these devices, Napier extended their potential to provide the capability of performing a number of additional arithmetic operations including root taking, and finding the diameters and side lengths of polygons.

BIBLIOGRAPHY

Biographical

Horsburgh, E.M., ed., *Handbook of the Napier Tercentenary Celebration or Modern Instruments and Methods of Calculation,* G. Bell & Sons, Edinburgh, 1914; reprinted as Volume 3, Charles Babbage Institute Reprint Series for the History of Computing, foreword by M.R. Williams, Tomash Publishers, Los Angeles, 1982.

Napier, Mark, *Memoirs of John Napier of Merchiston, His Lineage, Life and Times, With a History of the Invention of Logarithms,* William Blackwood, Edinburgh (and Thomas Cadell, London), 1834.

Tomash, Erwin, "The Madrid Promptuary," *Ann. Hist. Comp.,* Vol. 10, No. 1, 1988, pp. 35–69.

Significant Publications

Napier, John, *A Plaine Discovery of the Whole Revelation of Saint John,* private printing, Edinburgh, 1593.

Napier, John, *Mirifici logarithmorum canonis descripto,* private printing, Edinburgh, 1614.

Napier, John, *Rabdologia,* private printing, Edinburgh, 1617; reprinted as Vol. 15, Charles Babbage Institute Reprint Series for the History of Computing, MIT Press, Cambridge, Mass., 1990.

ROGER M. NEEDHAM

*Born February 9, 1935, Birmingham, UK; successor to Maurice Wilkes as the
director of the Cambridge University Computer Laboratory, who maintained
the level and quality of research and innovation.*

Education: BA, Cambridge University, 1956; PhD, Cambridge University, 1961.

Professional Experience: Cambridge Computer Laboratory, 1963–present; head
of department, 1980–present.

Honors and Awards: fellow, Royal Society, 1985; fellow, ACM, 1994.

Roger M. Needham has worked in the Cambridge Computer
Laboratory, and been on the faculty, since 1963, becoming head of the
department in 1980. He worked on the design automation programs
for the Titan computer, and subsequently on its operating system,
being in charge of the multiple-access project at the time of its completion. As part of the Titan system development, Needham developed
the first use of a one-way function to protect the user's password file, a
tactic that has since become almost universally used in secure systems.
Later he led the project to design and build the CAP computer and its
operating system, and after that the Cambridge Distributed
Computing System. In the 1980s he was concerned with major projects
in distributed computing and communications. He was elected to the
Royal Society in 1985.

ALLEN NEWELL

*Born March 19, 1927, San Francisco, Calif.; died July 19,
1992, at Montefiore Hospital in Pittsburgh, Pa.; with
Herbert Simon and John Shaw in 1957, first articulated a
rule-based model of human and computer problem solving.*

Education: BS, physics, Stanford University, 1949;
postgraduate studies, Princeton University,
1949–1950; PhD, industrial administration, Carnegie
Institute of Technology, 1957.

Professional Experience: research scientist, Rand
Corporation, 1950–1961; Carnegie-Mellon University: associate professor, 1961–1976, professor, 1976–1992.

Honors and Awards: AFIPS Harry Goode Award, 1971; ACM Turing Award, 1975; Alexander C. Williams Jr. Award, Human Factors Society, 1979; IEEE Computer Society Pioneer Award, 1980; Distinguished Research Contribution Award, American Psychological Association, 1985; Research Excellence Award, International Joint Conference on Artificial Intelligence, 1989; IEEE Emanuel R. Piore Award, 1990; Louis E. Levy Medal, Franklin Institute, 1992; National Medal of Science, 1992; honorary doctor degrees, University of Pennsylvania, Groeningen University (Netherlands); member, National Academy of Science; member, National Academy of Engineering; member, American Academy of Arts and Sciences; fellow, IEEE.

Newell earned an international reputation for his pioneering work in artificial intelligence, the theory of human cognition, and the development of computer software and hardware systems for complex information processing.

Newell's career spanned the entire computer era, which began in the early 1950s. In computer science, he worked on areas as diverse as list processing, computer description languages, hypertext systems, and psychologically based models of human-computer interaction.

A native of San Francisco, Newell received a bachelor's degree in physics from Stanford University in 1949. He spent a year at Princeton University doing graduate work in mathematics, and worked for the Rand Corporation as a research scientist from 1950 to 1961. While at Rand, he met Nobel Laureate Herbert A. Simon, then a professor of industrial administration at Carnegie Institute of Technology, now Carnegie Mellon University. Their discussions on how human thinking could be modeled led Newell to go to Pittsburgh so the two could collaborate. Newell earned a doctor's degree in industrial administration from CIT's business school in 1957.

Newell joined the CIT faculty as a professor in 1961. He played a pivotal role in creating Carnegie Mellon's School of Computer Science and elevating the school to world-class status.

The fields of artificial intelligence and cognitive science grew in part from his idea that computers could process symbols as well as numbers and, if programmed properly, would be capable of solving problems in the same way humans do. In the 1960s (in particular) Newell and Herb Simon created computer models of human problem-solving. This work was one of the major forces behind the "cognitive revolution" in psychology.

Throughout his research career, his work touched on architectures to support intelligent action in humans and machines. Since the early 1980s his research interests were centered on the development of SOAR, a cognitive architecture realized as a software system capable of solving problems and learning in ways similar to human beings. As a proposed unified theory of cognition, the goal of SOAR is to provide an underlying structure that would enable a computer system to perform the complete range of mental tasks. SOAR has been in use since 1986 as a framework for intelligent system design at research institutions around the world.

Newell, a professor of psychology and Helen Whitaker professor of computer science at the time of his death, wrote and coauthored more than 250 publications, including ten books. He coauthored *Human Problem Solving* with Simon in 1972, and coauthored *The Psychology of Human-Computer Interaction* with two colleagues in 1983. His last book, *Unified Theories of Cognition*, published by Harvard University Press in 1990, is based on the thesis that tools are at hand that will allow psychologists to start to develop a unified theory describing many different types of behavior, instead of building separate theories to cover isolated aspects, as has long been the practice.

Newell's awards and honors include the Harry Goode Award of the American Federation of Information Processing Societies (1971); the A.M. Turing Award of the Association for Computing Machinery, jointly with Simon (1975); the Alexander C. Williams Jr. Award of the Human Factors Society (1979); the Distinguished Research Contribution Award of the American Psychological Association (1985); the Research Excellence Award of the International Joint Conference on Artificial Intelligence (1989); the Emanuel R. Piore Award of the Institute for Electrical and Electronic Engineers (1990); and the Franklin Institute's Louis E. Levy Medal (1992). He was awarded honorary doctoral degrees by the University of Pennsylvania and Groeningen University in the Netherlands.

Newell was a member of the National Academy of Sciences, the National Academy of Engineering, and the American Academy of Arts and Sciences. He was the first president of the American Association for Artificial Intelligence and president of the Cognitive Science Society. In 1987 he delivered the William James Lectures to the Department of Psychology at Harvard. Those lectures formed the basis for his book *Unified Theories of Cognition*.

BIBLIOGRAPHY

Biographical

Anon., "Awards for Scientific Contributions: 1985—Allen Newell," *J. American Psychological Association*, Vol. 41, No. 4, Apr. 1986, pp. 347–353.

Simon, Herbert, and Allen Newell, "Information Processing Language V on the IBM 650," *Ann. Hist. Comp.*, Vol. 8, No. 1, Jan. 1986, pp. 47–49.

Significant Publications

Bell, C.G., and A. Newell, *Computer Structures: Readings and Examples*, McGraw-Hill, New York, 1971.

Newell, Allen, J.C. Shaw, and H.A. Simon, "Chess-Playing Programs, and the Problem of Complexity," in Feigenbaum, Edward A., and Julian Feldman, eds., *Computers and Thought*, McGraw-Hill, New York, 1983, pp. 39–70.

Newell, Allen, J.C. Shaw, and H.A. Simon, "Empirical Explorations with the Logic Theorem Machine: A Case Study in Heuristics," in Feigenbaum, Edward A., and Julian Feldman, eds., *Computers and Thought*, McGraw-Hill, New York, 1983, pp. 109–133.

Newell, Allen, and Herbert A. Simon, *Human Problem Solving*, Prentice-Hall, Englewood Cliffs, N.J., 1972.

EDWARD ARTHUR NEWMAN

Born April 27, 1918, London, England; died August 7, 1993, Surrey, England; computer engineer responsible for significant implementation contributions to the ACE system designed by Alan Turing, and later for work in pattern recognition.

Education: BSc, physics, University College, London, 1940.

Professional Experience: Masteradio, 1940–1941; EMI Research Laboratories, 1941–1947; National Physical Laboratory, 1947–1983.

After graduating in physics at University College, London, Newman spent some time doing postgraduate research and a short period at Masteradio before joining EMI Research Laboratories in 1941. There he worked with the legendary genius of electronics, A.D. Blumlein, on radar including the airborne system H2S. Newman was noted for cycling to Worcestershire where the test flights were carried out. On one of these flights Blumlein and some of his colleagues were killed in a crash.

After World War II, EMI resumed the development of television and the pulse technology from radar proved invaluable. Newman developed advanced circuits for improved cameras that served BBC television for many years. His advice on circuits was much sought after and his ability in lateral thinking is remembered.

Newman moved to the National Physical Laboratory in 1947 to join the project initiated by Alan Turing to build ACE, one of the world's first electronic computers. The engineering of these machines was a puzzle in which there were no guidelines and precious little relevant experience. A "test assembly" was then being built, using dubious electronic designs. Newman was quick to point out their faults, in strong terms, and how to do it better.

He seized the initiative and rapidly translated designs from television and radar into digital circuits. Nothing at the time could match them. This one contribution was a main reason that the ACE project began, at last, to flourish. Together with a colleague from EMI, David Clayden, he made the memory work—the first step towards a complete machine. Newman also produced a new logical design for the machine's central control which was probably the biggest single advance over Turing's original design.[1]

When the machine building ended there was a change of direction in the group, under the leadership of A.M. Uttley (an unsung pioneer of neural networks). Newman undertook to lead the work on pattern recognition and he demonstrated multispeaker recognition of words and phrases, culminating in successful tests for use by military helicopter pilots who needed a "third hand" to set instruments. Newman had an abiding interest in understanding the human brain and kept in touch with Alan Turing who was at Manchester University and was fascinated by this problem. Using the new computer technology to try to understand the brain was a bold and imaginative step, although ahead of its time. Newman had a novel idea about dreaming—that it is a process of reviewing and tidying the short-term memory.

Those early computers were intended for scientific and engineering calculations, and using them for office work, administration, or commerce seemed farfetched; indeed it was a very difficult transition to make. With characteristic vigor Newman set out to make "office automation" a reality. His collaboration with Michael Wright culminated in an influential report for the (UK) Treasury that stimulated the use of computers in Whitehall. The subsequent leaders in the government use of computers all came to the National Physical Laboratory for their training. The practical effect of this second pioneering effort by Newman was immense.

---

[1]See also the biography of Harry Huskey.

During the late 1960s and early 1970s, NPL provided the technical leadership for a large government sponsorship scheme called the Advanced Computer Technology Project. Newman chaired the committee, which vetted new proposals.

Newman was a stimulating colleague, around whom there was always argument and discussion. It is notable that in all his main achievements, there were close collaborators who could develop his ideas and pass them on.

BIBLIOGRAPHY

Biographical

Davies, Donald, "Edward Newman," *The London Times*, Aug. 17, 1993.[2]

MAXWELL (MAX) HERMAN ALEXANDER NEWMAN[3]

Born February 7, 1897, Chelsea, England; died February 22, 1984; leader of the Enigma codebreakers at Bletchley Park during World War II, whose group developed the concept of Colossus; later worked on the Manchester Mark I computer.

Education: BA and MA, St. John's College, Cambridge, 1924.

Professional Experience: Cambridge University: fellow, St. John's College, 1923–1945, university lecturer in mathematics, 1927–1945, honorary fellow, St. John's College, 1973–1984; Manchester University: Fielden Professor of Mathematics, 1945–1964, professor emeritus, 1964–1984; visiting professor, Australian National University, 1964–1965 and 1967; visiting professor, University of Warwick, *and* Michigan State University, 1964–1969; visiting professor, University

---

[2]Written by Donald Davies, but published anonymously.
[3]Changed by deed poll in 1916 from Neumann.

of Wisconsin, Madison, University of Utah, *and* Rice University, 1965–1966; George A. Miller Visiting Professor, University of Illinois, 1969–1970.

Honors and Awards: fellow, Royal Society, 1939–1984; president, London Mathematical Society, 1950–1952; president, Mathematical Association, 1960; De Morgan Medal, London Mathematical Society, 1962; Sylvester Medal, Royal Society, 1968; DSc, University of Hull, 1968.

Maxwell Herman Alexander Newman, known to all his friends as "Max," was born in Chelsea, London, on February 7, 1897, and died on February 22, 1984. His family name was originally Neumann, his father having come from Germany. Max changed his name by deed poll in 1916.

He went to school in Dulwich from 1904 to 1908 and from there to the City of London School. He went up to Cambridge in 1915, having won an entrance scholarship to St. John's College. He remained in residence till December 1916, and then spent the next three years in various forms of national service, including service in the British Army as a paymaster and a stint as a schoolmaster at a school in Epping Forest.

Newman returned to Cambridge in the autumn of 1919. In 1921 he was a wrangler in part II of the mathematical tripos, obtaining a distinction in what was then the equivalent of part III. He was elected a fellow of St. John's College in November 1923, and retained that position until 1945. He had spent the year 1922–1923 in Vienna, where he was strongly influenced by Reidemeister, among others. He was appointed university lecturer at Cambridge in 1927. He visited Princeton as a Rockefeller Research Fellow in 1928–1929 and returned, to the Institute for Advanced Study, in 1937–1938. The School of Mathematics was, at that time, still housed in Fine Hall, and it is interesting to remark that, on the list of permanent and visiting members of the institute, Max Newman's is the only name carrying the simple prefix "Mr."

In September 1942, Newman joined the Government Code and Cipher School (GCCS) at Bletchley Park and remained there for the rest of the war. He was in charge of a section concerned with the machine decipherment of secret German signals. The machines in question (the Bombe and the Colossus) may not inaccurately be described as the forerunners of today's computers.

In September 1945 Newman, already released from his war service, resigned his Cambridge positions to take up his appointment, in succession to Mordell, as Fielden Professor of Mathematics in the University of Manchester, and remained there till his retirement in 1964. During that time he built up a very strong research department and also played a major part in ensuring the university's leading role in the design, development, and scientific utilization of the computer. Not least of his achievements in this direction was his appointment of Alan Turing as reader in mathematics in October 1948.

Newman was largely instrumental, with Hodge and Whitehead, in launching the British Mathematical Colloquium, an institution of vital significance to the mathematicians of the UK. The inaugural meeting of the colloquium was in Manchester in 1949, and Newman was able to call on the cooperation of the members of his department, especially Walter Ledermann, to ensure the success of the enterprise.

In 1962 Newman gave an invited address to the International Congress of Mathematicians, which met in Stockholm in that year. It should be emphasized that such invitations are made in recognition of current work, not past achievements, so that it was a rare event for such an invitation to be received by a person at the age of 65.

On retirement, Newman spent three years (1964–1967) as visiting professor; the first and third years he was at the Australian National University, at the invitation of his erstwhile Manchester colleague, Bernhard Neumann, while the year 1965–1966 was spent at Rice University in Houston, Texas. During this period he remained active in research.

Newman was elected a fellow of the Royal Society in 1939, and was awarded the Sylvester Medal in 1959. He was president of the London Mathematical Society for the years 1950–1951 and was awarded the De Morgan Medal in 1962. He was president of the Mathematical Association in 1959. In 1968 he was given the honorary degree of DSc by the University of Hull, and in 1973 he was elected to an honorary fellowship of his college, St. John's.

In 1934 Newman married Lyn Irvine; they had two sons, Edward and William. His wife was an author and continued to write under her maiden name. Her book *Field with Geese* was a delightful study of the social life of these fascinating birds, based on her experience with the geese living on the farm at Comberton, near Cambridge, which was their home. Lyn died in 1973 and, later that year, Newman married Margaret Penrose, the widow of Lionel Penrose, who survived him.

Max Newman was a man of deep culture and sensitivity. His knowledge ranged over a broad field and he showed a great love of the arts. He was a very accomplished musician and a fine pianist. Bernhard Neumann recalls that when Newman went to the Australian National University on his retirement from the chair at Manchester University, he was scheduled to play a Beethoven piano concerto with a local orchestra—but, unfortunately, the orchestra disbanded.

Newman's Mathematical Contributions

Max Newman's principal contribution to mathematics was in the field of combinatorial topology, where he did pioneering work. He was almost certainly inspired by a desire to prove the *Hauptvermutung,* and it is perhaps not too fanciful to assert that, had it been true, Newman would have proved it. He improved very significantly the notion of a combinatorial move, designed to generate an equivalence relation between combinatorial manifolds. (Incidentally, it is interesting that Newman spoke of the "combinatory method" and "combinatory topology" rather than use the word "combinatorial." This insistence on etymological rectitude is also to be found in his habit of pronouncing the first syllable of "homotopy" with a long vowel, and in his rejection of the neologism "onto," which, if he did encounter it, he humorously pronounced "on-toe.")

Newman's ideas in combinatorial topology exercised a profound influence on Henry Whitehead, whose elementary moves were simply the adaptation of Newman's moves to the more general topological situation he was studying. Thus Whitehead's *simple homotopy theory* was a direct offshoot of Newman's pioneering work. Indeed, Newman's influence on Whitehead went even further, and Whitehead was often heard to testify of his great debt to Max Newman. These two giants of twentieth-century mathematics were the warmest of friends, and all who knew them both recall Newman's profound sadness at Henry's premature death in 1960.

Newman's interest in topology persisted throughout his mathematical career and was rejuvenated by the renaissance of combinatorial, or *geometric,* topology, which began in the 1950s. He gave an invited talk entitled "Geometric Topology" at the Stockholm Congress in 1962, and published an important paper on the engulfing theorem in the *Annals of Mathematics* in 1966. It is important to remark of this later work that Newman showed not only his own mathematical virtuosity unimpaired by age but also a very impressive and unusual mastery of highly sophisticated contemporary ideas.

Newman's original contributions were not confined to topology. He also contributed to mathematical logic, which we may see as the bridge between his early interests in topology and his later interest in computer science.

Newman wrote only one book, *Elements of the Topology of Plane Sets of Points,* which was first published (by the Cambridge University Press) in 1939. A second edition appeared in 1951, and was then reprinted, with fairly minor changes, in 1961. It is beautifully written in the limpid style one would expect of one who combined clarity of thought, breadth of view, depth of understanding, and mastery of language. Newman saw, and presented, general topology as part of the whole of mathematics, not as an isolated discipline, and many must wish he had written more.

Bletchley Park (BP), Government Code and Cypher School (GCCS), 1942–1945

Max Newman was approached in May 1942 to do secret work at Bletchley Park and started work there in September of that year. Turing had been recruited to BP much earlier and Newman fully appreciated the significance of Turing's ideas for the design of high-speed electronic machines for searching for wheel patterns and placings on the highest-grade German enciphering machines, and the result was the invention of the "Colossus" and its systematic exploitation for cryptanalytical purposes. On the other hand, it was not envisaged that the entire process of "setting" a message in the wheels of the encoding machines would, in practice, be mechanized (actually, this was done at the very end of the war, rather to establish an "existence proof" for the method). So the total effort required the cooperation of those who exploited certain statistical biases in the language with the aid of Colossus (that is, the Newmanry), and those who used hand methods to exploit German procedural weaknesses or, in other ways, to complete the task (that is, the Testery).

It does not seem possible to overestimate the importance of Newman's contribution, even though one does not associate the most conspicuous features of the success of the total effort with him in any direct or immediate way. To use an American term, Newman was the great "facilitator"; he ensured that those who worked in this section had the best possible conditions for success and the greatest possible freedom from interference. He was uncannily good at anticipating future needs, with respect to both equipment and personnel. Unobtrusively but with supreme effectiveness, he ensured that no effort of any member of his team was wasted. Anyone familiar with normal civil service procedures will appreciate how remarkable was his success—and therefore ours—and how unusual were the circumstances he created. None of us lacked his encouragement and he understood our needs and met them.[4]

---

[4]Newman died several years *after* the much belated release of information about the work of the GCCS. Newman wrote the Royal Society biography for Alan M. Turing in 1953, several years *prior* to that release of information about the work at Bletchley Park. Of that period Newman was only able to write: ". . . in 1939 war broke out. For the next six years he (Turing) was fully occupied with his duties for the Foreign Office."

University of Manchester

When Newman assumed the Fielden chair at Manchester University in the autumn of 1945, he immediately set to work to create an outstanding mathematics department. He brought to bear two great gifts—on the one hand, his profound knowledge of and excellent taste in mathematics and, on the other hand, his extraordinary administrative flair, which had been in evidence, to such decisive effect, during his war service at Bletchley Park. He shared the responsibility for building up mathematical activity at Manchester University with Sydney Goldstein, the professor of applied mathematics, and they worked very harmoniously together. It should also be remarked that Newman carried with him to Manchester from BP a deep awareness of the potential importance of electronic computers; it was one of his finest achievements to ensure Manchester's leading role in this field. With Turing recruited in 1948 and F.C. Williams and T. Kilburn already on the faculty, Manchester indeed had a formidable team. Newman once again was the "facilitator," the man with the broadest vision, and thus Ferranti was commissioned to build a pioneering machine. One recalls a typical example of Newman's good sense in orchestrating this endeavor—at a certain stage he said, "We are now ready to build Mark I. Any further bright ideas will go into Mark II." For Newman recognized that it would be essential to have a working model in order to know what the operational snags, the "bugs," might be.

Newman, as a fine research mathematician himself, naturally appreciated the role of research in a mathematics department. There was no doubt that research talent and potential constituted the primary criteria for appointment to his department. However, Newman fully recognized that there was a continuity in the spectrum of professional duties of a university mathematician that encompassed both teaching and research.

Newman made it perfectly clear that it was important to try to ensure good teaching. He paid a great deal of attention to course curricula, which were very explicit without, of course, being totally prescriptive; and he was very careful about assigning teaching duties. He introduced the system whereby the entire department scrutinized the proposed examination questions, which had to be accompanied by model answers. His control of the operations of the department was, however, achieved by quiet diplomacy rather than by diktat; he was, in many respects, the model of how a head of department should function.[5]

---

[5]Edited with permission from Hilton 1986.

BIBLIOGRAPHY

Biographical

Adams, J.F., "Maxwell Herman Alexander Newman," *Biographies of Fellows of the Royal Society*, Vol. 31, 1985, pp. 437–452.

Hilton, Peter, "Obituary—M.H.A. Newman," *Bull. London Math. Soc.*, Vol. 18, 1986, pp. 67–72.

Hinsley, Sir Harry H., and Alan Stripp, *Code Breakers: The Inside Story of Bletchley Park*, Oxford Univ. Press, Oxford, UK, 1993.

Randell, Brian, "The Colossus," in Metropolis, N., J. Howlett, and Gian-Carlo Rota, *A History of Computing in the Twentieth Century*, Academic Press, New York, 1980, pp. 47–92.

Ritchie, David, *The Computer Pioneers*, Simon and Shuster, New York, 1986.

Significant Publications

Newman, M.H.A., *Elements of the Topology of Plane Sets of Points*, Cambridge Univ. Press, Cambridge, UK, 1939, 1951, 1961.

RALPH A. NIEMANN

Born 1921, Centralia, Ill.; died June 28, 1988, Springfield, Ohio; early computer user of the Harvard Mark III and supervisor of the NORC and STRETCH installations at the Naval Surface Weapons Center, Dahlgren, Va.

Education: AB, mathematics, DePauw University, 1941; MA, mathematics, University of Illinois, 1942; rector scholar, DePauw University; graduate of the Federal Executives Institute, 1970.

Professional Experience: Naval Surface Weapons Center, Dahlgren, Va.: staff member, 1947–1955, head, Warfare Analysis Department, 1955–1970, assistant technical director, 1970–1972, head, Warfare Analysis Department, 1972–1977, head, Strategic Systems Department, 1977–1979.

Honors and Awards: Navy Meritorious Civilian Service Award, 1970; Admiral John A. Dahlgren Award, 1974; Navy Distinguished Civilian Award, 1975.

"I went to DePauw University and got an AB degree in mathematics in 1941 and in 1942 went to the University of Illinois to get a master's degree in mathematics. Then I got taken into the Army for about 42 months, and after I got out of the Army I worked as a personnel officer at Valley Forge Hospital for about six months. One day I was reading *Popular Mechanics* and I saw that Aiken was building the Mark II computer for the Navy. I gave him a call. He said 'Yeah, come on up for an interview,' and when I got up there first I thought I was going to talk to Aiken. It turned out to be Dr. Bramble who was head of the Computation Department at Dahlgren. Aiken came in later and said, 'Can you use a pair of pliers and a screwdriver?' I said, 'Yes, I think so.' He said, 'Well, there are too damn many mathematicians that can't use a screwdriver and a pair of pliers.' He actually meant it, because over in the Gordon-McKay Laboratory there were people putting the Mark II together. So he had some petty cash there and he insisted on giving me some of it to go down to Dahlgren and get sworn in. I rode the Greyhound bus to Dahlgren and I said to myself, 'Boy, what am I getting into here?' I finally got to Dahlgren and got sworn in by the Personnel Office. Then I went back to Penneysville, Pennsylvania, where I was living at the time, and packed up and moved up to Harvard for six months. Later on I went back for another month when the Mark III was being built.

"They only had one programming manual. In fact they were using it all day so I would slip it out and make copies of it. So I made my own programming manual so that I could study at home at night.

"So then we moved to Dahlgren in February 1948—I came down with the computer. And then during the succeeding months there was a guy by the name of Heizer who used to be at the Census Bureau at one time, and he got a job offer somewhere and he left. And it turns out that everybody was leaving ahead of me and I kept getting promoted. Finally, I became department head and served about 22 years [in that position]. The Mark II is probably the one where I did most of my programming and then on the Mark III I did a little bit, but I didn't do any on the NORC."[6]

Niemann recognized the early potential for using computers to solve massive technical problems and led the implementation of cumbersome exterior ballistics calculations on a succession of "super" computers. Under Niemann's direction the department at Dahlgren led

---

[6]From an unpublished interview by J.A.N. Lee and Henry S. Tropp, 1986.

the field in the Fleet Ballistic Missile Program, and is credited with major contributions to the Polaris, Poseidon, and Trident programs.

QUOTATION

Regarding the Harvard Mark II: "It filled a whole room, and you could look at it, and see things going on, with a paper tape moving like a bicycle chain. You could hear all the clacking, and it was more impressive, in some ways, than modern computers."

BIBLIOGRAPHY

Biographical

Niemann, Ralph A., "Dahlgren's Participation in the Development of Computer Technology," Report #NSWC MP 81–416, Naval Surface Weapons Center (now Naval Surface Warfare Center), Dahlgren, Va., 1982.

DAVID L. NOBLE

Born 1928; led the early development of the floppy disk storage units within IBM, beginning with the first read-only version "Minnow" delivered in 1971.[7]

Education: BS, electrical engineering, Rensselaer Polytechnic Institute, 1940.

Professional Experience: taught at RPI, served in the naval reserve, and was one of the founding engineers of Engineering Research Associates in 1946; 1956 joined IBM in Poughkeepsie; worked on magnetic ink character sensing equipment for banking equipment.

---

[7]Based on Pugh, Emerson W., Lyle R. Johnson, and John H. Palmer, *IBM's 360 and Early 370 Systems,* MIT Press, Cambridge, Mass., 1991.

ROBERT N. NOYCE

Born 1927, Denmark, Iowa; died June 3, 1990, Austin, Texas; with Gordon Moore, the developer of the integrated circuit (or microchip) and semiconductor chips; chairman of the board of Intel Corp.

Education: BS, Grinnell College, 1949; PhD, physical electronics, MIT, 1953.

Professional Experience: Philco Corp., Philadelphia, 1953–1956; research assistant, Shockley Semiconductor Laboratories, 1956–1957; Fairchild Semiconductor Corp., 1957–1968; cofounder and vice chairman, Intel Corp., 1968–1990.

Honors and Awards: Ballantine Medal, Franklin Institute, 1966; Medal of Honor, IEEE; Faraday Medal, IEEE, 1979; National Medal of Science, 1979; National Medal of Technology, 1987; IEEE Computer Society Pioneer Award, 1980; member, National Academy of Science; member, National Academy of Engineering; member, American Academy of Arts and Sciences.

The son of a Congregational minister, Noyce attended Grinnell College, graduated Phi Beta Kappa in 1949, and continued his education at MIT, receiving a PhD in physical electronics in 1953. Noyce's coinvention of the integrated circuit in 1959 transformed Santa Clara Valley's orchards into the world center of high-tech industry, and launched what some people call the second industrial revolution. Fairchild Semiconductor Corporation was the first successful semiconductor company in the valley, and was the training ground for many of the entrepreneurs who later founded other valley companies.

Soon after Noyce and other Shockley engineers founded Fairchild Semiconductor Corporation, his patent application on behalf of the chip was challenged by the Texas Instruments application with Jack Kilby. In 1969 the courts ruled in favor of Noyce. It is generally agreed, in hindsight, that Kilby built the first integrated circuit while Noyce provided a practical implementation that could be commercialized.

BIBLIOGRAPHY

Biographical

Bylinsky, Gene, *The Innovative Millionaires,* Charles Scribner's, New York, 1976.

Caddes, Carolyn, *Portraits of Success: Impressions of Silicon Valley Pioneers,* Tioga Publishing Co., Palo Alto, Calif., 1986.

Noyce, Robert N., and Marcian E. Hoff, Jr., "A History of Microprocessor Development at Intel," *IEEE Micro,* Vol. 1, Feb. 1981, pp. 8–21.

Reid, T.R., *The Chip: How Two Americans Invented the Microchip and Launched a Revolution,* Simon and Schuster, New York, 1984.

Slater, Robert, *Portraits in Silicon,* MIT Press, Cambridge, Mass., 1987.

Wolfe, Tom, "The Tinkerings of Robert Noyce," *Esquire,* Dec. 1983, pp. 346–374.

ROY NUTT

Born 1931, Marlborough, Mass.; died June 14, 1990, Seattle, Wash.; one of two non-IBM contributors to the development of Fortran, and the one who introduced FORMAT into the language as part of his input/output section; later founder and vice president of Computer Sciences Corporation.

Education: BS, mathematics, Trinity College, 1953.

Professional Experience: Programming Research and Development, United Aircraft Corp., 1953–1959; Computer Sciences Corp., founder and vice president, 1959–1988.

Upon graduation with a degree in mathematics from Trinity College, Hartford, Conn., in 1953, Nutt joined the United Aircraft Corporation to work in programming research and development. Shortly thereafter United Aircraft received the ninth model of the IBM Defense Calculator (IBM-701), and when the SHARE user organization was created, Nutt became the company representative. Through this organization he designed and developed the symbolic assembly program (SAP) and was invited to join the IBM team led by John Backus which was developing the original Fortran compiler for the IBM-704. Nutt took charge of the input/output facilities and contributed the concept of FORMAT to the field.

Foreseeing the demand for increasingly sophisticated systems software from computer manufacturers anxious to broaden their markets, he joined with Fletcher Jones to found Computer Sciences Corporation (CSC) in 1959. The two men, each 28 years old, capitalized the company with $100 each. Their first major contract came from Honeywell to build a commercial compiler; the result was FACT (Fully Automatic Commercial Translator).

CSC was successful from the outset, largely due to the innovative solutions that Nutt found to solve technical complexities generated by the rapidly advancing hardware technology. His development of a commercial programming language FACT substantially influenced the design of Cobol. Within a few years the young company was called to developed the entire software suite for the new Univac 1107. The company continued to grow, although Nutt steadfastly resisted the management aspects of the work. Fletcher Jones was unfortunately killed in an airplane accident in 1972; Nutt recruited a new president for the company, William Hoover, but Nutt's influence on the technical aspects of their products was never absent.

BIBLIOGRAPHY

Biographical

Backus, John, "The History of Fortran I, II and III," in Wexelblat, Richard L., ed., *History of Programming Languages,* Academic Press, New York, 1981, pp. 25–74.

Computer Sciences Corporation, "He Wrote Software Like a Song," *CSC World,* Vol. 3, 1990, pp. 2–10.

Nutt, Roy, "Compiler Techniques Available in 1954," *Ann. Hist. Comp.,* Vol. 6, No. 1, Jan. 1984, pp. 20–22.

Weiss, Eric, "Obituary: Roy Nutt," *Ann. Hist. Comp.,* Vol. 12, No. 4, 1990.

KRISTEN NYGAARD

*Born 1926, Oslo, Norway; with Ole-Johan Dahl, the developer of the program-
ming language SIMULA, which introduced the basic concept of "classes" into
the field.*

Education: MS, 1956.

Professional Experience: Norwegian Defense Research
Establishment: staff member, 1948–1960, head, operation research groups, 1957–1960; Norwegian
Computing Center: staff member, 1960–1975, director of research, 1962–1975; professor, Aarhus
University, 1975–1976; professor, University of Oslo,
1976–present.

Nygaard became director of research at the
Norwegian Computing Center in 1962 with the
responsibility of building up the center as a research institute, and
later added the responsibilities for work in operations research and
the development of SIMULA I and SIMULA 67. After working on SIM-
ULA 67, he did research for the Norwegian trade unions on planning,
control, and data processing, all evaluated in the light of the objectives
of organized labor. Other research and development work included
the social impact of computer technology, the general system description language DELTA, and the programming language BETA. His
work at Aarhus and Oslo included research and education on systems
development and the social impact of computer technology. He is a
member of the research committee of the Norwegian Federation of
Trade Unions and has cooperated with trade unions in several countries.[8]

QUOTATION

"We often quoted the story about the two businessmen debating
whether to locate an important software project in the US or in
Europe, the question being settled by the remark 'We have to locate
the project in Europe since in the US it is not possible to put together
a sufficiently small team.'" (Nygaard and Dahl 1981)

---

[8]From Nygaard and Dahl 1981.

BIBLIOGRAPHY

Biographical

Nygaard, Kristen, and Ole-Johan Dahl, "The Development of the SIMULA Languages," in Wexelblat, Richard L., ed., *History of Programming Languages*, Academic Press, New York, 1981.

Significant Publications

Dahl, O., and K. Nygaard, "SIMULA—An Algol Based Simulation Language," *Comm. ACM*, Vol. 9, No. 9, Sept. 1966, pp. 671–682.

HOMER R. (BARNEY) OLDFIELD

Born August 28, 1916, Mount Vernon, N.Y.; as manager of General Electric's Computer Department, put the company into position to become a significant player in the computer business; later, as president of Searle Medidata, introduced the first computerized medical-history taker and associated on-line automated multiphasic health testing system.

Education: BS, aeronautical engineering, MIT, 1938; MS, instrumentation, MIT, 1939.

Professional Experience: research associate, MIT Instrument Laboratory, 1939–1941; US Army, Coast Artillery Board, Project Officer, Microwave Radar 1941–1943; US Army Air Force, 1943–1945; visiting professor, Cornell University, 1951–1952; General Electric Company: Air Force Sales, Gov't. Division, Syracuse, 1945–1948; manager of sales, Gov't. Division, 1948–1949; operations manager, GE Advanced Electronics Center, Cornell University, 1950–1952; director, GE Microwave Laboratory, Stanford, Calif., 1952–1955; general manager, Computer Department, Phoenix, Ariz., 1955–1958; Raytheon: general manager, Equipment Division, Wayland, Mass., 1959–1960; senior vice president, Electronic Components (including two years as general manager, Raytheon Europe, Rome), 1960–1964; DASA Corp., Andover, Mass: general manager and vice president, Data Communications Systems, 1964–1968; G.D. Searle: president, Searle Medidata, Lexington, Mass. (Hospital Information Systems and Multiphasic Health Testing Systems), 1968–1974; Medidata Health Services, Rockville, Md.: part owner and senior vice president, 1975–1989, Far East representative, Kailua-Kona, Hawaii, 1989–1991; semiretired and consultant, 1991–present; free-lance writer, 1989–present.

Honors and Awards: Legion of Merit with Palms; Commendation Ribbon; European Theater Medal with Star; fellow, Institute of Radio Engineers; fellow, International Health Evaluation Association; member, American Medical Informatics Association.

While with the General Electric Company, Oldfield founded two research and development laboratories in association with two major universities. One was the GE Advanced Electronics Center at Cornell University, devoted to radar, countermeasures, and communications R&D for the US government; the second was the General Electric Microwave Laboratory at Stanford, which developed microwave tubes and associated microwave devices. These two laboratories were among the first to establish close industry-university relationships.

Also, with General Electric, Oldfield formed a team including GE, Stanford Research Institute, and the Bank of America to produce the ERMA[1] system for automating the checking account bookkeeping

---

[1]Electronic Recording Machine Accounting

process. The ERMA computer was one of industry's first transistorized computers. The data entry technique of magnetic ink character reading (MICR) direct from checks became the worldwide standard, still in use today after almost 35 years.

Later, as president of Searle Medidata, Inc., a subsidiary of G.D. Searle & Co. (pharmaceuticals), he organized a team of engineers, programmers, biochemists, physicians, and paramedicals to develop a line of computer-based systems for the medical profession. Several of the systems utilizing DEC's PDP-8I and PDP-11, installed in the mid-1970s, were still in active use a quarter of a century later. During this period, he organized the International Health Evaluation Association, which continues to bring together preventive medicine experts from all over the world, and is active in promoting computerized health evaluation techniques.

QUOTATION

"Invented in 1819, the stethoscope was not accepted by physicians for half a century. The computer takes a little longer, but its day will come."

BIBLIOGRAPHY

Biographical

McKenney, James, and Amy Fisher, "The Manufacture of the ERMA," *Ann. Hist. Comp.*, Vol. 15, No. 4, 1993.

ADRIANO OLIVETTI

Born April 11, 1901, Ivrea, Italy; died February 27, 1960, Aigle, Switzerland; Italian manufacturer of Olivetti typewriters, calculators, and computers.

Education: degree in industrial chemical engineering, Turin Polytechnic, 1924.

Professional Experience: Olivetti Company: factory hand, 1924–1925, general manager, 1933–1938, chairman, 1938–1960.

Honors and Awards: Compasso d'Oro, 1955; Architecture Prize, Cercle d'Etudes Architecturelles (Paris), 1956; Edward O. Seits Memorial Award, National Association of Foremen, 1957; honorary doctorate in political and social science, University of Florence, 1962 (posthumous).

Olivetti was an entrepreneur and innovator who transformed shop-like operations into a modern factory. In and out of the factory, he both practiced and preached the utopian system of the "community movement," but he was not an astute enough politician to have a mass following.

The Olivetti empire was begun by his father Camillo, an Italian of Spanish origin; his ancestors, escaping the Inquisition, arrived in Turin in around 1600. Initially the "factory" (30 workers) concentrated on electric measurement devices. By 1908 (25 years after Remington in the US) Olivetti started to produce typewriters.

Camillo, an engineer and innovator, believed that his children could get a better education at home. Adriano's formative years were spent under the tutelage of his mother, an educated and sober woman. Also, as a socialist, Camillo emphasized the nondifferentiation between manual and intellectual work. His children, during their time away from study, worked with and under the same conditions as his workers. The discipline and sobriety Camillo imposed on his family induced rebellion in Adriano's adolescence, manifested by a dislike of "his father's" workplace and by his studying at a polytechnic school subjects other than the mechanical engineering that his father wanted.

Nevertheless, after graduation in 1924, he joined the company for a short while. When he became undesirable to Mussolini's Fascist regime, Camillo sent Adriano to the US to learn the roots of American industrial power. For the same reasons he later went to England. Upon his return he married Paolo Levi, a sister of a good friend, a marriage that produced three children but did not last long.

His visit to the US at various plants and especially at Remington convinced Adriano that productivity is a function of the organizational system. With the approval of Camillo, Adriano organized the production system at Olivetti on a quasi-Taylorian mode and transformed the shop into a factory with departments and divisions. Possibly as a result of this reorganization, output per man-hour doubled within five years. Olivetti, for the first time, sold half of the typewriters used in Italy in 1933. Adriano Olivetti shared with his workers the productivity gains, by increasing salaries, fringe benefits, and services.

His success in business did not diminish his idealism. In the 1930s he developed an interest in architecture, as well as urban and community planning. He supervised a housing plan for the workers at Ivrea (a suburb of Turin, where the Olivetti plant is still located) and a zoning proposal for the adjacent Valle d'Aosta. Under Fascism, patronizing workers at work and at home was in line with the corporative design of the regime. While Adriano showed distaste for the regime, he joined the Fascist Party and became a Catholic. Yet during World War II he participated in the underground anti-Fascist movement, was jailed, and at the end sought refuge in Switzerland. There he was in close contact with intellectual émigrés, and he was able to develop further his socio-philosophy of the community movement.

During the immediate postwar years, the Olivetti empire expanded rapidly, only to be briefly on the verge of bankruptcy after the acquisition of Underwood in the late 1950s. During this period, first calculators and then computers replaced typewriters as the prime production focus. Adriano shared his time between business pursuits and attempts to practice and spread the utopian ideal of community life. His belief was that people who respect each other, and the environment, can avoid war and poverty.

In his enterprises, Adriano Olivetti's attempts at utopia translated in practice as actions of an enlightened boss or a form of corporatism. He decreased the hours of work and increased the salaries and fringe benefits. By 1957 Olivetti workers were the best paid of all in the metallurgical industry, and Olivetti workers showed the highest productivity. His corporatism also succeeded in having his workers accept a company union not tied to the powerful national metallurgical trade unions.

During the 1950s, in a limited way, the community movement succeeded politically in Ivrea. But the utopia at the factory and in Italy at large began withering away even before Adriano's death in 1960.[2]

BIBLIOGRAPHY

Biographical

Anon., "Adriano Olivetti," *Time*, New York, Feb. 8, 1954.

Kent, George, "The Man Who Saves Villages," *Reader's Digest*, New York, Jan. 1957.

---

[2]Based on documents provided by Olivetti Research, Ltd.

Significant Publications

Olivetti, Adriano, "Reflections on the Management of Complex Mass-Production Industry," *Technica ed Organizzione*, No. 3, Ivrea, Italy, May 1937.

Kenneth H. Olsen

Born 1926, Stratford, Conn.; arguably the most successful entrepreneur in the history of American business.[3]

Education: SB, electrical engineering, MIT; SM, electrical engineering, MIT.

Professional Experience: Digital Computer Laboratory, MIT, 1950–1957; founder and president, Digital Equipment Corporation, 1957–1993.

Honors and Awards: Government Computer News Award for Excellence in Information Management, 1986; first IEEE Computer Society Computer Entrepreneur Award, 1987; fellow, Institute of Electrical and Electronics Engineers; member, American Academy of Arts and Sciences; member, National Academy of Engineering; Young Electrical Engineer of the Year, Eta Kappa Nu, 1960; Businessman of the Year, *Bay State Business World*, 1970; Executive of the Year, Society for the Advancement of Management, Boston Chapter, 1970; first person to receive the "President's Award," New England Chapter, Electronic Representatives Association, 1970; New Englander of the Year Award, New England Council, 1977; Entrepreneurial Hall of Fame, Babson College, 1978; Business/Statesman Award, Columbia Business School Club of Boston, 1978; Vermilye Medal, Franklin Institute, 1980; New England Award, Engineering Societies of New England, 1986; first IEEE Engineering Leadership Award; Yale School of Management Award for Entrepreneurial Excellence, 1986; John Ericsson Award, American Society of Swedish Engineers, 1988; American Manager of the Year, National Management Association, 1988; National Inventors Hall of Fame, 1990; MCI Communications Information Technology Leadership Award for Innovation, The Computerworld Smithsonian Awards, June 1992.

Prior to founding Digital Equipment Corporation, Olsen was on the staff of the Massachusetts Institute of Technology's Digital Computer

---

[3]*Fortune* magazine, 1986.

Laboratory for 7 years. His activities there included serving as a leader of the section of MIT Lincoln Laboratory that designed and built the Memory Test Computer (MTC) used in the SAGE Air Defense Computer design program, and supervising the building of the high-performance transistorized digital computers, the TX-0 and TX-2, which set the standard of comparison for transistor circuit performance.

Olsen founded Digital Equipment Corporation in 1957 and served as its president until 1993. Under his direction, DEC grew from three employees in 8,500 square feet of leased space in a corner of an old woolen mill, to become the world's leading manufacturer of network computer systems and associated peripheral equipment, and the leader in systems integration with its networks, communications, and software products. In 1994, DEC had 119,500 employees and 41.4 million square feet of space in over 800 locations throughout the world.

Olsen is a member of the board of directors of Polaroid Corporation and Ford Motor Company; the Corporation of MIT, Cambridge, Mass.; Gordon College, Wenham, Mass.; and the Corporation of Wentworth Institute, Boston, Mass.

He is also a member of the corporation and advisory vice president of the Joslin Diabetes Foundation, Inc., Boston; a member of the corporation of the Museum of Science, Boston; and a deacon of the Park Street Church, Boston.

He has served on the Computer Science and Engineering Board of the National Academy of Sciences, Washington, D.C., and the President's Science Advisory Committee.

A World War II US Navy veteran, Olsen is a fellow of the Institute of Electrical and Electronics Engineers, Inc., and the American Academy of Arts and Sciences, Boston; and is a member of the National Academy of Engineering.

BIBLIOGRAPHY

Biographical

Rifkin, Glenn, and George Harrar, *The Ultimate Entrepreneur: The Story of Ken Olsen and Digital Equipment Corporation*, Contemporary Books, Chicago, Ill., 1988.

ELLIOTT IRVING ORGANICK

Born February 25, 1925, Brooklyn, N.Y.; died December 21, 1985,
Shreveport, La.; foremost expository writer of computer science; a modern-day
Menabrea.

Education: BS, chemical engineering, University of Michigan, 1944; MS, chemical engineering, 1947; PhD, chemical engineering, University of Michigan, 1950.

Professional Experience: chemist, Manhattan Project, 1944–1945; chemical engineer, M.W. Kellogg Co., 1945–1946; United Gas Corp.: senior engineer, 1950–1953, senior research engineer, 1953–1955; University of Houston: associate professor and director, Computing Center, 1955–1963, professor, computer science and chemical engineering, 1963–1971, chairman, Department of Computer Science, 1967–1969; associate director, Ford Foundation Project, University of Michigan, 1960; visiting professor, Project MAC, MIT, 1968–1969; professor, University of Utah, 1971–1980; visiting professor, electrical engineering, Stanford University, 1977–1978; member staff, Inferno Manufacturing Corp., 1980–1985.

Honors and Awards: ACM/SIGCSE Award for Outstanding Contributions to Computer Science Education, 1985.

Elliott was a native of New York City, and received a classical education in Manhattan. He left that island, possibly for the first time, to enroll in chemical engineering at the University of Michigan in 1941. Foreshadowing his capacity for intensive work, he earned the bachelor's degree in three years (1944); then followed two years in industry with the Manhattan Project and the M.W. Kellogg Company. He returned to the University of Michigan and received a master's degree in 1947 and a doctorate in chemical engineering in 1950.

His early industrial work and his university research formed a good basis and the motivation for his career. He was introduced to the complexity of property calculations with the Benedict-Webb-Rubin (BWR) equation by Leo Friend and Walter Lobo of M.W. Kellogg Company. His doctoral research, with professors George Granger Brown and Donald L. Katz in the field of complex hydrocarbon vapor-liquid equilibrium, involved the tabulation, manipulation, and correlation of masses of both coherent and scattered data. As almost a recreational sideline, he and a fellow student, Walter Studhalter, published a complete thermodynamic chart for benzene using the BWR equation of state. All of this work was accomplished with the assistance only of graph paper and mechanical desk calculators. Thus, he finished his student career fully persuaded of the value of such work, but aware of the relentless tedium of longhand calculations with their inherent possibility of errors. He was ready for the appearance of large computers.

During his employment with the United Gas Pipeline Company (1950–1955) his interest turned in good part to computer applications in predicting phase behavior and in chemical engineering in the petroleum industry. Another significant event of this period was the marriage of Elliott and Betty Blanchard in Shreveport, La., in July 1953. In 1955 he enjoyed a brief term as a consultant in computer applications. However, at the urging of his doctoral research adviser he returned to academic life by joining the Computing Center at the University of Houston. Within five years he was director of that center.

In 1959, in response to a joint proposal from the University of Michigan Computing Center and the engineering faculty, the Ford Foundation established a major project to introduce the engineering faculty to the use of computers in engineering education and practice. In the program, released time and expenses were provided to bring faculty from the nation's engineering schools to Ann Arbor for a semester's study and practice with computers. Professor Donald L. Katz, the project director, after a nationwide search for technical leadership in computing, invited Elliott to return to Ann Arbor as associate director. There his responsibility was the organization of all instruction and the selection of teachers for the project.

At that time the available computers included the IBM-650 and the Bendix G-15. His first book, *A Fortran Primer*, was initially published in 1961 and later revised in 1966 and 1974; as the language improved his books kept up. His tenure at Michigan provided him with an insight to the programming language MAD.[4] The result was the *MAD Primer*, which although narrowly circulated, somehow seemed to reach the hands of almost every programming language designer of the next generation. After his year in Ann Arbor, he returned for the summers of 1961 and 1962 to broaden the project with National Science Foundation support to embrace engineering design study.

The Ford Foundation project was exceedingly successful in stimulating the growth of computer use in engineering. Perhaps not until the availability of low-cost microcomputers has such a steep change in computer use occurred again.

During 1968–1969 Elliott took a sabbatical leave at MIT with Project MAC and produced a textbook on the Multics system design, thereby establishing him further as an expository writer. His description

[4]Michigan Algorithm Decoder.

of the design of Multics far exceeded in clarity the technical publications of the implementers.

In 1971 Elliott was attracted to the University of Utah as professor of computer science, with the mandate to shape an innovative undergraduate computer science curriculum. His commitment to learning and professional service led him to assume a variety of leadership positions in ACM. He served six years on the ACM Education Committee and was instrumental in founding the Special Interest Group for Computer Science Education (SIGCSE). He was editor of the education section of the *Communications of the ACM* for two years and editor-in-chief of *Computing Surveys* during six of its formative years, building its circulation to over 30,000.

In the late 1970s Organick became convinced that he had not as yet made a lasting contribution to his profession. He resolved to put aside his book writing and to devote his prodigious energies to research. With his typically uncanny vision, he grasped a way to do this: by hastening the convergence he foresaw between design techniques for hardware and software. In particular he was convinced that the complexity-taming ideas of modern high-level languages, such as top-down design, abstract data types, and tasking, could be used to reap similar benefits for hardware design. He obtained sizable funding and achieved significant results under the banner "Ada to Silicon."

One factor of Organick's urgency was the diagnosis of leukemia about a decade before his death.[5]

QUOTATIONS

"I am such a slow learner that once I understand something I might as well write it down!"

"This is great stuff, but does it *have* to be so complicated?"

BIBLIOGRAPHY

Biographical

Lindstrom, Gary, "Elliott I. Organick: 1925–1985," *Comm. ACM*, Vol. 29, No. 3, Mar. 1986, p. 231.

---

[5]From Lindstrom 1986, and notes provided by Brice Carnahan, Donald L. Katz, Brymer Williams, and J.O. Wilkes.

Significant Publications

Organick, Elliott Irving, *Fortran IV Primer,* Addison-Wesley, New York, 1966.

Organick, Elliott Irving, *Fortran Primer,* Addison-Wesley, New York, 1965.

Organick, Elliott Irving, *Interpreting Machines: Architecture and Programming of the B-5000,* North-Holland, Amsterdam, 1978.

Organick, Elliott Irving, *Multics System: An Examination of Its Structure,* MIT Press, Cambridge, Mass., 1972.

Organick, Elliott Irving, and Loren P. Meissner, *Fortran IV,* 2nd ed., Addison-Wesley, Reading, Mass., 1974.

Organick, Elliott Irving, Alexandra I. Forsythe, and Robert P. Plummer, *Programming Language Structures,* Academic Press, New York, 1978.

DAVID PACKARD

Born September 7, 1912, in Pueblo, Colo.; with William Hewlett, creator of the computer company that bears their names; financial supporter and designer, Monterey Aquarium.

Education: BA, Stanford University, 1934; MS, electrical engineering, Standford University, 1939.

Professional Experience: GE, Schenectady, NY, 1934–1938; cofounder, Hewlett-Packard Corp., 1939; deputy secretary of defense, 1969–1972; chairman, President Reagan's Blue Ribbon Committee Commission on Defense Management, 1985–1986; member, US-USSR Trade and Economic Council Committee on Science and Technology, 1975–1982; chair, US-Japan Advisory Commission, 1983–1985; member, President's Council of Advisors on Science and Technology, 1990, 1991.

Honors and Awards: Honorary degrees from Colorado College, the University of California, Pepperdine University, South Colorado State College, University of Notre Dame, and Catholic University; Founders Medal, the Institute of Electrical and Electronics Engineers (IEEE), to Hewlett and Packard, 1973; Industrialist of the Year, to Hewlett and Packard, California Museum of Science and Industry and California Museum Foundation, 1973; SAMA (Scientific Apparatus Makers Association) Award, to Hewlett and Packard, 1975; Vermilye Medal, to Hewlett and Packard, the Franklin Institute, Philadelphia, 1976.

As a Stanford freshman in 1930, David Packard met fellow engineering student William Hewlett. Their friendship led to founding one of America's most successful companies. From its beginning in 1939, Hewlett-Packard has been a solid partnership, with both men sharing technical and organizational responsibilities. The company was incubated in a garage behind Packard's Palo Alto home.[1] Packard's wife, Lucile, served as secretary and bookkeeper.[2]

David Packard was born September 7, 1912, in Pueblo, Colorado, the son of a lawyer. He avidly read library books on science and electricity as a boy and built his first radio while he was in elementary school. After graduating from his local public high school, Packard enrolled as an electrical engineering student at Stanford University in California. There he met William Hewlett, a fellow student who shared his interest in electronics and the out-of-doors. In college he was a varsity athlete and president of his fraternity; he received a BA with honors in 1934.

After a few months of further work at Stanford, Packard went to Schenectady, New York, to work in the vacuum tube engineering

---

[1]367 Addison Street, Palo Alto, Calif.
[2]From Caddes 1986.

department of General Electric Company. He returned to Stanford in 1938 to study the theory of the vacuum tube.

In 1939 Packard finished his electrical engineering degree under Stanford professor Frederick Terman. By then he had renewed his friendship with Hewlett, who had developed considerable expertise on negative feedback circuits. Hewlett and Packard set up a laboratory in the Packard family garage and soon were taking orders for apparatus ranging from air conditioning control units to electronic harmonica tuners to exercise machines. In 1939 Hewlett-Packard turned its emphasis from custom orders to mass-produced instruments. Particularly important were its audio oscillators, devices that generate a controlled signal at a predetermined frequency, and are generally used to check the performance of amplifiers and broadcast transmitters. Some provided sound effects for Walt Disney's movie *Fantasia.*

During World War II Hewlett-Packard expanded rapidly to meet the needs of various defense projects. Packard ran the company alone, as Hewlett was in the US Army. Business declined sharply at the end of the war, and Hewlett-Packard was forced to lay off employees for the only time in Packard's career. Demand rebounded by 1950; in 1957 the company's stock began to trade on the open market. Hewlett-Packard's product line grew to include not only thousands of electronic measuring devices for a wide range of frequencies but, from 1972, hand-held scientific calculators. The company had done custom work in computer manufacture as early as the 1940s, but did not begin to market its own computers until the late 1960s. Experienced in supplying engineers and scientists, Hewlett-Packard had some difficulty with wider business and consumer markets. Nonetheless, it developed a wide range of programmable calculators, minicomputers, and microcomputers.

Hewlett-Packard was one of the first and largest electronics companies in the region of California now called Silicon Valley. It gradually expanded its sales force from a handful of representatives into a national and then an international network. Manufacturing facilities also extended out of California, not only to Colorado and Oregon but to Europe, South America, and Asia. At the same time, staff trained at Hewlett-Packard came to have important posts at other electronics firms. For example, Stephen Wozniak, cofounder of Apple Computer, first worked at Hewlett-Packard.

With Packard as manager and Hewlett as technical expert, Hewlett-Packard followed conservative but unconventional business practices. Profits were reinvested in the company so that debt was low. Following General Electric's example, the company preferred to hire employees directly out of school. Staff received generous benefits and were entrusted with considerable responsibility. Hewlett and Packard set general objectives, assisted those who carried them out, and chose not to flaunt their wealth and power. Engineering, sales, and management were done by men, while women did much of the actual assembly work. Emphasis was on high quality. To retain the atmosphere of a small business when the staff came to number thousands, Hewlett and Packard divided the company according to product types, with each division having its own marketing, production, and research groups. Support functions such as sales and advertising often were handled by outside contractors.

In addition to his business activities, Packard took an active interest in civic affairs. From 1948 until 1956 he chaired the Palo Alto School Board. In 1968 he favored Nelson A. Rockefeller as the Republican candidate for president. When Richard M. Nixon was nominated and elected instead, the new president sought a skilled administrator to serve as deputy secretary of defense. Packard agreed to take the position, decreasing his salary from nearly a million dollars a year to about $30,000 annually. Congressional critics pointed out that Packard owned about one-third of the stock in Hewlett-Packard and that the company did about $100 million in defense-related business each year. To avoid conflicts of interest, Packard put his stock in a trust fund, with all dividends and capital increases going to charity.

In 1977 Packard returned to Hewlett-Packard as chairman of the board. He also served on the boards of directors of corporations such as Caterpillar Tractor, Standard Oil of California, and Boeing, and was a trustee of the Herbert Hoover Foundation and of the American Enterprise Institute conservative research groups. He was named as one of President Ronald Reagan's informal advisers.

Packard held several patents in the area of electronics measurement and published papers in that field. He received honorary degrees from Colorado College, the University of California, Catholic University, and elsewhere.[3]

BIBLIOGRAPHY

Biographical

Caddes, Carolyn, *Portraits of Success: Impressions of Silicon Valley Pioneers,* Tioga Publishing Co., Palo Alto, Calif., 1986.

---

[3]Based on a biography by Margaret Paull, longtime secretary to David Packard.

DONN B. PARKER

Born October 9, 1929, San Jose, Calif.; SRI International promoter of security measures against computer crime and renowned expert on computer abuses and intrusions.

Education: BA, mathematics, University of California at Berkeley, 1952; MA, mathematics, University of California at Berkeley, 1954.

Professional Experience: programmer, manager of programming, computer operations, General Dynamics Corp., 1954–1962; manager, computer services and computer research, Control Data Corporation, 1962–1969; senior management consultant, director of computer resources, SRI International, 1969–present.

Honors and Awards: Individual Achievement Award, Information Systems Security Association, 1991–1992.

Donn B. Parker is a senior information systems management consultant and researcher on information and computer security and crime, as well as an international lecturer on these topics. He has published *Computer Security Management* (Reston 1983), *Crime by Computer* (Scribner's 1976), *Ethical Conflicts in Computer Science and Technology* (AFIPS Press 1978 and 1988), *Criminal Justice Resource Manual on Computer Crime, Computer Security Techniques* (US Government Printing Office, 1980 and 1989), and *Fighting Computer Crime* (Scribner's 1983). Numerous papers, articles, and reports by Parker have been published in leading journals, trade and news magazines, encyclopedias, edited books, newspapers, and conference proceedings. He consults for leading business organizations, the US Congress and state legislatures, and government agencies on information security. He is the creator of the International Information Integrity Institute (I-4) at SRI International, providing ongoing services to 60 of the largest corporations in the world, those most advanced in the protection of their information assets.

Research on computer abuse has been funded in part by the US National Science Foundation for nine years, for six years by the US Department of Justice, and more recently by the US Department of Defense. Research includes the collection of hundreds of reported cases of computer abuse and crime and field investigation of these incidents to identify vulnerabilities, criminal methods, and security problems. Parker believes that the increasing use of computers and networks, and advances in security, are generally making businesses and their customers far safer from the frequency of losses than ever before, while loss per case is rising dramatically. However, there are many sophisticated criminal methods, such as using Trojan horses and logic bombs, superzapping, leaking data, and using computer viruses and worms, for which effective preventive controls are still lacking. Security must be treated as a "people" problem as well as a technological problem, to preserve u.'ity and availability, integrity and authenticity, and confidentiality of inforι. ~ion through avoidance, deterrence, prevention, detection, mitigation, transference, sanctions, recovery, and correction of accidental and intentional loss.

He has been active in the Association for Computing Machinery and American Federation of Information Processing Societies as a national officer and chairman of the committee on professional standards and practices. He has BA and MA degrees in mathematics from the University of California at Berkeley (1952 and 1954). He has over 40 years experience in the computer field in computer programming, computer systems management, and research, including 22 years at SRI in information security. Recent lecturing, at the rate of 30 presentations per year, covers the subjects of computer abuse, crime, and information security, and their impacts on business, government, and society. He is listed in *Who's Who in the West* and other such publications, was the subject of two articles in *People Magazine*, has appeared on national and international television including *60 Minutes*, *NOVA*, and *20/20*, and is frequently quoted in news and business media.

BIBLIOGRAPHY

Significant Publications

Parker, Donn B., *Crime by Computer*, Scribner's, New York, 1976.

Parker, Donn B., *Ethical Conflicts in Computer Science and Technology*, AFIPS Press, 1978.

Parker, Donn B., *Criminal Justice Resource Manual on Computer Crime*, US Department of Justice, 1980, reprinted 1989.

Parker, Donn B., *Fighting Computer Crime*, Scribner's, New York, 1983.

Parker, Donn B., *Computer Security Management*, Prentice-Hall, Englewood Cliffs, N.J., 1983.

Parker, Donn B., "Applied Research Notes and Baseline Recommendations Reports," SRI/I-4, 1987–1990.

Parker, Donn B., "New Baseline Methodology in Reviewing Security," *Information Age*, 1989.

Parker, Donn B., "Computer Misuse Techniques," National Computer Security Conference, 1989.

Parker, Donn B., "17 Information Security Myths Debunked," IFIP International Conference, Helsinki (1990) and ISSA National Conference (1990), North-Holland, Amsterdam.

Parker, Donn B., "Ethical Conflicts in Computer Science and Technology," AFIPS Press, Arlington, Va., 1979.

JOHN E. PARKER

Born October 26, 1900, Danvers, Mass.; died December 22, 1989; financial member of the group of four who founded the pioneer computer firm Engineering Research Associates (ERA), and later a top executive in a succession of other computer companies.

Education: BS, US Naval Academy, 1922.

Professional Experience: US Navy, 1922–1925; John L. Edwards and Co., 1925; G.M.P. Murphy and Co., 1938; Auchincloss, Parker, and Redpath, 1938–1952; president, Engineering Research Associates, Inc. (ERA), 1946–1951; Remington-Rand: ERA Division, 1952–1953, Electronic Computer Sales Department, 1953–1955; Sperry-Rand, 1955; chairman of the board and chief executive officer, Teleregister, 1955–1969.

Born on October 26, 1900 in Danvers, Mass., John E. Parker was brought up in farming communities in Maine where his family had deep roots. After grade school in Rockland, Maine, and Danvers, his family moved to Boston where he went to the English High School for almost three years, with expectations of going to MIT. Instead, with the aid of a private tutor, he passed the examinations for the US Naval Academy, from which he graduated in 1922. After three years in the Navy, having advanced from ensign to the rank of lieutenant junior grade, he resigned his commission to take over the Washington stock brokerage firm of his dying father-in-law, John L. Edwards and Company.

To learn the brokerage business he started as a runner with Hornblower and Weeks, one of the Edwards' New York correspondents, and went to Washington when his father-in-law died. The Edwards firm was sold to G.M.P. Murphy and Company and within three years Parker had become a partner.

The principal partner was Colonel Grayson M.P. Murphy, a West Point classmate and close personal friend of General Douglas MacArthur, then the Army chief of staff. The Murphy firm had participated in the forming and financing of Pan American Airways, United Airlines, and Northwest Airlines, among other pioneer aviation manufacturing and air transport companies. When Colonel Murphy died in 1938, his firm was liquidated. Parker, now 38, merged the Murphy offices in Philadelphia, Baltimore, and Washington into Auchincloss, Parker, and Redpath, in which he was a partner until 1952.

In his new investment partnership Parker continued the aviation connections. Just at the beginning of World War II, Parker foreclosed on debt-ridden Porterfield Aircraft Company, a tiny, struggling builder of light aircraft in Kansas City, with an Air Corps training airplane proposal. Porterfield, the company founder, resigned and took with him his experienced employees. Parker was unable to interest the Air Corps in a proposal to build troop-carrying wooden gliders, since he had little staff and facilities. To get around this lack he took advantage of his financial connection and board membership in Northwest Airlines and struck a deal with the airline. He formed Northwestern Aeronautical Corporation (NAC) with a capital of $10,000 ($1,000 of his cash and $9,000 of Porterfield equipment). He contracted with Northwest to furnish NAC with staff and space. The advantages to Northwest were that they could participate in the just-starting defense effort and protect their staff from the draft. The advantage to Parker was that he now had a sufficiently credible organization to get a government contract. NAC started building wooden gliders in a leased Northwest Airlines hanger at the Minneapolis airport. A year later the company moved to a government-owned 140,000-square-foot plant at 1902 West Minnehaha Ave. in St. Paul.

By the end of the war, NAC was building 15 gliders a day. Of the 14 firms that had built such gliders during the war, only Ford and NAC were still producing them at the war's end, and NAC had become one of the two or three largest war contractors in the Twin Cities area. When, in the summer of 1945, his wartime contracts were being canceled, Parker had to find some peacetime business for NAC.

Starting ERA

How and why fate selected Parker for the role of ERA's financial angel are obscure, but this was how in 1985 he reconstructed the probable path:[4]

---

[4]Norberg, Arthur L., transcript of "An Interview with John E. Parker," conducted on December 13, 1985 and May 6, 1986 in Washington, D.C., housed in the archive at the Charles Babbage Institute.

At that time, as the war wound down, three Naval Reserve commissioned civilians, Howard T. Engstrom, William C. Norris, and Ralph I. Meader, who had been designing, building, and operating the primitive computers used in cracking and creating codes for the Navy in its secret Communication Supplementary Activity Washington (CSAW), were trying to start their own postwar company to continue the secret work of CSAW outside the Navy and free of civil service restrictions. They were searching for financial backing for a firm that would build computers, and other things, and do computing, and other things, for the Navy, and others. The backing had to satisfy the Navy requirements of secrecy and their own requirements of ownership and scientific freedom. They had tried American Airlines, Socony-Vacuum, Raytheon, Goodyear Rubber, National Cash Register, and many others including New York and English financiers. Nothing had worked. Toward the end of the year, Colonel Nelson Talbot, a Dayton resident, who had administered the Army's glider program, who knew Meader through his National Cash Register connections in Dayton, told Meader to talk to Parker.

The three, Engstrom, Norris, and Meader, told Parker that they had been doing some very classified work in the Navy during the war and they would like to continue to carry on this work and be together. They said if they could get someone to finance the start-up of the company who would give them a half-interest, and certify that he wouldn't try to direct any of their scientific research activities, they would agree to bind themselves to the firm for three years.

Apparently they did not tell Parker precisely what they were doing so, to make sure of what he was getting into, Parker consulted some prominent Navy friends, including the assistant secretary of the Navy and the Judge Advocate's office, about CSAW, its importance, and the qualifications of its three leaders. He said that as far as he was concerned the most significant endorsement came from Admiral Nimitz, chief of Naval Operations, who told him, "I've looked into your background and there's a job that I would like to have you do. It may be more important in peacetime than it was in wartime." To which Parker replied, "Aye, aye, sir!"

Parker always maintained that he never really knew what CSAW was doing, or how they did it, but took on faith the assurances the Navy gave him. Indeed, he took pride in this attitude. When asked how he decided that Engstrom, Norris, and Meader could actually do what they said they could do, Parker said:

There was no judgment on my part as to whether or not they could perform. It was the fact that they had been performing over a period of time, all these years during the war, and they made these accomplishments, and the Navy wanted them to be kept together. I had no way of knowing. It was like taking on the Symphony Orchestra without knowing a note.[5]

The Navy assured Parker that if he could put the firm together, he would get a Navy contract. In his later dramatic description of these negotiations Parker said that he had declared his St. Paul plant surplus and was just moving out of it when he got a call to come to Washington, where he was finally asked if he would take over the as yet unnamed firm.

Parker told this story of how he got the whole CSAW group together in Washington:[6]

> One day I reserved the fourth floor of the Metropolitan Club, main dining room, and I invited, through Norris, and Meader, and Engstrom, all of them to come. I think 92 came with their wives, to meet my wife and me so we could see each other, to see that they were really human beings. They were agreeable to binding themselves together and signing this contract to spend three years. . . . I always give my wife a great amount of credit for this, that we made a fairly favorable impression on them, as they did on me. And this was the start of it. And if I had to do it over again, I wouldn't know how to do it.

In January 1946 Engineering Research Associates, Inc. (ERA) was incorporated. Parker and his investor partners owned half and the technical partners, headed by Engstrom, Norris, and Meader, owned the other half. Total equity invested was $20,000, represented by 200,000 shares of stock at $0.10 per share. Parker and his investor partners arranged for a $200,000 line of credit. In June of that year the Navy, without competitive bidding, issued two cost-plus-fixed-fee contracts; a small one to ERA and a much larger one to NAC, both of which had the same management and occupied the same facilities. The larger one called for the development of special-purpose data processing equipment and specialized communication devices as the Navy would specify. The smaller one was for research studies, consulting services, and training programs, which allowed for the recruiting of personnel not yet cleared for classified work. By the next year, August 1947, when ERA could be considered to be an established company, the NAC contract was replaced by one issued directly to ERA, and NAC was phased out. This contract was Navy Task 13, the design on paper of a general-purpose stored-program computer so highly classi-

---

[5]Ibid.
[6]Ibid.

fied that it was said that, except for those engineers working on the computer's logical design, no one else at ERA knew even the smallest detail about the project. It appears that even Parker was not privy to the whole story.

Parker's Opinions of the Founders

Parker's relations with Meader were always strained for Meader had hoped to control the new enterprise. Parker told Norberg:[7]

> Well, Meader was not a help. He was not one of the scientific people. He was an administrative man. He had run the Navy's Computing Machine Laboratory at National Cash Register during the war and he was a difficult man to handle. He didn't get along with Norris. Engstrom was afraid of him. He was a trial for me too, and I finally bought him out. . . . In early 1950 Meader did his best to get us to sell the company to IBM. He was going to sue me because I could have sold the company and gotten $3 a share. So instead of that, I bought his stock at $3 a share and that's how I got him out of the company. I made the offer available to everybody in the company, every stock holder. Nobody else wanted to pay $3 a share for the stock at that time. And it wasn't worth $3 a share at that time. In my book, it was my contribution to making the company stronger. But it was on the basis that Meader felt that we should have gone with IBM, and that he could get money out of it then. So that's how I happened to buy him out. It turned out all right because when we traded the stock in for Remington-Rand, we got eight dollars and a half in stock for each share. He [Meader] wanted to remain a captain in the Navy and he wanted to be an officer of ERA and he just couldn't serve those two masters. He did get out of the Navy, and although I must give him credit for being one of the three people who put the group together, he was the one person who was a real problem.

Within a week after Meader had been bought out for $30,000, the muck-raking newspaper column "Washington Merry-Go-Round" published an exposé of ERA, charging the Navy and the founders of ERA with self-dealing and conflicts of interest. Parker and his associates suspected Meader of planting the story. The press did not pursue the charge, which never came up again.

Parker had these comments about Engstrom, Norris, and himself:[8]

> Engstrom was a very fine man in many, many ways. He probably was one of the best educated men I ever knew. I looked to him for leadership with the technical group. Bill Norris was really the administrative

---

[7]Ibid.
[8]Ibid.

vice president and did an excellent job in every way. My interactions with Norris were always excellent. He had enough engineering background to be able to communicate with the technical people, although Engstrom was really the leader in that. I always used to feel that this group of people sort of felt sorry for me, this poor fellow sitting up in that front office who didn't know what was going on, you know, and didn't understand any of these really technical things and so forth. I wasn't technically capable of really understanding. I used to go out to every place and I always tried to go through the factory—I call it the factory because that's really what it was—once a day and stop everywhere. Sometimes I'd have Bill Norris, sometimes Howard Engstrom, sometimes Meader, and then I'd have whoever were the other heads of things, and I'd try to assimilate as much as I could. I'll give you an example of what we were doing. When our first complete on-line system was built, Jack Hill was the engineer in charge. . . . I'd say, "Jack, why are you doing this that way?" He'd say, "Don't ask me, go ask Arnold Cohen. He's the one who said to do it this way." And there he is, he's the top engineer! All I'm saying is that this was done by absolute pioneers; a lot of this had never been done before. So, there wasn't anything to compare it with. There wasn't any background. What we had to be able to do was to come up with a finished product to satisfy the customer, which in this case was the Naval Communication Annex and then, of course, the NSA, which is now out at Fort Meade.

ERA History

Erwin Tomash and Arnold Cohen have recorded the history of ERA in detail.[9] As much as possible we do not repeat their story, but confine the story to Parker's role in that history, a role which was chiefly concerned with finance.

The first year, 1946 to 1947, was profitable, not because of the Navy contracts, but because of what Parker called "these little things . . . that we had gotten into." These included a refueling truck for light aircraft, a truck to siphon out airplane septic tanks, a bore-hole camera, a system that weighed railroad cars in motion, a machine that assembled candy bars, an aircraft antenna coupler, and a self-recording accelerometer.

By the end of its first fiscal year, October 1947, ERA reported revenues of $1.5 million and a profit of $34,000. Employment had jumped from 145 to 420. But long-term debt had also increased to $330,000. Parker said:[10]

---

[9] Hakala Associates, Inc., *Engineering Research Associates, The Wellspring of Minnesota's Computer Industry*, in commemoration of ERA's 40th anniversary, Communications Department, Sperry, St. Paul, Minn., undated; no copyright notice.

[10] See note 4.

There were many problems to deal with, most having to do with lack of capital, and it was a constant job keeping everyone happy. I looked upon the company as a symphony orchestra in which a few strings would break now and then. I was just trying to keep the melody going.

As a consequence of Parker's wartime experience with government cost-plus-fixed-fee contracts, he insisted from the very beginning that there be both Navy auditors and General Accounting Office auditors resident on site to approve billable expenses. As an example of how he worked to keep the ERA melody going without upsetting the auditors, he told this story:[11]

In order to keep this group together and to keep happiness as best I could, I took every good excuse I had for giving a dinner. When I got somebody coming out from Washington, for instance, from the Navy headquarters which is now NSA, I would give a dinner. I would have everybody to it, all the engineering, all the technical staff, and I would pay for it myself. None of that ever went into expenses. But having seen that we had those dinners, we got attacks from others because we must have done something wrong. But I'm so happy that I did it that way. Oh, I just know that it made a contribution to keeping those people together.

In a further discussion of the auditing of billable expenses Parker said:[12]

It's the trivial things that kill you, really, on these kind of contracts. For example, Bill Norris and I were coming up from Chicago to Minneapolis together, a four-hour trip by train. We were working on a proposal for another contract. So we took a room on the train for an extra $8 or so. We were working on classified documents that we did not want to expose in the open, and so forth. But this is the type of thing the auditors would seize. It was nit-picking but it was the little things that hurt you, not the big ones. Everybody did the big ones all right.

How Management Functioned

The ERA management committee took up two different kinds of topics. The first kind were all personnel matters: the determination of a health program, a pension program, a vacation policy. The second kind involved the financial aspects of new proposals. Should a proposal be bid on? What price? What profit should be expected? Parker participated in both of these kinds of discussions.

Parker did not participate in technical discussions. Norris, without Parker, would meet with the next lower level of people (Rubens, Hill,

---

[11]See note 4.

[12]See note 4.

Mullaney, and Cohen, for example) to discuss the research and the technical possibilities that could be achieved. Their decisions would be passed up to Parker who, when asked by Norberg if he ever had an effect on any of these decisions, said: "I don't believe so. The only thing I might have had some negative reaction to would be in the financial side of it."[13]

Financial Difficulties

Tomash and Cohen describe how ERA always did splendidly technically, increasing its staff and growing, but always suffering from being under-capitalized.[14] In early 1951 Parker estimated that at least $5 million and perhaps as much as $10 million was needed for ERA to seriously enter the computer business. An internal evaluation of ERA's prospects and needs at that time resulted in the consideration by the management committee of four alternative solutions: slow growth, borrow more money, sell stock to the public, or merge with a stronger company.

The alternatives did not come as a surprise to Parker. His prewar experience with early airlines had taught him that for their first 10 years of growth they had to have more and more money, which they would get on the basis of projections of future growth. He said:[15]

> I was doing the same thing about ERA. We were going to be in the computer business and we were going to need a lot of money. I said, "We can get it. We'll become a public company. We'd have to project and we'd have to do it by little leaps, but we could do it." We got to the point that if we were going to go commercial, we needed lots of money. We could have sold our stock. We had enough background, except the devilish thing at that time was that we were still under wraps about the things for which we had been formed, which was to carry on our secret code work. So we couldn't go into the SEC and show them the background of all these things, and it was a real problem.

Slow growth was not acceptable to the enthusiastic ERA management, and Parker did not consider it feasible to borrow even more money. Thus he saw ERA's only option to be a merger.

According to Tomash and Cohen:[16]

> From 1948 onward he [Parker] had maintained contact with possible purchasers. ERA was never explicitly for sale, but such companies as

---

[13]See note 9.

[14]See note 9.

[15]See note 4.

[16]See note 9.

IBM, ARMA, Burroughs, Honeywell, National Cash Register, and Raytheon were all kept informed of ERA's progress.

When asked specifically about IBM, Parker later said:[17]

> IBM never made an offer, although they gave me every indication in the world that if I would come to them and say I'd like to merge with them, yes. I always said that as long as we were doing what we were and as well as we were, we'd always have IBM as a background. . . . I'm sure that IBM was looking at ERA. There was quite a good deal of pressure for ERA to discuss a possible association with IBM. Engstrom and I met with Mr. Watson, Sr., and the head of his patent department, who later became one of the officers of ERA. Meader and Talbot urged me to deal with IBM. IBM never actually made an offer. They were restricted by antitrust.

In a private communication J.W. Birkenstock, retired IBM vice president to whom the patent department then reported, expressed doubts about this story of a meeting with Watson and of the head of IBM's patent department later joining ERA, and disagreed with some of Parker's criticisms of IBM.

While talking about IBM, Parker gave an opinion about doing business with them:[18]

> For several years I did my best to acquire some business from IBM. Several times we came down to almost having a major contractual product arrangement with IBM, but I always came up against the same block from the IBM standpoint that "it wasn't invented here." Whatever we had, they thought they could do better and they did have the power. . . . It was always my opinion that we had real possible good legal action against IBM, but it came down to points where we could hire one lawyer and they could hire ten.

Sale to Remington-Rand

In the fall of 1951 Parker got a call from a brokerage firm in Boston saying that their client would like to make an offer to buy ERA. Parker met with the Remington-Rand management: James H. Rand, the president; General Douglas MacArthur, chairman of the board; and their chief financial officer. Parker had never courted that company because it already owned Eckert-Mauchly, and because he was annoyed about a personnel raid it had made on ERA in 1949. Negotiations were complicated by the lack of security clearance for any of the Remington-Rand

---

[17]See note 4.

[18]See note 4.

executives, which made it impossible to disclose the nature of most of ERA's products and programs. Final closing of the deal was delayed for some months, due to an investigation by the Federal Trade Commission and antitrust inquiries from the Department of Justice. Parker spent about four months in Washington with the FTC, who finally, "after being educated in the computer business, qualified that they [Remington-Rand] weren't violating antitrust laws and so forth."[19]

In December 1951, Parker announced to a surprised and somewhat dismayed group of ERA shareholder/engineers that he had accepted an offer for the purchase of the company. The price was 73,000 common shares of Remington-Rand worth about $1.7 million. ERA shareholders had their original investment multiplied by 85 in a little more than five years.

The distress of Parker's associates because of the sale was real and, in some cases, permanent. For example, in a private communication in response to Weiss' request for obituary comments on Parker, William C. Norris wrote:[20]

> After he left Univac, we virtually lost contact. I can recall only briefly seeing him twice, and on both occasions at reunions. John Parker and I had deep differences over the future of Engineering Research Associates . . .

In his interview with Norberg, Parker said that part of his reason for accepting the Remington-Rand offer was that ERA would stay as an intact organization, something that would have been impossible if it had been swallowed up by IBM. Parker also said:[21]

> After it was over with [the sale to Remington-Rand] both Burroughs and the Cash Register and others all said, "Gee, why didn't you let us know you were for sale and so forth?" and I said, "Well, it wasn't for sale until somebody came in with an offer that I put up to the stockholders and we felt this was in the best interest of the company to go." I took the position that I would never offer our company for sale but that, if somebody made us a bona fide offer, then I would have to put it up to my stockholders. The professional staff owned 50% of the stock and I owned 50%.

After the sale Parker remained as president of ERA, which was at first a wholly owned subsidiary of Remington-Rand and, about six

[19]See note 4.
[20]Norris, William C., July 9, 1990; private communication.
[21]See note 4.

months later, transformed into a division. ERA, like all the Remington-Rand divisions, operated independently and was in competition in every respect with the Eckert and Mauchly division in Philadelphia and the Norwalk laboratories; most of the computer personnel at Norwalk were former ERA employees acquired by Remington-Rand in the 1949 personnel raid.

At the beginning of 1953, Parker moved to New York to head a newly established Electronic Computer Sales Department. Here is how he described starting in New York:[22]

> I was immediately taken in and introduced to the manager of the New York office. The manager of the real estate division had just passed on and his office was vacant and his secretary was without an assignment, so I was introduced to Miss Quinn and they said this is going to be my secretary and this is going to be my office. The treasurer's office, the general counsel's office, and that type of management was in New York, in this very large building. Eventually, we grew from that one office to three. We had one floor in which we had a Univac system where we did work for hire and used it as a demonstrator for people we were negotiating with. We ran a school for our customers including a two-week introductory course in computers for senior management. We had a three-month programming course and a six-month maintenance course. This, I think, was one of our real contributions to the development of the business.

In New York Parker dealt on a regular basis with the top executives of the merged companies, including Art Rumbles, vice president of sales for the entire Remington-Rand organization; Al Sears, vice president in charge of the New York area, who had close relationships with the financial people; Frank McNamara, general counsel; and patent attorney George Elgroth. He had unlimited contact with General MacArthur, Remington-Rand chairman, to whose New York apartment he took most of his leading prospects. Sometimes he used Jim Rand as his authority for his promises of what Remington-Rand would do, but he preferred to use MacArthur.

Here is Parker's description of how both he and his potential customers would be impressed with a meeting in MacArthur's Waldorf Towers apartment:[23]

> Sometimes Mrs. MacArthur made it, depending on the group of people. And she'd take the people around and show them these mementos that he had gathered all around the world. It was dramatic the way

---

[22]See note 4.
[23]See note 4.

he would come in. His aide would come in first and, you know, everybody would be around the room somewhere, and he'd walk right over to me the first thing and shake hands with me and ask me about my wife, to show that this was a personal relationship, which, fortunately, it was. This goes way back to his mother and my wife's grandmother, who were intimate friends here in Washington. When he [MacArthur] was chief of staff, my senior partner in my banking firm, G.M.P. Murphy and Co., [was MacArthur's] classmate, and they used to come down and use our apartment for private visits. So this goes way back and, I must say, he was magnificent.

Parker's staff grew to 40 or 50 people. He considered himself to be vice president of all electronic computer sales and was independent, from a sales point of view, of Philadelphia, Norwalk, and St. Paul, although he had in his department representatives from each of these fiefdoms. His sales presentations to customers included seminars on products from all three locations, although he said that Norwalk really supplied practically nothing. In addition to Parker's central sales organization, each of the three subdivisions had sales organizations with representation in the principal US cities.

Parker said that there was a very good working relationship between his staff and the laboratories and, when asked about the relationship between Philadelphia and St. Paul, he replied:[24]

> Well, I think the best answer to that is the Univac II, which was a product of a cooperation between St. Paul and Philadelphia. Primarily, I give credit for the development of Univac II to St. Paul.

When pressed further on the question of friction between the two divisions, Parker responded with an anecdote about J. Presper Eckert of the Philadelphia division:[25]

> I don't really think so. Do you know Eckert? . . . There's just no way that anybody could deal consistently with him without having some friction, but nothing, nothing that I took seriously. . . . He's a very unusual man. Very unusual. . . . For instance, once upon a time I invited him to come to a meeting I was having with the senior people of the Metropolitan Life Insurance Company: the chairman, the president, several officers. He came in and talked about the future. He made everything that Metropolitan Life had, obsolete. Why did they already have this, when what "Pres" was proposing was going to be so much better. This was typical. He was primarily a developer, an engineer. Not a salesman.

---

[24]See note 4.

[25]See note 4.

Parker met resistance to the computer business from other Remington-Rand divisions. For example, he said:[26]

> Within the management there were people who just didn't believe. People like the president himself [James Rand], who said that he didn't see any future in the computer business. As an example, the president of the shaver division—that used to be a very profitable unit of the company—didn't want to see any moneys spent for development work, research and development, in this field [computing]. At one meeting we had in front of the management, he made the statement that if we ever sold five of these machines that he would have a statue built for me in the front yard.

Merger with Sperry

As Tomash and Cohen point out, under Parker's sales leadership Remington-Rand had computers in place, ahead of IBM, at General Electric, US Steel, Westinghouse, and Metropolitan Life, but, because it was primarily a rental and service business, the more Parker succeeded, the more cash Remington-Rand required.[27] By 1955 James Rand belatedly recognized that his firm did not have the resources necessary to maintain a position of market leadership and sought a stronger partner. In June 1955 the Sperry Corporation and Remington-Rand merged to form the Sperry-Rand Corporation.

When Sperry bought Remington-Rand, Parker recalled that the president of Sperry said he was never going to put another cent into the development of the computer business. He didn't think it was necessary. Parker remarked:[28]

> This was where Remington-Rand lost its lead with IBM and it took ten years for them to get back into business.

Soon after this merger, Parker left the company. This is how he described that step:

> I said, "I've made speeches all across this country about Remington-Rand and our staff and our ability, that we were always going to continue to keep pace with the advancement of the technology. I just can't go back and say that we're not going to do any of these new things." I asked for a hearing before the board, which Harvey Vickers, president of Sperry, didn't grant me, but I did appear before part of the executive committee.

---

[26]See note 4.

[27]See note 9.

[28]See note 4.

Parker made a rather impassioned plea that the only way that Univac could maintain its market preeminence over IBM was to continue to invest capital and persist in funding research and development. Faced with a choice of backing Parker, then a senior vice president, or the chairman and chief executive officer, the committee chose to defer to Vickers and follow what proved to be his short-sighted judgment.

That fall, Norris was moved from being head of the ERA Division to be the first general manager of a newly consolidated Univac Division that now included all the previously independent divisions. Parker commented:[29]

> When they put Bill Norris in, I told them that they couldn't find a finer man in every respect to do this, but if he had to work under the conditions under which I had had to work, I didn't give him two years to stay with the company. Bill only stayed about eight months.

Life after Univac

After leaving Univac, Parker was an independent consultant for several years and became well known to Charles and Herbert Allen, who controlled Allen & Company, a New York City investment banking firm that indirectly controlled Teleregister.[30] Teleregister had been a pioneer in the airline reservation systems after having installed the early railroad reservation systems; in 1947 Teleregister provided American Airlines with the first on-line real-time reservation system at their Boston and New York terminals. In 1961 Teleregister was the principal supplier of stock quotation systems in the form of large "tote" boards in brokerage offices. At that time the business was just beginning to utilize desktop access devices, and Teleregister was in the forefront of these developments.

Under its previous CEO, Teleregister encountered technical and financial problems, causing the Allens to seek outside help. They hired Parker as chairman of the board and chief executive officer because of his expertise in the data-processing industry and his background in finance.

In 1964 the Bunker Ramo Corporation, then a defense contractor engaged in the military data processing and process control business

---

[29]See note 4.

[30]Sheehan, Dennis W., September 27, 1990; private communication.

and owned jointly by Martin Marietta and Thompson Ramo Wooldridge, was merged with Teleregister. Parker continued as chairman of the board and was the principal executive officer of the merged company. The company grew, through mergers and acquisitions, from approximately $35 million in 1964 to $359 million in 1974. Parker retired from the firm in 1969, when almost 70, and from the board of directors, because of the age policy at Bunker Ramo, in 1973 or 1974.

In a personal letter to Eric Weiss, Mrs. Marshall Pritchett, Parker's last personal secretary, listed from memory the boards on which he served in the period that she knew him (late 1960s to 1989): Northwest Airlines, Hall-Scott, Brown Co., Slick Airways, Airlift International, Ambac (now United Technologies), Martin-Marietta, National Savings and Trust Co. (now Crestar Bank N.A.), and Zeigler Coal Co.[31]

Prior to his retirement, the Parkers had a principal residence in Washington but spent most of each week in their New York apartment, which they gave up in 1972. In the mid-1970s Parker was much taken up with the protracted lawsuits that resulted from Howard Hughes' acquisition of Air West. Parker's primary outside interest was the Finance Committee of the US Naval Academy Foundation, on which he served until a few months before his death.

In the late 1970s the Parkers retired to the St. Andrews Club in Florida.

For the last few years of his life Parker wintered in Delray, Fla., a few miles from J.W. Birkenstock of IBM. Parker told Norberg in 1986:[32]

> We had a very pleasant relationship through Birkenstock. He's now retired, lives in Delray, where I live in the winter, and I'll be seeing him in the next couple of weeks. And every time we get together we reminisce about why, you know, it hadn't gone that way.

Summary

A Sperry commemoration of ERA summarized Parker:[33]

> Parker was a capitalist by experience, a dynamic, personable extrovert who rolled over problems or tiptoed around them in equally deft fashion.

---

[31]Pritchett, Juliette A., September 10, 1990; private communication.

[32]See note 4.

[33]See note 9.

Tomash and Cohen, both participants in the birth of ERA and both of whom knew Parker personally, describe him in these words:[34]

> A genial extrovert, he was well-connected and moved easily in the Washington political and military milieu. Parker was a personable salesman, a resourceful entrepreneur and an energetic businessman. Beneath a hearty, bluff exterior he was observant, shrewd, and pragmatic.

History has shown that his vision of the future of the computing industry was far better than that of his superiors in Sperry and Univac.[35]

BIBLIOGRAPHY

Biographical

Tomash, Erwin, and Arnold A. Cohen, "The Birth of an ERA, Engineering Research Associates, Inc., 1946–1955," *Ann. Hist. Comp.*, Vol. 1, No. 2, Oct. 1979, pp. 83–97

Weiss, Eric, "John E. Parker—Obituary," *Ann. Hist. Comp.*, Vol. 14, No. 4, 1992.

---

[34]See note 4.
[35]From Weiss 1992.

JOHN T. PARSONS

Born January 7, 1913, Detroit, Mich.; the father of numerical control.

Professional Experience: president and owner, Parsons Corp., Traverse City and Detroit, Mich., and Stockton, Calif., 1954–1968; president/owner, The John T. Parsons Co., Traverse City, Mich., 1968–1986.

Honors and Awards: first recipient, Joseph Marie Jacquard Award, Numerical Control Society, "for outstanding technical contributions" as the "Father of Numerical Control," 1968; Medal, Society of Manufacturing Engineers Engineering, "presented to John T. Parsons, industrialist and inventor whose brilliant conceptualization of numerical control marked the beginning of the second industrial revolution and the advent of an age in which the control of machines and industrial processes would pass from imprecise craft to exact science," 1975; National Medal of Technology from President Reagan, 1985; charter fellow, Society of Manufacturing Engineers, 1986; DEng (Hon.), University of Michigan, 1988; member, National Inventors' Hall of Fame, 1993.

Parsons' activities involved the direction of the design (test static, dynamic, and flight), the development of unique manufacturing processes, and the tooling, including brazing and adhesive bonding, for the first all-composite airplane (for the Office of Naval Research), and many other composites and metal structures for aerospace industries. He directed the design and construction of the first numerical control milling machine, under a US Air Force contract, and now has 30 years' experience designing and applying computers to manufacturing and administration operations, leading to random sequence "just-in-time" manufacture. Among his accomplishments related to the application of computers to numerical control (N/C) were:[36]

1944   Devised manufacturing system for producing 22' Sikorsky R-5 rotor blades in an old mill-construction furniture factory with 12' × 12' bays and 7' headroom. Quality and costs were such that the US Army refused to approve Sikorsky's request for a second source, even when the schedule increased to 405 blades per month. (Parsons' first aircraft job.)

1945   Conceived/installed first production facility in the world for metal-to-metal adhesive bonding of primary aircraft structures—R-5 Sikorsky rotor blade spars. Redesigned spar from spot-weld to adhesive bonded construction.

---

[36]From a biographical outline which accompanies the collection of his papers archived at the Special Collections Division, Newman Library, Virginia Tech.

1946   Tooled rotor blade plant to also produce 1,260 pair of "Ercoupe" airplane wings per month. Directed program to use punched-card machines for the solution of engineering problems (probably the first company in the US to do this).

1947   Devised and implemented a system for producing airfoil templates on manually controlled boring mill, using machine tool table settings calculated and tabulated on IBM accounting machines.

1948   Conceived a machine tool for producing aircraft structural shapes automatically from punched-card/tape input.

1949   Negotiated and executed the contract on behalf of Parsons Corporation with US Air Force to build the first numerical control milling machine. Coordinated its development with Parsons staff and principal subcontractors: IBM, Snyder Corporation, and Massachusetts Institute of Technology. Monitored design and completion of machine, 1950–1952.

1950   Conceived/installed a modular tooling system for aircraft plants, resulting in great reduction in tooling costs and floor space requirements.

1951   Designed the layout of a new rotor blade manufacturing plant, including materials laboratories for ferrous and nonferrous metals, resins and reinforced plastics, and test laboratories for structural, dynamic, and flight test.

1952   Took leave from Parsons Corporation. Purchased all rights in numerical control patents he had originally assigned to the corporation.

1954   Devised and installed Operations Control System at Parsons Corporation using single source document to control total engineering, manufacturing, quality, and service functions.

1955   Granted exclusive license to N/C patent to Bendix, and was signatory to its sublicenses to General Electric, TRW, Sundstrand, Milacron, Allen-Bradley, IBM, Fujitsu, Bosch, and so on.

1956   Doubled the size of the rotor blade plant; installed the first electronic blade tracker in the world (furnished by Chicago Aerial Industries). Conceived and installed a hydraulic adhesive bonding press with a 2' × 22' platen with automated load/unload system. Conceived and installed programmable salt bath furnaces for heat-treating 25'-long alloy steel tubes.

1957   Conceived badge-activated time clock, directed design and construction of breadboard model; directed preliminary design of point-of-sale machine, portable inventory recorder, and badge-activated vending machine.

1959   Conceived the unique process, did the plant layout, and directed the installation of a production facility for 55′ diameter fiberglass geodesic radomes.

1961   Evaluated vendor proposals, then purchased and directed the installation of facilities for producing seamless metal tubes up to 26-$\frac{1}{2}$″ diameter × 125′ length. Produced tubes with wall thicknesses as low as .007 plus or minus .0002″ for the Minuteman Missile. Directed plant-wide psychological testing to select employees to be entrusted with the operation of this very expensive equipment, which was the sole source for Saturn booster fuel lines.

1962   Conceived, designed, and directed the installation of a programmable, totally enclosed surface preparation system integrated with white room techniques, for adhesive bonding stiffener rings to tubes up to 30″ diameter × 56′ long used in projects such as the fuel lines for the Saturn Booster for the Apollo moon shot program. Conceived the complete facilities and plant layout for producing 7′ fiberglass turbine-type blades for a supersonic wind tunnel at US Air Force's Arnold Engineering Development Center.

1963   Designed the complete facility for producing monoblock ship's propellers up to 28′ diameter. Subcontracted the foundry design to Lester B. Knight Associates. US Navy used these concepts to upgrade its Propeller Shop at the Philadelphia Naval Shipyard.

1964   Conceived and directed the installation of a special 4-axis N/C machine tool for helicopter rotor blades.

1965   Participated in the blade design and conceived the manufacturing process and tooling for the first tapered metal helicopter rotor blade (Lockheed AH-56 helicopter). Not even one blade was scrapped during the entire program.

1967   Conceived a programmable surface preparation system for adhesive bonding stainless, titanium, aluminum, and alloy steel aircraft structures up to 35′ long in random sequence.

1969   Devised N/C techniques and tooling for producing polystyrene foam patterns for aluminum, bronze, iron, and steel castings marketed under "ComputerBilt" trademark. (Sold 300 castings produced from such patterns to various machine tool builders.)

1969   Conceived a unique N/C part-programming machine, and directed the prototype construction.

1970   Developed the theory and commercially exploited the process for machining thin section forgings in one cut per surface, without distortion.

1971   Conceived and used in production the N/C system for the automatic inspection of turbine blades.

1973   Initiated design studies on rotor blades for large wind energy systems.

1977   Conducted design studies on N/C ball-screw presses to replace crank, eccentric, and hydraulic presses for many uses.

1978   Conducted extensive design studies on advanced CRT and terminal keyboards.

QUOTATION

Burt Raynes, a manufacturing engineer who became chairman, president, and chief executive officer of Rohr Corporation, after inspecting Parsons' Traverse City plants, stated, "There aren't 25 people in the United States capable of understanding the magnitude of John Parsons' accomplishments."

BIBLIOGRAPHY

Biographical

Ward, J.E., "Numerical Control of Machine Tools," *McGraw Hill Yearbook of Science and Technology*, McGraw-Hill, New York, 1968, pp. 58–65.

BLAISE PASCAL

Born 1623, Rouen, France; died 1666, France; French mathematician and philosopher who invented an adding machine with automatic carry between digits, and the "Pascal Triangle" of coefficients of the binomial series; also the inventor of the wheelbarrow, the omnibus, and the roulette wheel.[37]

Son of a tax collector, Pascal was a child prodigy who discovered the proof of Euclid's 32nd Proposition at the age of 12: "La somme des angles d'un triangle quelconque est égale à deux angles driots." Four years later, he developed a fundamental theorem of projective geometry, such that the projections of the opposing sides of a hexagon inscribed in a conic section intersect to define a single line named the "droite de Pascal" (figure below).

In assisting his father he became impressed by the need for a mechanical device for performing arithmetic operations and, in 1642, developed his adding (and subtracting) machine. The primary innovation of the calculator was its ability to automatically carry the "tens" digit from one position to the next.

During the next decade he built almost 50 copies of the machine, but most of them were used as parlor curiosities of their rich purchasers rather than working machines. After this period he returned to his studies of mathematics, and in 1654 presented two papers that form the basis of integral calculus and the theory of probability. In the

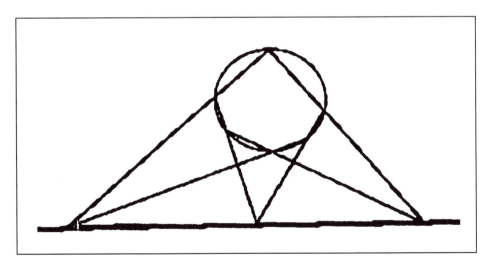

La droite de Pascal

---

[37]From "Trivial Pursuit," original version.

1	1	1	1	1	1	1	1	1	1
1	2	3	4	5	6	7	8	9	
1	3	6	10	15	21	28	36		
1	4	10	20	35	56	84			
1	5	15	35	70	126				
1	6	21	56	126					
1	7	28	84						
1	8	36							
1	9								
1									

Pascal Triangle

same year he introduced his triangle of binomial coefficients—the Pascal Triangle—which predated the concepts of computation of the values of polynomial functions by differences.

The method of computation is quite simple. The first row and column consist simply of unit values. The entry in any interior cell is then simply the sum of the entry in the cell to the left and the cell above. The diagonal elements (top right to lower left) then constitute the coefficients of the polynomial $(x + y)^n$, where $n + 1$ is the index of the diagonal. Thus $(x + y)^4$ can be read off from the 5th diagonal (in bold above):

$$x^4 + 4x^3y + 6x^2y^2 + 4xy^3 + y^4$$

The powers associated with the free variables x and y sum to n in each term and change monotonically.

In 1658 Pascal challenged his fellow mathematicians to a contest; he entered the contest himself under a pseudonym and when he awarded the prize to himself his colleagues were (perhaps justifiably) enraged.

QUOTATION

Je n'ai fait celle-çi plus longue que parceque je n'ai pas en le loisir de la faire plus corte. [I have made this letter longer than usual, because I lack the time to make it short.] (*Lettres Provençiales*, 1657)

BIBLIOGRAPHY

Biographical

Bishop, M., *Pascal: The Life of a Genius,* Bell & Sons, London, 1937.

Devaux, Pierre, "Cet Amateur de Genie: Pascal," *Sciences et Avenir,* No. 188, Paris, Oct. 1962, pp. 678–682.

Jones, C.V., "Pascal, Blaise," in Ralston, Anthony, and Edwin D. Reilly, Jr., *Encyclopedia of Computer Science and Engineering,* Van Nostrand Reinhold Co., New York, 1983.

JOHN R. PASTA

Born 1918, New York City; died June 5, 1981, Washington, D.C.; mathematician, computer scientist, and science administrator who started programming at Los Alamos Scientific Laboratory and finished his career as the leading proponent of computer science research as director of the Division of Mathematical and Computer Sciences of the National Science Foundation; with S.M. Ulam and Enrico Fermi, the originator of the Fermi-Pasta-Ulam (FPU) problem.

Education: BS, City College of New York, 1946.

Professional Experience: real estate title examiner, Title Guarantee and Trust Co., 1938–1941; patrolman, New York City Police Department, 1941–1942; officer, Signal Corps, US Army, and cryptographical security officer, radar officer, 29th Tactical Air Command, Ninth Air Force, 1942–1946; Los Alamos Scientific Laboratory, 1951–1956; Mathematics and Computer Branch, Atomic Energy Commission Division of Research, Washington, D.C., 1956–1961; research professor of physics, Digital Computer Laboratory, University of Illinois, 1961–1970; National Science Foundation, Washington, D.C., 1970–1981.

Honors and Awards: Bronze Star; Belgian Fourragere.

John was born in New York City in 1918, the eldest of four children, and grew up in Queens. He attended the New York public schools and became interested in physics at an early age when an uncle gave him some of his old college books. After graduating from Townsend Harris High School, he entered City College of New York in 1935 and completed three years. The depression forced him to drop out of college at that stage to take a job as a real estate title examiner for Title Guaranty and Trust Company. In 1941 he took the examinations for the New York City police department, entered the police academy, and became a patrolman in August 1941. In 1942, he was drafted into the US Army, became an officer in the Signal Corps, and took courses on electronics and radar at Harvard and MIT. He married Betty Ann Bentzen at the Little Church Around the Corner in New York City in May 1943. After the war, John and Betty had two children: Diane, now a lawyer in Seattle, and David, completing his doctoral dissertation in statistics at Stanford and president of a statistical computing firm in Palo Alto.

John's tour of duty with the Army during World War II was spent in the European theater, mostly as cryptographical security officer and radar officer for the 29th Tactical Air Command, Ninth Air Force, for which he was awarded the Bronze Star and the Belgian Fourragere. After being discharged from the Army in 1946, he took advantage of the GI Bill to finish his undergraduate work at City College that same year and enter graduate school at New York University to study mathematics and physics.

As a graduate student he became a research fellow in the Department of Physics at Brookhaven National Laboratory, the beginning of a long and rewarding association with Brookhaven, and completed his thesis on "Limiting Procedures in Quantum Electrodynamics" in 1951 under the guidance of Hartland Snyder.

He became a staff member of the Los Alamos Laboratory in August 1951. The MANIAC was in its final stage of construction and testing, and like many others, John was mesmerized by this marvelous toy that offered so much potential for gaining an insight into nonlinear physics. Trained as a theoretical physicist, he came to grips with "hands-on" computing, dealing directly with all its aspects.

John's most cherished interaction was with Fermi. In the summer of 1953 Fermi raised the question of the nature of approach to describing the equilibrium of a vibrating nonlinear string initially in a single oscillatory mode. Together with Ulam, they formulated some preliminary test problems. As expected, the computations showed that the initial vibrational energy gradually transferred into neighboring modes, and the system seemed to achieve equilibrium—the time taken being the so-called relaxation time. The completely unexpected happened one day when a typical problem was being computed. Owing to a very energetic, distracting discussion, the computations continued beyond the usual cutoff. The results were so strange and mysterious that everyone around was quick to assume that the computer, the traditional whipping boy, had gone awry. The vibrational energy had returned to the initial mode, within a few percent. The rest is history—the stimulation that work provided to soliton theory, the enormous literature that emerged globally. Today it is well known as the FPU (Fermi-Pasta-Ulam) problem.

He joined the AEC in 1956, and he performed two important functions. The first was to serve as the sole computer expert and adviser at AEC headquarters for unclassified work involving computing.

John's second task was to institute a contract-research program in mathematics and computers. By 1956 the mechanism for the support of research in the basic sciences, as mandated by the Atomic Energy Act of 1946, was well established, but it was believed that there was no need for a separate and independent program of research in mathematics, since relevant mathematics research was implicit in the theoretical physics program.

Early in the 1960s a major concern of the AEC was the availability of computer systems capable of handling the anticipated future loads of the weapons laboratories and, to a lesser extent, the requirements of its reactor and high-energy physics programs. In retrospect, it is somewhat amusing to note that the absence on the horizon of a "machine ten times STRETCH" was taken as cause for great concern. In consequence, the major manufacturers were invited to discuss their future plans at a meeting hosted by Oak Ridge National Laboratory in May 1962.

Shortly after that meeting, with the concurrence of the AEC, a small informal group consisting of Pasta, Nicholas Metropolis, John Richardson, Jerome A.G. Russel, Yoshio Shimamoto, and, later, Daniel L. Slotnick was organized to discuss and explore some of the newer computer technologies that were beginning to make the news.

The members felt that the meetings were instructive and worthwhile, however, so they continued to meet at a rate of once every 9 to 10 months. At one of the meetings, Slotnick was asked to discuss his SOLOMON computer and was invited to become a member of the group shortly thereafter. This association was influential in the subsequent research and development leading to the ILLIAC IV.

Around 1965, John returned to his first love—nonlinear physics—and his time at Brookhaven was devoted to numerical experimentation. The Brookhaven staff also benefited from his managerial talents, for he was constantly drawn into planning and management discussions. When the decision was made to connect minicomputers, located at the various experimental facilities, to the CDC 6600 of the Central Scientific Computing Facility, John was also involved in the initial planning stage of the project.

After spending approximately four years in the Division of Research of the Atomic Energy Commission as head of the mathematics and computer branch, John had developed that branch into a vital part of the Division of Research's programs and had completed the task for which von Neumann had prevailed upon him to come to Washington. He felt ready for a change in career. After some discussion, John accepted a position as research professor of physics in the Digital Computer Laboratory, the Graduate College, and the Department of Physics in the College of Engineering at the University of Illinois, effective September 1, 1961.

His early research career at Illinois involved the programming of the ILLIAC II, which became operational in August 1962. As was often the case in those early days, most attention was paid to developing the hardware aspects of a computer system. Only when the machine was near completion was work begun on the operating system and compilers that would be needed before even talented users could exploit the machine. In two years they produced an operating system and Fortran compiler for the ILLIAC II that first ran in August 1964.

Cordial relations with the Department of Mathematics permitted a bachelor's degree called mathematics and computer science to be formulated; it contained a heavy component of mathematics as well as computer science. The tedious approval process was carried out in record time; the bachelor's program became official in 1965 and immediately enrolled 41 students. The graduate degrees became available in 1966 and immediately attracted 10 students. By 1970, when Pasta left Illinois, these programs had grown to 302 undergraduates and 141 graduates. Pasta felt that this facet of his stay at Illinois was personally the most rewarding.

Another significant development during Pasta's leadership was the consolidation and growth of the ILLIAC II project. The pilot study yielded promising results, and by 1964–1965 the AEC had agreed to fund the full development of a computer whose cost would be on the order of several million dollars. Naturally, the computer was called the ILLIAC III. Unfortunately, disaster in the form of a fire struck ILLIAC III before it was completed, and its ideas could not be tested. Nevertheless, it was pioneering work in parallel computer architectures.

Other research on parallel architectures during Pasta's tenure at Illinois involved the ILLIAC IV project and its originator, Daniel L. Slotnick. Slotnick's initial ideas about parallel computers go back to the mid-1950s. Pasta prevailed on Slotnick to join the Department of Computer Science at Illinois in May 1965.

Ivan Sutherland, who was in charge of computing activities in the Advanced Research Projects Administration (ARPA) of the Department of Defense, visited Illinois shortly after Slotnick's arrival to discuss building such a machine. A positive decision was made, and the ILLIAC IV project was born. Within a few months, a $10 million contract with ARPA was executed.

Another activity that should be mentioned, especially in connection with his Illinois period, is John Pasta's participation in international science. He participated in the IFIP conferences beginning in the 1950s and was the American delegate to IFIP in 1965–1966.

If John's personal feelings about his position at Illinois in 1969 were similar to those he had had about his AEC position in Washington in 1961, the situation he met when he returned to Washington was much like the one he had found at the AEC when he first went there in 1956. There was widespread bewilderment, doubt, insecurity, and downright skepticism in government circles about the role of computers in education and research, and computer science as a discipline had almost no recognition at all. NSF's university computer-facilities program was under attack and being reduced; its computer-research program had never grown. His credentials as a physicist often served him well in battles with physicists and other scientists to protect the fledgling computer-research activities, and he always loved the fight.

It is not surprising that John's first few years at NSF were ones of retrenchment and rebuilding. First, the university computer-facilities program was phased out; its mission was declared accomplished. The educational activities of the Office of Computing Activities were the next to go, moved into the foundation's Directorate for Science Education as a more natural organizational home for all of NSF's educational functions. John fought that move bitterly and lost. The Office of Computing Activities was then renamed the Division of Computer Research.

A final change took place in 1975 when the Division of Computer Research was merged with the mathematics section of NSF to form the Division of Mathematical and Computer Sciences, with John as division director and with one section for computer sciences and one for mathematics.

An area John worked on steadily from the time he came to NSF was computer networking. He advocated formation of a national computer network among research groups in computer science, but was stymied by skepticism at higher levels of NSF, and reluctance by the government to take on responsibility for an operation of unknown but possibly frightening magnitude. Unfortunately, although he lived long enough to see the National Science Network (CSNET) project, he was unable to participate in it.

Throughout his professional life, John was fascinated by the deep impact computer technology was having, first on science and then on the whole fabric of social organization and intercourse. It was natural for him to include in the spectrum of activities supported by his Division of Computer Research at NSF a group of projects performing research on the social impact of computing technology. He undertook to alert the branches of government that have primary responsibility for law enforcement, to the dangers of criminal activity using computer technology. NSF still carries on fundamental research in data and computer-system privacy and security.

Although his research funds at NSF were for scientific studies, and another (weakly funded) program in the foundation had responsibility for the history of science, John took the opportunity to work with that program and supplement the resources available for the history of science on several occasions when strong proposals were submitted to NSF. Two examples were the first History of Programming Languages Conference in 1978 and the Convocation of Computer Pioneers, organized in Los Alamos in 1976.

John was fascinated by the world around him and never missed the opportunity to better himself. Thus, while he was at Illinois, he availed himself of the facilities provided by the university to resume his childhood piano lessons, which had long been abandoned, and to take flying lessons and qualify for a pilot's license.

Above all, he was a man of considerable courage. He suffered a long, painful illness and had considerable time to contemplate death, yet he maintained the grace to joke on the subject. He served the NSF even after he was no longer able to walk. Until the very end, he was the tough New York City cop whose primary concern was the well-being of science and his country.[38]

---

[38]From Curtis et al. 1983.

BIBLIOGRAPHY

Biographical

Cortada, James W., "Pasta, John R.," in *Historical Dictionary of Data Processing: Biographies,* Greenwood Press, Westport, Conn., 1987, pp. 208–210.

Curtis, Kent K., N.C. Metropolis, William G. Rosen, Yoshio Shimamoto, and James N. Snyder, "John R. Pasta, 1918–1981: An Unusual Path Toward Computer Science," *Ann. Hist. Comp.,* Vol. 5, No. 3, July 1983, pp. 224–238.

ALAN J. PERLIS

Born April 1, 1922, Pittsburgh, Pa.; died February 7, 1990, New Haven, Conn.; computer pioneer; leader in establishing computer science as a legitimate discipline; longtime developer of programming languages and programming techniques; author of classic one-liners.

Education: BS, chemistry, Carnegie Institute of Technology (now Carnegie Mellon University), 1943; MS, mathematics, MIT, 1949; PhD, mathematics, MIT, 1950.

Professional Experience: research mathematician, Aberdeen Proving Grounds, 1951; Project Whirlwind, MIT, 1952; assistant professor, mathematics, Purdue University, 1952–1956; Carnegie Mellon University: associate professor of mathematics, 1956–1960, director of the Computation Center, 1956–1971, professor and chairman, Mathematics Department, 1960–1965, codirector, Graduate Program in Systems and Communications Science, 1962–1965, head, Graduate Department of Computer Science, 1965–1971; Eugene Higgins Chair in Computer Science, Yale University, 1971–1990.

Honors and Awards: ACM Turing Award, 1966;[39] AFIPS Education Award, 1984; IEEE Pioneer Award, 1985; member, National Research Council Assembly of Engineering, 1978–1990; member, National Academy of Engineering, 1976–1990; member, American Academy of Arts and Sciences; honorary doctorates: Davis and Elkins College, University of Waterloo, Purdue University,

---

[39]The first ACM Turing Award.

and Sacred Heart University; editor-in-chief, *Communications of the ACM*, 1958–1962, president, ACM, 1962–1964.

In 1951 Perlis was employed as a research mathematician at Aberdeen Proving Grounds, and in 1952 at Project Whirlwind. Later that year Perlis became an assistant professor of mathematics at Purdue and was responsible for forming the university's digital computer laboratory. In 1955 he organized an effort to build the IT compiler for the Datatron 205 at Purdue and this work continued on the IBM-650 when he took the position of associate professor of mathematics and director of the computation center at Carnegie in 1956. Along with Joseph Smith, Harold van Zoernen, and Arthur Evans, he designed and built a succession of algebraic language compilers and assemblers for the IBM-650. A course on programming, distinct from numerical analysis, was instituted in 1958 and made accessible to undergraduates at all levels. Also in 1958, Professor Perlis became one of 8 people to define the programming language Algol 58, and in 1960 he was one of 13 international scientists involved in the definition of Algol 60.

Alan Perlis was named professor and chairman of the Mathematics Department at Carnegie in 1960 and he also remained as director of its computation center. Then, in 1962, he became codirector of a graduate program in systems and communications science, whose goal was the development of a graduate program in what has now become computer science. In 1965, the graduate department of computer science was founded at Carnegie, and he became its first head.

Throughout the 1960s he was involved in the definition and extensions of Algol, that is, Formula Algol, a version for manipulating formal mathematics expressions, and LCC, a version adapted to interactive incremental programming. He joined the new Computer Science Department at Yale University as Eugene Higgins Professor of Computer Science in 1971, a position he held until his death.

His research was primarily in the area of programming language design and the development of programming techniques. He was the author or coauthor of many published articles, and two books, *Introduction to Computer Science* and *A View of Programming Languages*. He was the founding editor of the *Communications of the ACM* and served as president of the association from 1962 to 1964.

In 1981 Perlis was asked to give a talk on "Computing in the Fifties" at the ACM National Conference in Nashville, Tenn. The transcript of his talk follows:[40]

---

[40]Perlis had submitted this transcript for consideration for publication in the *Annals of the History of Computing*. It was being edited at the time of his death.

One has to understand that computing after World War II was largely concentrated in a few locales under the support of agencies of the federal government. Whirlwind at MIT and the Mark I, II, III computers at Harvard were both supported, by and large, by the Office of Naval Research. The Ordnance Department of the US Army supported a large activity at the University of Illinois. A few other smaller efforts were under way in other places. Within universities as such, however, there was no computing, other than some small punched-card calculations being done in various statistical departments around the country. Almost all computing was essentially funded by the federal government and aimed at developing computers that would be directly used within the defense effort.

In 1952 I was fortunate to be invited to Purdue University, where the director of the Statistical Laboratory, an unsung hero of our profession named Carl Cossack, decided that an engineering school should have a computer that would be used by its students and faculty as part of its educational and research program. I accepted a position at Purdue and went out there to start a computing center. There were no computer science departments in those days; everybody who worked around computers was either an electrical engineer or a numerical analyst. The courses on the computer usually were of two kinds: courses in circuitry taught within the engineering department, or courses in numerical analysis taught under the aegis of the mathematics department.

At Purdue we searched for one year for a computer—the university having given us $5,000 and a Purdue automobile to travel through the eastern and middle-western part of the country. We saw some very strange computers. One I will never forget was being developed by Facsimile in New York City in a loft, in the Lower East Side, on the third floor that one reached by going up on a rickety freight elevator. The machine was called the Circle Computer. It had one important attribute: there was a socket on the top of the computer into which one could plug an electric coffee pot. The Circle Computer showed me that machines really do have a personality and a spectrum of emotions over which they run; the Circle Computer would only run when one of its designers was in the same room. As soon as he happened to leave the room the computer would stop. National Cash Register, for some strange reason, bought this computer and used it as the basis of their incursion into the computer field, starting out on the West Coast in Hawthorne, California.

We found a small computer firm in Minneapolis that was only distinguished by the fact that the president of the firm had a clock in back of him with the face reversed. There was a mirror on the other wall. He was very fond of saying to people when they came in that a good executive never turns his back on his work. He looked at the mirror to find out what the time was. Needless to say, his computers weren't any good. I did try to get a clock like that later on, however.

Ultimately we found a computer for Purdue in California called the Datatron 205. It was manufactured by a firm called Consolidated Electrodynamics. The computer cost about $150,000, which in those days was an awful lot of money.

Behind every computer development at a university, one finds an administration, either an administration that objects to and rebels against and postpones all growth and development, or an administration that fosters. Generally, we don't find them being neutral. At Purdue, the president at that time was Frederick Hutde, an ex-All American football player from the University of Minnesota, who unfortunately was ahead of his time; otherwise he might be running for president today. In any event, I walked in with the three other members of our committee to see the president and told him the sad news: the computer that Purdue needed would cost $125,000 (we had gotten a small discount). I expected the president to throw up his hands and say, "Impossible! No one spends that kind of money on a piece of equipment that no one really understands the benefits of." Instead, he said, "Give me two days." In two days he called me on the phone and said, "You have $125,000 from the Purdue Research Foundation. Get the machine."

From that point on, my attitude has always been that if you are expert, if you are right, the administrators will accede to your wishes. I haven't been disappointed. It's a principle by which I think all of us should operate. By and large, administrators are always looking for people to tell them what they ought to be doing, rather than being confronted with a decision that they have to make on which they have no information with which to make that decision, so the natural technique is to postpone or form another committee. Instead, one really ought to go to them and say, "Do this because it's right."

The computer arrived at Purdue in 1952, and we began to teach computing in a university to the students and the faculty. But the education then was quite primitive: numerical analysis and electronic circuitry. There was no such subject as programming, and programming languages did not exist as such. We knew of Grace Murray Hopper's work at Univac, but programming languages as such were for the future.

I was interested in a problem in numerical analysis in those days: [Chebychev] approximation. I came up with some potential algorithms that required a great deal of programming experimentation and decided that it was impossible to write these programs in machine language. So we began at Purdue the development of a compiler, which I continued when I moved on to Carnegie in 1956.

In the meantime, IBM decided in marketing the IBM 650 computer to offer a resounding 60% discount for that machine, which made it extraordinarily attractive. The initial budget at Carnegie—and I think the budgets for 650s were similar at that time in other universities—for operating the 650, for supplies, for personnel, and for rental of the machine, was $50,000 per year. With that $50,000 we were able to develop a computer center. We continued work on the compiler, which became known as "IT" (Interpretative Translator). I will never forget the miracle of seeing the first program compiled, when an eight-line Gaussian elimination program was expanded into 120 lines of assembly language, which we took as evidence of the power of the compiler, rather than its weakness. It was with absolute amazement that we witnessed this process of generation.

Shortly after that there began a very fruitful exchange between Carnegie and Case and Michigan. The three universities collaborated on the development of a whole sequence of languages based on "IT," all of the successors being far superior to the original. These successors came cascading out over a period of about a year and a half. Don Knuth developed a series at Case Institute; Bernie Galler, Bruce Arden, and Bob Graham developed a series at Michigan.

In 1957 we taught for the first time (although I won't claim at all that there was no previous course offered in the US) a course in programming, independent of numerical analysis and independent of circuitry. The chief issue of this course was: how do you program? In the course we used one of our compiler languages, and we also taught assembly language. We developed what I called structured programming. What we meant by *structure* was: if you were to write a program in assembly language, write out the structure in a high-level language and then use templates or macros (although we didn't call them that then) to reduce the program to machine language. We were able to reduce the errors tremendously in the resulting programs.

In teaching a course on programming in those days, one of our major problems was: what do you do in such a course and what kind of exercises do you give? There is little point in a course in programming to give exercises in doing square roots by Newton-Raphson or Gaussian elimination or interpolation. They do not reveal the issues in programming. We developed a series of exercises that were based on geometry, where the problems given to students were of a very simple kind that had the blessed virtue that the students did not have to know any deep mathematics at all to understand the intent of the program or the problem and the goal they were to reach. Problems were very simple, such as: if we give you the coordinates of the endpoints of n line segments, how do you tell if these line segments form the consecutive sides of a polygon? The students understood exactly what they were supposed to do, and yet nowhere in their education had they ever been supplied with the techniques, or algorithms as we now call them, by which these tasks could be accomplished. So they were therefore forced to think in what we might call pure programmatic terms. These courses were very successful, and now, of course, such courses are taught everywhere.

The way one used the computer in those days was to line up on Monday morning to sign up for time in blocks half an hour to an hour or even two hours after midnight. A cot was always kept next to the computer, and in the air-conditioning unit of the computer there was a small chamber where one kept beer and Coca-Cola. I lived across the street from Carnegie at that time. One night I received a call, as I often did, at 2 o'clock in the morning, saying, "Come quick! The machine is broken down, and I'm in the middle of the last calculations of my PhD thesis." I walked over to the Computing Center, which was in the basement of the Graduate School of Industrial Administration building. The hall was dark, but I knew my way along. Suddenly I fell over something. I heard a curse in the dark. I remembered where the light switch was and turned it on. There, to my amazement, were stretched out 20 yards down one corridor and two yards at a right angle, one body after another lying on the floor—including women! I said, "What's going on here?" "Oh, we're waiting to sign up for time on Monday morning." I recognized a graduate student's wife. I said, "What are you doing here?" "Well, my husband's at home working on the thesis and taking care of the kid. I'm holding his place in line."

I was appalled. It turns out, as is always the case, that the people in charge are the last to know when things are going bad. The next day I went to see the president and said we needed a new computer. The president said, "Fine, as long as it doesn't cost too much."

In those days, how did one decide what kind of computer to get? The choices were rather sparse. Nevertheless, in looking around, we decided there was really no computer around that was worth getting as a second-generation machine to replace the 650. At an ACM meeting at MIT at that time, I met a man named Dave Evans, who is now the president of Evans and Sutherland. At that time he was the chief engineer of Bendix. We were walking along the Charles River, and he said, "We are building a new machine. Let me describe it to you." He did, and it was the G-20, which was based on the idea of a collection of processors tied together in a communications net—works we now hear a great deal of—all the processors operating independently, being controlled by interrupt sequences.

I listened to him, and I said, "We'll take it." Indeed, Carnegie then received delivery of the first G-20 shipped from California, and that machine worked quite well for about five years. When the machine arrived at Carnegie, it came with a full load of software: one binary load routine used by the engineers for testing memory. That was the sole extent of the software. Back in California, they were working on Algol compilers, Fortran compilers, assembly systems—all kinds of things—but none of it was available for us. So we had to build a piece of software for the machine.

At that time we were using at Carnegie a compiler language that was an extension of one developed at Michigan called GAT; we called it GATE (GAT Extended). That came over several steps from "IT." This excellent language predated BASIC in a way and was much better than BASIC: about the same size, about the same speed.

How could one build a compiler quickly? We were fortunate at that time to have with us a visitor from Denmark, Jorn Jensen, who was with the Regnecentralen. Jorn was a magnificent programmer. We conceived of the idea of building a piece of software as though we were carrying out the execution of a program. We put into one room the three programmers who had built the system, with their desks at the vertices of a triangle, if you will. Jensen sat at one desk; he was building the assembler. Arthur Evans sat at another desk; he was building the parser. Harold Van Zoren sat at the third desk; he was building the code generator. All three were being defined simultaneously.

The method of construction worked as follows. Jensen would decide that a certain construction ought to be in assembly language, and he would broadcast to the other two. He would then start independent processes to determine how and where these ideas would be embedded in the code they were writing. When they decided how they would work or what changes would be required, working in good code-team fashion, they suspended and broadcast back to Jensen their proposals. Jensen would drop what he was doing and start another independent process. The amount of code that each wrote turned out to be of the order of about 2,000–3,000 machine language instructions. It turned out that at that size of code, such a technique worked magnificently. Each of the programmers could keep two to four processes in the air simultaneously, and changes progressed very fast. All three parts were completed at the same time. Jensen debugged the assembly language on the computer, simultaneously with the debugging of the parser and the code generator. We had here an example of the construction of a piece of software as though we were executing a real-time multiprocessor program.

About that time in the late 1950s, Algol came into being. Algol has never turned out to be as successful a language in the US as we would have liked at that time. Maybe that's a blessing in disguise. In any event, the Algol process in the 1950s was extraordinarily important in that it brought together computer scientists (although we didn't go by that name then) from the US and Europe who worked closely together to produce something that would be, it was hoped, an international standard. We now know more about the difficulties of getting people to accept programming languages and programming systems. Saul Rosen has amply demonstrated the slowness with which people are going to change what they have been doing. Algol as such never flew in the US; it did in Europe, however, and a great deal of Europe's success in computing is a consequence of the Algol effort in the 1950s.

One of the things about the 1950s that was pronounced was the sparseness of people. In almost every university you could find one—and if they were fortunate two—persons who knew anything at all about computing. They had to carry the burden of teaching everyone else at the university the benefits of computing in those days. Now everybody knows about computing. I used to use as a yardstick the conversations I would hear on airplanes. In the late 1950s, when you would take a flight, you would never hear anyone on the airplane speaking to anyone else about Fortran or Cobol, about software, or anything of that sort. Nowadays, 50% of the people on airplanes are writing programs, or reading computing books, or traveling to a computing meeting, or coming back from one. Another yardstick we used to use in those days was an estimate of the largest population of a city in the US that had no computers in it. It was about 15,000 in the late 1950s. Today, I doubt if that number would even reach 300. We really are in the computer age.

In the 1950s we learned, I think, a great deal. At the time we weren't aware that we were learning it, but the things we learned in those days have become the basis of computer science as we now know it, the basis of the use of computers in industry as we now see it. It is too bad that we didn't know what we were learning at the time, because we might have saved everyone a lot of grief and prevented people from going down the wrong path—except that in computing there is no wrong path. One of the things we learned about computing in the 1950s was that there are no bounds to the subject. It cannot be put into a tidy receptacle. Everywhere that computing has been embedded in some other discipline, it has not flowered. Computing is not part of electrical engineering; it is not part of mathematics; it is not part of industrial administration. Computing belongs by itself. The reason this *is* the computer age is precisely because of that.

One of the things we have learned since the 1950s is that computer science is really nothing more or less than the study of all the phenomena that arise around computers. These phenomena are generated from preceding phenomena, and one cannot predict what they will be. I have been collecting a number of epigrams about computing. One of them is that if a professor tells you that computer science is *x* but not *y*, have compassion for his students.

Herb Simon, when he said that there would be a chess champion in the 1960s, had no idea that this would not occur. He believed that it would. Since that time we have learned that there is a tremendous difference between the ease with which we can master syntax and the difficulty with which we take care of semantics. I am fond of saying that many a good idea is never heard from again once it embarks on a voyage in the semantic gulf.

Certainly, one of our goals in developing chess programs—programs that understand natural language, programs that play any kind of game—is to write programs that learn. What we have found is this: when we write programs that learn, it turns out that we do and they don't.

A previous speaker mentioned VLSI, the great new hope. All that comes to my mind when I hear about VLSI is, "Isn't it wonderful we can now pack 100 ENIACs in one square centimeter?" VLSI is going to turn out to be of enormous value in special-purpose computers. We all know that computers are ubiquitous, and soon they will sink beneath notice, like the electric motor. How many of you know how many electric motors you have in your kitchen? In five years the same question will be asked: how many computers do you have in your home?

Almost all of them you won't see. But the general-purpose computers are going to measure the future of computing, not the special-purpose ones. VLSI places a tremendous burden on those of us who are concerned with imaginative uses of computing to find out how to control and to utilize the great benefit that comes from microcircuitry.

In the 1950s we often asked ourselves, "What are our goals?" As computers were applied in new areas, as new computers kept coming out, as we saw that there were waves of students who wanted to learn about computers, we visualized a world in which everything would be done by computers, everyone would be literate in computers, but what is the goal? I don't really know whether a science depends on having a major problem. Physicists are very fortunate in that they can create their major problems quite easily; all they do is say that there must be some new fundamental particle. Society, because of nuclear energy, has cheerfully paid for this search. Biologists, of course, have suddenly come up with a major problem: genetic engineering.

What is the major problem in computer science? Is there one? Can there ever be any? In thinking about it, I have come to the conclusion that if there is any major problem, it is the problem of bridging the gap between neuroscience and psychology. If one looks at neuroscientists, one finds that they work very deep inside the nervous system at an extremely primitive level; they work on neurons. It is as though computer scientists spent all their time looking at gates. On the other end of the spectrum is the psychologist, who sees man as an entity, as a totality, trying to understand what makes him tick. The psychologist's weapons are gross and very, very macroscopic. How can we create a bridge between neuroscience and psychology? My conclusion is that computer science is the discipline that will provide this bridge, and the bridge will come from the study of software. *There* is a major problem worth sinking your teeth into. Software—collections of symbols that execute processes—is our external way of trying to model the way thinking goes on. Of course, we are very primitive. Nevertheless, it seems to us that is the clue: computer science—if any discipline will—will ultimately provide us the bridge that tells us how the neurons, working as gates, pass signals by the billions in such a way that our brain causes us to behave in a way that psychologists can say, "Ah! I understand."

We've learned some other things, too. Some of them are so trivial and so obvious that we've ignored them. For instance, syntax is extraordinarily expensive. Nothing slows programming down as a plethora of syntax. When one looks at a new language such as Ada, one observes that the disease is in its final stages there. It's a language that is redolent with syntax. Why is syntax so expensive? Well, when you build systems that include other systems in which you wish to generate programs, every time you work with heavy syntax you must build heavy parsers and all the software that has to be carried along. Everything slows to a crawl. It is obvious why a language like LISP has proved so fruitful in artificial intelligence. It has no syntax. Parsing is automatic, and when one wishes to build up languages within, systems within, they all look the same. The same thing that has happened in the human body—that has worked so well in the development of all complex organisms—happens there. Why is it that we have not extended the same point of view toward other programming languages? The reason, of course, is that in these other programming languages, we always think of having built systems at the design table, that once having been built they will stay that way forever. All of our bitter experience tells us they do not. I think we learned some of those lessons in the 1950s, and we neglected our role as teachers in not passing them along.

I would like to close with one last remark. We live in a country in which computers have flowered. When I ask people, "Why is it that computers have flowered in the United States?" the answer is usually "Lots of bucks; the Defense Department; IBM"—as if these are natural phenomena that existed all the time. In point of fact, I think there is another reason. I think computers have flowered in this country because of our national style for accomplishing things. This country has always supported entrepreneurial activities—people who have ideas and are willing to sweat to bring them about. Computers flower in such an environment because on a computer everything is possible, although we have since learned that nothing is easy. Compare that with, for example, the Soviet Union. The Soviet Union, having a large centralized society, needs computers much worse than we do. Yet they are totally unable to produce them, totally unable to apply them in anywhere near the profusion that we find here. They have the wrong kind of society for the instrument they most badly need. Tony Hoare, in his Turing Award lecture, also talked of a style of life. The European style has always worked very hard at producing elegant constructions—devices that fit. Holland, for example, is a very small country, and when going to Holland one finds that the instruments they use are also small. Russia is an enormous country; they use large instruments. So it never surprised me that the Russians decided to build a compiler once that would simultaneously compile PL/1, Cobol, and Algol. Holland gave us Edsger Dijkstra, with structured programming and natural Dutch construction.

Computers really are an explanation of what *we* are. Our goal, of course, ought to be to use this tool of our age—as Saul Rosen has said, the computer age—to help us understand why we are the way we are, today and forever.

QUOTATIONS[41]

"Any noun can be verbed."

"People in charge are the last to know when things go bad."

"It is easier to get forgiveness than permission."

---

[41]Perlis made a habit of adding pithy sayings to his talks, lectures, and presentations, and thus may be one of the most quoted computer pioneers—along with Richard Hamming.

"The goal of computation is the emulation of our synthetic abilities, not the understanding of our analytical ones."

"The best is the enemy of the good." (Perlis 1981)

"Fools ignore complexity;
Pragmatists suffer it;
Some can avoid it;
Geniuses remove it." (Perlis 1982)

"Both knowledge and wisdom extend man's reach. Knowledge led to computers, wisdom to chopsticks."

"If a professor tells you that computer science is x but not y, have compassion for his students."

"When we write programs that learn, it turns out that we do and they don't."

BIBLIOGRAPHY

Biographical

Anon., "Alan J. Perlis, 1922–90," *Comm. ACM*, Vol. 33, No. 5, May 1990, pp. 604–605.

Perlis, Alan J., "The American Side of the Development of Algol," in Wexelblat, Richard L., ed., *History of Programming Languages*, Academic Press, New York, 1981.

Perlis, Alan J., "Two Thousand Words and Two Thousand Ideas—The 650 at Carnegie," *Ann. Hist. Comp.*, Vol. 8, No. 1, Jan. 1986, pp. 62–65.

Significant Publications

Carr, John W., III, and Alan J. Perlis, "A Comparison of Large-Scale Calculators," *Control Engineering*, Vol. 3, Feb. 1956, pp. 84–96.

Perlis, Alan J., et al., *Software Metrics*, MIT Press, Cambridge, Mass., 1981.

Perlis, Alan J., "Epigrams on Programming," *ACM SIGPLAN Notices*, Vol. 17, No. 9, Sept. 1982, pp. 7–13.

Charles A. Phillips

Born 1906, Hastings, Neb.; died March 8, 1985, Washington, D.C.; chairman of the CODASYL committee and leader in the creation of Cobol; recipient of Howard Bromberg's tombstone.

Education: Hastings College and University of Nebraska.

Professional Experience: Colonel, US Air Force, 1941–1946; US Treasury Department, US State Department, Department of Defense, 1946–1962; vice president, Computer and Business Equipment Manufacturer's Association (CBEMA), 1962–1972; director, Management Consulting Services, Lybrand, Ross Brothers, and Montgomery, 1972–1976; consultant, CBEMA, 1976–1980; real estate agent, Begg Realtors, Bethesda, Md., 1980–1985.

Phillips was the first chairman of the executive committee of the Conference on Data Systems Languages (CODASYL), which initiated the development of the programming language Cobol. He was also past chairman of American National Standards Committee X3, Information Processing Systems, which pioneered the concept of common industry standards for the computer industry. Under his chairmanship Committee X3 developed standards for the programming languages Fortran and Cobol, the American Standard Code for Information Interchange (ASCII), punched cards, and several other firmware standards.

QUOTATION

Phillips coined the phrase "do not fold, spindle or mutilate!"

BIBLIOGRAPHY

Biographical

Phillips, Charles A., "Recollections on the Early Days of Cobol and CODASYL: Reminiscences (Plus a Few Facts)," *Ann. Hist. Comp.*, Vol. 7, No. 4, Oct. 1985, pp. 304–309.

Bromberg, H., " . . . the Story of Sending the Cobol Tombstone to Charlie Phillips," *Ann. Hist. Comp.*, Vol. 7, No. 4, October 1985, pp. 309–310.

John Robinson Pierce

Born March 27, 1910, Des Moines, Iowa; aka science fiction author J.J. Coupling, Bell Telephone Laboratories namer of the transistor and early promoter of communications satellites.

Education: BS, California Institute of Technology, 1933; MS, California Institute of Technology, 1934; PhD, California Institute of Technology, 1936.

Professional Experience: Bell Telephone Laboratories: member, technical staff, 1936–1952; director, electronics research, 1952–1955; director of research, Electronic Communications, 1955–1958; director of research, Communications Principles, 1958–1961; executive director, 1961–1963, executive director of research, Communications Principles and Systems Division, 1962–1965, executive director of research, Communications Science Division, 1961–1963; California Institute of Technology: professor of engineering, 1971–1980, emeritus professor of engineering, 1980–present; chief technologist, Jet Propulsion Laboratory, 1979–1982.

Honors and Awards: Morris Liebman Memorial Prize, Institute of Radio Engineers, 1947; Stuart Ballantine Medal, Franklin Institute, 1960; H.H. Arnold Trophy, Aerospace Man of the Year, Air Force Association, 1962; Golden Plate Award, Academy of Achievement, 1962; General Hoyt S. Vandenberg Trophy, Arnold Air Society, 1963; National Medal of Science, 1963; Edison Medal, Institute of Electrical Engineers, 1963; Valdemar Poulsen Gold Medal, 1963; H.T. Cedergren Medal, 1964; John Scott Award, Franklin Institute, 1974; Marconi Award, 1974; Medal of Honor, Institute of Electrical and Electronics Engineers, 1975; Founders Award, National Academy of Engineering, 1977; Marconi International Fellowship, 1979; Microwave Career Award, Microwave Theory and Techniques of IEEE, 1984; Japan Prize, 1985; Arthur C. Clarke Award, 1987; International Telemetering Conference, Pioneer Award, 1990.

Honorary Degrees: DEng, Newark College of Engineering, 1961; DSc, Northwestern University, 1961; DSc, Yale University, 1963; DSc, Polytechnic Institute of Brooklyn, 1967; DSc, Columbia University, 1965; ED, Carnegie Institute of Technology, 1964 ; DSc, University of Nevada, 1970; LLD, University of Pennsylvania, 1974; DEng, University of Bologna (Italy), 1974; DSc, University of Southern California, 1978.

As executive director, Research, Communication Sciences Division at Bell Telephone Laboratories, Dr. Pierce was in charge of work on mathematics and statistics, speech and hearing, behavioral science, electronics, radio, and guided waves. His chief work was in electronic devices, especially traveling wave tubes, microwaves, and various aspects of communication.

He proposed unmanned passive and active communication satellites in 1954. The Echo I satellite launched in 1960 embodied his ideas; he was instrumental in initiating the Echo program, and the East Coast ground station was constructed in his division. Telstar resulted from satellite work that he had initiated.

At Cal Tech he was concerned with energy consumption in personal transportation, satellite systems, synthetic aperture radar, quantum effects in communication, and auditory perception.

At Stanford he has been concerned with a new musical scale (in collaboration with M.V. Mathews), and with various aspects of musical sound and perception.

BIBLIOGRAPHY

Significant Publications

Inose, Hiroshi, and John R. Pierce; with a foreword by Koji Kobayashi, *Information Technology and Civilization*, W.H. Freeman, New York, 1984.

Mathews, Max V., and John R. Pierce, eds., *Current Directions in Computer Music Research*, MIT Press, Cambridge, Mass., 1989.

Pierce, John Robinson, *Almost All About Waves*, MIT Press, Cambridge, Mass., 1974.

Pierce, John Robinson, *An Introduction to Information Theory: Symbols, Signals, and Noise*, 2nd rev. ed., Dover Publications, New York, 1980.

Pierce, John Robinson, and Arthur G. Tressler, *The Research State: A History of Science in New Jersey*, Van Nostrand, Princeton, N.J., 1964.

Pierce, John Robinson, and Edward C. Posner, *Introduction to Communication Science and Systems*, Plenum Press, New York, 1980.

Pierce, John Robinson, *Signals: The Telephone and Beyond*, W.H. Freeman, San Francisco, 1981.

Pierce, John Robinson, *Symbols, Signals, and Noise: The Nature and Process of Communication*, 1st ed., Harper, New York, 1961.

Pierce, John Robinson, *The Science of Musical Sound*, Scientific American Library, San Francisco, 1983.

Pierce, John Robinson, *Theory and Design of Electron Beams*, 2nd ed., Van Nostrand, New York, 1954.

Pierce, John Robinson, *Theory and Design of Electron Beams*, Van Nostrand, New York, 1949.

JOHANNA (HANSI) PIESCH

Born June 6, 1898, Innsbruck, Tyrol, Austria; died September 28, 1992,
Vienna, Austria; one of the earliest authors on the subject of switching alge-
bra; after Shannon but prior to Russian pioneers who often quoted her work.

Johanna Piesch had never been loud, and now she has left us in total
silence at the biblical age of 94. She never published an autobiography, or even talked about herself. She was one of the earliest authors
on switching algebra, and she appears as such in the international literature on the subject.

Johanna (Hansi) Piesch studied physics at the University of Vienna
and then joined the Austrian PTT service. Her first publications were
written in Berlin in 1938 (where she had been moved by the German
administration), the second of which proposes an original simplification method. After World War II she expanded on her thesis, and then
in cooperation with H. Sequenz, then head of the Vienna University of
Technology, on the history of the switching algebra in Austria.

After her retirement, Piesch turned to social work and gave 30
years of service to others. She died on September 28, 1992, in a Vienna
hospital.[42]

BIBLIOGRAPHY

Biographical

Zemanek, Heinz, "Johanna Piesch," *Ann. Hist. Comp.*, Vol. 15, No. 3, 1993,
p. 72.

Significant Publications

Piesch, H., "Begriff der Allgemeinen Schaltungstechnik (Concept of General
Switching Theory)," *Archiv für Elektrotechnik*, Vol. 33, 1939, pp. 672–686.

Piesch, H., "Über die Vereinfachung von Allgeneinen Schaltungen (On the
Simplification of General Switching Circuits)," *Archiv für Elektrotechnik*, Vol. 33,
1939, pp. 733–746.

Piesch, H., "Systematik der Automatischen Schaltung (Systematics of
Automatic Switching)," *OFT*, Vol. 5, 1951, pp. 2–43.

Piesch, H., "Die Matrix in der Schaltungsalebgra zur Planung
Relaisgesteuerter Netzwerke (Matrices in Switching Algebra for the Design of

---

[42]From Zemanek 1993.

Relay Controlled Networks)," *Archiv für elektrische Übertragung*, Vol. 9, 1955, pp. 460–468.

Piesch, H., "Beiträge zur Modernen Schaltalgebra (Contributions to Modern Switching Algebra)," *Conference in Como*, 1956, pp. 16–25.

Piesch, H., and H. Sequenz, "Die österreichischen Wegbereiter der Theorie der Elektrischen Schaltungen (The Austrian Pioneers of the Theory of Electrical Switching)," *Elecktrotechnik & Maschinenbau*, Vol. 75, 1958, pp. 241–245.

JOHN M. M. PINKERTON

Born August 2, 1919, London; took a leading role in the design and construction of the LEO I at J. Lyons & Co. in Great Britain.

Education: BA, natural sciences, Cambridge University, 1940; PhD, Cavendish Laboratory, Cambridge University, 1948.

Professional Experience: engineer, LEO Computers Ltd., 1948–1963; head, research, English Electric Computers, 1963–1968; ICL, 1968–1984.

Honors and Awards: fellow, British Computer Society; fellow, Institution of Electrical Engineers; DSc (Hon.), Loughborough University, 1990.

John M.M. Pinkerton was educated at King Edward VI School, Bath, and at Clifton College, Bristol. He entered Trinity College, Cambridge, in 1937 to read for the natural sciences tripos, graduating in 1940. He spent the war years on radar research. Returning to Cambridge in 1945 he studied ultrasonic absorption in liquids, using a pulse technique at the Cavendish Laboratory; he submitted a PhD thesis in 1948.

He was in charge of the engineering aspects of the development of LEO I, LEO II, and LEO III, and a director of LEO Computers Ltd. when it merged with the Computer Department of English Electric in 1963. LEO (Lyons Electronic Office) was inspired by and based on Maurice V. Wilkes' pioneering EDSAC and was one of the first electronic computers designed specifically for commercial rather than scientific use. Until 1968 he was head of research for English Electric Computers and, from 1968 until retiring in 1984, worked for ICL. He was a member of the team planning ICL's 2900 range and later acted as technical consultant on marketing strategy. He was the representative until retiring, first of LEO Computers, then English Electric Computers, and finally ICL, to the European Computer Manufacturers Association, of which he was twice president.

As an independent consultant since retiring, he has edited a series of books on information technology for a British publisher and now acts as editor of the *ICL Technical Journal.* He is a fellow of the British Computer Society, and of the Institution of Electrical Engineers, and a liveryman of the Company of Information Technologists, a recently formed livery company in the city of London. In 1990 he received an honorary DSc from Loughborough University.

BIBLIOGRAPHY

Biographical

Bird, Peter J., *LEO: The First Business Computer,* Hasler Publ., Wokingham, Berks., UK, 1994.

Evans, Christopher, "Conversation: J.M.M. Pinkerton," *Ann. Hist. Comp.,* Vol. 5, No. 1, Jan. 1983, pp. 4–72.

Lavington, Simon, *Early British Computers,* Digital Press, Bedford, Mass., 1980. See Chapter 13: "LEO and English Electric."

Pinkerton, John M.M., "The Evolution and Design in a Series of Computers, LEO I-III," *Computer Journal,* Vol. 4, Apr. 1961, pp. 42–46.

Pinkerton, John M.M., "Taming Leo," *IEEE Review,* Jan. 1991, pp. 13–17.

Simmons, J.R.M., *LEO and the Managers,* MacDonald, London, 1962; reviewed in *Ann. Hist. Comp.,* Vol. 2, No. 4, 1962, p. 382.

Significant Publications

Pinkerton. J.M.M., "Operating and Engineering Experience Gained with LEO," *Automatic Digital Computation, Proc. Symp. Held at NPL, March 25–28, 1953,* H. M. Stationary Office, London, 1954, pp. 21–34.

Walter Pitts

Inventor, with Warren McCulloch in 1943, of the binary neuron that bears their names, which has strongly influenced basic concepts in AI.

BIBLIOGRAPHY

Significant Publications

McCulloch, Warren S., and Walter Pitts, "A Logical Calculus of the Ideas Immanent in Nervous Activity," *Bull. Mathematical Biophysics*, Vol. 5, 1943, pp. 115–133.

James (Jim) H. Pomerene

Born June 22, 1920, Yonkers, N.Y.; design engineer for the IAS computer with John von Neumann, and the IBM HARVEST system.

Education: BS, electrical engineering, Northwestern University, 1942.

Professional Experience: design engineer, Hazeltine Corp., 1942–1946; Electronic Computer Project, Institute for Advanced Study: staff member, 1946–1951, chief engineer, 1951–1956; IBM Corp.: senior engineer, 1956–1976, IBM Fellow, 1976–present.

Honors and Awards: fellow, IEEE, 1971; Computer Pioneer Award, IEEE Computer Society, 1986; member, National Academy of Engineering, 1988; IEEE Edison Medal, 1993.

James H. Pomerene was born in Yonkers, New York, on June 22, 1920. After receiving his BS degree in electrical engineering from Northwestern University in June 1942, he joined the Hazeltine Corporation and was involved with the design of IFF radar, working in both the microwave and pulse modulator areas.

In April 1946 he accepted an invitation from John von Neumann and Herman Goldstine to join the newly organized Electronic Computer Project at the Institute for Advanced Study in Princeton, New Jersey. This project was to build a parallel stored-program computer that would be the prototype for a number of machines such as the MANIAC, ORACLE, ILLIAC, AVIDAC, and so on. Pomerene designed the adder portion of the arithmetic unit and then was entirely responsible for the development and construction of the electrostatic (Williams tube) memory. In August 1951 he was appointed chief engineer of the project, a position he held until the project was disbanded in 1956.

In July 1956 he joined the IBM Corporation in Poughkeepsie, New York, to work on the STRETCH project. He and several others conducted a study that began the development of the HARVEST computer, and he was subsequently put in charge of the design team. HARVEST was a special system built for the National Security Agency. It consisted of a STRETCH computer to provide standard computer processing, plus a byte vector pipeline unit for processing large amounts of nonnumeric data. HARVEST was unusual in several ways. It had two levels of program control: one level set up a process, including the pattern for fetching and storing bytes from and to memory; and the second level operated on the process set up by the first. It also had a remarkable tape and tape library system that was fully automatic and of great capacity.

Following the completion of HARVEST in 1962, Pomerene spent a year in IBM Research studying the use of multiple processors as a way to increase both computer capacity and system availability. He returned to Poughkeepsie to help with several contract proposals to the government, including a possible second HARVEST and a multiprocessor system, starting a chain of events that led to IBM's first commercial MP system, the Mod 65MP. In 1965 he headed a team doing the preliminary design of the Parallel Network Digital Computer (PNDC), an early SIMD machine proposal. The PNDC was not built, but work on it led Pomerene to the idea of making a highly available memory system out of a number of memory units, each storing but one bit position of a word.

With top management support Pomerene began, in 1966, a special study of a highly available system based on this memory. As envisioned, the memory would read out a block of words on every access and it was conjectured that such a block readout could be useful if each processor in the system were provided with a local memory capable of holding a number of recently used blocks. This arrangement, now known as a cache, was simulated and the results were much better than expected. Subsequently the cache was incorporated in the Model 85 processor.

In 1967 Pomerene was promoted to the position of senior staff member on the Corporate Technical Committee at corporate headquarters in Armonk, New York. He was appointed an IBM fellow in 1976 and soon transferred to the Research Division. He helped to found the High End Machine project in Research and is currently heading a group investigating a number of improvements in high-end 370 processor organization. Results of this work have contributed to high-end processor developments and have led to several important patents.

BIBLIOGRAPHY

Biographical

Pomerene, J.H., "Historical Perspectives on Computers—Components," *Proc. Fall Joint Computer Conf.*, AFIPS Press, Montvale, N.J., pp. 977–983.

Significant Publications

Pomerene, J.H., "Institute for Advanced Study Williams Memory," *Proc. Symp. on Large Scale Digital Computing Machines*, Argonne Nat'l Laboratory, pp. 37–46.

Gilchrist, B., J.H. Pomerene, and S.Y. Wong, "Fast Carry Logic for Digital Computers," *IRE Trans. Electronic Computers*, Vol. EC-4, No. 4, Dec. 1955, pp. 133–136.

Herwitz, P.S., and J.H. Pomerene, "The Harvest System," *Proc. Western Joint Computer Conf.*, San Francisco, Calif., Spartan Books, Baltimore, Md., pp. 23–32.

Pomerene, J.H., "An Approach to Parallel Processing," *Proc. IFIPS Congress 65*, New York, North-Holland, Amsterdam, p. 322.

A. PORTER

Designer, with Douglas Hartree, of the Manchester Meccano differential analyzer.

EMIL POST

Mathematician who in 1936 independently introduced a concept essentially identical to the Turing Machine; credited by John Backus of having introduced him to the basic ideas which led to the development of the Backus-Normal Form (predecessor of Backus-Naur Form).

JOHN POWERS

Bureau of the Census engineer who in about 1910 devised mechanical sensing of card perforations as an improvement of Hollerith's electrical sensing method, and who later founded the Power Accounting Machine Company, which became part of Remington-Rand, then Univac, Sperry-Rand, and eventually UNISYS.

EMERSON WILLIAM PUGH

Born May 1, 1929, Pasadena, Calif.; president of IEEE and leader of the IBM History Project.

Education: BSc, physics, Carnegie Mellon University, 1951; PhD, physics, Carnegie Mellon University, 1956.

Professional Experience: assistant professor of physics, Carnegie Mellon University, 1956–1957; IBM Corp.: staff member, IBM Research, 1957–1958, manager of metal physics group, IBM Research, 1958–1961, visiting scientist at IBM Zurich Laboratory, 1961–1962, senior engineer, IBM Components Division, 1962–1965, IBM Group Director of Operational Memory, 1965–1966, director, Technical Planning, IBM Research Division, 1966–1968, special assistant to IBM vice president and chief scientist, 1968–1971, consultant to the IBM director of research, 1971–1973, research manager of exploratory magnetics, 1975–1980, member, research review board, 1981–1982, member of IBM Technical History Project, 1983–1993; manager of IBM Technical History Project, 1985–1993; executive director of the National Academy of Sciences' study of Motor Vehicle Emissions and Fuel Economy (on leave from IBM), 1974.

Honors and Awards: fellow, American Physical Society, 1962; fellow, Institute of Electrical and Electronics Engineers (IEEE), 1972; president, Magnetics Society, IEEE, 1973–1974; fellow, American Association for the Advancement of Science, 1977; distinguished lecturer, Magnetics Society, IEEE, 1980; IEEE Centennial Medal, 1984; distinguished visitor, IEEE Computer Society, 1984–1986; president elect, president, and past president, IEEE, 1988–1990; Merit Award, Carnegie Mellon University Alumni Association, 1990; Achievement Award, IEEE Magnetics Society, 1991; IEEE Literary Award, 1992.

Emerson W. Pugh was a research staff member at the IBM T.J. Watson Research Center, Yorktown Heights, New York. Technology assessment, the history of computers, information storage technologies, and technology policy are his primary interests.

He has held senior management positions at IBM, including director of memory development for the Data Processing Group and director of technical planning for the Research Division. Earlier he managed the development of the highest-performance main-memory array shipped with System/360 computers. He has initiated and led research and development studies in laboratories in Switzerland, Japan, and the US. On leave in 1974, he served as executive director of a National Academy of Sciences study of automobile emissions and fuel economy conducted for the Environmental Protection Agency and the US Congress.

Pugh was president of the Institute of Electrical and Electronics Engineers (IEEE), the world's largest professional technical society. Previously, he has held numerous IEEE positions, among them executive vice president, vice president for technical activities, president of the Magnetics Society, editor-in-chief of the *Transactions on Magnetics*, and distinguished visitor for the Computer Society. He is also a member of the United Engineering Trustees Board, which is the governing body for the Engineering Societies Library, the Engineering Foundation, and the United Engineering Center in New York City.

Pugh is chairman of the Friends Committee of the IEEE History Center, a director of the IEEE Foundation, and a trustee of the Charles Babbage Foundation.

P

BIBLIOGRAPHY

Significant Publications

Bashe, C.T., L.R. Johnson, J.H. Palmer, and E.W. Pugh, *IBM's Early Computers,* MIT Press, Cambridge, Mass., 1986.

Pugh, E.M., and E.W. Pugh, *Principles of Electricity and Magnetism,* 2nd ed., Addison-Wesley, Reading, Mass., 1970.

Pugh, E.W., "Thin Metallic Films," in Slonczewski, J.C., ed., *Magnetic Materials Digest,* National Academy of Sciences—National Research Council, 1960, pp. 91–101.

Pugh, E.M. and E.W. Pugh, *Principles of Electricity and Magnetism,* Addison-Wesley, Reading, Mass., 1960.

Pugh, E.W., and H.B. Michaelson, eds., "Thin Films," *IBM J. Research and Development,* 1960, pp. 94–205.

Pugh, E.W., "Magnetic Films of Nickel-Iron," in Hass, George, ed., *Physics of Thin Films,* Vol. 1, Academic Press, New York, 1963, pp. 277–334.

Pugh, E.W., and T.O. Mohr, "Properties of Ferromagnetic Films," in Wilsdorf, H.G.F., ed., *Thin Films,* American Society for Metals, Metals Park, Ohio, 1964, pp. 195–226.

Pugh, E.W., *Memories That Shaped an Industry—Decisions Leading to IBM System/360,* MIT Press, Cambridge, Mass., 1984.

Pugh, E.W., L.R. Johnson, and J.H. Palmer, *IBM's 360 and Early 370 Systems,* MIT Press, Cambridge, Mass., 1991.

JACOB RABINOW

Born January 8, 1910, Kharkov, Russia; inventor at the National Bureau of Standards who, in August 1952, reported experimental work on a notched-disk memory, the predecessor of the IBM disk memory.

Education: BS, engineering, City College of New York, 1933; graduate degree, electrical engineering, 1934.

Professional Experience: National Bureau of Standards: mechanical engineer to chief of the Electro-Mechanical Ordnance Division, 1938–1954, chief research engineer, National Engineering Laboratory, 1972–1989, consultant, 1989–present; own engineering company, 1954–1964; vice president, Control Data Corporation, 1964–1972; head, Rabinow Advanced Development Laboratory, 1964–1972; founder, RABCO Company,[1] 1968.

Honors and Awards: The Exceptional Service Award, Department of Commerce, 1949; President's Certificate of Merit, 1948; Certificate of Appreciation, War Department, 1949; Naval Ordnance Development Award, 1945; Certificate of Commendation, NDRC, 1945; Edward Longstreth Medal, Franklin Institute, 1959; 50th Anniversary Medal, CCNY Engineering School, 1969; Jefferson Medal Certificate, American Patent Law Association, 1973; Harry Diamond Award, IEEE, 1977; Industrial Research and Development Scientist of the Year, 1980; doctor of humane letters, Towson State University, 1983; fellow, IEEE; fellow, American Association for the Advancement of Science; fellow, Audio Engineering Society.

Jacob Rabinow was born in Kharkov, Russia, on January 8, 1910. After what he calls a too eventful life as a child in European Russia and Siberia during the revolution, his family moved to China in 1919 and finally came to the US in 1921. He was educated in the schools of New York and graduated from the City College of New York in 1933 with a BS in engineering, and with a graduate degree in electrical engineering in 1934.

Jacob Rabinow spent the depression years at various jobs and finally was appointed as a mechanical engineer to the National Bureau of Standards in 1938. Here he worked on a great many ordnance devices during the war and rose rapidly through the ranks to become chief of the Electro-Mechanical Ordnance Division.

In 1954 he left the government to form his own engineering company. Ten years later, in 1964, his company joined Control Data Corporation; until 1972 he was vice president of that company and head of the Rabinow Advanced Development Laboratory. In 1968 he also formed the RABCO Company to manufacture his straight-line

---

[1]This company was later acquired by the Harmon Kardon Corporation.

phonographs. This company was later acquired by the Harmon Kardon Corporation.

In March 1972 he rejoined the National Bureau of Standards and held several positions, among them that of chief research engineer, National Engineering Laboratory.

In April 1989 Rabinow retired from the government service and is now a consultant at the National Institute of Standards and Technology (formerly NBS). His main duty is the evaluation of inventions submitted to the Office of Energy-Related Inventions.

Jacob Rabinow holds 226 US patents on a very wide variety of mechanical and electrical devices. Among these are the automatic regulation of clocks and watches formerly used in all American automobiles, the automatic letter-sorting machine used by the US Post Office, the magnetic particle clutch, formerly used in several European automobiles, now used in a Subaru car, in airplanes, in servomechanisms and in a great many other machines, the "best-match" principle in optical- and magnetic-character-reading machines, many safety mechanisms for ordnance devices, and the straight-line phonograph.

In addition his patents concern such diverse arts as photography, computer equipment (the world's first magnetic disk memory), card punches and card sorting equipment, and a wide variety of optical, electromagnetic, and mechanical inventions.

He is a member of the National Academy of Engineering, the Cosmos Club, the Philosophical Society of Washington, and the Sigma Xi. He is a fellow of the IEEE, of the American Association for the Advancement of Science, and of the Audio Engineering Society.

In addition to his technical work, Jacob Rabinow has delivered literally hundreds of talks on specific technologies and on invention in general. He was a Regent's Lecturer at the University of California at Berkeley, a frequent guest on radio and TV programs, and the author of many papers. His only full-length book, entitled *Inventing for Fun and Profit,* was published in 1989 by San Francisco Press.

BIBLIOGRAPHY

Significant Publications

Rabinow, J., *Inventing for Fun and Profit,* San Francisco Press, San Francisco, 1989.

GEORGE RADIN

Member of the IBM group that developed the language and the compiler technology in support of the programming language PL/I.

Education: BA, English literature, Brooklyn College, 1951; MA, English literature, Columbia University, 1952; MS, mathematics, New York University; 1961.

Professional Experience: manager, NYU College of Engineering Computer Center; manager, Applications Programming, Columbia University; IBM Corp.: instructor, IBM Systems Research Institute, member, Advanced Computer Utilization Department, manager, Product Planning and Advanced Technology, manager, Advanced Systems Architecture and Design, senior manager, T.J. Watson Research Center.

Honors and Awards: fellow, IBM Corp., 1980.

After joining the IBM Advanced Computer Utilization Department in 1963, Radin has been intimately involved with the development of the programming language PL/I, and has been a member of the design teams for OS/360 and TSS.

BIBLIOGRAPHY

Biographical

Radin, George, "The Early History and Characteristics of PL/I," in Wexelblat, Richard L., ed., *History of Programming Languages,* Academic Press, New York, 1981.

JAN A. RAJCHMAN

Born August 10, 1911, London, UK; died April 1, 1989, Princeton, N.J.;
RCA inventor of the Selectron, which was used in the JOHNNIAC as the
memory system; inventor of the basic concepts of core memories.

Education: DiplEE, Swiss Federal Institute of Technology, 1935; DSc, Swiss Federal Institute of Technology, 1938.

Professional Experience: Radio Corporation of America: student engineer, Testing Department, 1935, member, technical staff, RCA Laboratories, 1936–1958, associate director, Research Systems Laboratory, 1958–1961, director, Computer Research Laboratory, 1961–1967, staff vice president, Data Processing Research, RCA Laboratories, 1967–1969, staff vice president, Information Science, 1969–1976; Mackay Professor, University of California, Berkeley, 1976–1977; consultant, 1977–1989.

Honors and Awards: Levy Medal, Franklin Institute, 1947; Liebman Award, IEEE, 1960; Edison Medal, 1974; Harold Pender Award, University of Pennsylvania, 1977; member, National Academy of Engineering; fellow, American Physical Society; fellow, IEEE; fellow, American Association for the Advancement of Science; member, New Jersey Inventors Hall of Fame.

Born in London, England, where his father was engaged in medical research, at the age of 7 Rajchman returned with his parents to their native Poland, and three years later to Geneva. He graduated from the College de Geneve in 1930, and in 1934 obtained the diploma of electrical engineering from the Swiss Federal Institute of Technology in Zurich; in 1938 he graduated from the same institution with a doctor of science degree.

He emigrated to the US in early 1935, hoping to do research at the RCA Laboratories. After a summer at MIT, RCA employed him in the Testing Department, where he matched the variable condensers for superheterodyne radio receivers to standards, by bending plates by hand. In January 1936 he joined Vladimir K. Zworykin's laboratory in Camden, N.J.

His first research was in electron photomultiplier tubes, to which he applied electrostatic rather than magnetic focusing. The determination of the electron trajectories in the fields of complex electrodes was beyond the computational capabilities of the day, and he resorted to modeling the electron paths by rolling small steel ball bearings on stretched rubber sheets. He designed an intricate system of dynodes to keep gas ions from feeding back to the cathode, which removed the main causes of dark current that set the lower limit of light detection for these phototubes. His designs, which formed the basis of his doctoral thesis, are still the mainstay of present-day multipliers.

At this time Rajchman made informal suggestions to many particle and radiation physicists that they could make a detector out of a sealed-off photomultiplier by putting some phosphor on its face. Thus, he is probably the father of the scintillation counter.

During World War II the laboratory was asked to work on the directors for anti-aircraft guns, using electronic digital systems. The first work was to develop counters, shift registers, and arithmetic units. Under Rajchman's direction the laboratory developed a vacuum tube capable of binary arithmetic, which was dubbed the "computron." A second invention was the function generator, consisting of a large matrix of resistances, which created what would now be known as a read-only memory. The capability for building a complete computer existed, but the laboratory turned down the opportunity to build one, fearing the lack of reliability of the large number of vacuum tubes involved. Rajchman then spent some time consulting with the Moore School at the University of Pennsylvania, transferring much of their know-how to the developers of the ENIAC.

In 1946 John von Neumann asked RCA Laboratories to assist in the development of a memory for the IAS machine. Rajchman developed the selective electrostatic storage tube, which represented the first truly digital, random-access high-speed memory. The storage capacity for each tube was 256 bits. Later Rajchman began to look at magnetic devices, and conceived of the use of the hysteresis loop of toroids as a memory system. The cores were squeezed into shape using a converted aspirin tablet press. Jay Forester and the group at MIT (including An Wang) achieved a similar result and eventually got into a patent dispute with the RCA Laboratories. The early core memory matrices contained 10,000 bits, which Rajchman termed a *myriabit*.

In 1961 Rajchman became director of the Computer Research Laboratory, but eventually RCA departed from the computer field and Rajchman, after spending a year at UC Berkeley, became an independent industry consultant, continuing to make inventions and receive patents.[2]

---

[2]Based on Weiss 1989 and the interview by the staff of the *RCA Engineer*, 1973.

QUOTATION

"I have experienced the great thrill in conceiving an idea and actually implementing it myself, a thrill that I imagine inventors share with artists."(Rajchman, 1973 interview)

BIBLIOGRAPHY

Biographical

Anon., "An Interview with Jan Rajchman," *RCA Engineer,* Vol. 19, No. 2, Sept. 1973; reprinted in part in *Ann. Hist. Comp.,* Vol. 12, No. 2, 1990, pp. 142–146.

Burks, Arthur W., and Alice R. Burks, "The ENIAC: First General Purpose Electronic Computer," *Ann. Hist. Comp.,* Vol. 3, No. 4, 1981, pp. 310–399.

Rajchman, Jan A., "Early Research on Computers at RCA," in Metropolis, N., J. Howlett, and Gian-Carlo Rota, *A History of Computing in the Twentieth Century,* Academic Press, New York, 1980, pp. 465–469.

Weiss, Eric, "Jan A. Rajchman," *Ann. Hist. Comp.,* Vol. 11, No. 4, 1989, p. 328.

Significant Publications

Rajchman, Jan A., et al., *Report on the Development of Electronic Computer,* Research Labs, RCA Manufacturing Co., Inc., Camden, N.J., 1941.

Rajchman, Jan A., "Report on Electronic Predictors for Anti-Aircraft Fire," reprinted in Randell, Brian, *Origins of Digital Computers: Selected Papers,* Springer-Verlag, Berlin, 1982, pp. 345–348.

Rajchman, Jan A., "The Selectron—A Tube for Selective Electrostatic Storage," *Math. Tables and Other Aids to Comp.,* Vol. 2, No. 20, Oct. 1947, pp. 359–361.

Rajchman, Jan A., "The Selective Electrostatic Storage Tube," *RCA Review,* Mar. 1951, pp. 53–87.

Rajchman, Jan A., "Static Magnetic Matrix Memory and Switching Circuits," *RCA Review,* Vol. 13, 1952, pp. 183–201.

Rajchman, Jan A., "A Myriabit Magnetic-Core Matrix Memory," *Proc. IRE,* Vol. 41, 1953, pp. 1407–1421.

ANTHONY RALSTON

Born 1930, New York City; computer educator, numerical analyst, author.

Education: SB, mathematics, MIT, 1952; PhD, mathematics, MIT, 1956.

Professional Experience: member, technical staff, Bell Telephone Laboratories, Whippany, N.J., 1956–1959, supervisor, 1959; lecturer, Department of Mathematics, University of Leeds, Leeds, England, 1959–1960; manager of technical computing, American Cyanamid Company, New York, 1960–1961; Stevens Institute of Technology, Hoboken, N.J.: associate professor of mathematics, 1961–1964, professor of mathematics, 1964–1965, director of the Computing Center, 1961–1965; visiting senior research fellow, Institute of Computer Science, University of London, 1971–1972; visiting professor, Department of Statistics and Computer Science, University College, London, 1978–1979; visiting professor, Department of Computing, Imperial College of Science and Technology, London, 1985–1986; State University of New York at Buffalo: professor, computer science, 1967–present, chairman, 1967–1980, professor, mathematics, 1965–present, director, Office of Computer Services, 1967–1970, director, Computing Center, 1965–1967.

Honors and Awards: ACM Distinguished Service Award, 1982; fellow, American Association for the Advancement of Science, 1989; fellow, ACM, 1994.

Ralston was born in New York City in 1930, graduated from the Bronx High School of Science in 1948, and then attended MIT, where he graduated with an SB in mathematics in 1948 and a PhD in mathematics in 1952. He spent three years at the Bell Telephone Laboratories as a member of technical staff and then supervisor (interrupted by a six-month sojourn in the US Army) working on military systems, mainly the Nike Zeus antiballistic missile system. During this time he was awarded his only patent, on a "track initiator" for sorting and categorizing the trajectories of incoming missiles. While at Bell Telephone Laboratories he published his first book, *Mathematical Methods for Digital Computers* (co-edited with H.S. Wilf), the first of a series of three books and an encyclopedia.

Following a year as a lecturer at the University of Leeds, England, he became manager of technical computing for the American Cyanamid Corporation in 1960. Thinking better of the world of industry, however, he left after five months to become associate professor of mathematics and director of the Computer Center (initially an IBM-1620 and, later, the last manufactured Univac 1105) at the Stevens Institute of Technology. He has been an academic ever since.

Before leaving Stevens in 1965, he was promoted to professor and published *A First Course in Numerical Analysis,* which for some years was a standard text in this subject. In 1965 he left Stevens for the State

University of New York at Buffalo, where he has been ever since, except for four sabbatical years at the University of London. Originally professor of mathematics and director of computer services (until 1970), he founded the Department of Computer Science at Buffalo in 1967 and remained its chair until 1980.

Service on the editorial boards of the *Journal of the ACM* and *Computing Reviews* in the late 1960s led to an invitation from George Forsythe to run for the ACM Council as Northeast regional representative in 1968. Election to this post led to further elections as ACM vice president (1970–1972) and president (1972–1974). During those years some progress was made on putting ACM on a firmer organizational and financial footing. Following service on the AFIPS board of directors ex officio as ACM president, Ralston became AFIPS president in 1975 and spent a rather stormy year in that post trying unsuccessfully to wean AFIPS away from dependence on the National Computing Conference and into new ventures such as publishing a popular journal of computing, a project which AFIPS never embraced but which was resurrected outside AFIPS later (see below). After urging more activity by ACM in the human rights field for some years, Ralston became the first chair of the Committee on Scientific Freedom and Human Rights in 1980 and served in that post for eight years.

During the 1970s Ralston moved away from numerical analysis to more specifically computer science pursuits, which included publication of a textbook (*An Introduction to Programming and Computer Science*) and the editing of the *Encyclopedia of Computer Science* (first edition, 1976, second edition, 1982, third edition, 1992), which for 15 years was the only reference of its kind and still is the major one-volume reference in computer science. During this period he served a term on the Computer Science and Technology Board of the National Research Council.

Starting in the late 1970s and continuing until the present, his interests turned to education, first the mathematical aspects of computer science education, then college and university mathematics education generally and, for the past few years, elementary and secondary mathematics education. He has been at the forefront of those calling for more emphasis on discrete mathematics in undergraduate mathematics and computer science education, beginning with a paper "Computer Science, Mathematics and the Undergraduate Curricula in Both" and culminating in 1991 with a book, *Discrete Algorithmic Mathematics* (coauthored with Stephen B. Maurer).

Ralston's increasing interest in mathematics education in the 1980s led to a term on the board of governors of the Mathematical

Association of America, as well as a term on the newly chartered Mathematical Sciences Education Board of the National Research Council. During the 1980s he also became the founding (and, as it turned out, only) editor of *Abacus,* a magazine intended to be a popular journal of computing, but which never achieved a wide audience, and which ceased publication when Ralston resigned as editor after five years in that post.

His current interests are in precollege education broadly, with a particular focus on mathematics education.

QUOTATION

"Questions about education arouse strong feelings. For this reason and because seldom, if ever, can propositions about education be proved or even strongly supported with evidence, they provoke strong statements. . . . Our essential proposition is simple and not immodest. It is time to consider (i.e., try) an alternative to the standard undergraduate mathematics curriculum, which would give discrete analysis an equivalent role to that now played by calculus in the first two years of the undergraduate curriculum."

BIBLIOGRAPHY

Significant Publications

Ralston, A., and H.S. Wilf (coeditor and author of two chapters), *Mathematical Methods for Digital Computers,* John Wiley and Sons, New York, 1960. [French, German, and Japanese translations].

Ralston, A., *A First Course in Numerical Analysis,* McGraw-Hill, New York, 1965. [Hungarian, Polish, Spanish, Czech, and Bulgarian translations].

Ralston, A., and Stephen B. Maurer, *Discrete Algorithmic Mathematics,* Addison-Wesley, Reading, Mass., 1991.

Ralston, A., et al., *Encyclopedia of Computer Science,* 3rd ed., Van Nostrand Reinhold, New York, 1992.[3]

---

[3] 2nd edition was entitled *Encyclopedia of Computer Science and Engineering;* the 3rd edition returned to the original title.

Brian Randell

Born April 16, 1936, Cardiff, UK; developer with Lawford Russell of the Whetstone KDF9 Algol compiler, and the coauthor of the first significant textbook on compilers.

Education: Cathays High School, Cardiff; BSc, ARCS, mathematics, Imperial College of Science and Technology, University of London, 1957; DSc, Imperial College of Science and Technology, University of London, 1989.

Professional Experience: Atomic Power Division, English Electric Company Ltd., Whetstone, Leicester, 1957–1964; IBM Corp., 1964–1969; professor of computer science, University of Newcastle upon Tyne, 1969–present.

Honors and Awards: British Computer Society Award, 1977; fellow, British Computer Society; honorary doctorate, University of Rennes, France, 1991.

On leaving Imperial College in 1957 Randell joined the Atomic Power Division of the English Electric Company Ltd., Whetstone, Leicester. His first work was programming neutron diffusion and reactor kinetic problems on a DEUCE computer. With a colleague, Mike Kelly, Randell wrote the EASICODE compiler for DEUCE.[4]

By 1964 Randell was head of the automatic programming section and had written, or had supervised the writing of, six compilers, most notably the Whetstone KDF9 Algol Compiler with Lawford Russell (described in their book *Algol 60 Implementation*). This compiler was aimed at fast compilation and the provision of good diagnostics and debugging aids, and was developed in conjunction with a project at English Electric, Kidsgrove, led by Fraser Duncan, on the design of an optimizing compiler for Algol.

In 1964 Randell joined the IBM T.J. Watson Research Center at Yorktown Heights, N.Y., to work on a research project with John Cocke and Herb Schorr, concerned with the design of an ultra-high-speed computer. However, Randell was then able to take up an invitation, received some years earlier, to join the IFIP Algol Committee.

With twelve others from IBM Research, in 1965 Randell transferred temporarily to California, where they formed the nucleus of the newly formed Advanced Computer Systems Department of the Systems

---

[4]This compiler was initially bootlegged, and nearly led to the authors' being fired from the company, since their manager viewed it as a diversion from their work on applications programming; later he accepted that it provided a cost-effective means of helping many users to write their own programs.

Development Division, and where Randell worked on CPU architecture and in particular the design of look-ahead units with Don Senzig, but also somehow got involved in the design of a high-speed divider.

In 1966 Randell wrote a memorandum entitled "Clean Machine Design" (about the need to make sure that an architecture was coherent, and not merely the sum of a set of individually defensible design decisions), and shortly thereafter found it appropriate to return to the IBM Research Center; there, Randell became manager of the System Modeling and Evaluation Group in Project IMP, an investigation, led by Manny Lehmann, of the design of both the hardware and software of a large multiprocessing system. During this time Randell worked on dynamic storage allocation (with Carl Kuehner) and on system design methodology (with Frank Zurcher).

In 1968 Randell was one of the group of IFIP Algol Committee members who resigned over Algol 68. Shortly afterwards Randell took part in, and coedited with Peter Naur the report on, the first NATO Software Engineering Conference, an event which had a major effect on his future research thinking. These two experiences led to his involvement in the group that set up the IFIP Working Group on Programming Methodology.

In 1969 Randell returned to the UK to take up a position of professor of computing science in the Computing Laboratory (now Department of Computing Science) of the University of Newcastle upon Tyne. Influenced no doubt by his experiences at the NATO Conference, Randell set up a research project at Newcastle, funded by the UK Science Research Council, and later also the Ministry of Defence, on Fault-Tolerant Computing Systems.

This research interest has continued ever since. In the early days of the research he investigated with colleagues the possibility of software fault tolerance, and introduced the "recovery block" concept. Subsequent major developments have included, with Lindsay Marshall and others, the Newcastle Connection (a transparently distributed Unix system, developed in 1982) and, with John Rushby, the prototype Distributed Secure System, an architecture for multilevel secure systems, later taken up by the Ministry of Defence.

Currently Randell leads the ESPRIT Basic Research Project on "Predictably Dependable Computing Systems." This project, initiated in 1988, involves a number of the main European researchers who, like Randell, were founder-members of the IFIP Working Group on Dependability and Fault Tolerance.

In 1980 Lawford Russell's and Randell's paths crossed again. By this time the former was technical director of CAP, one of the major UK software houses. Together they set up MARI (the Microelectronics

Applications Research Institute), a contract research, development, and training organization in Newcastle, jointly owned by the university, CAP, and Newcastle Polytechnic. Randell remained an associate director of MARI for some 10 years, until it became an independent organization with over 300 staff, involved in a large number of European collaborative research projects.

Randell's other research interest is the history of computing. He first started to pursue this interest actively soon after he reached Newcastle, prompted by his coming across the work of Percy Ludgate, the little-known Irish computer pioneer, while Randell was preparing material for his inaugural lecture. The main results of this research interest have been the book that Randell edited entitled *The Origins of Digital Computers,* and his unveiling of the Colossus machines—code-breaking computers that were developed secretly in the UK during World War II.[5]

Since arriving at Newcastle, Randell has had brief sabbaticals and visiting professorships at the University of Toronto, Canada, the University of Otago, New Zealand, the Universities of Kaiserslautern and of Karlsruhe, Germany, and CNRS-LAAS, Toulouse, France.

BIBLIOGRAPHY

Significant Publications

Naur, P., and Brian Randell, eds., *Software Engineering—Report on a Conference Sponsored by the NATO Science Committee, Garmisch, Germany, 7 to 11 October, 1968,* NATO Scientific Affairs Div., Brussels, 1968.

Randell, B., and L. J. Russell, *Algol 60 Implementation,* Academic Press, London, 1964. (Russian translation published by the State Publishing Organization, Moscow, 1967).

Randell, B., and F.W. Zurcher, "Iterative Multi-Level Modelling: A Methodology for Computer System Design," *Proc. IFIP Congress 68,* North-Holland, Amsterdam, 1968, pp. D138–142.

Randell, B., "A Note on Storage Fragmentation and Program Segmentation," *Comm. ACM,* Vol. 12, 1969, pp.365–369.

Randell, B., *Origins of Digital Computers: Selected Papers,* 3rd ed., Springer-Verlag, Berlin, 1982.

---

[5]See the biographies of I. J. Good, Max Newman, Donald Michie, and Alan Turing.

Randell, B., and J. J. Horning, "Process Structuring," *Computing Surveys,* Vol. 5, No. 1, Feb. 1974, pp. 69–74.

Randell, B., "System Structure for Software Fault Tolerance," *Proc. Int'l Conf. on Reliable Software,* reprinted in *IEEE Trans. Software Engineering,* Vol. SE-1, No. 2, June 1975, pp. 220–232.

Randell, Brian, "Colossus: Godfather of the Computer," in Randell, Brian, *Origins of Digital Computers: Selected Papers,* Springer-Verlag, Berlin, 1977, pp. 349–354.

Randell, B., "The COLOSSUS," in Metropolis, N., et al., eds., *A History of Computing in the Twentieth Century,* Academic Press, New York, 1980, pp. 47–92.

Randell, B., D.R. Brownbridge, and L.F. Marshall, "The Newcastle Connection, or, Unixes of the World Unite," *Software Practice & Experience,* 1982, pp. 1147–1162.

Randell, B., and J.M. Rushby, "A Distributed Secure System," *Computer,* July 1983, pp. 55–67.

Randell, B., and R.H. Campbell, "Error Recovery in Asynchronous Systems," *IEEE Trans. Software Engineering,* Vol. SE-12, No. 8, Aug. 1986, pp. 811–826.

Randell, B., J.P. Black, and L.F. Marshall, "The Architecture of Unix United," *Proc. IEEE,* Vol. 75, No. 5, May 1987, pp. 709–718.

Randell, B., and J.E. Dobson, "Formal Verification: Public Image and Private Reality," *Comm. ACM,* Vol. 32, No. 4, Apr. 1989, pp. 420–422.

MINA REES[6]

Born August 2, 1902, Cleveland, Ohio; director of the mathematical section of the Office of Naval Research who, in the 1950s, used Navy resources to support the fledgling computing community.

Education: AB, Hunter College, 1923; AM, Columbia University, 1925; PhD, mathematics, University of Chicago, 1931.

Professional Experience: Hunter College: instructor to professor, mathematics, 1926–1961, dean, faculty, 1953–1961, emeritus professor of mathematics, 1972–present; City University of New York: founder and dean, Graduate

[6]aka Mrs. Leopold Brahdy.

Studies, 1961–1968, provost, Graduate Division, 1968–1969, president, 1969–1972, emeritus president, 1972–present; technical aide and executive assistant, chief, Applied Mathematics Panel, National Defense Research Committee, Office of Science Research and Development, 1943–1946; Office of Naval Research: head, Mathematics Branch, 1946–1949, director, Mathematics and Science Division, 1949–1952, deputy science director, 1952–1953; National Research Council: member, Mathematics Division, 1953–1956, member, executive committee, 1954–1956.

Honors and Awards: King's Medal for Service in Engineering, 1948; fellow, American Association for the Advancement of Science (president, 1971, chairman of board, 1972); Public Welfare Medal, National Academy of Sciences, 1983; IEEE Computer Society Pioneer Award, 1989; 18 honorary degrees from US colleges and universities.

Mina Rees, after receiving her PhD in mathematics at the University of Chicago in 1931 and serving her academic apprenticeship on the faculty of Hunter College, received her initiation into the military applications of mathematics during World War II when she served as assistant to the chief of the Applied Mathematics Panel of the Office of Scientific Research and Development. For her work, she was honored by both Britain and the US. At the end of the war, the Navy invited her to establish the mathematical research program in the newly created Office of Naval Research. This proved to be a surprisingly effective effort that expanded the horizons of mathematical research in the US and strengthened programs in mathematics throughout the country. Her work was recognized in 1962 when the Mathematical Association of America gave her its first Award for Distinguished Service to Mathematics.

Among Rees' activities in Washington, one that proved particularly significant was her participation, on behalf of the Navy, in the government sponsorship that proved critical in the infancy of computers. In addition to providing wide support for university research of basic importance to the emerging computer field, ONR collaborated with the National Bureau of Standards in supporting and directing its program. This program claims, as one of its achievements, funding the production of the first commercially produced electronic, stored-program computer, the Census Univac that was delivered in 1951 and used in analyses of the 1950 census data.

When, in 1953, Rees left Washington to become dean of the faculty of Hunter College, she continued her support of the Bureau of Standards as chairman of the Bureau's Advisory Committee on Mathematics, and was a member of the Mathematics Division of the National Research Council, where she was chairman of the

Subcommittee on Applied Mathematics of the Commission on a Survey of Research in Mathematics in the United States, 1954–1956. There followed public service activities for the Defense Department, for several academic organizations, and for the American Association for the Advancement of Science, of which she became the first woman president in 1971.

With her assumption of the position of dean of graduate studies and, later, first president of the Graduate School and University Center of the newly established City University of New York, Rees' activities became focused on the strengthening of graduate education in her own institution and throughout the US. In 1970, she was chairman of the Council of Graduate Schools in the United States. From 1964 to 1970 she was a member of the National Science Board.

Since her retirement in 1972, Rees has continued to serve on boards that are concerned with applications of research to social problems, including the delivery of health care. She is a member of visiting committees in two universities and works with a number of foundations concerned with improving the effectiveness of the educational establishment.

BIBLIOGRAPHY

Biographical

Rees, Mina, "The Computing Program of the Office of Naval Research, 1946–53," *Ann. Hist. Comp.*, Vol. 4, No. 2, 1982, pp. 102–120.

Rees, Mina, "The Federal Computing Machine Program," *Ann. Hist. Comp.*, Vol. 7, No. 2, 1985, pp. 156–163.

Significant Publications

Rees, Mina, *Theory of Air Warfare*, Vol. II, Summary Technical Report, Applied Mathematics Panel, McGraw-Hill, New York, 1947.

Rees, Mina, "Warren Weaver," *Biographical Memoirs*, Vol. 57, National Academy of Sciences, 1983, pp. 493–530.

MARIAN REJEWSKI

Born August 16, 1905, Bydgoszcz, Poland; died February 13, 1980, Warsaw, Poland; Polish cryptographer who helped break the Enigma codes prior to the work at Bletchley Park.

Education: MPhil, University of Poznan, 1929.

Professional Experience: insurance underwriting, Göttingen, 1929–1930; lecturer, Institute of Mathematics, University of Poznan, 1930–1932; Polish Cipher Bureau, 1932–1945; Clerk, Bydgoszcz, 1945–1967.

BIBLIOGRAPHY

Biographical

Rejweski, Marian, "How Polish Mathematicians Deciphered the Enigma," *Ann. Hist. Comp.*, Vol. 3, No. 3, 1981, pp. 213–234.[7]

IDA RHODES (HADASSAH ITZKOWITZ)

Born May 15, 1900, between Nemirow and Tulcin, Ukraine; died February 1, 1986, Rockville, Md.; mathematician, pioneer programmer, and language translation specialist.

Education: BA, mathematics, Cornell University, 1923; MA, mathematics, Cornell University, 1923.

Professional Experience: Mathematical Tables Project, New York City, 1940–1947; National Applied Mathematics Laboratories, NBS, 1947–1964.

Honors and Awards: Exceptional Service Gold Medal, Department of Commerce, 1949; Certificate of Appreciation, Department of Commerce, 1976; Univac I Pioneer, AFIPS National Computer Conference, Chicago, 1981.

Ida Rhodes was born Hadassah Itzkowitz on May 15, 1900, in a Jewish village between Nemirow and Tulcin in the Ukraine about 150 miles

---

[7]Includes afterwords by Cipher A. Deavours and I. J. Good.

southwest of Kiev. Her stories of her youth were not those of the poverty described in *Fiddler on the Roof*. Instead she told of a Russian countess who owned, she said, about 99 communities. "She [the countess] was a great naturalist and set up a school for the poor of the area. She was very kind and wanted to adopt me. I said that was impossible, that I already had a family. Nevertheless she often had me as a house guest and arranged for the finest of kosher food for me. She took me riding and showed me plants and explained what I could expect of the plants' development by the next time we visited. There was an island we visited in one of her parks where the swans nested. The lady was careful to instruct me never to touch the swan eggs or the mother would disown them." Later, after Rhodes had left Russia, at the time of the Bolshevik revolution, the local communities sent a delegation to the local soviet, urging good treatment for the countess, and for a while she was spared.

Rhodes' parents, David and Bessie Sinkler Itzkowitz, brought her to the US in 1913, where she attended Cornell University (1919–1923). She was elected to Phi Beta Kappa in 1922 and received her BA in mathematics in February 1923 and her MA in September of the same year. She later studied at Columbia University (1930–1931).

One of the stories she told about these years involved Albert Einstein. About 1936 she joined a group of mathematicians who each weekend piled into their cars to race to Princeton to spend weekends in informal seminars with Einstein (she carefully pronounced it "Einshtein"). When she entered with the others, Einstein looked at her a moment and said, "It must have been in 1922 that we first met at Cornell. Have you learned to talk since then?" At the earlier meeting Rhodes had been so impressed with Einstein's reputation that she had said practically nothing.

She held several positions involving mathematical computations before she joined the Mathematical Tables Project (MTP) in New York City in 1940. The MTP was a particular effort of the New Deal within the Works Projects Administration to relieve unemployment among mathematicians by setting them to work creating mathematical tables using pencil, paper, and desk calculators.[8] It was sponsored by the National Bureau of Standards and later supported by the Office of Scientific Research and Development. Rhodes' major work for MTP was as a planner and supervisor of the preparation of the *Handbook of Mathematical Functions*, Number 55 in the Applied Mathematics Series of the NBS.

---

[8]Salzer, H.E., "New York Mathematical Tables Project," *Ann. Hist. Comp.*, Vol. 11, No. 1, 1989, p. 52.

In 1947 Rhodes' boss in New York told her to go to the NBS in Washington and learn what she could about the new efforts by NBS to develop electronic computers. After a week there, she was so disappointed with her own incapacity, as she saw it, that she returned to New York and scolded her boss for having humiliated her. He told her to pack again, that the Washington people had been very much impressed and wanted her to work with them in the bureau's development and procurement of automatic electronic digital computers.

The purpose and first five years of progress of this part of NBS, set up in July 1947 as the National Applied Mathematics Laboratories (NAML), are recited in a contemporary paper (1953) by John H. Curtiss, its chief.[9] In this paper Curtiss specifically identifies Rhodes as one of those in the Machine Development Laboratory (MDL) of NAML who was most active in offering consulting and advisory service to the many government agencies needing it. (In this period Rhodes was moved from MDL to the administration of the NAML as a consultant.) In addition to her consulting work, she was a pioneer in the analysis of systems of programming. She designed the C-10 language in the early 1950s for the Census Bureau Univac I, and designed the original computer program used by the Social Security Administration. She was a pioneer in the application of computers to language translation, being one of the first to recognize the importance of parsing sentences and separating the roots of words from their prefixes and suffixes as initial steps in the process.

As mentioned by Curtiss, she gave orientation lectures on computers to government agencies and private firms, explaining how computers could enable them to do their work better, more easily, and faster. She taught computer coding techniques, including special classes for the physically handicapped, that is, deaf mutes and the totally blind. She also taught Russian within NBS. She lectured widely on computers and their applications.

In 1949 the Department of Commerce awarded her an Exceptional Service Gold Medal for "significant pioneering leadership and outstanding contributions to the scientific progress of the nation in the functional design and application of electronic digital computing equipment."

She formally retired from NBS in 1964 but continued to be active as a consultant in the Applied Mathematics Division until 1971. In

---

[9]Curtiss, John H., "The National Applied Mathematics Laboratories of the National Bureau of Standards," *Ann. Hist. Comp.*, Vol. 11, No. 2, 1989, pp. 69–98.

retirement Rhodes maintained an immense worldwide correspondence.

In 1976 the Department of Commerce gave her a Certificate of Appreciation "on the occasion of the 25th anniversary of Univac I in recognition of your services to the Information Revolution." At the 1981 National Computer Conference in Chicago she was cited as a Univac I Pioneer.

Her long interest in the Hebrew calendar culminated in her paper, "Computation of the Dates of the Hebrew New Year and Passover," *Computers and Mathematics with Applications,* Vol. 3, 1977, pp. 193–196.

Her benevolences went beyond generous gifts to Hebrew charities to the extent of a 1977 gift to the NBS for azaleas and rhododendrons to be planted near the Administration Building in honor of the three directors under whom she served: Lyman J. Briggs, Edward U. Condon, and Allen V. Astin.

A friend of Rhodes reported that Golda Meir, later Prime Minister of Israel, who used to live in her New York apartment house, had urged her to go to Israel. The friend remarked that if it had not been for her dedication in caring for her aging parents she might have done her main work in Israel.

As she aged, her heart condition required that she conserve her energy, so she cut back on phone calls and correspondence, finally moving to a nursing home. As reading became more tiring, she comforted herself with the comment that the dimming of her eyes had a compensatory benefit: she couldn't see so many of the wrinkles on her face.[10]

BIBLIOGRAPHY

Biographical

Blanch, Gertrude, and Ida Rhodes, "Table Making at NBS," in Scaife, B.K., ed., *Studies in Numerical Analysis, Papers in Honor of Cornelius Lanczos,* Royal Irish Academy, Dublin, and Academic Press, New York, 1974, pp. 1–6.

Weiss, Eric, "Ida Rhodes," *Ann. Hist. Comp.,* Vol. 14, No. 2, 1992, pp. 58–59.

---

[10]From Weiss 1992.

Louis Robinson

Born May 7, 1926, Chelsea, Mass.; died March 28, 1985, White Plains, N.Y.; computer manager who used his talents and corporate resources for the benefit of the community.

Education: BS, University of Massachusetts (Amherst), 1949; MA, Syracuse University, 1951; PhD, mathematics, Syracuse University, 1953.

Professional Experience: instructor, mathematics, Syracuse University, 1952–1953; IBM Corp.: Applied Science representative, 1953–1956, manager, Mathematics and Applications Department, 1956–1958, Market Development Department, 1958–1959, market analyst, 1959–1961, systems engineer, 1961–1962, scientific computing, 1963–1965, manager, Systems Development, 1965–1969, director, Standards and Systems Evaluation, 1969–1972, Standards and Systems Analysis, 1972–1975, director, Science Centers, 1975–1982, director, University Relations, 1982–1985.

A longtime IBM employee, "Lou" Robinson made significant impacts in several areas as he traveled through the corporation. He was among the first to advocate the use of computers for statistical modeling and simulation in business applications. Also sensitive to the human side of information processing, he was responsible for the application of computers to Braille translation. He managed the original NASA Vanguard satellite tracking project for IBM, and he advised government groups on privacy and security legislation relating to computers. As director of standards and systems evaluation, he represented IBM in the American National Standards Institute committee X3 (Information Processing), encouraging the development of industry-wide standards. During his last assignment as director of University Relations, he provided a strong interface between IBM and university computer programs.

QUOTATION

"The computer is a tool for the realization of ideas, and it carries with it a challenge for all of us. We have started to change the way people work, the way people live, the way people think. . . . The challenge for us is to learn how to apply information-processing machines so that they are used to improve the human condition in different ways." (1983 EDUCOM Annual Conference)

BIBLIOGRAPHY

Biographical

Anon., "Louis Robinson," *Perspectives in Computing*, IBM, White Plains, N.Y., 1985, p. 48.

NATHANIEL ROCHESTER

Born January 14, 1919, Buffalo, N.Y.; chief architect of IBM's first scientific computer and of the prototype of its first commercial computer, and developer of symbolic assembly language programming.

Education: BS, MIT, 1941.

Professional Experience: MIT Radiation Laboratory, 1941–1943; Sylvania Electric Products, 1943–1948; IBM: 1948–1992, engineering manager, 700 series, 1954–1959, director, Experimental Machine Research, 1959.

Honors and Awards: fellow, IEEE,[11] 1958; IBM Fellow, 1967; Computer Pioneer Award, IEEE Computer Society, 1984.

Rochester worked on radar at the MIT Radiation Laboratory from 1941 to 1943 and for Sylvania Electric Products until he joined IBM in 1948. After being chief architect of IBM's first scientific computer and of the prototype of its first commercial computer (IBM-701, Defense Calculator), and in 1953 having developed symbolic assembly language programming, in 1954 he was appointed engineering manager of the 700 series, which included both. He was made director of experimental machine research in 1959 and became an IBM fellow in 1967. He is also a fellow of IEEE.

---

[11]At the time of the award the organization was the IRE.

BIBLIOGRAPHY

Biographical

Rochester, N., "The 701 Project as Seen by Its Chief Architect," *Ann. Hist. Comp.*, Vol. 5, No. 2, Apr. 1983, pp. 202–204.

Significant Publications

Astrahan, M.M., and N. Rochester, "The Logical Organization of the New IBM Scientific Calculator," *Proc. ACM*, 1952, pp. 79–83.

Rochester, Nathaniel, "Symbolic Programming," *IRE Trans. Electronic Comp.*, Vol. EC-2, 1953, pp. 10–15.

SAUL ROSEN

Born February 8, 1922, Port Chester, N.Y.; died June 9, 1991, West Lafayette, Ind.; chief software designer for the Philco Transac S-2000, the world's first transistorized computer.

Education: BS, City College, 1941; MA, University of Cincinnati, 1942; PhD, University of Pennsylvania, 1950.

Professional Experience: instructor, mathematics, University of Delaware, 1946–1947; lecturer, University of California, Los Angeles, 1948–1949; assistant professor, Drexel Institute of Technology, 1949–1951; Burroughs Corp.: associate research engineer, 1951–1952, manager, Eastern Applied Mathematics Section, Electrodata Division, 1956–1958; assistant professor, University of Pennsylvania, 1952–1954; associate professor, Computational Laboratory, Wayne University, 1954–1956; Philco Corp.: manager, Computer Programming and Service, 1958–1960, consultant, Computer and Programming Systems, 1960–1962; Purdue University: professor, mathematics and computer science, 1962–1966 and 1967–1991; director, Computing Center, 1968–1987; professor of engineering, associate director of computing, State University at Stony Brook, 1966–1967.

Honors and Awards: ACM Distinguished Service Award,[12] 1984.

---

[12]"For his continued dedication to extending the frontiers of computer science."

Born in Port Chester, N.Y., Rosen graduated from the City College of New York in 1941 with a BS in mathematics. He received an MS in mathematics from the University of Cincinnati in 1942 and then served in the Army Signal Corps in Europe until 1946. After the war he attended the University of Pennsylvania, where he earned his PhD in mathematics in 1950; after two years at Drexel and a year at Burroughs, he returned to the Moore School of Electrical Engineering, working on the successor machines to ENIAC. In 1954 he left Philadelphia and spent two years at Wayne (now Wayne State) University in Detroit. He returned to Philadelphia in the fall of 1956 as manager of the Eastern Applied Mathematics Section of the ElectroData Division of Burroughs Corporation. The work of this section would now be called software support.

In 1947 he became involved in the activities of the fledgling Association for Computing Machinery, first on the languages committee that eventually led to Algol, and then as first managing editor of the *Communications of the ACM*.

In the spring of 1958 he declined an offer from his employer, the ailing Burroughs Corporation, to move to California, and instead joined the Philadelphia-based Philco Corporation to be manager of programming systems at $18,000 per year. Philco was about to enter the general-purpose scientific computer field with its as yet unbuilt Transistorized Automatic Computer, TRANSAC S-2000. In many ways it was considered at that time to be a modern version of the IAS computer. It was to be faster and more powerful than the IBM-704 or the IBM-709 and would have all the advantages that transistors gave over vacuum tubes.

Rosen had misgivings about Philco's ability to successfully attack IBM head-on but felt that, although the programming management task he himself had undertaken was extremely difficult, he could handle it and handle it well. He later wrote (1991) that he was probably "Quixotic," a word which he applied to the whole Philco computer effort.

Just before his death Rosen finished writing, from memory, a detailed account of his career at Philco, "Philco: Some Recollections of the Philco TRANSAC S-2000."

In it he summarized his two years at Philco in these words. "I had started from scratch and had built up a good programming systems department. We had designed and built and delivered software products, an assembler, a Fortran compiler, subroutine libraries, and service routines that were being used by . . . customers on a daily basis. I received praise and good increases in pay from Philco management."

He left Philco in 1960 chiefly because he had lost confidence in Philco's long-term prospects in the computer field. He remained in the Philadelphia area, working as an independent consultant. In 1962 he joined the initial faculty of the Computer Sciences Department at Purdue University, a department that is the oldest such department in the US, and probably in the world.

For one year in the mid-1960s he was a professor of engineering at the Computing Center of the State University of New York at Stony Brook, returning to Purdue in the fall of 1967, as a faculty member and director of the Purdue University Computing Center until 1987, and a member of the faculty until his death.

He wrote extensively on practical systems programming, and in 1967 produced his major book, *Programming Systems and Languages,* a carefully selected collection of articles from computer journals and conferences ranging from the historical to the technical details of preparing compilers and operating systems. In one chapter, Rosen organized excerpts from the series of opaque IBM manuals concerning Operating System/360 into a comprehensible description, the first available at that time. Rosen demonstrated his interest in the history of computing in his introduction to the book, which is a historical survey of programming systems and languages.

In 1979 he participated in the founding of the AFIPS *Annals of the History of Computing,* contributed to it, and served as one of its editors for the rest of his life. Most recently he was studying and writing about the controversies surrounding the invention of the automatic electronic digital computer. In 1991 *Computing Reviews* published his "The Origins of Modern Computing," in which he retold the story of the start of ENIAC and EDVAC, and critically reviewed the publications, both contemporary and current, that deal with their history. Because of the widely differing interpretations of the events of this era, the editors of *Computing Reviews* felt it necessary to attach eight responses, both pro and con, to this paper.

His professional memberships included the Institute of Electrical and Electronic Engineers and ACM, from which he received the Distinguished Service Award in 1984.

BIBLIOGRAPHY

Significant Publications

Rosen, Saul, ed., *Programming Systems and Languages,* McGraw-Hill, New York, 1967.

Rosen, Saul, "The Origins of Modern Computing," *Computing Reviews*, Vol. 31, No. 9, Sept. 1990, pp. 449–481.

Rosen, Saul, "Philco: Some Recollections of the Philco TRANSAC S-2000," Purdue University Computer Sciences Department Report, CSD-TR 91-051, June 1991.

Douglas T. Ross

Born December 21, 1929, Canton, China; developer of the programming language APT.

Education: AB cum laude, mathematics, Oberlin College, 1951; SM without course specification, MIT, 1954.[13]

Professional Experience: MIT: head of the Computer Applications Group, Electronics Systems Laboratory, lecturer, Electrical Engineering Department, project engineer, MIT Computer-Aided Design Project; SofTech Corp.: founder and president, 1969–1975, chairman, board of directors, 1975–present.

Honors and Awards: Joseph Marie Jacquard Award, Numerical Control Society, 1975; Prize Paper Award, AFIPS Spring Joint Computer Conference for "Theoretical Foundation for the Computer-Aided Design System," coauthored with J.E. Rodriguez, 1963; Prize Paper Award, 20th Anniversary National Meeting, Association for Computing Machinery (ACM) for the paper "AED Approach to Generalized Computer-Aided Design," August 1967; Distinguished Service Award, Society for Manufacturing Engineers, 1980.

Ross has held many positions at MIT, including head of the Computer Applications Group at the Electronics Systems Laboratory, lecturer in the Electrical Engineering Department, and project engineer for the MIT Computer-Aided Design Project. His activities include:

- directing development of an integrated system of program development, integration, and testing tools for production of large-scale military programs;

---

[13] He completed the course requirements for the degree of PhD in mathematics at MIT in 1956.

- creating and directing development of the APT System for automatic programming of numerically controlled machine tools, now an international standard;
- leading the MIT Computer-Aided Design Project including research and development in language theory, language design, generalized compiler construction, computer graphics hardware and software, and design applications.

In 1969, SofTech was founded. Ross was president from 1969 to 1975 and is now chairman of the board of directors.

He was an organizer and participant in the NATO Software Engineering Conferences in Germany (1968) and Italy (1969).

BIBLIOGRAPHY

Biographical

Ross, Douglas T., "Origins of the APT Language for Automatically Programmed Tools," in Wexelblat, Richard L., ed., *History of Programming Languages,* Academic Press, New York, 1981.

Significant Publications

Ross, Douglas T., and J.E. Rodriguez, "Theoretical Foundation for the Computer-Aided Design System," *Proc. AFIPS Spring Joint Computer Conference,* Spartan Books, Baltimore, Md., 1963.

Ross, Douglas T., "AED Approach to Generalized Computer-Aided Design," *Proc. 20th Ann. National Meeting ACM,* ACM, New York, Aug. 1967.

J. BARKLEY ROSSER

Born December 6, 1907, Jacksonville, Fla.; died September 5, 1989, Madison, Wis.; mathematical logician who contributed the Church-Rosser theorem to the study of computer science.

Education: BS, physics, University of Florida; MS, physics, University of Florida; PhD, logic, Princeton University, 1934.

Professional Experience: Proctor Research Fellowship, Princeton; National Research Council Fellowship, Harvard University, 1935–1936; Cornell University, 1936–1963; director, Mathematics Research Center (MRC), University of Wisconsin, 1963–1978.

Honors and Awards: Presidential Certificate of Merit; Commendations from the Department of the Army and the Secretary of the Navy.

J. Barkley Rosser, professor emeritus of mathematics and computer science at the University of Wisconsin and former president of SIAM, died on Tuesday, September 5, 1989, at the age of 81.

Rosser was born in Jacksonville, Florida, on December 6, 1907. (He was to claim later that he owed his interest in scholarship to the enforced rest that had accompanied the periodic bouts of malaria he experienced while living in Florida.) He graduated from the University of Florida with BS and MS degrees in physics, and received a PhD in logic from Princeton University in 1934 under Alonzo Church. He held a Proctor Research Fellowship at Princeton and a National Research Council Fellowship at Harvard University (1935–1936), after which he moved with his wife Annetta to Cornell University, which remained his academic home until 1963.

Initially, the focus of Rosser's mathematical research was on the foundations of mathematical logic, and he had a parallel interest in number theory. Over the years, Rosser wrote three books on logic: *Many-Valued Logics* (1952), *Logic for Mathematicians* (1953), and *Simplified Independence Proofs* (1969).

The world events of 1939 and 1941 affected Rosser as they did many pure mathematicians. Turning to his early interest in physics and applications, in 1944 he went to the Allegheny Ballistics Laboratory to work on rocket theory and design. Several books emerged from this experience: two dealing with the mathematical aspects of rocket flight and ballistics, and the three-volume *Space Mathematics,* which appeared in 1966 under his editorship. This wartime experience also left him with a respect for those who support the security of the nation and a personal acceptance of the possibility that he could be called on to fill similar roles in the future.

As a logician, Rosser could appreciate the exciting possibilities that lay ahead for the primitive computers he had seen and used. Accordingly, he was well prepared when approached in 1949 to become director of research at the newly created Institute for Numerical Analysis, located at UCLA and sponsored by the National Bureau of Standards. At this early stage in the history of computing, Rosser was able to assemble a stellar group of mathematicians whose ultimate impact on the future of computing would be impressive. In addition, he saw the potential of the computer for research in many areas of pure mathematics. One example is the project on rigorous computation of the zeros of the Riemann zeta function; while the final report by Rosser, Lowell Schoenfeld, and James Michael Yohe appeared in 1969, the project had been conceived and planned much earlier.

Rosser continued to make Cornell his base; he served as department chair and directed a total of nine doctoral students, mostly on topics in logic and related areas. With a joint Guggenheim-Fulbright fellowship, he spent the academic year 1953–1954 in Europe, devoting much of his time to research on topics in logic.

Because able scientific administrators are rare, however, he continued to receive requests to fill administrative posts. In addition to serving on many panels and committees connected with the space program and related projects, he also held other key professional scientific positions, among them director of the Institute for Defense Analysis, chair of the mathematics division of the National Research Council, and chair of the conference board of the Mathematical Sciences.

In 1963 Rosser accepted an invitation to move from Cornell to the University of Wisconsin as director of the Mathematics Research Center (MRC), replacing the retiring founding director, Rudolph Langer. MRC, then seen as one of a number of similar semi-autonomous research centers on the campus, was operating under a contract from the US Army originally awarded to the university in 1956. After an initial period, Rosser modified the center's organization to integrate it more closely into the normal departmental structure of the university. He adhered to his policy of bringing in the best possible persons in an important field, with tenure when available, and providing them with an environment in which they were free to carry out research. Consultation with government mathematicians was a voluntary choice, as for mathematicians elsewhere.

The events of 1965 to 1969 produced tensions on many college campuses, and MRC was an obvious target for protest. Once Rosser realized that reason was of no avail with the opponents of MRC, he continued on the path he felt was right and bore the affronts with stoicism.

In 1970, a misdirected bombing that killed a young physicist who had no affiliation with MRC brought the period of protest to a halt. Yet the incident did not end the productive work of MRC or that of Barkley Rosser; two of his papers on the zeta function were yet to appear. He retired from the University of Wisconsin in 1978 as professor emeritus of both mathematics and computer science.

It is interesting that at different times Rosser served as president of both the Association of Symbolic Logic and SIAM, two organizations whose stated goals might seem rather far apart. His invited address at the end of his term as president of SIAM was titled "A Runge-Kutta for All Seasons," and his last publications dealt with number theory. His public service record was recognized by a Presidential Certificate of Merit and other decorations and commendations from the Department of the Army and the Secretary of the Navy.[14]

BIBLIOGRAPHY

Biographical

Buck, R.C., S.V. Parter, and L.B. Rall, Obituary, *SIAM News*, 1989.

HEINZ RUTISHAUSER

Early Swiss computer scientist who worked on Konrad Zuse's Z4 and developed his own two-dimensional programming system Plankalkul—not to be confused with Zuse's own earlier system of the same name.

BIBLIOGRAPHY

Biographical

Bauer, Friedrich L., "Between Zuse and Rutishauser—The Early Development of Digital Computing in Central Europe," in Metropolis, N., J. Howlett, and Gian-Carlo Rota, *A History of Computing in the Twentieth Century*, Academic Press, New York, 1980, pp. 505–524.

---

[14]From Buck et al. 1989.

Schwartz, H.R., "The Early Years of Computing in Switzerland," *Ann. Hist. Comp.*, Vol. 3, No. 1, 1981, pp. 121–132.

Significant Publications

Rutishauser, H., et al., *Programmgestuerte Digitale Rechengerate (Elektronische Rechenmaschinen),* Mitt. Aus dem Inst. f. Angewandte Mathematik an der E. T. H., Zurich, Vol. 2, 1951.

James M. Sakoda

Developer of the "dynamic storage allocator" DYSTAL, based on the Fortran language.

Sakoda studied psychology at the University of California at Berkeley and received a PhD in 1949. From 1958 to 1962 he represented the University of Connecticut at the MIT Computation Center. From 1962 to 1981 he was professor in the Department of Sociology at Brown University; he is now professor emeritus. He was director of the Social Science Computer Laboratory from 1962 to 1975 and of the Social Science Data Center from 1975 to 1981. He was on the NIH Computer Advisory Committee from 1960 to 1965. Developer of the "dynamic storage allocator" DYSTAL, he has published works on DYSTAL and even one on origami.

BIBLIOGRAPHY

Biographical

Sakoda, James M., "DYSTAL: Non-numeric Applications of Fortran," *Ann. Hist. Comp.*, Vol. 6, No. 1, Jan. 1984, pp. 37–38.

Gerard Salton

Born May 8, 1927, Nuremberg, Germany; longtime leader in practical information retrieval.

Education: BA, Brooklyn College, 1950; MA, Brooklyn College, 1952; PhD, applied mathematics, Harvard University, 1958.

Professional Experience: instructor to assistant professor, Harvard University, 1958–1965; Cornell University, Computer Science: associate professor, 1965–1967, professor, 1967–present, department chairman, 1971–1977.

Honors and Awards: Guggenheim Fellow, 1963; first ACM-SIGIR Award for Contributions to Information Retrieval, 1983; Humboldt Foundation Senior Scientist Award, 1988; Award of Merit, ASIS, 1989.

Salton was the last of Howard Aiken's PhD students at the Harvard Computation Laboratory in the 1950s, and he was one of the first programmers for the Harvard Mark IV computer. He became interested in natural-language processing, especially in information retrieval, and in the early 1960s he designed the well-known SMART retrieval system which, for some 30 years, has been a test-bed for the evaluation of large numbers of information retrieval techniques and strategies. Under the SMART umbrella, many well-known information retrieval concepts were introduced, including the vector processing model replacing the standard Boolean processing systems, sophisticated statistical term-weighting schemes that distinguish concepts important for text representation from other more marginal concepts, and the widely used "relevance feedback" technique for query optimization.

From 1965 to 1968, Salton was editor-in-chief of *Communications of the ACM*, and from 1969 to 1970, editor-in-chief of the *Journal of the ACM*. Between 1972 and 1978, he served on the ACM Council as Northeast regional representative. Currently, Salton is an editor of *Information Systems* and of the *ACM Transactions on Database Systems*. He was a Guggenheim Fellow in 1963 and has received the first ACM-SIGIR Award for contributions to information retrieval in 1983, as well as a Humboldt Foundation Senior Scientist Award in 1988 and the ASIS Award of Merit in 1989. He has published a large number of articles and several books on information retrieval and related areas. The most recent text is *Automatic Text Processing* (Addison-Wesley, 1989).

BIBLIOGRAPHY

Significant Publications

Salton, Gerard, *Automatic Information Organization and Retrieval*, McGraw-Hill, New York, 1968.

Salton, Gerard, ed., *The SMART Retrieval System: Experiments in Automatic Document Processing*, Prentice-Hall, Englewood Cliffs, N.J., 1971.

Salton, Gerard, *Dynamic Information and Library Processing*, Prentice-Hall, Englewood Cliffs, N.J., 1975.

Salton, Gerard, and Michael J. McGill, *Introduction to Modern Information Retrieval*, McGraw-Hill, New York, 1983.

Salton, Gerard, ed., *Research and Development in Information Retrieval: Proceedings*, Springer-Verlag, Berlin, 1983.

Salton, Gerard, *Automatic Text Processing: The Transformation, Analysis, and Retrieval of Information by Computer,* Addison-Wesley, Reading, Mass., 1989.

Salton, Gerard, "Developments in Automatic Text Retrieval," *Science,* Vol. 253:5023, 1991, pp. 974–980.

Jean E. Sammet

Born March 23, 1928, New York, N.Y.; member of the CODASYL Cobol committee, chairman of the Short Range Subcommittee, which developed all the statements of the language; originator and developer of FORMAC, one of the earliest formula manipulation languages; leader in language systematization and historian of computer languages.

Education: BA, mathematics, Mount Holyoke College (magna cum laude, Phi Beta Kappa), 1948; MA, mathematics, University of Illinois, 1949.

Professional Experience: teaching assistant, mathematics, University of Illinois, 1948–1951; dividend technician, Metropolitan Life Insurance Co., 1951–1952; teaching assistant, mathematics, Barnard College, Columbia University, 1952–1953; engineer, Sperry Gyroscope Co., 1953–1958; Sylvania Electric Products: section head, MOBIDIC Programming, 1958–1959, staff consultant, Programming Research, 1959–1961; IBM Corp.: manager, Boston Advanced Programming, 1961–1965, Programming Language Technology manager, 1965–1968, manager, Programming Technology Planning, 1968–1974, manager, Programming Language Technology, 1974–1979, Software Technology manager, Federal Systems Division, 1979–1983, manager, Programming Language Technology, 1983–1986, senior technical staff member, 1986–1988.

Honors and Awards: IBM Outstanding Contribution Award, 1965; Mount Holyoke College Alumnae Association Centennial Award, 1972; member, National Academy of Engineering, 1977; honorary doctor of science, Mount Holyoke College, 1978; ACM Distinguished Service Award, 1985; Augusta Ada Lovelace Award, the Association for Women in Computing, 1989; ACM Fellow (initial group), 1994.

Miss Sammet organized and supervised the first scientific programming group for Sperry Gyroscope Company, 1955–1958. She worked at Sylvania Electric Products, 1958–1961, first as section head for MOBIDIC Programming, and then as staff consultant for Programming Research.

She joined IBM in 1961 to organize and manage the Boston Programming Center in the IBM Data Systems Division to do advanced development work in programming. She initiated the concept, and directed the development, of the first FORMAC (FORmula MAnipulation Compiler), for which she received an IBM Outstanding Contribution Award in 1965. (FORMAC was the first widely used general language and system for manipulating nonnumeric algebraic expressions.) She also started and directed work on other language projects.

In 1965 she became programming language technology manager in the IBM Systems Development Division to enable her to write a book on programming languages. In 1969 her book *Programming Languages: History and Fundamentals* was published by Prentice-Hall and has been described by others as "the standard work on programming languages" and an "instant computer classic."

Between 1968 and 1978 she held various positions in the IBM Federal Systems Division involving planning, internal consulting, and lecturing on programming languages. In 1978 she became the divisional program manager for Ada, with responsibility for coordinating the strategy and actions for IBM's Federal Systems Division to start the use of Ada. She initiated the concept of, and managed the development of, PDL/Ada and its usage in the division. In 1981 she was also assigned corporate responsibility for IBM's activities in Ada standardization.

In 1979 she became software technology manager for FSD; in that capacity she continued her general and Ada language responsibilities and also managed a department to assess and advise on software technology for the division. In 1983, she returned to the position of programming language technology manager to concentrate on programming languages; she continued her involvement with Ada standardization, both internally and externally. In 1986 she was named senior technical staff member, a title she retained until her formal retirement from IBM in December 1988. She is doing consulting and also working on the second edition of her programming languages book.

She taught mathematics at the University of Illinois and Barnard College, and programming courses at Adelphi College, Northeastern University, UCLA, Mount Holyoke College, and IBM's Systems Research Institute. She organized and directed a two-week Programming Technology Symposium for IBM customers under the auspices of the IBM System Sciences Institute in September 1972.

She has given numerous lectures and talks on the subjects of non-numerical mathematics, symbolic computation, and programming languages (general, specific, and historical). She has published over 50 papers on these subjects.

She has been very active in the Association for Computing Machinery and was the ACM president from June 1974 to July 1976. From 1972 to 1974 she served as ACM vice president. In those positions she played a key role in restoring ACM to a healthy financial condition. Prior to that time she was involved in numerous ACM activities: She organized and was the first chairman of the ACM Special Interest Committee on Symbolic and Algebraic Manipulation (SICSAM), 1965–1968. She served as conference and program chairman for the very successful Symposium on Symbolic and Algebraic Manipulation, held in March 1966. She was elected Northeast regional representative (and therefore ACM Council member) 1966–1968. She served as an ACM lecturer from 1967 to 1968 and again in 1972. From August 1968 to September 1970 she served as chairman of the ACM Committee on Special Interest Groups and Committees, responsible for coordinating activities of 26 technical committees organized by the members. In June 1971 she was elected chairman of the ACM Special Interest Group on Programming Languages (SIGPLAN). After finishing the term as ACM president in 1976, she was chairman of the ACM Awards Committee and the Fellowship Investigation Subcommittee for a year. She conceived the idea and served as both general and program chairman for the very successful ACM SIGPLAN History of Programming Languages Conference (HOPL) held June 1978. From January 1979 to January 1987 she was editor-in-chief of ACM *Computing Reviews* and of the *ACM Guide to Computing Literature*. She was the program chairman for the ACM SIGPLAN Second History of Programming Languages Conference (HOPL-II) held in April 1993.

She has also been active in various other professional organizations and committees in the language and standards areas. She was a key member of the group which first developed Cobol in 1959, serving as chairman of the Statement Language Task Group and the Editing Committee. She was a member of the CODASYL Language Structure Group from 1960 until its dissolution in 1964. She was a charter member of USASI X3.4 Committee on Programming Languages from its formation in 1960, and was a member of USASI X3.4.2 Committee on Language Specifications, until the dissolution of each in 1969. She was a consultant to the ANSI X3K5 (Vocabulary) Committee. She was a member of the first DOD-organized Ada Distinguished Reviewers group throughout its existence and was an original member of the DOD-organized Ada Board (a federal advisory committee) from its inception until her resignation in 1989. She organized and chaired the ACM SIGAda Policy Committee for several years. She was a member of the ISO Working Group on Ada for many years.

She has been involved in various other activities involving computing history. Her book *Programming Languages: History and Fundamentals* contained a description of the histories of many languages, as well as significant technical material. In her work on preparing a second edition of that book she is concentrating heavily on the histories of the more modern languages. Her work on the two ACM SIGPLAN Conferences on the History of Programming Languages (1978 and 1993) is mentioned above.

From 1977 to 1979 she organized, and served as first chairman of, the AFIPS History of Computing Committee. In that capacity she initiated numerous projects, including major concerns with archiving material. She assisted in creating the AFIPS journal, *Annals of the History of Computing* in 1978, and was on its editorial board for many years. She initiated and produced the Self-Study Department in that journal through 1991.

From 1983 to 1993 she was on the board of directors of the Computer Museum. She is also on its collections committee. She served on the original executive committee of the Software Patent Institute (1991–) and was its education committee chairman, 1992–1993.

Miss Sammet has voluminous historical files on programming languages, including material from the mid-1950s. Her files have been characterized by two museums as the best in the world for that subject. She also has other files of historical, computer-related material.

QUOTATION

". . . I do not consider an assembly language (even a sophisticated one) to be a programming language. This view differs from that held by some people who maintain that *anything*[1] in which programs are written is a programming language." (Sammet 1969)

BIBLIOGRAPHY

Biographical

Sammet, Jean E., "The Early History of Cobol," in Wexelblat, Richard L., ed., *History of Programming Languages,* Academic Press, New York, 1981.

---

[1]Emphasis added.

Sammet, Jean E., "The Beginning and Development of FORMAC," *ACM SIGPLAN Notices*, Vol. 28, No. 3, 1993, pp. 209–230.

Significant Publications

Sammet, Jean E., "A Method of Combining Algol and Cobol," *Proc. WJCC*, Vol. 19, 1961, pp. 379–387.

Sammet, Jean E., "Survey of Formula Manipulation," *Comm. ACM*, Vol. 9, No. 8, 1966, pp. 555–569.

Sammet, Jean E., "Formula Manipulation by Computer," in Alt, F.L., and M. Rubinoff, eds., *Advances in Computers*, Academic Press, New York, Vol. 8, 1967, pp. 47–102.

Sammet, Jean E., "Revised Annotated Descriptor Based Bibliography on the Use of Computers for Non-Numerical Mathematics," in Bobrow, D.G., ed., *Symbol Manipulation Languages and Techniques, Proc. IFIP Working Conf. Symbol Manipulation Languages*, North-Holland, Amsterdam, 1968, pp. 358–484.

Sammet, Jean E., *Programming Languages: History and Fundamentals*, Prentice-Hall, Englewood Cliffs, N.J., 1969.

Sammet, Jean E., "Software for Non-Numerical Mathematics," in Rice, J.R., ed., *Mathematical Software*, Academic Press, New York, 1971.

Sammet, Jean E., "Roster of Programming Languages," *ACM SIGPLAN Notices*, Vol. 13, 1978, pp. 56–85.

Sammet, Jean E., "The Early History of Cobol," in Wexelblat, Richard L., ed., *History of Programming Languages*, Academic Press, New York, 1981.

Sammet, Jean E., "Why Ada is Not Just Another Programming Language," *Comm. ACM*, Vol. 29, No. 8, Aug. 1986, pp. 722–732.

Sammet, Jean E., "Some Approaches to, and Illustrations of, Programming Language History," *Ann. Hist. Comp.*, Vol. 13, No. 1, 1991, pp. 33–50.

Sammet, Jean E., "Software History," in Ralston, Anthony, and Edwin D. Reilly, Jr., eds., *Encyclopedia of Computer Science and Engineering*, 3rd ed., Van Nostrand Reinhold, New York, 1993, pp. 1224–1229.

Sammet, Jean E., "Key High-Level Languages," in Ralston, Anthony, and Edwin D. Reilly, Jr., eds., *Encyclopedia of Computer Science and Engineering*, 3rd ed., Van Nostrand Reinhold, New York, 1993, pp. 1471–1477.

Sammet, Jean E., "The Beginning and Development of FORMAC," *ACM SIGPLAN Notices*, Vol. 28, No. 3, 1993, pp. 209–230.

Sammet, Jean E., and E. Bond, "Introduction to FORMAC," *IEEE Trans. Electronic Computers*, Vol. EC-13, No. 4, 1964, pp. 386–394.

Arthur Lee Samuel

Born 1901, Emporia, Kan.; died July 29, 1990, Menlo Park, Calif.; pioneer in machine learning.

Education: BS, College of Emporia; MS, MIT, 1926; graduate work, physics, Columbia University.

Professional Experience: instructor, electrical engineering, MIT, 1926–1928; Bell Telephone Laboratories, 1928–1946; professor, electrical engineering, University of Illinois, 1946–1949; IBM, 1949–1966; Stanford University: lecturer and research associate, 1966–1982.

Honors and Awards: IEEE Computer Society Pioneer Award, 1987; fellow, Institute of Electrical and Electronic Engineers; fellow, American Physical Society; fellow, Institute of Radio Engineers; fellow, American Institute of Electrical Engineers; DSc (Hon.), College of Emporia.

Professor Emeritus Arthur L. Samuel died July 29, 1990, at Stanford Hospital from complications related to Parkinson's disease.[2] A pioneer of artificial intelligence research (best known for his program that played championship level checkers), his life spanned a period of broad scientific advancement. Arthur Samuel was born in 1901 in Emporia, Kansas. He graduated from the College of Emporia, and while also working intermittently at General Electric Company in Schenectady, he went on to earn a master of science degree from MIT in 1926. He later did graduate work in physics at Columbia University. In 1946 the College of Emporia awarded him an honorary doctorate.

After his master's degree he stayed on at MIT as an instructor in electrical engineering until 1928, when he joined Bell Telephone Laboratories. At "Bell Labs" he worked mainly on electron tubes. Particularly notable was his work on space charge between parallel electrodes, and his wartime work on TR-boxes, switches that disconnect the receiver of a radar when it is transmitting and prevent the sensitive receiver from being destroyed by the high power transmitter.

In 1946 Samuel became professor of electrical engineering at the University of Illinois, and was active in their project to design one of the first electronic computers. It was there he conceived the idea of a checkers program capable of beating the world champion, to demonstrate the power of electronic computers. Apparently the program was not finished while he was at the University of Illinois, perhaps because the computer was not finished in time.

---

[2]From Tajnai 1991.

In 1949 Samuel joined IBM's Poughkeepsie Laboratory. This move was seen by IBM's competitors as a commitment by IBM to vacuum-tube-based computing. However, as his autobiography describes it, he had to fulfill a dual role there: pushing research on switching transistors and keeping engineers going with the available tube technology. Tubes were used for logic and memory in IBM's first stored program computer, the 701. The memory was based on Williams tubes, which stored bits as charged spots on the screen of a cathode ray tube. Samuel managed to increase the number of bits stored from the customary 512 to 2,048 and to raise the mean time to failure to half an hour. Memory capacities of those machines eventually grew to 8K words. He completed the first checkers program, apparently the world's first self-learning program, on the 701. When it was about to be demonstrated, Thomas J. Watson, Sr., the founder and president of IBM, remarked that the demonstration would raise the price of IBM stock 15 points. It did.

The Samuel Checkers-Playing Program is a very early example of a method now commonly used in artificial intelligence (AI) research, that is, to work in a complex yet understandable domain. Programs for playing games fill the role in AI research that the fruit fly (drosophila) plays in genetics. Drosophilae are convenient for genetics because they breed quickly, and games are convenient for AI because it is easy to compare computer performance with that of people.

Samuel took advantage of the fact that the checker players have access to many volumes of annotated games with the good moves distinguished from the bad ones. Samuel's learning program replayed the games presented in *Lee's Guide to Checkers* to adjust its criteria for choosing moves so that the program would choose as often as possible those moves thought good by checker experts.

In 1961, when Ed Feigenbaum and Julian Feldman were putting together the first AI anthology (*Computers and Thought*), they asked Samuel to give them, as an appendix to his splendid paper on his checker player, the best game the program had ever played. Samuel used that request as an opportunity to challenge the Connecticut state checker champion, the number-four-ranked player in the nation. Samuel's program won. The champion provided annotation and commentary to the game when it was included in the volume.

Because his checkers work was one of the earliest examples of nonnumerical computation, Samuel greatly influenced the instruction set of early IBM computers. The logical instructions of these computers were put in at his instigation and were quickly adopted by all computer designers because they are useful for most nonnumerical computation.

Samuel was a modest man, and the importance of his work was widely recognized only after his retirement from IBM in 1966. He did not relish the politics that would have been required to get his research more vigorously pursued. He was also realistic about the large difference between what had been accomplished in understanding intellectual mechanisms and what will be required to reach the level of human intelligence.

Samuel's papers on machine learning are still worth studying. With great creativity and working essentially alone, doing his own programming, he invented several seminal techniques in rote learning and generalization learning, using such underlying techniques as mutable evaluation functions, hill climbing, and signature tables. One still hears proposals for research in this area less sophisticated than his work of the 1950s. Besides engineering and computer science, Samuel did important management work at IBM. He played a large role in establishing IBM's European laboratories and setting their research directions, especially in Vienna and Zurich. (The Vienna Laboratory did important work in computer language specifications and the Zurich Laboratory in physics, leading to several Nobel prizes.) He became the editor of the influential IBM *Journal of Research and Development*.

Samuel retired from IBM in 1966 and went to Stanford University as a lecturer and research associate, starting yet another life. In 1974 he became a research professor there. He continued his work on checkers until his program was outclassed. He also worked on speech recognition until the funding agency decided to concentrate its speech work on developing a single approach. Samuel was actively teaching up to 1982. He supervised several PhD theses at Stanford.

Arthur Samuel remained an active computer programmer long after age forced him to give up active research. His contributions included work on the SAIL operating system, on software for the Livermore S-1 multiprocessor, and on the TEX typesetting system. His last work, continued up to the age of 86, involved modifying programs for printing in multiple type fonts on some of the Stanford Computer Science Department's computers. We believe he was the world's oldest active computer programmer. The Stanford computer he used tells us that he last logged into it on February 2, 1990, and his home computer was still used throughout the summer.

One of Samuel's talents was understanding inadequate documentation of complicated programs and writing clear and attractive manuals. In 1989 his *First Grade TEX* was translated into Japanese. He started an autobiography, which, unfortunately, takes us only to the middle 1960s.

Arthur Samuel was a fellow of the Institute of Electrical and Electronic Engineers, the American Physical Society, the Institute of Radio Engineers, and the American Institute of Electrical Engineers, and a member of the Association for Computing Machinery and the American Association for the Advancement of Science.

As a person, Samuel was distinguished by his objectivity and his kindness in helping people, especially in sharing his knowledge.

BIBLIOGRAPHY

Biographical

Tajnai, Carolyn E. "Samuel Was Artificial Intelligence Pioneer," *Computing Research News,* Jan. 1991.

Weiss, Eric, "Arthur Samuel," *Ann. Hist. Comp.,* Vol. 14, No. 3, 1992, pp. 55–68.

Significant Publications

Samuel, A.L., "Artificial Intelligence: A Frontier of Automation," *Ann. American Acad. Political and Social Science,* Vol. 340, Mar. 1962, pp. 10–20.

Samuel, Arthur L., "Some Studies in Machine Learning Using the Game of Checkers," in Feigenbaum, Edward A., and Julian Feldman, eds., *Computers and Thought,* McGraw-Hill, New York, 1983, pp. 71–105.

JOSÉ GARCIA SANTEMASES

Born 1907, Spain; died October 23, 1989, Madrid, Spain; Spanish pioneer in informatics and founding member of the International Federation for Information Processing (IFIP).

Honors and Awards: Gran Cuz de Alfonzo X El Sabio; Medalla de Fisica de la Real Sociedad Espanola de Fisica y Quimica; Premio Leorando Torres Quevedo; Medalla de Oro al Mérito en el Trabajo; fellow, IEEE; Medallade Oro del Premio Echegaray de la Real Academia de Ciencias Exactas; Fisicas y Naturales; Silver Core, IFIP; Presidente de Honor de la AEIA (Spanish Association of Informatics and Automation); Miembro de Honor de la FESI (Spanish Federation of Informatics Societies); Medalla de Honor de la Universidad Complutense.

Professor Santemases devoted his life to cultivating and promoting automation and informatics in Spain. His interest in computers was born after meeting Maurice Wilkes in Cambridge in 1949. In 1951 he worked in the Computation Laboratory at Harvard University with Howard Aiken, who was then directing the construction of the Harvard Mark IV computer.

When he returned to Madrid, he promoted the study of computers from his chair at the Universidad Complutense and from the Departmento de Electricidad del Consejo Superior de Investigaciones Cientificas (CSIC) [the Superior Council of Scientific Research]; later he became the director of the Instituto de Electricidad y Automática [the Electricity and Automation Institute]. He studied extensively the work of Leonardo Torres Quevedo, the Spanish pioneer of automata.

In 1952 he delivered the first lectures on computers in Spain at the Universidad Complutense. In 1962 he directed courses on automation for graduates. These courses, transformed into international offerings in 1965 and sponsored by UNESCO, OEA, Instituto de Cultura Hispánica, CSIC, and Universidad Complutense, were repeated until 1970, when specializations in computer sciences were introduced as the last two courses for undergraduates in physics and mathematics at the Universidad Complutense.

In 1958 Santemases was the president of the organizing committee of the International Automation Congress held in Madrid. Present at the congress were Howard Aiken, Sam Alexander, Andrew Booth, Samuel Caldwell, Antonin Svoboda, Maurice Wilkes, Hideo Yamashita, Konrad Zuse, and Heinz Zemanek. This collection of pioneers reveals his preoccupation with the universal dimension of scientific activities.

The following year, a congress sponsored by UNESCO concerning the same subjects was held in Paris, France. During the congress the creation of IFIP was proposed; one of the 13 founding national organizations was Spain, represented by Santemases.[3]

QUOTATION

About Santemases: "Both Professor Santemases and his wife were highly cultured and endearing people. He will be long remembered for his efforts to advance the teaching and development of computer technology in his country." (Isaac Auerbach, first president, IFIP)

---

[3]From an obituary provided by Antonio Vaquero.

BIBLIOGRAPHY

Biographical

Santemases, José Garcia, "Early Computer Developments in Madrid," *Ann. Hist. Comp.*, Vol. 4, No. 1, 1982, pp. 31–34.

Weiss, Eric A., "José Garcia Santemases," Obituary, *Ann. Hist. Comp.*, Vol. 12, No. 4, 1990, p. 277.

Significant Publications

Santemases, José Garcia, "Sobre ciertos aspectos de la ferror-resonancia de un circuito," *Anal. Real Soc. Esp. Fis. y Quim.*, Vol. 31, 1942, p. 21.

Santemases, José Garcia, "Switching Research in Spain," *Proc. Int'l Symp. Theory of Switching*, Harvard University, Cambridge, Mass., 1957.

Santemases, José Garcia, "A Few Aspects of the Impact of Automatics on Society," *Impact of Science on Society*, UNESCO, Vol. 11, No. 2, 1961, pp. 107–126.

ALLAN L. SCHERR

Born November 18, 1940, Baltimore, Md.; pioneer in the development of operating systems for large-scale computers and systems for defining and automating business processes.

Education: SB, SM, electrical engineering, MIT, 1962; PhD,[4] electrical engineering, MIT, 1965.

Professional Experience: IBM Corp.: computer hardware architect, 1965–1968, manager, Programming Systems, executive in programming and systems development, 1968–1991, vice president, technology, IBM Consulting Group, 1991–present.

Honors and Awards: IBM Outstanding Contribution Award for TSO Design and Development, 1971; ACM Grace Murray Hopper Award for pioneering work in performance analysis (of time-sharing systems), 1975; fellow, IEEE, 1983;

---

[4]Thesis: "An Analysis of Time-Shared Computer Systems."

IBM Fellow for his development of IBM's general-purpose time-sharing system, the large-scale operating system, MVS, and software support for distributed processing and communications networks, 1984.

Scherr was born in Baltimore in 1940 and in 1958 graduated from the Baltimore Polytechnic Institute. He then went on to MIT, where in 1959 he was first exposed to computers in a programming course taught by John McCarthy (the inventor of LISP) and Nat Rochester (a future IBM fellow). Scherr's concentration during his undergraduate and master's degree studies was a computer logic design. During this period he also worked as a cooperative student with IBM doing logic design with their advanced technology groups. This work resulted in several patented inventions.

In 1963 he was part of the original group of graduate students at MIT's Project MAC (which later became the laboratory for Computer Science). His PhD research involved measuring and modeling the performance of the world's first general-purpose time-sharing system, CTSS. This work, still referenced in system performance analysis literature, earned him the ACM's Grace Murray Hopper Award in 1975, and was published as a research monograph by the MIT Press.

Scherr joined IBM as a staff engineer in 1965 and worked on the architecture for what became the IBM System/370 line. His work in simulating program-addressing patterns and memory allocation were instrumental in establishing IBM's virtual storage architecture and the direction for memory allocation in OS/360.

In 1967 he led a series of studies to create a time-sharing system strategy for IBM. His proposal for a general-purpose time-sharing system was accepted and he became the manager of the group that designed and led the implementation of TSO (Time Sharing Option), today's most widely used time-sharing system.

In 1971 he participated in the IBM task force that proposed the creation of MVS, a multiple virtual storage, multiple coupled processor, high-visibility operating system for IBM's large computer systems. Scherr became the overall manager for the project until its shipment in 1974. This was the largest single software release ever produced, consisting of nearly two million lines of new and changed code on a base of over three million lines.

In 1977 he took over the management of the development of a new operating system for distributed processing (DPPX) for IBM's minicomputer line, the 8100. In 1980, after successfully shipping the first release of DPPX, Scherr was named a director of programming in the Systems Communications Division, supervising the development of IBM's networking software (VTAM, TC, NCP) and its premier transac-tion processing system (CICS). After a two-year assignment on the corporate engineering and programming staff, in 1983 Scherr directed the early design work for what later evolved into AS/400, IBM's midrange system line. During this period he also developed an approach to achieving unprecedented levels of productivity from engineering and programming teams.

In 1986 Scherr moved to IBM's Application Solutions Line of Business, where he directed engineering and programming groups developing products for specific application by IBM customers in various industries. In 1989 he directed the technical staff overseeing development for the entire line-of-business and coordinated the creation of an overall application architecture. He represented the application layer of software in the creation of IBM's System Application Architecture and was instrumental in setting its distributed-processing and intelligent-workstation direction.

In 1991 he became vice president of technology in the IBM Consulting Group, responsible for providing leading-edge tools and methodologies for consultants in advising clients on information technology strategy, business process reengineering, and quality.

During the last few years, Scherr has led a research effort in the definition, automation, and management of business processes. His group has developed a new approach to defining business processes that promises to revolutionize the way computers are used in business.

QUOTATION

"Most of the work I've done has been to [bring] things into existence that didn't exist before. . . . In a sense, my whole career's been about building organizations that didn't exist before, creating processes to do things that have never been done before, and solving technical problems that hadn't been solved before. The work I did at MIT was that way as well. There was no real foundation to build on, and I had to make it up as I went along. That's characterized, if not my whole career, at least the parts of my career that I consider the most rewarding. Pioneers are also the people that get arrows shot through them. That's the downside, and I've had my share of arrows pulled out of my hide."[5]

---

[5]Frenkel 1987.

BIBLIOGRAPHY

Biographical

Frenkel, Karen A., "Allan L. Scherr: Big Blue's Time-Sharing Pioneer," Profiles in Computing, *Comm. ACM*, Vol. 30, No. 10, Oct. 1987, pp. 824–828.

Significant Publications

Auslander, Larkin, and A.L. Scherr, "The Evolution of the MVS Operating System," *IBM J. Research & Development*, Vol. 25, No. 5, 1981, pp. 471–482.

Scherr, A.L., *An Analysis of Time-Shared Computer Systems*, MIT Press, Cambridge, Mass., 1966.

Scherr, A.L., "Time-Sharing Measurement," *Datamation*, Apr. 1966.

Scherr, A.L., "Functional Structure of IBM Virtual Storage Operating Systems; Part II: OS/VS2-2 Concepts and Philosophies," *IBM Systems J.*, Vol. 12, No. 4, 1973, pp. 382–400.

Scherr, A.L., "Distributed Data Processing," *IBM Systems J.*, Vol. 17, No. 4, 1978, pp. 324–343.

Scherr, A.L., "A Perspective on Communications and Computing," *IBM Systems J.*, Vol. 22, Nos. 1&2, 1983, pp. 5–9.

Scherr, A.L., "Structures for Networks of Systems," *IBM Systems J.*, Vol. 26, No. 1, 1987, pp. 4–12.

Scherr, A.L., "SAA Distributed Processing," *IBM Systems J.*, Vol. 27, No. 3, 1988, pp. 370–383.

Scherr, A.L., "Managing for Breakthroughs in Productivity," *Human Resource Management*, Vol. 28, No. 3, 1989, pp. 403–424.

Scherr, A.L., "A New Approach to Business Processes," *IBM Systems J.*, Vol. 32, No. 1, 1993.

EDVARD RAPHAEL SCHEUTZ

Born September 13, 1821, Stockholm, Sweden; died January 28, 1881, Stockholm, Sweden; son in the Swedish father-and-son team who in 1853 constructed the world's first commercially available, operational Difference Engine after the style of Charles Babbage.

Education: qualified as an engineer, Technological Institute, Stockholm, 1841.

Honors and Awards: Medaille d'Honneur, L'Exposition Universelle de Paris, 1855.

Around 1830 Edvard's father, Georg Scheutz, first learned of Babbage's work on the Difference Engine. Through the publication of Dionysius Lardner[6] in 1834, he received more detailed information. Georg began to experiment with models of wood, pasteboard, and wire, and soon developed some improvements with the assistance and ingenuity of his son Edvard, then a teenager. By 1842 they had built a calculating unit which was capable of third-order differences; they completed their first engine in 1843, including the printing unit. With funding from the Swedish Academy of Sciences, a second Difference Engine was built according to the Scheutz' plans by Johan Bergström. It was completed in 1853, and was sold to the Dudley Observatory in New York in 1857. A copy of this engine was ordered by the General Register Office in London. Built by Bryan Donkin and Co., this machine was delivered in 1859 and was put to work to produce life-time tables. The Scheutzes and Babbage met for the first time in late 1854, by which time Babbage was deeply involved in his design of the Analytical Engine, his Difference Engine never having been completed. Babbage, however, undertook to publicize the Scheutz machines, designating his son Prevost to develop a notation for describing their second engine.

Edvard went on to complete two other inventions of his own: the rotary steam engine and a methodology for the printing of postage stamps.

The "difference engine business" did not bring the Scheutz family the expected financial returns. Edvard died in 1881 at the age of 59, bankrupt; the Difference Engine's notoriety died with him.[7]

---

[6]Lardner, Dionysius, "Babbage's Calculating Engine," *Edinburgh Review*, No. 120, July 1834.

[7]Reviewed and corrected by Michael Lindgren, National Museum of Science and Technology, Stockholm.

BIBLIOGRAPHY

Biographical

Chase, George C., "History of Mechanical Computing Machinery," *Ann. Hist. Comp.*, Vol. 2, No. 3, 1980, pp. 198–226.

Lindgren, Michael, *Glory and Failure: The Difference Engines of Johann Müller, Charles Babbage, and Georg and Edvard Scheutz*, MIT Press, Cambridge, Mass., 1990.

(PEHR) GEORG SCHEUTZ

Born September 23, 1785, Jönköping, Sweden; died May 22, 1873, Stockholm, Sweden; father in the Swedish father-and-son team who in 1853 constructed the world's first commercially available, operational Difference Engine after the style of Charles Babbage.

Education: law degree, University of Lund, 1805.

Professional Experience: probationer, Göta Hovrätt, 1805–1811; Justitie-Revisionen för Sjöärendena, 1811; deputy actuary, Jönköping, 1812; second auditor, Svea Artillery Regiment, 1812–1816; owner/editor, *Anmärkaren* (newspaper), Stockholm, Sweden, 1816–1836.

Honors and Awards: Medaille d'Honneur, L'Exposition Universelle de Paris, 1855; Swedish Order of Wasa, 1856; Russian Order of St. Anne, 1858.

Georg Scheutz originally had ideas about becoming a mining engineer, but his university did not have the courses necessary to fulfill the requirements, and thus he graduated with a degree in law. He practiced law in various capacities for about 11 years, when his finances, buoyed by inheritances, were sufficient for him to set himself up in business as a newspaper publisher. In 1834 Georg Scheutz published a small book containing an invention which was an improvement on Napier's "bones." In the same year Scheutz learned the details of Babbage's work on the Difference Engine through the publication of

Dionysius Lardner.[8] Scheutz began to experiment with models of wood, pasteboard, and wire, and soon developed some improvements with the assistance and ingenuity of his son Edvard, then a teenager. By 1842 they had built a calculating unit which was capable of third-order differences; they completed their first engine in 1843, including the printing unit. With funding from the Swedish Academy of Sciences, a second Difference Engine was built according to the Scheutz' plans by Johan Bergström in 1853; it was sold to the Dudley Observatory in New York in 1857.

A copy of this engine was ordered by the General Register Office in London. Built by Bryan Donkin and Co., this machine was delivered in 1859 and was put to work to produce life-time tables. The Scheutzes and Babbage met for the first time in late 1854, by which time Babbage was deeply involved in his design of the Analytical Engine, his Difference Engine never having been completed. Babbage, however, undertook to publicize the Scheutz machines, designating his son Prevost to develop a notation for describing their second engine.

Although well known for 30 years, the "difference engine business" did not bring the Scheutz family the expected financial returns. Georg died virtually bankrupt in 1873.[9]

BIBLIOGRAPHY

Biographical

Chase, George C., "History of Mechanical Computing Machinery," *Ann. Hist. Comp.*, Vol. 2, No. 3, 1980, pp. 198–226.

Lindgren, Michael, *Glory and Failure: The Difference Engines of Johann Müller, Charles Babbage, and Georg and Edvard Scheutz*, MIT Press, Cambridge, Mass., 1990.

---

[8]Lardner, Dionysius, "Babbage's Calculating Engine," *Edinburgh Review*, No. 120, July 1834.

[9]Reviewed and corrected by Michael Lindgren, National Museum of Science and Technology, Stockholm.

WILHELM SCHIKARD

Born April 22, 1592, Herrenberg, Wüttemberg; died October 23, 1635, Tübingen; created an adding machine preceding that of Pascal, and using logarithms of Napier; it could perform multiplication and division.

Wilhelm Schickard was professor of Hebrew, professor of Oriental languages, professor of mathematics, professor of astronomy, professor of geography, and, in his spare time, a Protestant minister in the German town of Tübingen during the early 1600s. He has been compared to Leonardo da Vinci in that both had far-ranging interests and inquiring minds. Besides being an excellent mathematician who developed some methods that were still in use well into the nineteenth century, he was a good painter, a good enough mechanic to construct his own astronomical instruments, and an engraver skilled enough to provide some of the copper plates used to illustrate Kepler's great work *Harmonices Mundi.*

It is known that Schickard and Kepler not only knew each other well but also collaborated on several occasions. It was one of these joint efforts that resulted in Schickard's producing the first really workable mechanical adding machine. Kepler and Schickard were both born in the same town; they shared an interest in mathematics and astronomy, and both had associations with Tübingen University. It was only natural that they saw each other whenever possible, and wrote back and forth discussing the problems each was attempting to solve. When Kepler's mother was accused of being a witch and thrown into jail, Kepler returned to Tübingen to help in her defense and, while there, was known to have associated with Schickard. Kepler and Schickard were known to have discussed John Napier's various inventions as early as 1617. During Kepler's stay in Tübingen he shared with Schickard some results he had obtained using Napier's "bones" and logarithms. This seems to have inspired Schickard to consider the design of a machine that would incorporate both a set of Napier's "bones" and a mechanism to add up the partial products they produced in order to completely automate the multiplication process. On September 20, 1623, Schickard wrote to Kepler saying (in translation):

> What you have done in a logistical way (i.e., by calculation), I have just tried to do by mechanics. I have constructed a machine consisting of eleven complete and six incomplete (actually "mutilated") sprocket wheels which can calculate. You would burst out laughing if you were present to see how it carries by itself from one column of tens to the next or borrows from them during subtraction.

Kepler must have written back asking for a copy of the machine for himself because, on February 25, 1624, Schickard again wrote to Kepler giving a careful description of the use of the machine, together with several drawings showing its construction. He also told Kepler that a second machine, which was being made for his use, had been accidentally destroyed when a fire leveled the house of a workman Schickard had hired to do the final construction.

These two letters, both of which were found in Kepler's papers, give evidence that Schickard actually constructed such a machine. However, the drawings of the machine had been lost and no one had the slightest idea of what the machine looked like or how it performed its arithmetic. Then some scholars who were attempting to put together a complete collection of Kepler's works were led to investigate the library of the Pulkovo Observatory near Leningrad. While searching through a copy of Kepler's *Rudolphine Tables*, they found a slip of paper which had seemingly been used as a bookmark. It was this slip of paper which contained Schickard's original drawings of the machine.

Little detail can be seen, but with the hints given in the letters it became possible to reconstruct the machine. The reconstruction was done by Professor Bruno Baron von Freytag Loringhoff, now retired from the post of professor of philosophy at the University of Tübingen. The baron was able to figure out the details of the machine because, among other things, he is an expert on the techniques used by seventeenth-century clockmakers. This reconstruction was featured on a stamp issued by West Germany in 1971 to honor the 350th year of its invention.

In the stamp illustration, the upper part of the machine is set to show the number 100722 being multiplied by 4. The result of this multiplication would be added to the accumulator, using the lower portion of the machine. The upper part is simply a set of Napier's "bones" (multiplication tables) drawn on cylinders in such a way that any particular "bone" may be selected by turning the small dials in Schickard's drawing. Moving the horizontal slides would expose different sections of the "bones" to show any single-digit multiple of the selected number; the fourth multiple is shown exposed in the stamp illustration. The very bottom of the machine contains a simple *aide-memoire*. By turning the small knobs it was possible to make any number appear through the little windows, eliminating the need to have pen, ink, and paper handy to note down any intermediate results in the computation.

The mechanism used to effect a carry from one digit to the next was very simple and reliable in operation. Every time an accumulator wheel rotated through a complete turn, a single tooth would catch in an intermediate wheel and cause the next highest digit in the accumulator to be increased by one. This simple-looking device actually presents a host of problems to anyone attempting to construct an adding machine based on this principle. The major problem is caused by the fact that the single tooth must enter into the teeth of the intermediate wheel, rotate it 36 degrees (one tenth of a revolution), and exit from the teeth, all while only rotating 36 degrees itself. The most elementary solution to this problem consists of the intermediate wheel being, in effect, two different gears, one with long and one with short teeth, together with a spring-loaded detente (much like the pointer used on the big wheel of the gambling game generally known as crown and anchor) which would allow the gears to stop only in specific locations. It is not known if Schickard used this exact mechanism, but it certainly works well on the reproductions constructed by von Freytag Loringhoff.

The major drawback of this type of carry mechanism is the fact that the force used to effect the carry must come from the single tooth meshing with the teeth of the intermediate wheel. If the user ever wished to do the addition 999,999 + 1, it would result in a carry being propagated right through each digit of the accumulator. This operation would require enough force that it might well do damage to the gears on the units digit. It appears that Schickard was aware of this weakness, because he constructed machines with only six-digit accumulators even though he knew that Kepler undoubtedly needed more figures in his astronomical work. If the numbers became larger than six digits, he provided a set of brass rings that could be slipped over the fingers of the operator's hand in order to remember how many times a carry had been propagated off the end of the accumulator. A small bell was rung each time such an "overflow" occurred to remind the operator to slip another ring on his finger.

Although we know that the machine being made for Kepler was destroyed in a fire, there is some mystery as to what happened to Schickard's own copy of the device. No trace of it can be found in European museums. It may well turn up one day in some dusty forgotten corner of an old building, but the more likely situation is that it has simply been lost. This is particularly likely in that Schickard and all his family died during one of the great plagues that swept Europe. As he left no living heirs, the machine was probably taken by someone who could not understand its workings and found its last use as firewood in some family kitchen.[10]

---

[10]Reproduced with permission from Williams 1985.

BIBLIOGRAPHY

Biographical

Möhring, Manfred, "Wilhelm Schickard: Erfinder der Ersten Mechanischen Rechenmaschine (1623)," *J. Wissenschaft und Fortschritt*, GDR Academy of Sciences, Vol. 38, No. 10, 1988.

Williams, Michael R., "From Napier to Lucas: The Use of Napier's Bones in Calculating Instruments," *Ann. Hist. Comp.*, Vol. 5, No. 3, July 1983, pp. 279–296.

Williams, Michael R., *A History of Computing Technology*, Prentice-Hall, Englewood Cliffs, N.J., 1985, pp. 123–128.

HELMUT SCHREYER

Born July 4, 1912; died December 12, 1984, Sao Paulo, Brazil; German engineer who helped Konrad Zuse and experimented with using vacuum tube circuits to perform arithmetic pre-World War II.

Schreyer assisted in the design and construction of Konrad Zuse's pioneering mechanical and electromechanical computers, which were built in Germany during the late 1930s and 1940s, but remained virtually unknown elsewhere until much later. Zuse credits Schreyer with the idea of replacing electromechanical relays with vacuum and neon tubes.

Schreyer began the design of such an electronic computer in 1937. A model was almost completed during World War II, but the work was abandoned and the model was lost.

BIBLIOGRAPHY

Biographical

Bülow, Ralf, "Three Inventors—Scenes from Early German Computing History," *Ann. Hist. Comp.*, Vol. 12, No. 2, 1990, pp. 109–126.

Ceruzzi, Paul E., "The Early Computers of Konrad Zuse, 1935 to 1945," *Ann. Hist. Comp.*, Vol. 3, No. 3, 1981, pp. 241–262.

Significant Publications

Schreyer, H., "Technical Computing Machines," reprinted in Randell, Brian, *Origins of Digital Computers: Selected Papers,* Springer-Verlag, Berlin, 1982, pp. 171–174.

Schreyer, H., "An Experimental Model of an Electronic Computer," *Ann. Hist. Comp.*, Vol. 12, No. 3, 1990, pp. 189–189.

JULES I. SCHWARTZ

Developer of JOVIAL, *Jules Own Version of IAL.*

While attending graduate school at Columbia University, Schwartz became acquainted with some early computing devices at the T.J. Watson Center in New York. He joined the Rand Corporation in 1954 where he worked on the JOHNNIAC computer, primarily in the development of utilities, and on the IBM-704, where his major work was on the PACT compiler (one of the early high-level language efforts). He joined the SAGE System development at Lincoln Laboratory in late 1955, where his major contribution was to the Lincoln Utility System. After Systems Development Corporation (SDC) was split off from Rand, he became involved with various system efforts, which eventually led to language work and the development of JOVIAL (Jule's Own Version of IAL)[11] in 1959–1960. After JOVIAL, beginning in the early 1960s, he became responsible for a wide variety of projects, including early time-sharing efforts on the AN/FSQ-32, database management, continued language efforts, and other activities. By the end of the 1960s, he was director of technology at SDC. In 1970 he joined Computer Sciences Corporation, where his primary responsibilities were consulting, managing, auditing, and working on a variety of commercial and government systems. In the process, he has been responsible for the design of several general- and special-purpose languages.[12]

---

[11]International Algebraic Language
[12]From Schwartz 1981.

BIBLIOGRAPHY

Biographical

Schwartz, Jules I., "The Development of Jovial," in Wexelblat, Richard L., ed., *History of Programming Languages*, Academic Press, New York, 1981.

Dana Stewart Scott

Born October 11, 1932, Berkeley, Calif.; logician; joint creator with Christopher Strachey of a theoretical system for the study of program properties and language definitions—denotational semantics; joint recipient of the 1976 ACM Turing Award with Michael Rabin.

Education: BA, University of California, Berkeley, 1954; PhD, Princeton University, 1958.

Professional Experience: instructor, University of Chicago, 1958–1960; assistant professor of mathematics, University of California, Berkeley, 1960–1962; associate professor of mathematics, University of California, Berkeley, 1962–1963; associate professor of logic and mathematics, Stanford University, 1963–1967; professor of logic and mathematics, Stanford University, 1967–1969; visiting professor of mathematics, University of Amsterdam, 1968–1969; professor of philosophy and mathematics, Princeton University, 1969–1972; professor of mathematical logic, Oxford University, 1972–1981; University professor of computer science, mathematical logic, and philosophy, Carnegie Mellon University, 1981–present (on leave); Hillman Professor of Computer Science, Carnegie Mellon University, 1989–present (on leave); Osterreich University Professor, symbolic computation and logic, University of Linz, 1992–present.

Honors and Awards: Bell Telephone fellow, Princeton University, 1956–1957; Miller Institute fellow, University of California, Berkeley, 1960–1961; Alfred P. Sloan research fellow, 1963–1965; Guggenheim Foundation fellow, 1978–1979; visiting scientist, Xerox Palo Alto Research Center, 1978–1979; professorial fellow, Merton College, Oxford, 1972–1981; LeRoy P. Steele Prize, American Mathematical Society, 1972; Turing Award, Association for Computing Machinery (with Michael Rabin), 1976; Drhc, Rijksuniversiteit Utrecht, the Netherlands, 1986; Harold Pender Award, University of Pennsylvania, 1990; Academy Fellowships: American Association for the Advancement of Science, American Academy of Arts and Sciences, British Academy, Finnish Academy of Sciences and Letters, New York Academy of Sciences, US National Academy of Sciences; fellow, ACM, 1994.

Dana Scott's work in logic has concerned the theories of models, automata, and sets, modal and intuitionistic logic, constructive mathematics, and connections between category theory and logic. His interests in philosophy concern the foundations and philosophy of logic and mathematics and the semantical analysis of natural language. Scott's work in computer science has been directed principally toward the development of denotational semantics of programming languages and the mathematical foundations of a suitable theory of computability. His current projects aim at unifying the semantical approach with constructive logical formalisms to be able to give rigorous and machine-implementable proof methods and development tools for the inferential construction of correct programs. Part of the technique is based on modeling computational structures as partially ordered sets in special categories enjoying extensive closure conditions (the theory of domains). Other current projects involve work in information retrieval, electronic publishing (and generally studies on the structure of electronic text), computational linguistics, and computer algebra. Scott has supervised 36 PhD theses within this range of subjects.

QUOTATIONS

"Learn as much as you can while you are young, since life becomes too busy later."

"Try to regard mathematics as an experimental science."

BIBLIOGRAPHY

Significant Publications

Scott, Dana, and J. Kalicki, "Equational Completness of Abstract Algebras," *Koninkl. Nederl. Akademie van Wetenschappen, Proceedings, Series A*, Vol. 58, 1955, pp. 650–659.

Scott, Dana, and A. Tarski, "The Sentential Calculus with Infinitely Long Expressions," *Colloquium Mathematicum*, Vol. 6, 1958, pp. 165–170.

Scott, Dana, and Patrick Suppes, "Foundational Aspects of Theories of Measurement," *J. Symbolic Logic*, Vol. 23, 1958, pp. 113–128.

Scott, Dana, "Existence and Description in Formal Logic," in Schoenman, R., ed., *Bertrand Russell: Philosopher of the Century*, George Allen & Unwin, London, 1967, pp. 181–200.

Scott, Dana, "Some Definitional Suggestions for Automata Theory," *J. Computer and System Sciences*, Vol. 1, 1967, pp. 187–212.

Scott, Dana, "Outline of a Mathematical Theory of Computation," *Proc. Fourth Annual Princeton Conference on Information Sciences and Systems*, 1970, pp. 169–176.

Scott, Dana, "The Lattice of Flow Diagrams," in Engeler, E., ed., *Semantics of Algorithmic Languages,* Springer-Verlag, Berlin, Vol. LNM 188, 1971, pp. 311–368.

Scott, Dana, and C. Strachey, "Toward a Mathematical Semantics for Computer Languages," *Proceedings of the Symposium on Computers and Automata,* Polytechnic Press, Brooklyn, N.Y., Microwave Research Institute Symposia Series, Vol. 21, 1971, pp. 19–46.

Scott, Dana, "Lattice Theory, Data Types and Semantics," in Rustin, R., ed., *Formal Semantics of Programming Languages,* Prentice Hall, Courant Computer Science Symposia, Vol. 2, 1972, pp. 65–106.

Scott, Dana, "Continuous Lattices," in Lawvere, F.W., ed., *Toposes, Algebraic Geometry and Logic,* Springer-Verlag, Berlin, Vol. LNM 274, 1972, pp. 97–136.

Scott, Dana, "Mathematical Concepts in Programming Language Semantics," *AFIPS Conference Proc.*, AFIPS Press, Montvale, N.J., Vol. 40, 1972, pp. 225–234.

Scott, Dana, "Axiomatizing Set Theory," in Jech, T.J., ed., *Proc. Symposia in Pure Mathematics,* American Mathematical Society, Providence, R.I., Vol. 13, Part 2, 1974, pp. 207–214.

Scott, Dana, "Data Types as Lattices," *Proc. Int'l Summer Institute and Logic Colloquium,* Muller, G., et al., eds., Springer-Verlag, Keil, Vol. LNM 499, 1975, pp. 579–651.

Scott, Dana, "Logic and Programming Languages," *Comm. ACM*, Vol. 20, 1975, pp. 634–641.

Scott, Dana, "Relating Theories of the Lambda-Calculus," in Seldin, J.P., and J.R. Hindley, eds., *To H.B. Curry: Essays on Combinatory Logic, Lambda Calculus and Formalism,* Academic Press, New York, 1980, pp. 403–450.

Scott, Dana, "Domains for Denotational Semantics," in Nielsen, M., and E.M. Schmidt, eds., *Automata, Languages and Programming,* Springer-Verlag, Vol. LNCS 140, 1982, pp. 577–610.

Scott, Dana, and C. A. Gunter, "Semantic Domains," in Van Leeuwen, Jan, ed., *Handbook of Theoretical Computer Science; Formal Models and Semantics,* Vol. B, Elsevier/MIT Press, 1980, pp. 633–674.

CLAUDE ELWOOD SHANNON

Born April 30, 1916, Gaylord, Mich.; inventor of information theory and first use of the word "bit."[13]

Education: BS, University of Michigan, 1936; SM, MIT, 1940; PhD, mathematics, MIT, 1940.

Professional Experience: assistant, electrical engineering and mathematics, 1936–1939; National Research Council fellow, Princeton University, 1940; research mathematician, National Defense Research Committee, 1940–1941; research mathematician, Bell Telephone Laboratories, 1941–1957; MIT: Donner professor of science, 1958–1980, professor, electrical engineering, 1957–present; emeritus Donner professor of science, 1980–present.

Honors and Awards: Noble Prize, Institute of Electrical Engineers, 1939; Leibmann Prize, Institute of Radio Engineers, 1949; Ballantine Medal, Franklin Institute, 1955; MSc, Yale University, 1954; DSc, University of Michigan, 1961; Life Achievement Prize, Marquis *Who's Who*, 1984; Kyoto Prize, 1985; member, National Academy of Sciences; member, American Academy of Arts and Sciences.

Claude Shannon was a contemporary of the originators of computers such as John von Neumann, Howard Aiken, and Alan Turing, working in the field of communications at the Bell Telephone Laboratories during World War II. While Turing and von Neumann recognized the application of mathematical logic to computer design, it was the 1948 paper of Shannon that set the stage for the recognition of the basic theory of information which could be processed by the machines the other pioneers developed. As part of that theory, Shannon also considered the problems of information distortion, redundancy, and noise, thus providing a means for the measurement of information. This theory of communication was based on the identification of the bit as the fundamental unit of data, which coincidentally was the basic unit of computation. Thus, while aimed at explaining communication, Shannon's theory provided the bridge between communications and computers.

QUOTATION

"The best is yet to come. We've only scratched the surface. Computers can only do what we tell them now, but it will be different in the future."

---

[13]See Tropp 1984.

BIBLIOGRAPHY

Biographical

Slater, Robert, *Portraits in Silicon*, MIT Press, Cambridge, Mass., 1987.

Tropp, Henry S., "The Origin of the Term Bit," *Ann. Hist. Comp.*, Vol. 6, No. 2, 1984.

Significant Publications

Shannon, Claude E., "A Mathematical Theory of Communication," *Bell System Tech. J.*, Vol. 27, 1948, pp. 379–423, 623–656.

Shannon, Claude E., *Programming a Computer for Playing Chess*, Bell Tel. Labs., Murray Hill, N.J., 1948.

Shannon, Claude E., and W. Weaver, *A Mathematical Theory of Communication*, Univ. of Illinois Press, Urbana, 1949.

Shannon, Claude, "A Chess-Playing Machine," *Scientific American*, Vol. 182, Feb. 1950, pp. 48–51.

Shannon, Claude, and John McCarthy, *Automata Studies: Annals of Mathematical Studies*, Princeton Univ. Press, Princeton, N.J., 1956.

JOHN CLIFFORD SHAW

Born 1922; died February 9, 1991, Los Angeles, Calif.; the "father of JOSS," the well-known and landmark personal-computing, time-sharing system developed on Rand's JOHNNIAC machine. Cliff was also part of the Newell-Shaw-Simon consortium, innovators of the Information Processing Languages (IPL I through IPL V), which today we would call artificial intelligence languages.

Shaw was born and raised in California, serving in the US Navy during World War II as an aircraft navigator. Following his return to civilian life he worked as an actuary for an insurance company, taking advantage of his early training and mathematical skills. Cliff joined Rand as a programmer in 1950 on the JOHNNIAC. He collaborated with Allen Newell to develop a radar simulator and, while he was primarily involved in administrative matters, he looked to the means of improving the processes of company management as well as improving the techniques of computation. With Newell and Herbert Simon, he assisted in the development of the "Logic Theory Machine," which provided the first symbolic and list-processing computation system, and formed the base for the development of later "artificial intelligence" languages. The three—Newell, Simon, and Shaw (NSS)—went on to develop a sequence of Information Processing Languages (IPL I through IPL V), and the "General Problem Solver" (GPS).

With the advent of batch processing and closed shop systems, Shaw wanted to preserve the personal contact between the programmer and the computer, and led the development of the JOSS (JOHNNIAC Open-Shop System), a contemporary of Corbató's Compatible Time-Sharing System (CTSS). JOSS was restricted to a primary language that was specifically designed to support interactive computing, rather than providing a platform for the execution of existing (batch-oriented) language systems. There is a precious factual story that concerns a booby trap that Cliff put in JOSS; it was really a first Trojan horse. Rand had a mathematician named Oliver Gross, who worked extensively on JOSS, but was a poor typist and made frequent mistakes. Cliff put in a trap that waited for Oliver (no other user could spring the trap) and after he had made some number of typing mistakes, it printed on the typewriter terminal "Damn it, Oliver, can't you get anything right?" Then the Trojan horse destroyed itself, never to appear again. Oliver was much taken aback, and spent long hours trying to make JOSS repeat the event, but without success.

Cliff worked at Rand from 1950 to 1973 in the Numerical Analysis Department, later the Computer Sciences Department. Upon leaving Rand, he acted as a consultant and devoted himself to church activities.

QUOTATION

Shaw was a stickler for care and precision in his work. As he pointed out on one occasion, the success and impact of JOSS was careful attention to "a million details, each of them decided properly and with care."

BIBLIOGRAPHY

Biographical

Baker, C.L., "JOSS—JOHNNIAC Open-Shop System," in Wexelblat, R.L., *History of Programming Languages*, Academic Press, New York, 1981, pp. 495–513.

Cortada, James W., "Shaw, J. Cliff (1922–)," *Historical Dictionary of Data Processing: Biographies,* Greenwood Press, Westport, Conn., 1987, pp. 236–237.

Shaw, J.C., *JOSS: A Designer's View of an Experimental On-Line Computing System,* Rand Corporation, Rep. No. P-2922, Santa Monica, Calif., 1964.

Significant Publications

Newell, Allen, J.C. Shaw, and H.A. Simon, "Chess-Playing Programs, and the Problem of Complexity," in Feigenbaum, Edward A., and Julian Feldman, eds., *Computers and Thought,* McGraw-Hill, New York, 1983, pp. 39–70.

Newell, Allen, J.C. Shaw, and H.A. Simon, "Empirical Explorations with the Logic Theorem Machine: A Case Study in Heuristics," in Feigenbaum, Edward A., and Julian Feldman, eds., *Computers and Thought,* McGraw-Hill, New York, 1983, pp. 109–133.

Donald Lewis Shell

Born March 1, 1924, Worth Township, Sanilac County, Mich.; inventor of the sorting method that bears his name.

Education: BS, Michigan Technological University, 1944; MS, University of Cincinnati, 1951; PhD, mathematics, University of Cincinnati, 1959.

Professional Experience: instructor, mathematics, Michigan Technological University, 1946–1949; General Electric Co.: mathematician, 1951–1952, numerical analyst, 1952–1953, supervisor, Systems Analysis & Synthesis, 1953–1954, manager, Computer Technology Development, 1954–1956, manager, Evendale Computing, 1956–1957, computer consultant specialist, 1957–1959, manager, Digital Analysis & Computing, Knolls Atomic Power Laboratory, 1960–1961, engineering mathematician, Advance Technology Laboratory, 1961–1963, manager, Computing Applications & Processing Telecommunications & Information Processing Operations, 1963–1966, manager, Information Service Department, 1966–1968, manager, Automation Studies, Research & Development Center, 1968–1969, manager, Information Services Quality Assurance, 1971–1972; Robotics Inc.: chairman of the board and general manager, 1972–1975, manager, File Systems, 1975–1976, manager, Technical Systems, 1976–1978, manager, Application Systems, 1978–1980; manager, Mark II Systems, General Electric Information Services Company, 1980–present.

Peter B. Sheridan

Died August 25, 1992, Greenwich, Conn.; a mathematical logician with a special interest in automatic coding and natural language translations by computer; he was a member of the original Fortran development team, responsible for the compilation of arithmetic expressions.

Education: BS, City College of New York; MS, Fordham University.

Professional Experience: research scientist, IBM Corp., 1952–1992

In referring to the development of the section of the original Fortran compiler, Backus (1984) said:

> When I say that somebody "wrote a section of the compiler," it is important to remember that what I really mean is that they *invented* it—they developed all the groundbreaking techniques used in it. It is a great understatement to say only "somebody wrote a section." Peter Sheridan wrote Section One, which parsed algebraic expressions, translated them into code, and optimized that code.

Roy Nutt (1984) termed the technique of inserting parentheses into an algebraic expression (initially "concocted" by John Backus and Irving Ziller) to be a "dubious technique." Peter Sheridan, in his impressive paper in 1959, proved this to be a viable scheme, although some people did not particularly care for his notation.

BIBLIOGRAPHY

Biographical

Backus, John, "Afterword," *Special Issue on the 25th Anniversary of Fortran, Ann. Hist. Comp.*, Vol. 6, No. 1, 1984, pp. 26–27.

Nutt, Roy, "Compiler Techniques Available in 1954," *Special Issue on the 25th Anniversary of Fortran, Ann. Hist. Comp.*, Vol. 6, No. 1, 1984, pp. 20–22.

Significant Publications

Backus, J.W., R. J. Beeber, S. Best, R. Goldberg, L.M. Haibt, H.L. Herrick, R.A. Nelson, D. Sayre, P.B. Sheridan, H. Stern, I. Ziller, R.A. Hughes, and R. Nutt, *Programmer's Reference Manual, The Fortran Automatic Coding System for the IBM 704 EDPM*, IBM Corporation, New York, 1956.

Sheridan, P.B., "The Automatic Translator-Compiler of the IBM Fortran Automatic Coding System," *Comm. ACM*, Vol. 2, No. 2, Feb. 1959, pp. 9–21.

WILLIAM BRADFORD SHOCKLEY

Born February 13, 1910, London, UK; died 1989, Santa Clara, Calif.; with Walter Brattain and John Bardeen, inventor of the transistor in 1947; the 1956 Nobel laureate.

Education: BS, physics, California Institute of Technology, 1932; PhD, physics, MIT, 1936.

Professional Experience: Bell Telephone Laboratories: member, Technical Staff, 1936–1942 and 1945–1954, director, Transistor Physics Research Facility, 1954; director of research, Antisubmarine Warfare Operations Research Group, US Navy, 1942–1944; founder, Shockley Semiconductor Laboratory, 1954–1989; Stanford University: lecturer, 1958–1963, Alexander M. Poniatoff Professor of Engineering Science and Applied Science, 1963–1975, professor emeritus, 1975–1989.

Honors and Awards: Nobel Prize in physics,[14] 1956.

Coinventor of the transistor in 1947 with John Bardeen and Walter Brattian, Shockley participated in one of the most important discoveries of the century. They applied for a patent in 1948; this device was described as a germanium "transfer resistance" unit, from which the name "transistor" was derived. Shockley continued his research on the device to create the germanium junction transfer transistor, which was much more reliable than the first unit. From this start he founded Shockley Semiconductor Laboratories in Santa Clara Valley in 1954. After he received the Nobel Prize in 1956, disenchantment with Shockley's management style and his propensity for pure research led to the defection of the "Fairchild Eight" in 1957, and the deterioration of his company. His controversial views on genetics and his racist theories have shocked the society around him, but he has continued his research into "grave world problems."

QUOTATION

"The only heritage I can leave to Billy is the feeling of power and joy of responsibility for setting the world right on something." (Shockley's mother, about her 8-year-old son)

---

[14]Jointly with John Bardeen and Walter H. Brattain.

BIBLIOGRAPHY

Biographical

Caddes, Carolyn, *Portraits of Success: Impressions of Silicon Valley Pioneers*, Tioga Publishing Co., Palo Alto, Calif., 1986.

Slater, Robert, *Portraits in Silicon*, MIT Press, Cambridge, Mass., 1987.

Significant Publications

Bardeen, John, Walter Brattain, and William Shockley, *Nobel Lectures—Physics*, Elsevier, New York, 1964.

Shockley, William, *Electrons and Holes in Semiconductors, With Applications to Transistor Electronics*, Van Nostrand, New York, 1950.

Herbert A. Simon

Born 1916, Milwaukee, Wis.; Nobel Prize winner in economics and leader in AI and cognitive psychology who in 1956, with Allen Newell and J.C. (Cliff) Shaw, first articulated a model of human and computer problem-solving based on heuristic search, and invented list processing languages to implement it.

Education: PhD, political science, University of Chicago, 1943.

Professional Experience: Int'l City Managers' Assoc., Chicago, 1936–1939; University of California, Berkeley, 1939–1942; Illinois Institute of Technology, 1942–1949; Carnegie Institute of Technology (later renamed Carnegie Mellon University): Graduate School of Industrial Administration, 1949–1965, Richard King Mellon University Professor of Computer Science and Psychology, 1965–present.

Honors and Awards: Award for Distinguished Scientific Contributions, American Psychological Association, 1969; ACM A.M. Turing Award (with Allen Newell), 1975; Nobel Prize in economics, 1978; ORSA/TIMS John von Neumann Award, 1984; National Medal of Science, 1986; member, National Academy of Sciences; fellow, ACM, 1994.

Simon's research career has been focused on the nature of intelligence, especially as exhibited in problem-solving and decision-making.

As this topic cuts across many fields, it is difficult to identify his contributions with particular disciplines. His major awards in four areas—psychology, economics, management science, and computer science—attest to his breadth of interest and expertise. Prior to his early contacts with computers, he studied the informational and computational limits on the rationality of human decision makers, especially in organizations. His initial contributions to computer science were made in collaboration with Allen Newell and Cliff Shaw in the development of the first heuristic programs, the first list-processing languages (a series of IPLs [Information Processing Languages]), and the establishment of the field of artificial intelligence, which they preferred to call "complex information processing." Simon and Newell continued their collaboration through most of the 1960s, and remained in close association at Carnegie Mellon (although not engaged in joint research projects) until Newell's death in 1992. Their joint work on problem-solving was reported in *Human Problem Solving* (1972), which contains some of the first examples of the use of production systems to model human thought.

In the 1960s and subsequently, Simon's main research effort was aimed at extending the boundaries of artificial intelligence, with particular concern for the simulation of human thought processes, moving from the well-structured tasks addressed in early AI programs to wider ranges of tasks that call on substantial bodies of knowledge and that are relatively loosely structured. Among the important early programs were the General Problem Solver (GPS), jointly with Newell, and the Elementary Perceiver and Memorizer (EPAM), with Edward A. Feigenbaum, Lee W. Gregg, and Howard B. Richman.

The work on GPS led to a sustained program of research, with graduate students and colleagues, on human problem-solving, involving laboratory experimentation paired with computer modeling of human performance in various problem environments. One line of work, with William G. Chase, explored the role of knowledge-based recognition processes based in expert performance (using chess as the principal domain of study). Recognition processes, modeled by production systems, have provided one important basis for the expert systems now common in AI applications.

The work on EPAM has also continued to the present time, producing a system that simulates human behavior over a wide range of the perceptual, learning, and concept induction tasks that have been studied in the psychological laboratory, thereby constituting a theory of unmatched generality in this domain. Among the important phenomena implemented by EPAM's discrimination (sorting) mechanisms is learning by chunking—the assembly, through learning, of small units into larger entities, performed recursively to produce structures of arbitrary size and complexity. The discrimination net of EPAM was a progenitor of the Rete nets used to access productions in modern production system languages. Many of the papers reporting the research on problem-solving and on EPAM have been collected in the two volumes of *Models of Thought*.

A third line of research, with Kenneth Kotovsky and subsequently with Pat Langley, Gary Bradshaw, and Jan Zytkow, has built systems for discovering lawful patterns in empirical data, initially in sequences of letters or numbers (the Thurstone letter series completion tasks). In the past decade and a half, this research has expanded into the computational study of the processes of scientific discovery, producing such well-known discovery programs as BACON, DALTON, KEKADA, and LIVE. This research, too, has moved from highly structured but simple "toy" tasks to important discovery tasks taken from the history of science.

Simon has been deeply concerned with problems of knowledge representation and their relation to language understanding processes. The dissertation of his student Laurent Siklóssy demonstrated a model that learned language by matching linguistic sentences with their semantic interpretations. This and related work was collected in Simon and Siklóssy (eds.), 1972. With John R. Hayes, Simon built the UNDERSTAND program, which reads task descriptions in natural language and constructs representations of the task suitable as inputs to GPS. The research on representation has led to inquiries into computational procedures for reasoning from diagrams, and for automatic generation of representations.

In this research, the construction of intelligent systems has been closely linked with the development of a computational theory of human intelligence. The two chess programs Simon has constructed with colleagues (the NSS program with Newell and Shaw [1958], and the MATER program with George W. Baylor) contrast with more powerful programs like DeepThought and HighTech, the former modeling highly selective humanoid search rather than relying on massive computing power to compensate for lack of chess knowledge.

Simon has also made a series of contributions to "pure" computer science, not directly related to psychology. His Heuristic Compiler (1961, in Simon and Siklóssy 1972) was apparently the first system with (simple) capabilities for automatic programming. He has applied theories and techniques that originated in other disciplines to research problems in computer science. Methods of decomposing large systems into hierarchies of subsystems in order to simplify their analysis were developed by Simon and Ando (1961) for application to problems in economics, then transported by Courtois into computer science for the analysis of operating systems and other applications. A formal approach to causal ordering developed by Simon in the 1950s has been shown by Iwasaki and Simon to have broad applicability to research in qualitative physics, and generally, to the automatic induction of causal structures within AI.

At a theoretical level, Simon (1983) has examined the computational equivalence and inequivalence of different knowledge representations. He has shown the disadvantages of modal logic, compared with ordinary predicate logic and standard mathematics, as representation languages in AI, and has examined the computational differences among natural language, logical, diagrammatic, and schema-like representations as tools of inference. With J. Kadane, he proved an important theorem on optimal all-or-none search. He has discussed problems of parallel architecture and programming in terms of our knowledge of hierarchical organization (1969), and has addressed other foundational issues in computational AI.

The rapid development of computer science has demanded of its early practitioners a considerable investment of effort in institution building. Alan Perlis, Allen Newell, and Herbert Simon played the central roles in bringing computers to the campus of what was then Carnegie Institute of Technology, and building there the strong programs and faculties in computation that now exist not only in the School of Computer Science, but also in the Psychology Department, the Engineering Research Design Center, the Philosophy Department, and elsewhere on the campus. Simon has also been active in science policy at the national level, primarily through the council and committees of the National Academy of Sciences and its associated National Research Council, and (1968–1972) the President's Science Advisory Committee.

BIBLIOGRAPHY

Biographical

Baars, Bernard J., *The Cognitive Revolution in Psychology*, Guilford Press, New York, 1986.

McCorduck, Pamela, *Machines Who Think*, W.H. Freeman & Co., San Francisco, 1979.

Newell, Allen, "Simon, Herbert A.," in Ralston, Anthony, and Edwin D. Reilly, *Encyclopedia of Computer Science and Engineering*, Van Nostrand Reinhold Co., New York, 1983, pp. 1324–1325.

Simon, Herbert A., *Models of My Life*, Basic Books, New York, 1991.

Simon, Herbert A., and Allen Newell, "Information Processing Language V on the IBM 650," *Ann. Hist. Comp.*, Vol. 8, No. 1, Jan. 1986, pp. 47–49.

Significant Publications

Newell, Allen, J.C. Shaw, and H.A. Simon, "Empirical Explorations of the Logic Theory Machine," *Proc. Western Joint Computer Conf.*, 1957, pp. 218–239.

Newell, Allen, J.C. Shaw, and H.A. Simon, "Chess-Playing Programs, and the Problem of Complexity," *IBM J. Research and Development*, Vol. 2, No. 4, 1958, pp. 320–335.

Newell, Allen, and Herbert A. Simon, *Human Problem Solving*, Prentice-Hall, Englewood Cliffs, N.J., 1972.

Simon, Herbert A., *The Sciences of the Artificial*, MIT Press, Cambridge, Mass., 2nd ed., 1981.

Simon, Herbert A., *Models of Thought*, Yale Univ. Press, New Haven, Conn. Vol. 1, 1979; Vol. 2, 1989.

Simon, Herbert A., "Search and Reasoning in Problem Solving," *Artificial Intelligence*, Vol. 21, 1983, pp. 7–29.

Simon, Herbert A., and Laurent Siklössy, eds., *Representation and Meaning*, Prentice-Hall, Englewood Cliffs, N.J., 1972.

DANIEL L. SLOTNICK

Significant developer of the concept of the processor array.

Slotnick developed the concept of the processor array from his time with the IAS project with von Neumann. Whereas von Neumann could not accept the concept, Slotnick developed the idea into the SOLOMON scheme, which eventually evolved into the ILLIAC IV at the University of Illinois. However, funding restrictions only permitted the construction of a small portion of Slotnick's scheme.[15]

BIBLIOGRAPHY

Biographical

MacKenzie, Donald, "The Influence of the Los Alamos and Livermore National Laboratories on the Development of Supercomputing," *Ann. Hist. Comp.*, Vol. 13, No. 2, 1991, pp. 179–202.

Slotnick, D.L., "The Conception and Development of Parallel Processors—A Personal Memoir," *Ann. Hist. Comp.*, Vol. 4, No. 1, Jan. 1982, pp. 20–30.

R. BLAIR SMITH

Head of the project within the Advanced Systems Development Division of IBM that developed the first airline reservation systems (SABRE) for American Airlines.

Smith joined the sales department of IBM in 1950 after nearly 11 years as an IBM customer. In 1952–1953 he was senior salesman in the Santa Monica office and was then promoted to headquarters as one of the first special representatives in EDPM. He served as manager of market analysis and field testing for all proposed IBM products, director of corporate methods and operations research, and head of the airline systems (SABRE) for the Advanced Systems Development Division. Until forced to take early retirement because of a broken neck and major surgery, he was in charge of IBM's work with the airline industry.

---

[15]See biography of John Pasta.

SAMUEL S. SNYDER

Born August 18, 1911, Baltimore, Md.; computer scientist who had consider-able influence on the acquisition of computing capabilities in US governmen-tal agencies; founding member of ACM.

Education: BS, chemistry, George Washington University, 1939.

Professional Experience: National Security Agency, 1934–1964; supervisor, automation activities, Library of Congress, 1964–1966; Research Analysis Corporation, 1967–1970.

From 1936 to 1964 Snyder's work with the National Security Agency and its predecessors included assignments as punched-card equipment supervisor, cryptologist, and computer programmer and planner. He played a leading part in the agency's acquisition of a number of com-puters, including the specially modified model of IBM's STRETCH series, known as the HARVEST project. In 1964 he was appointed as the first supervisor of the Library of Congress automation activities, retiring from government service in December 1966. From 1967 to 1970 he worked at the Research Analysis Corporation. *Man and Computer,* coauthored by Snyder and anthropologist Ashley Montagu, was published in 1973. For several years Snyder served as a part-time consultant at the National Security Agency. He is a charter member of ACM (1947) and senior member of IEEE.

BIBLIOGRAPHY

Biographical

Snyder, Samuel S., "Computer Advances Pioneered by Cryptologic Organizations," *Ann. Hist. Comp.*, Vol. 2, No. 1, 1980, pp. 60–70.

Thomas B. Steel

SHARE representative who was deeply involved in the development of basic software for the IBM-700 series of computers, including the SHARE Operating System (SOS), and a universal language named UNCOL; later a pioneer in the promulgation of industry standards in information processing.

Honors and Awards: ACM Distinguished Service Award, 1977; fellow, ACM, 1994.

The announcement that Steel was to receive the ACM Distinguished Service Award in 1977 stated:[16]

> It is hard to avoid mentioning Steel's many areas of technical activity, especially in programming languages and in the theory of information handling, but those are not the areas for which he is now being honored. His most important area of service has been Standards, an area in which he has worked continuously and productively since he was a member of the SHARE 709 Standards Committee in 1957–1959 and a member of the ASA X3.4.2 Language Standards Committee in 1960–1961. He was chairman of the USASI X3.4 Subcommittee on Common Programming Languages (1965–1969), and was a member of the ACM Standards Committee (1963–1975) and of its Steering Committee (1963–1968). He was chairman of the ANSI X3 Standards Planning and Requirements Committee (SPARC) (1969–1974) and has been the SHARE representative to ANSI X3 since 1971. He has chaired the ANSI/X3/SPARC Data Base Study Group since 1973.
> He has been the AFIPS (and hence the US) representative to IFIP TC-2 (Programming Languages) since 1963, and the chairman of that group since 1969. He has been the AFIPS (and hence the US) member of the IFIP TC-2 Working Group 2.2 (Formal Languages Description) since 1966, and chairman of that group from 1966–1972.

Tom Steel was one of the founders of SHARE, the first and still the most prestigious user group. He served SHARE in many capacities, including membership on its executive board (1965–1966) and its board of directors (1973–1975). He was on the committee that produced the well-known SHARE study of data processing in the period 1980–1985.

In addition to his work on the ANSI Standards Committee previously mentioned, he was a member of the ACM National Program Committee (1963–1966) and an ACM National lecturer in 1968–1969. He was the first chairman of ACM SICSoft (1975–1976).

---

[16] *Comm. ACM*, Vol. 20, No. 9, 1977, pp. 682–683.

BIBLIOGRAPHY

Significant Publications

Steel, T.B., "UNCOL: The Myth and the Fact," in Goodman, R., ed., *Ann. Rev. Automatic Programming*, Pergamon Press, London, Vol. 2, 1961, pp. 325–344.

GEORGE ROBERT STIBITZ

Born April 30, 1904, York, Pa.; Bell Telephone Laboratories inventor of several pre-World War II relay computers, and the first demonstrator of remote telecomputing.

Education: AB, mathematics and physics, Denison University, 1926; MS, physics, Union College, 1927; PhD, mathematics, Cornell University, 1930.

Professional Experience: General Electric Company, Schenectady, 1926–1927; Bell Telephone Laboratories, New York City, 1930–1941; technical aide, Division 7 (Fire Control), NDRC (later OSRD), 1941–1945; private consultant, 1945–1964; research associate, Department of Physiology, Dartmouth Medical School, 1964–1974; professor emeritus active, 1974–present.

Honors and Awards: AFIPS Harry Goode Award, 1965; IEEE Emmanuel Piore Award, 1977; National Academy of Engineering, 1981; IEEE Computer Pioneer Award, 1982; honorary degrees from Denison University, 1976, Keene State College, 1978, Dartmouth College, 1986.

George Stibitz grew up in Dayton, Ohio, where his father taught ancient languages at a theological seminary of the German Reform Church. He entered the seventh grade at the Moraine Park School, an experimental school newly founded by Charles Kettering and Col. Edward Deeds. Its flexible curriculum and small classes provided an excellent environment for intellectual investigation and exploration.

Stibitz developed an interest in mathematics and physics while in high school, and after graduating in 1922, he received a scholarship to Denison University. At Denison he continued his studies in mathematics and physics. He also enjoyed his English classes and out of them grew not only an appreciation for literature, but an intolerance for the abuse of language.

Upon graduation from Denison in 1927 with a major in mathematics, Stibitz enrolled in the graduate program at Union College, where he received his MS degree in physics in 1926. He then took a year off and went to work for the General Electric Company in Schenectady, N.Y. In 1928, he enrolled in the PhD program at Cornell University. Under the tutelage of Wallie Hurwitz and Kennard, he generalized his interest in the vibrations of the loudspeaker diaphragm into his dissertation study of the differential geometry of a nonplanar membrane.

In the summer of 1929 he met his future wife, Dorothea Lamson, and they were married in September 1930 after he had completed his PhD and had accepted a position as a "mathematical engineer" with Bell Telephone Laboratories on West Street, New York City.

One weekend at home in 1937, observing the similarity between two-state positions of telephone relays and the binary notation, Stibitz decided to experiment. He fastened two relays from the Bell Telephone Laboratories scrap pile to a piece of plywood, cut strips from a tobacco can, bought two dry cell batteries and some flashlight bulbs, and with some electrical work constructed a one-digit binary adder. His colleagues were amused when he showed it to them in the laboratory, but this simple exercise might have ended there, except for Stibitz' penchant for generalization. Further evenings were spent sketching circuits for other arithmetic operations. He presented his ideas to Thornton Fry, head of the mathematical section at the laboratory, who indicated a curiosity as to whether these little relay calculators could do complex arithmetic, which then involved a number of human computers (computists) in the laboratory. With this challenge, Stibitz began to design relay binary circuits for calculations with complex numbers. The designs were completed in February 1938 and Stibitz began to work in earnest with Sam Williams, a switching engineer. In 1939 the Complex Calculator was completed and put to use in the laboratory.

The machine was capable of performing all four basic arithmetic operations, and was capable of being operated by remote access from any of three Teletype machines located in different parts of the laboratory. The first public demonstration of the Complex Calculator (and coincidentally the first remote control of a computer) occurred at a meeting of the American Mathematical Society (AMS) and the Mathematical Association of America at Dartmouth College in September 1940. Stibitz presented a paper describing the machine, followed by Dr. Fry showing how a problem could be introduced to the calculator in New York through a Teletype and telephone line, the computation performed, and the answer returned to the same Teletype. Attendees, among them Norbert Wiener and John Mauchly, were then able to participate in using the complex calculator.

In 1940 Stibitz proposed that the laboratory construct a general-purpose automatic computational device. He had developed circuit drawings to provide for interchangeable taped programs, an assembly language (as it would now be called), an error-detection representation code, and a design for floating-point arithmetic operations. Initially the laboratory management showed no interest in the development of a general-purpose computational device, but the onset of World War II provided the necessity for the design and construction of automatic computing machines. The first of a series of relay devices, the Relay Interpolator, was installed on West Street in September 1943. Late in the war it was moved to the Naval Research Laboratory, where it remained until 1961. The Relay Ballistic Computer, which was replicated in 1943 and 1944, was a general-purpose device as was its successor, the Model 4, or in Naval terminology, the Error Detector Mark 22. This sequence of relay calculators was later renamed Models 1, 2, 3, and 4. Models 5 (in two copies) and 6, the most ambitious of the relay devices, were completed in 1946, 1947, and 1950, respectively. Model 3 (and its successors) contained error-detection, halting-trouble diagnosis, and an assembly language. Model 5 was the first to implement floating-point arithmetic.

Each copy of the Model 5 incorporated a system of two arithmetic units and four problem positions. Problems were loaded into any positions that were idle, and upon completion of one problem the computer automatically picked up another. When the models were redesignated, Dorothea Stibitz suggested that the original one-digit binary adder should be called the Model K—for the kitchen table on which it was constructed. The kitchen table sits today in a screened-in porch in the Stibitz' home in Hanover, N.H. The Model 5 may still exist—in 1960 one was shipped to the Bihar Institute of Technology in Bihar, India. Correspondence with that institution suggests that it was never uncrated and may still be on the premises.

During World War II, Stibitz took a leave of absence from Bell Telephone Laboratories and joined Division 7 (Gun-Fire Control) of the National Defense Research Committee (NDRC), later the Office of Scientific Research and Development (OSRD), as a technical aide. The Dynamic Tester, a device developed by Division 7 to test and guide the design of newly developed antiaircraft gun control directors, made great demands on the computers. Model 2 reduced the number of fundamental calculations for the early Dynamic Testers by an order of magnitude (10), and later models of the relay series further increased the speed and reliability of the calculations, thereby making possible enormous savings in human labor.

Stibitz did not return to Bell Telephone Laboratories at the end of the war, but instead established himself as a private consultant to government and industry. One of his projects during this period grew out of his wartime association with Duncan Stewart, later president of the Barber-Coleman Company. Beginning in 1946, Stibitz began the design of a desk-size electronic digital computer for use in the business world. Two working prototypes of the Barber-Coleman computer were completed, but in 1954 the project was abandoned for financial reasons. In 1964 Stibitz was invited to join the Department of Physiology at Dartmouth Medical School as a research associate. In his new career, Stibitz did significant pioneering work in a field that is now called "biomedicine." In the next quarter of a century, Stibitz worked on a variety of biophysical problems, including the modeling of the renal exchange processes, the computer display of brain cell anatomy, and a mathematical model of capillary transport phenomena. He retired as a professor emeritus in 1974, but remained active as a consultant to the medical school.[17]

BIBLIOGRAPHY

Biographical

Daubenspeck, J. Andrew, *Dartmouth Medical School Alumni Magazine,* Spring 1978, pp. 12–13.

Luebbert, William F., "Commemoration of 1940 Remote Computing Demonstration by Stibitz," *Ann. Hist. Comp.,* Vol. 3, No. 1, 1981, pp. 68–70.

Ritchie, David, *The Computer Pioneers,* Simon and Schuster, New York, 1986.

Stibitz, George R., "The Relay Computers at Bell Labs," *Datamation,* Apr. 1967, pp. 35–44.

Stibitz, George R., "The Relay Computers at Bell Labs," *Datamation,* May 1967, pp. 45–49.

Stibitz, George R., "Early Computers," in Metropolis, N., J. Howlett, and Gian-Carlo Rota, *A History of Computing in the Twentieth Century,* Academic Press, New York, 1980, pp. 479–483.

---

[17]Prepared by Henry S. Tropp, November 1991.

Stibitz, George R., *The Zeroth Generation*, private printing, 1994.

Tropp, Henry S., *An Inventory of the Papers of George Robert Stibitz Concerning the Invention and Development of the Digital Computer,* Dartmouth College, Hanover, N.H., 1973.

Tropp, Henry S., "New Stibitz Exhibit," *Ann. Hist. Comp.,* Vol. 13, No. 1, 1991, pp. 81–82.

Significant Publications

Stibitz, George R., "Computer," reprinted in Randell, Brian, *Origins of Digital Computers: Selected Papers,* Springer-Verlag, Berlin, 1982, pp. 247–252.

Stibitz, George R., *Relay Computers,* Appl. Math. Panel Report 171.1R, National Defense Research Council, Washington, D.C., Feb. 1945.

Stibitz, George R., "A New Class of Computing Aids," *Math. Aids and Other Aids to Computation,* Vol. 3, No. 23, July 1948, pp. 217–221.

CHRISTOPHER STRACHEY

Born November 16, 1916, Hampstead, London, UK; died May 18, 1975, Oxford, England; early English programmer who in 1959 proposed a form of time-sharing, illuminated the understanding of programming languages, and developed denotational semantics.

Education: Gresham's School, Norfolk, 1930–1935; lower second, natural sciences tripos, King's College, University of Cambridge, 1938.

Professional Experience: physicist, Standard Telephones and Cables, 1938–1945; physics/mathematics master, St. Edmund's School, Canterbury, 1945–1949; master, Harrow School, 1949–1952; technical officer, National Research and Development Corp. (NRDC), 1952–1959; private consultant, 1959–1966; University Mathematical Laboratory, Cambridge, 1962–1966; Programming Research Group, Oxford University, 1966–1975.

Honors and Awards: distinguished fellow, British Computer Society, 1972.

Born in 1916 into one of England's more prominent families, Christopher Strachey was educated at Gresham's School, Norfolk, and at King's College, Cambridge. He spent the war years in radar research, after which he spent several years as a schoolmaster. His career in computing did not effectively begin until 1951 when he started to program the machines at the National Physical Laboratory and Manchester University, while still a master at Harrow School.

In 1962 he also began work in the University Mathematical Laboratory, Cambridge, where, in the nominal position "part-time research assistant," he worked on the CPL programming language. In 1965 he wound up his consultancy and resigned from Cambridge in order to form the Programming Research Group at Oxford University. Under his leadership the group quickly established an international reputation in the theory of programming. At Oxford, in collaboration with Dana Scott, he produced the work of which he was most proud, the foundation of denotational semantics; this work was just beginning to bear fruit when he died in 1975.

Returning to King's in October 1938 for a fourth and final year, he graduated in the summer with a "lower second" in the natural sciences tripos. This mediocre result was a considerable disappointment, and it dashed any hopes he had entertained of a research studentship. Obliged to find an occupation of some kind, he accepted a post as a physicist with Standard Telephones and Cables Limited (STC) at a salary of £4 per week.

Strachey began work in the Valve Development Laboratories of STC, London, in August 1939, just a month before the declaration of war with Germany.

Most of his time at STC was spent as one member of a small team led by J.H. Fremlin (later a professor at the University of Birmingham), investigating the theoretical design of centimetric radar valves. Strachey's particular contribution was the derivation of analytical formulas for valve parameters and their experimental verification. His mathematical work involved the integration of differential equations, some of which proved particularly intractable; so, with colleague P.J. Wallis, he began to obtain numerical solutions using a differential analyzer. He later came to regard this experience with a computing machine as being something of a turning point, and his interests in computing were aroused generally at this time; he began to read the literature on the subject, and from time to time he also assisted STC colleagues in computational tasks.

In July 1944 Strachey left Fremlin's group and was transferred to London to work in the STC Radio Division. This work was concerned with electrical and mechanical design, which he found much less to his taste than the theoretical work. Strachey had never liked the atmosphere of the STC laboratories (either at Ilminster or at London), which he found "rather narrow-minded and sordid."

Strachey began as "physics-cum-mathematics" master at St. Edmund's in October 1945, at a salary of £335 per annum.

He seems to have been a thorough schoolmaster: his lessons were meticulously prepared, and he spent much effort coaching his pupils for public examinations. After many applications to other schools, he was finally offered a position at Harrow School and left St. Edmund's in the spring of 1949.

Strachey began teaching at Harrow School in September 1949, at a salary of £600 a year. Securing a post at Harrow, one of Britain's leading public schools, was a real advancement to his career.

Strachey spent many of his evenings organizing societies and clubs. He was particularly keen on the science society and gave talks on topics such as interplanetary travel and the surface tension of soap films. He also played bassoon in the school orchestra, an instrument he had taught himself at St. Edmund's.

Against this background of busy "schoolmastering," Strachey's interest in computing had been largely dormant since leaving STC. Of course, computers were very much in the air in the late 1940s, and he no doubt read the semipopular articles.

His first exposure to a stored-program computer occurred in January 1951 when, through a mutual friend, he obtained an introduction to Mike Woodger of the National Physical Laboratory (NPL).

Back at Harrow, he began to write a program to make the Pilot ACE play draughts. This was typical of his early attempts at programming: anyone with more experience or less confidence would have settled for a table of squares. He got the idea of using the machine to play draughts largely from an article by Donald Davies of NPL, "A Theory of Chess and Noughts and Crosses," that had appeared in the June 1950 issue of *Penguin Science News*.

The following spring, Strachey learned from Woodger of the Ferranti Mark I computer that had just been installed at Manchester University. This machine had a much larger store than the Pilot ACE, with correspondingly greater scope for Strachey's kind of programming. Alan Turing, who was then assistant director of the Manchester University Computing Machine Laboratory, had written the programmer's handbook for the machine, and Strachey had known him just well enough at King's College that he could ask for and receive a copy.

He visited the Manchester Mark I for the first time in July 1951. When Strachey explained his ideas for a draughts-playing program, Turing was much impressed and suggested that another interesting problem would be to make the machine simulate itself, in the fashion of the interpretive trace routines developed for the Cambridge

University EDSAC. Strachey was attracted by this idea and temporarily put the draughts program to one side. The final trace program was some 1,000 instructions long—by far the longest program that had yet been written for the machine, although Strachey was unaware of this.

Shortly after, Strachey received a letter from M.H.A. Newman, professor of pure mathematics at Manchester, complimenting him on the quality of his programs (which had been reported by Turing), and saying that he hoped to be able to offer him a post in the laboratory when one became available. Before he could do so, however, Strachey came to the notice of Lord Halsbury, managing director of the National Research and Development Corporation (NRDC). In November 1951 he was formally offered a post as technical officer with NRDC at a salary of £1200. Strachey formally began as an employee of NRDC on June 3, 1952.

During the first week of September 1952, Strachey attended the second ACM National Conference, held at the University of Toronto. The conference was timed to coincide with the inauguration of the FERUT, the second Ferranti Mark I, which had been installed in the Computation Centre of the university.

NRDC had agreed to loan Strachey to the University of Toronto to help with programming the calculations for the St. Lawrence Seaway project.[18] Strachey spent all of October and November, and part of the following spring, on the program. The program was very long—about 2,000 instructions—and the input data tape was estimated to be one and a half miles in length.

During his stay in North America, Strachey visited several research laboratories and computer manufacturers in the US, making a detailed study of the order codes (instruction sets) of different computers. He was perhaps the first person in Britain to realize that this subject deserved more than casual thought.

Early 1954 also saw the first of many meetings with Ferranti concerning the design of a new machine, the Ferranti Packaged-Circuit Computer (FPC, later marketed as Pegasus). He persuaded Ferranti to set up a small department to produce a programming system for the machine, and he personally took a major part in its specification. The Pegasus programming system was a high point in programming in Britain during the 1950s and had great influence.

Strachey, although a relative newcomer to computing, was 38 years old when he began work on Pegasus and was at the height of his

---

[18]Williams, M.R., "UTEC and Ferut: The University of Toronto's Computation Centre," *Ann. Hist. Comp.*, Vol. 16, No. 2, 1994, pp. 4–12.

energies and maturity; the project was undoubtedly borne along by his confidence, and he never subsequently showed such strong leadership.

In the late 1950s multiprogramming (then confusingly also known as time-sharing) was very much in the air. What Strachey proposed in his concept of time-sharing was an arrangement that would preserve the direct contact between programmer and machine, while still achieving the economy of multiprogramming. Strachey filed a patent application for time-sharing in February 1959. At the time, there was some friction between Strachey and Kilburn's group at Manchester, for much of his exposition was based on the Atlas development and preempted their own publications.

In March 1959, having been with NRDC for eight years, Strachey announced his intention of resigning in order to work as a freelance director and consultant.

Strachey formally started activities as a private consultant on June 1, 1959, operating from his private address of 9 Bedford Gardens, Kensington. As part of his consultancy agreement with Ferranti, Strachey undertook to deliver a scientific autocode for the new ORION computer. To do this work, he took on a full-time employee, Peter Landin, in January 1960. Landin spent only part of his time on the autocode; with Strachey's encouragement, he spent the remainder of his time on a theoretical study of programming languages. It gave Strachey a certain ironic satisfaction that he was financing "the only work of its sort being carried out anywhere (certainly anywhere in England)" (Strachey 1971). Landin's work, which concerned the application of Church's lambda calculus to programming language semantics, was described in a classic paper, "The Mechanical Evaluation of Expressions."

As well as financing Landin's theoretical studies, Strachey was also prominent in the public debate on programming languages, particularly Algol. For example, at the 1959 UNESCO conference in Paris, he was in fine form, holding forth on the deficiencies of Algol while perched on the edge of a table on the platform, his legs swinging.

Strachey became well known for his outspoken view that Britain had fallen seriously behind the US in the field of programming. The main reason for the poor progress in Britain, Strachey perceived, was the small size of British machines. It was simply not possible to implement a LISP compiler on a machine the size of Pegasus, which was then the workhorse of most university computer centers.

In June 1962 Wilkes invited Strachey to work full-time in the University Mathematical Laboratory, Cambridge, to participate in the development of a new programming language and compiler for the

Titan computer. Strachey accepted enthusiastically and began work the following month. A considerable financial sacrifice was involved, for the salary that Wilkes was able to offer was very modest by comparison with the consultancy fees he was then able to command.

The CPL (Cambridge Programming Language) project got off to a most promising start. By mid-August, the project group, which consisted of Strachey, Baron, and David F. Hartley, had produced an outline proposal. In the autumn, the group began to collaborate with Eric Nixon and John N. Buxton of the London University Computer Unit, so that CPL could also be used on the London University Atlas.

Concurrent with the CPL activity at Cambridge, it must be recalled that Strachey was also in business as a private consultant, with an office, a secretary, and his principal assistant Peter Landin to support. From mid-1963 he was actively seeking an opportunity to lead a university research group in the theory of programming. At first it was hoped to set up a research unit in the Mathematical Laboratory at Cambridge, but this proved unsuccessful. In January 1964 Strachey also unsuccessfully competed for the chair of Computing Science at Imperial College, University of London. Finally, he secured the support of Leslie Fox, who succeeded in obtaining a DSIR grant to set up a programming research group at Oxford University in July 1965.

Although DSIR support for the Programming Research Group (PRG) ran from July 1965, Strachey did not take up residence at Oxford until April 1966. The work on CPL continued. In June, Strachey convened a meeting of the full CPL group, which decided— no doubt as a result of his lack of restraint in revising earlier drafts— that Strachey should edit and distribute the final version of the CPL reference manual. During the remainder of 1966, Strachey and David Park continued to work on CPL and prepare the reference manual, entitled the *CPL Working Papers.*

During the second half of 1967, Strachey wrote "Fundamental Concepts in Programming Languages," one of his most important and lengthy papers, which (typically) remains unpublished in its original form. Like much of Strachey's work at Oxford, however, the paper had an influential private circulation.

Since taking up his appointment at Oxford, Strachey had limited his external activities so as to detract as little as possible from his academic work. For example, he resigned his directorship of CAP in 1967, although he remained a shareholder and a consulting fellow. He now took little active part in British Computer Society affairs. He did serve on the computer science subcommittee of the SRC, and he still gave occasional external lectures and did a little consulting; but these activities were on a much reduced scale compared with the early 1960s. On one notable occasion he joined forces with Stanley Gill and Alex d'Agapeyeff to address a Labour Party Science and Technology Committee, and on another in July 1973 he took part in a television debate on the Lighthill report on AI research in Britain.

Strachey's own research into mathematical semantics took an important step forward during 1969 as a result of his collaboration with Dana Scott. Scott, a mathematical logician then at Princeton University, was halfway through a year's sabbatical leave in Europe when he first saw Strachey at a lively meeting of IFIP Working Group 2.2 in Vienna at Easter.

Scott's contribution was to provide a sound mathematical basis for the lambda-calculus models that Strachey used in his formal semantics. Strachey had first used this device in 1964 in his paper "Towards a Formal Semantics," but now conceded it was "gravely lacking in mathematical rigour."

Strachey decided, early in 1973, to submit an essay for the Adams Prize of Cambridge University, an award that has secured the reputation of many distinguished British mathematicians over the years. The subject for the Adams Prize for 1973–1974 was "Computer Science excluding Hardware," and the competition was open to persons admitted to a degree of the university. Apart from its obvious practical value as the kind of tangible evidence that would impress a Royal Society election committee, winning the Adams Prize perhaps meant something deeper to Strachey in terms of recognition from the alma mater. The essay for the Adams Prize dominated the remainder of his life.

The Adams essay included an important historical account of the development of the Oxford semantics and a final reworking of his "Fundamental Concepts in Programming Languages." The essay, with a few sections still unwritten, was finally dispatched to the Cambridge University Registry at the very end of 1974. The effort of writing the Adams essay took its toll on Strachey, and early in 1975 he spent several weeks away from Oxford resting. He returned to Oxford in the spring, where he continued to work with Milne at completing the essay and revising it into book form. In a matter of weeks, however, he contracted an illness diagnosed as jaundice; he obeyed the usual dietary restrictions and made an apparent recovery, but the illness quickly returned. He died of infectious hepatitis on May 18, 1975. The winner of the Adams Prize was announced shortly after Strachey's death. The submission of Strachey and Milne did not win.

Strachey made three important technical contributions to computing in Britain: the logical design of computers, the design of programming languages, and the development of denotational semantics.

Strachey was responsible for a strong current of influence in the design of programming languages. Perhaps more important than any details of a particular language was the example that Strachey set: his whole approach to the subject and his way of going about things. Donald Michie made this point well when he wrote in 1971:

> Today an "invisible college" of programming theory exists throughout the Universities of Britain. Almost every member of this "college" was guided along the path at some stage by Strachey's direct influence. Developments of theory may in the long run prove decisive in helping to clear the hurdles of software engineering which still lie ahead (Michie 1971).[19]

QUOTATIONS

"Work out what you want to say before you decide how you want to say it." (Strachey's First Law of Logical Design)

"Computing Science: The study of the use and sometimes construction of digital computers. It is a fashionable, interesting, difficult, and perhaps useful activity."

BIBLIOGRAPHY

Biographical

Alton, J., et al., *Catalogue of the Papers of Christopher Strachey (1916–1975)*, Contemporary Scientific Archives Center, Oxford, UK, 1980.

Campbell-Kelly, Martin, "Christopher Strachey, 1916–1975: A Biographical Note," *Ann. Hist. Comp.*, Vol. 7, No. 1, Jan. 1985, pp. 19–42.

Michie, D., "Computing: Can Britain Set the Pace?," *University of Edinburgh Bulletin*, Vol. 8, No. 3, 1971, pp. 1–2.

Significant Publications

Scott, Dana, and Christopher Strachey, "Towards a Mathematical Semantics for Computer Languages," *Proc. Symp. on Computers and Automata*, Polytechnic Institute of Brooklyn, Apr. 1971, pp. 19–45.

Strachey, C., "Programme-Controlled Time Sharing," *Proc. IEE*, Vol. 106, Part B, 1959, p. 462.

---

[19]Extracted from Campbell-Kelly 1985.

Strachey, C., "Time-Sharing in Large Fast Computers," *Proc. Int'l Conf. Information Processing,* UNESCO, Paris, 1960, pp. 336–341.

Strachey, Christopher, and Maurice V. Wilkes, "Some Proposals for Improving the Efficiency of Algol 60," *Comm. ACM,* Vol. 4, No. 11, 1961, pp. 488–491.

Strachey, Christopher, "Systems Analysis and Programming," *Scientific American,* Vol. 25, No. 3, 1966, pp. 112–124.

Strachey, Christopher, and R.E. Milne, *A Theory of Programming Language Semantics,* 2 Vols., Chapman and Hall, London, 1976.

IVAN EDWARD SUTHERLAND

Born May 16, 1938, Hastings, Neb.; inventor of the 1963 interactive graphics system—Sketchpad; later commercial developer of graphical systems and recipient of the 1988 ACM Turing Award.

Education: BS, electrical engineering, Carnegie Mellon University, 1959; MS, electrical engineering, California Institute of Technology, 1960; PhD, electrical engineering, MIT, 1963.

Professional Experience: consultant, Lincoln Laboratory, MIT, 1961–1964; director, Information Processing Technology, Advanced Research Projects Agency, Department of Defense, 1964–1966; associate professor, electrical engineering, Harvard University, 1966–1968; University of Utah: associate professor, 1968–1972, professor, electrical engineering, 1972–1976; Fletcher Jones Professor and department head of computer science, California Institute of Technology, 1976–1980; cofounder, vice president, and chief scientist, Evans and Sutherland Computer Corp., 1968–1976; founded Sutherland, Sproull, and Associates, a consulting firm, and Advanced Technology Ventures, a venture capital firm, Palo Alto, Calif., 1980–1990; vice president and fellow, Sun Microsystems Laboratories, Inc., 1990–present.

Honors and Awards: Valdimir K. Zworykin Award, National Academy of Engineering, 1972; Outstanding Accomplishment Award, Systems, Man and Cybernetics Society, 1975; IEEE Computer Society Pioneer Award, 1985; IEEE Emmanuel R. Piore Award, 1987 (joint with David C. Evans); ACM Turing Award, 1988; member, National Academy of Sciences; member, National Academy of Engineering; honorary degrees from Harvard University, California Institute of Technology, and the University of North Carolina; fellow, ACM, 1994.

Ivan E. Sutherland received the 1988 ACM A.M. Turing Award for his pioneering contributions to the field of computer graphics:

For his pioneering and visionary contributions to computer graphics, starting with Sketchpad, and continuing after. Sketchpad, though written twenty-five years ago, introduced many techniques [which are] still important today. These include a display file for screen refresh, a recursively traversed hierarchical structure for modeling graphical objects, recursive methods for geometric transformations, and an object-oriented programming style. Later innovations include "Lorgnette" for viewing stereo and colored images, and elegant algorithms for registering digitized views, clipping polygons, and representing surfaces with hidden lines.

Sutherland is the inventor and developer of the interactive computer graphics field 25 years ago. Sketchpad's many innovations include a display file for screen refresh, a recursively traversed hierarchical structure for modeling graphical objects, recursive methods for geometric transformations, and an object-oriented programming style.

From 1976 to 1980, Sutherland was the Fletcher Jones Professor and chair of computer science at CalTech. Prior to joining the CalTech faculty, Sutherland and David C. Evans founded Evans and Sutherland Computer Corporation, where Sutherland served as vice president and chief scientist. Both he and Evans taught at the University of Utah during this period, and were instrumental in establishing Salt Lake City as a premier center for computer graphics. He remains actively involved in E&S as a major shareholder and board member.

Sutherland moved to Utah from Harvard University, where he was Gordon McKay Associate Professor of Computer Science. Earlier, he served as director of the Information Processing Techniques Office of the Defense Advanced Research Projects Agency, overseeing DARPA's funding of academic computer science during an exceptionally productive and influential period.

QUOTATION

"I like everything you say but I think it's all bull."

BIBLIOGRAPHY

Biographical

Frenkel, Karen A., "An Interview with Ivan Sutherland," *Comm. ACM*, Vol. 32, No. 6, June 1989, pp. 712–718.

ANTONIN SVOBODA

*Born October 14, 1907, Prague, Czechoslovakia; died May 18, 1980,
Oregon; Czech computer scientist who was instrumental in the development of
computer research in his native country through the design and construction
of the SAPO and EPOS computers. Rejected by his own country, he returned to
the US in 1965 to teach at UCLA.*

Education: degree in electrical engineering, Czech Institute of Technology,
Prague, 1931; doctor of technical sciences, Czech Institute of Technology,[20]
Prague, 1936.

Professional Experience: active duty, Czechoslovak Army, 1936–1938; assistant
professor, mathematics, Czech Institute of Technology, 1938–1939; consultant,
French Ministry of War, Paris, 1939–1940; Radiation Laboratory, MIT,
1941–1946; National Enterprise Aritma, Prague, 1946–50; Central Institute of
Mathematics (later the Research Institute of Mathematical Machines),
Czechoslovakian Academy of Sciences, 1950–1965; professor, University of
California at Los Angeles, 1966–1977.

Honors and Awards: US Naval Ordnance Development Award, 1948.

Antonin Svoboda commenced his work in the field of computing in
the mid-1930s while undertaking to improve antiaircraft fire-control
devices for the Czechoslovakian Army. Chased out of Czechoslovakia
and France by the advancing German armies, he found his way to the
US where he joined the Radiation Laboratory at MIT; he was able to
continue his work on his computational devices while also working on
radar equipment. In 1948 he published a book on his work at MIT
entitled *Computing Mechanisms and Linkages.*

In 1946 he returned to Czechoslovakia with the intention of establishing a computer industry. After several years of development in
cooperation with the National Enterprise Aritma on punched equipment, he established a laboratory within the Central Institute of
Mathematics (later the Research Institute of Mathematical Machines)
of the Czechoslovakian Academy of Sciences. The researchers within
the institute, under Svoboda's direction, developed two major computing devices—the SAPO and the EPOS. The former was a classic relay
computer equipped with a magnetic drum, somewhat akin to the
Harvard Mark III, but with added stored-program capabilities and a
unique design involving fault-tolerant systems. SAPO contained three
arithmetic units that operated simultaneously on a computation and
compared the results to ensure correctness. Realizing the shortcom-

---

[20]The work which he reported in his thesis was completed at Charles University, Prague.

ings of a relay machine, the institute then developed the EPOS machine, which relied on vacuum tubes, germanium diode logic units, delay-line registers, and ferrite core memory. It was also built with fault-tolerant capabilities.

By this time the political climate in Czechoslovakia turned against the use of western technologies, and Svoboda chose to return to the US in order to continue his work. He joined the faculty at UCLA in 1966, teaching computer engineering until his retirement in 1977.

BIBLIOGRAPHY

Biographical

Oblonsky, Jan G., "Eloge: Antonin Svoboda, 1907–1980," *Ann. Hist. Comp.*, Vol. 2, No. 4, 1980, pp. 284–292.

Svoboda, Antonin, "From Mechanical Linkages to Electronic Computers: Recollections from Czechoslovakia," in Metropolis, N., J. Howlett, and Gian-Carlo Rota, *A History of Computing in the Twentieth Century,* Academic Press, New York, 1980, pp. 579–586.

Significant Publications

Svoboda, Antonin, *Computing Mechanisms and Linkages,* McGraw-Hill, New York, 1948.

HIDETOSHI TAKAHASHI

Died June 1985; one of the most eminent figures in the development of Japanese computing.

Honors and Awards: National Person of Cultural Merit, Government of Japan.

Hidetoshi Takahashi played an important role, not only in the development of Parametron computers, but also in the field of general numerical calculations. He influenced all who worked in the computer field in Japan.

BIBLIOGRAPHY

Biographical

Takahashi, Hidetoshi, "Some Important Computers of Japanese Design," *Ann. Hist. Comp.*, Vol. 2, No. 4, Oct. 1980, pp. 330–337.

ALFRED TARSKI

Born January 14, 1901, Warsaw, Poland; died October 27, 1983, Berkeley, Calif.; one of the four greatest logicians of all time.

Education: PhD, University of Warsaw, 1924.

Professional Experience: instructor, logic, Pedagogical Institute, Fical, Warsaw, 1922–1925; docent (and later adjunct professor), the University of Warsaw, 1925–1939; research associate, Harvard University, 1939–1941; member, Institute for Advanced Study, 1942; Guggenheim Fellow, 1941–1942 and 1955–1956; University of California at Berkeley: lecturer, 1942–1946, professor, 1946–1968, emeritus professor of mathematics, 1968–1983.

Honors and Awards: Alfred Jurzykowski Foundation Award, 1966; member, National Academy of Sciences; member, Royal Netherlands Academy of Science; honorary member, Netherlands Mathematical Society; UC Berkeley Citation, 1981.

Emeritus professor of mathematics Alfred Tarski, widely regarded as one of the four greatest logicians of all time (along with Aristotle,

Gottlob Frege, and Kurt Gödel), passed away on October 27, 1983, at the age of 82.

A great teacher and influential scientific leader as well as a profound thinker, Tarski arrived in Berkeley in 1942 at the age of 41 and built up what is often cited as the outstanding center for research in logic and the foundations of mathematics in the world. His mathematical treatment of the semantics of languages and the concept of truth has had revolutionary consequences, which can be drawn from the possibility of giving a general treatment of the concept of truth in formal mathematical languages in a rigorous mathematical way. Among such consequences is his celebrated theorem that the set of true sentences of any sufficiently expressive formal language cannot be defined in that language itself (although it can be defined in a richer language).

Born in Warsaw, Poland, in 1901, Tarski was educated in Polish schools and received his PhD at the University of Warsaw in 1924. His education was rather more rigorous and demanding than most American students receive today: as he recalled in 1981 (when Chancellor Heyman presented him with the Berkeley Citation in a ceremony honoring his 80th birthday), his high school curriculum involved the study of six foreign languages (in addition to logic—the subject in which he received a grade of B!). Nor were his early teaching duties light: as a professor in Zeromski's Lycee and docent (and later adjunct professor) at the University of Warsaw, he sometimes taught as many as 29 hours a week. As was the case with many now-famous workers in the then-budding discipline of mathematical logic, broad recognition came to Tarski slowly: appointed as a lecturer at Berkeley in 1942, he became a full professor only in 1946 at age 45.

Of his numerous investigations, outlined in seven books and more than 300 other publications, Tarski was most proud of his works on truth or falsity of any sentence of the elementary theory of high school Euclidean geometry. Today this work is viewed as a pioneering landmark, resulting in the burgeoning branch of theoretical computer science, which considers what problems can or cannot be settled, either practically or in principle, by computers.

But the influence of Alfred Tarski on the development of logic, mathematics, computer science, and the philosophy of science was due not only to his own research but also to his prodigious activity as a teacher and as an organizer and leader in the international scientific community for over 60 years. Visitors came from many countries to study and collaborate with him. Among his more than 20 doctoral students are many (including Andrzej Mostowski, Bjarni Jonsson, Julia

Robinson, Robert Vaught, C.C. Chang, Solomon Feferman, Richard Montague, and Jerome Keisler) who have become leading logicians in their own right; their students have further spread Tarski's vision of logic throughout the world.

What was his secret as a teacher? Perhaps it was his dogged insistence on precision and clarity in the way his students expressed their ideas. In a seminar he would never be satisfied with an "almost" clear account accompanied by a wave of the hand to indicate "you see what I mean." "No," he would rejoin, "you must say what you mean." His longtime colleague and collaborator Leon Henkin, now acting chair of California's Department of Mathematics, states that "Tarski's emphasis on absolute standards of intellectual communication was exemplified in his own lectures, whose ideas became more firmly rooted in the minds of his audience because of their brilliant clarity. The training he gave us in precise expression of ideas, with an accompanying clarification in the perception of our own ideas, was one of the great legacies he bequeathed to colleagues and students alike."

Tarski's early work on semantics led in time to his development of "the theory of models," now one of the four major fields of research in a mathematical logic. It treats the often beautiful and deep relationships between the grammatical form of a sentence expressing a concept and the mathematical properties of the abstract structures which are models of the sentence. His lifelong interest in the theory of sets (another of the major fields of research in logic) culminated in work around 1960 that led to hundreds of new publications studying the role of exotic and mysterious "large" infinite cardinal numbers.

But Tarski was more than just a logician. He made important contributions to branches of mathematics other than logic, including algebra, analysis, and geometry. His 1924 theorem with fellow Pole Stefan Banach—that one can divide a solid sphere into a finite number of "pieces" (five pieces actually suffice, as was shown later) and then put the pieces together again to form two solid spheres, each of the same size as the original one—became known as the Banach-Tarski paradox, and illuminates limitations of any mathematical theory of volume applying to all "pieces" of space. (An irate citizen once demanded of the Illinois legislature that they outlaw the teaching of this result in Illinois schools!) Referring to his tremendous body of work in many different parts of mathematics, Julia Robinson, MacArthur Fellow and current president of the American Mathematical Society, calls Tarski "one of the greatest mathematicians of the twentieth century."

Tarski was the founder at Berkeley of the pioneering interdisciplinary Group in Logic and the Methodology of Science. In 1981

Chancellor Heyman, speaking for the regents, officially named the group's common room in Evans Hall "The Alfred Tarski Room," and unveiled a bronze plaque citing Tarski as a "great logician and inspiring teacher." As future generations of logic students at Berkeley study the portrait of Tarski that hangs in the room and reflect upon his career, they may well add the epitaph, "He Sought Truth and Found It."[1]

BIBLIOGRAPHY

Biographical

Addison, J.W., "Eloge: Alfred Tarski, 1901–1983," *Ann. Hist. Comp.*, Vol. 6, No. 4, Oct. 1984, pp. 335–336.

ORRIN EDISON TAULBEE

Born October 18, 1927, Taulbee, Ky.; died May 4, 1987, Pittsburgh, Pa.; organizer of the computer science employment register and founding member of the Computer Science Conference.

Education: BS, Berea College, 1950; MA, Michigan State University, 1951; PhD, mathematics, Michigan State University, 1957.

Professional Experience: research mathematician, Univac Division, Sperry-Rand Corp., 1955–1958; mathematical specialist, Lockheed Aircraft Corp., 1958–1959; associate professor, Michigan State University, 1959–1961; manager, Information Science, Goodyear Aerospace Corp., 1961–1966; University of Pittsburgh: director, Management Information Systems and Computing Center, 1966–1970, professor of computer science, 1966–1987, chairman, Computer Science Department, 1966–1984.

Honors and Awards: ACM Outstanding Contribution Award, 1984.

---

[1]Taken from the eloge by J.W. Addison; reprinted, with permission, from the December 1983 *California Monthly*, the alumni magazine of the University of California at Berkeley, where Addison is chairman of the group in Logic and the Methodology of Science.

[2]See also the biography of Ken Olsen.

After 11 years in the computer industry, Orrin Taulbee went to the University of Pittsburgh in 1966 as director of the Computer Center and professor of computer science, mathematics and information science. He was also chairman of the Department of Computer Science until 1984. He served as a visiting scientist at the National Bureau of Standards in 1971 and was a consultant to many industries and universities.

Orrin's concern for computer science student education was appropriately epitomized in the establishment of the "Employment Register" in connection with the annual ACM Computer Science Conference, which he operated with support and assistance from his wife Margaret up until the time of his death.

Orrin Taulbee was a charter member of the Computing Science Board, now called the Computer Research Association. As a member of the board, he was the indefatigable tabulator of the PhDs in "computer science supply and demand." The data he gathered were of the highest quality and have been widely utilized. His data were frequently used in assessing newly proposed PhD programs. In a continuing tribute to his efforts, the annual survey of characteristics of graduating computer scientists, published by ACM and IEEE Computer Society, bears his name, "The Taulbee Survey."

BIBLIOGRAPHY

Biographical

Hamblen, John W., Seymour Wolfson, and Marshall C. Yovits, "Orrin Edison Taulbee, 1928–1987," *Comm. ACM,* Vol. 30, No. 8, Aug. 1987, p. 687.

NORMAN H. TAYLOR

Whirlwind computer and SAGE system engineer.

Education: BA, Bates College, 1937; MSEE, MIT, 1939.

Professional Experience: Whirlwind project, MIT Digital Computer Laboratory, 1947–1952; Lincoln Laboratory: associate head, Computer Division, 1952–1958, manager, SAGE Weapons Integration, 1958–1959; Itek Corp.,

Control Data Corporation, and Arthur D. Little, 1958–1969; founder, president, Corporate-Tech Planning, 1969–1982; independent consultant, 1982–present.

Honors and Awards: fellow, IEEE; Electronic Reliability Award, IEEE.

Taylor worked on the Whirlwind project at the MIT Digital Computer Laboratory from 1947 to 1952 and was associate head of Lincoln Laboratory's Computer Division, where he was in charge of the MTC, the FSQ-7, and the TX-0 and TX-2 computers.[2] By 1958 to 1959 he was manager of SAGE weapons integration. From 1958 to 1969 he worked for Itek Corporation, Control Data Corporation, and Arthur D. Little. In 1969 he founded and until 1982 was president of Corporate-Tech Planning. He is now an independent consultant. He helped run the first Joint Computer Conferences in 1950–1951.

KENNETH THOMPSON

Born February 4, 1943, New Orleans; Bell Telephone Laboratories developer with Dennis Ritchie of Unix; joint recipient of the 1983 ACM Turing Award.

Education: BS, University of California, Berkeley, 1965; MS, University of California, Berkeley, 1966.

Professional Experience: member, technical staff, Bell Telephone Laboratories, 1966–present.

Honors and Awards: member, National Academy of Engineering; A.M. Turing Award, ACM, 1983.

Thompson started work after his master's degree with Bell Telephone Laboratories. At that time BTL was involved with MIT and General Electric in the development of the Multics operating system through Project MAC, but when it became clear that the system was not going to meet the expectations of the laboratory, Thompson and Dennis Ritchie chose to build their own (lesser) version, which they named Unix as a "take-off" on the Multics name. After several years of development, Unix was made portable through the use of the programming language C that had been developed incidentally by Ritchie. This feature made Unix available on a variety of machines, and the decision by AT&T to make it freely available to academic institutions still furthered its acceptance.

QUOTATION

"I used to be an avid hacker in an electrical sense, building things. And ever since computers, I find it very similar. Computing is an addiction. Electronics is a similar addiction but not as clean. Much dirtier. Things burn out. (Slater 1987, p. 277)

BIBLIOGRAPHY

Biographical

Slater, Robert, *Portraits in Silicon*, MIT Press, Cambridge, Mass., 1987.

JOHN TODD

Born May 16, 1911, Carnacally, Ireland; British numerical analyst who joined John Curtiss at NBS post World War II; chief of the Computer Laboratory when the SEAC was delivered.

Education: BSc, Queen's University, Belfaşt, 1931; research exhibitioner, 1931–1932, Strathcona Research Student, 1932–1933, St. John's College, Cambridge.

Professional Experience: lecturer, Queen's University, Belfast, 1933–1937; lecturer, King's College, London, 1937–1949; scientist, British Admiralty (Admiralty Computing Service), 1939–1946; National Bureau of Standards: expert, applied mathematics, 1947–1948, chief, Computation Laboratory, 1949–1954, chief, Numerical Analysis, 1954–1957; professor, mathematics, California Institute of Technology, 1957–present.

Honors and Awards: Fulbright professor, Vienna (1965); Governor, Math. Assoc. 1980–1983; SIAM National Lecturer, 1960; International Linear Algebra Society has instituted the "Olga Taussky—John Todd Lecture" beginning in 1993; Cal Tech has instituted the Olga Taussky—John Todd Instructorships, beginning in 1993.

BIBLIOGRAPHY

Biographical

Todd, John, "The Prehistory and Early History of Computation at the US National Bureau of Standards," in Nash, Stephen G., *A History of Scientific Computing*, ACM Press History Series, New York, 1990, pp. 251–268.

Todd, John, and Magnus R. Hestenes, "Mathematicians Learning to Use Computers—The Institute for Numerical Analysis, UCLA 1947–1954," *Math. Assoc. of America*, AMA, Washington, D.C., 1991.

Significant Publications

Todd, John, and D.H. Sadler, "The Admiralty Computing Service," *MTAC*, Vol. 2, 1947, pp. 289–297.

Todd, John, "A Table of Rational Arctangents," *American Math. Soc.*, #11, US General Printing Office, 1950: paperback, US GPO, 1965.

Todd, John, ed., *Survey of Numerical Analysis*, McGraw-Hill, New York, 1962.

Todd, John, Chapters 3 "Analysis" (pp. 22 –58) and 7 "Numerical Analysis" (pp. 90–125) in *Handbook of Physics,* Condon, E.U., and Hugh Odishaw, eds., 2nd ed., McGraw-Hill, New York, 1967.

Todd, John, "Numerical Analysis at the NBS," *SIAM Rev.,* Vol. 17, 1975, pp. 361–370.

LEONARDO TORRES Y QUEVEDO

Born 1852, Santander, Spain; died 1936; 1920 Spanish computer inventor.

Born in Santa Cruz in the province of Santander in Spain in 1852 and educated as a civil engineer, Torres became director of a major laboratory, president of the Academy of Sciences of Madrid, a member of the French Academy of Sciences, and famous as a prolific and successful inventor. Some of his earliest inventions took the form of mechanical analog calculating devices of impressive originality.[3] He was a pioneer of radio control, and in 1906 successfully demonstrated a radio-controlled model boat operating in Bilbao harbor before an admiring crowd that included the king of Spain. He received similar acclaim for his invention of a semirigid airship that was manufactured in quantity and used by both sets of military forces during World War I. One of his inventions is still thriving as a tourist attraction at Niagara Falls: the Spanish Aero Car, originally installed in 1916.

In 1911 he made and successfully demonstrated a chess-playing automaton for the endgame of king and rook against king.[4] This chess automaton, believed to have been the world's first, was fully automatic, with electrical sensing of the pieces on the board and what was in effect a mechanical arm to move its own pieces.[5] Some years later Torres made a second chess automaton, which used magnets underneath the board to move the pieces. Like a number of his other inventions, this one still exists and is still operational.

Torres y Quevedo's major motivation in all his work appears to have been to exploit, to the full, the new facilities the electromechanical techniques offered, and to challenge accepted thinking as to the limitations of machines. His attitude was well summarized in the *Scientific American* account (1915) of the first chess automaton:

> There is no claim that [the chess player] will think or accomplish things where thought is necessary, but its inventor claims that the limits within which thought is really necessary need to be better defined, and that an automaton can do many things that are popularly classed with thought. It will do certain things which depend upon certain conditions, and these according to arbitrary rules selected in advance.

Torres' major written work on this subject is the fascinating "Essays on Automatics" (1913), which well repays reading even today. The paper provides us with the main link between Torres and Babbage. Torres gives a brief history of Babbage's efforts at constructing a mechanical Difference Engine and Analytical Engine. He describes the Analytical Engine as exemplifying his theories as to the potential power of machines, and takes the problem of designing such an

---

[3]See Eames, Charles, and Ray Eames, *A Computer Perspective*, Harvard Univ. Press, Cambridge, Mass., 1973, pp. 66–68.

[4]Anon., "Torres and His Remarkable Automatic Devices," *Scientific American Supplement*, Vol. 80, No. 2079, 1915, pp. 296–298.

[5]The one earlier apparent chess automaton, exhibited by von Kempelen, turned out to have a small human operator hidden inside; see Chapuis, A. and E. Droz, 1958. *Automata: A Historical and Technological Study*, Basford, London.

engine as a challenge to his skills as an inventor of electromechanical devices. The paper in fact contains a complete design (albeit one that Torres regarded as theoretical rather than practical) for a machine capable of calculating completely automatically the value of the formula $a^x (y - z)^2$, for a sequence of sets of values of the variables involved. It demonstrates cunning electromechanical gadgets for storing decimal digits, for performing arithmetic operations using built-in function tables, and for comparing the values of two quantities. The whole machine was to be controlled from a read-only program (complete with provisions for conditional branching), represented by a pattern of conducting areas mounted around the surface of a rotating cylinder. Incidentally, the paper also contains, almost casually, what is believed to be the first proposal of the idea of floating-point arithmetic.

The paper ends with a comparison of the advantages of electromechanical devices that were all that were available to Babbage. It establishes that Torres y Quevedo would have been quite capable of building a general-purpose electromechanical computer more than 20 years ahead of its time, had the practical need, motivation, and financing been present.

This opinion need not rest solely on the fact that Torres documented a plausible theoretical design, however, because it turns out that he went ahead to prove his point with a series of working prototypes. Possibly the first was a demonstration machine, capable of evaluating $p \times q - b$. How successful this was in practice we do not know. In 1920 Torres must have removed any uncertainty, because he startled the attendees at a Paris conference, marking the centenary of the invention of the first really practical calculating arithmometer (Torres y Quevedo 1920). This machine consisted of an arithmetic unit connected to a (possibly remote) typewriter, on which commands could be typed and the results printed automatically. Torres apparently had no thought of making such a machine commercially, viewing it instead as a means of demonstrating his ideas and techniques. Thus we can only speculate on what might have happened if he had gone ahead and made a full-scale computer, or even if his writings had become better known to the English-speaking world. As it turned out, his work had little discernible effect on later developments leading to the modern computer. In all other respects, his career must surely be judged as a very successful one, and one that deserves much wider appreciation outside Spain, where a laboratory has been named after him, books have been written about him (Rodriguez Alcalde 1966, 1974; Santesmases 1980), and a number of his machines, some still in working order, are on exhibition at the Colegio di Ingenieros do Caminos, Canales, y Puertos, in Madrid.[6]

BIBLIOGRAPHY

Biographical

Chase, George C., "History of Mechanical Computing Machinery," *Ann. Hist. Comp.*, Vol. 2, No. 3, 1980, pp. 198–226.

Randell, Brian, "From Analytical Engine to Electronic Digital Computer: The Contributions of Ludgate, Torres, and Bush," *Ann. Hist. Comp.*, Vol. 4, No. 4, 1982, pp. 327–341.

Rodriguez Alcalde, L., *Torres Quevedo y la Cibernetica*, Ediciones Cid., Madrid, 1966.

Rodriguez Alcalde, L., *Biografia de D. Leonardo Torres Quevedo*, Institucion Cultural de Cantabria, Consejo Superior de Investigaciones Cientificas, Duputacion Provicial de Santander, Madrid, 1974.

Santesmases, J.G., *Obra e Inventos Torres Quevedo*, Instituto de Espana, Madrid, 1980.

Significant Publications

Torres y Quevedo, "Arithmometre Electromechanique," *Bull. de la Societe d'Encouragement for l'Industrie Nationale*, Vol. 119, 1920, pp. 588–99, reprinted in Randell, Brian, *Origins of Digital Computers: Selected Papers*, Springer-Verlag, Berlin, 1982.

JACK TRAMIEL

Founder of Commodore International, which he sold while successful to buy Atari from Warner Communications in 1984.

---

[6]Extracted from Randell 1982.

Joseph Frederick Traub

Born June 24, 1932, Karlsruhe, Germany; leader in the study of computational complexity.

Education: BS, City College of New York, 1954; PhD, applied mathematics, Columbia University, 1959.

Professional Experience: Mathematics Research Center, Computer Science Research Center, Bell Laboratories, Murray Hill, New Jersey, 1959–1971; head, Carnegie Mellon University, Computer Science Department, 1971–1979; Columbia University: Edwin Howard Armstrong professor and chairman, Computer Science Department, 1979 to 1986, professor of mathematics, 1979–1986; New York State Center for Computers and Information Systems: director, 1979–1986, chairman, Computer Science Department, 1987–1989, Edwin Howard Armstrong Professor, Computer Science Department, 1987–present; Princeton University: professor of computer science, 1986–1987, John von Neumann National Supercomputer Center, Consortium for Scientific Computing, president 1986–1987; chair, Computer Science and Telecommunications Board, 1986–1992.

Honors and Awards: member, National Academy of Engineering, 1985; fellow, American Association for the Advancement of Science, 1971; distinguished lecturer, MIT, February 1977; Edwin Howard Armstrong Memorial Lecture, Columbia University, 1980; First Annual BMAC Distinguished Lecture, Colorado State University, October 1982; University Lecture, Columbia University, February 1985; board of governors, New York Academy of Sciences, 1986–1989 (executive committee, 1987–1989); board of trustees, Charles Babbage Institute, 1989–present; Second Annual Charles Babbage Foundation Lecture, October 1989; chairman, Computer Science and Technology Board, National Research Council, 1986–1990; Lecture, Presidium, Academy of Sciences, Moscow, USSR, May 1990; chairman, Computer Science and Telecommunications Board, National Research Council, 1990–1992; First Prize, Ministry of Education, Poland, for the research monograph *Information-Based Complexity*; distinguished lecture, UCLA, November 1991; distinguished lecture, UCSD, February 1991; Emanuel R. Piore Gold Medal, IEEE, 1991; Sherman Fairchild Distinguished Scholar, California Institute of Technology, 1991–1992; Distinguished Service Award, Computer Research Association, 1992; Distinguished Senior Scientist Award, Alexander von Humboldt Foundation, 1992; Lezioni Lincee, Accademia Nazionale dei Lincei, Rome, 1993; Computing Research Association Award for Service to Computing Research, 1993; fellow, ACM, 1994.

Starting in 1959, Traub pioneered research in what is now called information-based complexity, which studies the computational complexity of problems with partial and contaminated information. Such information is all that is available for many real-world problems. Information-based complexity is being used to solve the continuous problems typical of science, engineering, economics, and finance.

He was the founding chairman of the Computer Science Department at Columbia University from 1979 to 1989. From 1971 to 1979, he was head of the Computer Science Department at Carnegie Mellon University and led it from a critical period to eminence. He was founding chairman of the Computer Science and Telecommunications Board of the National Academy of Sciences. The board produces studies on matters of national concern related to computers and telecommunications.

He is the author or editor of eight books and some 100 journal articles. He is the founding editor of the *Journal of Complexity*, which began publication in 1985. Traub has served as adviser or consultant to the senior management of numerous organizations, including IBM, Hewlett-Packard, Schlumberger, Stanford University, IRIA (Paris), the Federal Judiciary Center, and the National Science Foundation.

BIBLIOGRAPHY

Significant Publications

Traub, J.F., *Iterative Methods for the Solution of Equations,* Prentice-Hall, New York, 1964; reissued Chelsea Publishing Company, 1982; Russian translation, MIR, 1985.

Traub, J.F., ed., *Complexity of Sequential and Parallel Numerical Algorithms,* Academic Press, New York, 1973.

Traub, J.F., ed., *Analytic Computational Complexity,* Academic Press, New York, 1975.

Traub, J.F., ed., *Algorithms and Complexity: New Directions and Recent Results,* Academic Press, New York, 1976.

Traub, J.F., and H. Wozniakowski, *A General Theory of Optimal Algorithms,* Academic Press, New York, 1983; Russian translation, MIR, 1980.

Traub, J.F., G. Wasilkowski, and H. Wozniakowski, *Information, Uncertainty, Complexity,* Addison-Wesley, New York, 1983; Russian translation, MIR, 1988.

Traub, J.F., ed., *Cohabiting with Computers,* William Kaufman, Inc., New York, 1985.

Traub, J.F., G. Wasilkowski, and H. Wozniakowski, *Information-Based Complexity,* Academic Press, New York, 1988.

IRVEN TRAVIS

Born March 30, 1904, McConnelsville, Ohio; died October 1, 1986;
University of Pennsylvania, Moore School of Electrical Engineering professor
who went from the ENIAC project to lead the Burroughs Corporation into com-
puters.

Education: BS, Drexel Institute of Technology, 1926; MS, University of Pennsylvania, 1928; DSc, electrical engineering, University of Pennsylvania, 1938.

Professional Experience: University of Pennsylvania: professor, electrical engineering, 1928–1949, supervisor, research, Moore School of Electrical Engineering, 1946–1948; chief, fire-control research, Navy Bureau of Ordnance, 1941–1945; Burroughs Corp.: director, research, 1949–1952, vice president, 1952–1969, member, board of directors, 1950–1971; management consultant, 1969–1986.

Honors and Awards: DEng, Drexel Institute of Technology; fellow, American Association for the Advancement of Science; fellow, IEEE.

JOHN WILDER TUKEY

Born June 16, 1915, New Bedford, Mass.; with James Cooley, the creator of
the fast Fourier transform (FFT) and possible creator of the word "bit."[7]

Education: ScB, chemistry, Brown University, 1936; ScM, Brown University, 1937; MA, Princeton University, 1938; PhD, mathematics, Princeton University, 1939.

Professional Experience: Princeton University: instructor, mathematics, 1939–1941, research associate, Fire Control Research Office, 1941–1945, professor, statistics, 1965–present, Donner Professor of Science, 1976–present; Bell Telephone Laboratories: member, technical staff, 1945–1948, assistant director, Research Communication Principles, 1958–1961, associate executive director, Research Communication Principles Division, 1961–present.

Honors and Awards: DSc (Hon.), Case Institute of Technology, 1962; DSc (Hon.), Brown University, 1965; S.S. Wilks Medal, American Statistical

---

[7]See Tropp 1984.

Association, 1965; DSc (Hon.), Yale University, 1968; DSc (Hon.), University of Chicago, 1969; National Medal of Science, 1973; IEEE Medal of Honor, 1982; member, National Academy of Sciences; member, American Academy of Arts and Sciences; honorary member, Royal Statistical Society.

BIBLIOGRAPHY

Biographical

Tropp, H.S., "Origin of the Term Bit," *Ann. Hist. Comp.,* Vol. 6, No. 2, Apr. 1984, pp. 152–155.

Significant Publications

Cooley, J.W., and J.W. Tukey, "An Algorithm for the Computation of Complex Fourier Series," *Math. of Computation,* Apr. 1965.

ALAN MATHISON TURING

Born June 23, 1912, London, England; died June 7, 1954, Manchester, England; creator of the concept of the "universal machine," the concepts of early computational machines, and computer logic.

Education: Sherborne School, 1926–1931; wrangler, mathematics tripos, Kings College, Cambridge; PhD, Princeton University, 1938.

Professional Experience: fellow, King's College, 1935–1945; Princeton University, 1936–1938; British Foreign Office, Bletchley Park, 1939–1945; National Physical Laboratory, 1945–1948; University of Manchester, 1948–1954.

Honors and Awards: Smith's Prize, Cambridge University, 1936; Order of the British Empire (OBE), 1946; fellow, Royal Society, 1951.

Alan Turing's interest in science began early and never wavered. Both at his preparatory schools and later at Sherborne, which he entered in

1926, the contrast between his absorbed interest in science and mathematics, and his indifference to Latin and "English subjects," perplexed and distressed his teachers, bent on giving him a well-balanced education. Many of the characteristics that were strongly marked in his later life can already be clearly seen in remembered incidents of this time: his particular delight in problems, large or small, that enabled him to combine theory with the kind of experiments he could carry out with his own hands, with the help of whatever apparatus was at hand; and his strong preference for working everything out from first principles instead of borrowing from others—a habit which gave freshness and independence to his work, but also undoubtedly slowed him down, and later on made him a difficult author to read.

In 1931 he entered King's College, Cambridge, as a mathematical scholar. A second class in Part I of the tripos showed him still determined not to spend time on subjects that did not interest him. In Part II he was a wrangler, with "b*," and he won a Smith's Prize in 1936. He was elected a fellow of King's in 1935 for a dissertation on the central limit theorem of probability (which he discovered anew, in ignorance of recent previous work).

It was in 1935 that he first began to work in mathematical logic, and almost immediately started on the investigation that was to lead to his best known results, on computable numbers and the "Turing machine." The paper attracted attention as soon as it appeared and the resulting correspondence led to his spending the next two years (1936–1938) in Princeton, the second of them as Procter Fellow, working with Professor Alonzo Church.

In 1938 Turing returned to Cambridge; in 1939 the war broke out. For the next six years he was fully occupied with his work at the Government Code and Cypher School, otherwise known as Bletchley Park. His application of logic to code breaking has still not been well documented, though his influence on the development of Colossus is well known. But the loss to his published scientific work of the years between the ages of 27 and 33 was a cruel one. Three remarkable papers written just before the war, on three diverse mathematical subjects, show the quality of the work that might have been produced if he had settled down to work on some big problem at that critical time. For his work at Bletchley Park he was awarded the OBE.

At the end of the war many circumstances combined to turn his attention to the new automatic computing machines. They were in principle realizations of the "universal machine" which he had described in the 1937 paper for the purpose of a logical argument, although their designers did not yet know of Turing's work. Besides this theoretical link, there was a strong attraction in the many-sided nature of the work, ranging from electric circuit design to the entirely new field of organizing mathematical problems for a machine. He decided to decline an offer of a Cambridge University lectureship, and join the group that was being formed at the National Physical Laboratory for the design, construction, and use of a large automatic computing machine. In the three years (1945–1948) that this association lasted, he made the first plan of the ACE,[8] the NPL's automatic computer, and did a great deal of pioneering work in the design of subroutines. The machine was still incomplete when he left.

In 1948 he was appointed to a readership in the University of Manchester, where work was beginning on the construction of a computing machine by F.C. Williams and T. Kilburn. The expectation was that Turing would lead the mathematical side of the work, and for a few years he continued to work, first on the design of the subroutines out of which the larger programs for such a machine are built, and then, as this kind of work became standardized, on more general problems of numerical analysis. From 1950 onward he turned back for a while to mathematics and finally to his biological theory. But he remained in close contact with the Computing Machine Laboratory, whose members found him ready to tackle the mathematical problems that arose in their work, and what is more, to find the answers, by that combination of powerful mathematical analysis and intuitive shortcuts that showed him at heart more of an applied than a pure mathematician.

After the war, feeling in need of violent exercise, he took to long distance running, and found that he was very successful at it. He won the 3-mile and 10-mile championships of his club (the Walton Athletic Club), both in record time, and was placed fifth in the Amateur Athletic Association Marathon race in 1947. He thought it quite natural to put this accomplishment to practical use from time to time, for example, by running some 9 miles from Teddington to a technical conference at the Post Office Research Station in North London, when the public transport proved tedious.

In conversation he had a gift for comical but brilliantly apt analogies, which found its full scope in the discussions on "brains v. machines" of the late 1940s. He delighted in confounding those who, as he thought, too easily assumed that the two things are separated by an impassable gulf, by challenging them to produce an examination paper that could be passed by a man, but not by a machine.

---

[8]Automatic Computing Engine.

Robin Addie and Maurice Wilkes were students together at Cambridge University in the years before World War II. They were both active in the Cambridge University Wireless Society, and were both keen radio hams. Their later careers took different directions. Addie held a Royal Signals commission in the Territorial Army Volunteer Reserve, and was mobilized soon after the outbreak of the war on September 3, 1939. He found himself, at the age of 23, in command of the Wireless Section of the 52nd (Lowland) Divisional Signals in France. Later in the war, when attached to the "Y" service, Addie met Alan Turing:

One of my wartime activities was to be involved in the planning, design, and construction of a large radio receiving station at Hanslope Park a few miles from Bletchley. It was known as a "Y" station and was intended for the interception of enemy radio signals. The project was aimed at setting a new standard for intercept stations. It was a green field exercise involving a new station building, and much of the equipment for it had to be specially designed and made. To this end, workshop and laboratory space was provided. The antenna system consisted of numbers of 3-wire rhombics spaced radially round the main building which housed banks of receivers fed from wide band amplifiers to whose inputs selected antennas could be connected. Dedicated land lines fed outgoing signals to Bletchley Park, which was only a few miles away, and to other places. The engineering section, with which I was associated, undertook all constructional and maintenance work in the technical field.

It was in 1944, when the station was operational, that I was asked to provide facilities for Alan Turing so that he might pursue his ideas on speech encryption. Thus I came to know him well and appreciate his intellectual qualities, which clearly dwarfed those of us who were trying to help him.

His aim was to develop active elements for his computer ideas, largely NOR/AND gates, etc. I gave him room and assistants, and supplied him with chassis, components, power supplies, etc.

My vivid memories are of a man of medium build with a round head of crewcut hair bending over what we used to describe as an "electrified bird's nest" of resistors, capacitors, and odd components insecurely fixed to a prototype chassis. All components were held aloft by little blobs of solder, hence the "nest." At one end was a power supply delivering several hundreds of volts. I would watch fascinated as Turing plunged a hot soldering iron in the midst of this wonderwork. Needless to say, calamities happened; sparks flew, fuses blew, and things got hot, but Turing just pressed on in the sure knowledge of what he wished to achieve. Working on experimental gear with the power on was a common practice in those days, but not everybody was as reckless as Turing.

It had been arranged to find him digs locally, to and from which he rode an ancient bicycle. He seemed impervious to weather and, on more than one occasion, arrived soaked to the skin. On these occasions, he was coaxed into removing his trousers and given a lab coat in which he marched throughout the complex, regardless of his hairy legs and sock suspenders (garters) being on general view. He decided that our impregnating oven was the place to dry his garments, and on one occasion, with his mind on other weightier matters, he caused a minor fire. Clothes were then rationed in the UK, and we had to have a collection of ration coupons to help him buy a new pair of trousers.

In the Mess, he was both lively and amusing, and would engage in all manner of discussions on all kinds of diverse topics. I recall a most interesting tete-à-tete between Turing and Professor Stratton (the astrophysicist), then Colonel Stratton, which went on for a long time, way above my head, as can be imagined.

Turing was indeed a most dedicated man, totally oblivious of the wherewithal required for his own comfort. He took it for granted that all would somehow be provided, and we did provide it as far as we could. The girls at Hanslope took him in hand, calling him "prof," which he seemed to like. He was pleasant to me, and I always kept close touch with the work he did, and showed that I was interested. He always took trouble to explain his thoughts, which I appreciated.

Unfortunately, I did not see the outcome of Turing's experiments, since I was posted to the Far East to help mastermind the communications for Mountbatten in India and beyond. I was particularly distressed at the manner of his death in 1954, and the utter waste of a brilliant mind.

Much has been made of the homosexuality of Alan Turing. The biography by Andrew Hodges was initially intended (according to the publishers) to be a celebration of his sexual preference, but they were able to convince Hodges that there was more to the story than just that aspect of his life. Similarly, the play by Hugh Whitemore makes homosexuality the central theme, and a recent (1992) video play by the British Broadcasting Corporation, entitled "The Strange Life and Death of Dr. Turing," followed the same thread.

In a set of interviews in 1992 with I. Jack Good and Donald Michie,[9] both colleagues of Turing during his Bletchley Park sojourn, I led them to discuss their knowledge of Turing's homosexuality:

Good: . . . when we walked down King's Parade [in 1947] that was the first time I discovered that he was homosexual. That was when he said that he was going to Paris to "see a boy." It was obvious that he was admitting or proclaiming his homosexuality.

Lee: He was very open about it?

Good: Yes, at that time.

---

[9]Sponsored in part by the National Science Foundation.

Michie: He certainly wasn't during the war, for some of us, including both of us, were quite unaware. . . . I took quite seriously his engagement to . . .

Good: Joan Clarke?

Michie: At the same time I was thoroughly aware that the whole problem of converse with women was a great burden, and a problem, for him. And I recall his explaining to me once, I didn't think he was homosexual as a result of this conversation, because I [saw him through] the eyes of a rather priggish young person (me) who had just left school and just experimenting with female company—I had grown up to look on women as undereducated relative to men, which to put it that way, was perhaps to some extent in those days was the case. But he put it in a very grotesque way to me and said "you know, the problem is that you have to talk to them," "If you take a girl out, you have to talk to her. And then so often when a woman says something, to me it is as though a frog has suddenly jumped out of her mouth." It was an extremely unpleasant metaphor.

Lee: Peter Hilton [1991] quotes you, Jack, as saying, "It was fortunate that the authorities did not know during the war that Turing was a homosexual, otherwise the Allies might have lost the war."

Good: Yes . . .

Michie: Oh but that's absolute nonsense, because Bletchley had some flamboyant homosexuals—Peter's ideas that security people were down on homosexuality itself, is absolute nonsense. I can't think how he could write that. The most flamboyant case was Angus Wilson—he later became a very successful novelist, and he had a boyfriend called Beverly, and these two, Angus was about that high [indicating small] with flowing yellow hair (I remember it went white later) and Beverly (I forget his second name) was very "weed-like," very tall. They could be seen shambling along the horizon, a daily sight, as they took their walk around lawns after lunch.

Good: I never knew that. I know that Angus Wilson ran around the pond in the nude, when he had a nervous breakdown.

Michie: He was also said to have poured ink on his head on another occasion; it was the first sign he was going nuts again. I had not heard about the nude bit.

Good: I assumed they were down on homosexuality.

Michie: I think that's a retrospective coloring actually. Because Henry Reed,[10] you remember Henry Reed, you knew he was a homosexual didn't you?

Good: No!

Michie: I must have known him better than you. He was always complaining to me about how his current affair was, or was not, prospering.

Good: Well, I was in digs with him, and with David Rees. . . . He never said anything about his affairs.

Michie: I had some links to a more literary set. There was a literary set in Bletchley, and I was fresh from a *wholly* arts education. There were these two cultures—the mathematicians' culture was another—I worked all my time in the mathematicians' culture but I retained, certainly for a year or two, quite a lot of social links to various classics dons and literary people like Henry Reed. And in that group, things like whether Henry Reed was a homosexual—everybody knew. And the same with Angus Wilson.

Good: I had no idea.

In 1952 Turing was convicted by a British court for his involvement in "unnatural acts" and was required to take female hormones in an effort to rid him of his preferences. The physical result was the development of Turing's breasts, and apparently his accompanying depression. This was the time of Turing's life when he was studying the chemical theory of morphogenesis. His "experimental methodology" was what Newman termed his "rules of the game," in which he attempted to solve problems using only the materials immediately at hand or which he could construct in his mind. Turing died by his own hand in 1954 by eating an apple dipped in strychnine. It is unknown whether this was an experiment which had an unfortunate result or whether his death was intentional. Either way, the world lost a mathematical genius at the height of his intellectual power.

QUOTATION

"It is of course important that some efforts be made to verify the correctness of the assertions that are made about a routine. There are essentially two types of method available, the theoretical and the

---

[10]Reed was a poet who had composed a poem entitled "Naming of Parts"—see Lewin, Ronald, 1978, *Ultra Goes to War*, Hutchinson & Co., Ltd., London, 490 pp.

experimental. In the extreme form of the theoretical method a watertight mathematical proof is provided for the assertion. In the extreme form of the experimental method the routine is tried out on the machine with a variety of initial conditions and is pronounced fit if the assertions hold in each case. Both methods have their weaknesses."

(*Manchester Mark I Programming Manual,* 1951)

BIBLIOGRAPHY

Biographical

Addie, Robin, "Memories of Alan Turing," *Ann. Hist. Comp.*, Vol. 15, No. 1, 1992, pp. 59–60.

Aspray, William F., *From Mathematical Constructivity to Computer Science: Alan Turing, John von Neumann, and the Origins of Computer Science in Mathematical Logic,* unpublished PhD dissertation, University of Wisconsin, Madison, 1980.

Britton, J.L., ed., *Pure Mathematics; with a Section on Turing's Statistical Work by I. J. Good,* North-Holland, Amsterdam, 1992.

Campbell-Kelly, Martin, "Programming the Pilot ACE: Early Programming Activity at the National Physical Laboratory," *Ann. Hist. Comp.*, Vol. 3, No. 2, 1981, pp. 133–162.

Carpenter, B.E., and R.W. Doran, eds., *A.M. Turing's ACE Report of 1946 and Other Papers,* MIT Press, Cambridge, Mass., 1986.

Herken, Rolf, ed., *The Universal Turing Machine: A Half-Century Survey,* Oxford Univ. Press, Oxford, UK, 1988.

Hilton, Peter, "Working with Alan Turing," *Mathematical Intelligencer*, Vol. 13, No. 4, 1991, pp. 22–25.

Hinsley, Sir Harry H., and Alan Stripp, *Code Breakers: The Inside Story of Bletchley Park,* Oxford Univ. Press, Oxford, UK, 1993.

Hodges, Andrew, *Alan Turing: The Enigma,* Simon and Schuster, New York, 1983.

Huskey, Harry, "From ACE to G-15," *Ann. Hist. Comp.*, Vol. 6, No. 4, Oct. 1984, pp. 350–371.

Lavington, Simon, *Early British Computers,* Digital Press, Bedford, Mass., 1980; see Chapter 5: "The ACE, the British National Computer," and Chapter 8: "The NPL Pilot ACE."

Michie, D., "Machines that Play and Plan," *Science Journal,* Oct. 1968, pp. 83–88.

Michie, D., "The Disaster of Alan Turing's Buried Treasure," Letter to the editor, *Computer Weekly,* Mar. 1977, p. 10.

Michie, D., "Turing and the Origins of the Computer," *New Scientist*, Vol. 85, No. 1195, 1980, pp. 580–583.

Newman, M.H.A., "Alan Mathison Turing, 1912–1954," *Biographical Memoirs of Fellows of the Royal Society*, Vol. 1, 1955, pp. 253–263.

Randell, Brian, "The Colossus," in Metropolis, N., J. Howlett, and Gian-Carlo Rota, *A History of Computing in the Twentieth Century*, Academic Press, New York, 1980, pp. 47–92.

Ritchie, David, *The Computer Pioneers*, Simon and Schuster, New York, 1986.

Slater, Robert, *Portraits in Silicon*, MIT Press, Cambridge, Mass., 1987.

Turing, Sara, *Alan M. Turing*, W. Heffer & Sons, Cambridge, UK, 1959.

Wilkinson, J.H., "Turing's Work at the National Physical Laboratory and the Construction of Pilot ACE, DEUCE, and ACE," in Metropolis, N., J. Howlett, and Gian-Carlo Rota, *A History of Computing in the Twentieth Century*, Academic Press, New York, 1980, pp. 101–114.

Whitemore, Hugh, *Breaking the Code*, A Play in Two Acts, Samuel French, New York, 1987.

Significant Publications

Carpenter, B.E., and R.W. Doron, eds., *A.M. Turing's ACE Report of 1946 and Other Papers*, MIT Press, Cambridge, Mass., 1986.

Morris, F.L., and C.B. Jones, "An Early Program Proof by Alan Turing," *Ann. Hist. Comp.*, Vol. 6, No. 2, Apr. 1984, pp. 139–143.

Turing, Alan M., "On Computable Numbers with an Application to the Entscheidungs-problem,"[10] *Proc. London Math. Soc.*, Vol. 42, 1937, pp. 230–265.

Turing, Alan M., "Machine Intelligence," submitted to National Physical Laboratory, reprinted in Meltzer, Bernard, and Donald Michie, eds., *Machine Intelligence 5*, Halstead Press, John Wiley & Sons, New York, 1970, pp. 3–23.

Turing, Alan M., "Computing Machinery and Intelligence,"[11] *Mind*, Vol. 59, 1950, pp. 433–460.

Turing, Alan M., *Proposal for the Development of an Electronic Computer, Nat'l. Phys. Lab. Report, Computer Science 57*, London; reprint from original with foreword by D.W. Davies, 1972.

---

[10]This paper defined the concept of the universal machine.

[11]It is in this paper that Turing proposed the test of intelligence which we now know as the "Turing Test."

S. M. Ulam

Born April 13, 1909, Lwów, Poland; died May 13, 1984, Santa Fe, N.M.; colleague of John von Neumann and collaborator in the development of innovative programs for early computers and the solution of problems related to atomic energy.

Education: MA and DSc, mathematics, Polytechnic Institute, Lwów, 1933; subsequent postdoctoral studies in Vienna, Zurich, and Cambridge.

Professional Experience: Institute for Advanced Studies, Princeton University, 1935; junior fellow, Harvard Society of Fellows, lecturer, mathematics, Harvard University, 1936–1940; assistant professor, University of Wisconsin, 1941–1943; Los Alamos Scientific Laboratory: staff member, 1944–1967, consultant, 1967–1984; professor and chairman, Department of Mathematics, University of Colorado, Boulder, 1965–1977; visiting professor, MIT, 1972; visiting professor, University of Paris, 1972; graduate research professor, University of Florida, Gainesville, 1974–1984; professor, biomathematics, University of Colorado Medical School, Denver, 1979–1984; visiting professor, University of California, Davis, 1982.

Honors and Awards: member, American Academy of Arts and Sciences; member, National Academy of Sciences; DSc (Hon.), University of New Mexico, 1965; DSc (Hon.), University of Wisconsin, 1978; DSc (Hon.), University of Pittsburgh, 1978; Polish Millenium Award, Jurzykowski Foundation; Polish Heritage Award.

Goldstine (1974, p. 295) has attributed the concept of the Monte Carlo method to Ulam: "One of the most important projects [at IAS] was the development of the now well-known Monte Carlo Method, which was apparently first suggested by Ulam to von Neumann."

QUOTATION

Regarding his arrival at Los Alamos in 1943: "When I arrived . . . the blackboard was filled with very complicated equations. . . . This sight scared me out of my wits; looking at these I felt that I should never be able to contribute even an epsilon to the solution of any of them."

(Ulam 1980)

BIBLIOGRAPHY

Biographical

Goldstein, Herman H., *The Computer from Pascal to von Neumann,* Princeton Univ. Press, Princeton, N.J., 1972, p. 295.

Ulam, S.M., *Adventures of a Mathematician*, Charles Scribner's Sons, New York, 1976.

Ulam, S.M., "Von Neumann: The Interaction of Mathematics and Computing," in Metropolis, N., J. Howlett, and Gian-Carlo Rota, *A History of Computing in the Twentieth Century*, Academic Press, New York, 1980, pp. 93–99.

Significant Contributions

Bednarek, A.R., and Francoise Ulam, eds., *Analogies between Analogies: The Mathematical Reports of S.M. Ulam and His Los Alamos Collaborators*, Univ. of California Press, Berkeley, 1990.

ADRIAAN[1] VAN WIJNGAARDEN

Born November 2, 1916; died February 7, 1987; leader in programming linguistics and language translation; contributor to Algol 60 and 68 development, and versatile supporter of IFIP.

Education: mechanical engineering, Technical University of Delft; PhD, Technical University of Delft.

Professional Experience: various positions, including director, Amsterdam Mathematisch Centrum, 1947–1981.

Honors and Awards: member, Royal Dutch Academy of Sciences, 1959; first honorary member, Dutch Computer Society, 1972; IFIP Silvercore Award, 1974; IEEE Computer Society Pioneer Award, 1986.

Born on November 2, 1916, Adriaan van Wijngaarden was educated as a mechanical engineer at the technical University of Delft, where he obtained his PhD. He joined the Amsterdam Mathematisch Centrum on January 1, 1947, later becoming its director, and remained there until he retired in 1981.

His first assignment was to tour the UK and the US in an attempt to determine to what extent the newly invented automatic calculating machine would influence the work of the Centre. Upon his return he convinced the Centre's management that computing power is essential to applied mathematics, and stimulating to the emerging discipline of computer science. In those days there was no way to acquire such power other than building one's own machine. The result, commissioned in 1952, was ARRA. The group who built this machine contained people such as G.A. Blaauw, Edsger W. Dijkstra, and W.L. van der Poel, themselves to become trailblazers in the world of computing. After constructing ARRA, the group went on to build ARMAC and finally the fully transistorized X1.

In the meantime, van Wijngaarden pursued two other main activities. While he was a late-joining member of the joint ACM/GAMM group that developed Algol 60, he was very active in the subsequent development of Algol 68. Initially the proposal for an update to Algol was Algol X, with Algol Y being the name reserved for the corresponding metalanguage. Van Wijngaarden produced a paper for the 1963 IFIP programming language committee, entitled "Generalized Algol," which contained the basic concepts which were eventually incorporat-

---

[1]There seems to be some disagreement regarding van Wijngaarden's first name. Naur (Wexelblat 1981) refers to him as "Aad." Cortada (1987) uses the first name "Arie."

ed into Algol 68. During this period he was a central figure in the organization of the International Federation for Information Processing (IFIP) serving as Congress vice president, general assembly member, vice president, and chairman of Technical Committees 1 and 2.

After his retirement, Professor van Wijngaarden lived more or less hidden in his home, following computer developments closely but only occasionally appearing at an event. His declining health kept him ever more closely tied to his home; he died on February 7, 1987.[2]

BIBLIOGRAPHY

Biographical

Verrijn-Stuart, A.A., "Obituary, A. van Wijngaarden,"*IFIP Newsletter*, Vol. 4, No. 3, 1987.

Zemanek, Heinz, "The Role of Professor A. van Wijngaarden in the History of IFIP," in de Bakker, J.W., and J.C. van Vliet, eds., *Algorithmic Languages*, North-Holland, Amsterdam, 1981, pp. +xxvi.

Zemanek, Heinz, "Eloge: Adriaan van Wijngaarden (1916–1987)," *Ann. Hist. Comp.*, Vol. 11, No. 3, 1989, pp. 210–225.[3]

Significant Publications

van Wijngaarden, A., "The State of Computer Circuits Containing Memory Elements," in Aiken, H., ed., *Proc. Int'l Symp. on the Theory of Switching, Cambridge MA*, Vol. 30, *Annals of the Computation Laboratory*, Harvard Univ. Press, Cambridge, Mass., 1959, pp. 231–224.

van Wijngaarden, A., "Generalized Algol," *Symbolic Languages in Data Processing, Proc. Symp. Int'l, Computation Center Rome*, Gordon & Beach, New York, 1962, pp. 409–419.

van Wijngaarden, A., "Recursive Definition of Syntax and Semantics," in Steel, T.B., ed., *Formal Language Description Languages for Computer Programming, Proc. IFIP Working Conference*, North-Holland, Amsterdam, 1966, pp. 13–24.

van Wijngaarden, A., B.J. Mailloux, J.E.L. Peck, and C.H.A. Koster, eds., "Report of the Algorithmic Language Algol 68," *Numerische Mathematik*, Vol. 14, 1969, pp. 79–218.

---

[2]From Zemanek 1989.

[3]This obituary contains an extensive list of publications of van Wijngaarden.

John[4] Louis von Neumann

Born December 28, 1903, Budapest, Hungary; died February 8, 1957, Washington, D.C.; brilliant mathematician, synthesizer, and promoter of the stored-program concept, whose logical design of the IAS became the prototype of most of its successors—the von Neumann architecture.

Education: University of Budapest, 1921; University of Berlin, 1921–1923; chemical engineering, Eidgenössische Technische Hochschule [ETH] (Swiss Federal Institute of Technology), 1923–1925; doctorate, mathematics (with minors in experimental physics and chemistry), University of Budapest, 1926.

Professional Experience: Privatdozent, University of Berlin, 1927–1930; visiting professor, Princeton University, 1930–1953; professor of mathematics, Institute for Advanced Study, Princeton University, 1933–1957.

Honors and Awards: DSc (Hon.), Princeton University, 1947; Medal for Merit (Presidential Award), 1947; Distinguished Civilian Service Award, 1947; DSc (Hon.), University of Pennsylvania, 1950; DSc (Hon.), Harvard University, 1950; DSc (Hon.), University of Istanbul, 1952; DSc (Hon.), Case Institute of Technology, 1952; DSc (Hon.), University of Maryland, 1952; DSc (Hon.), Institute of Polytechnics, Munich, 1953; Medal of Freedom (Presidential Award), 1956; Albert Einstein Commemorative Award, 1956; Enrico Fermi Award, 1956; member, American Academy of Arts and Sciences; member, Academiz Nacional de Ciencias Exactas, Lima, Peru; member, Acamedia Nazionale dei Lincei, Rome, Italy; member, National Academy of Sciences; member, Royal Netherlands Academy of Sciences and Letters, Amsterdam, Netherlands; member, Information Processing Hall of Fame, Infomart, Dallas Texas, 1985 (posthumous).

Von Neumann was a child prodigy, born into a banking family in Budapest, Hungary. When only 6 years old he could divide eight-digit numbers in his head. He received his early education in Budapest, under the tutelage of M. Fekete, with whom he published his first paper at the age of 18. Entering the University of Budapest in 1921, he studied chemistry, moving his base of studies to both Berlin and Zurich before receiving his diploma in 1925 in chemical engineering. He returned to his first love of mathematics in completing his doctoral degree in 1928. He quickly gained a reputation in set theory, algebra, and quantum mechanics. At a time of political unrest in central

---

[4]Originally named Johann, but called Jancsi by the family.

Europe, he was invited to visit Princeton University in 1930, and when the Institute for Advanced Studies was founded there in 1933, he was appointed to be one of the original six professors of mathematics, a position which he retained for the remainder of his life. At the instigation and sponsorship of Oskar Morganstern, von Neumann and Kurt Gödel became US citizens in time for their clearance for wartime work. There is an anecdote which tells of Morganstern driving them to their immigration interview, after their having learned about the US Constitution and the history of the country. On the drive there Morganstern asked them if they had any questions which he could answer. Gödel replied that he had no questions but he had found some logical inconsistencies in the Constitution that he wanted to ask the Immigration officers about. Morganstern strongly recommended that he was not to ask questions, just to answer them.

During 1936 through 1938 Alan Turing was a visitor at the institute and completed a PhD dissertation under von Neumann's supervision. Von Neumann invited Turing to stay on at the institute as his assistant but he preferred to return to Cambridge; a year later Turing was involved in war work at Bletchley Park. This visit occurred shortly after Turing's publication of his 1934 paper "On Computable Numbers with an Application to the Entscheidungs Problem," which involved the concepts of logical design and the universal machine. It must be concluded that von Neumann knew of Turing's ideas, although whether he applied them to the design of the IAS machine 10 years later is questionable.

Von Neumann's interest in computers differed from that of his peers by his quickly perceiving the application of computers to applied mathematics for specific problems, rather than their mere application to the development of tables. During the war, von Neumann's expertise in hydrodynamics, ballistics, meteorology, game theory, and statistics was put to good use in several projects. This work led him to consider the use of mechanical devices for computation, and although the stories about von Neumann imply that his first computer encounter was with the ENIAC, in fact it was with Howard Aiken's Harvard Mark I (ASCC) calculator. His correspondence in 1944 shows his interest with not only the work of Aiken but also the electromechanical relay computers of George Stibitz, and the work by Jan Schilt at the Watson Scientific Computing Laboratory at Columbia University. By the latter years of World War II, von Neumann was playing the part of an executive management consultant, serving on several national committees, applying his amazing ability to rapidly see through problems to their solutions. Through this means he was also a conduit between groups of scientists who were otherwise shielded from each other by the requirements of secrecy. He brought together the needs of the Los Alamos National Laboratory (and the Manhattan Project) with the capabilities of, first, the engineers at the Moore School of Electrical Engineering who were building the ENIAC and, later, his own work on building the IAS machine. Several "supercomputers" were built by national laboratories as copies of his machine.

Postwar von Neumann concentrated on the development of the Institute for Advanced Studies (IAS) computer and its copies around the world. His work with the Los Alamos group continued, and he continued to develop the synergism between computer capabilities and the needs for computational solutions to nuclear problems related to the hydrogen bomb.

Any computer scientist who reviews the formal obituaries of John von Neumann of the period shortly after his death will be struck by the lack of recognition of his involvement in the field. His Academy of Sciences biography, written by Salomon Bochner (1958), for example, includes but a single short paragraph in 10 pages ". . . in 1944 von Neumann's attention turned to computing machines and, somewhat surprisingly, he decided to build his own. As the years progressed, he appeared to thrive on the multitudinousness of his tasks. It has been stated that von Neumann's electronic computer hastened the hydrogen bomb explosion on November 1, 1952." Dieudonné (1981) is a little more generous with words but appears to confuse the concept of the stored program with the wiring of computers:

> Dissatisfied with the computing machines available immediately after the war, he was led to examine from its foundations the optimal method that such machines should follow, and he introduced new procedures in the logical organization, the "codes" by which a fixed system of wiring could solve a great variety of problems.

Among the views of von Neumann's contributions to the field of computing, including the application of his concepts of mathematics to computing, and the application of computing to his other interests such as mathematical physics and economics, perhaps the most comprehensive is by Herman Goldstine (1972). There has been some criticism of Goldstine's perspective since he personally was intimately involved in von Neumann's computing activities from the time of their chance meeting on the railroad platform at Aberdeen in 1944 through their joint activities at the Institute for Advanced Studies in developing the IAS machine.[5]

---

[5]Goldstine 1972, p. 182.

There is no doubt that his insights into the organization of machines led to the infrastructure which is now known as the "von Neumann architecture." However, von Neumann's ideas were not along those lines originally; he recognized the need for parallelism in computers but equally well recognized the problems of construction, and hence settled for a sequential system of implementation. Through the report entitled *First Draft of a Report on the EDVAC* (1945), authored solely by von Neumann, the basic elements of the stored-program concept were introduced to the industry. A retrospective examination of the development of this idea reveals that the concept was discussed by J. Presper Eckert, John Mauchly, Arthur Burks, and others in connection with their plans for a successor machine to the ENIAC.[6] The "Draft Report" was just that, a draft, and, although written by von Neumann, was intended to be the joint publication of the whole group. The EDVAC was intended to be the first stored-program computer, but at the summer school at the Moore School in 1946, there was so much emphasis on the EDVAC that Maurice Wilkes, Cambridge University Mathematical Laboratory, conceived his own design for the EDSAC, which became the world's first operational, production, stored-program computer.

In the 1950s von Neumann was employed as a consultant to IBM to review proposed and ongoing advanced technology projects. One day a week, von Neumann "held court" at 590 Madison Avenue, New York. On one of these occasions in 1954 he was confronted with the Fortran concept; John Backus remembered von Neumann being unimpressed and that he asked, "Why would you want more than machine language?" Frank Beckman, who was also present, recalled that von Neumann dismissed the whole development as "but an application of the idea of Turing's 'short code.'" Donald Gilles, one of von Neumann's students at Princeton, and later a faculty member at the University of Illinois, recalled that the graduate students were being "used" to hand-assemble programs into binary for their early machine (probably the IAS machine). He took time out to build an assembler, but when von Neumann found out about it he was very angry, saying (paraphrased), "It is a waste of a valuable scientific computing instrument to use it to do clerical work."

One last anecdote about von Neumann's brilliant mathematical capabilities: the von Neumann household in Princeton was open to many social activities and on one such occasion someone posed the

---

[6]See Aspray, W.F., "Pioneer Day '82: History of the Stored Program Concept," *Ann. Hist. Comp.*, Vol. 4, No. 4, 1982, pp. 358–361.

"fly and the train" problem to von Neumann.[7] Quickly von Neumann came up with the answer. Suspecting that he had seen through the problem to discover a simple solution, he was asked how he solved the problem. "Simple," he responded, "I summed the series!"

QUOTATIONS

"If people do not believe that mathematics is simple, it is only because they do not realize how complicated life is."

"Anyone who considers arithmetical methods of producing random numbers is, of course, in a state of sin."

BIBLIOGRAPHY

Biographical

Aspray, William F., *From Mathematical Constructivity to Computer Science: Alan Turing, John von Neumann, and the Origins of Computer Science in Mathematical Logic,* unpublished PhD dissertation, University of Wisconsin, Madison, 1980.

Aspray, William, "The Mathematical Reception of the Modern Computer: John von Neumann and the Institute for Advanced Study Computer," in Phillips, Esther R., ed., *Studies in the History of Mathematics,* Vol. 26, Math. Assoc. of America, Washington, D.C., 1987, pp. 166–194.

Bigelow, Julian, "Computer Development at the Institute for Advanced Study," in Metropolis, N., J. Howlett, and Gian-Carlo Rota, *A History of Computing in the Twentieth Century,* Academic Press, New York, 1980, pp. 291–310.

Birkhoff, G., et al., "Memorial Papers on John von Neumann," *Bull. AMS,* Vol. 64, No. 3, 1958, Pt. 2.

Bochner, Salomon, "John von Neumann," *Biographical Memoirs,* Vol. 32, National Academy of Sciences, 1958, pp. 456–451.

Dieudonné, J., "Von Neumann, Johann (or John)," in Gillespie, Charles C., *Dictionary of Scientific Biography,* Charles Scribner's Sons, New York, 1981, pp. 88–92.

Godfrey, M.D., "The Computer as von Neumann Planned It," *Ann. Hist. Comp.* Vol. 15, No. 1, 1993, pp. 11–21.

Goldstine, Herman H., *The Computer from Pascal to von Neumann,* Princeton Univ. Press, Princeton, N.J., 1972.

---

[7]Suppose two trains on the same track are 20 miles apart, heading towards each other, each traveling at 20 miles per hour. Suppose a fly, capable of flying at 60 miles per hour, leaves the first train, flies to the other, turns around and flies back and forth until the two trains collide. How far will the fly travel before it is squashed between the crashing trains?

Hurd, Cuthbert, "Early IBM Computers: Edited Testimony," *Ann. Hist. Comp.*, Vol. 3. No. 1, 1981, pp. 163–182.

Ritchie, David, *The Computer Pioneers,* Simon and Schuster, New York, 1986.

Slater, Robert, *Portraits in Silicon,* MIT Press, Cambridge, Mass., 1987.

Stern, Nancy, *From ENIAC to Univac: An Appraisal of the Eckert-Mauchly Computers,* Digital Press, Bedford, Mass., 1981.

Stern, Nancy, "John von Neumann's Influence on Electronic Digital Computing, 1944–46," *Ann. Hist. Comp.*, Vol. 2, No. 4, 1980, pp. 349–362.

Tropp, H.S., "John von Neumann" in Ralston, Anthony, and Edwin D. Reilly, Jr., *Encyclopedia of Computer Science and Engineering,* Van Nostrand Reinhold Co., New York, 1983, pp. 1564–1565.

Ulam, S.M., "Von Neumann: The Interaction of Mathematics and Computing," in Metropolis, N., J. Howlett, and Gian-Carlo Rota, *A History of Computing in the Twentieth Century,* Academic Press, New York, 1980, pp. 93–99.

Ulam, S., "John von Neumann, 1903–1957," *Ann. Hist. Comp.*, Vol. 4, No. 2, Apr. 1982, pp. 157–181.

Von Neumann, Nicholas A., *John von Neumann—As Seen by His Brother,* private printing, Meadowbrook, Pa., 1988.

Significant Publications

Charney, J.G., R. Fjörtoft, and John von Neumann, "Numerical Integration of the Barotropic Vorticity Equation," *Tellus*, Vol. 2, 1950, pp. 237–254.

Taub, A.H., ed., *John von Neumann: Collected Works, 1903–1957,* 6 Vols., Pergamon Press, Oxford, UK, 1961–1963.

von Neumann, John, and Oskar Morganstern, *Theory of Games and Economic Behavior,* Princeton Univ. Press, Princeton, N.J., 1944.

von Neumann, John, *First Draft of a Report on the EDVAC,* Contract No. W-670-ORD-492, Moore School of Electrical Engineering, Univ. of Pennsylvania, Philadelphia, June 1945; reprinted (in part) in Randell, Brian, *Origins of Digital Computers: Selected Papers,* Springer-Verlag, Berlin, 1982, pp. 383–392; reprinted with corrections, *Ann. Hist. Comp.*, Vol. 15, No. 4., 1993, pp. 25–75.

von Neumann, John, "The Principles of Large-Scale Computing Machines," reprinted in *Ann. Hist. Comp.*, Vol. 3, No. 3, 1981, pp. 263–273.

von Neumann, John, *The Computer and the Brain,* Yale Univ. Press, New Haven, Conn., 1958.

von Neumann, John, and Arthur W. Burks, *Theory of Self-Reproducing Automata,* Univ. of Illinois Press, Urbana, 1966.

V

EDWARD A. VOORHEES

Los Alamos scientist who was a member of the team that developed the IBM STRETCH.

Education: BA, Maryville (Tenn.) College, 1947; MA, Vanderbilt University, 1949.

Vorhees was an instructor in mathematics until 1952, when he joined the Los Alamos Scientific Laboratory as a staff member in the 701 Programming Section of Group T-1. In 1954 he became section leader and assistant group leader in T-1. From 1956 to 1961 he worked on the IBM-LASL effort that produced the STRETCH (IBM-7030) computer. From 1966 to 1978 he was the laboratory's coordinator, ADP (CADP). He retired from LASL in 1982.

AN WANG

Born February 7, 1920, Shanghai, China; died March 24, 1990, Boston, Mass.; developer of the basic concept of the ferrite core memory, and founder of Wang Laboratories, which developed the first desktop computer.

Education: BS, engineering, Chiao Tung University, Shanghai, China, 1940; MS, applied physics, Harvard University, 1946; PhD, applied physics, Harvard University, 1948.

Professional Experience: research fellow, Harvard Computation Laboratory, 1948–1950; founder, president, Wang Laboratories, 1950–1987.

Honors and Awards: 23 honorary degrees; Medal of Liberty, 1986; National Inventors Hall of Fame, 1988.

Early life in China[1]

Wang was born in Shanghai, China, on February 7, 1920, the second child and eldest son of the five children of Yin Lu Wang, a teacher of English and a practitioner of traditional Chinese medicine, and Z.W. Chien, his wife. His name, An Wang, means "peaceful king." Until he was 6 he lived in the Shanghai compound of his mother's family. Then his family moved to his father's ancestral city, Kun San (Kunshan), about 30 miles west of Shanghai. Here Wang started his formal education in the private elementary school where his father taught. Because the school lacked the first two grades, he had to start in the third. As a consequence, for the rest of his education in China, he was always two years younger than his classmates, a situation which he said put him at a great disadvantage but from which, in the long run, he benefited because he found that he could quickly learn to swim when faced with the alternative of sinking.

He discovered early that he was good at mathematics but had difficulty with subjects requiring rote memorization, and he always had a hard time concentrating on subjects, such as political doctrine, that did not interest him. His father started teaching him English at home when he was 4. His paternal grandmother diligently tutored him in Confucianism, which he later called "the practical philosophy that has profoundly influenced Chinese character," and which embodied the principles of moderation, patience, balance, and simplicity that he

---

[1]This material is drawn largely from Wang's 1986 didactic autobiography (Wang 1986), which is also a triumphant recounting of the founder's view of the history of Wang Laboratories, and in turn from Weiss 1993. To avoid clutter, the autobiography will not be referenced again.

later concluded were important to success in business. Wang also ascribed to Confucianism his belief that a sense of satisfaction comes from service to one's community.

During these school years he found that, although he did poorly during the term in the nonscientific subjects that did not interest him, by concentrating at the term-end he could always perform well enough on the final exams to get by. This success added to his confidence that he could rise to the occasion when the situation demanded it.

By the time Wang was 11 the bloody struggle with the Communists had left the Nationalist Government barely in control of China. In 1931 the Japanese seized Manchuria and repeatedly bombed Nationalist-held Shanghai. The Nationalists directed an overwhelming program of relentless propaganda at its school children between the ages of 8 and 12. Wang remembered being forced to join in at least five political mass rallies a year. This experience turned him against political activism, an attitude that he retained all his life.

When he was 13 he enrolled at Shanghai Provincial High School, about 10 miles outside the city, where he boarded and where he was taught entirely from American textbooks. Wang's two-year age disadvantage kept him out of team sports but he found that he had a talent for table tennis. At the age of 16 he entered the university his father had attended for one year, Chiao Tung University in Shanghai, then the MIT of China. He had the highest entrance examination scores of his class. Here for the next four years he studied electrical engineering with an emphasis on communications. The subject, again taught from American textbooks, was easy for him. He later said that he spent more time at table tennis (he was on the university team) than he did studying engineering.

In late 1936, during Wang's first year at Chiao Tung, his mother, broken by years of fear and conflict, died in Kun San. After the Japanese invasion of China, the university was moved into the French concession of the Shanghai International Settlement. This gave protection from the devastation, because for the first few years of the war the invaders respected the territorial integrity of the foreign concessions. In the midst of this chaos Wang's family made its way from Kun San to temporary safety in the concession.

After graduation in 1940 Wang spent a year in Chiao Tung as a teaching assistant. In the summer of 1941 he joined a small project to provide radios for the Nationalist troops. His group of eight went by boat from occupied Shanghai to still-British Hong Kong, and then to Kuan Chou Wan, an isolated French concession on the Lui-Chow peninsula between the South China Sea and the Gulf of Tonkin. From here they slipped through the Japanese line and marched for three nights to a river where they took a boat and then a train to Nationalist-held Kweilin (now Guilin), 300 miles inside China.

In Kweilin, 21-year-old Wang was put in charge of a group scrounging and scavenging parts and improvising the designs to build radios for military use. In late 1944 Wang and his group were evacuated to Chungking just before the Japanese took Kweilin. Wang did not hear until much later that, in this period, both his father and his older sister Hsu had died as a result of the war. His younger sister Yu and his two brothers Ping and Ge survived, although he did not see them for 40 years.

Going to Harvard

In March 1945, with Japan in retreat, Wang placed second in a competitive examination to enter a Nationalist government program to give two years of advanced training in the US to several hundred young engineers. In April he was flown "over the Hump" in a US DC-3 to Ledo in India, went by train to Calcutta and, after a wait of a month, made a month-long voyage to Newport News, Virginia, where he arrived in June. By this time, he writes, "the notion that there were things I could not or should not attempt to accomplish was utterly foreign to me."

Because, Wang says, he looked for cultural similarities, not differences, he claims that he suffered no culture shock. The US was exciting but not strange, and to him seemed a lot like China. Wang's group was housed temporarily at Georgetown University in Washington, D.C. Its campus struck Wang as "not unlike that of Chiao Tung." While some in the group immediately accepted offers to serve their two-year apprenticeships as technical observers with firms such as Westinghouse and RCA, Wang conceived the novel idea of applying for admission to Harvard. By luck, he applied at the only time that Harvard would have considered a case like his. In the early summer of 1945, although Germany had surrendered, at least a year of further war with Japan seemed certain. Most American young men were still in uniform, and even Harvard had more openings than potential students. It turned out that getting into Harvard was easier for several in the group of Chiao Tung graduates than finding an apprenticeship in industry. In September 1945 Wang entered Harvard as a graduate student in applied physics.

Here, although his spoken English was poor, he felt comfortable. He could read and write English well. The university setting suited him, there were a number of other Chinese associated with Harvard, and a laboratory seemed a second home to him. He found the work relatively easy and in two semesters he satisfied the requirements for a master's degree in applied physics, getting two A+'s and two A's in his first term—Wang always had a clear and proud recollection of his many academic successes.

After the summer of 1946, Wang's monthly $100 stipend from the Chinese government ended as the Nationalists turned all their resources to the civil war with Mao Tse-tung. At first Wang took a clerical job with the Chinese purchasing mission in Ottawa. This was a mistake. The work was routine and boring, and the fall weather was extremely cold with worse to come in the winter. Wang applied to Harvard for admission to the PhD program in applied physics. He was accepted and given a $1,000 a year teaching fellowship and, later, a Benrus Time Fellowship. By February 1947 he was back in Cambridge determined to get his degree as promptly as possible.

In May he chose his thesis topic not for its importance but because he knew he could do it quickly and it would satisfy his PhD committee. It was in nonlinear mechanics, and involved the determination of the effects on a mass with a nonlinear response of two forces simultaneously oscillating at different frequencies. He later said it was one of the few problems he ever approached without concern for its practical application—although its practical purpose was to enable him to get a PhD. He did some experimentation in the summer, started to write up his results in September, finished his thesis in December, submitted it in February, defended it at the oral exam in the spring, and obtained his degree at the ceremony in June 1948.

After seeing the pile of security forms that Hughes Aircraft sent to him in reply to his job inquiry, he walked across the Harvard campus to see if he could get a job in the Harvard Computation Laboratory, then consisting of Howard Aiken, five or six research fellows, and a few assistants in a new but undistinguished two-story brick building that still housed the glass-enclosed Mark I on the ground floor. Aiken was working on the Mark IV for the US Air Force, his first purely electronic computer, which turned out to be the last computer that he, and Harvard, built. Wang applied to the Computation Laboratory not because he was eager to work on computers but because it was nearby. While his graduate education had nothing to do with computers, he had taken courses in digital electronic circuitry and this, as well as his newly minted PhD and his personality, appeared to qualify him, for soon after being interviewed by Aiken he started work as a research fellow, although his appointment was delayed until July 1.

Invention of Magnetic Core Storage

On May 18, 1948, within a day or two of starting work, Aiken gave him the problem of finding a way to record and read magnetically stored information without mechanical motion. Later Wang wrote, "After struggling with the question for about 3 weeks, the solution presented itself to me." He agreed with many others in the then small computer community who were considering the same problem, that the best way to store information magnetically was by magnetizing a toroid or core of magnetic material which had a strong residual magnetic flux. The problem was how to read the stored information out without destroying it by demagnetizing the core. One day, while he was walking through Harvard Yard, the idea came to him in a flash, that the destruction did not matter if, immediately after reading the information, it was rewritten back into the magnetic toroid. His June 29, 1948, notebook entry reads, ". . . It is very possible that the information can stay there [in the core in the form of a particular magnetic direction] and be transferred many times before the information [is lost or muddied]. . . ." As Wang later put it, "The idea is that by destroying the information—I know it."(Pugh 1984)

This simple, novel, and elegant concept, applied to all the magnetic core memories that followed, which were, as Pugh (1984) said, these "memories that shaped an industry," was Wang's greatest technical achievement. Although these devices are now fast becoming only a memory, their importance to the development of computers in the period from 1950 to 1970 was second only to that of transistors. Indeed Pugh (1984) goes further, saying, "Development of reliable, high-speed ferrite core memories that could be mass-produced at low cost was probably the most important innovation that made stored-program computers a practical, commercial reality." It was Wang's concept that set this development in motion.

This conceptual breakthrough left him with the practical problem of finding the right materials and implementing his design. He found a Navy publication that described a suitable magnetic material developed by the Germans during the war, Permanorm 5000-Z (the US copy of this material was called Deltamax, made by Arnold Engineering, a subsidiary of Allegheny-Ludlum). To put the toroids into a memory system, he linked them in series so they became the magnetic core delay line used in the Mark IV, but in almost no other computer.

In June 1949 Wang first discussed the idea of patenting his device with his fiancée, Lorraine Chiu, whom he had been courting for a year and whom he married the following month. Wang had met Lorraine in 1948 at a Boston area get-together for Chinese students and academics. She was distantly related to Yung Wing, the first Chinese to study at and graduate from Yale (1854). Her parents had been born in Hawaii before its annexation but had moved back to Shanghai, where Lorraine was born and where she had her undergraduate education at St. John's College. She had come to the US to study Shakespeare at Wellesley, where the civil war in China marooned her. The conflict also prevented the couple from following the traditional procedure of seeking her parents' approval of their marriage.

Chiu saw the value of a patent based on the concept and encouraged Wang to get it. No one else at the Computation Laboratory had taken any patents and at that time there was a feeling at some universities that patents were evil and should not be taken out on inventions made by academics.[2]

Wang wanted to avoid Aiken's legendary wrath, although he had never personally encountered it, so he first explored the question of patents with the Harvard administration. At that time Harvard only reserved patent rights to itself for those inventions that applied to public health. The Harvard administrator he consulted advised Wang to file for it himself at his own expense, and recommended Harvard's own firm of patent attorneys, Fish, Richardson, and Neave. Within a month, on October 21, 1949, Wang filed his patent application, titled "Pulse Transfer Controlling Devices," with 34 claims, most of which are directed toward "an information delay line." The application resulted in Patent 2,708,722, issued May 17, 1955 (Wang 1955). The most important claim, number 24, stating Wang's concept in the arcane language of the Patent Office, allowed the patent owner, ultimately IBM, to demand and usually obtain royalties from all who made core memories, that is to say, the entire computer industry.

This monopoly existed for the patent's 17-year life, that is, until 1972, after which Wang's invention entered the public domain and could be freely used by anyone. Since Wang's work at Harvard had been funded by the Air Force, the US government always had a nonexclusive license to use what the patent claimed.

---

[2]At this time only a few universities, chiefly those with strong departments of engineering, had established policies about the patent rights of their staff members. Just a few years earlier the acrimonious split between the University of Pennsylvania and the inventors of the ENIAC had been caused by a difference of opinion about valuable academic patents. MIT, on the other hand, had a policy of turning such patents over to the closely linked Research Corporation which made arrangements to reward the inventors, exploit the patents, and pass the resulting funds to MIT. It is interesting that Harvard and Pennsylvania, two universities that denigrated staff patents, quickly lost and never regained their original computing eminence, while MIT, with the opposite patent policy, has always been at the forefront of computing research. (Editor)

Here is the claim:

24. A pulse transfer controlling device including a core of magnetic material in which the residual magnetic flux density is a large fraction of the saturation flux density, winding means on said core, current pulse generator means operatively connected to said winding, means to apply current pulses of opposite polarity to said winding means, said pulses of one polarity acting to saturate said core in one direction to read in information, and of the opposite polarity acting to read out said information by inducing voltage in said winding means as controlled by the state of residual magnetic flux density of said core and to reset said core.

After filing his patent application Wang suffered a rare sleepless night as he braced himself to inform Aiken, who, to his surprise, while not overjoyed, did not react at all. Aiken later gave Wang another substantial raise in pay and in the year and a half that Wang stayed at the lab he noticed no difference in his relationship with Aiken, which had always been correct but never close or cordial.

On September 29, 1949, just before filing his application, Wang described his invention at a Harvard computing symposium and later wrote technical papers about it for the *Journal of Applied Physics* and the *Proceedings of the Institute of Radio Engineers*, making his concept well known to those in the computer memory field. Others already working on the problem (notably Ralph E. Meager, Munro K. Haynes, Jan Rajchman, and Jay W. Forrester) devised and sometimes patented improvements, releasing a storm of patent litigation out of which Wang's patent emerged virtually unscathed as controlling over all later patents in the field, because of its priority and breadth.

Jay W. Forrester at MIT devised a different way of organizing the cores. His scheme, which Wang called "brilliant" and always regretted not thinking of himself, was to arrange the cores not in a line but in a matrix with wires strung so each one could be individually selected (Forrester 1951). This system, combining the concepts of Wang and Forrester and ascribed by some to Haynes, dominated computer memories until cores were replaced by solid-state devices.

It is remarkable that while Pugh (1984) in his description of these times gives full credit to Wang, writers about Forrester's Whirlwind, which used magnetic core storage (Redmond and Smith 1980), and the MIT Institute Archives Staff (1990), manage to ignore Wang and his controlling patent completely, giving full credit for the core memory to Forrester.

It was clear to Wang in 1950 that Harvard was soon going to deemphasize basic computer research in line with its policy of staying out of fields that had commercial applications. He later wrote that Harvard was ill-advised to abandon its eminence in computer development.

Since Harvard was not going to do basic computer research it was easy for him to decide to leave the Computation Laboratory. He treasured independence and did not want to work for someone else's company. What he really wanted to do was to try something on his own.

Start of Wang Laboratories
His innovations with memory cores had given him the status of an expert in digital electronics, a status which he thought he might exploit by starting his own business to make and sell memory cores, a business for which little capital would be needed. He had been making $5,400 a year; he hoped to earn $8,000 or so in his first year on his own. He did not anticipate great wealth. He discussed the plan with his wife, but she later said that she had been so preoccupied with the birth complications of their first son, Frederick, that she did not appreciate the importance of the step that Wang was taking. In April 1951 he gave his notice to the Computation Laboratory and in June he set up Wang Laboratories as a sole proprietorship with his six hundred dollars of savings as capital, no orders, no contracts, and no office furniture.

An Wang's life was so intimately intertwined with his creation, Wang Laboratories, that their histories must be considered as one. Thus what follows is as much about Wang Laboratories as about Wang himself. It is plain that in his mind, there was no clear distinction.

His Chinese friends, sensitive to anti-Asian discrimination, did not think it wise to start a business in an area dominated by the Caucasian establishment. His success encouraged other Chinese in academia to follow his example.

Wang began methodically telephoning or writing to everyone in universities, government, and industry whom he thought might be interested in buying memory cores. Within three weeks he began to get responses to his offer of cores at $4 each. The lump sum payment to him of his Harvard pension fund gave him a year's cushion, but even so, his finances were precarious. To supplement his income he taught an electrical engineering evening course at Northeastern University. In the last six months of 1951 he earned $3,253.60, somewhat more than the $2,700 he would have earned at Harvard. In the fall of 1952 the Laboratory for Electronics gave him a contract to develop a pulse synchronizer and counter. He got more and more consulting contracts to design specialized digital equipment, which developed his facility with digital electronics. The contracts also taught him about the marketplace and the essentials of running a business. His approach was to be concerned with innovation only insofar as it served the marketplace, an approach which he said characterized his company as long as he lived.

Bargaining with IBM

One of the first steps he took after starting Wang Laboratories was to ask IBM if they were interested in buying a license to his pending patent. Over a period of a year IBM corresponded, sent visitors, and asked for detailed information, which Wang, on the advice of his lawyer, declined to furnish without an agreement. Then Wang proposed doing some consulting work for IBM, and after another year of dickering, an agreement was reached in November 1953 under which he agreed both to consult for IBM and to grant them a three-year option to buy a nonexclusive license to his as yet unissued patent. The resultant thousand-dollar-a-month income gave Wang Laboratories financial stability.

It was Wang's impression that IBM was much less interested in the specific project they gave him than in their option and their access to his thinking about the applications of magnetic cores. At that time he was surprised by IBM's slowness to grasp the importance of magnetic core storage and it occurred to him that this characteristic slowness of the giant might make it possible for a smaller, quicker company to compete against them.

There was intense activity at IBM in the development of ferrite core memories and by mid-1954 IBM was developing such memories for commercial computers (Pugh 1984). In May 1955, when Wang's patent was issued, IBM opened negotiations about royalties. They flatly declined to confirm an earlier oral suggestion of a royalty of one cent per bit. Wang offered to sell them the patent for $2.5 million, to be told that "even half of $2.5 million is too high." In October 1955, IBM offered $500,000 plus 70% of all royalties from the licensing to third parties. Wang was prepared to accept but objected to clauses regarding the validity of the patent and the consequences of any patent interferences. After Wang replied to a list of 58 questions attacking his patent from every conceivable angle, IBM unleashed its thunderbolt. They had discovered an inventor, Frederick W. Viehe, a Los Angeles public works inspector, who had been in several patent interference battles with large companies in the past, who had a pending 1947 patent application that IBM believed would "certainly lead to an interference." IBM would not reveal the content of the application which, as usual, the Patent Office held secret. Now IBM wanted to move immediately to an agreement with Wang. He later wrote, "Later events suggested that IBM knew more about Mr. Viehe's patent application than they were telling at the time."

In spite of these feelings, in March 1956 Wang assigned his patent to IBM under the October terms but with the provision of certain conditions under which the final $100,000 payment might be withheld. One of the conditions was "the declaration of interference of the patent or any of its claims." Two weeks before the deadline for an interference, in May 1956, the Patent Office declared an interference with the Viehe patent. In November 1957, while the patent interference hearings were going on, IBM bought the Viehe patent application, reputedly for a million dollars, and hired the inventor as a consultant. In spite of the fact that the opposing parties in the interference case were now IBM vs. IBM, it went to a decision a year later. The decision gave Viehe only one of Wang's claims, a minor one. The decision could not be further argued or appealed since IBM now owned both patents. Wang forfeited the $100,000 and stored in his memory a lifelong grudge against IBM.

When Viehe died in 1960 he left an estate of $625,000. His widow's attorney said he made his fortune through the sale of an invention about which he was sworn to secrecy but Viehe's son identified IBM as the buyer. It was Wang's belief that IBM decided that buying both patents might be cheaper than buying one of them should one patent emerge as dominant. Before buying, IBM used each patent to drive down the price of the other and to force both inventors to an early agreement.

In 1975 the continuing legal struggles over the various patents on a matrix magnetic core memory brought to light an internal memo by the late J. William Hinkley of the Research Corporation recounting a 1962 meeting involving IBM, MIT, and the Research Corporation, during which James W. Birkenstock, an IBM vice president, was said to have commented "that they had probably underpaid Wang or Viehe for their patents . . . in view of the tremendous increase in the size of the computer industry. Birkenstock apparently put this forward as an example of how good a negotiator he was, but was severely taken to task by Watson" (Gardner 1976). It is interesting that Fish, Richardson, and Neave, the Boston law firm recommended to Wang in 1949, was patent counsel to IBM in these 1962 negotiations.

Wang later wrote: "I am sure that much of what my lawyers and I perceived as attempts at intimidation, IBM would argue was merely the exercise of due diligence in determining the worth of the property they sought to buy. Nonetheless, timing and bluff played an important role in our negotiations, and they were affected at the eleventh hour by an event totally unanticipated by me or my lawyers, and which to this day I remain convinced was instigated by IBM."

After the settlement, Wang put his energies into developing new ideas and new directions for his company rather than becoming obsessed with any injustices concerning the patent. In spite of this surface appearance of forbearance, he took pride in the fact that tiny Wang Laboratories later competed directly against IBM's greatest strength, remarking that he had frequent encounters with IBM's no-holds-barred style of competition, and often won.

On April 18, 1955, just before the patent was issued, Lorraine and Wang gave up their Chinese citizenship and became naturalized US citizens.

Wang Laboratories Grows

During the following years Wang Laboratories gradually changed from a consulting firm into a company that developed and sold its own products. It was in this period that Wang's associates started to refer to him as "the Doctor," a title which his own family came to use.[3]

In 1954 Wang Laboratories moved to Cambridge. In the next year, in the midst of the negotiations with IBM, the Doctor incorporated Wang Laboratories. Its assets were $25,000 and all the stock was held by Wang, some of which he gave to his wife and family. In 1958, when he employed 10 people, he bought land along Route 128 for expansion, land which the Commonwealth soon took for road widening, causing him to expand into Natick instead.

At first Wang vigorously pursued government contracts. Some of these led to commercial products such as transistor logic cards called Logiblocs, and control units for machine tools, called Weditrol. In 1959, for financial reasons, he sold 25% of his company for $50,000 to Warner and Swasey, a much larger company and one of his Weditrol customers. He regretted the deal almost at once. The alliance caused problems of management and financing far in excess of any benefits. In short, for the first time Wang was not in full and unquestioned control of his creation.

Compugraphic, a small Cambridge firm, proposed that Wang design and build a photo-typesetting machine, which Compugraphic would market. In one year Wang Laboratories, then 20 people strong, designed, patented, and built a semiautomated justifying typesetter called Linasec, for each of which Compugraphic paid Wang $30,000. Sales soared through the early 1960s, reaching the million-dollar mark in 1964. At this point Compugraphic took advantage of its right to manufacture the machine itself, putting Wang out of the typesetting business.

---

[3]Informal titles for the leader were not unusual in small technical organizations. Howard Aiken was first known as "the Commander" and later as "the Boss."

From these two mistakes, neither fatal and both educational and profitable, Wang learned not to release control of his company to anyone else and not to design and manufacture a product for another company to market.

In the mid-1970s, the Wang stock carried on the Warner and Swasey books at cost, a hidden asset worth scores of millions, attracted that aggressive acquirer of companies, William Agee, then president of Bendix. He saw that he could buy Warner and Swasey and pay for the acquisition by selling the Wang stock. Wang declined to play white knight, and the famous old machine tool company fell to the raider and into oblivion.

While Wang Laboratories was flourishing with Linasec, Wang devised a factor-combining method for finding logarithms using logic circuits requiring fewer than 300 transistors. In 1964 he applied for a patent and designed a desktop calculator, LOCI, using the principle and selling for a base price of $6,500. The user had to have some familiarity with logarithms and programming but LOCI was vastly easier to use than a computer. It could be programmed from its console or with punched cards or with a teletypewriter, which could be both terminal and printer. It could serve several keyboards. By 1966 Wang was selling about 10 a month through manufacturers' representatives, and LOCI was becoming his major source of revenue. Although Wang was ultimately issued more than 40 patents, LOCI appears to be the last commercial product based on one of them.

In 1964 Wang purchased an 85-acre site in Tewksbury and moved his total work force of 35 there from Natick.

LOCI was a transitional product that led to the Wang 300 calculator, the first Wang product that could be used by everybody. It was priced with the principal competition, Friden, at $1,695, yielding a gross profit margin of 65–70 percent. It had a small desktop unit with a numerical keyboard and a 10-digit electronic display. It performed the arithmetic functions now expected of a pocket calculator. The larger electronic unit sat on the floor and could be multiplexed to several keyboards. The Wang 300 reached the market 10 months after LOCI. Sales rose from $2.5 million in 1965 to $3.8 million in 1966 and $6.9 million in the next year when the laboratories had grown to 400 people.

With the Wang 300 the laboratories had moved from serving the scientific world into the open marketplace in which marketing, sales, and service were more important than inventions. At this time the firm also went international, selling in the UK, Belgium, and Taiwan. Some of the labor-intensive aspects of manufacturing were moved to Taiwan.

Wang developed a network of salesmen to take the place of independent manufacturers' representatives, and by mid-1967 he had 80 of his own people selling in 40 cities. He established a sales commission curve that grew according to the square root of the increase in sales, a curve later modified when his firm no longer owned the calculator market as it did when the Wang 300 was new and without real competition.

Although Wang liked to take his own risks and be in full control, he decided to take his company public, raising the money to retire his short-term debt without diluting the stock to the point where he would lose control. The firm had good earnings and had had rapid growth. Furthermore it was well known on Wall Street because of the wide use of the Wang 300 in brokerage houses. The Wang 300 had gained a legendary reputation there when it was used to reveal an error in the Salomon Brothers' bond trading tables that had been in unquestioned use for 30 years. Furthermore, in the summer of 1967 the hot new issues market was receptive to computer stocks at relatively high prices. The issuance of the stock changed Wang Laboratories from a company which had a net worth of about one million dollars to one with a market capitalization of about seventy million. Wang's own holdings rose to a paper value of about fifty million. Wang claimed no credit for going public at exactly the right time; he said it was just luck.

Wang was happy to have shown to be wrong those who warned him that a Chinese name would impede him.

While the Wang 300 and its improvements which permitted some programming were selling well, it became clear that Wang would have to replace it with something more than a mere improvement. The advent of BASIC, the first computer language that Wang considered user-friendly, convinced him that he should consider making a general-purpose computer.

When, in the spring of 1968, he saw the first proposed design, the Wang 4000, using the electronics of his more sophisticated calculators and bulk storage based on magnetic cassettes, he saw that it could not compete with DEC's PDP-8 and rejected it. Now Wang went outside his company to get the needed design expertise in computer hardware and software. In the late summer of 1968 he simultaneously launched two new efforts to develop a general-purpose computer, the Wang 700 and the Wang 3300 BASIC.

The Wang 700 was, at first, to be a computer with an architecture like that of the IBM 360 using microcoding. When Hewlett-Packard announced their new calculator, the HP 9100, with a CRT display and individual magnetic cards, Wang's sales of his top-of-the-line calculators, the Wang 370 and the Wang 380, were hurt. To protect Wang's share of the calculator market the development of the Wang 700 was changed to make it a calculator to directly challenge the HP 9100. Those were the days of "paper machines" that were announced at conception rather than birth. The Wang 700 was announced in December 1968, promised for delivery in June 1969, and reached the market a few months later. This calculator was Wang's last successful product to use magnetic core memory.

Although the Wang 3300 BASIC reached the market as a computer, it too was a false start. It was to be a true minicomputer with the capabilities of the PDP-8 but specialized for BASIC. Programs were loaded with paper tape, which often took 40 minutes per program. Furthermore it used a teletypewriter as a terminal instead of a CRT. Not many were sold.

By 1971 market price pressure had pushed the base price of the low end of the Wang 300 series to $600. Semiconductor chips, using large-scale integration (LSI) that contained all the circuits of a calculator, came to the commercial market from the laboratories that had developed them with military contracts. At Christmas Bowmar introduced the first LSI-based pocket calculator for $250 and soon afterwards a host of other similar products appeared. At that time Wang made the much too conservative estimate that their prices would soon drop to $100. Although 70% of Wang's revenues came from calculators, he decided to get out of that market, first leaving the lowest priced field. Wang claimed that this decision to move out of the calculator business was a product of reasoning and decisiveness, not luck.

His first general-purpose computer was the Wang 2200, although it was actually called a "computing calculator" to keep from frightening customers. It was first shipped in late 1972. BASIC and its interpreter were stored in ROM. The Wang 2200 continued to evolve and was still being sold in 1986 when more were sold than in 1973, although by then it accounted for only a small fraction of Wang's sales.

Word Processing
In November 1971 Wang announced the Wang 1200, his entry into the word processing market. He was deliberately attacking IBM's MTST (Magnetic Tape Selectric Typewriter). The Wang 1200 was based on the Wang 700 calculator, with rewritten firmware.

In use, a letter would be typed on a terminal and recorded on a tape cassette. Editing involved command codes. Printing was at 175 words per minute. By today's standards the Wang 1200 was extremely primitive but it was vastly superior to an electric typewriter, cutting the cost of a business letter in half. Although IBM controlled 80% of the market, MTST was only a tiny part of their business. Wang was attacking their little finger, not their right arm. As he anticipated, IBM was slow to react. It took Wang several years to develop a product that was clearly superior to IBM's and in that time, 1972 to 1975, IBM might have ended the threat altogether but, by not developing their own word processing technology they gave Wang time to learn, grow, correct his mistakes, and acquire some market share.

Although the Wang 1200 never really fulfilled the Doctor's expectations, one of its significant limitations being the lack of a CRT display, by 1975 Wang was well positioned in the word processing market. At this time Xerox came out with the 800, no easier to use than the Wang 1200 but with a Diablo printer, twice as fast as Wang's. To meet this threat the Doctor ordered the design of a word processor that did not simply copy existing automatic typewriters but offered features that reflected the desires and limitations of the user. Its specifications were drawn not from what could be done with electronics but from what secretaries, then almost all women, wanted in their machines. It would be CRT- rather than typewriter-based, and it would be driven by a series of user-guiding menus. It was called the WCS (Wang Computer System).

It was introduced in June 1976 at the New York Syntopican trade show by demonstrating the only model, so much a prototype that it even lacked a printer. People lined up ten deep to see text editing done on a screen for the first time on a commercial product. The list price was $30,000 and one customer ordered a million dollars worth on the basis of an advance look. Wang separated the sale of word processing from the rest of the sales department and, to indicate how seriously he took the new product, appointed his older son Frederick A. Wang, then 26, to head the new department.

In the midst of these events the oil crisis stopped automobile sales in 1975 and pushed Wang's earnings, which were greatly dependent on sales of his calculators to automobile dealers, down by one third. Wang had to lay off 40 people, his first layoff ever. By 1976 Wang's characteristic unusual growth started again, stimulated by sales of the Wang 2200 and the WCS, both of which represented Wang's timely move into the office market.

Wang, now the 32nd largest computer company in the country, undertook to confront IBM directly with an advertisement. IBM was the only computer company that advertised on TV. To establish Wang as a well-known name, a firm from which it would be prudent for cautious managers to buy office products, Wang doubled its yearly advertising budget to mount a three-month TV campaign based on a single advertisement. The advertisement was a David vs. Goliath motif set in a corporate board meeting. It raised Wang's name recognition from 4.5 to 16 percent among businessmen. The Doctor recalled that following his example DEC, Data General, Prime, and Apple later turned to TV with similar anti-IBM themes, but "not always as successfully."

Having outgrown the space in Tewksbury, in 1976 Wang bought land and a building in Lowell and moved his headquarters there, leaving manufacturing in Tewksbury. Growth and building in Lowell were by leaps and bounds, and Wang quickly became the largest employer in this previously severely depressed area. In the following few years, this move was said to have sparked the "Massachusetts Miracle" of the 1980s, rejuvenating Lowell.

By 1978 Wang was the largest worldwide supplier of CRT word processing systems, with fifty thousand users. In a few years 80% of the 2,000 largest US firms had bought Wang equipment. At one time, it was said, every secretary in America swore by Wang products.

In 1975 the financial state of the company had become as critical as when it had gone public. It had a great deal of debt and needed a lot more cash to exploit the projected WCS. The market value of its stock had dropped close to its issuing price. If Wang was to seize the opportunity he saw in word processing he would have to return to the capital market, but he wanted to retain his personal and exclusive voting control. To do this he recapitalized, issuing a class B common stock with a higher dividend but only one-tenth the voting power of class A common stock. The New York Stock Exchange would not stretch its rules to allow this (they have since changed their rules), so Wang delisted his firm from the New York Exchange and moved it to the American Exchange, where the rules would stretch. Trading was heavy in class A but light in class B, just the opposite of what the Doctor wanted. He concluded that orders to brokers to "Buy Wang" were being executed on the first Wang in the list. By changing the name of class A to class C and thus getting it listed in the newspapers below class B, the Doctor solved that problem.

Wang had also solved the problem of personal control. With 52% of the votes, Wang Laboratories remained all his. At this time the value of the Wang family trust which the Doctor had established in 1957 was $1.6 billion.

The Wang Institute of Graduate Studies was established in 1979 in Tyngsboro. Wang gave $6 million. Classes started in 1981 with five students and high hopes. It was to demonstrate how enlightened industry could advance education. Its program was for a master's degree in software engineering. It attracted an excellent staff, put a good program in place that addressed the needs of the software development industry, grew, and achieved a good reputation in a short time among practitioners and educators. Its program addressed the entirety of the systems development life cycle and acknowledged the difficult human aspects of systems analysis and project management (Fairley 1989). The institute also supported Chinese studies with graduate fellowships.

In late 1982 Wang tried to remove himself from the details of day-to-day operations, and in 1983 designated John Cunningham, a Wang sales veteran, as president. This move didn't work, for the Doctor never really let go and in late 1984 he took back the reins and Cunningham left. Wang stock peaked in 1984 at $42.5, a level never reached again. At about the same time, realizing that Wang Laboratories had missed the start of the personal computer revolution, Frederick Wang, then in charge of product development, announced a series of 14 dazzlingly innovative products. Most of them did not exist. As customers realized this, they started switching to IBM in droves.

Wang saw that an important company problem was communications, chiefly with him, so he set out on a program of traveling, which he hated, throughout the company to listen and talk to employees and customers. His talking was legendary, but some employees questioned the effectiveness of his listening.

In the decade before 1983, Wang Laboratories' annual growth had been 40%. By 1986, when Wang's autobiography ends, his company did more business in two weeks than it had done in all of 1976. It was a $3 billion dollar enterprise employing 30,000 people. The Doctor considered Wang Laboratories to be not only an example of a phenomenal success but one well situated for the future.

As the company developed in the 1980s it both confronted IBM in some areas and adapted to it in others. It was careful to stay out of the battle between corporate MIS departments, usually in IBM's pocket, and departmental decision makers who buy word processors and PCs. Toward the end of his autobiography Wang points out that when he negotiated the sale of his patent to IBM, it was ten thousand times his size but in 1986 it was only twenty times.

Wang recognized an even more formidable competitor than IBM: Japan. In his autobiography he says, "Having both observed and experienced Japan's economic aggressiveness, I am led to the conclusion that they learned little from their experiences in World War II, and instead of tempering their imperial ambitions, they are merely pursuing their goal in the economic arena rather than the military one."

Wang Laboratories Stumbles

Just before 1986, although its revenues climbed, reaching a peak in 1988 of $3.07 billion, the earnings went into a decline from which they have not recovered. Wang had moved too slowly in product development and had gradually bogged down his company with short-term debt. Wang's word processors, built around expensive minicomputers, became dinosaurs as smaller, cheaper, more capable personal computers took over office functions. Wang's own PCs were priced too high and were not compatible with industry standards, notably IBM's dominant products. Service was poor and expensive. Almost half Wang's orders were delivered late and more than half those entered at the factory were wrong. The company had developed the reputation with its customers of being hard to do business with. Of 800 R&D projects under way only 72 had been subjected to feasibility studies.

Now with sharply reduced earnings Wang had to cut back on his contributions. In 1987, after fewer than 10 years of life, the Wang Institute of Graduate Studies closed as its funding was abruptly cut off (Fairley 1989).

In 1987 Wang made Frederick, now 38, president and chief operating officer. Frederick moved too slowly to cut costs and shift product strategy. After a modest rebound, sales stalled and losses mounted. His father rated his performance as president at 75%. In the fall of 1989, at the end of his first day back at work after undergoing surgery for esophageal cancer, and after his firm reported a $424 million loss for the previous fiscal year, An Wang, in a last ditch effort to save his company, fired his son. The firing was done in a stoical and businesslike fashion, Fred Wang, like a true Chinese son, accepting from his dying father his public humiliation with grace and dignity.

After a hectic 10-day search Wang replaced his son with 48-year-old Richard W. Miller, a Harvard MBA from General Electric with no computer industry experience. Miller faced a debt of $900 million. He ended cash dividends, sold some operations, cut staff by 27%, but still lost $715.9 million in his first year. In the next year he stabilized the firm but it has still not recovered. Its stock, which had fallen below $4 in 1990, remains at about that level today.

While the first of these wrenching changes were being made in Wang Laboratories, its founder, father, and alter ego died in Boston's Metropolitan General Hospital.

The decline in the fortunes of Wang Laboratories, especially its staff reductions, was disastrous to Lowell, where the unemployment rate, 4.3% in 1984, rose to 12.5% in 1991.

Why?

Just as the Doctor must be given full credit for the astonishing and unprecedented success of his firm, it is natural to look to him and his actions for the reasons for the decline of Wang Laboratories while he was still in charge, for even while the son was president, the father continued to exercise control. He could not let go.

One author who has studied Wang's decline, Charles C. Kenney (1991), lists what he considers the following major reasons:

1. Wang was determined to pass his personal control of his company to his older son in keeping with Chinese tradition. He groomed Frederick for this from the time he was 26 and ignored the evidence that his son was not equal to the tasks he was assigned. Wang Laboratories' serious problems started with Frederick's move to the top. When directors objected, pointing out he had made a botch of his last job, product development, the Doctor replied, "He is my son."

2. Wang was convinced that his products were so good that customers would always wait months for them and he simply refused to listen to the entreaties of his staff to develop a personal computer early. When he did, it was too expensive, too late.

3. Today, customers recognize paper machines as signs of weakness and incompetence. Product announcements must be supported by existing products. Frederick's brazen 1982 announcement of imaginary machines, unlike his father's similar 1968 ploy, backfired.

4. An Wang's personality had changed. He describes himself in his autobiography, and those who knew him before 1986 confirm this, as always avoiding the slightest hint of pomp, having only two suits, both gray, accepting a chauffeur only because he caught himself thinking while driving, and generally avoiding pomp and ceremony. In the last years of his life these things changed. He surrounded himself with security guards, bought corporate jets, and moved into a 3,000-square-foot office with a marble fireplace and whirlpool bath. In the words of deposed president Cunningham, "The Doctor had become a humble egomaniac."

Contributions

An Wang, his family, his family trust, and Wang Laboratories gave generously in time and money to education and charity. Wang himself served as a member of the Massachusetts Board of Higher Education and the Massachusetts Board of Regents, as trustee of Northeastern University and of Boston College, and as an overseer of Harvard, to which he gave $4 million. In 1983 the Wangs donated $4 million to save the Boston Metropolitan Center, renamed the Wang Center for the Performing Arts. The Wangs were major funders of the nine-story Ambulatory Care Center of the Massachusetts General Hospital, giving it $4 million. Wang was a major funder of the Fairbanks Center for Asian Studies at Harvard. He supported China scholars and studies at MIT, Harvard, and the Chinese Cultural Institute.

Honors

Wang was awarded 23 honorary degrees. Those he prized most were from Harvard and Chiao Tung, now in Taiwan. In 1986 he received the US Medal of Liberty; in 1987 *Datamation* entered him in its Hall of Fame; and in 1988 he was entered into the National Inventors' Hall of Fame.

QUOTATION

Four years before his death, An Wang ended his autobiography with his own epilogue:

> My days are spent doing the things I really want to do. The satisfaction of turning an idea into something real never diminishes, and the great gift of change is that it continually replenishes the stock of new ideas that might be brought to life. The thrill of this challenge more than compensates for the setbacks that are the price of learning and growth. There are still many lessons to be learned.

Some may be learned from the Doctor's life.

BIBLIOGRAPHY

Biographical

Fairley, Richard E., "A Post-Mortem Analysis of the Software Engineering Programs at Wang Institute of Graduate Studies," in Fairley, R., and P. Freeman, eds., *Issues in Software Engineering Education*, Springer-Verlag, New York, 1989, pp. 19–35.

Forrester, J.W., "Multicoordinate Digital Information Storage Device," US Patent 2,736,880, filed May 11, 1951, issued Feb. 28, 1956.

Gardner, W.D., "An Wang's Early Work in Core Memories," *Datamation*, Mar. 1976, pp. 161–164.

Kenney, Charles C., *Riding the Runaway Horse*, Little-Brown, Boston, Mass., 1991.

MIT Institute Archives Staff, "The Magnetic Core Memory Collection at the MIT Institute Archives and Special Collections," *IEEE Center for the History of Electrical Engineering Newsletter*, No. 23, Spring 1990, pp. 6–7.

Pugh, Emerson W., *Memories That Shaped an Industry*, MIT Press, Cambridge, Mass., 1984.

Redmond, Kent C., and Thomas M. Smith, *Project Whirlwind, The History of a Pioneer Computer*, Digital Press, Bedford, Mass., 1980.

Salton, Gerard, "Howard Aiken's Children: The Harvard Computation Laboratory and Its Students," *Abacus*, Vol. 1, No. 3, Spring 1964, p. 28.

Wang, An, and Eugene Linden, *Lessons*, Addison-Wesley, Reading, Mass., 1986.

Weiss, Eric, "An Wang, Obituary," *Ann. Hist. Comp.*, Vol. 15, No. 1, 1993, pp. 60–69.

Significant Publications

Wang, An, "Pulse Transfer Controlling Devices," US Patent 2,708,722, filed Oct. 21, 1949, issued May 17, 1955.

WILLIS HOWARD WARE

Born August 31, 1920, Atlantic City, N.J.; computer engineer who assisted John von Neumann to develop the IAS machine, and who took charge of the subsequent development of the JOHNNIAC at Rand Corporation.

Education: BS, electrical engineering, Moore School of Electrical Engineering, University of Pennsylvania; SM, electrical engineering, MIT, 1942; PhD, electrical engineering, Princeton University, 1951.

Professional Experience: research engineer, Hazeltine Electronics Corporation, Little Neck, N.Y., 1942–1946; Institute for Advanced Study, Princeton University, 1946–1951; North American Aviation Corp., 1951–1952; Rand Corp., 1952–present; adjunct professor, University of California at Los Angeles, 1955–1968.

Honors and Awards: Atwater Kent Prize, Moore School of Electrical Engineering, University of Pennsylvania, 1941; National Fellowship, Tau Beta Pi, 1941–1942; Achievement Award, Los Angeles Chapter, IRE, 1957; fellow, IRE, 1962; Distinguished Service Award, AFIPS, 1963 and 1986; Computer Sciences Man of the Year, Data Processing Management Association, 1975; Exceptional Civil Service Medal, US Air Force, 1979; Centennial Award, IEEE, 1984; member, National Academy of Engineering, 1985; Computer Pioneer Award, IEEE Computer Society, 1993; fellow, ACM, 1994.

THOMAS J. WATSON, JR.

Born January 8, 1914, Dayton, Ohio; died December 31, 1993; IBM president who led his father's firm to total domination of the computer world and industry.

Education: BA, Brown University, 1937.

Professional Experience: IBM Corp.: Rising from trainee to president, 1937–1973; Lieutenant Colonel, US Army Air Corps, 1940–1946; US Ambassador, Soviet Union, 1979–1988.

Honors and Awards: Applause Award, New York Sales Executives; Drexel Institute Business Administration Award; New York University C. Walter Nichols Award; Prometheus Award—the highest honor in the electrical manufacturing industry; National Foreign Trade Council's Captain Robert Dollar Award; *Saturday Review* Businessman of the Year Award; Pace College's Man in Management Award; Silver Quill Award, *American Business Press.*

Watson, Jr., was born in the period while his father was a sales manager at the National Cash Register Corporation but, by the time he had graduated from Brown, his father had aspirations for him to take over IBM one day. But that had to wait until after World War II. In the late 1940s Watson, Jr., became convinced that IBM should get into the business of building and marketing computers, but had to convince his father of the efficacy of this move. The involvement of IBM in the card-processing and unit record business was strong, and Watson, Sr., was not willing to take away from this strength to invest in a venture that he regarded not only as risky but also with a much more limited market.

IBM had been involved in the construction of the Harvard Mark I computer, which they had dubbed the "Automatic Sequence Controlled Calculator" or ASCC. However, a reluctance on the part of

Howard Aiken to share the spotlight led IBM to construct the SSEC as its showcase "supercomputer."[4] However, it was the onset of the Korean War that led IBM to offer to build the Defense Calculator, a decision which led to the development of a production line of machines starting with the 700 series. In 1952 Watson, Jr., took over as president of the corporation and began to consolidate IBM's position in the computer field. By the time his father died in 1956, he had also introduced changes in the management of the company, giving managers and executives more power and responsibility. At this time he agreed to sign a consent decree with the US government, thereby restricting IBM's almost monopolistic hold on the card-processing industry, and offsetting the possibility of antitrust litigation. By that time, however, the card-processing portion of the company's business was rapidly being replaced by the computer business. In 1913 his father had been fired for refusing to sign a similar agreement regarding NCR's business practices.

Watson, Jr., remained as president of IBM through to the commitment to build the System/360 machines, on which base IBM has developed almost all mainframe systems for 30 years. After serving for 10 years as chairman of the board until 1971, he continued to serve as the chairman of the executive committee of the corporation until 1979, by which time IBM's annual sales had reached $23 billion.

Although retired in 1979 Watson, Jr., accepted the nomination of President Carter to serve as the ambassador to the Soviet Union. He served through the remainder of the Carter presidency and continued to serve in that position under President Reagan.

BIBLIOGRAPHY

Biographical

Hurd, Cuthbert, "Early IBM Computers: Edited Testimony," *Ann. Hist. Comp.*, Vol. 3. No. 1, 1981, pp. 163–182.

Significant Publications

Watson, Jr., Thomas J., and Peter Petre, *Father, Son & Co,* Bantam Books, New York, 1990.

---

[4]See biography of Howard Aiken.

Thomas J. Watson, Sr.

Born February 17, 1874, Cambell, N.Y.; died 1956; the towering figure
whose lengthening shadow was IBM, which he reluctantly allowed to be
dragged from punched cards to computing; creator of IBM's motto "Think."

Education: Addison Academy, New York; School of Commerce, Elmira, N.Y.

Professional Experience: salesman, pianos and sewing machines, Painted Post, N.Y., 1892–1896; salesman to general sales manager, National Cash Register (NCR) Corp., Dayton, Ohio, 1896–1914; general manager to chief executive officer, Computing-Tabulating-Recording Corp., 1914–1924; chief executive officer to president, IBM Corp., 1924–1956.

Thomas J. Watson, Sr., is one of those figures in the history of computing whose contributions are by no means technological but without whom the technologists would not have been able to proceed. After his somewhat controversial stint as general manager with the National Cash Register Corp., and the subsequent growth of IBM out of the Computing-Tabulating-Recording Corporation, Watson set the stage for the introduction of the computer in the corporation.

The first step was the construction of the Harvard Mark I calculator designed by Howard Aiken. IBM was selected as the "prime contractor" company but also had to provide expertise and experience from its card processing and unit record business to supplement Aiken's ideas and to complete the project. At the dedication ceremony Aiken snubbed Watson and IBM's contributions, and a never-to-be-mended rift developed between the two men.[5] Although Columbia University had been influential in its promotion of mechanical computing systems in the T.J. Watson Astronomical Computing Bureau, IBM had never taken advantage of this expertise to move into the computer business.[6] Subsequently IBM constructed the Selective Sequence Electronic Computer (SSEC) machine, installed it in its headquarters on Madison Avenue, New York, and opened a service bureau to provide computing utilities to the public. The Korean War provided an impetus to allow IBM to show its nationalistic pride by offering to build a "Defense Calculator" to serve the war effort. This machine, later designated as the Type 701 machine, became the first of the two major series of mainframe computers central to its success.

Watson, Sr., has been labeled as having been reluctant to depart from the business that had stood him in good stead for almost 40 years

---

[5]See biography of Howard Aiken.
[6]See biography of Wallace Eckert.

and to commit the corporation to build electronic computers. By the time that this opportunity was being pressed on him, Watson, Sr. was relying more and more on the judgment and advice of his eldest son to make decisions. But the stage was set, the line of succession was established, and the technology was ready. Watson had contributed the environment within which the commercialization and marketing of the computer constituted a profitable venture. Throughout Watson's career he had profited from the "waiting game"; although rarely the first to introduce a new product, he was able to build on the experience of others. He did it with the computer; his son did it with System/360; the company did it with the personal computer.

QUOTATION

"I think there's a world market for about five computers." (Attr. [1943]—probably apocryphal)

BIBLIOGRAPHY

Biographical

Hurd, Cuthbert, "Early IBM Computers: Edited Testimony," *Ann. Hist. Comp.*, Vol. 3. No. 1, 1981, pp. 163–182.

Slater, Robert, *Portraits in Silicon,* MIT Press, Cambridge, Mass., 1987.

Watson, Jr., Thomas J., and Peter Petre, *Father, Son & Co,* Bantam Books, New York, 1990.

WARREN WEAVER

Born July 17, 1894, Reedsburg, Wis.; died November 24, 1978, New Milford, Conn.; World War II director of the Applied Mathematics Panel of the NDRC,[7] whose work showed the full possibilities of the applications of mathematics to the problems of war—and in turn the application of computational devices to myriad applications; originator in 1946, in a discussion with Andrew Booth, of the idea of translating languages with a computer.

Education: BS, mathematics, University of Wisconsin, 1916; CE, University of Wisconsin, 1917; PhD, mathematical physics, University of Wisconsin, 1921.

Professional Experience: assistant professor, Throop College of Technology, 1917–1918; assistant professor, California Institute of Technology, 1919–1920; University of Wisconsin: assistant professor, associate professor, 1920–1928, professor, and department chairman, 1928–1932; Rockefeller Foundation: director, Natural Science, 1932–1955, vice president, Natural and Medical Sciences, 1955–1959, vice president, 1959–1964; consultant, Science Affairs, Alfred P. Sloan Foundation, 1964–onwards.

Honors and Awards: LLD, University of Wisconsin, 1948; ScD, University of Sao Paulo, 1949; ScD, Drexel Institute, 1961; DEng, Rensselaer Polytechnic, 1962; LHD, University of Rochester, 1963; ScD, University of Pittsburgh, 1964; ScD, New York University, 1964; US Medal for Merit, 1948; officer, Legion of Honour, France, 1950; Public Welfare Medal, National Academy of Sciences, 1957; British King's Defense Freedom Medal, 1965; Kalinga Prize and Arches of Science Award, 1965; fellow, American Physical Society; member, National Academy of Sciences.

Warren Weaver started his career as a teacher of mathematics. But before his 38th birthday he became a foundation executive, when he accepted the post of director of the Division of Natural Sciences of the Rockefeller Foundation. In that role he exercised a profound influence on the development of biology worldwide, and it was probably for this that he was best known during his lifetime. During his years as an officer of the Rockefeller Foundation, however, and during his service as an officer of the Sloan Foundation after his retirement from his Rockefeller post, his influence on many other aspects of science expanded and its impact was broadly felt.

Weaver was born on July 17, 1894, in the little town of Reedsburg, Wisconsin. As a child he was shy, introspective, unskilled in sports, and often lonesome. When he was a youngster, his father, who was a pharmacist, made an annual buying trip to purchase the drugstore's supply of Christmas toys for the coming holiday season. It was traditional for him to return with a gift for each of the boys in the family. After one of

---

[7]National Defense Research Committee.

these trips, Warren received a small electric motor powered by a dry cell battery. It was labeled "Ajax" and cost a dollar. From experiments with this motor, which included taking it apart and rewiring and rebuilding it, Weaver was first exposed to science and engineering. From this experience he assumed without question that he was destined to be an engineer.

It was at the University of Wisconsin that Warren, studying "Advanced Mathematics for Engineers," realized that his enthusiasm was for science rather than for engineering. He decided to pursue a graduate degree in mathematics and theoretical physics as soon as this proved feasible. Immediately after receiving a degree in civil engineering in 1917 (he had earned a BS in mathematics in 1916), he accepted an invitation from Robert A. Millikan to become an assistant professor of mathematics at Throop College (soon to be renamed the California Institute of Technology). Weaver had been at Throop less than a year when he was drafted into the Army at the request of Charles E. Mendenhall, chairman of the Physics Department at Wisconsin. Mendenhall was then serving as a major in the Army's unit associated with the newly formed National Research Council. Weaver was assigned to participate in one of the technical efforts to develop effective equipment to assist US aviators in the air battles of World War I.

After a brief interlude at Wisconsin and a year at Pasadena, as the end of the 1920 academic year approached a letter from Madison invited Weaver to join the faculty at the University of Wisconsin. There was also a most important letter from Max Mason, who urged Warren to accept Wisconsin's offer, and suggested that they work together on a book on electromagnetic field theory.

In 1921 Weaver earned his PhD; his collaboration with Mason began promptly and was vigorously pursued. In 1925, however, Mason left to become president of the University of Chicago, while Weaver carried on alone in Madison, sending drafts to Mason in Chicago. In 1928 Weaver succeeded Edward Burr Van Vleck as chairman of the Department of Mathematics. The Mason-Weaver book *Electromagnetic Field* was published in 1929. For some years thereafter, it was the book from which many graduate students in physics learned Maxwell's field equations and the associated theory. For occasional physicists whom he met in later years, Warren became the "Weaver, of Mason and Weaver."

In the fall of 1931 Mason invited Weaver to visit him in New York to discuss the possibility of his joining the staff of the Rockefeller Foundation as head of its program in natural sciences. The Rockefeller Foundation had recently been reorganized, absorbing several other Rockefeller agencies that had been founded for special purposes but no longer required separate settings. The foundation's aim "to promote the well-being of mankind throughout the world" was interpreted by the trustees as being served, in the immediate future, by support of the scientific research of individuals.

From the beginning, Weaver's duties at the Rockefeller Foundation required fairly regular travel to Europe, and later to other parts of the world. During his trips in the early 1930s he became acquainted with many of Europe's leading scientists whose work lay in the areas of the foundation's interest. His conversations with German scholars in those years convinced him of the imminence of worldwide conflict.

In 1940 at the invitation of President Roosevelt, Vannevar Bush set up an organization, the National Defense Research Committee (NDRC), to aid the military services with their scientific problems. Weaver wrote to Bush offering his services on a full-time basis. He also took a step motivated by his memory of World War I and the destruction of European libraries that ensued. With the support of the Rockefeller Foundation trustees, he arranged for the American Library Association to administer a grant "for the purchase or reproduction of American scholarly journals for institutions in areas of war damage, chiefly in Europe and Asia." A first-rate librarian was employed, and a large empty loft was rented in Washington. The librarian made a list of university libraries in Europe and the developing countries, including those of Socialist governments, and entered subscriptions for all the professional journals in the US. As the journals were published, copies were deposited in bins marked "Library of the Sorbonne," Library of the University of Heidelberg," "Library of the University of Louvain," and so on. At the end of the war, the complete series of journals was boxed and ready for shipment to these libraries as the rubble was being cleared.[8]

In July 1940 Bush invited Weaver to set up the fire-control section of NDRC. Weaver accepted and planned to resign from the Rockefeller Foundation. But he was persuaded to retain his appointment there, carrying on some of his usual duties while giving first priority to the NDRC functions.

The NDRC fire-control unit was working on sighting systems to be used for directing the guns of an airplane against enemy aircraft, and on bombsights for such uses as low-level attacks on submarines. But the largest and most useful of the projects sponsored by the section was the design and development of a successful antiaircraft director. In

---

[8]Interestingly, some of the losses to library holdings in eastern Europe may have been the result of Soviet "reparations" at the end of the war.

February 1942 the revolutionary instrument was accepted by the Army as the M-9 Director. It was ready in time to join radar and the proximity fuse, which was also developed by Bush's organization, in reversing the tide of the later parts of the Battle of Britain—saving London from the worst destruction threatened by the German V1 devices (buzz-bombs [doodle bugs]) that began to rain on the city in 1944.

By late 1942, Bush had identified the increasing need for sophisticated mathematical studies, and the greatly expanded need for mathematical assistance in NDRC. He established the Applied Mathematics Panel (AMP) with Weaver as its chief; Harold Hazen of MIT became chief of the fire-control division. Weaver's skill in the administration of research and his effectiveness in dealing with military officers and with the Washington bureaucracy greatly facilitated the work of the AMP. During the war, the panel received many letters of appreciation from military commands; at war's end, several of the war-born research projects were continued with support from interested military agencies. For his war work, Weaver received the King's Medal for Service in the Cause of Freedom from Great Britain, and the Medal of Merit of the US. In 1950 he was made an officer of the Legion of Honour of France. The citation that accompanied the US Medal of Merit read, in part: "He revolutionized anti-aircraft fire control. He made brilliant contributions to the effectiveness of bomber aircraft. The work of his Panel showed the full possibilities of the applications of mathematics to the problems of war."

Warren Weaver was a man whose company was a constant source of stimulation to those who were closely associated with him. He was a prodigious worker and a man for whom the conquest of a new and difficult idea, particularly in science, was an event of importance. He viewed science as the most successful of man's intellectual adventures, and in some senses his whole life was devoted to science.[9]

QUOTATION

"The most imaginative and powerful movements in the history of science have arisen not from plans, not from compulsion, but from the spontaneous enthusiasm and curiosity of capable individuals who had the freedom to think about the things they considered interesting."

---

[9]Extracted from Rees 1983.

BIBLIOGRAPHY

Biographical

Rees, Mina, "Warren Weaver," *Biographical Memoirs,* Vol. 57, National Academy of Sciences, Washington, D.C., 1983, pp. 493–530.

Significant Publications

Weaver, Warren, "A Scientist Ponders Faith," *Saturday Review,* Jan. 3, 1959.

Weaver, Warren, "Careers in Science," in Love, Albert, and James Saxon Childers, eds., *Listen to Leaders in Science,* Tupper & Love/David McKay, Atlanta, 1965, p. 276.

GERARD P. WEEG

Born October 29, 1927, Davenport, Iowa; died April 10, 1977, Iowa City, Iowa; educator who contributed significantly to the development of early computer science curriculum.

Education: BS, St. Ambrose College, 1949; MS, Oklahoma State University, 1950; PhD, mathematics, Iowa State University, 1955.

Professional Experience: teaching assistant, Oklahoma State University, 1949–1950; teacher, mathematics, St. Ambrose College, 1950–1951; teaching assistant, Iowa State University, 1951–1955; Remington-Rand, Univac Corp., St. Paul, Minn., 1955–1956; Department of Mathematics and the Computer Laboratory, Michigan State University, 1956–1964; University of Iowa: director, University Computer Center, 1964–1977, chairman, Department of Computer Science, 1965–1977.

Gerard P. Weeg, a pioneer in the field of academic computing, died in Iowa City, on April 10, 1977, after a long illness. Gerry's career in computing began shortly after he received a PhD degree in mathematics from Iowa State University in 1955. He spent nearly two years working at the Remington-Rand Corporation, Univac Division, in St. Paul,

Minn., on the Univac 1101—a machine which later proved to be the forerunner of a long line of Univac products. Then in 1956 he moved to Michigan State University and served in a joint appointment between the Department of Mathematics and the Computer Laboratory. Soon after his arrival on the MSU campus, he became intimately involved in the university's efforts to build its own computer—a copy of the widely known ILLIAC I designed at the University of Illinois. His interests in the project were concentrated in the area of numerical analysis. Over the next few years he published several papers in the area and co-authored a well-received textbook, *Introduction to Numerical Analysis*. Attracted by earlier developments in the use of algebraic models to approach the problems of design and analysis of digital circuits, Gerry soon turned his attention to that topic. He published several early papers in algebraic automata theory, which have been, and continue to be, widely referenced works.

Gerry went to the University of Iowa in 1964 as director of the University Computer Center. He had always voiced strong ideas concerning the administration of a campus computing resource, and shortly after his arrival he began to vigorously assert those ideas. At the same time he initiated efforts to establish an academic-degree-granting program in computer science. Thus, in 1965, Iowa became one of the earliest institutions to formalize such a department. Gerry was named chairman of the new department, and he held these dual administrative responsibilities for many years.

As a teacher and computer science educator, Gerry's contributions were both universal and personal. Known as "Doc" Weeg to all, with the title signifying affection as well as honor, he attracted many bright young minds into the new discipline. As chairman of the department, Gerry guided the development of a sound academic program with solid academic standards through a difficult period of uncertainty as to which direction the new science should take. To his students, he was a superb teacher. His technical expertise and preparation combined with a natural enthusiasm and flair for humor made his classes both an education and a delight. To his colleagues, he was the epitome of a good friend, always supportive and concerned, his boundless energy immediately turned in their direction by the simplest request.

As director of the Computer Center, Gerry was instrumental in the development of grant proposals that brought funding to the university for major equipment additions, and the establishment of a regional computer center to meet the data processing needs of about 15 smaller educational institutions in eastern Iowa and western Illinois. He so forcefully advocated networking as a means of making computing resources available on a broad scale that he was frequently called upon to consult in other states attempting a similar undertaking. He was also instrumental in establishing a computer-to-computer link between Iowa State University and the Iowa campus. His leadership was strong yet flexible and his efforts resulted in the potential of academic computing being reached on the Iowa campus and others, especially as a service to many other disciplines.

Gerry Weeg's ability, expertise, and experience in computing brought recognition throughout the world to him and to the university. At the national level, he was a participant in many ACM activities, serving as a visiting ACM lecturer, 1968–1969; a visiting ACM scientist, 1969–1970, and an ACM consultant, 1970–1972. He was particularly active in SIGUCC (the Special Interest Group in University Computer Centers), having been one of the early promoters of its annual User Services Conference. In addition, Gerry was one of the founders of CONDUIT, a national organization whose mission is the generation and distribution of educational computing materials; and he was a major contributor to the initiation and success of the annual Conference on Computers in Undergraduate Curricula.[10]

After he became ill with a brain tumor he wrote a set of rules for his children to follow:

> Rules that my kids would receive to see them through to a happy old age:
>
> 1. Be pleasant, though this does not mean to be pleasant should another person consistently overbear upon you.
> 2. Be good. That is, be truthful, patient, and kind.
> 3. Be forth-right. In other words, be honest and sincere.
> 4. Be upstanding, that is, be a courageous leader; at least, be a courageous follower.
> 5. Be not lascivious. That is, be neither an unmarried person that carries romancing too far; not a married person who seeks a divorce.
> 6. Be chaste, that is, clean and pure.
> 7. Be holy, which encompasses all the above.

---

[10]From Fleck 1977.

In 1978 the University of Iowa named its new computing center on campus "The Gerard P. Weeg Computer Center" in recognition of his distinctive and outstanding contributions to the university.

BIBLIOGRAPHY

Biographical

Fleck, Arthur C., "A Special Tribute to Gerard P. Weeg," *ACM/SIGUCC Newsletter,* Vol. 7, No. 2, 1977, pp. 14–15.

Joseph H. Wegstein

Chairman of the Short Range Committee of CODASYL that developed the programming language Cobol, and a longtime supporter of information processing standards; member of the joint ACM/GAMM committee that developed Algol.

BIBLIOGRAPHY

Biographical

Sammet, Jean E., "The Early History of Cobol," in Wexelblat, Richard L., ed., *History of Programming Languages,* Academic Press, New York, 1981.

Significant Publications

Wegstein, Joseph H., and Samuel N. Alexander, "Programming Scientific Calculators," *Control Engineering,* Vol. 3, May 1956, pp. 89–92.

JAMES A. WEIDENHAMMER

IBM employee and the inventor with Walter S. Buslik of the vacuum column[11] and numerous other features widely used on magnetic tape drives.[12] First project with IBM was to design the paper tape stepping mechanism for the ASCC (Harvard Mark I).

Education: BS, mechanical engineering, Lehigh University, 1938.

Professional Experience: Joined IBM Endicott Laboratory and transferred to Poughkeepsie in 1949 to work on magnetic tape drives.

GERALD M. WEINBERG

Discoverer of the psychology of computer programming announced in his book of that name.

QUOTATION

On dumps: "How truly sad it is that just at the very moment when the computer has something important to tell us, it starts speaking gibberish."(Weinberg 1971)

BIBLIOGRAPHY

Significant Publications

Weinberg, Gerald M., *The Psychology of Computer Programming*, Van Nostrand Reinhold, New York, 1971.

---

[11]US Patent 3,057,568, filed May 28, 1952: Tape Feed Mechanism.

[12]Based on Pugh, Emerson W., Lyle R. Johnson, and John H. Palmer, *IBM's 360 and Early 370 Systems,* MIT Press, Cambridge, Mass., 1991.

JOSEPH WEIZENBAUM

Born January 8, 1923, Berlin, Germany; inventor in 1965 of ELIZA, the mechanical psychiatrist, who first warned of the dangers of confusing computers with people and vice versa.

Education: BS, Wayne University, 1948; MS, Wayne University, 1950.

Professional Experience: systems engineer, Computer Development Laboratory, General Electric Corp., 1955–1963; MIT: visiting associate professor, electrical engineering, 1964, associate professor, 1964–1970, professor, computer science and engineering, 1970–present.

Honors and Awards: fellow, American Association for the Advancement of Science.

Weizenbaum started his professional career with the General Electric Corp. at the time that they were working on the project under Barnie Oldfield to create an automated banking operation for the Bank of America, the computer system of which was named ERMA. He developed a programming language which (retrospectively) had the qualities of artificial intelligence (AI). This work led him to an interest in the subject being promulgated by John McCarthy and eventually he joined the faculty at MIT where he could pursue these interests. In the early 1960s, working with the emerging technology of time-sharing, interactive computers, he developed a mechanical psychiatrist named ELIZA, which appeared to be capable of conducting meaningful conversations. In fact the system (Weizenbaum 1965) used keywords in the responses of the user to create commonly used questions that gave the appearance of understanding and responsiveness. In some ways, ELIZA may have been one of the early approaches to the solution of the Turing test for intelligence.

In the 1970s Weizenbaum found himself on the outside of the mainstream of AI for his views on the ultimate limits of computation. He criticized his colleagues for overselling AI and for not reaching their professed goals in a reasonable time span. Promises had been made by the profession that were not being fulfilled, and he had the temerity to tell the world of their shortcomings.

BIBLIOGRAPHY

Significant Publications

Weizenbaum, Joseph, "ELIZA—A Computer Program for the Study of Natural Language Communication Between Man and Machine," *Comm. ACM*, Vol. 9, No. 1, Jan. 1965, pp. 36–45.

Weizenbaum, Joseph, *Computer Power and Human Reason: From Judgment to Calculation,* W.H. Freeman & Co., New York, 1976.

DAVID J. WHEELER

Born February 9, 1927; professor of computer science, University of Cambridge; fellow of Trinity College, Cambridge, who worked on the EDSAC in 1951 with Maurice Wilkes and Stanley Gill, and introduced the concept of the subroutine, invented the subroutine (or mark place and return) "jump," then called the "Wheeler jump."

Education: BA, mathematics, Cambridge University, 1948; PhD, mathematics, Cambridge University, 1951.

Professional Experience: Mathematical Laboratory (now Computer Laboratory), Cambridge University, 1948–present.

Honors and Awards: fellow, British Computing Society in 1970; fellow, Royal Society, 1981; IEEE Computer Society Pioneer Award, 1985; fellow, ACM, 1994.

David J. Wheeler is professor of computer science at Cambridge University, where he has spent most of his career. He started computer work as an undergraduate in 1947, and his PhD dissertation titled *Automatic Computing with the EDSAC* was accepted in 1951. During Wheeler's work at the Mathematical Laboratory on the development of the EDSAC, he invented the concept of "initial orders," which were the code sequence that initialized the machine and permitted additional programs to be introduced and executed directly. In 1951 he was elected as a fellow of Trinity College, Cambridge, but he spent the next two years at the University of Illinois, helping design the programming systems for the ORDVAC and the ILLIAC. Returning to Cambridge in 1953, he designed extensions to the EDSAC such as the index register and the programming system for EDSAC 2. Since then he has worked on the Cambridge Titan computer, extensions for on-line working, the CAP computer, and the Cambridge Ring.

He has spent time at the University of Illinois, the University of California, and the University of Sydney, Australia, and acted as consultant to various companies including Bell Telephone Laboratories at Murray Hill, and DEC at the Western Research Laboratory.

BIBLIOGRAPHY

Biographical

Wilkes, M.V., "Early Programming Developments in Cambridge," in Metropolis, N., J. Howlett, and Gian-Carlo Rota, *A History of Computing in the Twentieth Century*, Academic Press, New York, 1980, pp. 497–501.

Wheeler, David J., "Programmed Computing at the Universities of Cambridge and Illinois in the Early Fifties," in Nash, Stephen G., *A History of Scientific Computing*, ACM Press History Series, New York, 1990, pp. 269–279.

Wheeler, David J., "The EDSAC Programming Systems," *Ann. Hist. Comp.*, Vol. 14, No. 4, 1992, pp. 34–40.

Significant Publications

Wheeler, D.J., "Program Organisation and Initial Orders for the EDSAC," *Proc. Royal Soc.*, London, Vol. A, No. 202, Aug. 1950, pp. 573–589.

Wilkes, M.V., D.J. Wheeler, and Stanley Gill, *The Preparation of Programs for an Electronic Digital Computer*, Addison-Wesley, New York, 1951.

NORBERT WIENER

Born November 26, 1894, Columbus, Miss.; died March 18, 1964, while on tour in Stockholm, Sweden; logician, scholar, and consultant who invented the concept of cybernetics.

Education: BA, mathematics, Tufts College, 1909; MA, Harvard University, 1912; PhD, Harvard University, 1913.

Professional Experience: docent, Harvard University, 1915–1918; "Computer," Aberdeen Proving Ground, 1918–1919; MIT: professor, 1919–1960, Institute Professor Emeritus, 1960–1964.

"I became a scholar partly because it was my father's will but equally because it was my internal destiny." Thus did Norbert Wiener in his autobiography sum up the forces that directed him to become the mathematical genius whose work achieved international reputation. He is noted for his contributions in the communications sciences, in the realm of nonlinear problems in random theory, in the analysis of brain waves, and in the evolution of cybernetics, where he explored the similarities between the human brain and the modern computing machine capable of memory association, choice, and decision making.

Norbert Wiener was born in Columbus, Mississippi, on November 26, 1894. Signs of his genius appeared early. He began to read at age 4, and by 7 his reading ranged from Darwin and Kingsley to the psychiatric writings of Charot and Janet. He entered Tufts College at age 11 and graduated at 14 with a BA in mathematics and considerable study in philosophy. He entered Harvard University and received his MA at age 17 and his PhD at 18. With a traveling fellowship from Harvard, he studied in England and Germany under, among others, Bertrand Russell and G.H. Hardy. Upon his return to the US in 1915, he studied philosophy under John Dewey at Columbia University and served as a docent at Harvard.

Poor eyesight prevented him from enlisting in World War I, but in 1918 he was accepted into the military and assigned to duty as a "computer" at Aberdeen Proving Ground. He began his career at MIT in 1919. During World War II, he worked with the Operational Research Laboratory at Columbia on antiaircraft predictors. After 42 years on the faculty he retired in 1960 as Institute Professor Emeritus. Following his retirement, he lectured around the world and died on March 18, 1964, while on tour in Stockholm.

Wiener coined the word *cybernetics* from the Greek *kybernetes* ("steersman") and wrote *Cybernetics—Control and Communication in the Animal and the Machine* (1948) and *The Human Use of Human Beings* (1950). In cybernetics he sought to discover the degree to which the human nervous system is a mechanized process as it carries stimuli to the brain—in other words, how much in a human is unconsciously a machine. The question led him to considering automation and how like a human a machine could become—could a machine assume human intellectual capabilities, and when could it exceed and replace a human? In *The Human Use of Human Beings* he discussed the desirable features of automation—relief of repetitive drudgery such as assembly-line production, thus freeing people for pursuits that would make greater claim on their creative abilities.

Wiener's awareness of the economic and social dangers stimulated him repeatedly to warn of the necessity for planned control of automation's progress.[13]

---

[13]Extracted from Brown and Wiener 1955.

QUOTATIONS

"We are not the stuff that abides, but patterns that perpetuate themselves. A pattern is a message. . . . We are but whirlpools in a river of everflowing water."

"This piece of work is an example of the value and even necessity of combining the machine and the living organism, of combining control and communication too, into a unified subject. I've called it *cybernetics*."

BIBLIOGRAPHY

Biographical

Brown, G.S., and Norbert Wiener, "Automation 1955: A Retrospective," reprinted in *Ann. Hist. Comp.*, Vol. 6, No. 4, 1984, pp. 372–383.

Masani, P., ed., *Norbert Wiener: Collected Works*, 4 Vols., MIT Press, Cambridge, Mass., 1976–1986.

Masani, Pesi, Brian Randell, David K. Ferry, and Richard Seeks, "The Wiener Memorandum on the Mechanical Solution of Partial Differential Equations," *Ann. Hist. Comp.*, Vol. 9, No. 2, 1987, pp. 183–198.

Masani, Pesi, *Norbert Wiener 1894–1964*, Birkhäuser, Boston, 1992.

Tropp, H.S., "Norbert Wiener," in Ralston, A., and C.L. Meeks, eds., *Encyclopedia of Computer Science*, Pertrocelli/Charter, New York, 1976, pp. 1557–1558.

Wiener, Norbert, *I am a Mathematician: The Later Life of a Prodigy*, Doubleday, Garden City, N.Y., 1956.[14]

Significant Publications

Wiener, Norbert, "Cybernetics: New Field of Study Looks into Processes Common to Nervous Systems and Mathematical Machines," *Scientific American*, Vol. 1979, Nov. 1948, pp. 14–19.

Wiener, Norbert, *Cybernetics*, 2nd ed., MIT Press, Cambridge, Mass., 1961.

Wiener, Norbert, *God and Golem Inc.*, MIT Press, Cambridge, Mass., 1966.

Wiener, Norbert, *The Human Use of Human Beings*, Avon Books, New York, 1969.

---

[14]The cover of this book explains that this is a "continuation of the account of his childhood in *Ex-Prodigy*."

C. ROBERT WIESER

Designer and developer of the Cape Cod Air Defense and SAGE systems, which introduced the first concepts of multiprogramming and interactive input.

Education: BSEE and MSEE, MIT, 1940.

Professional Experience: Boston Edison Company, 1940–1942; MIT Servomechanisms Laboratory, 1942–1951; Lincoln Laboratory: leader, Cape Cod Air Defense Direction Center, 1951; head of the Systems Division (changed to the Data Systems Division in 1963), assistant director, deputy director, Office of the Secretary of Defense, 1968–1971; director, Advanced Weapons Programs, Douglas Astronautics Company, 1971–1982; vice president and general manager, Western Division of Physical Dynamics, Inc., RES Operations.

Wieser worked with the Boston Edison Company from 1940 to 1942, after which he joined the MIT Servomechanisms Laboratory, developing in 1949 the application of the Whirlwind I to air traffic control and then air defense. In 1951 he joined the Lincoln Laboratory and was leader of the group designing and testing the Cape Cod Air Defense Direction Center, and preparing the operational and mathematical specifications for the SAGE system. At Lincoln he became head of the Systems Division (changed to the Data Systems Division in 1963), assistant director, and deputy director. In 1968 he joined the Office of the Secretary of Defense and in 1971 went to the Douglas Astronautics Company as director of Advanced Weapons Programs. Since 1982 he has been vice president and general manager of the Western Division of Physical Dynamics, Inc., RES Operations.

BIBLIOGRAPHY

Biographical Publications

Everett, Robert R., "Whirlwind," in Metropolis, N., J., Howlett, and Gian-Carlo, Rota, *A History of Computing in the Twentieth Century*, Academic Press, Inc., New York, 1980, pp. 365–384.

Redmond, Kent C., and Thomas M. Smith, *Project Whirlwind: The History of a Pioneer Computer*, Digital Press, Burlington, Mass., 1980.

MAURICE VINCENT WILKES

Born June 26, 1913, Dudley, Worcestshire, England; director of the Cambridge Computer Laboratory throughout the whole development of stored-program computers starting with EDSAC; inventor of labels, macros, and microprogramming; with David Wheeler and Stanley Gill, the inventor of a programming system based on subroutines.

Education: St. John's College, Cambridge, 1931–1934; PhD, Cambridge University, 1936.

Professional Experience: Cambridge University: university demonstrator, Mathematical Laboratory, 1937, member of staff, Mathematical Laboratory (later the Computer Laboratory), 1937–1939, head, Mathematical Laboratory, 1945–1980, fellow, St. John's College, 1950–present, professor of computer technology, 1965–1980, emeritus professor, 1980–1989; senior consulting engineer, Digital Equipment Corp., Maynard, Mass., 1980–1986; adjunct professor, electrical engineering and computer science, MIT, 1981–1985; Olivetti Research Board: member for research strategy, 1986–1989, adviser on research strategy, 1989–present.

Honors and Awards: fellow, Royal Society, 1956; first president, British Computer Society, 1957–1960; ACM Turing Award, 1967; Harry Goode Memorial Award, AFIPS, 1968; distinguished fellow, British Computer Society, 1973; member, Fellowship of Engineering, London, 1976; foreign associate, US National Academy of Engineering, 1977; foreign corresponding member, Royal Spanish Academy of Sciences, 1979; foreign associate, US National Academy of Sciences, 1980; ACM/IEEE Eckert-Mauchly Award, 1980; IEEE Computer Society Pioneer Award, 1980; McDowell Award, IEEE Computer Society, 1981; Faraday Medal, IEE, London, 1981; Pender Award, University of Pennsylvania, 1982; C&C Prize, Tokyo, 1988; ITALGAS Prize for Research and Innovation,[15] 1991; Kyoto Prize, 1992; Honorary Degrees: Universities of Newcastle, Hull, Kent, London, Amsterdam, Munich, Bath, Linköping, and Cambridge; fellow, ACM, 1994.

Wilkes received a PhD from Cambridge University in 1936 for a thesis on the propagation of very long radio waves in the ionosphere. In 1937 he was appointed to a junior faculty position at Cambridge in connection with the establishment of a computing laboratory.

---

[15]This prize is awarded on the recommendation of the Academy of Sciences of Turin, an academy of respectable antiquity (according to Wilkes), having been founded by Lagrange. It was held in high regard by Babbage, who at one time hoped that the academy would endorse his work. This did not happen, but Wilkes was enormously gratified that the academy did for him what it could not do for Babbage. Coincidentally, Wilkes gave a short address before the award ceremony, probably in the same room in which Babbage lectured in 1840.

The university gave formal approval on February 20, 1937, for the creation of a computer laboratory. The laboratory was to be called the "Mathematical Laboratory" and was to be equipped with an eight-integrator differential analyzer, the model differential analyzer, the "Mallock Machine"—an electrical analog calculating device built in 1933 to solve linear simultaneous equations—and a variety of desk calculators. John Lennard-Jones, Plummer Professor of Theoretical Chemistry at Cambridge University, was appointed part-time director of the Mathematical Laboratory for a period of five years from October 1, 1937, and Wilkes was appointed as university demonstrator (a post approximately equivalent to assistant professor in the US). Wilkes' initial brief was to supervise the construction of the new differential analyzer and visit Manchester University to gain experience on the differential analyzer there.

He left for war service on the outbreak of war in 1939 and worked in radar and operational research.

When he returned to Cambridge in September 1945, he was appointed head of the laboratory. In May 1946 Leslie Comrie returned from a visit to the US with a copy of von Neumann's *First Draft of a Report on the EDVAC*. Wilkes was given the opportunity of one night in which to read and digest the document that described the stored-program computer concept. Wilkes "recognized this at once as the real thing, and from that time on never had any real doubt as to the way computer development would go."

Following this opportunity to read von Neumann's "First Draft," Wilkes received an invitation to attend a series of lectures on the "Theory and Techniques for Design of Electronic Digital Computers," given at the Moore School of Engineering at the University of Pennsylvania July 8 to August 31, 1946. Wilkes jumped at the chance to go and, although he arrived late owing to postwar shipping shortages, he was in time for the detailed description of the ENIAC and the discussion of the EDVAC principle.

Hartree provided Wilkes with introductions to Howard Aiken at Harvard, Sam Caldwell, who was responsible for the differential analyzer at MIT, and Herman Goldstine, von Neumann's associate. In addition to meeting these people, Wilkes also got to know John Mauchly and J. Presper Eckert, who were the principal instructors on the course, and he discussed the future of computing machines with them.

By the time Wilkes returned to Cambridge in October 1946 he was determined to build a stored-program computer—a project which was well within the province of the Mathematical Laboratory. The laboratory had sufficient funds to get the project started without

Wilkes needing to apply to anyone for permission or funding. The next few years were spent in intense activity setting up an electronics laboratory and building the EDSAC, which was operational in June 1949.

Later Wilkes was responsible for the construction of EDSAC 2. EDSAC 2, which came into operation early in 1958, was designed by the team that had successfully built and operated EDSAC 1, and embodied the experience obtained with that machine. EDSAC 2 was the first computer to have a microprogrammed control unit and it established beyond doubt the viability of microprogramming as a basis for computer design—this in spite of the fact that vacuum tubes were far from ideal for the purpose. At the mechanical level of organization, EDSAC 2 was packaged in a bit-sliced manner, with interchangeable plug-in units. This method of packaging was well matched to the vacuum tube technology of the period, and its expected advantages, arising from the replication of units, were fully realized.

Around 1960 it was evidently necessary to consider what should come after EDSAC 2. After much discussion it was decided to enter into a collaboration with Ferranti Ltd. to develop a reduced-scale version of the Atlas machine, a joint effort between Manchester University and Ferranti. The Atlas was a large and very expensive machine, and the plan, born of financial necessity, was to make a more modest but largely compatible computer. The main differences were the lack of virtual memory and the concomitant drum, the omission of the fixed store, and a different approach to the control of magnetic tapes. A joint team from Ferranti and Cambridge designed the new hardware, which was built by Ferranti, and also designed an operating system intended to give high-performance multiprogrammed computing. The Atlas operating system had been built without much computer support, and one of the contributions of the joint group working on the Titan, as the Cambridge machine was called, was the Titan Supervisor Assembly System. This was very early in the field of version control systems, and had a useful feature in that it distinguished two sorts of changes to the source text of a module. These were corrections and improvements, the former being essential to a working system and the latter usually incompatible with the other.

Design work on the supervisor was well under way when first Wilkes and then others became aware of the development at MIT of the Compatible Time-Sharing System (CTSS). It was clear that this was the way of the future, and Wilkes successfully negotiated with ICT (which now incorporated much of Ferranti's civil computer business) for the provision of a disk on which a filing system could be based. The disk was supplied free of charge in the first instance, but was later paid for. One of the main differences between the Cambridge system and the CTSS was what became known as "normal mode." This was a simple way of running programs from a terminal, which depended on the observation that a very common structure was to have initial input from the terminal, and final output to the terminal without interaction in between. It was very usual for visitors not to notice that the service was not actually fully interactive. Naturally some of the main utilities such as editors were fully interactive. The filing system, designed by A.G. Fraser, was very similar to that of the CTSS, though with considerably more flexible arrangements for access control. In particular it was possible to use the identity of a program as a parameter for access control decisions as well as or instead of the identity of the user, a feature which Cambridge people have ever since regarded as strange to omit. The Titan system was also the first to make use of a one-way function to protect its password file, a tactic, due to R.M. Needham, which has since become almost universal.

The Titan had to give a round-the-clock conventional service to the university, and there was accordingly a certain amount of trepidation about the effects, both technical and political, of running the multiple-access system at the same time. In the event the multiple-access system did not adversely affect the conventional service and quickly became regarded as an integral part of it.

In 1965 an effort under the leadership of Charles Lang started up in mechanical CAD. It originally used a DEC PDP-7 computer with a type 340 display (which was the first such system in the country) as an interface to the Titan Multiple-Access System. A high-performance link was therefore built between the PDP-7 and the Titan, so that the interactive graphics user could have the mainframe filing system and other utilities readily at his command as well as the display. The work led to a 15-year effort in CAD, including major advances in solid modeling.

As the 1960s drew to a close there was an obvious question as to what to do next. The university decided to set up the Computing Service as a separate organization still within the laboratory (which was renamed the Computer Laboratory at the same time). The traditions of the Titan were continued in the shape of innovations and enhancements to commercially supplied computer systems. Meanwhile Wilkes and Needham considered all kinds of possible projects. Wilkes recalls in his *Memoirs* (1985) how they contemplated and rejected what would now be called a multi-microprocessor project as a way of making a mainframe. Eventually they became fascinated by capability-based computers, and in 1970 they set out to design and build one. The Cambridge CAP, as it became known, had a hardware cache for evaluated capabilities and microprogrammed evaluation on cache miss. There was much debate about its instruction set, which was resolved in favor of a very conventional one when it was realized that easy transfer of compilers to CAP was essential. The operating system was almost entirely written in the local dialect of Algol 68. This was found very effective and the development of that system was very smooth by comparison with earlier experiences. It did, however, make it difficult to share the credit for the relatively painless implementation between the type-checking of the language and the memory protection of the hardware. Between the two, bad programs did not often survive very long. Algol 68C was at that time much used in the laboratory, in particular for the solid modeling work mentioned above. The CAP and its system are described in Wilkes and Needham's 1978 book.

In 1974 Wilkes was shown a digital communication ring working at the laboratories of Hasler A.G. in Switzerland, where it was regarded as a contribution to digital telephony. He immediately realized that such ideas had application to computer communication, and on his return put in hand as soon as possible the development of what became known as the Cambridge Ring. As implemented, it differed considerably from Hasler's register insertion ring. The Cambridge Ring was an empty-slot ring, which was believed to be easier to maintain. The data rate was 10 megabits per second. The original application of the ring was peripheral-sharing. They had been struck by the trouble and expense associated with having to have one printer per minicomputer, for example. About that time, however, modern ideas of distributed computing were becoming current, and it was clear that the Ring could serve as a basis for this concept.

This it did, and not only in Cambridge. Several companies began to market Ring equipment, and the Science and Engineering Research Council bought a quantity in support of an initiative in distributed computing. At that period practical experience of distributed computing was more common in British universities than anywhere else, which is directly attributable to the availability of the Ring on a commercial basis. In Cambridge an experiment was undertaken, reported in Needham and Herbert's 1982 book, to produce a distributed computing system based on a processor bank.[16] The idea was that users would have modest workstations, and when they needed more serious

---

[16]Needham, R.M., and A.J. Herbert, *The Cambridge Distributed Computing Systems*, Addison-Wesley, Reading, 1982.

computation a processor would be allocated to them from a pool. Because of lack of resources the implementation was a model one, with users having terminals only, and not very powerful machines in the pool. Nevertheless, the model system was practically useful, and has had its effects on subsequent developments, particularly of file servers.

In 1980 Wilkes retired from his professorship and from the laboratory of which he had been head since late 1945. He joined the central engineering staff of the Digital Equipment Corporation in Maynard, Massachusetts. Returning to England in 1986, he became a member for research strategy on the Olivetti Research Board. He is now a consultant to Olivetti.[17]

In 1993 Wilkes was presented with an honorary doctor of science degree by his alma mater, Cambridge University. In his presentation, the public orator (in Latin) introduced him as follows:

> A century and a half ago Charles Babbage, Lucasian Professor of Mathematics, devised his Analytical Engine, which embodied most of the concepts which we now take for granted in the digital computer. But those concepts were far ahead of the available technology. Here stands the man who finally brought to its fullest reality Babbage's dream, by providing the computer with the one vital organ which it still lacked: a capacious memory. He converted a program and its data, punched onto paper tape, into ultrasonic pulses, and he fed the pulses into a tube of memory, which delayed their progress, and he caused the pulses to circulate indefinitely. And so EDSAC was born, the Electronic Delay Storage Automatic Calculator, the first full operational computer with its own memory. As Virgil almost said,
>
> *A spirit nourishes the parts within,*
> *And mind moves matter in the mighty frame.*
>
> From all sides they flocked to admire it, and stayed to use it. Soon it was performing the vital calculations by which our chemists and radio-astronomers perfected their Nobel Prize-winning work. On those glorious pioneering days he has never ceased to build. With TITAN he took a further giant stride forward, enabling a multitude of users, instead of waiting their turn in a queue with their strip of punched tape, to key in their programs simultaneously from their own desks, at whatever distance. He has given us a computer laboratory which is a source of no small parochial pride and is the admiration and envy of the world outside.

---

[17]Extracted from the several articles in Campbell-Kelly 1992.

QUOTATION

Regarding developing programs: ". . . It would be more logical first to choose a data structure appropriate to the problem, and then to look around for, or construct with a kit of tools provided, a language suitable for manipulating the structure."

BIBLIOGRAPHY

Biographical

Campbell-Kelly, Martin, ed., *Special Issue—The University of Cambridge, Ann. Hist. Comp.*, Vol. 14, No. 4, 1992.

Gill, S., "Maurice Wilkes," in Ralston, Anthony, and Edwin D. Reilly, Jr., *Encyclopedia of Computer Science and Engineering*, Van Nostrand Reinhold Co., New York, 1983.

Lavington, Simon, *Early British Computers*, Digital Press, Bedford, Mass., 1980; see Chapter 6: "The Cambridge EDSAC."

Wilkes, M.V., "Early Programming Developments in Cambridge," in Metropolis, N., J. Howlett, and Gian-Carlo Rota, *A History of Computing in the Twentieth Century*, Academic Press, New York, 1980, pp. 497–501.

Wilkes, Maurice, *Memoirs of a Computer Pioneer*, MIT Press, Cambridge, Mass., 1985.

Wilkes, Maurice, "The Genesis of Microprogramming," *Ann. Hist. Comp.*, Vol. 8, No. 2, 1986, pp. 115–126.

Wilkes, Maurice V., "EDSAC 2," *Ann. Hist. Comp.*, Vol. 14, No. 4, 1992, pp. 49–56.

Significant Publications

Strachey, Christopher, and Maurice V. Wilkes, "Some Proposals for Improving the Efficiency of Algol 60," *Comm. ACM*, Vol. 4, No. 11, 1961, pp. 488–491.

Wilkes, Maurice V., "The Design of a Practical High-Speed Computing Machine," *Proc. Royal Soc.*, London, Vol. A, No. 195, 1948, pp. 274–279.

Wilkes, Maurice V., and W. Renwick, "An Ultrasonic Memory Unit for the EDSAC," *Electronic Engineering*, Vol. 20, No. 245, July 1948, pp. 208–213.

Wilkes, Maurice V., and W. Renwick, "The EDSAC, An Electronic Calculating Machine," *J. Scientific Instruments*, Vol. 26, Dec. 1949, pp. 385–391; reprinted in Randell, Brian, *Origins of Digital Computers: Selected Papers*, Springer-Verlag, Berlin, 1982, pp. 417–422.

Wilkes, Maurice V., D.J. Wheeler, and Stanley Gill, *The Preparation of Programs for an Electronic Digital Computer,* Addison-Wesley, Cambridge, Mass., 1951.

Wilkes, M.V., *Time-Sharing Computer Systems,* Macdonald/Elsevier, London, 1968; 2nd ed., 1972; 3rd ed., 1975.

Wilkes, M.V., and R.M. Needham, *The Cambridge CAP Computer and Its Operating System,* Elsevier, London, 1978.

Wilkes, Maurice V., "Pray, Mr. Babbage . . . , A Character Study in Dramatic Form," *Ann. Hist. Comp.*, Vol. 13, No. 2, 1991, pp. 147–154.

JAMES (JIM) HARDY WILKINSON

Born 1919; died October 5, 1986, London, UK; numerical analyst, developer of the so-called "backward" error analysis, and believer in the ability to work with large matrices.

Education: Graduated with first-class honors, Cambridge University, 1939.

Professional Experience: National Physical Laboratory (NPL), 1947–1980; professor, Computer Science Department, Stanford University, 1977–1984.

Honors and Awards: DSc, Cambridge University, 1963; fellow, Royal Society of London, 1969; A.M. Turing Award, Association for Computing Machinery (ACM), 1970; John von Neumann Award, Society for Industrial and Applied Mathematics (SIAM), 1970; honorary fellow, (British) Institute for Mathematics and Its Applications, 1977.

When he was 16 years old, Jim Wilkinson won an open competition scholarship in mathematics to Trinity College, Cambridge. He won two coveted prizes (the Pemberton and the Mathison) while he was an undergraduate there, and graduated with first-class honors before he was 20 years old. Throughout World War II he worked as a mathematician for the Ministry of Supply, and it was there that he met and married his wife, Heather. In 1946 he joined the recently formed group of numerical analysts at the National Physical Laboratory (NPL). He was to stay there until his retirement in 1980. Soon after his arrival he began to work with Alan Turing on the design of an electronic computer, in addition to his work with the numerical analysts using mechanical computing machines. That work led to the Pilot ACE machine, which executed its first scientific calculations in 1953.[18] Wilkinson designed the multiplication unit for ACE and its successor DEUCE.

One could say that the decade 1947–1957 was the exciting *learning* period in which Wilkinson and his colleagues at NPL discovered how automatic computation differed from human computation assisted by desktop calculating machines. By dint of trying every method that they could conceive and watching the progress of their computations on punched cards, paper tape, or even lights on the computer console, these pioneers won an invaluable practical understanding of how algorithms behave when implemented on computers.

Some algorithms that are guaranteed to deliver the solution after a fixed number of primitive arithmetic operations *in exact arithmetic* can produce, on some problems, completely wrong yet plausible output on a digital computer. That is the fundamental challenge of the branch of numerical analysis of which Wilkinson became the leader: matrix computations. He was the first to see the pattern in the bewildering mass of output.

The period 1958–1973 saw the development, articulation, and dissemination of this understanding of dense matrix computations. It was in 1958 that Wilkinson began giving short courses at the University of Michigan Summer College of Engineering. The notes served as the preliminary version of his first two books. The lectures themselves introduced his work to an audience broader than the small group of specialists who had been brought together in 1957 by Wallace Givens at Wayne State University, Michigan, for the first of a sequence of workshops that came to be called the "Gatlinburg" meetings. The year 1973 saw the beginning of the NATS project (at the Argonne National Laboratory), whose goal was to translate into Fortran and test in a most exigent manner the Algol algorithms collected in the celebrated *Handbook* of 1971. That book, written essentially by Wilkinson and Reinsch, embodied most of what had been learned about matrix transformations.

Wilkinson was honored for achieving an understanding of the effect of rounding errors during the execution of procedures that are used for solving matrix problems and finding zeros of polynomials. He managed to share his grasp of the subject with others by making error analysis intelligible, in particular by his systematic use of the

---

[18]See also the biographies of Harry Huskey and Edward Newman.

"backward," or inverse, point of view. This approach asks whether there is a tiny perturbation of the data such that execution of the algorithm in exact arithmetic using the perturbed data would terminate with the actual computed output derived from the original data. Wilkinson did not invent backward analysis but he put it to its best use. In spite of its apparent simplicity, the *significance* of backward error analysis did not occur to either Alan Turing or John von Neumann, despite the fact that both of them were thinking about related matters.

By 1973 Wilkinson had received the most illustrious awards of his career. He was awarded a doctor of science degree at Cambridge in 1963; he was elected to the Royal Society of London in 1969; in 1970 he was awarded the A.M. Turing Award by the Association for Computing Machinery, and the John von Neumann award of the Society for Industrial and Applied Mathematics. It was not until 1977 that he was made an honorary fellow of the (British) Institute for Mathematics and Its Applications.

The final period, 1974–1986, may be marked by Wilkinson's promotion to the Council of the Royal Society. He accepted a professorship in the Computer Science Department at Stanford University (1977–1984). He was able only to be resident for the winter quarters, and then not every year.[19]

The obituary the *Annals of the History of Computing*[20] published for Jim Wilkinson was one of the most interesting ever created. On Sunday, October 5, 1986, Gene Golub (golub@score.stanford.edu) sent out a message over the Internet, which announced:

> I'm sorry to tell you that our dear colleague Jim Wilkinson died today. He was in the garden and had a massive heart attack. . . . Let me invite you to send messages . . . giving your thoughts on Jim and retelling any encounters that you may have had with him.

The Numerical Analysis distribution list on the Internet then received a number of stories about Wilkinson of such interest that the *Annals* published the obituary as a part of its "Anecdotes" department rather than the usual place for obituaries—the "Biographies" department:

- Even after a glass or two, he still had an incredibly strong insight into people's motives—in their mathematical work and in other aspects of life. [He delivered conference talks] in the best English tradition, underplaying his own contribution.

---

[19]Based on Parlett 1990.
[20]Anon. 1987.

- He made you want to take him home with you.
- I always looked forward to his lectures. The image I remember is of his lecturing in shirt sleeves—sleeves held up by garters to achieve the correct length. Nevertheless, his lectures were always both interesting and informative. He had a great knack for working in an interesting historical anecdote that illuminated what he was trying to say.

QUOTATION

"Did I understand von Neumann? I could verify that each line was deduced from the one above, but if asked what he did, I couldn't answer. And when I probed my colleagues, I found I was losing friends fast."[21]

BIBLIOGRAPHY

Biographical

Anon., "James Wilkinson (1919–1986)," *Ann. Hist. Comp.*, Vol. 9, No. 2, 1987, pp. 205–210.

Parlett, B.N., "The Contribution of J.H. Wilkinson to Numerical Analysis," in Nash, Stephen G., *A History of Scientific Computing*, ACM Press History Series, New York, 1990, pp. 17–30.

Significant Publications

Wilkinson, J.H., *The Algebraic Eigenvalue Problem*, Oxford Univ. Press, Oxford, UK, 1965.

Wilkinson, J.H., and C. Reinsch, *Handbook for Automatic Computation, Volume II, Linear Algebra*, Springer-Verlag, New York, 1971.

Wilkinson, J.H., "Turing's Work at the National Physical Laboratory and the Construction of Pilot ACE, DEUCE, and ACE," in Metropolis, N., J. Howlett, and Gian-Carlo Rota, *A History of Computing in the Twentieth Century*, Academic Press, New York, 1980, pp. 101–114.

---

[21]Parlett 1990.

FREDERIC CALLAND WILLIAMS

Born 1911; died 1977; developer of the CRT electrostatic memories that bore his name, devised for the Manchester computers.

Education: BSc, Engineering, University of Manchester, 1932; MSc, Engineering, University of Manchester, 1933.

Professional Experience: Metropolitan-Vickers, 1933–1934; Oxford University, 1934–1936; assistant lecturer, University of Manchester, 1936–1939; Telecommunications Research Establishment, Radar Research, 1939–1946; chair of Electro-Technics, University of Manchester, 1947–1977.

F.C. Williams graduated in engineering from Manchester University in 1932. A year later he received his MSc and joined Metropolitan-Vickers for a short time before moving to Oxford University in 1934 to work on circuit and valve noise. Williams stayed two years at Oxford before returning to Manchester in September 1936 as an assistant lecturer. While lecturing at Manchester, Williams gave a new course called "Electro-technics," which combined physics and electrical engineering (Kilburn and Piggott 1978). Williams also collaborated with P.M.S. Blackett, Langworthy Professor of Physics at Manchester, to design a curve follower for Hartree's differential analyzer, situated in the basement of the Physics Department (Blackett and Williams 1939). Williams later recalled that Blackett had influenced his thinking throughout his career.[22]

By 1939, Williams had established his reputation with the publication of over 20 papers and, near the beginning of the war, Williams was "channeled" by Blackett (Lovell 1975) into radar research, first at Bawdsey and later at the Telecommunications Research Establishment (TRE), which moved to Malvern in 1942. One of the first projects Williams became involved in was the IFF system (Identification Friend or Foe), which used radar pulses to distinguish Allied aircraft. The device was manufactured by Ferranti. Williams later went on to do extensive radar research at TRE, where he was "prolific, enthusiastic and unselfish" (Kilburn and Piggott 1978) and confirmed his standing as an acknowledged expert in circuit design.

Toward the end of the war, Williams became involved in producing a series of definitive works in electrical engineering. The Radiation Laboratory at the Massachusetts Institute of Technology (MIT)

---

[22]Lovell, B., "Patrick Maynard Stuart Blackett, *Biographical Memoirs of Fellows of the Royal Society*, Vol. 21, 1975, pp. 1–115.

planned 24 volumes (published between 1947 and 1949) giving a comprehensive coverage of all aspects of electrical engineering. Williams was editor and a contributor to volumes 19 and 20, *Waveforms* and *Electrical Time Measurements,* respectively. Williams visited the Radiation Laboratory in his editorial capacity (in both November 1945 and June 1946), and learned of work being done at both the Radiation Laboratory and the Moore School (which he visited June 21 and 22, 1946) on using cathode-ray tubes as storage devices. Drath[23] quotes Williams as remarking that the end of the war "left many scientists and engineers at TRE searching for new projects to occupy themselves." Cathode-ray tube storage was such a project and, on his return from the US in July 1946, Williams began to study the problem. By October 1946 Williams was able to demonstrate that a single cathode-ray tube could regeneratively store a single binary digit. Tom Kilburn, a scientific officer at TRE, began to work with Williams.

As early as May 8, 1946, Womersley, superintendent of the NPL Mathematics Division, had written to TRE inquiring about the use of cathode-ray tubes as a possible alternative to delay-line storage for the ACE. When news of Williams' success in storing one binary digit reached the NPL, Sir Charles Darwin, director of the NPL, and E.S. Hiscocks, secretary of the NPL, visited TRE on October 15–17, 1946, to see the Williams tube demonstrated. This visit was followed up on November 22 with a meeting at the NPL attended by Hiscocks, Womersley, and Turing from the NPL and by R.A. Smith (director of TRE), Williams, and A.M. Uttley, also from TRE. The NPL, most notably Hiscocks and Womersley rather than Turing, pressed hard for TRE to agree to carry out much of the electronic development work needed to construct the ACE to Turing's designs. The NPL did not intend to build the machine in house, as none of the Mathematics Division staff had the relevant electronics experience.

At the meeting, Smith outlined the difficulties that TRE had concerning availability of staff with electronics experience. Williams, one of the TRE's most valuable assets as far as the NPL was concerned, was about to leave TRE to go to Manchester University. The majority of TRE's circuit technicians had been transferred to the United Kingdom Atomic Energy Authority, and any remaining staff with computing machine knowledge (but not valve experience) were already committed to a project for the Ministry of Supply concerning computers for military use. The amount of assistance TRE could give to the NPL was, therefore, very limited.

---

[23]Drath, P., *The Relationship Between Science and Technology: University Research and the Computer Industry, 1945–1962,* unpublished doctoral dissertation, Manchester Univ., UK, 1973.

The NPL did not, however, give up trying to persuade Williams to tailor his work on cathode-ray tube storage systems to the needs of the ACE project. In January 1947 the NPL prepared a draft contract under which Williams was to:

1. "develop an electronic storage tube for A.C.E. machine" and
2. "develop components of the arithmetical organ of the machine, e.g., adding circuit and multiplying circuit."[24]

Williams turned down the offer of such a binding contract, preferring to work within the relative freedom of TRE and Manchester University sponsorship. It was also obvious that the ACE as designed by Turing was very dependent on delay-line storage, and a major design change would have been necessary to use cathode-ray tube storage as an alternative.

In early October 1946, Williams was offered the chair of electrotechnics at Manchester University. Blackett and Max Newman both sat on the committee that appointed Williams. Blackett, through his familiarity with Williams' prewar work at Manchester and his wartime contributions to radar research from his position as director of Naval Operational Research, is credited (Lovell 1975) with influencing the appointment. Newman, too, when he learned of Williams' work with cathode-ray tubes, was keen to secure Williams for Manchester. Williams moved to Manchester (on January 14, 1947) and continued to work on his cathode-ray tube storage system.

Williams was appointed to the Edward Stocks Massey Chair of Electro-Technics at Manchester University in January 1947. Kilburn joined him from TRE. TRE was willing to continue to support Williams' work on cathode-ray tube storage systems not only by seconding Kilburn but also by supplying Williams with the components necessary for him to carry out his research. In postwar Britain, such components were not readily available. Newman was pleased that Williams had been appointed and decided to wait for Williams' work to come to fruition rather than rely on buying components from the US whenever they became available. Newman did not anticipate that Williams would produce a working memory unit in such a short time.

Williams and Kilburn spent 1947 perfecting the CRT memory unit and were joined on the project by A.A. Robertson and G.C. Tootill. While the work in the Electro-Technics Department went on independently of the Royal Society Computing Machine Laboratory, the engineers did seek advice from Newman and his staff. By autumn 1947, the

---

[24]National Physical Laboratory, *Draft Contract for Discussion between NPL and Manchester University*, Nat'l Archive for the History of Computing, NAHC/MUC/Series 1/B1a/(iii), Manchester, UK, u.d.

Williams tube was able to store 2,048 bits, and the next step was to develop a computer around it. It was at this stage that Newman was able to offer explanations as to what kind of machine Williams and Kilburn needed to build. Williams recalls that:

> They took us by the hand and explained how numbers could live in houses with addresses and how if they did they could be kept track of during a calculation. (Williams 1975)

I.J. Good also worked with Kilburn making suggestions for the design of the computer. For example, in May 1947 Good suggested 12 basic instructions that a prototype machine would need to include. He also pushed for two accumulators to be built into the machine. Good claims to have suggested microprogramming (which he called machine building) as early as February 1947.[25] The liaison between the Mathematics Department and the Electro-Technics Department was established.

The Royal Society Computing Machine Laboratory housed Williams' and Kilburn's work on a prototype computer being built around the Williams tube store. In reality, the Royal Society Computing Machine Laboratory was a 20 × 20-foot room in the Engineering Department, labeled "Magnetism." The laboratory had no staff paid for by the Royal Society. Newman, Good (who left Manchester in April 1948), and Rees were based in, and employed by, the Mathematics Department. Williams, Robertson, and Tootill were on the staff of the Electro-Technics Department. Kilburn was still a senior scientific officer with the Ministry of Supply. The equipment needed to carry out the research continued to be supplied through TRE. Consequently, the Royal Society grant remained almost untouched.

Throughout early 1948, work was done, principally by Kilburn,[26] on building a prototype (or baby machine) around the Williams tube to demonstrate the feasibility of building a much larger machine. Meanwhile, information about the Williams tube was disseminated. In December 1947, Kilburn produced a progress report[27] describing the storage system and included a description of a hypothetical computer.

---

[25]Good, I. J., "Early Computers at Manchester University," Nat'l Archive for the History of Computing, NAHC/MUC/Series 2/A4, Manchester, UK, Apr. 7, 1976.

[26]Manchester University, *Arrangements for Royal Society Computing Machine Laboratory,* Nat'l Archive for the History of Computing, NAHC/MUC/Series 2/C2, Manchester, UK, Oct. 15, 1948.

[27]Kilburn, T., "A Storage System for Use with Binary Digital Computing Machines," Dept. of Electro-Technics, Univ. of Manchester, UK, Dec. 1, 1947.

Fifty copies were made of this report (which was later published without the description of the hypothetical computer in 1949) and distributed to interested parties worldwide. On March 4, 1948, Williams described his store to the Royal Society during a "Discussion on Computing Machines."[28] Other contributors to this discussion were D. R. Hartree, M.V. Wilkes from the Cambridge Mathematical Laboratory, J.H. Wilkinson from the NPL, and A.D. Booth from Birkbeck College, London. Williams later recalled (Williams 1975) that during the discussion (which took place in March 1948) Newman stressed that the major question concerning the large computing machines being built in the US and in Britain was "if they work at all." This remark clearly illustrates the continued element of doubt about the feasibility of building stored-program computers.

However, by summer 1948 Williams, Kilburn, and Tootill had built a very small prototype computer—which has become known as the Manchester baby—using only 32 words of 32 bits each stored on a single Williams tube. Cathode-ray tubes were also used for the accumulator and the logical control, which stored the current instruction and its address. The only input mechanism was a series of switches. Output was read directly from the Williams tube. On June 21, 1948, the machine correctly ran its first program, which found the highest factor of an integer. It was the first program to run on an electronic stored-program computer. Simon Lavington states that Manchester folklore has it that Williams never wrote a program during his career and Kilburn "wrote just one—the world's first!"[29]

The baby machine served one purpose—to prove that a stored-program computer could be built around a Williams tube storage system. The machine carried out this function very well indeed. When Blackett saw the machine working, he suggested to Williams that it was an invention from which industry could benefit. Williams demurred, feeling that the project was still too immature to involve industry. Nevertheless, Blackett contacted Sir Ben Lockspeiser (chief scientist, Ministry of Supply), who came unannounced to visit Williams and see the machine for himself. The Ministry of Supply was interested in supporting computer development (which they were already doing through TRE's continuing supply of components to Williams) for three reasons: first, to promote scientific research; second, to open up further possibilities in defense research; and third, to support industry,

---

[28]Hartree, D.R., et al., "A Discussion on Computing Machines," *Proc. Royal Soc. A.*, Vol. 195, pp. 265–287.

[29]Lavington, S.H., *A History of Manchester Computers*, NCC Publications, Manchester, UK, 1975.

which was suffering from lack of orders and lack of investment in the postwar era. Lockspeiser felt that Ferranti, which was close to Manchester and had electronic experience, would be an ideal industrial partner for a joint computer venture. Although Williams had to be persuaded on this point (Drath 1973), Lockspeiser continued the negotiations with Ferranti and was able to commit £100,000 from the Treasury to support Ferranti in constructing "an electronic calculating machine to the instructions of Professor F.C. Williams" (Williams 1975).

A contract with Ferranti was not signed until February 19, 1949, but cooperation began in November 1948. D.G.B. Edwards and G.E. Thomas joined the computing effort at Manchester in October 1948, and in November Kilburn was officially appointed to the staff of Manchester University as lecturer in the Royal Society Computing Machine Laboratory. Turing moved to Manchester from the NPL in September 1948 as deputy director of the Royal Society Computing Machine Laboratory. Thus, by autumn 1948, work had started on building a larger prototype computer, the Manchester Mark I, the result of which was to be manufactured by Ferranti. The future of computers at Manchester was assured.[30]

BIBLIOGRAPHY

Biographical

Croarken, Mary, "The Beginnings of the Manchester Computer Phenomenon: People and Influences," *Ann. Hist. Comp.*, Vol. 15, No. 3, 1993, pp. 9–16.

Kilburn, T., and L.S. Piggott, "Frederick Calland Williams, 1911–1977," *Biographical Memoirs of Fellows of the Royal Society,* Vol. 24, 1978, pp. 583–604.

Lavington, Simon, *Early British Computers,* Digital Press, Bedford, Mass, 1980; see Chapter 4: "The Technology of Early Computers," and Chapter 7: "The Manchester Mark I."

Lavington, S.H., "Computer Development at Manchester University," in Metropolis, N., J. Howlett, and Gian-Carlo Rota, *A History of Computing in the Twentieth Century,* Academic Press, New York, 1980, pp. 433–443.

Williams, F.C., "Early Computers at Manchester University," *Radio and Electronic Engineer*, Vol. 45, No. 7, 1975, pp. 327–331.

---

[30]Extracted from Croarken 1993.

Significant Publications

Williams, F.C., and T. Kilburn, "Electronic Digital Computers," reprinted in Randell, Brian, *Origins of Digital Computers: Selected Papers,* Springer-Verlag, Berlin, 1982, pp. 415–416.

Williams, F.C., "Cathode Ray Storage," in Wilkes, M.V., ed., *Report on a Conf. on High Speed Automatic Computing Machines, July 22–25, 1949,* Univ. Math. Lab., Cambridge, UK, 1949.

Niklaus Wirth

Born February 15, 1934, Winterthur, Switzerland; early promoter of good programming practices; developer of the programming languages Pascal, Modula-2, and Oberon; recipient of the 1984 ACM Turing Award.

Education: undergraduate studies at ETH Zurich, Dept. of Electrical Engineering, 1954–1958; diploma, Electronics Engineer ETH, 1959; MSc, Laval University, Quebec, Canada, 1960; PhD, electrical engineering, University of California, Berkeley, 1963.

Professional Experience: assistant professor of computer science, Stanford University, 1963–1967; assistant professor of computer science, University of Zurich, 1967–1968; professor of computer science, University of Zurich and ETH Zurich, 1968–1972; professor of computer science, ETH Zurich, 1972–present; sabbatical leaves, Xerox Palo Alto Research Center, 1977 and 1985; head of Department of Computer Science, ETH Zurich, 1982–1984 and 1988–1990; head of Institute of Computer Systems, ETH Zurich, 1990–present.

Honors and Awards: ACM Programming Systems and Languages Paper Award for "Towards a Discipline of Real-Time Programming," 1978; honorary doctorate, University of York, England, 1978; honorary doctorate, Ecole Polytechnique Federale, Lausanne, Switzerland, 1978; Computer Design, Hall of Fame Award, 1982; Emanuel R. Piore Award, IEEE, for "achievement in the field of Information Processing contributing to the advancement of science and the betterment of society," 1983; A.M. Turing Award, ACM, "for developing a sequence of innovative computer languages Euler, Algol-W, Pascal, and Modula. Pascal has become pedagogically significant, and has provided a foundation for future computer languages, systems, and architectural research," 1984; ACM-SIGCSE Award, "for outstanding contributions to computer science education," 1987; honorary doctorate, Laval University, Quebec, Canada, 1987;

IEEE Computer Society Pioneer Award, 1987; Computer Pioneer Award, IEEE Computer Society, 1988; Prix Max Petitpierre, Bern, 1988; IBM Europe Science and Technology Prize 1988, "recognition of outstanding work in the field of computer science," 1989; Marcel Benoist Preis, "in Anerkennung der von ihm geschaffenen Computer-Sprachen, die neuartige Konzepte der strukturierten Programmierung verwirklichen und den vielseitigen Einsatz von Rechnern weltweit und auf allen Wissensgebieten nachhaltig beeinflusst haben," 1990; distinguished alumnus, University of California, Berkeley, 1992; foreign associate, US Academy of Engineering, 1993; fellow, ACM, 1994.

Professor N. Wirth received the degree of electronics engineer from the Swiss Federal Institute of Technology (ETH) in Zurich in 1958. Thereafter he studied at Laval University in Quebec, Canada, and received the MSc degree in 1960. At the University of California at Berkeley he pursued his studies, leading to the PhD degree in 1963. Until 1967 he was assistant professor at the newly created Computer Science Department at Stanford University, where he designed the programming languages PL360 and (in conjunction with the IFIP Working Group 2.1) Algol W. In 1967 he became assistant professor at the University of Zurich, and in 1968 he joined ETH Zurich, where he developed the languages Pascal between 1968 and 1970 and Modula-2 between 1979 and 1981.

Further projects include the design and development of the personal computer Lilith, a high-performance workstation, in conjunction with the programming language Modula-2 (1978–1982), and the 32-bit workstation computer Ceres (1984–1986). His most recent works produced the language Oberon, a descendant of Modula-2, which served to design the operating system with the same name (1986–1989). He was chairman of the Division of Computer Science (Informatik) of ETH from 1982 until 1984, and again from 1988 until 1990. Since 1990 he has been the head of the Institute of Computer Systems of ETH.

In 1978 Professor Wirth received honorary doctorates from York University, England, and the Federal Institute of Technology at Lausanne, Switzerland, in recognition of his work in the fields of programming languages and methodology. In 1983 he was awarded the Emanuel Priore prize by the IEEE, in 1984 the A.M. Turing Prize by the ACM, and in 1987 the Award for Outstanding Contributions to Computer Science Education by ACM. The ACM Turing Award cited Wirth for "developing a sequence of innovative computer languages Euler, Algol-W, Modula, and Pascal. Pascal has become pedagogically significant, and has provided a foundation for future computer language, systems, and architectural research." In 1987 he was awarded an honorary doctorate by the Université Laval, Canada, and in 1988 he was named a Computer Pioneer by the IEEE Computer Society.

In 1989 Professor Wirth was awarded the Max Petitpierre Prize for outstanding contributions made by Swiss noted abroad, and he received the Science and Technology Prize from IBM Europe. He was awarded the Marcel Benoist Prize in 1990. In 1992 he was nominated Distinguished Alumnus of the University of California at Berkeley. He is a member of the Swiss Academy of Technical Sciences and a Foreign Associate of the US Academy of Engineering.

QUOTATIONS

Regarding Pascal: "In the interest of increased quality of software products, we may be well advised to get rid of many facilities of modern, baroque programming languages that are widely advertised in the name of 'user-orientation,' 'scientific sophistication,' and 'progress.'"

In introducing Professor Wirth to present his Turing Award Lecture in 1984, ACM president Adele Goldberg commented: "In Europe he is called by name—Wirth (pronounced *virt*), while in America we know him by value—Wirth (pronounced *worth*)!"

BIBLIOGRAPHY

Significant Publications

Wirth, N., "The Programming Language Pascal," *Acta Informatica*, Vol. 1, June 1971, pp. 35–63.

Hoare, C.A.R., and N. Wirth, "An Axiomatic Definition of the Programming Language Pascal," *Acta Informatica*, Vol. 2, 1973, pp. 335–355.

Wirth, N., *PASCAL—User Manual and Report* (with Kathy Jensen), Springer-Verlag, Berlin, 1974.

Wirth, N., *Algorithms, Data Structures, Programs*, Prentice-Hall, Englewood Cliffs, N.J., 1975.

Wirth, N., *Programming in Modula-2*, Springer-Verlag, Heidelberg, New York, 1982.

Wirth, N., "The Programming Language Oberon," *Software—Practice and Experience*, Vol. 18, No. 7, 1985, pp. 671–690.

Wirth, N., *Programming in Oberon* (with M. Reiser), Addison-Wesley, Reading, Mass., 1992.

Wirth, N., *Project Oberon* (with J. Gutknecht), Addison-Wesley, Reading, Mass., 1992.

MICHAEL WOODGER

National Physical Laboratory designer of the Pilot ACE, later influential in the design of software and languages, most recently in the development of the programming language Ada.

BIBLIOGRAPHY

Biographical

Campbell-Kelly, Martin, "Programming the Pilot ACE: Early Programming Activity at the National Physical Laboratory," *Ann. Hist. Comp.*, Vol. 3, No. 1, 1981, pp. 133–162.

STEPHAN (STEVE) WOZNIAK (WOZ)

Born August 11, 1950, San Jose, Calif.; loner/whiz kid who developed a personal computer in his garage and, with the assistance of Steve Jobs, founded the Apple Corporation.

Education: electrical engineering, University of Colorado, 1968–1969; electrical engineering, De Anza College, 1969–1970; electrical engineering, University of California at Berkeley, 1970.

Professional Experience: Hewlett-Packard Corp.; founder, Apple Computer Corp.

Woz built his first computer when he was 13 and took top prizes in a science fair. At 19 he met 14-year-old Steve Jobs and the two built an electronic "blue box" enabling them to make free phone calls by seizing phone-company lines. The two entrepreneurs sold 200 boxes to fellow students at $80 each. Working at Hewlett-Packard Corporation and a member of the Homebrew Computer Club at the same time as Steve Jobs, Woz's involvement resulted in the design of their first Apple microcomputer (later called a personal computer). In 1976, the Byte Shop in Mountain View ordered 50 copies and the home computer business industry was founded. The following year Woz designed the Apple II and the incredible growth of the Apple started. After a near-fatal plane crash in 1981, Wozniak, using a pseudonym, entered the University of California at Berkeley to earn a degree in computer science. He gained notoriety by producing two rock festivals that lost $25 million and made generous donations of his Apple stock to employees.

QUOTATIONS

"I'd rather be liked than rich."

"I was self-taught; I discovered manuals about mini-computers. It was an internal puzzle for me—I didn't get a grade for it. . . . I sat down with a piece of paper and started to draw—with only imagination to guide me. I drew designs of various mini-computers. . . . My best friend and I . . . dreamed of owning our own computers—in those days, a mini-computer (consisting of 4k memory) cost almost as much as a house. . . . [When] I set out to design my own, I discovered something very shocking: the various components, connected together directly, came out to half as many as other computers. Here was a computer that could do as much as any other, was just as good, but had half the number of parts. . . . This principle of elegant, simple lines became my guiding force." (The Commonwealth Club, February 27, 1987)

About Wozniak: "In many ways, Woz was . . . Apple's conscience. When the company was up and running, and it became evident that some early employees had been treated more fairly than others in the distribution of stock, it was Wozniak who played the peacemaker, selling cheaply 80,000 of his own Apple shares to employees who felt cheated and even to those who just wanted to make money at Woz's expense."

(Robert X. Cringely 1992)

BIBLIOGRAPHY

Biographical

Caddes, Carolyn, *Portraits of Success: Impressions of Silicon Valley Pioneers,* Tioga Publishing Co., Palo Alto, Calif., 1986.

Levy, Steven, *Hackers: Heroes of the Computer Revolution,* Anchor Press/Doubleday, Garden City, N.Y., 1984.

Cringely, Robert X., *Accidental Empires,* Williams Patrick/Addison-Wesley, Reading, Mass., 1992.

HIDEO YAMASHITA

Born May 21, 1899, Kanda, Tokyo; died May 25, 1993, Bunkyo-ku, Tokyo; one of Japan's earliest computing pioneers, and founder of the Information Processing Society of Japan.

Education: BS, electrical engineering, Tokyo Imperial University, 1923; DEng, Tokyo Imperial University, 1938.

Professional Experience: lecturer and associate professor, Tokyo Imperial University, 1924–1938; professor, Tokyo Imperial University, which later became the University of Tokyo, 1938–1960; professor, Tokyo University, 1960–1975; president of the Institute of Electron Microscope of Japan, 1954–1955; president of the Institute of Electrical Engineers of Japan, 1956–1957; founder of the Information Processing Society of Japan and its first president, 1960–1961.

Honors and Awards: Japan Academy Award; honorary member of the Information Processing Society of Japan, the Institute of Electrical Engineers of Japan, the Institute of Applied Physics of Japan, and the Institute of Electrical and Electronic Engineers; member of the Japan Academy.

Born in Kanda, Tokyo, on May 21, 1899, Yamashita graduated from Tokyo Imperial University (now the University of Tokyo) with a BS degree in electrical engineering in 1923. Immediately after the graduation, he was appointed as a lecturer of the faculty of electrical engineering of the university. He became an associate professor in 1924. Yamashita's specialty was electric machinery.

In February 1938, he received a doctor's degree in engineering from the university, and two months later became a professor there. Prior to this, Yamashita spent one and half years in Europe and the US, mostly at MIT. His research interest changed after this to calculating machines, spurred by the need for them at the Bureau of Statistics of the Japanese government.

IBM punched-card machines were used in Japan for statistical calculations, and the demand for them had been rapidly increasing before 1940 when the US government banned exportation of these machines to Japan as war material.

Yamashita and his colleagues, Katsuji Ono and Ryosaku Sato, conceived a calculating machine based upon binary logic, and launched its development with the use of electric relays in 1940. The shortage of parts and materials during the war hampered the development, and it was 1948 before they completed the machine using relays and counters released from military use.

The machine used 4,000 relays and 2,000 counters, had 20 sets of keyboards for data input, and a dual arithmetic unit for statistical calculations. Input was made simultaneously through both keyboards of each pair. For verification purposes, they had to accept identical input, and, if not, the input was discarded and had to be reentered. The arithmetic unit was shared by 20 sets of inputs, and added them up one by one. The dual results of each addition were compared with each other, and, if not identical, they were discarded and the addition was automatically repeated.

This machine was used by Chuohtoukei-sha, a not-for-profit organization located in an annex building of the Ministry of Finance, Kasumigaseki, Tokyo, for statistical calculation services, which was the first attempt to provide computation services in Japan. It was eight years before the first commercial computation service bureau using a relay computer was offered in Tokyo by Fujitsu Ltd.

NEC and Fujitsu, following Yamashita's design, produced one machine each in 1951. They were put into practical use at the Bureau of Statistics of the Japanese government and the Department of Statistics of the metropolitan government of Tokyo, respectively. Unfortunately, Yamashita did not give any particular name to the machines. Several machines built following his design were generally called "statistical machines of the Yamashita type."

Yamashita became involved in the international aspects of computing in 1951, when UNESCO developed a plan to install a large-scale computer to be shared by all the nations of the world. At that time, computers were extremely expensive, and the plan was thought to be worth putting forward to provide computing power for the less prosperous nations. UNESCO held an international meeting to reach a treaty for this purpose in Paris in November 1951. Japan was invited, although she was not quite independent, being still under occupation. The Japanese government appointed Tohru Hagiwara of the Foreign Office as its representative, and named Yamashita as his adviser.

The meeting agreed to establish an International Computation Centre in Rome. The treaty needed endorsements by at least 10 nations to be effective, and Japan was the first to endorse it. While awaiting other endorsements, UNESCO started the Center, qualified as "Provisional." Yamashita was appointed to represent Japan on the board of trustees of the PICC (Provisional International Computation Centre).

After the meeting in Paris in 1951, Yamashita visited the universities and laboratories working on computers in Europe and the US as the very first Japanese ever to have such an opportunity. The information he brought back to Japan and the news of PICC spurred interest in computers at the Academic Congress of Japan, which resulted in its launching the Tokyo Automatic Computer (TAC) Project at the University of Tokyo in 1952.

TAC, a vacuum tube computer, was finally completed in 1959. By then several digital electronic computers had already been developed in Japan.[1,2] While the TAC project was not regarded as a success, as the first attempt to develop an electronic digital computer in the country, it stimulated interest in computers and increased the number of computer scientists and engineers in Japan. Yamashita was involved in this project from its beginning through its completion.

Yamashita was also active in the managing committee for the first international conference on information processing sponsored by UNESCO and held in Paris in June 1959. This conference was first proposed by Isaac L. Auerbach of the US at one of the board meetings of the PICC.[3] UNESCO accepted this proposal and appointed Jean A. Mussard, secretary general of the PICC, to run the managing committee in which Yamashita participated, representing Japan.

The conference was a success. It was UNESCO's policy to only trigger something, and if it was found worth continuing, somebody else had to run it. Auerbach proposed to establish the International Federation of Information Processing (IFIP), an international society of societies, to hold international conferences. This proposal was accepted by 12 nations including Japan, which Yamashita represented, and the IFIP came into existence on January 1, 1960. It has been holding a congress every two to three years since 1959.

Yamashita had a problem, since Japan did not then have any appropriate national society to participate in the IFIP. In collaboration with Hiroshi Wada, then the head of the Electronics Division of the Electrotechnical Laboratory of the Japanese government (now professor emeritus of Seikei University), Yamashita founded the Information Processing Society of Japan in 1960, and was elected its first president.

Yamashita published many distinguished papers in the field of electric machinery in his early days. In the field of computing he published a very informative 20-page survey paper in 1954 (Yamashita 1954) based on his visits to various universities and laboratories in Europe and the US after the Paris meeting of 1951 for the ICC treaty. He was the editor-in-chief for *Handbook of Electronic Computers* pub-

---

[1]Takahashi, Sigeru, "Early Transistor Computers in Japan," *Ann. Hist. Comp.*, Vol. 8, No. 2, 1986, pp. 144–154.

[2]Takahasi, Hidetosi, "Some Important Computers of Japanese Design," *Ann. Hist. Comp.*, Vol. 2, No. 4, 1980, pp. 330–337.

[3]Auerbach, Isaac L., "The Start of IFIP—Personal Recollections," *Ann. Hist. Comp.*, Vol. 8, No. 2, 1986, pp. 180–192.

lished by Korona-sha in 1960 (Yamashita 1960). It should be also noted that he introduced into Europe the status of computing in Japan as early as 1956 and 1958 (Yamashita 1956, 1957).

After his retirement from the University of Tokyo in 1960, Yamashita taught at Toyo University until 1975. He was a professor emeritus of both the University of Tokyo and Toyo University, and an honorary member of the Information Processing Society of Japan, the Institute of Electrical Engineers of Japan, the Institute of Applied Physics of Japan, and the IEEE. He was also a member of the Japan Academy.[1]

BIBLIOGRAPHY

Biographical

Takahashi, Sigera, "Obituary: Hideo Yamashita," *Ann. Hist. Comp.*, Vol. 16, No. 1, 1994.

Takahashi, Sigera, "Hideo Yamashita," *Ann. Hist. Comp.*, Vol. 16, No. 2, 1994, p. 72.

Significant Publications

Yamashita, Hideo, "Electronic Digital Automatic Computers" (in Japanese), *Proc. Symp. Calculating Machines,* Institute of Electrical Engineers of Japan, Tokyo, 1954.

Yamashita, Hideo, "Present Status of Electronic Computers in Japan," *Proc. Rome Symp. International Computation Centre*, UNESCO, Paris, 1956.

Yamashita, Hideo, "Recent Development of Automatic Computers in Japan," *Proc. Int'l Conf. Computers and Automation*, UNESCO, Madrid, 1958.

Yamashita, Hideo, ed., *Handbook of Electronic Computers* (in Japanese), Korona-sha, Tokyo, Japan, 1960.

---

[1]Takahashi 1994.

HEINZ ZEMANEK

Born January 1, 1920, Vienna, Austria; Austrian computer scientist who developed the MAILUFTERL computer, and while director of the IBM Laboratory, Vienna, directed the development of formal programming language descriptors.

Education: Dipl. Ing., Technical University of Vienna, 1944; Dr. Techn., engineering, Technical University of Vienna, 1951.

Professional Experience: lecturer, Army Communications School and Radar Research, German Army, (1939)–1945; assistant professor, Technical University, Vienna, 1947–1961; French Government Scholarship, Sorbonne, Ecolé Normale Supérieure, PTT Laboratories, 1948–1949; Head, MAILUFTERL development team, 1955–1959; Dozent, Technical University of Vienna, 1959; Professor, Technical University of Vienna, 1964–present; Director, IBM Laboratory, Vienna, 1964–1976.

Honors and Awards: Prize of the NTG, 1960; Goldene Stefan-Ehrenmedaille of Öve, 1969; fellow, IEEE, 1970; fellow, British Computer Society, 1970; President, IFIP, 1971–1974; Wilhelm-Exner-Medaille, 1972; Honorary Life Member, Computer Society of South Africa, 1972; Grosses Ehrenzeichen für Verdienste um die Republic Österreich, 1974; President, Austrian Computer Society, 1975–1976; Honorary Member, Information Processing Society, Japan, 1975; Honorary Member, Austrian Society for Cybernetic Studies, 1975; IBM Fellow, 1976; Honorary Member, IFIP, 1976; Silvercore Award, IFIP, 1976; Johann Josef Ritter von Prechtl Medal, 1978; Corresponding Member, Austrian Academy of Sciences, 1979; Ordinary Member, Austrian Academy of Sciences, 1984; Corresponding Member, Spanish and Bavarian Academy, 1984; Ordinary Member, Spanish and Bavarian Academy, 1985; Ordinary Member, European Academy, Salzburg, 1984; Computer Pioneer, IEEE Computer Society, 1986; Oskar von Miller Bronze Medal, Deutsches Museum, Munich, 1988.

Zemanek was born in Vienna in 1920; he studied low-voltage technology at the Technical University of Vienna, and was appointed as an assistant at the Institute for Low-Voltage Technology where he received his PhD in engineering. In 1959 he was appointed as an assistant professor of low-frequency communications technology, as an associate professor in 1964, and 20 years later (1984) as a full professor. He is a member of various academies of science and has received an honorary doctorate from several universities.

Starting in 1954, he was responsible for the development of the first fully transistorized computer in Europe, the legendary "MAILUFTERL," which is now in the Technical Museum of Vienna.

He was the originator of both teaching and research in the area of electronic data processing at the Technical University of Vienna.

Along with the rest of the MAILUFTERL team, Zemanek moved to IBM in 1961 to become the developer and director of the Viennese laboratory, with primary work in the area of programming languages and their formal definition, especially the programming language PL/I. In 1976 he was awarded the title of IBM fellow and undertook a project entitled "Abstract Architecture."

During his career, Zemanek has published more than 400 articles, and authored, coauthored, or edited more than 15 books, ranging from highly specialized journal articles to introductory articles of general interest, philosophical treatises, critical commentaries on the social implications of computers, and historical studies (among others, a presentation of the history of computers in a text-and-picture collage in the Technical Museum of Vienna).

He has been active in both national and international professional circles, with considerable contributions to IFIP beginning in the year of its founding in 1959, where he represented Austria's interests. He was also responsible for the 1975 founding of the OCG (die Österreichische Computer Gesellschaft) (Austrian Computer Society). Zemanek served as president of both organizations and has been recognized by many high honors and awards. Since 1985 the OCG has awarded the Heinz Zemanek Prize to young (computer) scientists.

On January 11, 1990, the Austrian Computer Society, the Austrian Society for Electronics (der Öseterreichische Verband für Elecktrotechnik), and the Technical Museum of Vienna (das Technische Museum Wien) honored Heinz Zemanek, editor and frequent author of the *Annals of the History of Computing*, on the occasion of his 70th birthday. The celebration at the Technical Museum of Vienna was also the occasion to present the Heinz Zemanek Award to a young Austrian computer scientist.

BIBLIOGRAPHY

Biographical

Eier, R., "Heinz Zemanek und sein Wirken," *Elektrotechnik und Informationstechnik*, Zeitschift des österreichischen Verbandes für Elektrotechnik (Journal of the Austrian Society for Electrotechnology), Vienna, 1990, pp. 584–588.

Zemanek, H., "Central European Prehistory of Computing," in Metropolis, N., J. Howlett, and Gian-Carlo Rota, *A History of Computing in the Twentieth Century*, Academic Press, New York, 1980, pp. 587–609.

Zemanek, H., "Aus meinem Leben," *Elektrotechnik und Informationstechnik*, Zeitschift des österreichischen Verbandes für Elektrotechnik (Journal of the Austrian Society for Electrotechnology), Vienna, 1990, pp. 588–594.

Significant Publications

Zemanek, H., "Semiotics and Programming Languages," *Comm. ACM*, Vol. 9, No. 3, Mar. 1966, pp. 139–143.

KONRAD ZUSE

Born June 22, 1910, Berlin-Wilmersdorf; German inventor of prewar electro-mechanical binary computer designated Z1 which was destroyed without trace by wartime bombing; developed two more machines before the end of the war but was unable to convince the Nazi government to support his work; fled with the remains of Z4 to Zurich, which was successfully used at ETH; developer of a basic programming system known as "Plankalkül," with which he designed a chess-playing program.

Education: By 1927 Konrad Zuse had enrolled at the Technical University in Berlin-Charlottenburg and began his working career as a design engineer (Statiker) in the aircraft industry (Henschel Flugzeugwerke) and by 1935 he had completed a degree in civil engineering. He remained in Berlin from the time he finished his degree until the end of the war in 1945, and it was during this time that he constructed his first digital computers.

Honors and Awards: honorary professor, Georg-August-Universität, Göttingen, 1966; honorary degrees: Dr.-Ing.E.h., T.U. Berlin-Charlottenburg, 1956; Dr.rer.nat.h.c., Universität Hamburg, 1979; Dr.rer.nat.h.c, T.U. Dresden, 1981; Dr.techn.h.c., Universität Reykjavik University, Iceland, 1986; Dr.rer.nat.h.c., Dortmund, 1991; Dr.h.c.sc.techn., ETH Eidgenössische Technische Hochschule, Zurich, 1991; Dr.-Ing.E.h., Hochschule f. Architektur und Bauwesen, Weimar, 1991; dottore ad honorem in matematica, Siena University, Italy, 1992; Inländische Auszeichnungen/Ehrungen: Werner-von-Siemens-Ring, Stiftung Werner-von-Siemens-Ring, 1964; Dieselmedaille in Gold, DEV Deutscher Erfinder-Verband/Nürnberg, 1969; Grosses Verdienstkreuz des Verdienstordens der Bundesrepublik Deutschland, 1972, (mit Stern, 1985); Ehrenmitglied der Deutschen Akademie der Naturforscher LEOPOLDINA, Halle/Saale, 1972; Aachener und Münchener Preis, Carl-Arthur-Pastor- Stiftung, Kuratorium der

Aachener und Münchener Versicherungs AG, 1980; Ehrenplakette der Stadt Bad Hersfeld, 1980; Konrad-Zuse-Medaille, ZDB/Zentralverband des Deutschen Baugewerbes), 1981; Bernhard-Weiss-Plakette, VDMA/Verband Deutscher Maschinen- und Anlagenbau e.V., Düsseldorf, 1983; Bayerischer Maximiliansorden, Bayerischer Ministerpräsident, 1984; Goldener Ehrenring, Deutsches Museum/München, 1984; Cothenius-Medaille, LEOPOLDINA, Deutsche Akademie der Naturforscher, Halle/Saale, 1985; Ernst-Reuter-Plakette, Senat Berlin, 1985; VDE-Ehrenring, Verband Deutscher Elektrotechniker e.V., Düsseldorf, 1986; Philip-Morris-Ehrenpreis, Philip Morris GmbH/DABEI, 1987; Wilhelm-Leuschner-Medaille, Hessischer Ministerpräsident, 1987; Ehrenmitglied: Deutsche Akademie der Naturforscher LEOPOLDINA, Halle/Saale, 1972; Akademischer Verein Motiv, 1982; Verein des Schleswig-Holsteinisches Museums für Rechen- und Schreibtechnik e.V., Altzenholz, heute: MICOM, 1983; Gesellschaft für Informatik e.V., GI, 1985; Verein isländischer Ingenieure, Reykjavik/Island, 1986; Deutsches Museum, München, 1990; Vereinigung der Freunde und Förderer der Ingenieurschule an der Fachhochschule Schmalkalden e.V., 1992; Ehrenbüraerrecht: Ehrenbürgerrecht der Stadt Hünfeld, 1975; Namensqebunq: Konrad-Zuse-Strasse, in Bad Hersfeld/Hessen, 1972; Konrad-Zuse-Schule, in Hünfeld/Hessen, 1978; Konrad-Zuse-Medaille, ZDB Zentralverband des Deutschen Baugewerbes und GI/Gesellschaft f. Informatik e.V., 1981; Konrad-Zuse-Zentrum für Informationstechnik Berlin/ZIB, in Berlin, 1984; Konrad-Zuse-Zertifikat, Freundeskreis der Berufl. Schulen e.V./Bad Hersfeld, 1985; Zuse-Raum, Berufliche Schulen/Bad Hersfeld, 1985; Konrad-Zuse-Gesellschaft, Gründung am 6.9.88 in Hünfeld, 1988; Konrad-Zuse-Haus, Fa. PDS Programm + Software GmbH, Rotenburg/Wümme, 1989; Konrad-Zuse-Programm, Förderung v. Gastdozenten ausländischer Hochschullehrer—DAAD/Deutscher Akademischer Austauschdienst, Bonn, 1990; Konrad-Zuse-Zimmer, Schelztor-Gymnasium, Esslingen, 1991; Zusestrasse, in 0-Hoyerswerda, 1991.

From 1936 to 1938 Konrad Zuse developed and built the first binary digital computer in the world (Zl). A copy of this computer is on display in the Museum for Transport and Technology (Museum für Verkehr und Technik) in Berlin.

The first fully functional program-controlled electromechanical digital computer in the world (the Z3) was completed by Zuse in 1941, but was destroyed in 1944 during the war. Because of its historical importance, a copy was made in 1960 and put on display in the German Museum (Deutsches Museum) in Munich.

Next came the more sophisticated Z4, which was the only Zuse Z-machine to survive the war. The Z4 was almost complete when, due to continued air raids, it was moved from Berlin to Göttingen, where it was installed in the laboratory of the Aerodynamische Versuchanstalt (DVL/Experimental Aerodynamics Institute). It was only there for a few weeks before Göttingen was in danger of being captured and the machine was once again moved to a small village "Hinterstein" in the Allgäu/Bavaria. Finally it was taken to Switzerland where it was installed in the ETH (Federal Polytechnical Institute/Eidgenössisch Technische Hochschule) in Zurich in 1950. It was used in the Institute of Applied Mathematics at the ETH until 1955.

Education and Experience

By 1927 Konrad Zuse had enrolled at the Technical University in Berlin-Charlottenburg and began his working career as a design engineer (Statiker) in the aircraft industry (Henschel Flugzeugwerke), and by 1935 he had completed a degree in civil engineering. He remained in Berlin from the time he finished his degree until the end of the war in 1945, and it was during this time that he constructed his first digital computers.

My First Computer and First Thoughts About Data Processing[1]

I started in 1934, working independently and without knowledge of other developments going on around me. In fact, I hadn't even heard of Charles Babbage when I embarked on my work. At that time, the computing industry was limited to mechanical calculators using the decimal system. Punched-card devices were slightly further developed and able to deal with relatively complex operations for statistical and accounting purposes. However, these machines were almost entirely designed for commercial application. This meant that mathematicians and engineers had to develop computers on their own, working independently from one another. I was no exception.

At the beginning of the 1930s, while studying civil engineering in Berlin, I decided to develop and build bigger calculating machines, more suitable for engineering purposes. I approached the problem from various angles:

> *First, from a logical and mathematical point of view:*
> This involved
> 1. program control,
> 2. the binary system of numbers, and
> 3. floating point arithmetic.

Today, these concepts are taken for granted, but at the time this was new ground for the computing industry.

> *Second, from the design angle:*
> 1. allowing fully automatic arithmetical calculation,

---

[1] "Computer Design—Past, Present, Future," talk given by Prof. Konrad Zuse, in Lund/Sweden, Oct. 2, 1987, previously unpublished.

2. a high-capacity memory, and
3. modules or relays operating on the yes/no principle.

My research was initially aimed at pure number calculation, but soon led on (1935/1936) to new ideas about "computing" in general. Personally, I believe that was the birth of modern computer science. I recognized that computing could be seen as a general means of dealing with data and that all data could be represented through bit patterns, generally speaking.

That led to my basic hypothesis that:

data processing starts with the bit.

At that time, of course, I didn't talk of "bits," but of "yes/no status." On the basis of this hypothesis I defined "computing" as

the formation of new data from input
according to a given set of rules.

This basic theory meant that all computing operations could be carried out by relays operating according to the dual-status principle just mentioned. The most suitable devices available at the time were telephone relays.

Now a link with mathematical logic had been forged. As an engineer I had no idea of the existence of such a discipline. I developed a system of "conditional propositions" for relays—something that corresponded approximately to what is known as Boolean algebra today. My former mathematics teacher showed me that this sort of calculation was identical with the propositional calculus of mathematical logic.

From the engineering point of view, the gap between this and pure mathematical logic was bridged in order to simplify the design and programming of computing machines. At roughly the same time in England, the mathematician and logician Alan Turing was in the process of solving this problem from a different angle. He used a very simple computer as a model in order to place theoretical logic on a more formal basis. Turing's work was of major importance for the theory of computer science. However, his ideas had little influence on the practical development of computing machines.

The theories needed to be put into practice. First of all high-capacity memories had to be designed. At that time (1935) memory consisted of single registers operating a system of numbered wheels using the decimal system. Typical problems were the input and retrieval of information, as well as the choice of counters. Capacity was fairly restricted, although some punch-card machines were able to deal with up to 20 counters. These machines generally functioned on the basis that a number could be "added on."

But a new problem had to be overcome: pure memory was needed without the adding-on facility, but with high capacity and a special selection facility, as well as an elegant way of communicating with the periphery. I thought it was a good idea to base such a memory device on binary numbers from the outset. My idea was to divide the machine up into cells which would be able to hold data for a complete number, in other words, the operational sign, exponent and mantissa (where a floating point was being used), as well as additional specifications. Using the yes-no principle a "word"—as we would call it today—could be formed from a series of bits. The memory elements only needed to store yes-no values.

One device that could deal with this type of operation was the electromagnetic relay, which can adopt two positions, "open" or "closed." However, at the time I felt that the problem could be better solved mechanically. I played around with all sorts of levers, pins, steel plates, and so on, until I finally reached what was a very useful solution, for those days. My device consisted mainly of pins and steel plates, and in principle could be extended to 1,000 words. A proper machine using telephone relays would have needed 40,000 relays and filled a whole room.

The basic principle was that a small pin could be positioned right or left of a steel lug, thus memorizing the value 0 or 1. Input and retrieval were also effected via a steel-plate construction, and the individual parts could be stacked on top of one another in a system of layers. The address system also used binary code.[2] These machines had the advantage of being made almost entirely of steel, which made them suitable for mass production.

Individual memory elements could be easily arranged in matrix form, which was very useful as far as constructing computers was concerned. Not only was a number memory now available, but it could also be used to store general data drawn from practically any source. Logic studies conducted at the same time had already shown that general calculations with any sort of data structure were possible, and that this data could be made up entirely of bit combinations. That is why I had already called the storage system a "combination memory" in the patent application.

This was something new on the Babbage designs. It was clear that programs could be stored provided they were composed of bit combinations—one reason why programmable memory had already been patented by 1936.

---

[2]Further details can be found in Patent no. 907 948, Kl. 42 m, Group 15 / May 1936 entitled "Mechanical Relay"; and Patent no. 924 107, Kl. 42 m, Group 15 / May 1936 "Mechanical Relay Memory."

In the course of pursuing the basic principles of mechanical memory, I developed a mechanical relay technology. This I applied to both programming and calculating parts. At the time it was not clear whether all operations could be run according to the yes-no principle, or even whether that was a good idea. That was something that was only discovered later after much hard work. Initially I developed various adding machines for binary numbers, which used elements providing up to three or four positions. This was done using both electromagnetic and mechanical relays. Finally I found a solution which worked on the yes-no principle alone. By this time the similarities between essentially very different technologies were becoming increasingly obvious. I was faced with the choice of using either telephone relays or mechanical technology for my computing machine. As mechanical memory had proved successful (I was able to build a working model in six weeks), and because of the frightening number of relays needed in the alternative system (around 1,000), I decided in favor of the mechanical version, at first.

Inventors are often faced with that sort of decision. Today, I know that opting for relays immediately would have been better. However, working on a completely private basis, with just the help of some friends, I started to construct a mechanical model of the computer. At first I thought it would be possible to produce it quickly. In fact it took two years to set up a half-way functioning machine that I could present to the experts. Unfortunately the surviving photos are not very good and the machine itself proved somewhat unreliable. In fact, with the help of switching algebra, it proved easy to convert mechanical relay circuits for use in electromagnetic relay technology.

At this point I would like to mention my friend Helmut Schreyer, who was working on the development of electronic relays at that time. Helmut was a high-frequency engineer, and was completing his studies (around 1936) at Professor Stäblein's Institute at the Technical University in Berlin-Charlottenburg. Helmut, who was a close personal friend of mine, suddenly had the bright idea of using vacuum tubes. At first I thought it was one of his student pranks—he was always full of fun and given to fooling around. But after thinking about it we decided that his idea was definitely worth a try. Thanks to switching algebra, we had already married together mechanics and electromagnetics, two basically different types of technology. Why not then with tubes? They could switch a million times faster than elements burdened with mechanical and inductive inertia.

The possibilities were staggering. But first the basic circuits for the major logical operations such as conjunction, disjunction, and negation had to be discovered. Tubes could not simply be connected in line like relay contacts. We agreed that Helmut should develop the circuits for these elementary operations first, while I dealt with the logical part of the circuitry. Our aim was to set up elementary circuits so that relay technology could be transferred to the tube system on a one-to-one basis. This meant the tube machine would not have to be redesigned from scratch. Schreyer solved this problem fairly quickly.

This left the way open for further development. We cautiously told some friends about the possibilities. The reaction was anything from extremely skeptical to spontaneously enthusiastic. Interestingly enough, most criticism came from Schreyer's colleagues, who worked with tubes virtually all the time. They were doubtful that an apparatus with 2,000 tubes would work reliably. This critical attitude was the result of their own experience with large transmitters, which contained several hundred tubes. Apart from that, conditions were not exactly propitious for the development of a fully tube-operated machine. The war had broken out in the interim, making the procurement of staff and material very difficult. Nothing could be done by private initiative. We therefore proposed the construction of a 2,000-tube computer for special use in antiaircraft defense to the military authorities. Although the reaction was initially sympathetic towards the project, we were asked simply, "How much time do you think you need for it?" We replied, "Around two years." The response to this was, "And just how long do you think it'll take us to win the war?" The outcome was considerable obstruction and delay in the development of a German electronic computing machine. Schreyer was by now fully engaged in other projects. By the end of the war he had constructed a small experimental machine for 10 binary digits and around 100 tubes. But this machine was also lost in the general confusion just after the war.

After the war was finally over, news of the University of Pennsylvania ENIAC machine went all round the world—"18,000 tubes!" We could only shake our heads. What on earth were all the tubes for? Schreyer and I parted company after the war. At that time it was prohibited to develop electronic equipment in West Germany. As Schreyer saw no means of continuing his very interesting research, he emigrated to Brazil to take up a university chair. Schreyer died in 1985.

The English development known as COLOSSUS was unheard of outside the circle of those working on it. It was only much later that the wraps came off this very interesting project. In 1980 Schreyer and I had the opportunity to speak to the COLOSSUS people in England. We compared our circuits and it turned out that there were considerable similarities. The English had also been working on logical operations and other similar design principles.

By the end of 1938 it seemed clear that electromagnetic relays offered the best chance of producing a reliable operating computer quickly. Before I redesigned the Z1 to operate completely with relays, I made a test with a small pilot machine, the Z2. I used the mechanical memory of the Z1 with a low storage capacity (16 words), as well as the card punch and reader to build a simple computer with 200 relays operating with 16 bits and on the basis of fixed-point arithmetic.

Young transmitter specialists, including Schreyer and other friends of mine, helped me design the circuits and choose the appropriate components. But although their advice was a great help, to a certain extent I expressly set out to explore new ground. The most important thing seemed to be to keep the frequency absolutely even, so that one cycle equaled one addition, itself comprising several steps. Frequency was set using rotating disks or rollers, which were covered in alternating strips of conducting and nonconducting material, contact being made via carbon brushes. This principle had many advantages. Tests could be run on the machine at any speed. Another advantage was that spark extinction took place at the brushes and not at the relay contacts when circuits were being shut down. Despite well-meaning advice from some friends, I did not make use of certain well-known telephone communication tricks such as delayed-response relays.

All in all, I was able to gather enough experience with the Z2 in order to convert the complete Z1 design for relay operation. What emerged was the Z3, which I consider to have been the first properly functioning computer in the world. In order to make fast progress the memory was also given a 64-word capacity, making use of relays.

The Z3's basic specifications were:

- a binary number system
- floating point arithmetic
- 22-bit word length, with 1 bit for the sign, 7 exponential bits, and a 14-bit mantissa
- 2,400 relays, 600 in the calculating and program section and 1,800 in the memory.

The calculations possible were addition, subtraction, multiplication, and division, taking the square root, as well as some ancillary functions. Construction of the machine was interrupted in 1939 when I was called up for military service. It was typical of the attitude prevalent in Germany at the time that I should be later released from active service, not to develop computers, but as an aircraft engineer. However, in my spare time, and with the help of friends, I was able to complete the machine. By 1941 it was working and I was able to show it to the aircraft construction authorities. The German Aircraft Research Institute in Berlin-Adlershof showed the greatest interest. Professor Teichmann, who had been working on the problem of wing flutter, was particularly attracted. Unlike aircraft stress, wing flutter results in critical instability due to vibration of the wings, sometimes in conjunction with the tail unit. Complex calculations were needed in order to overcome this design problem. The most difficult part was calculating the so-called "Küssner determinants" based on complex numbers and unknown quantities in the main diagonal. I achieved a breakthrough, using my equipment for this calculation. Unfortunately the Aircraft Research Institute had not been given a high enough priority for me to be released from military service. Only Professor Herbert Wagner, who was working on the development of remote-controlled flying bombs, and for whom I worked as a stress analyst, was in this enviable position. However, Wagner was very understanding, and helped as much as possible by allowing me to use some of my work time on the project. By then I had already set up my own small engineering business, the "Zuse-Ingenieur-Büro," in Berlin. The Z3 was later destroyed after bombing raids. Because of its historic importance we rebuilt it 20 years later; a replica now stands in the Deutsches Museum in Munich.

Around 1942 it was decided to build a more powerful, improved Z4. We thought that we would be able to have it ready within one to one and a half years. It was to have a mechanical memory with a capacity of 1,024 words, several card readers and punches, and various facilities to enable flexible programming (address translation, conditional branching).

Construction of the machine started well but it was not long before the war imposed its delays. In the end, construction was not completed until the close of the war. Procurement of staff and materials became increasingly difficult, and around 1943 the Berlin blitz began, with heavy bombing raids nearly every day. Several times we had to move the location of the machine. During the last few weeks of the war we found refuge in Göttingen. The Z4 was the only model we were able to save, and this in the face of considerable difficulties. On the 28 April 1945 we were able to demonstrate the Z4 to Professors Prandtl, Betz, and Küssner. But the Western and Eastern fronts were drawing closer daily and nobody could say whether Göttingen would be bombed or not, or whether the Z4 was safe there. The Ministry of Aviation ordered us to take the machine to the underground works in the Harz. It was there that we first learned of the terrible conditions under which the so-called reprisal weapons—the V1 and V2—were being built. We refused to leave the machine there and, with the help of Wernher von Braun's staff, we managed to get hold of a truck to transport it elsewhere. And so the Z4 odyssey continued. We then moved south, ending up in a small Alpine village called Hinterstein in the Allgäu, where we were finally able to find a good place to store the machine.

Around 1950, after a number of modifications, the machine was set up in the Technical University of Switzerland in Zurich, where it remained for several years, the only working computer in Continental Europe. Today it is a historic model and can be seen in the Deutsches Museum in Munich. Unfortunately it's no longer in full working order.

Another offshoot of computer research ought to be mentioned here, too. By that I mean process control. At the Henschel Aircraft Factory Professor Herbert Wagner, for whom I worked as a stress analyst, was involved in developing remote-controlled bombs. To this end, the tailplane and wings, which were constructed of metal with a relatively low degree of precision, were subjected to detailed measurements, using gauges at some 80 different points. The necessary adjustments were then calculated to allow for manufacturing inaccuracies. This required a rather complex calculation. Initially I constructed a special-purpose computer for a fixed sequence of operations using around 500 relays. This machine replaced a dozen calculators and worked very reliably for two years, two shifts a day. The procedure required a mechanic to read off the gauges. The values were then recorded and operators entered the figures into the computer. This led me to build an improved model, which could read the gauges automatically and transfer data directly into the computer. The heart of the machine was a device that today would be called an analog/digital transformer. Perhaps this was the first process control system in the world.

The machine itself had its own history. It completed trial tests on a production line in Sudetenland, but never reached full operational use as the war forced the whole factory to be relocated. The exact fate of the machine is unknown—it's possible the factory fell into the hands of the Russians, who must have been the only ones at the time to own a fully-operational computer. The Z3 had already been destroyed, the Z4 was not completed, and the first US machines, Mark I and ENIAC, were not operational at that time. However, it is unlikely that the Russians would have known what to do with the machine even if they had found it in an undamaged condition.

Alongside my practical work with various computer models I started to consider certain theoretical aspects. The breakthrough to a new computing age went hand in hand with new scientific ideas and the development of new components. Today we talk about hardware and software. These expressions were really only introduced much later by the Americans, although the terms have now become established. It was apparent that a special branch of "computer science" was needed. But shortage of time meant that I could only scratch the surface in this field. Initially I worked on my own, but towards the end of the war Herr Lohmeyer, an outstanding mathematician, was assigned to assist me. Lohmeyer was a product of Heinrich Scholz's school in Münster, the latter himself a famous logician. The link with mathematical logic had already been established. As a civil engineer I was attracted by the prospect of drawing on predicate and relational calculus and exploring the possibilities they offered as a basis for computing. Take the frameworks used in building construction for example—were they not similar to the graphs used in relational calculus? Using pair lists, it was relatively easy to digitalize the structure of a framework with the aid of relational calculus, in other words, to break it down into its component data. This could then be entered into the combination memory, which had been invented by this time, and serve as a basis for combination calculations. This ought to mean that not only purely numerical calculations could be dealt with, but construction design itself. Up till now only the human mind had been capable of this. The same idea applied to frameworks and other types of building design. I became extremely preoccupied with this new aspect of computing. I even went as far as learning to play chess in order to try to formulate the rules of the game in terms of logical calculus. Chess offered a mass of data structures within a limited space. A symbolic language (the expression "algorithmic language" was unknown to me at the time) that could describe chess problems seemed to me to be suitable for all computer machine problems. Plankalkül was later (1945) devised with this principle in mind.

This led to my first confrontation with what is known today as "artificial intelligence." Naturally I realized my computer would never be able to run that sort of calculation. But combination memory and the general circuitry were a step in the right direction. Many developments were predictable; of course, others were still in the realm of fantasy. I remember mentioning to friends back in 1938 that the world chess champion would be beaten by a computer in 50 years time. Today we know computers are not far from this goal.

But even in those days quite a lot was achieved at the drawing board. A diary extract from 1938 describes various principles of program control (starting with Babbage and the Z1 to the storage of numerical values, general data, and programs, all in the same memory). Today we call this computer architecture. The latter type of machine is known as the John von Neumann computer, after its namesake, who first produced it 10 years later together with Goldstine and Burks. We now know this was a very elegant solution.

The question is why I did not use this concept in 1939 if I already knew about it. Well, at that time it would have been senseless to try to build that sort of machine, as the necessary facilities were simply not available. For example, storage capacity was not big enough to cope; an efficient program memory needs to be able to store several thousand words. Speed was also too low. It's true that floating-point arithmetic can be performed by simply following a series of single instructions (as is the case today). But that means giving 10 to 20 times as many instructions. As long as the electronic prerequisites were not available, it was a waste of time. Two things were needed first: high storage capacity (around 8,000 words), as in the first magnetic-drum memories, and electronic speed. Towards the end of the 1940s this seemed possible, but as Germans we were not able to participate in this development at the time.

The possibility of a computer being able to deal with numeric calculations and logic organization was so exciting that I gave serious thought to a "logical computing machine." This led to the "program compiling machine" project. Work was to be split between numerical and logic computers. That included such areas as:

- construction of extensive programs made up of subprograms according to specific parameters
- address translation necessary for these programs
- capability of dealing with engineering structures (e.g., frameworks) using pair lists from which a numerical program could be developed.

This project was commissioned towards the end of the war by the Ministry of Aviation. However, the work soon proved to be too broadly based and the ideas never left the drawing board. Since then, the concept of dividing computers according to numerical or logical operation has failed to find favor anywhere. The dominance of electronics made this unnecessary. The high speeds obtainable meant that such operations could be carried out by a single machine. However, one aspect became clear to me in view of all this research between 1936 and 1946. Some means was necessary by which the relationships involved in calculation operations could be precisely formulated. My answer was "Plankalkül"—today it would be termed an "algorithmic" language. However, in those days, known mathematical and logical forms were not advanced enough. There were also several other differences compared with today's languages:

1. Plankalkül was not conceived as a means of programming the Z4 or other computers available at the time. Its true purpose was to assist in establishing consistent laws of circuitry, that is, for floating-point arithmetic, as well as in planning the sequence of instructions a computer would follow—what we would term "hardware" and "software" today.

2. It was meant to cover the whole spectrum of general calculating.

By contrast, the program languages developed around 10 years later were relatively one-sided. They were designed specifically for existing computing machines, in other words, for the first really flexible electronic computers. In the first instance, these languages were concerned with conditional branching, address translation, and suchlike. There was hardly any demand for logical operations, such as the application of predicate and relational calculus for engineering constructions, chess programs, and so on. That also applied to the breakdown of data into yes-no combinations. In other words, mathematicians did not consider my principle of "data processing starting with the bit" to be of any fundamental importance. Plankalkül's weakness was that it went into too much depth with regard to difficult calculations, which seemed better left to the future. The importance of my chess program, as an example of applied logic, was simply ignored. In addition to this, in the early 1950s, I was completely absorbed in building up my business at a time when program languages started to become more relevant. This meant I could not participate in the debate on Algol and so on. Plankalkül was later published out of historical interest (in English, too, although it is now unfortunately out of print).

As has already been mentioned, 1945 was a hard time for the Germans. Our Z4 had been transported with incredible difficulty to the small Alpine village of Hinterstein in the Allgäu. My group and my Berlin firm had been dissolved. All of us who had managed to get out of Berlin were happy just to have survived the inferno there. Work on Plankalkül now continued in the wonderful countryside, undisturbed by bomber attacks, telephone calls, visitors, and so on. Within about a year we were able to set up a "revamped" Z4 in full working order in what had once been a stable. Unlike research going on in the US, where every possible facility was available, our means were very limited.

There was no body or organization able to support our work at that time in Germany. Nevertheless, word got out abroad that some sort of machine was operating in South Bavaria. IBM/USA instructed the German firm Hollerith GmbH to see what this was all about. All sorts of promising discussions ensued about possible applications for computers in various areas. But as everything was decided on the other side of the Atlantic at the time, no contract was signed. Interest was only shown in the industrial property rights. It wasn't even possible to secure a promise that I would be able to continue work on development. At that time computers were simply not that important.

However, we did have more success with Remington-Rand, who commissioned us to continue development, initially in a special project dealing with mechanical relay technology. People didn't trust electronics fully at the time and wanted to have a second option. We ourselves were convinced that the future lay with electromagnetics and electronics. This meant working against our own convictions. Nevertheless the machine was interesting, as it became the first pipeline computer in the world—a punched-card machine with a series of mechanical adding devices using mechanical circuits incorporated between the card reader and the card punch. Multiplication was carried out by a series of adding operations. This resulted in a reasonable degree of accuracy despite the relatively slow mechanics. But the development of electronic alternatives was progressing; it was soon not worthwhile continuing with mechanical designs.

However, we were able to produce an interim solution based on our relays prior to the introduction of pure electronic machines, prototypes of which were being prepared by Remington-Rand in the US. The production run consisted of around 40 additional units for punched card machines, most of which were exported to Switzerland. About the same time, we had been able to set up the Z4 as a scientific machine in the Technical University in Zurich. Both contracts helped us reestablish the ZUSE KG company, which I founded near Bad Hersfeld in 1949 with two other partners.

The German market slowly began to develop and we started to receive orders from German companies. One of our first clients was Leitz, which, thanks to the world-famous "Leica Camera," had the necessary financial means to purchase a computer for optics calculations. Later other optics firms followed suit, so that by the mid-1950s we had a virtual monopoly in the field of scientific computers in the optics industry in central Europe.

By that time everyone was talking about electronic machines, but their reliability still left a lot to be desired. The first were built by scientific institutes for their own special purposes, as the commercially available machines were not good enough. We were able to bridge this gap with our relay computers. One thing in our favor was land consolidation, which was in full swing in Germany at the time. Computers were needed to calculate how fields and land were to be reallocated. To this end we developed the Z11, which was later further refined and used elsewhere in urban and agricultural surveying, optics, and so forth. This machine corresponded to what the users wanted—namely, to always know how the calculation was progressing, and to have everything under complete control. In the course of time full automation led to a maze of branches and impenetrable procedures, and software became an increasingly urgent problem. We also experienced and influenced this (not always happy) development with our machines.

After some years, electronic components achieved a degree of reliability that warranted their production in large numbers. Initially we developed a tube model, the Z22, moving later to the transistorized versions Z23, Z31, and Z25. These were based on analytical code, which meant they were extremely flexible as far as programming was concerned. These were the first types of machine where general calculation using any desired data structure and program storage could be carried out. The machines were very popular with scientists and engineers, as they were excellent to play around with, and all sorts of models for the most diverse problems could be tried out. Sadly, in most cases our machines could only serve to whet people's appetites. While our clients were very short of financial means during the early years of the electronic computer, research departments were later much better funded, allowing them to purchase much bigger, more expensive equipment. Unfortunately, my firm hardly profited from this, as we were oriented towards small and medium-sized companies. Nor did we have enough capital to take part in the development of larger machines. Our Z11, Z22, and Z23 are now sought after only as collector's pieces for museums and so on.

One development, which received much impetus from specialists working in the surveying field, was the automatic drafting board. The aim was the automatic representation of various maps which had been calculated beforehand by computer. It is interesting to note that the surveyors were looking for a very high degree of accuracy and initially only wanted to plot polygon-vertices. From this emerged the Graphomat, the first computer-controlled automatic drawing board. Many others were interested, too. These were our first tentative steps in the direction of CAD (computer-aided design). Little is known about this side of our work. Here, too, we found out that it is not always a good idea to be the early bird. As early as 1964 I was involved in negotiations with a major European carpet manufacturer to build a computerized control system for a large weaving machine. I proposed that we start at the design stage of the carpet pattern. The intention was not to make the artisan redundant, but simply to give him a new tool. But this suggestion met with complete opposition from all parties concerned, and the contract failed to come off.

Competition in the computer sector became increasingly tough. Not only were the costs of hardware constantly rising, software development costs were also growing. My company with its thousand-odd employees faced growing capital shortages, making it necessary to bring in new shareholders. This led, step by step, to the company being completely taken over by Siemens.

Today, this leaves me free to devote more time to purely scientific problems, and I still work on a free-lance basis for Siemens AG, Munich. I am currently involved in computer architecture, and am particularly interested in the parallel operation of machines. Back in the 1950s I designed a machine for the meteorological office that today would be termed a "cellular computer." Here, too, however, I was guilty of trying to run before I could walk.

Let me review a few of the ideas I have examined on paper without ever being able to turn them into reality.

"The Computing Universe" is based on the idea that the whole cosmos is a kind of cellular computer, something that some physicists are seriously considering today. This theory has yet to be confirmed, due to the lack of experimental evidence. A paper on the subject under the same title has also appeared in English.[3] I am sure the idea will gain considerable significance in the future and might help theoretical physics to solve a number of problems.

Another idea of mine was "The Self-Reproducing System." I approached this concept differently from John von Neumann, who dealt with it using pure mathematics in the context of cellular computers. As an engineer I was more interested in setting up the conditions necessary for actual construction. In essence, the idea envisages a tool factory which is capable of reproducing its own essential component parts. This idea has met with complete opposition. People have been reluctant to consider such a radical solution for all sorts of reasons. Today traditional means of production are being automated step by step. We have yet to build the factory of the future. But one day these farsighted developments will become reality, leading to a complete revolution in the production process throughout the economy.

QUOTATION

"Of one thing I am sure—computer development has still a long way to go. Young people have got plenty of work ahead of them yet!"

---

[3] *International Journal of Theoretical Physics*, 21st ed., Nos. 6–7, June 1982, p. 589.

BIBLIOGRAPHY

Biographical

Bauer, Friedrich L., "Between Zuse and Rutishauser—The Early Development of Digital Computing in Central Europe," in Metropolis, N., J. Howlett, and Gian-Carlo Rota, *A History of Computing in the Twentieth Century*, Academic Press, New York, 1980, pp. 505–524.

Ceruzzi, Paul E., "The Early Computers of Konrad Zuse, 1935 to 1945," *Ann. Hist. Comp.*, Vol. 3, No. 3, 1981, pp. 241–262.

Czauderna, Karl-Heinz, "Konrad Zuse, der Weg zu seinem Computer Z3" (Konrad Zuse, the Path to His Z3 Computer), Report 120, *Gesellschaft für Mathematik und Datenverarbeitung*, R. Oldenbourg, Munich, 1979.

Ritchie, David, *The Computer Pioneers*, Simon and Schuster, New York, 1986.

Schwartz, H.R., "The Early Years of Computing in Switzerland," *Ann. Hist. Comp.*, Vol. 3, No. 1, 1981, pp. 121–132.

Slater, Robert, *Portraits in Silicon*, MIT Press, Cambridge, Mass., 1987.

Speiser, A.P., "The Relay Computer Z4," *Ann. Hist. Comp.*, Vol. 2, No. 3, 1980, pp. 242–245.

Zemanek, Heinz, "Zuse, Konrad," in Ralston, Anthony, and Edwin D. Reilly, Jr., *Encyclopedia of Computer Science and Engineering*, Van Nostrand Reinhold Co., New York, 1983.

Zuse, Konrad, *Der Computer—Mein Lebenswerk*, Verlag Moderne Industrie, Munich, 1970.

Zuse, Konrad, "Some Remarks on the History of Computing in Germany," in Metropolis, N., J. Howlett, and Gian-Carlo Rota, *A History of Computing in the Twentieth Century*, Academic Press, New York, 1980, pp. 611–627.

Zuse, Konrad, "Installation of the German Computer Z4 in Zurich in 1950," *Ann. Hist. Comp.*, Vol. 2, No. 3, 1980, pp. 239–241.

VLADMIR ZWORYKIN

Born July 30, 1989, Mourom, Russia; RCA inventor of the iconoscope, the first really practical television image pickup tube.

Education: EE, Institute of Technology, Petrograd, Russia, 1912; PhD, physics, University of Pittsburgh, 1926.

Professional Experience: research engineer, Westinghouse Electrical and Manufacturing Corp., 1920–1929; director, Electronic Research, RCA Manufacturing Corp., 1929–1940; RCA Corp.: associate research director, RCA Laboratories, 1942–1945, director, electronic research, 1946–1954, vice president and technical consultant, 1947–1954, consultant, 1954–1978, honorary vice president, 1954.

Honors and Awards: Liebmann Prize, 1934; DSc (Hon.), Polytechnic Institute of Brooklyn, 1938; Overseas Award, (British) Institute of Electrical Engineers, 1939; Faraday Medal, 1965; Modern Pioneer Award, National Manufacturers Association, 1940; Rumford Medal, American Academy of Arts and Sciences, 1941; Certificate of Appreciation, US War Department, 1945; Potts Medal, Franklin Institute, 1947; Certificate of Commendation, US Department of the Navy, 1947; Chevalier Cross, Legion of Honour, France, 1948; Gold Medal of Achievement, Poor Richard Club, 1949; Lamme Award, IEEE, 1948; Progress Medal, Society of Motion Picture and Television Engineers, 1950; Medal of Honor, IEEE, 1951; Edison Medal, IEEE, 1952; Gold Medal, French Union of Inventors, 1954; Cristoforo Columbo Medal, Italian Government, 1959; Order of Merit, Italian Government, 1950; Trasenter Medal, University of Liege, 1959; Broadcast Pioneers Award, 1963; DSc (Hon.), Rutgers University, 1972; member, National Academy of Sciences; member, National Inventors Hall of Fame.

APPENDIX

Collections of Biographies and Memoirs

Anon., *Leaders in American Science,* Who's Who in American Education, Inc., Nashville, Tenn., 8 Vols., 1953–1969.

Anon., "Thanks for the Memories," *Datamation,* Vol. 28, No. 10, Sept. 1982, pp. 27–52.

Anon., *Who's Who in Computers and Data Processing 1971,* Quadrangle Books, New York, 5th ed., 1971.

Applied Computer Research, *Directory of Top Computer Executives,* Applied Computer Research, Phoenix, Ariz., 1983.

Azimov, Isaac, and Karen A. Frenkel, *Robots: Machines in Man's Image,* Harmony Books, New York, 1985.

Berkeley, Edmund C., *Who's Who in the Computer Field,* Berkeley Enterprises, Newtonville, Mass., 1963.

Caddes, Carolyn, *Portraits of Success: Impressions of Silicon Valley Pioneers,* Tioga Publishing Co., Palo Alto, Calif., 1986.

Cortada, James W., *Historical Dictionary of Data Processing: Biographies,* Greenwood Press, Westport, Conn., 1987.

Cringely, Robert X., *Accidental Empires,* Williams Patrick/Addison Wesley, Reading, Mass., 1992.

Debus, Allen G., *World Who's Who in Science,* Marquis-Who's Who, Inc., Chicago, 1968.

Levering, Robert, Michael Katz, and Milton Moskowitz, *Computer Entrepreneurs: Who's Making It Big and How in America's Upstart Industry,* New American Library, New York, 1984.

Levy, Steven, *Hackers: Heroes of the Computer Revolution,* Anchor Press/Doubleday, Garden City, N.Y., 1984.

Ralston, Anthony, and Edwin D. Reilly, Jr., *Encyclopedia of Computer Science and Engineering,* Van Nostrand Reinhold Co., New York, 1983.

Richie, David, *The Computer Pioneers,* Simon and Schuster, New York, 1986.

Rosenberg, Jerry M., *The Computer Prophets,* MacMillan Co., London, 1969.

Slater, Robert, *Portraits in Silicon,* MIT Press, Cambridge, Mass., 1987.

Tropp, Henry S., "The Effervescent Years: A Retrospective," *IEEE Spectrum,* Vol. 11, No. 2, 1974, pp. 70–79.

Zientara, Marguerite, et al., *The History of Computing: A Biographical Portrait of the Visionaries Who Shaped the Destiny of the Computer Industry,* CW Communications, Framingham, Mass., 1981.

BIOGRAPHIES IN:

Cortada, James W., *Historical Dictionary of Data Processing: Biographies,* Greenwood Press, Westport, Conn., 1987.

Ramon Lull (1235–1315)
John Napier (1550–1617)
Henry Briggs (1561–1630)
Wilhelm Schickard (1592–1635)
Rene Grillet (1600s)
Gaspard Schott (1608–1666)
Blaise Pascal (1623–1666)
Samuel Morland (1625–1695)
Gottfried Wilhelm von Leibniz (1646–1716)
Pierre Jacquet-Droz (1700s)
Wolfgang von Kempelen (1734–1804)
Joseph-Marie Jacquard (1752–1834)
Baron Jean-Baptiste–Joseph Fourier (1768–1830)
Pehr Georg Scheutz (1785–1873)
Charles Babbage (1791–1871)
George Boole (1815–1864)
Countess of Lovelace, Augusta Ada (1816–1852)
Martin Wiberg (1826–1905)
William Stanley Jevons (1835–1882)
Henry Adams (1838–1918)
Ramön Verea (1838–1899)
John Shaw Billings (1839–1913)
John Henry Patterson (1844–1922)
John K. Gore (1845–1910)
Willgodt Theophil Odhner (1845–1905)
Joseph Boyer (1848–1905)
George Barnard Grant (1849–1917)

Charles Ranlett Flint (1850–1934)
Emst Georg Fischer (1852–1935)
Leonardo Torres y Quevcdo (1852–1936)
Allan Marquand (1853–1924)
George Winthrop Fairchild (1854–1924)
William Seward Burroughs (1855–1898)
Lyman Frank Baum (1856–1919)
Alfred Blake Dick (1856–1934)
Carl George Lange Barth (1860–1939)
Herman Hollerith (1860–1929)
Vilhelm Bjerknes (1862–1951)
Maurice d'Ocagne (1862–1938)
Dorr Eugene Felt (1862–1930)
Annibale Pastore (1868–1936)
Leon Bollee (1870–1913)
Edward Andrew Deeds (1874–1960)
Thomas John Watson (1874–1956)
James Wares Bryce (1880–1949)
Percy E. Ludgate (1883–1922)
Clark Hull (1884–1952)
James Henry Rand (1886–1968)
Theodore Henry Brown (1888–1973)
Clair D. Lake (1888–1958)
Vannevar Bush (1890–1974)
William Frederick Friedman (1891–1969)
Leslie John Comrie (1893–1950)
Alfred Blake Dick, Jr. (1894–1954)
Norhert Wiener (1894–1964)
Leslie Richard Groves (1896–1970)
Douglas Rayner Hartree (1897–1958)
Ernest Galen Andrews (1898–1980)
Boris Artybasheff (1899–1965)
Howard Hathaway Aiken (1900–1973)
Donald Alexander Flanders (1900–1958)
Harold Locke Hazen (1901–1980)
Alfred Tarski (1901–1983)
Wallace John Eckert (1902–1971)
Mina Spiegel Rees (1902–)
John Vincent Atanasoff (1903–)
John von Neumann (1903–1957)
John Grist Brainerd (1904–1988)
Alston Scott Househoulder (1904–)

Derrick Henry Lehmer (1905–1991)
Grace Brewster Murray Hopper (1906–1992)
Reynold B. Johnson (1906–)
Gordon S. Brown (1907–)
John William Mauchly (1907–1980)
Antonin Svoboda (1907–1980)
James Franklin Forster (1908–1972)
John Hamilton Curtiss (1909–1977)
William Bradford Shockley (1910–)
Konrad Zuse (1910–)
Richard Goodman (1911–1966)
Cuthbert C. Hurd (1911–)
John Aleksander Rajchman (1911–1989)
Louis "Moll" Nicot Ridenour, Jr. (1911–1959)
Frederic Calland Williams (1911–1977)
David Packard (1912–)
Alan Mathison Turing (1912–1954)
Julian Bigelow (1913–)
Herman Heine Goldstine (1913–)
Simon Ramo (1913–)
Maurice Vincent Wilkes (1913–)
Dean Everett Wooldridge (1913–)
George Bernard Dantzig (1914–)
Walter W. Jacobs (1914–1982)
George Robert Stibitz (1914–)
Thomas John Watson, Jr. (1914–)
Arthur Walter Burks (1915–)
Borje Langefors (1915–)
Nicholas C. Metropolis (1915–)
Harry Douglas Huskey (1916–)
Claude Elwood Shannon (1916–)
Herbert Alexander Simon (1916–)
Christopher Strachey (1916–1975)
Jule Gregory Charney (1917–1981)
Dov Chevion (1917–1983)
Frank August Engel, Jr. (1917–)
Robert Mano Fano (1917–)
Ralph Ernest Meagher (1917–)
Andrew Donald Booth (1918–)
Jay Wright Forrester (1918–)
John R. Pasta (1918–1981)
John Presper Eckert, Jr. (1919–)

Niels Ivar Bech (1920–1975)
Robert William Bemer (1920–)
Frank Taylor Cary (1920–)
An Wang (1920–1990)
Willis Howard Ware (1920–)
Heinz Zemanek (1920–)
Isaac Levin Auerbach (1921–1992)
Robert Rivers Everett (1921–)
Gene Myron Amdahl (1922–)
Alan J. Perlis (1922–1990)
Saul Rosen (1922–1991)
J. Cliff Shaw (1922–1991)
John Weber Carr (1923–)
Victor Mikhaylovich Glushkov (1923–1982)
Jack St. Clair Kilby (1923–)
Herman Lukoff (1923–1979)
Joseph Weizenbaum (1923–)
John Backus (1924–)
Julien Green (1924–)
John R. Opel (1925–)
William Michael Blumenthal (1926–)
Fernando Jose Corbató (1926–)
John Diebold (1926–)
Stanley Gill (1926–1975)
Kristen Nygaard (1926–)
Kenneth Harry Olsen (1926–)
Richard Utman (1926–)
William Louis Van Den Poel (1926–)
Robert (Bob) Overton Evans (1927–)
Charles Katz (1927–)
John McCarthy (1927–)
Marvin Lee Minsky (1927–)
Allen Newell (1927–1992)
Robert Norton Noyce (1927–)
David John Wheeler (1927–)
Bernard Aaron Galler (1928–)
Peter Naur (1928–)
Jean E. Sammet (1928–)
Gordon E. Moore (1929–)
Emerson W. Pugh (1929–)
Frederick Phillips Brooks, Jr. (1931–)
Ole-Johan Dahl (1931–)

Andrei Petrovich Ershov (1931–1988)
Arie Van Wijngaarden (1933–1987)
Chester Gordon Bell (1934–)
Ralph E. Griswold (1934–)
Brian Randell (1936–)
Philip Don Estridge (1938–1985)
Donald Ervin Knuth (1938–)
Adam Osborne (1939–)
Gary A. Kildall (1942–1994)
Stephen Gary Wozniak (1950–)
William H. Gates (1955–)
Steven Paul Jobs (1955–)

Evans, Christopher, *Pioneers in Computing (audiocassettes)*, Science Museum, London, 1970.[1]

Donald W. Davies

J. Presper Eckert, Jr.

Tom Kilburn

F.C. Williams

Andrew D. Booth

Arthur W. Burks

Harry D. Huskey

M.H.A. Newman

Allen W.M. Coombs

Grace Murray Hopper

Herman H. Goldstine

Donald Michie

Gordon S. Brown

Harold L. Hazen

Michael Woodger

Konrad Zuse

Jay W. Forrester

J. Pinkerton

John W. Mauchly

James H. Wilkinson

Stanley M. Ulam

Ralph J. Slutz

Thomas H. Flowers

Cuthbert C. Hurd

Andrew Porter

I. J. Good

George R. Stibitz

John V. Atanasoff

Maurice V. Wilkes

Helmut Schreyer

Ralston, Anthony, and Edwin D. Reilly, Jr., eds., *Encyclopedia of Computer Science and Engineering,* Van Nostrand Reinhold Co., New York, 1983.

Ada (Augusta Ada King [née Byron] Countess of Lovelace)
Howard Aiken
John Vincent Atanasoff
Charles Babbage

---

[1]For a survey of contents, see Tropp, H.S., "Pioneers of Computing," *Ann. Hist. Comp.*, Vol. 3, No. 4, 1981, pp. 417–20. These interviews are biographical, but not complete by any means.

George Boole
J. Presper Eckert
Wallace Eckert
Herman Hollerith
Grace Murray Hopper
Gottfried Wilhelm von Leibniz
John William Mauchly
Blaise Pascal
Alan M. Turing
John von Nuemann
Maurice V. Wilkes
Konrad Zuse

Richie, David, *The Computer Pioneers,* Simon and Schuster, New York, 1986.

While not a collection of biographies, this book presents descriptions of the inventions and creations of:

Howard Aiken	John Vincent Atanasoff
Charles Babbage	Clifford Berry
Garrett Birkhoof	George Boole
Arthur Burks	Vannever Bush
Alan Coombs	J. Presper Eckert
Wallace Eckert	Jay Forrester
Herman Goldstine	I.J. Good
Herman Holerith	Grace Hopper
Harry Huskey	Thomas Kilburn
Derrick Henry Lehmer	Derrick Norman Lehmer
Gottfried Leibniz	John Mauchly
Max Newman	William Schockley
George Stibitz	Alan Turing
John von Neumann	Thomas Watson, Jr.
Thomas Watson, Sr.	Norbert Wiener
Maurice Wilks	J.H. Wilkinson
F.C. Williams	Konrad Zuse

Slater, Robert, *Portraits in Silicon,* MIT Press, Cambridge, Mass., 1987.

Charles Babbage	Alan Turing
John von Neumann	Claude Shannon
Konrad Zuse	John V. Atanasoff

John V. Mauchly	J. Presper Eckert
Howard Aiken	Jay W. Forrester
Thomas J. Watson, Sr.	William Norris
H. Ross Perot	William Shockley
Robert Noyce	Jack Kilby
Marcian E. (Ted) Hoff	Gene Amdahl
Seymour Cray	Gordon Bell
Grace Murray Hopper	John Backus
John Kemeny	Thomas Kurtz
Gary Kindall	William Gates
Dennis Ritchie	Kenneth L. Thompson
Daniel Bricklin	Nolan Bushnell
Steven Jobs	Adam Osborne
William Millard	Donald Knuth

Williams, Michael R., *A History of Computing Technology,* Prentice–Hall, Englewood Cliffs, N.J., 1985.

While not a collection of biographies, this book presents descriptions of the inventions and creations of:

Howard Aiken	John Vincent Atanasoff
Charles Babbage	Clifford Berry
René Grillet	Gottfried Wilhelm Leibnitz
Percy Ludgate	Samuel Morland
John Napier	Blaise Pascal
Wilhelm Schickard	Alan M. Turing
Konrad Zuse	

CHARLES BABBAGE INSTITUTE
ORAL HISTORY COLLECTION
AS OF JUNE 30, 1992

OH #	INTERVIEWEE	DATE	INTERVIEWER
211	ADRION, W.R.	10/29/90	Aspray
176	AMAREL, SAUL	10/5/89	Norberg
107	AMDAHL, GENE M.	4/14/86	Norberg
119	ANDERSON, WALTER L.	9/11/86	Norberg
059	ARMER, PAUL et al.	4/16/73	Mapstone
001	ARMER, PAUL	6/1/81	Green
002	AUERBACH, ISAAC	4/10/78	Stern
120	BABCOCK, DEAN	9/12/86	Norberg
182	BARAN, PAUL	3/5/90	O'Neill
213	BARNES, BRUCE	9/26/90	Aspray
128	BAUER, FRIEDRICH L.	4/17/87	Aspray
055	BAUER, WALTER	5/14/73	Mapstone
061	BAUER, WALTER	5/16/83	Norberg
047	BEMER, ROBERT	2/23/82	Lee
003	BIGELOW, JULIAN	8/12/80	Stern
004	BIRKENSTOCK, J.	8/12/80	Steu./Tom.
137	BIRKHOFF, GARRETT	8/19/87	Aspray
141	BITZER, DONALD	2/19/88	Hochheiser
166	BLAAUW, GERRITT	7/19/88	Aspray+
066	BLOCH, RICHARD	2/22/84	Aspray
173	BLUE, ALLAN	6/12/89	Aspray
005	BOOTH, ANDREW	X/X/76	Evans
006	BOWKER, ALBERT	5/21/79	McCorduck
230	BUCHANAN, BRUCE	6/11/91	Norberg
078	BURKS, ARTHUR W.	X/X/XX	Evans
075	BURKS, ARTHUR W.	6/20/80	Stern
136	BURKS, ARTHUR W.	6/20/87	Aspray
098	BURROUGHS B 5000	9/6/85	Galler
092	BUTLER, WILLIAM W.	11/8/84+	Norberg
067	CAMPBELL, ROBERT	2/22/84	Aspray
048	CANTRELL, HARRY	2/23/82	Lee
191	CERF, VINTON	4/24/90	O'Neill
007	CHAMBERS, CARL	11/30/77	Stern
223	CHERNIAVSKY, JOHN	9/26/90	Aspray

OH #	INTERVIEWEE	DATE	INTERVIEWER
195	CLARK, WESLEY	5/3/90	O'Neill
011	CLEAVER et al.	1/23/80	Stern
113	CLOVER, H. DICK	6/5/86	Norberg
058	COHEN, ARNOLD	1/20/83+	Ross
138	COHEN, ARNOLD A.	7/2/87	Norberg
079	COOMBS, A.W.M.	X/X/XX	Evans
162	CORBATO, F. J.	4/18/89	Norberg
209	CORBATO, F. J.	11/14/90	Norberg
134	CRITCHFIELD, C.	5/29/87	Aspray
233	CROCKER, STEPHEN	10/24/91	O'Neill
184	CROWTHER, WILLIAM	3/12/90	O'Neill
180	CSURI, CHARLES A.	10/23/89	Freedman
145	CURTIS, KENT	11/13/87	Minker
235	DANIEL, WILLIS	8/23/85	Ashmore
008	DAVIES, D.	X/X/75	Evans
189	DAVIES, D.W.	3/17/86	Campbell–Kelly
177	DENNIS, JACK B.	10/31/89	O'Neill
164	DERTOUZOS, MICHAEL	4/20/89	Norberg
144	DICK, GEORGE W.	2/19/88	Aspray
167	DIJKSTRA, EDSGER	7/22/88	Aspray+
009	DIRKS, GERHARD	9/22/78	Armer/TR
010	DIRKS, GERHARD	7/27/89	McCorduck
046	DRAKE, WILLIS	2/3/83	Ross
088	DUMEY, ARNOLD	10/9/84	Aspray
118	DUNCAN, HUGH	8/14/86	Norberg
153	DUNWELL, STEVEN	2/13/89	Aspray
193	ECKERT, J. PRESPER	X/X/75	Evans
013	ECKERT, J. PRESPER	10/28/77	Stern
165	FANO, ROBERT M.	4/20/89	Norberg
014	FEIGENBAUM, E.	6/12/79	McCorduck
157	FEIGENBAUM, E.	3/3/89	Aspray
015	FEIN, LOUIS	5/9/79	McCorduck
080	FLOWERS, T.H.	X/X/XX	Evans
148	FORREST, HENRY S.	8/17/88	Bruemmer
016	FORRESTER, JAY	X/X/75	Evans
017	FORSYTHE, ALEXANDRA	5/16/79	McCorduck
049	FOX, MARGARET	4/14/83	Ross
188	FRANK, HOWARD	3/30/90	O'Neill
236	GALLER, BERNARD A.	8/91	E. Galler
222	GALLIE, THOMAS	7/11/90	Aspray

OH #	INTERVIEWEE	DATE	INTERVIEWER
238	GECKEL, JEROME	10/27/86	S. Anderson
207	GOLDBERG, ROBERT	7/27/90	Cargo
018	GOLDSTINE, HERMAN	8/11/80	Stern
019	GOLDSTINE, HERMAN	12/2/81	Green
020	GOLUB, GENE	5/16/79	McCorduck
105	GOLUB, GENE	6/8/79	McCorduck
216	GRAD, ARTHUR	10/29/90	Aspray
201	GRISWOLD, R & M	7/25/90	Cargo
056	HAMMER, CARL	4/15/83	Ross
064	HAWKINS, ROBERT	2/20/84	Aspray
186	HEART, FRANK	3/13/90	O'Neill
221	HEDGES, HARRY	9/26/90	Nebeker
226	HEILMEIER, GEORGE	3/27/91	Norberg
111	HERR, ROBERT	1/17/87	Norberg
021	HERRIOT, JOHN	5/22/79	McCorduck
208	HERZFELD, CHARLES	8/6/90	Norberg
140	HERZSTARK, CURT	9/10/87	Tomash
101	HILL, JOHN LINDSAY	1/15/86	Norberg
050	HOLBERTON, FRANCES	4/14/83	Ross
168	HOLLANDS SIGNAAL	7/X/88	Aspray
081	HOPPER, GRACE	X/X/XX	Evans
022	HUGHES, THOMAS	11/6/80	Green
023	HUMPHREYS, ARTHUR	2/28/81	Tomash
082	HURD, CUTHBERT	X/X/XX	Evans
076	HURD, CUTHBERT	1/20/84	Stern
083	HUSKEY, HARRY D.	X/X/XX	Evans
215	INFANTE, ETTORE F.	11/14/90	Aspray
158	KAHN, ROBERT	3/22/89	Aspray
192	KAHN, ROBERT	4/24/90	O'Neill
217	KEENAN, THOMAS A.	9/28/90	Aspray
024	KILBURN, TOM	X/X/76	Evans
074	KILBY, JACK ST. C.	8/21/84	Norberg
190	KLEINROCK, LEONARD	4/3/90	O'Neill
219	LEHMANN, JOHN	9/26/90	Nebeker
150	LICKLIDER, J.C.R.	10/28/88	Aspray+
025	LLOYD, RICHARD	9/26/80	Humphreys
232	LUKASIK, STEPHEN	10/17/91	O'Neill
214	LYKOS, PETER	11/13/90	Aspray
069	MAGUIRE, TIMOTHY H.	2/27/84	Aspray
051	MARDEN, ETHEL	10/18/83	Aspray

OH #	INTERVIEWEE	DATE	INTERVIEWER
115	MASTERSON, EARL E.	6/30/86	Aspray+
044	MAUCHLY, JOHN	11/13/73	–NONE–
026	MAUCHLY, JOHN	X/X/76	Evans
027	MAXWELL, A.T.	2/25/81	Humphreys
156	McCARTHY, JOHN	3/2/89	Aspray
068	McCORMACK, JAMES	2/23/84	Aspray
045	McDONALD, ROBERT	12/16/82	Ross
057	McDONALD, ROBERT	5/4/83	Ross
185	McKENZIE, A.	3/13/90	O'Neill
028	MERZBACH, UTA	9/15/80	Green
135	METROPOLIS, N.C.	5/29/87	Aspray
029	MILLER, WILLIAM	5/22/79	McCorduck
179	MINSKY, MARVIN L.	11/1/89	Norberg
203	MITCHELL, WILLIAM	7/26/90	Cargo
234	MOLNAR, ANDREW	9/25/91	Aspray
224	MORGAN, GRANGER	11/27/90	Goldstein
110	MULLANEY, FRANK C.	6/2/86	Norberg
073	MUMMA, ROBERT	4/19/84	Aspray
227	NEWELL, ALLEN	6/10/91	Norberg
084	NEWMAN, M.H.A.	X/X/XX	Evans
155	NILSSON, NILS	3/1/89	Aspray
116	NORRIS, WILLIAM C.	7/28/86	Norberg
133	O'ROURKE, THOMAS J.	5/29/87	Bruemmer
175	OHLANDER, R. B.	9/25/89	Norberg
097	OLIVER, BERNARD M.	8/9/85	Norberg
106	OLIVER, BERNARD M.	4/14/86	Norberg
183	ORNSTEIN, SEVERO	3/6/90	O'Neill
095	PACKARD, DAVID	8/8/85	Norberg
095	PACKARD, DAVID	4/9/85	Norberg
099	PARKER, JOHN	12/13/85	Norberg
093	PENDERGRASS, JAMES	3/28/85	Aspray
052	PESSIN, FLORENCE	6/24/81	Lee
194	PINKERTON, JOHN	X/X/76	Evans
149	PINKERTON, JOHN	8/31/88	Self
031	POMERENE, JAMES	9/26/80	Stern
085	PORTER, ARTHUR	X/X/XX	Evans
142	PROPST, FRANK	2/18/88	Hochheiser
032	RANKINE, JOHN	9/11/80	Green
231	REDDY, RAJ	6/12/91	Norberg
072	RENCH, CARL	4/18/84	Aspray

OH #	INTERVIEWEE	DATE	INTERVIEWER
159	ROBERTS, L.G.	4/4/89	Norberg
147	ROBINSON, H.W.	7/13/88	Bruemmer
210	ROSE, MILTON	11/6/90	Aspray
065	ROSS, DOUGLAS	2/21/84	Aspray
178	ROSS, DOUGLAS T.	11/1/89	O'Neill
100	RUBENS, SIDNEY M.	1/6/86	Norberg
163	RUINA, JACK P.	4/20/89	Aspray
169	SCHOLTEN, C.G.H.	7/X/88	Aspray+
161	SCHWARTZ, JULES I.	4/7/89	Norberg
124	SCHWARZSCHILD, M.	11/18/86	Aspray
033	SERRELL, ROBERT	4/5/82	Saretzky
187	SIMPSON, ROBERT L.	3/14/90	Norberg
086	SLUTZ, R.	X/X/XX	Evans
034	SMITH, R. BLAIR	5/29/80	Mapstone
090	STEIN, MARVIN L.	10/29/84	Aspray
131	STRASSMANN, P.A.	5/15/87	Norberg
171	SUTHERLAND, IVAN	5/1/89	Aspray
121	SVENDSEN, EDWARD C.	9/16/86	Norberg
035	SVOBODA, ANTONIN	11/15/79	Mapstone
225	TARESKI, VAL	10/15/90	Aspray
154	TAYLOR, ROBERT	2/28/89	Aspray
143	TENCZAR, PAUL	2/22/88	Hochheiser
220	THALER, ALVIN	9/28/90	Aspray
239	THOMPSON, KEN, et al.	NA	Mahoney
125	THOMPSON, PHILIP	12/5/86	Aspray
062	THORNTON, JAMES	2/9/84	Norberg
146	THORNTON, JAMES	3/16/88	Hochheiser
053	TOMASH, ERWIN	3/30/73	Mapstone
060	TOMASH, ERWIN	5/15/83	Norberg
204	TOWNSEND, GREGG	7/26/90	Cargo
070	TRAUB, JOSEPH F.	4/5/84	Aspray
089	TRAUB, JOSEPH F.	10/12/84	Aspray
094	TRAUB, JOSEPH F.	3/29/85	Aspray
036	TRAVIS, IRVEN	10/21/77	Stern
129	TUCKER, ALBERT	5/8/86	Aspray
087	ULAM, STANISLAW	X/X/XX	Evans
174	UNCAPHER, KEITH	7/10/89	Norberg
200	UNIVAC CONFERENCE	5/17/90	Bruemmer
063	VERZUH, FRANK	2/20/84+	Aspray
054	VINCENT, RICHARD	3/8/83	Solomonson

OH #	INTERVIEWEE	DATE	INTERVIEWER
104	WAKELIN, JAMES H.	2/27/86	Norberg
181	WALDEN, DAVID	2/6/90	O'Neill
205	WALKER, KENNETH	7/26/90	Cargo
117	WALSH, JOSEPH	8/13/86	Norberg
202	WAMPLER, STEVEN	7/25/90	Cargo
037	WARE, WILLIS	1/9/81	Stern
038	WARREN, S. REID	10/5/77	Stern
109	WATSON/BIRKENSTOCK	4/25/85	Norberg
212	WEINGARTEN, F	9/26/90	Aspray
112	WESTBEE, ROBERT L.	6/5/87	Norberg
199	WESTERVELT, FRANK	5/15/90	O'Neill
132	WHEELER, DAVID J.	5/14/87	Aspray
130	WIGNER, EUGENE	5/12/87	Aspray
039	WILKINSON, JIM	X/X/76	Evans
040	WILLIAMS, F.C.	X/X/XX	Evans
206	WILLS, CHEYENNE	7/27/90	Cargo
237	WINOGRAD, TERRY	12/11/91	Norberg
196	WINSTON, PATRICK H.	4/18/90	Norberg
127	ZEMANEK, HEINZ	4/14/87	Aspray
152	ZEMLIN, RICHARD A.	5/16/88	Bruemmer
170	ZONNEVELD	7/X/88	Aspray+
198	ZRACKET, CHARLES A.	5/3/90	Norberg
041	ZUSE, KONRAD	X/X/75	Evans

PROFESSIONAL SOCIETY AWARDS

ASSOCIATION FOR COMPUTING MACHINERY

Distinguished Service Award

1970	Franz Alt
1971	J. Don Madden
1972	George Forsythe (posthumous)
1973	William Atchison
1974	Saul Gorn
1975	John Carr
1976	Richard Canning
1977	Thomas B. Steel, Jr.
1978	Eric A. Weiss
1979	Carl Hammer
1980	Bernard Galler
1981	Aaron Finerman
1982	Anthony Ralston
1983	Grace M. Hopper
1984	Saul Rosen
1985	Jean Sammet
1986	Clair Maple
1987	Fred Brooks
1988	Charlie Bradshaw
1989	Peter Denning
1990	Walter Carlson
1991	Gerald L. Engel
1992	Joyce Currie Little
1993	J.A.N. Lee

A.M. Turing Award

1966	Alan J. Perlis
1967	Maurice V. Wilkes
1968	Richard Hamming
1969	Marvin Minsky
1970	James H. Wilkinson
1971	John McCarthy
1972	Edsger W. Dijkstra
1973	Charles W. Bachman
1974	Donald E. Knuth
1975	Allen Newell and Herbert A. Simon

1976   Michael O. Rabin
1977   John Backus
1978   Robert W. Floyd
1979   Kenneth E. Iverson
1980   C. Anthony R. Hoare
1981   Edgard F. Codd
1982   Stephen A. Cook
1983   Dennis M. Ritchie
1984   Niklaus Wirth
1985   Richard M. Karp
1986   John Hopcroft
1987   John Cocke
1988   Ivan Sutherland
1989   William (Velvel) Kahan
1990   Fernando Corbató
1991   Robin Milner
1992   Butler W. Lampson
1993   Juris Hartmanis
         Richard E. Stearns

Outstanding Contribution Award

1976   Bruce W. Van Atta
1977   W. Smith Dorsey
1978   Kathleen Wagner
1979   M. Stuart Lynn
1981   J.A.N. Lee
1982   Fred H. Harris
1983   Richard Austin and Seymour J. Wolfson
1984   Orrin E. Taulbee
1985   Jack Minker
1986   Herbert Maisel
1987   Edward G. Coffman, Jr.
1988   Thomas A. DeFanti
1989   Monroe (Monty) Newborn
1990   William B. Poucher
1991   Allen Tucker
1992   James Adams
         Lorraine Borman
         Peter Neumann
1993   John H. Esbin
         Frank Friedman

Grace Murray Hopper Award

1970	Donald E. Knuth
1971	Paul E. Dirksen
1972	Paul H. Cress
1973	Lawrence Breed, Richard Lathwell, and Roger Moore
1974	George N. Baird
1975	Allen L. Sherr
1976	Edward A. Shortliffe
1978	Raymond Kurzweil
1979	Stephen Wozniak
1980	Robert M. Metcalfe
1981	Daniel S. Bricklin
1982	Brian K. Reid
1984	Daniel H.H. Ingalls, Jr.
1985	Cordell Green
1986	William N. Joy
1987	John K. Ousterhout
1988	Guy L. Steele
1989	W. Daniel Hillis
1990	Richard Stallman
1991	Feng–hsiung Hsu
1993	Bjarne Stroustrup

Eckert–Mauchly Award[2]

1979	Robert S. Barton
1980	Maurice V. Wilkes
1981	Wesley A. Clark
1982	C. Gordon Bell
1983	Tom Kilburn
1984	Jack B. Dennis
1985	John Cocke
1986	Harvey G. Cragon
1987	Gene M. Amdahl
1988	Daniel P. Siewiorek
1989	Seymour Cray
1990	Kenneth E. Batcher
1991	Burton Smith
1992	Michael J. Flynn
1993	David Kuck

---

[2]Jointly awarded by the Association for Computing Machinery and the IEEE Computer Society.

IEEE COMPUTER SOCIETY

Computer Pioneer Awards

Howard H. Aiken (1980[3])
Large-Scale Automatic Computation

Samuel N. Alexander (1980)
SEAC

Gene M. Amdahl (1980)
Large-Scale Computer Architecture

John Vincent Atanasoff (1984)
First Electronic Computer with Serial Memory

John W. Backus (1980)
Fortran

Robert S. Barton (1980)
Language-Directed Architecture

Freidrich L. Bauer (1988)
Computer Stacks

C. Gordon Bell (1980)
Computer Design

Frederick P. Brooks, Jr. (1980)
Compatible Computer Family System/360

Werner Buchholz (1990)
Computer Architecture

Arthur Burks (1982)
Early Work in Electronic Computer Logic Design

Jeffrey Chuan Chu (1981)
Early Work in Electronic Computer Logic Design

Wesley A. Clark (1980)
First Personal Computer

John Cocke (1989)
Instruction Pipelining and RISC Concepts

Fernando J. Corbató (1980)
Time-Sharing

Seymour R. Cray (1980)
Scientific Computer Systems

---

[3]When the Pioneer Award was instituted in 1980 a number of pioneers were recognized simultaneously.

Edsger W. Dijkstra (1980)
Multiprogramming Control

Stephen W. Dunwell (1992)
Project Stretch

J. Presper Eckert (1980)
First All-Electronic Computer ENIAC

Douglas C. Engelbart (1992)
Human-Machine Interaction

Bob O. Evans (1991)
Compatible Computers

Robert E. Everett (1987)
WHIRLWIND

Robert W. Floyd (1991)
Early Compilers

Jay W. Forrester (1980)
First Large-Scale Coincident Current Memory

Gordon D. Goldstein (1989)
Special Award for the Office of Naval Research

Herman H. Goldstine (1980)
Contributions to Early Computer Design

Jerrier A. Haddad (1984)
Lead IBM-701 Design Team

Richard W. Hamming (1980)
Error-Correcting Code

C.A.R. Hoare (1990)
Programming Language Definitions

Jean A. Hoerni (1980)
Planar Semiconductor Manufacturing Process

Marcian E. Hoff, Jr. (1988)
Microprocessor on a Chip

Grace M. Hopper (1980)
Automatic Programming

Alston S. Householder (1980)
Numerical Methods

David A. Huffman (1980)
Sequential Circuit Design

Cuthbert C. Hurd (1986)
Contributions to Early Computing

Harry D. Huskey (1982)
First Parallel Computer SWAC

Kenneth E. Iverson (1980)
APL

Reynold B. Johnson (1987)
RAMAC

John G. Kemeny (1985)
BASIC

Tom Kilburn (1980)
Paging Computer Design

Donald E. Knuth (1980)
Science of Computer Algorithms

Thomas E. Kurtz (1991)
BASIC

Herman Lukoff (1980)
Early Electronic Computer Circuits

John W. Mauchly (1980)
First All-Electronic Computer—Eniac

John McCarthy (1985)
LISP and Artificial Intelligence

Nicholas C. Metropolis (1984)
First Solved Atomic Energy Problems on Eniac

Gordon E. Moore (1980)
Integrated Circuit Production Technology

Peter Naur (1986)
Computer Language Development

Allen Newell (1980)
Contributions to Artificial Intelligence

Robert N. Noyce (1980)
Integrated Circuit Production Technology

Ralph L. Palmer (1989)
IBM 604 Electronic Calculator

Alan Perlis (1985)
Computer Language Translation

James H. Pomerene (1986)
IAS and Harvest Computers

Mina S. Rees (1989)
Special Award for the Office of Naval Research

Lawrence G. Roberts (1980)
Packet Switching

Nathaniel Rochester (1984)
Architecture of IBM 702 Electronic Data Processing Machines

Arthur L. Samuel (1987)
Adaptive Nonnumeric Processing

George R. Stibitz (1980)
First Remote Computation

Ivan Sutherland (1985)
Sketchpad

James A. Weidenhammer (1989)
High-Speed I/O Mechanisms

Willem L. van der Poel (1984)
Serial Computer—ZEBRA

F. Joachim Weyl (1989)
Special Award for the Office of Naval Research

David Wheeler (1985)
Assembly Language Programming

Adriann van Wijngaarden (1986)
Algol 68

Maurice V. Wilkes (1980)
Microprogramming

Samuel Winograd (1980)
Efficiency of Computational Algorithms

Nicklaus E. Wirth (1987)
PASCAL

Marshall C. Yovits (1989)
Special Award for the Office of Naval Research

Heinz Zemanek (1985)
MAILUEFTERL

Konrad Zuse (1980)
First Process Control Computer

AMERICAN ASSOCIATION FOR ARTIFICIAL INTELLIGENCE

Fellows (Elected 1990 and 1991)

James F. Allen

Ruzena Bajcsy

Wolfgang Bibel

Daniel G. Bobrow

Ronald J. Brachman

Rodney A. Brooks

Bruce G. Buchanan

Jaime Carbonell

Eugene Charniak

Alain Colmeraurer

Johan de Kleer

Richard Duda

Jerome Feldman

Mark S. Fox

Barbara J. Grosz

Patrick J. Hayes

Geoffrey E. Hinton

Aravind K. Joshi

Takeo Kanade

Robert A. Kowalski

Wendy G. Lehnert

Victor R. Lesser

Vladimir Lifschitz

Alan K. Mackworth

Drew McDermott

Donald Michie

Marvin Minsky

J. Strother Moore

Allen Newell (deceased)

Judea Pearl

C. Raymond Perrault

Robin Popplestone

Marc Raibert

Raymond Reiter

Edwina L. Rissland

Charles A. Rosen

Stanley J. Rosenschein

Arthur Samuel (deceased)

Saul Amarel

Hans Berliner

Woodrow W. Bledsoe

Robert S. Boyer

J. Michael Brady

John Seely Brown

Alan Bundy

B. Chandrasekaran

Allan Collins

Randall Davis

Jon Doyle

Edward Feigenbaum

Richard E. Fikes

Michael Genesereth

Peter Hart

Barbara Hayes–Roth

Berthold K.P. Horn

Robert Kahn

Elaine Kant

Casimir A. Kulikowski

Douglas B. Lenat

Hector Levesque

Tomas Lozano-Perez

John McCarthy

John McDermott

Jack Minker

Tom Mitchell

Robert C. Moore

Nils Nilsson

Fernando C. N. Pereira

Tomaso Poggio

J. Ross Quinlan

D. Raj Reddy

Elaine A. Rich

Alan J. Robinson

Azriel Rosenfeld

David Rumelhart

Erik J. Sandewall

Roger Schank
Edward H. Shortliffe
Herbert A. Simon
Aaron Sloman
Mark J. Stefik
Jay M. Tenenbaum
Donald E. Walker
Bonnie Lynn Webber
Yorick A. Wilks
Andrew Witkin
Lotfi A. Zadeh

Oliver G. Selfridge
Candace L. Sidner
James R. Slagle
Guy L. Steele, Jr.
Gerald Jay Sussman
Richard J. Waldinger
David L. Waltz
Robert Wilensky
Patrick H. Winston
William Woods

1992 Fellows:

Narendra Ahuja
William J. Clancey
Gerald Francis DeJong III
Lee D. Erman
Frederick Hayes-Roth
Laveen N. Kanal
Benjamin J. Kuipers
Matthew T. Mason
Ramakant Nevatia
Edward M. Riseman
Howard E. Shrobe
Mark E. Stickel
Peter S. Szolovits

Michael Anthony Arbib
Philip R. Cohen
Robert S. Engelmore
Kenneth R. Forbus
Jerry Robert Hobbs
Janet L. Kolodner
Mitchell P. Marcus
Ryszard S. Michalski
Charles Rich
Glenn R. Shafer
Robert F. Simmons
William R. Swartout
Leslie G. Valiant

AAAI Presidents (all are also Fellows)

Allen Newell 1979–1980
Marvin Minsky 1981–1982
John McCarthy 1983–1984
Patrick Winston 1985–1987
Daniel Bobrow 1989–1991
Barbara Grosz 1993–1995

Edward Feigenbaum 1980–1981
Nils Nilsson 1982–1983
Woodrow Bledsoe 1984–1985
Raj Reddy 1987–1989
Patrick Hayes 1991–1993

AMERICAN FEDERATION OF INFORMATION PROCESSING SOCIETIES (AFIPS)[4]

Harry Goode Memorial Award Recipients

1964	Howard Hathaway Aiken
1965	George Robert Stibitz and Konrad Zuse
1966	J. Presper Eckert and John William Mauchly
1967	Samuel Nathan Alexander
1968	Maurice Vincent Wilkes
1969	Alston Scott Householder
1970	Grace Murray Hopper
1971	Allen Newell
1972	Seymour R. Cray
1974	Edsger W. Dijkstra
1975	Kenneth E. Iverson
1976	Lawrence G. Roberts
1977	Jay W. Forrester
1978	Gordon E. Moore and Robert N. Noyce
1979	Herman H. Goldstine
1980	Fernando J. Corbató
1981	C.A.R. Hoare
1982	Kingsun Fu
1983	Gene M. Amdahl
1984	Ralph E. Gomory
1985	Carver A. Mead
1986	Robert E. Kahn
1992	Edward S. Davidson
1994	Azriel Rosenfeld

COMPUTING RESEARCH ASSOCIATION

Distinguished Service Award

1988	Kent Curtis
1989	Peter Denning
1990	Robert Kahn
1991	David Gries
1993	Joseph Traub
1994	William Wulf

[4]Dissolved 1991, award now administered by IEEE Computer Society.

INAMORI FOUNDATION

Kyoto Prizes[5]

1985	Claude E. Shannon (Basic Sciences)
1988	John McCarthy (Advanced Technology)
1990	Noam A. Chomsky (Basic Sciences)
1992	Maurice V. Wilkes (Advanced Technology)
1993	Jack St. Clair Kilby (Advanced Technology)

ACM FELLOWS

The Association for Computing Machinery Fellows Program was established by the Council in 1993 to recognize and honor outstanding ACM members for their achievements in computer science and information technology and for their significant contributions to the mission of the ACM. The ACM fellows serve as distinguished colleagues to whom the ACM and its members look for guidance and leadership as the world of information technology evolves.

Inducted at the 1994 ACM Computer Science Conference in Phoenix, Arizona, the 133 men and women honored as ACM fellows have made critical contributions towards and continue to exhibit extraordinary leadership in the development of the information age.

James M. Adams, Jr.
Frances E. Allen
Franz L. Alt
William F. Atchison
Richard H. Austing
Kenneth E. Batcher
C. Gordoll Bell
Michael W. Blasgen
Daniel G. Bobrow
David R. Boggs
Loraine Borman
Charles L. Bradshaw
Dalliel S. Bricklin
Fredrick P. Brooks
Douglas K. Brotz

Richard R. Burton
Richard G. Canning
Walter M. Carlson
Vinton G. Cerf
Donald D. Chamberlin
Edgar F. Codd
Edward G. Coffman, Jr.
Fernando J. Corbató
Harvey G. Cragon
Thomas A. D'Auria
Thomas A. DeFanti
Peter J. Denning
Jack B. Dennis
L. Peter Deutsch
Edsger W. Dijkstra

---

[5]Kyoto Prizes are given each year in three categories; recipients who are also computer pioneers are listed here.

Stephen W. Dunwell
J. Presper Eckert
Peter Elias
Gerald L. Engel
John H. Esbin
Bob O. Evans
Tse-Yun Feng
Aaron Finerman
Robelt W. Floyd
Michael J. Flynn
Robert M. Frankston
Frank L. Friedman
Bernard A. Galler
Charles W. Gear
Adele J. Goldberg
Calvin C. Gotlieb
Susan L. Graham
James Gray
Cordell Green
David J. Gries
Carl Hammer
Richard W. Hamming
David Harel
Juris Hartmanis
Fred H. Harris
W. Daniel Hillis
John E. Hopcroft
Thomas E. Hull
J.N.P. Hume
Harry D. Huskey
William M. Kahan
Ronald M. Kaplan
Richard M. Karp
Donald E. Knuth
David J. Kuck
Thomas E. Kurtz
Ray Kurzweil
Butler W. Lampson
Stephen S. Lavenberg
Joshua Lederberg
J.A.N. Lee
Meir M. Lehman

Bruce G. Lindsay
Joyce Currie Little
C.L. Liu
M. Stuart Lynn
Herbert Maisel
Zohar Manna
John McCarthy
Edward J. McCluskey
Daniel D. McCracken
Paul R. McJones
A.J.R.G. Milner
Jack Minker
Roger M. Needham
Peter G. Neumann
Monroe M. Newborn
John K. Ousterhout
Susan S. Owicki
David L. Parnas
David Patterson
William B. Poucher
Anthony Ralston
Ronald L. Rivest
Azriel Rosenfeld
Johns F. Rulifson
Jean E. Sammet
Dana S. Scott
Daniel Siewiorek
Herbert A. Simon
Barbara Simons
Martha A. Sloan
Donald R. Slutz
Burton J. Smith
Richard E. Stearns
Thomas B. Steel, Jr.
Guy L. Steele, Jr.
Harold S. Stone
Michael Stonebraker
William D. Strecker
Bjarne Stroustrup
Patrick Suppes
Gerald J. Sussman
Ivan Sutherland

Edward A. Tait
Robert E. Tarjan
Robert W. Taylor
Charles P. Thacker
Irving L. Traiger
Joseph Traub
Allen B. Tucker
Andries van Dam
Willis H. Ware
Stuart Wecker

Ben Wegbreit
Eric A. Weiss
David J. Wheeler
Maurice V. Wilkes
Shmuel Winograd
Niklaus E. Wirth
Seymour J. Wolfson
William W. Wulf
L.A. Zadeh

INDEX

BUILDING
~~USE~~
~~ONLY~~

13/98